DISTRIBUTION AGREEMENTS
UNDER THE EC COMPETITION RULES

Professor Korah's short monographs on specific topics within EC Competition law are well known and widely used. In this work, with Denis O'Sullivan, she follows the pattern of her previous books on group exemptions for technology transfer and parallel imports. It examines the Regulation on vertical agreements, starting with a chapter on the economic background, before developing, in a series of chapters, a careful analysis of vertical agreements and all the relevant case law. A further chapter deals with agreements which do not come within the Regulation, again paying careful attention to the case law.

Valentine Korah is Professor Emeritus of Competition Law, University College, London; Visiting Professor, Fordham Law School and College of Europe, Bruges, and a Barrister.

Denis O'Sullivan is a barrister specialising in competition law matters at the Centre for European Integration Studies in Bonn, and a former associate with the law firm Coudert Brothers in Brussels.

Distribution Agreements Under the EC Competition Rules

VALENTINE KORAH
and
DENIS O'SULLIVAN

·HART·
PUBLISHING

OXFORD – PORTLAND, OREGON
2002

Hart Publishing
Oxford and Portland, Oregon

Published in North America (US and Canada) by
Hart Publishing c/o
International Specialized Book Services
5804 NE Hassalo Street
Portland, Oregon
97213-3644
USA

Distributed in the Netherlands, Belgium and Luxembourg by
Intersentia, Churchillaan 108
B2900 Schoten
Antwerpen
Belgium

Hart Publishing is a specialist legal publisher based in Oxford, England.
To order further copies of this book or to request a list of other
publications please write to:

Hart Publishing, Salter's Boatyard, Folly Bridge,
Abingdon Road, Oxford OX1 4LB
Telephone: +44 (0)1865 245533 or Fax: +44 (0)1865 794882
e-mail: mail@hartpub.co.uk
WEBSITE: http//www.hartpub.co.uk

British Library Cataloguing in Publication Data
Data Available
ISBN 1–84113–239–X (hardback)

Typeset by Hope Services (Abingdon) Ltd.
Printed and bound in Great Britain on acid-free paper by
Biddles Ltd, www.biddles.co.uk

Preface

Valentine started to write this book in 2000, but decided that she had insufficient opportunities to advise on Regulation 2790/99 to know what businessmen want to do. She, therefore, persuaded her old friend, Denis O'Sullivan, to contribute chapter seven on how to treat agreements outside the scope of the regulation. We started to write our chapters separately, but have each read and commented upon those of the other, and hope that we have made adequate cross references to integrate the two parts.

Several people have kindly read drafts of Valentine's chapters. Margaret Booth of the UK's Office of Fair Trading made many helpful comments, especially on the economics chapter. Pat Massey, then working for the Irish Competition Authority and now consulting at CompEcon Limited (www.compecon.com), made suggestions about the economics chapter. Cani Fernandez of Cuatrecasas' Brussels office and Marissa Tierno Cantello of the Dutch Competition office read the whole some months ago and made helpful comments. None of these friends has seen the final version and none is responsible for remaining errors and infelicities.

When Valentine was teaching at Fordham University School of Law in the Spring of 2001, Mr. Christhoph Huetteroth, then an LL.M. student, kindly acted as a research assistant and was extremely helpful. He has since graduated *magnum cum laude* and become a US attorney. Not only was he good at downloading material and meticulous in checking citations etc., but he was also able to check the German version of the regulation, when the French and English differed. He rejects the wide view given at 3.3.9.1 about the application of the regulation to pure trademark or copyright licences on the ground that article 2(3) is a *lex specialis* taking priority over the more general provisions in article 2(1).

As always, Valentine is indebted to Fordham University School of Law for encouraging her to write, providing a computer and, far more important, competent assistance from the help desk cheerfully and courteously given. Fordham always provides funds for her research assistant. The law library at Fordham is good and the help obtained from librarians far exceeds what can be offered in the UK.

She is also indebted to University College for providing a Professor Emeritus with students, an office, computer and help with it.

Valentine listened to a perceptive and careful speech by Andrzej Kmiecik of Van Bael and Bellis at a conference organised by IBC in Brussels in May 2000. She cannot tell how many of the ideas in this book were derived from that talk and the discussion thereafter. She also learned much from debates with Luc Peeperkorn She would like to think both gentlemen.

Denis would like to thank his friends and colleagues at Coudert Brothers (www.coudert.com) for their very generous support. Jean-Yves Art, Pierre-Manuel Louis and Stephen Spinks in particular shared their practical insights into effective distribution agreements inside and outside Regulation 2790/99. Many of their helpful suggestions have found their way into this book.

We would like to thank all these people, without whom the book would never have been written. Naturally, the remaining errors, omissions and infelicities are our sole responsibility.

We are both indebted to Hart Publishing, which provided a splendid team to produce the book. This time Richard Hart copy-edited the script himself, demonstrating once again the kind of versatility and responsiveness which small publishers possess and which their larger rivals often appear to lack. The index was prepared by Debbie Harris and then revised and edited by Hannah Young, who also co-ordinated production of the book with her usual good cheer and helpfulness, and providing answers to a host of questions en route. The tables were compiled swiftly and very accurately by John Emory Corral, a former student who has now done this for Valentine several times and who is always thorough and meticulous. The typesetters, Hope Services, produced the page proofs very quickly, which enabled us to read proofs in-between other work commitments in the US and Germany.

Valentine Korah,
University College London,
Bentham House, Endsleigh Gardens,
London, WC1H 0EG
valentine.korah@ucl.ac.uk

Denis O'Sullivan,
Centre for European Integration Studies,
University of Bonn,
Walter-Flex-Str. 3
53113 Bonn.
http://www.zei.de

Contents

Table of Cases

NATIONAL

Australia

Germany

Ireland

New Zealand

United Kingdom

United States

Table of Legislation

EUROPEAN

Subordinate Legislation

Directives

Regulations

Guidelines

Notices

NATIONAL

United States

1

Economic Considerations

1.1 BUSINESS CONSIDERATIONS—WAYS OF BRINGING PRODUCTS TO THE MARKET

A supplier of products faces six problems: 1. how to find customers, 2. how to obtain the materials or components it needs to make its products, 3. how to make the product, 4. how to get the finished product to its customers, 5. how to finance its operations and 6. how to provide against the unknown. This book is mainly concerned with the fourth task, but includes some consideration of the others.

If the firm is large enough or the product simple enough, it can perform all six functions itself. The alternative is to agree with independent firms that they should carry out some or all of these tasks. Perceived in this way, distribution is a service that may be bought by the supplier, the cost of which must be included in the final price to consumers. In some situations, it is more efficient to perform the functions within the firm, in others to buy in the services.

Unless there is good reason, businessmen should be left to select the most cost effective method with as little distortion as possible induced by the competition rules and other kinds of legal measure.[1]

Unless the distributor was a competitor of the supplier before it became a distributor, the relationship is said to be vertical.[2] Competition between the parties is not restricted by exclusive contracts, although competition between one of the parties and independent firms may be.

The seminal insight of the Chicago school of economics was that in a vertical relationship, the services provided are complementary: the supplier or licensor benefits from additional services by the buyer or licensee at lower prices and *vice versa*. Whereas, in a horizontal relationship, each competitor benefits from the other producing less at higher prices. This led to a less hostile attitude to vertical restrictions and to the US definition of vertical relationships depending on the firms not being

---

[1] The seminal article is by **Ronald Coase**, "The Nature of the Firm," (1937) *Economica* 386. **Oliver E. Williamson**, *Markets and Hierarchies: Analysis and Antitrust Implications*, (New York, Free Press, 1975) *passim* and other publications have filled it out more recently. See 1.1.1 below.

[2] Under Regulation 2790/99 an agreement is said to be vertical even if the parties could have competed but for their arrangement, but most agreements between actual or potential competitors are excluded from the regulation—an inelegant and complex way to draft a block exemption from Article 81(1).

actual or potential competitors.[3] This is accepted by the Commission in Guideline 100,[4] subject to qualifications in the next two paragraphs.

The favourable view of vertical agreements was challenged by **Robert L. Steiner**.[5] It perceives retailers of "must stock" brands as extremely competitive. They may earn virtually nothing on those brands directly, but must stock them to attract customers who are likely to know their price elsewhere. Where the brands are less strong however, dealers may have some negotiating power against the supplier. Customers may be willing to buy another brand within the same store. So the brand owner may want widespread distribution.

In relation to less valuable brands where there is some market power, supplier and dealer may compete with each other to reap the maximum of any monopoly profit ("rent") there may be for the product. Since Steiner's article was written, supermarket chains have gained more buying power.

Some economists went so far as to argue that vertical restraints would not be imposed unless they led to greater efficiency. This view is changing as possible anticompetitive effects may be the objective of vertical agreements.[6] A consensus is developing that one should balance the anticompetitive effects against any efficiencies: that exclusionary restraints will harm consumers only if there is significant market power.

Distribution has been changing with the revolution in information technology, which enables distributors using bar coding techniques at the till to re-order the products as they are sold without waiting for stock taking. "Just in time" delivery requires considerable joint control between brand owner and manufacturer on the one hand and the retailer on the other to instal the network of equipment and require its use for specified items. It is increasingly found in franchising, selective distribution networks and supermarket chains. Production is pulled by demand rather than being determined by manufacturers' decisions of the previous years and pushed towards consumers. Stocks can be reduced and far fewer unfashionable or obsolescent products have to be disposed of cheaply at the end of the season. The cost and risk of holding stocks have been greatly reduced.

The efficiencies due to this revolution was one of the factors causing the Commission to become less worried about restrictions on the conduct of retailers,

---

[3] According to the US agencies, where the licensee or customer competes with the licensor or supplier before the agreement is made, or could easily have done so, the relationship is horizontal and is more likely to restrict competition. Each may be interested in suppressing competition from the other—in the other restricting production to raise price. Even vertical relationships may have horizontal effects, see 1.2.3.2 below.

[4] Appendix 5 and 3.2 below.

[5] "The Nature of Vertical Restraints," (1985) XXX *The Antitrust Bulletin* 143.

[6] See, for example, **Peter C. Carstensen**, "The Competitive Dynamics of Distribution Restraints: the Efficiency Hypothesis Versus the Rent-seeking, Strategic Alternatives," (2001) 69 *Antitrust Law Journal* 569.

and prepared not to interfere with control in the absence of significant market power.[7]

This chapter starts with an introductory discussion of various ways of bringing products to the market. It continues by discussing the pros and cons from the consumers' viewpoint of freedom to protect dealers and suppliers from competition.

1.1.1 Markets and Hierarchies

A producer of goods or services which requires services at the distribution level may avoid the need for contracts with other undertakings by doing everything itself and instructing its employees or subsidiaries. Some firms operate directly in another member state through a branch, but for various reasons, many firms which intend to keep their distribution in-house set up subsidiaries in each member state. Such forms of organisation have the legal advantage that no agreement between undertakings independent of each other subject to the prohibition of Article 81 (1) needs to be negotiated.[8]

---

[7] **David Deacon**, "Vertical Restraints under EU Competition Law: New Directions," [1995] *Fordham Corporate Law Institute—International Antitrust Law and Policy* 307, and **Lucas Peeperkorn**, "Commission's Policy Review on Vertical Restraints," in J. Grayston (ed.), *European Economics and Law*, (London, Palladian Law Publishing, 1999) p. 2 at 3.

Complaints are made, e.g., *Financial Times*, 11 September 2001, that too often the information about point of sale transactions is used to order the goods from afar, but not to send them to the particular warehouse or outlet that requires a replacement.

[8] Article 81 prohibits agreements between undertakings that may affect trade between member states and have the object or effect of restricting competition. In *Centrafarm* v. *Sterling*, Case 15/74 [1974] ECR 1147, paras. 38–41, the ECJ held that the allocation of tasks within a group of companies did not constitute an agreement subject to Article 81(1).

In *Viho* v. *Commission*, Case C-73/95P, [1996] ECR I-5457, the ECJ held that instructions from a parent to its wholly owned subsidiary not to poach on the territories of other subsidiaries or dealers did not amount to an agreement between undertakings independent of each other and subject to Article 81, whether or not they amounted to the allocation of tasks.

See also *Hydrotherm Gerätebau GmbH* v. *Compact de Dott. Ing. Mario Andreoli e C. Sas*, Case 170/83 [1984] ECR 2999, where the ECJ held that for the purposes of competition law:

the term "undertaking" must be understood as designating an economic unit for the purpose of the subject-matter of the agreement in question even if in law that economic unit consists of several persons, natural or legal (paragraph 11).

See **Wouter P.J. Wils**, "The Undertaking as Subject of EC Competition Law and the Imputation of Infringements to Natural or Legal Persons," (2000) 25 *ELRev* 99.

Article 82 prohibits "as incompatible with the common market" the abuse of a dominant position within the common market, or a substantial part of it. This book will deal only incidentally with this provision, since the group exemptions relate to Article 81 and not to Article 82. In *Tetra Pak Rausing*, Case T-51/89 [1990] ECR II-309, the Court of First Instance (CFI) confirmed that an agreement subject to a group exemption may infringe Article 82. Tetra Pak owned one kind of technology protected by patent for filling milk cartons aseptically. When it acquired a firm which held an exclusive licence for the only other technology being developed, the Commission condemned it for abusing a dominant position contrary to Article 82, although the licence enjoyed the benefit of a group exemption for patent licences under Reg. 2349/84, OJ 1984, L219/15, corrections OJ 1985, C113/34, [1984] 2 CLE 389 (now expired).

On the other hand, vertical integration within the firm is not always efficient. First, many economists and management specialists believe that as a firm gets bigger dis-economies of scale in management begin to outweigh any economies of scale in production and marketing. In a very large firm, it is difficult for the people making decisions to know what is actually happening throughout the whole organisation or even in the parts directly involved. There are problems in devising appropriate incentives for employees to work effectively. This is far too complex a problem to be dealt with here.[9]

Secondly, a manufacturer that distributes its own products has to cope with local conditions unaided by an independent distributor which may be more familiar with them. Thirdly, the option may not be available to small firms which may lack sufficient resources to do all their own distribution. Fourthly, under the law of most EC countries, employees are entitled to various sorts of benefit—minimum wage levels, protection against unfair dismissal, redundancy payments, etc. Senior employees can be appointed at a salary that varies with turnover or profit, but the protection enjoyed by employees tends to make them less resourceful than independent distributors are likely to be. Tax considerations and capital control also play an important role and affect such decisions.

Few brand owners can do their own retailing throughout the common market. The resources required to organise a network of retail outlets may be large and the time taken to penetrate a market too long when a firm first has a product to bring to the market. The supplier may well want its products sold together with other products that attract shoppers. For products that can be sent by post and do not need to be inspected, internet sites may enable manufacturers to do more of their own retailing than used to be practicable, although organising the logistics of mailing punctually may be complex. Wholesalers may also operate at the retail level through such sites.

The degree of control over the distribution system required by suppliers has been increasing where "just in time" delivery systems are set up using bar coding techniques (1.1 above).

In the absence of government distortions, firms may be expected to buy in goods or services when it is more efficient to do this than to produce within the firm and vice versa.[10] Consequently, it is important that competition authorities should not intervene to prevent firms from adopting the level of vertical integration within the firm without good reason. Otherwise costs will rise. To induce firms to produce within the firm rather than have long term contracts with indepedent dealers solely to avoid Article 81 of the EC Treaty is likely to result in higher costs or less good products.

---

[9] If incentives to invest be particularly important at a given level in the chain of production and distribution, economists generally believe that ownership of the "product" should be vested at that level. On the complicated nature of the trade offs between incentives, governance and firm size, see especially **Williamson**, *The Economic Institutions of Capitalism*, (Free Press, New York, 1985) chapter 6.

[10] **R.H. Coase**, "The Nature of the Firm," [1937] *Economica* 386, 393.

1.1.2 Agency (2.8.4 and 7.1.1.1.1 below)

One method of performing the task almost in-house is to use agents. Indeed, a company, having no physical attributes, can act only through agents. The Commission considers that an exclusive agreement with an Agent is not made between undertakings independent of each other and subject to Article 81 because the agent constitutes part of its principal's undertaking. This has been confirmed by the ECJ (2.8.4 and 7.3.1.2 below).

To come within the concept of agency recognised by EC competition law, which however is narrower than that of commercial law generally, it is not sufficient to comply with the requirements of national law. In particular, it is not enough to ensure that title to the goods should remain with the principal until it passes to a third party since in EC competition law an agent is defined by reference to its commercial functions and not merely by reference to its legal position.[11] The Commission now considers that genuine agents should not bear much of the financial and commercial risks not only of unsold stocks, but also of other considerable sunk costs.[12]

The use of integrated agents to avoid the competition rules has the disadvantage that the law of many member states makes it very expensive ever to dismiss an agent once it has acted for a few years. For example, commercial agents enjoy considerable protection under German law. The wish to have independent entrepreneurs promoting one's products may be a stronger reason for not taking the agency route. National law has also been harmonised under a Council directive.[13]

1.1.3 Technology Licensing (3.4.9–3.4.10.2 and 7.2.4.1 below)

At the other end of the spectrum, a holder of technology may decide to license it and not to manufacture, at least in some member states. If it can license a single firm to make the product throughout the common market, it may need to impose few contractual restrictions on its licensee, although the licensee may use distributors and have to protect one against the other if each is expected to invest in ways that cannot be recouped if it leaves the market.

If several different licensees or sub-licensees are needed to exploit the whole of the common market, the licensor may have to protect each licensee from the others if each is to be induced to make the investment necessary to develop the technology, tool up and develop a market.[14]

[11] *Pittsburg Corning Europe (Re)* JO 1972, L272/35, [1973] CMLR D2 and the *Sugar Cartel—Cooperatiëve Vereniging Suiker Unie' UA and others* v. *Commission,* Joined Cases 40–48, 50, 54–56, 111 & 113–114/73 [1975] ECR 1663, paras. 537–554.

[12] Investments that have less value outside the operation for which they were made (1.2.4.1.1 below).

[13] Directive 86/653, OJ L 382/17 (2.8.4 below).

[14] For the free rider argument, see 1.2.4.1–1.2.4.1.5 below. Territorial restraints in a pure sales license are treated by the Commission as if it were a distribution agreement to which the Technology Transfer regulation does not apply, although Regulation 2790/99 may. See 3.4.9–3.4.9.2.4 below.

This book is not concerned with these problems save in so far as a dealer in one Member State may need protection from a licensee in another if it is to invest in marketing and vice versa (4.3.1 below).[15]

1.1.4 Independent Distributors

This book is mainly concerned with distribution agreements. These may be negotiated at several levels. A brand owner may appoint a single distributor for, say, the whole of France, responsible for national importation, warehousing, advertising, promotion and distribution. That distributor may agree to sell exclusively to a wholesaler for, say, the South of France and the latter may be required to organise a network of retail outlets throughout the region, organise repair shops and depots to ensure rapid delivery and so on.

The retailers may also be required to supply services to customers, such as stocking a full range of products for customers to inspect, employing skilled personnel capable of giving technical advice or providing an elegant ambience. Dealers at each level may be required to invest in these and other services before they begin selling and generating revenue and each must expect to be able to appropriate the benefits of its investment if the transaction is to be viable.[16] Such services may continue to be required throughout the relationship, and protection be required beyond a start up period. So at each level, the supplier may promise not to supply any other dealer or consumers within the dealer's territory.[17]

Nevertheless, an exclusive territory is often granted only for the higher levels of distribution as brand owners may want to retain the right to supply more retailers if demand should increase locally.

Dealers may be protected from other dealers taking a free ride on their services by other kinds of restriction, such as resale price maintenance (rpm), but the EC Commission, national competition authorities and courts are hostile to price restrictions.

As explained at 1.1 above, the need for tight control over dealers has increased where bar coding techniques enable retailers not only to itemise the customer's invoice, but also to re-order products as they are sold, both from the local warehouse and the place where they are made. When such systems are used, there are often only two levels of trade—the brand owner and its franchisees or selected retailers.

---

[15] See, **Valentine Korah**, *Technology Transfer and the EEC Competition Rules*, (Oxford, OUP, 1996).
[16] For the concept of sunk costs, see 1.2.4.1.1 below.
[17] We will use the term "dealers" generically to refer to re-sellers at any level of trade.

1.1.5 Franchising (2.8.2 and 7.2.4.2 below)

Franchising is a chameleon word and should always be explained when precise understanding is desired. One method of bringing products to market is what, in *Pronuptia*,[18] the Court has called "distribution franchising" and is known in the US as "retail format franchising." A firm that has developed a good sales formula, usually at the retail level, may exploit this idea by franchising retailers in other areas. In the Court's eyes, the essence of franchising is twofold, the licence of a trade mark or trade name and the transfer of confidential marketing know-how.

Tight control may be required in order to ensure the reputation and uniformity of all the outlets. Some franchisees supply only services and not goods, others buy their wares from third parties, but franchisees may be required to buy only from the franchisor or other designated source, at least for a period, and may be given some element of territorial protection from the franchisor and other franchisees.

Such agreements came within the words of the former group exemption, Regulation 67/67,[19] but in *Pronuptia*, (paras. 28–34) the Court held that such agreements were so different from exclusive distribution that they did not qualify under Regulation 67/67. They may now be brought within the group exemption granted by Regulation 2790/99. Between February 1989 and the end of 1999 they could be brought within Regulation 4087/88.[20]

From a commercial perspective, franchising may be a good compromise between operating through a hierarchy—doing one's own distribution—and operating through independent dealers who may have a greater incentive to try hard. With the popularity of just-in-time delivery, which reduces the amount of capital tied up in stocks and the cost of disposing of obsolete or unfashionable goods (1.1 above), franchising can be very useful. For this purpose, control may be needed over retail outlets. Retailers may be required to stock only the contract goods, ordered from a specified source and to use the organisation and equipment set up by the franchisor.

1.1.6 Selective Distribution (2.8.1–2.8.1.5, 4.3.3, 4.4, 5.2.3 and 7.4.4.3.2 below)

Where the quality of the premises, equipment or services at the point of sale is important to a supplier, it may want to limit dealers to selling only to the public or to approved retailers. A system whereby the supplier not only selects its retailers

---

[18] *Pronuptia*, Case 161/84 [1986] ECR 353; [1986] 1 CMLR 414; CMR 14245, para. 13, 2.8.2 below.

[19] Commission Regulation 67/67—Group exemption for exclusive dealing OJ Spec Ed 1967, 10, expired and replaced by Commission Regulation 1983/83, OJ 1983, L173/1, corrections OJ 1984, C101/2, [1983] 2 CLE 255. Commission Regulation 2790/99, on the application of Article 81(3) of the Treaty to vertical agreements and concerted practices, OJ 1999, L336/21, [2000] 4 CMLR 398, [2000] ECLR supp. to May issue.

[20] The former group exemption for franchising, OJ 1988, L359/46. This regulation has expired and will not be considered in this book, as Valentine wrote a monograph on it, *Franchising and the EEC Competition Rules: Regulation 4087/88* (Oxford, ESC/Sweet and Maxwell, 1989).

carefully, but also permits each of them to sell only to final buyers or other selected dealers is called by the Community institutions "selective distribution." Since it is often expensive to qualify, each qualified retailer is likely to need protection from other retailers selling the same brand nearby.

Such systems may enable the control required for just in time delivery to be organised. This is one of the reasons why selective distribution is exempted by the new group exemption in wider terms than the old formula developed by the European Court of Justice (ECJ).

On the other hand, if one believes that the most important competitive developments come from new ways of trading, selective distribution, with the accompanying refusals to supply, may be anti-competitive. It may be more efficient for a brand owner to provide consumer information by television advertising or a web site, and to require a different range of services from those of traditional outlets. Often the new low cost methods of retailing enjoy an unfavourable reputation at their birth. If those providing them cannot expand rapidly to the minimum efficient size to justify the capital invested, it may take a long time for them to become established and increase efficiency (1.2.3.4 below).[21]

1.1.7 Internet Trading

It is too early to say how internet trading will develop. The first firm to establish a successful site where others may pay to advertise their products and enable customers to click to order them has a large first mover advantage as the more people who use such a site, the more valuable it is—what economists call "the network effect" (1.2.1.2.3 below). There have been several reports on internet trading.[22]

1.1.8 Combination of Various Methods

Often a supplier which makes goods or has goods made for it will use several of these methods of getting products to markets within the EC. It may well sell down to the level of the larger retail outlets in its home territory, using wholesalers to

[21] See Robert Steiner, "The Nature of Vertical Restraints," (1985) XXX *The Antitrust Bulletin*, 143.
[22] The Federal Trade Commission (FTC) held a public workshop in June 2000 to consider whether to control e-commerce to ensure that everyone has access. The FTC held another public workshop on 7 and 8 May 2001. See www.ftc.gov/ftc/antitrust.htm.
The OECD websites for roundtables on internet trading are: http://www1.oecd.org/dsti/sti/1t/ec/act/paris_ec/index.htm for the forum on internet trading it held in Paris on 12/13 October 1999; see http://www1.oecd.org/subject/e_commerce for the *Emerging Market Economy Forum on Electronic Commerce* held in Dubai on 16/17 January 2001.
The OFT published a paper "E-commerce and the Implications for Competition Policy," prepared by Frontier Economics, which also published a shortened version on its web site: *Competition Bulletin* June 2000, p. 2, www.frontier-economics.com.
See also http://europa.eu.int/Ispo/legal/en/commerc.html, the website of European Commission Information Society.

supply smaller retailers. In some areas, or in the larger towns, it may franchise retailers. In some other member states it may sell through an exclusive distributor, who will organise a network of dealers for each part of it. Many manufacturers and brand owners are starting to sell either on their own web sites or on those managed by an independent third party.

If transport be a significant cost, or the brand owner has not got the resources to build a second factory, it may license someone else to make the product using its technology and to sell in specified countries. Problems may arise if it wants to get each of these agreements within an appropriate group exemption for the European Community and it needs to protect, for instance, a distributor from a licensee in another territory or vice versa (4.3.1.1 below).

1.2 ECONOMIC CONSIDERATIONS

This book is mainly concerned with the use of independent dealers, selected distributors or franchisees to provide a brand owner's needs for distribution. They are subject to two sorts of competition. One kind is from other suppliers of the product derived from the same producer, sometimes called intra-brand competition: competition between dealers selling the same brand of the same product.

The other is competition from products made by rival suppliers, sometimes called inter-brand competition: competition between dealers selling different brands of competing products. There may also be non-branded substitutes, but the phrase "inter-brand competition" is often used to embrace them.

Except by providing better value for money, a supplier is seldom able to save its dealers from inter-brand competition if such competition exists.[23] To do so, it would have to enter into a horizontal agreement with its competitors and this would clearly be contrary to the competition laws in most countries and, in particular, to Article 81 of the EC treaty for which heavy fines are likely to be imposed.[24]

In some markets, there may be little effective inter-brand competition. For instance, in network industries, the winner of the latest technological race may supply virtually the whole market but be subject to potential competition as the result of the next technological race (1.2.1.2.3 below). The supplier may be the only firm providing a product for which there are no close substitutes and shielded by barriers to entry. Vertical restraints in such market may have adverse effects on competitors, but provide benefits to consumers who want to connect with as many consumers as possible.

---

[23] Sometimes protection may be conferred through a licensing requirement imposed by law. If planning permission is required to install petrol tanks on a garage forecourt and, as in the UK, such permission is not given unless there is a long stretch of road without a garage, the retailers already licensed may enjoy considerable protection because of the cost to the motorist of driving far for petrol. See the report of the UK Monopolies Commission on the supply of Petrol cited at 1.2.5.2 below.

[24] Notice on the method of setting fines imposed pursuant to Article 15(2) of Regulation 17 and Article 65 of the ECSC Treaty, 14 Jan 1998, OJ 1998, C9/3, [1998] 4 CMLR 472.

Vertical restraints, such as those between a supplier and its dealer, may increase efficiency and competition between the brands of different manufacturers by enabling a supplier to induce its dealers to supply services that may benefit the brand as a whole but which, otherwise, it would not pay any individual dealer to provide. The "incentive" is created by offering the dealer some degree of protection against intra-brand competition.

For example, an exclusive territory may ensure that a dealer who invests in providing valuable pre-sale services such as skilled, trained sales staff and expensive display facilities does not find its investment undermined by a discount store nearby which does not provide similar services.

Where there is vigorous inter-brand competition it may ensure that the "protected" dealer is forced to provide services desired by consumers as effectively as possible. Where there is less vigorous inter-brand competition such vertical restraints may not only reduce intra-brand competition, but may also delay innovatory, lower cost methods of distribution by others (1.2.3.4 below).

Vertical restraints on the supplier and those the supplier imposes on one dealer to protect another affect intra-brand competition and may interfere with the integration of the common market. Where prices differ substantially in different member states and exclusive territories with a supporting ban on dealers actively seeking customers outside the territory as defined by state boundaries, the export ban may make it more difficult for customers in the Member State where prices are higher to buy their products from dealers in the Member State where prices are lower. If such sales were allowed, they would reduce the price differences.

Where justifications, such as the free rider argument (1.2.4.1–1.2.4.1.5 below), do not apply there is no reason to divide the common market in this way and restrict competition between dealers in the same brand. Rpm may also have such an effect.

Restraints requiring the dealer to buy mainly from a particular source or to handle only a particular brand may affect inter-brand competition by making it harder for a new supplier to enter the market on an efficient scale, but only in narrowly defined circumstances (2.7.3 below).

In the rest of this chapter, some of the economic considerations that underlie the policy that is or may sensibly be adopted towards the legality and validity of agreements for exclusive distribution and purchasing will be identified. The grouping of different kinds of restrictions used in the Commission's *Follow Up to the Green Paper*[25] and its guidelines to Regulation 2790/99 will then be explained shortly. The guidelines tend to give conclusions; there is more argumentation for and against possible conclusions in the *Follow Up*.

---

[25] *Communication on the Application of the EC Competition Rules to Vertical Restraints—Follow-Up to the green paper on vertical restraints*—OJ 1998, C365/3. Unfortunately, it has been removed from DG Comp's website.

1.2.1 Market Power—Substitutes and Entry Barriers

1.2.1.1 Substitutes

In appraising the effects on the market of vertical restrictions, the concepts of market power, substitutes on the demand side and barriers to entry are crucial. If markets are closed and monopolistic, the dangers created by vertical restraints are increased. They are greatly reduced if markets are open and competitive.[26] Suppliers who give too much protection to incumbent dealers will be punished by the market—by losing market share.

Market power presupposes not merely that there are few suppliers of a particular product. The only supplier of fish and chips would not be able to earn monopoly profits if consumers thought that Chinese takeaways or an omelette at home were good substitutes. A proper definition of the market must include substitutes on the demand side.

1.2.1.2 Entry conditions

Market power also depends on a matter more often neglected by lawyers—the lack of other firms who could start to produce the product or its substitutes if high profits are to be made. The only producer of a product for which there is no substitute would have power to earn monopoly profits only in the short term if someone else could quickly build or rent a factory and compete with it. Within the economics profession, however, what constitutes an entry barrier has been the subject of considerable debate although there is a growing consensus.[27]

1.2.1.2.1 Bain

Joe Bain of Harvard developed the concept of entry barriers in the 1950s and included many factors that would not generally now be regarded as entry barriers. He argued in *The Importance of the Conditions of Entry*[28] that conditions of entry are to be evaluated by

---

[26] This is now accepted by the Commission in accordance with the more economic approach it is adopting. See recital 7 of Regulation 2790/99 (Appendix 1 below) and Guidelines 6, 119(1), 123–129 and 164 (Appendix 2 below).

[27] Some of the best articles were conveniently collected in (1983) XIV, (1) *The Journal of Reprints for Antitrust Law and Economics*. In Europe, **P. Geroski**, **R. Gilbert** and **Alexis Jacquemin**, *Barriers to Entry and Strategic Competition*, Working paper no. 8910, Department des Sciences Economiques, Université Catholique de Louvain, 1989, consider the tests given by Stigler, Bain and others.

A recent summary of the various views and identification of the areas of consensus is contained in **Paul W. Dobson** and **Michael Waterson**, *Vertical Restraints and Competition Policy*, OFT Research Paper No. 12, December 1996. This contains a useful summary of the games theories that are beginning to be used in antitrust cases. Summaries tend to be tough reading for those skilled in other disciplines, but lawyers who have been working with economists should be able to manage. It has been written for non-economists.

[28] 1956, p. 3.

the advantages of established sellers in an industry over potential entrant sellers, these advantages being reflected in the extent to which established sellers can persistently raise their prices above a competitive level without attracting new firms to enter the industry.

He treated as entry barriers such factors as the need for capital, a good distribution network, technology, etc. although these may well be no more expensive or difficult for the newcomer to acquire than they were for the incumbent. In which event, they would not now be treated as barriers to entry by most economists. If incumbents had to incur these costs in the past, the newcomer is no worse off and the incumbent cannot earn a monopoly profit without attracting competitors.[29] If the investments are specific to the trade in question and cannot be used otherwise, the incumbent may be able to charge up to a price that does not attract new entry.

1.2.1.2.2 *Stigler and others*

The narrowest definition of an entry barrier is that by George Stigler, a Nobel prize winner, in *The Organization of Industry*.[30] He defined entry barriers as costs that must be incurred by the newcomer but were not necessary for existing firms. His theory is that if the existing suppliers were to charge prices higher than needed to cover costs including servicing the original investment, it would pay a normally efficient firm to enter. The existing suppliers could not, therefore, profitably restrict supply to raise price.

On Stigler's definition almost the only entry barriers are some form of government regulation or licensing requirements.[31] A newcomer might have to finance its factory, but so did the incumbent. Both have to service their finance.[32] If, however, the product, or the method of making it is protected by patents or copyright, the incumbent may enjoy market power for a considerable period although this is not always the case.

Stigler did not include even a minimum efficient scale of operation that is large in relation to the demand or its expected increase. Many economists would. Entry by the incumbent might have been comparatively safe, but a newcomer would know that its entry would result in surplus capacity and that both it and the incumbent would be likely to make losses. A newcomer might decide not to enter, even if the incumbent was earning monopoly profits unless demand was expected to increase sufficiently fast to make it worthwhile.

---

[29] See, e.g., the OFT guideline on assessment of market power, OFT 415, issued September 1999.

[30] (Homewood, Illinois, Irwin, 1968) at p. 67.

[31] It would also include the example of an incumbent who obtained some scarce resource before it disappeared, such as the railway line that was built through the only narrow valley between the mountains. A newcomer would have to build a tunnel or go higher up. Or a newcomer might have to compete with a supplier of gas or electricity, who built its retail network before the roads were paved, and so did not have to dig through the hard surface and re-instate it.

[32] The cost of finance is another controversial issue. Efficient small firms may have to pay higher interest charges even if capital markets function well, as they have fewer assets to cushion the risk to lenders. This problem will not be explored here.

There are few markets for final products in the whole of the European Economic Area (EEA) which can support only a single supplier, but in many component markets there may be only a few suppliers, because the research and development has to be recouped from a large turnover and the minimum efficient scale is large in relation to the demand.

More recently, Baumol suggested that ease of exit was as important as ease of entry. An example is waste disposal. Even a town that is so small that there is sufficient demand only for one garbage truck operator could not be held to ransom by the operator of that truck. If it overcharged, waste disposal firms in other localities could bid for the job when the next contract is put out for tender and bring a garbage truck from another area. The newcomer could also remove its truck and personnel with little cost should the incumbent react by reducing its charges.[33]

This theory, however, is of limited application. If the incumbent can respond to new entry fast, there may be little incentive to enter. The original example given of a contestable market was an air route between two cities. A plane could be brought in and out by someone else without much expense. In practice, however, it was found that the cost of establishing hubs was considerable and the markets less contestable than had been thought. The theory is not flawed, but even minor departures from perfect contestability have been found to alter the outcome.

Other economists have suggested that government regulation and a minimum efficient scale large in relation to the market are not the only kinds of entry barriers.[34]

1.2.1.2.3 *Network externalities*

Network markets are those where the addition of extra customers increases the value of a service to existing customers. There is little point in owning a telephone unless there are other people with phones to be contacted. The first successful entrant has a huge advantage over later entrants. This externality might be called a barrier to the entry of further suppliers. As the network expands, its value increases exponentially.

The network may be increased by a single firm increasing its customer base or by inter-connection between competing networks using harmonised protocols. In telecommunications, a subscriber to BT can phone a subscriber to Deutsche Telecom and the owner of the local loop, the pair of wires going from the final

---

[33] See **William J. Baumol**, "Contestable Markets: An Uprising in the theory of Industrial Structure," (1982) 72 *American Economic Review*, expounded at greater length in **W.J. Baumol**, **John C. Panzar** and **Robert D. Willig**, *Contestable Markets and the Theory of Industrial Structure* (New York, Harcourt Brace Jovanovich, 1982). Baumol's insight is that it is the height of the barriers to entry and exit and not the degree of concentration which determines whether conditions are competitive.
Jonathan B. Baker, "Recent Developments in Economics that Challenge Chicago School Views," (1989) 58 *Antitrust LJ* 645, 647 and the works cited at note 10 therein suggest that the theory of contestable markets is marginal. Most markets have more sunk costs than was originally realised.
Richard Schmalensee, "Ease of Entry: Has the Concept been Applied Too Readily?" (1987) 56 *Antitrust LJ* 41.
[34] See **Baker**, note 33 above; **Richard Schmalensee**, note 33 above; **Thomas G. Krattenmaker** and **Steven C. Salop**, "Anticompetitive Exclusion: Raising Rivals Costs to Achieve Power over Price," (1986) 96 *Yale LJ* 209.

switch to the hand set, has an interest in making possible such inter-connection with networks already established. Often established network markets are subject to regulation at a national level, and the regulator may require that new suppliers should be entitled to inter-connection.

Since suppliers in a newer network industry are likely to be trying to extend their networks fast, they are less likely to be over-charging than suppliers in the older kinds of networks, most of which require expensive infrastructure. On the other hand, unless they expect to be able to charge more than their average variable costs there will be no incentive to enter the industry. In some network markets, the capital costs of establishing the network are vast, and variable costs close to zero. It is not possible to define satisfactory criteria for finding what the competitive price would be.

New network markets are often characterised by very rapid technical progress, and any actual or potential competitors will be racing to develop the next generation of technology and protect it by intellectual property rights, such as patents or copyright. Some economists call this competition *for* the market rather than competition *in* the market. Microsoft won the race for computer operating software in the 1990s, but alternative operating systems like Linux may win the next race. The monopolist of today meets potential competition by those racing to develop the next major improvement.

Such markets are often characterised by successive monopolies, as one supplier after another wins a technology race. IBM computers have lost out to Microsoft windows and telephone companies are now subject to fierce competition from internet service providers. Regulators have ensured that the latter have access to phone lines at local rates.[35]

Network industries give rise to problems because excluding new competitors may lead to economies of scale that may benefit consumers more than would the entry of new providers, at least in those markets where harmonised protocols do not permit several providers to enjoy the benefits of scale. It is also clear that definitions of the relevant market based on a hypothetical rise in price of 5 or 10 per cent (2.4.1.2 below) are not appropriate to such a market. It is innovation rather than price that wins market share.

1.2.1.2.4 *Time dimension*

Assessment of market power also involves a time dimension. In the *Merger Guidelines*, 1992,[36] the Antitrust Division of the US Department of Justice proposed

---

[35] This may, however, reduce the incentives to enter the next technological race. It is not clear that such regulation is desirable in the long term.

[36] Conveniently reproduced in XIV, (2) *The Journal of Reprints for Antitrust Law and Economics* 1173. and on the web site of the FTC: www.ftc.gov.bc/guidelin.htm and DoJ, www.usdoj.gov/atr/public.

The EC Commission applies a similar test for mergers; see the notice on the definition of the relevant market for the purposes of Community competition law, OJ 1997, C372/5, [1998] 4 CMLR 177 (2.4.1.2 below). It applies this test also to Article 81 and 82 but, in the context of Article 82 and of cartels that infringe Article 81, there is a basic fallacy. If it would be profitable to raise the price of the product in question by 5% or 10%, this will probably have been done. Consequently, one should probably take as the basic price what would have been charged in a more competitive market and this it is seldom possible to determine.

a short term test for defining the product markets in merger cases, looking to pre-
dicted reactions in the market over a period of six months to a "small but significant" price rise. Economists are more likely to assess reactions over the period it
usually takes to build a new plant on a commercial scale because it takes time for
competition to work.[37]

1.2.1.2.5 *Objectives of competition law*

The debate over the objectives of competition law has great practical and theoretical importance. If one is concerned to protect consumers, government licensing
requirements and something the new entrant has to pay for and which the incumbent did not, are relevant entry barriers. Many are concerned also about sunk costs
and property rights. The first mover may be able to obtain assets at lower cost and
risk than subsequent entrants. Nevertheless, there are fewer entry barriers than
Bain perceived in that it is only when these costs are higher for the new entrant
than the incumbents that they create problem. Incumbents may raise rivals' costs
(1.2.5.2 below). Many markets are sufficiently competitive for intervention not to
be sensible.

   If, however, one is concerned also about the interest of smaller firms entering a
market of their choice, matters of the kind that were of concern to Bain constitute
entry barriers, even when the cost to the newcomer (multiplied by a factor to provide for risk) are no higher than they were to the incumbent. Examples are the need
to raise finance, arrange for distribution, to establish a brand after a competing firm
has obtained a reputation and to obtain technology. They are pervasive and many
firms enjoy some market power. Vertical contracts, especially those that are exclusive, may extend that power. Many economists take an intermediate position.

   If a long time frame be adopted, there are fewer barriers to entry and exit than
in the short term, when firms will be tied into existing manufacturing processes
and plant, their current suppliers and the need to satisfy existing contractual
obligations.

   Historically European competition law has been concerned not only by the possible restriction of production to raise prices to the detriment of consumers. Fair
competition and the interests of small and medium-sized firms are mentioned in

---

[37] Although the Antitrust Division focuses primarily on firms that currently produce and sell the
relevant products, it will sometimes include additional firms that could use their existing plant to produce the relevant product. It said that:

> If a firm has existing productive and distributive facilities that could easily and economically be used
> to produce and sell the relevant product within six months in response to a small but significant and
> non-transitory increase in price, the Department will include those facilities in the market. As a first
> approximation, the Department will hypothesise a price increase of five per cent and ask how many
> firms would be likely to change to the production and sale of the relevant product within six months.
> Firms that must construct significant new productive or distributive facilities in order to produce
> and sell the relevant product will not be included in the market, although the department will con-
> sider their competitive significance in evaluating entry conditions generally. [heading II, B, 1]

The EC Commission also considers entry conditions in the short term when defining the market and
says that it considers competition in the longer term when considering consideration within it.

the preamble of the EC Treaty. The law has also been concerned that traders should be able to enter the market of their choice, although this view is changing.[38]

Particularly in the early years, the Community institutions perceived the competition rules as being concerned to support the principle of free movement. They were hostile towards any restraint or disincentives to trade between member states. Vertical agreements, such as an exclusive territory given to a dealer covering the whole of a member state were seen as restrictive of competition, although some agreements of that kind were exempted provided parallel trade was not entirely eliminated.

1.2.1.2.6 *Case law on market power*

The European Court of Justice ("ECJ") seldom uses the term "barriers to entry", but refers to factors other than market shares when deciding whether a firm has sufficient economic power to enjoy a dominant position. In several judgments relating to Article 82, it has referred to problems a newcomer would have to overcome without considering whether an equally efficient firm would find it more difficult or expensive than did the incumbent.

For instance, in *Continental Can* v. *Commission*,[39] the Court mentioned that to establish a dominant position the Commission had relied on "the financial and technical difficulties involved in entering a market characterized by a strong concentration." The Court did not object to this, although it quashed the finding of dominance over the market for non-cylindrical cans used for meat and fish on the ground that the Commission had not given sufficient reasons for its narrow definition of the relevant market. In particular, the Commission had ignored the possibility of producers of cylindrical cans starting to make non-cylindrical cans with little change to their existing activities.

In *Michelin*,[40] the Court stated that:

> Due weight must also be attached to the importance of Michelin NV's network of commercial representatives, which gives it direct access to tyre users at all times.

An equally efficient firm might well have been able to create such a network. Most producers of tyres are large companies with significant market shares. The Court also referred to the cross elasticities of supply and demand and to the possibility of a tyre manufacturer entering the market by building a new factory, but dismissed the latter on the ground that it would take too long.

In *AKZO Chemie BV* v. *Commission*[41] the Court said that a dominant position may be rebuttably presumed with a 50 per cent share of the market.

---

[38] Guideline 7, quoted at 1.2.2 below, Advocate General Jacobs in *Oscar Bronner GmbH & Co. KG* v. *Mediaprint Seitungs- und Zeitschriftenverlag GmbH & Co. KG and others*, Case C-7/97 [1998] ECR I-7817, para. 58.

[39] Case 6/72 [1973] ECR 215, para. 30.

[40] Case 322/81 [1983] ECR 3461, [1985] 1 CMLR 282, CMR 14,031, para. 58.

[41] Case 62/86, 3 July 1991 [1991] ECR I-3359, [1993] 5 CMLR 215, [1993] 2 CEC 115.

61. Moreover, the Commission rightly pointed out that other factors confirmed AKZO's predominance in the market. In addition to the fact that AKZO regards itself as the world leader in the peroxides market, it should be observed that, as AKZO itself admits, it has the most highly developed marketing organization, both commercially and technically, and wider knowledge than that of their competitors with regard to safety and toxicology.
. . .

On the other hand, in recent cases, the Court has also looked at the possibilities of suppliers in other markets or of other products challenging the existing producer. See, for instance, *Alsatel* v. *Novasam*,[42] and *Ahmed Saeed.*[43]

In many cases, the ECJ has insisted that agreements should be appraised in their legal and economic context before being found to infringe Article 81(1) (2.7.3 below). This seems to mean that in the absence of market power, vertical agreements are unlikely to restrict competition significantly.

In 1997, the Commission published a notice on the definition of the relevant market for the purposes of Community competition law[44] (2.4.1.2 below).

1.2.2 The Commission's Guidelines

The Commission published guidelines in connection with its group exemption for distribution agreements.[45] Guidelines 21–70 express its views on the application of the new group exemption which is analysed in chapters 3–6 below, but other guidelines apply to agreements that do not come within the group exemption.

The guidelines start by asserting that vertical restrictions may have positive as well as negative effects on competition (Guideline 5), although the Commission will appraise efficiencies only under Article 81(3) and the onus will be on those alleging legality to establish that the restraints are needed and no wider than necessary.[45a] Nevertheless, it accepts that competition is distorted contrary to Article 81(1) only if there is insufficient competition from substitute products. It goes on to focus on benefits to consumers rather than to competitors.

7. The protection of competition is the primary objective of EC competition policy, as this enhances consumer welfare and creates an efficient allocation of resources. In applying the EC competition rules, the Commission will adopt an economic approach which is based on the effects on the market; vertical agreements have to be analysed in their legal and economic context. . . . Market integration is an additional goal of EC competition policy. Market integration enhances competition in the Community. Companies

---

[42] Case 247/86 [1988] ECR 5987, para. 17.

[43] Case 66/86 [1989] ECR 803, paras. 39–41. For further discussion of the concept of a dominant position and its abuse see **Valentine Korah**, *An Introductory Guide to EC Competition Law and Practice,* 7th ed., (Oxford, Hart Publishing, 2000) chapter 4.

[44] OJ 1997, C372/5, [1998] 4 CMLR 177, [2000] 5 CMLR 1074.

[45] OJ 2000, C 191/1, [2000] 5 CMLR 1074. For the status of the Guidelines see 3.2 below.

[45a] *Matra Hachette SA* v. *Commission,* Case T-17/93 [1994] ECR–II 595, para. 105 and *Métropole Télévision SA and Others* v. *Commission,* Case T-112/99 [2001] 12 CMLR 1236, paras. 131 and 158 (7.2.2–7.2.3 below).

should not be allowed to recreate private barriers between member States where State barriers have been successfully abolished.

The goal of market integration creates differences from US antitrust philosophies and some contractual provisions cause problems in Europe that would not do so in the US.

As in the USA, Guideline 7 speaks of of the primary objective being the protection of consumers rather than competitors. Unfortunately, the Commission rather easily finds that the exclusion of competitors may harm consumers in the long run without giving as much weight to short term benefits due to efficiencies made possible by a restraint, as is given in the US. Efficiencies will be considered only under Article 81(3), where the onus is on the parties alleging legality rather than under Article 81(1) where the onus of proof is on the person alleging illegality (7.4.5 below). Moreover, the onus under Article 81(3) is heavy in view of the language in the Treaty. The restriction must be "indispensable" and not merely reasonable as under US law,[46] and proof is often required that part will be passed on to consumers.

From Guidelines 104–114, the Commission divides vertical restrictions into four groups and lists the harms that may be done to competition by each group. Each group includes not only direct contractual prohibitions, but also provisions that indirectly have similar, if attenuated, effects.

1.2.2.1 Single branding group (1.2.5–1.2.5.4, chapter 5, 7.2.3 and 7.4.4.3.1 below)

The "single branding group" embraces provisions that make it unlikely that a dealer will handle competing products: what was previously called "a non-compete provision," under which a dealer agrees to handle the products of only a single supplier or to take a large proportion of a specified product from that supplier. It also includes provisions with a similar, if attenuated effect, such as fidelity rebates, a duty to take a specific quantity of product where that is a large in relation to its requirements ("quantity forcing"), or a two part tariff such as a fixed sum plus lower marginal prices or progressive discounts. The group also includes tying (2.9 below): refusing to supply one item unless some other product is paid for.

The Commission states that this group of restrictions may have four anti-competitive effects when there is insufficient competition at the supplier's level of trade (1.2.5–1.2.5.4 below). First, the foreclosure of other suppliers may keep them out of the market. Secondly, not only may this make the market more concentrated, it may also make it more rigid so that it is harder for the more efficient suppliers to expand at the expense of those less efficient. This has long been recognised as a problem by economists, but hitherto has not been expressed in the case law. Thirdly, buyers of final goods may not be able to make comparisons between brands at the same shop and, fourthly, tying one product to another may make the tied product more expensive.

---

[46] Although, the difference may be more literal than substantive in practice.

The Commission does not mention raising rivals' costs as those who tie the first dealers probably pay far less for the tie than those who adopt a single branding policy later when there are few dealers left, at least if there are high barriers to entry at the dealer level (1.2.5.2). Nor does it mention the theory from Chicago that there is only one monopoly profit to be made, and that few sellers tie in order to increase the price of the tied product (2.9 and 4.6.2 below).

The Commission accepts in Guideline 108 that there may be competition *ex ante*, when the dealer agrees to buy mainly from a designated source.

1.2.2.2 Limited distribution group

This group of restrictions limits the number of buyers for a particular territory or group of customers (Guideline 109). It includes exclusive distribution (I will sell only to you within a territory) and exclusive customer allocation as well as indirect ways of limiting the number of dealers such as an obligation or incentive scheme agreed between the supplier and buyer which induces the former to sell only or mainly to one buyer and after-market sales restrictions which limit a component supplier's sales possibilities.

According to Guideline 110, the limited distribution group of restraints has three main negative effects on competition: (1) other buyers within that market can no longer buy from that particular supplier and this may lead, in particular in the case of exclusive supply, to foreclosure of the purchase market, (2) when most or all of the competing suppliers limit the number of retailers this may facilitate collusion, either at the supplier's or the distributor's level, and (3) since fewer distributors will offer the product it will also lead to a reduction of intra-brand competition.[47] In the case of wide exclusive territories or exclusive customer allocation, the result may be total elimination of intra-brand competition. This reduction of intra-brand competition can in turn lead to a weakening of inter-brand competition.

Steiner objects also that widespread exclusive distribution agreements might make it hard for new low cost kinds of distributor to grow fast enough to a minimum efficient scale and thus harms inter-brand competition (1.2.3.4 below).

1.2.2.3 Resale price maintenance group (rpm) (2.8.5–2.8.5.4 and 4.2–4.2.6)

Guideline 112 indicates two main negative effects of rpm on competition: a reduction in intra-brand price competition and increased transparency on prices. Even a maximum or recommended price may work as a focal point for resellers, leading to a more or less uniform application of that price level.

Increased transparency on price and responsibility for price changes makes horizontal collusion, express or tacit, between manufacturers or between distributors

---

[47] This objection seems to Valentine to be only a different way of expressing the first, and not separate.

easier, at least in concentrated markets. The reduction in intra-brand competition, as it leads to less downward pressure on the price for the particular products, may have as an indirect effect a reduction of inter-brand competition.

This grouping and the next have probably been separated by the Commission from the limited distribution group because there is case law treating rpm and absolute territorial protection of dealers as "by their very nature" having the object of restricting competition (2.7.1 and 4.1 below). This has led to the group exemption for distribution not applying to any provisions in an agreement if there is fixed or minimum rpm. Much of the more general economic literature relating to the limited distribution group applies also to the rpm group of restrictions.

1.2.2.4 Market partitioning group

This group consists of agreements directly or indirectly limiting a buyer to buy or sell a particular product in a particular area. It includes exclusive purchasing, where an obligation or incentive scheme agreed between the supplier and the buyer induces the latter to buy its requirements for a particular product, for instance beer of brand X, exclusively from the designated supplier, but leaves the buyer free to buy and sell competing products, for instance competing brands of beer. It also includes territorial resale restrictions, the allocation of an area of primary responsibility, restrictions on the location of a distributor and customer resale restrictions.

According to Guideline 114, the main negative effect on competition is a reduction on intra-brand competition that may help the supplier to partition the market and thus hinder market integration. This may facilitate price discrimination.[48] When most or all of the competing suppliers limit the sourcing or resale possibilities of their buyers this may facilitate collusion, either at the distributors' level or at the suppliers' level.

The general economic literature usually treats the two middle groups—limited distribution and rpm—together, because either or both may be used to encourage dealers to invest for the benefit of the brand as a whole and the economic literature is seldom concerned about market partitioning.

---

[48] In some circumstances, economists welcome price discrimination as inducing a supplier with market power to supply even those who would not buy at a single monopoly profit maximising price. The benefit of discrimination is likely to be greatest when there are large fixed costs, and marginal costs are low. In such an industry even the lower prices may make some contribution to the overheads for the benefit also of those who pay more.

The benefit may be outweighed by the cost of determining what each group of customers is willing to pay and of preventing those buying at low prices selling to those who would buy at higher prices. In that event discrimination is unlikely.

Discrimination may also make it difficult for those paying more to compete downstream and distort competition in that market.

1.2.2.5 Justifications

Guidelines 115 stresses that there is no cause for concern when the firm has no market power and Guideline 116 lists various justifications for vertical restraints generally, without dividing them between the four groups (1.2.4.1–1.2.4.3 below). The first five justifications are based on free rider arguments.

1.2.3 Causes of Concern about Protection from Intra-Brand Competition

Economists have differed widely over time and between countries as to whether vertical rpm and territorial protection are anti-competitive. The practices may alleviate the free rider problem (1.2.4.1–1.2.4.1.5 below) in as much as a dealer providing pre-sales services may be protected from under-cutting by those that do not. Rpm may restrain intra-brand competition less than an exclusive territory since competition on non-price items, such as holding stocks and other services within the same area is permitted. Moreover, dealers can obtain the brands so protected, even if they cannot cut their price.

1.2.3.1 Concern for market integration

The most important difference between the policies pursued in the US and in the EC is the European concern for market integration. Article 2 of the EC Treaty states that the objectives of the Community are to be obtained through the mechanism of a common market. In competition cases this has been elevated by Commission and Court to an objective in itself.[49]

In the US, markets were already largely integrated before the Sherman Act was passed in 1890. There was a single currency, intellectual property rights were federal and English was the language spoken by most citizens. In the nineteenth century immigrants were encouraged to embrace the American language and culture in "the melting pot."

In Europe, not only do we still have national currencies with high charges for converting small amounts, although this is changing with the introduction of the physical euro in 12 member states in 2002. Euros have operated as a currency of account for some years. We also have national intellectual property rights[50] and

---

[49] See *Consten and Grundig—Re the Agreement of Grundig Verkaufs-GmbH* JO 2545/64, [1964] CMLR 489, Appeal—*Etablissements Consten SA and Grundig-Verkaufs-GmbH* v. *EEC Commission,* Joined cases 56 & 58/64 [1966] ECR 299 (2.2 below).

[50] Benelux trade mark and design rights apply in Belgium, the Netherlands and Luxembourg.

The Council trade mark Regulation 40/94, OJ 1994, L11/1, amended by Regulation (EC) 3288/94, OJ 1994, L349/83 provides for a Community trademark obtainable from the office in Alicante, although national trademarks also persist.

The Commission has submitted a proposal to the Council to create a unitary Community patent, proposal for a Council Regulation on the Community patent, COM(2000) 412 final—2000/0177(CNS), OJ 2000, C337 E/278.

several Member States depress prices, especially for medicines, through some form of price control leading to significant price differentials imposed by law.

The Commission and Courts have relied on parallel trade to provide arbitrage and reduce price differences by enabling dealers in the high priced state to buy where prices are lower.

Perceived *ex post*, when a dealer has made investments,[51] an exclusive territory, coupled with export bans, clearly isolates one member state from another and interferes with any arbitrage that might reduce prices in the high price area and lead to greater demand. It may also reduce the number of dealers of the brand throughout the common market. The Commission considers that the maintenance by a brand owner of resale prices at different levels in different member states may well have a similar effect.

Even if transactions are perceived *ex ante*, some scholars would enquire whether the protection is greater than the minimum reasonably necessary to induce sufficient investment by dealers and whether parallel importers would have been interested in the product even if the dealer had not invested for the benefit of all dealers in the brand.[52] If the answer to either question is positive, the justification fails, unless one takes the view that the supplier is better placed than a competition authority to make the decision. Even so the benefits to the supplier may not be the same as those of the economy as a whole.[53]

Rpm was pervasive in the UK until it was made illegal, and embraced many products for which free riding was not a problem as little sunk investment was required from retailers. The extent to which the abolition resulted in lower prices is not known as other factors changed at the same time, but it may have been by about 5 per cent.[54]

EC officials allege that the Common Market differs from the integrated markets of North America. Quite apart from the less competitive tradition in much of Europe, it is customary to appoint exclusive distributors for one or more member states of the European Communities. For many products, it is not merely one manufacturer, but all who do so. As long as the dealers in the high price countries are protected by their supplier from imports from places where prices are lower, price differences along national boundaries seem to persist even in the absence of government distortions or significant entry barriers.

It is difficult to persuade officials that if such regional oligopolies are unusually profitable, they are vulnerable to new manufacturers entering the market, or that

---

[51] See 1.2.4.1.1 below where the problem created by sunk costs is analysed and 2.2 and 2.7 below for the distinction between analysis *ex post* and *ex ante*. See also, **Valentine Korah**, *An Introduction to EC Competition Law and Practice*, 7th ed. (Oxford, Hart Publishing 2000) 257–8.

[52] See **Michel Waelbroeck**, "Vertical Agreements: Is the Commission Right not to Follow the Current U.S. Policy?" (1985) 25 *Swiss Review of International Competition Law* 45.

[53] See, however, **Robert Steiner**, "The Nature of Vertical Restraints," (1985) XXX *The Antitrust Bulletin* 143. They fear that a brand owner may be interested in marginal customers and may induce the dealers to provide pre-sales services that only a few marginal customers require, at the cost of those who do not require them.

[54] **J.F. Pickering** in "The Abolition of RPM in Great Britain," (1974) 26 *Oxford Economic Papers* 120 considered various estimates and their methodology.

ignoring government measures that lead to price differences between member states and attacking the symptom rather than the cause may increase the isolation of national markets.[55] So, it is not surprising that they sometimes intervene to protect those wanting to compete with existing dealers.

Entry barriers are also more pervasive in Europe than in America, since the costs of exit are higher.[56] For example, there is more social legislation making it expensive to employ people or to dismiss redundant workers. This increases the costs of failure when a risky market is entered and makes new entry less attractive. National markets are also more regulated than those in the USA, although considerable liberalisation has taken place during the last decade. Exclusive rights conferred by government create entry barriers, even on the narrowest definition used by Stigler.

1.2.3.2 Output restricting effects of vertical restrictions

Vertical arrangements may have horizontal anti-competitive effects, even according to economists of the Chicago school. Where markets are concentrated, vertical agreements may support horizontal collusion, actual or tacit, parallel behaviour that has similar effects to collusive price fixing, at either the producers' or the dealers' level of trade. In many trades, rpm originated as a horizontal cartel at the dealers' level. Horizontal price fixing either between producers or between dealers[57] is now illegal wherever there is a competition law, although, it may be difficult to detect it.

A more sophisticated version of the argument is that vertical agreements enable producers in oligopolistic markets to operate more effectively as if there were an illegal cartel agreement without having to organise one and infringe Article 81.

If there are only a few suppliers of a product for which there is no satisfactory substitute protected by entry barriers, each may charge considerably more than the cost of producing and marketing (including a normal return on capital) for extended periods. Each of the others knows that if any of them were to undercut in order to increase its market share, the others would soon discover this, and each reduce its prices. Each may act as if there were a price fixing or market allocation agreement although there is none.

---

[55] **Charles Baden Fuller**, "Economic Issues Relating to Property Rights in Trademarks: Export Bans, Differential Pricing, Restrictions on Resale and Repackaging," (1981) 6 *ELRev* 162.

Derek Ridyard and **David Lewis**, "Parallel Trade in Patented Medicines—Economics in Defence of Market Segmentation", [1998] *Int TLR* 12.

Concepión Fernández Vicién, "Why Parallel Imports of Pharmaceutical Products Should be Forbidden" [1996] *ECLR* 219.

[56] See **Baumol**'s insights, cited at 1.2.1.2.2 above.

[57] In *Metro II*, Case 75/84 [1986] ECR 3021, at 3064; Advocate General Verloren van Themaat was concerned that if a large part of the market was supplied by specialist dealers, manufacturers might be forced to operate a selective distribution system, refusing supplies to lower cost outlets, for fear of a collective boycott.

This would create a problem if entry at the dealer level was difficult, and might delay new low cost methods of distribution.

Such oligopolistic interdependence is fragile and depends on each supplier real-ising that its competitors are likely to notice if it chisels its prices and punish a price cutter. Rpm and exclusive dealing make it easier for everybody to discover price cutting by rivals and to enable them to react. It also reduces the incentive for deal-ers to cut their prices. Rpm, therefore, reduces the likelihood of price cutting.

It may be silly for a competition authority to attack parallel pricing directly because there are no appropriate remedies.[58] To the extent, however, that parallel pricing leads to prices that exceed costs including a normal return on capital, it may have the same effects of distorting competition as horizontal price fixing. It is, therefore, desirable to discourage facilitating devices that enable firms to avoid competition over extended periods.[59]

Parallel pricing practices are more likely to break down if three conditions are satisfied: if 1) price cutting is not easily detectable, 2) penalties for discounting are low and 3) discounting would enable the producer to increase its market share. Even purely vertical rpm which prevents a dealer from passing on any secret dis-counts and so prevents the discounter increasing its market share, may help to reduce price cutting by any of the producers,[60] and so may help suppliers to raise prices above competitive levels for extended periods.

Where rpm helps parallel pricing to endure, it is widely agreed that it is anti-competitive, but Comanor doubts whether resale prices are often maintained for this reason.[61] This may be because rpm is illegal not only in the EC, but also in the USA.

Similarly, if, in a market where supply is concentrated, most of the suppliers adopt limited distribution policies, the distribution market may be concentrated too and it may be easier to behave as if there was collusion even though there be none.

Another possible inefficiency resulting from vertical restraints such as rpm or limited distribution that lead to the restriction of output, is that if the practice

---

[58]   To make it illegal for each firm to announce a price rise as its costs rise might lead to the market becoming more concentrated as one firm after the other leaves it.

[59]   See Report of the UK Monopolies Commission on *Parallel Pricing*, June 1973, Cmnd. 5330. It rec-ommended that the government should watch mergers that make fairly concentrated industries more so.

Jonathan B. Baker, "Recent Developments in Economics that Challenge Chicago School Views," (1989) 58 *Antitrust LJ* 645 suggests other reasons why firms might engage in vertical restrictions.

Facilitating devices include:

1) announcing price rises well in advance, which makes it less risky for the price leader to announce the rise—it can rescind it if its competitors do not follow;

2) promising many large customers to extend to them any more favourable terms given to others, which discourages secret discounts;

3) exchanging recent information about bargains at special prices etc.

[60]   **Lester Telser**, "Why Should Manufacturers want Fair Trade?" (1960) 3 *Journal of Law and Economics* 86, 97. Where a dealer handles several products, a secret discount might encourage it to push the sale of the discounted item even if it cannot pass on the discount. Sometimes rpm is coupled with an obligation on the dealer to handle no other goods, and then it may reinforce interdependent pric-ing between manufacturers.

[61]   **William S. Comanor**, "Vertical Price Fixing, Vertical Market Restrictions, and the New Antitrust Policy," (1985) 98 *Harv L Rev* 983, 1155.

becomes widespread, discount merchandisers may have difficulty obtaining high quality branded products. The most important kinds of competition often come from innovatory ways of doing things, and new methods of distribution often enjoy a low reputation at their birth. Discounters may need the reputation provided by stocking some prestigious brands and selling them more cheaply than the traditional stores (1.2.3.4 below).

Rpm may prevent large discounters from surmounting threshold barriers to rapid growth, at least until one prestigious brand owner ceases the practice, when its competitors may have to follow suit, as happened with Levi jeans.[62] Moreover, some brand owners may continue to restrict intra-brand competition even after it has ceased to be profitable, partly because their dealers expect it, and partly from inertia.

Where several brands are subject to rpm, the supplier of one may hesitate to permit discounting in the knowledge that its competitors would follow suit.

Buyers with market power, such as big multiple retailers, may require a supplier not to supply its competitors. They might require to be protected from intra-brand competition. As supermarkets have been gaining ever larger market shares, and there have been mergers between them, there has been greater concern about buyer power leading to discriminatory discounts and refusal to stock more than two premium and one in-house brand for each category[63] (1.3 below).

It is also argued that suppliers who have grown used to protecting their dealers may hesitate to cease. Some suppliers who are not subject to strong inter-brand competition may opt for a quiet life. They may fear that changes would ensue if new dealers entered the market. Large discounting chains would obtain market power. Supermarkets might require their products to be packed differently; friends might be driven out of business and even in the absence of barriers to entry at the dealer level, the new large buyers would be able to demand higher discounts.[64]

---

[62] **Robert L. Steiner**, "The Nature of Vertical Restraints," (1985) 30 *The Antitrust Bulletin* 143–97, summarised by **Scherer** and **Ross**, *Industrial Market Structure and Economic Performance*, 3rd. ed. (Houghton Mifflin Company, Boston, 1990) p. 553–54.

Levi abandoned enforcing rpm under pressure from the FTC and its competitors followed suit. Initially sales of jeans increased, especially those of the Levi brand, as they were sold in cheaper outlets, but later they declined. Was the decline due to a change in fashion, or to prestigious shops no longer carrying its brand? New brands of designer jeans were developed to fill the up market gap left when denim ware was sold in mass market outlets. See 1.2.4.1.5 below.

[63] For a convenient summary of the concerns, see **Julian Maitland Walker**, "Buyer Power" (2000) *ECLR* 176 and 4.1 below.

In the concentration between *Rewe Internationale Beteiligsgesellschaft mbh, Rewe-Verkaufsgesellschaft mbh and Julis Meinl AG*, IV/M.1221, OJ 1999, L 274/1, [2000] 5 CMLR 256, the Commission cleared a merger of super market chains, only on condition that some of the stores were hived off to reduce buying power.

[64] See **Charles Baden Fuller**, "Rising Concentration: The UK Grocery Trade 1970–1980," in **K. Tucker** (ed.), *Firms and Markets* (London, Croom Helm, 1986). He relies in part on the Monopolies and Mergers Commission's report on *Discounts for Retailers*, 1981 HCP 311 to show that, despite the absence of barriers to entry, large multiple grocers were able to obtain better discounts and passed them on to shoppers.

1.2.3.3 No need to intervene if considerable inter-brand competition

Where a brand owner is subject to lively competition from other brands, there may be no need to intervene to prevent the protection of one dealer from another in the same brand even if dealers who have incurred no sunk costs are protected. If more protection is given than is necessary to induce the services wanted by consumers, the brand is likely to become too expensive and suppliers of other brands competing more intensively on price will expand their sales at its expense. The market punishes entrepreneurs who make stupid decisions, or even wrong ones.

If, on the other hand, monopoly profits are earned, new entry may be attracted unless there are barriers to entry. So, there is no need for officials or courts to consume their scarce resources by intervening. Excessive intervention increases the costs to business too, since antitrust advice is expensive and the Commission may not always evaluate free rider arguments correctly. This leads to uncertainty and increases the risks of investment.

1.2.3.4 Importance of inter-type competition

Joseph Schumpeter[65] concluded that the competition that matters most has been provided by new forms of operation rather than by rivalry among conventional operators of a similar type. Robert L Steiner took up the theme in relation to retailing.[66] He observed that discount stores are not only cheaper, they also provide a different, but not inferior, range of services from conventional stores: wider choice with the convenience of one stop shopping, longer hours of operation and free parking as well as low prices.

Major innovations in retailing have been the department stores and general mail order houses of the mid-nineteenth century, the various chain organisations at the turn of the century, followed by twentieth century supermarkets and discount stores. New kinds of retailers entered the fray as price cutters to exploit their comparative cost advantage to capture trade from the traditional outlets of the day. Although there were fewer sales assistants, information was provided upstream by the manufacturers' advertising often on a national basis, which was cheaper than sales assistants providing information individually.

To obtain the advantage of the new management methods discounters needed economies of scale and prestigious brands to attract customers. Since at first they usually had a poor reputation, it was difficult to obtain supplies. The conventional outlets were protected either by the best brands being sold only to a few outlets or by rpm. If the new discounters were unable to slash prices, they could not achieve

---

[65] *Capitalism, Socialism and Democracy*, 24–25, 1st ed. (New York, Harper & Brothers,1942).
[66] "The Nature of Vertical Restraints," (1985) XXX *The Antitrust Bulletin*, 143, 152. Most of 1.2.3.4 is taken from Steiner's article. The point is summarised by **Scherer** and **Ross**, *Industrial Market Structure and Economic Performance*, 3rd. ed. (Boston, Houghton Mifflin Company, 1990) p. 553.

their scale economies fast and new retailing methods were delayed. Nevertheless, rpm tends to last less long than selective distribution, which prevents discounters obtaining the products at all.[67]

Manufacturers and dealers compete with each other for their shares of any monopoly profit there may be.[68] This was assumed away by the Chicago economists who treated retailing as perfectly competitive. It nearly is for some products, but not all. A rule of thumb is that if consumers are more willing to switch brands within a store, retailers will have negotiating power and enjoy higher margins than if consumers are more willing to switch stores to obtain their favoured brand. Manufacturers compete with retailers by promoting their brands often on television. Retailers usually earn low margins on these items: the market for retailers to obtain the top brands is very competitive.

As new low cost methods of retailing emerged, traditional stores applied pressure on manufacturers to protect their top brands either by imposing minimum prices or by selling only to a few prestigious stores. Rpm tended to delay new developments less than limited distribution practices, as the new discounters could obtain stocks, which attracted customers even if the dealers could not cut prices. As the discounters grew in size and number, the power of traditional outlets to require protection broke down and price cutting broke out.[69]

1.2.4 Justifications for Restrictions of Intra-Brand Competition

Economists often treat distribution as a service bought by the producer (1.1 above). The margin earned by the dealer is, therefore, an additional cost borne by the producer which must be met from the price charged downstream. Viewed in this way, the producer's interest lies in keeping distribution costs to a minimum because they either raise the price of the product, eat into the profit earned by the producer from each sale, or a bit of both.

Hence, if the brand owner wants to maximise its profit, it will grant each dealer no more protection from other dealers in the same brand than is necessary to induce the investment in services that it thinks is optimal.[70] Any margin allowed the dealer which is greater than necessary to induce the desired level of investment

---

[67] See **Partick Massey** and **Paula O'Hare**, *Competition Law and Policy in Ireland* (Dublin, Oak Tree Press, 1996) at pp. 105–13 for a discussion of how rpm influenced the development of the grocery market in Ireland and delayed the advent of supermarkets.

[68] **Robert L. Steiner**, "The Nature of Vertical Restraints", (1985) 30 *The Antitrust Bulletin* 143, pp 156–160.

[69] *Ibid.*, pp. 152–56 and 165–83.

[70] See the seminal article by **Lester Telser**, "Why Should Manufacturers Want Fair Trade?" (1960) 3 *J of Law & Economics* 86. He returned to the subject in "Why Should Manufacturers Want Fair Trade II?" (1990) 33 *J of Law & Economics* 409. At p. 410 he clarified his position. He never considered that rpm should always be legal, merely that it should be subject to the rule of reason.

by the dealer in location, ambience and other services that the supplier thinks will increase demand for its product will cut into the brand owner's profits.

This view is controversial, however, even among economists.[71] Both Scherer and Comanor point out that the efficiency justification for vertical restraints assumes that all customers value the pre-sales services equally. If only marginal customers value the services, efficiency could well be reduced because all other customers will have to pay for services that have no, or little, value for them.[72] Moreover, it assumes that there is strong competition between dealers.

1.2.4.1 Free rider justification

The prospect that a brand owner may wish to provide its dealers with incentives to invest in developing a market and to the dangers of free riding were mentioned at 1.2. Restrictions of intra-brand competition may arise (1.1.4 above) in relation to complex products such as electronic consumer goods or vehicles about which customers seek information and require pre-sales service at the point of sale.

Each retailer may be required to undertake investments in skilled personnel, demonstration models, spare parts and equipment for repairs and maintenance. They may be required to sell fashion and glamorous articles in a luxurious ambience. It would be stupid for a dealer to agree to make such investments if it could not charge separately for the services and another dealer nearby does not supply the service and so can sell at lower prices. Many customers would make their selection at the expensive shop that provides the service, but order the main product from the cheaper shop that does not. The "cheap" shop would be able to take a "free ride" on the services provided at the "expensive" shop.

There may be no way that two kinds of retailer of high priced products for which pre-sales services are important can co-exist selling the same brands, one providing expensive services and the other not if their shops are nearby or if the brand is sold by mail order or the internet. When consumers need, but are resist-

---

[71] For strongly Chicago views, see **R. Bork**, *The Antitrust Paradox A Policy at War with Itself* (New York, Basic Books, 1978), chapter 13, p. 290; **R. Posner**, "The Next Step in the Antitrust Treatment of Restricted Distribution," (1981) 48 *U Chi L Rev* 6.

Jonathan B. Baker, "Recent Developments in Economics that Challenge Chicago School Views," (1989) 58 *Antitrust LJ* 645 suggests other reasons why firms might engage in vertical restrictions.

Michel Waelbroeck, "Vertical Agreements: Is the Commission Right not to Follow the Current US Policy?" (1985) 25 *Swiss Review of International Competition Law* 45, states that in Europe dealers are frequently protected when the free rider argument does not apply.

[72] **F.M. Scherer**, "The Economics of Vertical Restrictions", (1983) 52 *Antitrust LJ* 687, 700. See also **Scherer** and **Ross**, *Industrial Market Structure and Economic Performance*, 3rd. ed. (Boston, Houghton Mifflin Company, 1990), pp. 542–48 for analysis of vertical restraints and pp. 522–27 for vertical integration as a source of monopoly power; and **William S. Comanor**, "Vertical Price Fixing, Vertical Market Restrictions, and the New Antitrust Policy," (1985) 98 *Harv L Rev* 983 990–1000.

Scherer, in particular, notes that this discrepancy is less worrying where (a) inter-brand competition is vigorous and (b) rival suppliers use different distribution plans, (1983) 52 *Antitrust LJ* at 704–07 and 731–34. In those circumstances, customers should be able to chose to buy equivalent products at lower prices where the unwanted services are not provided.

ant to paying independently for, pre-sales services, the shop providing the services would have to cease doing so.

As discussed at 1.2.3.3 above, if the market be competitive, the brand owner has no interest in granting dealers more protection from other dealers than it thinks is necessary to induce the investment in services which it thinks is optimal. Indeed, its business may fail if it grants too much protection. The brand owner is more likely to get this assessment right than an official or court looking at the matter years later. It is risking its profits and livelihood when it makes decisions, so has an incentive to make them carefully. It probably understands the product and market conditions better than an official or a court. Consequently, some economists have recommended that vertical rpm should be automatically legal and the arguments apply generally to other forms of protection.[73]

Perceived *ex ante*, before the brand is well known in the dealer's territory, it may be expensive and risky for the dealer to promote the products. Without sufficient protection it may not be prepared to do so. If the dealer has not invested in promotion, parallel importers may not be interested in the product. In those circumstances, if protection from intra-brand competition is forbidden by the competition rules, both competition and the integration of the market may be impeded. In the *Green Paper on Vertical Restraints in EC Competition Policy*,[74] the Commission accepts that, without protection, dealers would tend to under-invest in pre-sales services. Where the market is competitive and there is a diversity of choice, there may be no danger in allowing individual firms considerable latitude.

One qualification to this view is that the supplier may be interested in attracting marginal customers, and may provide sufficient protection to induce services that they require, at the expense of most customers who do not (1.2.4 above). Another is the increased buying power of major super market chains (1.3 below).

1.2.4.1.1 *Sunk costs*

The investment in the pre-sales services that creates the free-rider problem is an example of a sunk cost.[75] Whenever a firm has had to make an investment in something that has no other equally valuable use, it needs contractual protection from opportunistic behaviour by its supplier. The costs sunk in the investment create an inequality in bargaining power and hence allow unilateral appropriation

---

[73] **Richard Posner**, "The Next Step in the Antitrust Treatment of Restricted Distribution: *per se* Legality," (1981) 48 *U Chi L Rev* 6, 22–26. See also **Bork**, *The Antitrust Paradox: A Policy at War with Itself* (New York, Basic Books, 1978). Contrast **Scherer** and **Ross**, *Industrial Market Structure and Economic Performance*, 3rd. ed. (Boston, Houghton and Mifflin Company, 1990) 542–58.

Posner's lucid introductory book, *Antitrust Law—An Economic Perspective* (Chicago, University of Chicago Press, 1976) from p. 147, is helpful in understanding the economics of vertical restraints. The language is not at all technical.

For some of the considerations raised by different forms of protection, see 1.2.4.1.3 below.

[74] COM(96) 721 final, [1997] 4 CMLR 519, para. 59 and Guideline 116.

[75] On the problem of sunk costs, see e.g., **Benjamin Klein**, **Robert Crawford** and **Armen Alchian**, "Vertical Integration, Appropriable Rents and the Competitive Contracting Process," (1978) 21 *JL & Econ* 297, 308 *et seq.*

of the benefit of that investment unless the investor protects himself by a contract that is enforceable.

An extreme example of a sunk cost is a fixed pipeline. If a distributor ("D") decides to build a pipeline to take the oil it is buying from the oil company's ("O") refinery to the market where it is selling, it must ensure that its supplier will continue to sell oil to it once the pipeline is built at a price which allows it to cover not only its operating costs but also enough to compensate it with a surplus to offset the risk of sinking its capital into building the pipeline in the first place.

Once the pipeline is built, it may be that no one else will be able to ship the oil as cheaply as can D and it might expect to buy at the market price of the oil at the place where it enters the pipeline. In the absence of an enforceable long-term contract, however, O could threaten to charge up to the amount at which it would cease to be worth D's time and trouble to pump any oil to the market. The price that emerges may lie anywhere between these two levels depending on the skill of the parties at negotiating. In the economic literature, this is commonly called "the hold-up problem."[76]

D may not be prepared to risk its capital in building the pipeline unless it expects that its returns from the pipeline's use will at least match those of any alternative use of its capital, such as investment in other activities or in government bonds.[77] D may require O to promise to supply it for decades at the price at which it sell to others near the refinery.

The argument from sunk costs can, however, be carried too far. Virtually all costs are partly sunk—one can seldom sell a used vehicle for what it cost less the value of its use. Nevertheless, until it is worn out, it can be used on routes other than those for which it was bought. The danger of hold-up is significant only where the investment has no alternative use or the next best use is much less valuable.

It is costly to build a pipeline, but its next best use might be as scrap, worth a tiny part of the cost of negotiating rights of way, making and erecting the pipeline. If, however, D had invested in a tanker to carry the oil, the problem would be much less significant because, if O were to raise its price, after some disruption, the carrier could refuse to buy and use its tanker to bring oil from elsewhere or, possibly, even to ship some other cargo or sell the vehicle which would retain significant market value. So, in the latter case, only a small part of the investment would be "sunk".

---

[76] E.g., Guideline 116(4). The Commission observes that for there to be a problem the investment must be specific to one supplier, the investment must be recouped only in the long term and must be asymmetric. It devotes a separate paragraph to the hold-up problem that arises after the transfer of secret know-how.

In Valentine's view, the Guideline goes rather too far.

[77] The Commission recognises that a solution to "the hold-up problem," may be justified, but only for a period of up to five years, guidelines 116(4) and 155. Where the investment has to be financed over a period of decades, this may be insufficient.

In *European Night Services* v. *Commission*, the CFI pointed out that the Commission should have given reasons for not granting an exemption for as long as a very large investment had been financed.

The free rider argument should not be pushed too far. In the United States, Comanor alleges that "the empirical evidence that vertical restraints have been imposed to avoid free riding is somewhat thin."[78] Furthermore, it may be argued that it is seldom necessary to protect dealers from each other in order to induce post-sales service since this can usually be charged for separately, either by the brand owner paying for the guarantee service or by the retailer making a normal charge for it to the customer. Even for pre-sales services, it may be possible to charge customers, possibly with a deduction from the purchase price for those who buy in the same shop.[79] In the *Follow Up to the Green Paper*[80] and in Guideline 116, the Commission accepts the free rider argument, but only where there is a significant problem and no less restrictive solution

Although the free rider argument applies only where the dealer has to invest in providing something for which it is difficult to charge, some manufacturers protect dealers of products for which pre-sales services are not required. In the US this seems to have happened most often for prestigious new brands (1.2.4.1.5 below). This may be because the higher margins the distributor can obtain will encourage it to stock and recommend the goods.

Other possible explanations are that the supplier is lazy and giving way to dealer requests against its own interest in minimising the price of its product to consumers; the dealers in a particular brand may illegally have conspired together in their own interest to persuade the supplier to protect each of them from competition from each other or the manufacturers may have entered into an illegal cartel or be colluding tacitly and want to avoid pressure from low cost outlets[81] (1.2.3.2 above).

1.2.4.1.2 *Ways of avoiding the problem*

There are various ways of overcoming the free rider problem where it does exist, but they may be more costly or less effective than providing protection for the dealer making the investment from dealers who do not. The supplier may itself build the pipeline or pay part of its cost if it has the resources. To avoid opportunistic behaviour, the sunk cost is often incurred by a joint venture between the parties, but there seems little point in forcing the supplier rather than the dealer to make part of the investment. A joint venture still leaves each party at risk if the other decides to operate differently and abandon its investment. Each may still

---

[78] **William S. Comanor**, "Arrangements and Antitrust Analysis," (1987) 62 *NYULR* 1153, 1156, **Scherer** and **Ross**, *Industrial Market Structure and Economic Performance*, 3rd. ed. (Boston,Houghton Mifflin Company, 1990) pp. 550–58.

[79] **Scherer** and **Ross**, *ibid.*, 555, record the interesting emergence of car dealers charging for entry to showrooms and for "test drives", Often these charges are deducted from the purchase price of those who buy there. This raises the interesting question of how often pre-sales services cannot be charged for separately. It may be easier to charge when the cost of pre-sales service is substantial.

[80] OJ 1998, C365/3, section III, 3.

[81] See **F.M. Scherer**, 52 *Antitrust LJ* 687, 694; **Comanor**, note 46 above; **Robert Steiner** "The Nature of Vertical Restraints," (1985) XXX *The Antitrust Bulletin* 143–97.

need a long term contract to supply at least fixed quantities by reference to a formula to set the price.

A brand owner may set up a demonstration centre in each town where customers can try the products and obtain specialist advice. Dealers, even from other areas, will not be able to take a free ride, since the brand owner can recoup its costs through the price it charges them for each item.

A supplier setting up such a centre may have to decide whether to enable customers to compare other brands and demonstrate them too,[82] in which case, it may be difficult to persuade the other brand owners to make a fair contribution to the cost. Alternatively, the centre may demonstrate only one brand, and customers have to travel to other outlets to compare what is available. This creates a greater cost in remote areas than in cities.

The problem may be overcome by a trade association or a third party organising national or international exhibitions at which all the manufacturers may exhibit, but these may enable only business buyers[83] to compare products every few years and, in any case, they do not provide information for consumers on a continual basis.

Through lack of resources, such as information, appropriate skills and, perhaps, even capital, smaller suppliers may not be able to set up such centres. It amounts to doing much of one's own retailing.

Another possibility is for the brand owner to pay a fee to those dealers who provide the services, but this may be less efficient in that someone must then monitor the dealers to ensure that the fee is spent on providing the services and that it is well spent. The brand owner might also have to specify the services, although the dealer is closer to the market and may be better placed to decide on what it is worth spending.[84] The threat of terminating a dealer for skimping on services, may be more serious if the dealer is able to make more than a normal profit (1.2.6.5 below),[85] but threats to terminate are not always possible under national law in Europe where exclusive dealers and agents may have rights against termination.

[82] This would amount to a horizontal agreement that might well be caught by Article 81. The Commission, however, has exempted decisions of several trade associations to organise large international trade exhibitions. Formerly the members agreed not to display at other exhibitions, and the Commission persuaded the trade associations to reduce this restriction to, e.g., a year before or after the international exhibition leaving a year or two in the middle when members were entitled to enter smaller exhibitions, e.g., *UNIDI* OJ 1975, L228/14, [1975] 2 CMLR D51, exemption renewed OJ 1984, L322/10 [1985] 2 CMLR 38, *SMM&T Exhibition Agreement*, OJ 1983, L376/1, [1984] 1 CMLR 611. See generally, **A. Brown**, "Trade Fairs and Fair Trade: The Commission's Exemption Policy," [1992] *ECLR* 66.

[83] Nevertheless, it is now common, for example, for trade shows to be organised annually and to admit consumers as well as trade buyers.

[84] **Jean Tirole**, *The Theory of Industrial Organization* (Cambridge Mass, MIT Press, 1989) at chapter 1 comments that often, compliance with contractual obligations may be neither observable nor enforceable. See also **Benjamin Klein**, **Robert Crawford** and **Armen Alchian**, "Vertical Integration, Appropriable Rents and the Competitive Contracting Process," (1978) 21 *JL & Econ* 297, 308 *et seq.* at p. 308 *et seq.* for an example from the automobile industry.

[85] Where a consumer may not be able to tell whether the services have been provided properly by the retailer, it may think that the product is less good than it ought to be. So the brand owner has a large incentive to ensure that the services are rendered. See the explanation of the FTC's case of *Coors*, discussed at 1.2.6.3 below.

1.2.4.1.3 *Problem may be overcome by giving incentives to dealers to provide the services*

These problems may be avoided by making it worth while for a dealer to make the investment. The dealer, who may be most familiar with local customs and demand, can exercise its judgement in deciding what services to provide.

For these purposes, various kinds of protection from free riders may be given.

First, the supplier may agree to supply only a particular dealer within an exclusive territory. A promise by the supplier not itself to sell in the area, may be of little value, unless it also promises not to permit other dealers to sell in the territory. Such obligations not to poach may be limited or absolute. The restriction on other dealers may relate only to actively seeking customers outside their territories which maybe allowed under the new block exemption. It may also embrace passively accepting orders in its own territory for delivery outside it or to dealers likely to export, but this prevents the application of the new group exemption. For an exclusive territory to provide effective protection, the supplier may have to promise also not to sell to dealers outside the area who do not provide the services.

Since many brand owners appoint a single distributor to supply a whole member state, or even several member states, an exclusive territory with associated export bans may insulate one member state from another and, given the Commission's interest in market integration, it is hardly surprising that it has objected strongly to absolute territorial protection. Where the territory is large and transport costs important, an exclusive territory, even without export bans imposed on dealers, may remove all intra-brand competition save near to the borders.[86] In the absence of strong inter-brand competition, this may reduce the pressures on the dealer to be efficient.[87]

Surprisingly, the Commission does not often distinguish sharply between exclusive distribution for a large territory covering one or more member states and at a more local level within a single member state.[88] It is often more difficult for consumers to travel far, or abroad,[89] to obtain cheaper products or better service. Where the territory is only part of a town, or a small country region, exclusivity will not enable very different prices to be charged net of VAT and excise duties. If

---

[86] That large territories increase the protection is noted in the *Communication on the Application of the EC Competition Rules to Vertical Restraints—Follow-up to the Green Paper on Vertical Restraints—* OJ 1998, C365/3 at page 10.

[87] The supplier may be expected to bear this in mind when deciding how much protection to give a dealer from intra-brand competition.

[88] In the draft of Regulation 1983/83 published for comment in OJ 1978, C31/3, the Commission blacklisted territories with a population exceeding 100 million. It was persuaded, however, that for some products larger territories were required and this requirement was eventually omitted.

[89] It may be easier in the centre of the Community. No part of Luxembourg is far from a border. Greece, however, is cut off from other member states, as are Ireland, and the UK. Germany is a huge Member State. When the euro exists in physical form from 2002 the need to convert currencies will cease and shopping abroad will present one less cost. The increased use of internet shopping will also increase competition for products where prior inspection is not important.

the territory is small, any restrictions would also seem unlikely to have perceptible effects on trade between member states.

Secondly, rather similar protection, although less strong, is a location clause without an exclusive territory, whereby each dealer is permitted to sell only from specified premises and requires express consent if it wants to move or to sell also in another location.[90] Each dealer may be able to rely on its supplier not permitting anyone else to move too close to its principal sales area unless demand increases sufficiently to support two retail outlets.

Thirdly, a different kind of protection may be given through maintaining the prices at which retailers may resell—rpm. In an EC context, rpm has the great theoretical advantage that, provided the price is similar throughout the EC, it does not divide the Common Market geographically. In practice, however, even if prices are originally set at the same level, currencies in a few member states fluctuate, although this problem has diminished with the introduction of a single currency, the Euro, in most member states.[91]

Rpm prevents retailers who do not provide services from undercutting those who do, but enables retailers to compete in other ways, providing services, ambience, parking or one stop shopping. It does not act as a complete ban on new entrants to a territory, although it may prevent low price retailers from adopting their normal strategy for entry. So rpm might be thought to restrict competition less than does an exclusive territory. It may also save the supplier from incurring considerable expense in having to monitor many retailers to ensure that sufficient and appropriate services are rendered.

There is, however, no assurance that the dealer given a firm margin over the price it pays will use it to provide the services the supplier hopes to induce. The dealer may prefer to promote less, but keep the high margin, relying on other dealers to provide the pre-sales services.

Comanor argues[91a] that rpm does not prevent dealers from competing in ways other than price. Consequently, competition between them will lead to all of the higher margin being devoted to the services wanted by the supplier. Prices may have to rise less than they would if limited distribution were the mechanism to induce the services.

On the other hand, because rpm reduces the pressure to minimise costs, there may be insufficient incentive on the dealer to provide the services efficiently.[92] If

---

[90]   E.g., the famous US case of *Continental TV, Inc.* v. *GTE Sylvania Inc.*, 433 US 36 (1977).

For the EC, see *Pronuptia*, Case 161/84 [1986] ECR 353, paras. 19 and 24, a case concerned with distribution franchising where the location clause itself was cleared but found to restrict competition and, consequently, require exemption, when used in combination with the grant of an exclusive territory to confer absolute territorial protection.

[91]   Not Denmark, Sweden or the UK.

[91a] **William S. Comanor**, "Vertical Agreements and Antitrust Analysis", (1987)62 *NYULR* 1153, 1160.

[92]   Most of the issues relating to rpm and competition were analysed by **Basil S. Yamey**, *The Economics of Resale Price Maintenance* (London, Pitman, 1954). Unfortunately it has long been out of print, but his analysis is clearly repeated for laymen in *Resale Price Maintenance and Shoppers' Choice*, Hobart Paper I (Institute of Economic Affairs, 1960). He considered the effect of the practice in increasing costs at pp. 16 *et seq.* of the Hobart paper.

delivery is provided free, why should a customer carry bulky goods out to its car, even if it is on the road outside the shop? The proliferation of services worth less than they cost seems to have been a problem when rpm was legal, although one might have expected brand owners to react by ending the practice.

Historically, however, rpm has frequently been adopted at the instigation of dealers acting collectively,[93] in which case, few economists would support it, but manufacturers would need courage to terminate it.[94]

Where a brand owner thinks that it is more effective to compete in services than in price, it may decide to protect each of its dealers in one or more of these ways. The protection may be justified on the ground that it increases inter-brand competition, which is generally more important than that between dealers in the same brand.

Nevertheless, the Commission has largely denied this in the past. The restriction of intra-brand competition may delay the entry of new, low cost methods of distribution. The free rider argument was rejected by the Court in *Consten & Grundig v. Commission*,[95] and not addressed in *The Distillers Company Ltd.*,[96] although it was unusually strong in those cases. In some of its later decisions, described at 2.7.1 below, the Court has allowed some intra-brand restrictions, such as a restriction on actively seeking customers, in order to induce investments that increased inter-brand competition or where there was intense inter-brand competition.

In too many of its decisions, however, the Commission has tended to perceive matters *ex post*, after the investment has been made and the product has become popular (2.6 below). By then it may be hard to persuade the Commission that the project was risky at the start. The *ex post* method by definition catches only the successful investments ignoring those where the distributors lost their investment or most of it. If the transaction is perceived *ex post*, it is usually more competitive to forbid protection from intra-brand competition.

More than once,[97] the Commission has stated that the product was introduced to the market years earlier, and seems to assume that soon after a product has been launched, protection from intra-brand competition ceases to be justified. A dealer, however, may not expect to recover all its sunk costs soon after launch. Moreover, it may continue to invest in promoting a brand throughout the period of its relationship with the supplier. That continuing investment will also be a sunk cost if it can be put to no alternative use.

---

[93] See **Scherer** and **Ross**, *Industrial Market Structure and Economic Performance*, 3rd. ed. (Boston, Houghton Mifflin Company, 1990), 548–50 for the history in the US and **Basil S. Yamey**, above n. 92, p. 11, for the UK.

[94] See 1.2.3.2 above.

[95] Cases 56 & 58/64, [1966] ECR 299, described at 2.2 below.

[96] 78/163/EEC, OJ 1978, L50/16, [1978] 1 CMLR 400. On appeal, *The Distillers Co. Ltd.* v. *Commission*, Case 30/78, [1980] ECR 2229, where the free rider argument was accepted by Advocate General Warner, but avoided by the ECJ.

[97] E.g., *Agfa Gevaert* and the Commission's decisions on know-how licensing made shortly before it adopted Regulation 556/89, considered in **Valentine Korah**, *Know-how Licensing and the EEC Competition Rules: Regulation 556/89*, 1.5.2.3.

If such incentives cannot legally be provided, manufacturers may integrate vertically and operate downstream, too. Cosmetic manufacturers may hire part of a department store and use their own employees to provide demonstrations. Sometimes, manufacturers supply part of the services, providing racks, displays and other forms of promotion. Frequently, they advertise directly on television.

Brand owners are most likely to operate downstream when the service desired is large in relation to the value of the product and a shirking dealer can easily expand output.[98]

1.2.4.1.4 *Both the concerns and justifications apply also to customer restrictions*

The Commission now accepts that these arguments apply equally to groups of customers. Under Article 2 of Regulation 2790/99 (4.3.1 below) the Commission permits a little protection of dealers' exclusive customer groups as well as territorial protection. This enables a supplier to grant an exclusive territory to one dealer for the supply of drugs for use in hospitals or to be sold in pharmacies and the same or another exclusive territory for another dealer to sell to the vets in the same area. This may enable the supplier to provide incentives to each dealer to invest in exploiting its customer group, when a single supplier might not be in a position to exploit both.

1.2.4.1.5 *Certification free rider issue*

There are many free rider problems that may be avoided by granting protection to dealers downstream.[99] When a supplier is introducing a new brand, it may want to have it sold in a prestigious shop until it gains a reputation so that other retailers will want to sell it. The prestigious shop may well refuse to handle the brand unless it is given an exclusive right to do so.[100]

This justification is listed by the Commission in Guideline 116(3)—

> 3) *The certification free-rider issue.* In some sectors, certain retailers have a reputation for stocking only "quality" products. In such a case, selling through these retailers may be vital for the introduction of a new product. If the manufacturer cannot initially limit his sales to the premium stores, it runs the risk of being de-listed and the product introduction may fail. This means that there must be a reason for allowing for a limited duration a restriction such as exclusive distribution or selective distribution. It must be enough to guarantee introduction of the new product but not so long as to hinder large-scale dissemination. Such benefits are most likely with "experience" goods or complex goods that represent a relatively larger purchase for the final consumer.

---

[98] **Klein** and **Murphy** "Vertical Restraints as Contract Enforcement Mechanisms," (1988) 31 *JL Econ* 265, 293, reprinted in *The Journal of Reprints for Antitrust Law and Economics,* Vertical Restraints (Part II) p. 293.

[99] Many are explained by **Klein** and **Murphy**, above n. 98.

[100] **Robert L. Steiner**, "The Nature of Vertical Restraints," (1985) 30 *The Antitrust Bulletin* 143, 171–74 and **Scherer** and **Ross**, *Industrial Market Structure and Economic Performance*, 3rd. ed. (Boston, Houghton Mifflin Company, 1990) 552–55. Scherer and Ross explain several limitations to the certification free rider argument.

This is part of the free rider argument. The prestigious shop may not want to share its prestige with the new brand owner unless promised exclusive rights for a period. Discounters, however, usually need some famous brands to attract customers, so, in the longer term, the limitation of the vertical restriction in time may enable new discounters to reach a minimum efficient scale sooner (1.2.3.4 above).

1.2.4.2 Avoiding double marginalisation

Where there is some market power, and the supplier sells to a dealer promised an exclusive territory at its profit maximising price, the dealer may take that as a fixed cost and sell at its profit maximising price. The final price from the dealer may be greater than the profit maximising price would be if the supplier were to do its own distribution. Maximum rpm may reduce the dealer's possibility of adding another monopoly margin. This argument, however, does not justify fixed or minimum rpm.

A possible justification for maximum rpm is to enable a brand-owner to charge different wholesale prices depending on demand. *Ex ante,* the brand owner may not know the level of demand in different areas. **Dernecke, Marvel** and **Peck**[101] show that the average quantity sold with rpm could be greater than without, as the resale price can be fixed later, when the demand is better known, and could come nearer to the profit maximising price.

1.2.4.3 Savings on transaction costs—fewer people
with whom brand owner has to deal

In recital 5 of Regulation 1983/83 (now expired and replaced by Regulation 2790/99) the Commission gave an unusual justification for exclusive distribution, which is based on the problems of terminating an exclusive dealer under some European national laws. It states:

> Whereas exclusive distribution agreements lead in general to an improvement in distribution because the undertaking is able to concentrate its sales activities, does not need to maintain numerous business relations with a larger number of dealers and is able, by dealing with only one dealer, to overcome more easily distribution difficulties in international trade resulting from linguistic, legal and other differences;

This is an example of what is sometimes called minimising the transaction costs of doing business.[102]

The problem of avoiding a proliferation of dealers used to be more acute in some European countries than elsewhere. In France it was, until recently, a crime to refuse to supply dealers prepared to order in normal commercial quantities, but the existence of an exclusive distribution agreement was a defence. Consequently,

---

[101] "Demand Uncertainty and Price Maintenance: Markdowns as Destructive Competition", (1997) 87 *American Economic Review* 619–41.

[102] See generally **Oliver E. Williamson**, *Markets and Hierarchies* (New York, Free Press, 1975).

suppliers were encouraged to grant exclusive territories in order to avoid having to supply any other reputable dealer. The position is not very different in Germany,[103] Italy and some other European countries. In the common law countries, there is no general duty to deal. It may be that the law criminalising refusals to sell has led to the grant of exclusive territories even where no distribution efficiency arguments apply. This seems to be avoidance of a regulatory distortion rather than a justification.

A related argument applies when the brand owner does not sell directly to retailers and it becomes difficult for the brand owner to ensure that point of sales services are supplied because it has no easy way to monitor. **Klein** and **Murphy**[104] argue that increasing the retailer's margin by maintaining resale prices increases the incentive of the retailer to provide the services. Withholding supplies to non-performing retailers becomes a more serious threat.

1.2.5 Concerns about Single Branding (1.2.2.1, above and chapter 5 below)

The converse practice, obligations accepted by dealers to handle a single brand in a line of products and other contractual provisions having a similar, if attenuated, effect may restrict competition between suppliers in various ways (1.2.2.1 above and chapter 5 below). The Commission, in Guideline 138 to Regulation 2790/99, calls these "single branding" arrangements.

1.2.5.1 Foreclosure

The concern of the ECJ about an obligation accepted by a dealer to handle a single brand, formerly called "a non-compete" or "exclusive purchasing" clause, is that it may foreclose other suppliers. In other words, competition from rival suppliers may be restricted. An outlet that has agreed for a long period to take much of its total requirements of a product or group of products from a particular supplier will not be free to take much of that product from anyone else. Other suppliers are shut off or "foreclosed" from that outlet. This, however, does not affect competition on the market when there are many free outlets through whom a new or expanding supplier could dispose of its output.[105]

In *Stergios Delimitis* v. *Henninger Bräu*,[106] the ECJ confirmed that the possible competitive concern about exclusive purchasing agreements was foreclosure, but observed that third parties would be foreclosed only if insufficient real and

---

[103] **D. Brault**, "Refusals to Supply: Should the French Rules be Harmonised with those of the EEC?" (1981) 3 *Northwestern J Int'l L & Bus* 384.

[104] "Vertical Restraints as Contract Enforcement Mechanisms," (1988) 31 *JL Econ* 265, 266. See the discussion of the FTC action against *Coors* at 1.2.6.5 below.

[105] In *Langnese-Iglo GmbH & Co. KG* v. *Commission*, Case T-7/93 [1995] ECR II-1533, the CFI criticised the Commission's decision for failing to decide how serious the foreclosure was under Article 81(1), but leaving the market analysis until it was considering Article 81(3).

[106] Case C-234/89 [1991] ECR I-935, para. 14 *et seq.* (7.2.3 below).

concrete possibilities remained for them to enter the market on an efficient scale or to expand. Competitors might be able to do this by opening new outlets or buying a competitor who already had a chain of tied outlets. It would be less easy to enter if the market were saturated or if there were a few well known brands to which consumers were loyal.

The Court added that even if there were barriers to entry at the level downstream and so many outlets were tied by exclusive purchasing obligations to one or other supplier for so long that others were foreclosed, it would be only the agreements made by the suppliers who contributed substantially to the foreclosure that would be illegal. So, it seems that a larger brewer might be allowed to tie for a short period. The Court did not indicate how long or how large the ties might be, save to refer to what was normal in the trade. This criterion has the grave disadvantage of penalising innovation.[107]

At Guideline 107, the Commission observes that not only does keeping other suppliers out make the supplier's market more concentrated, it makes it more rigid. It will be more difficult for the more efficient suppliers to expand at the cost of those less efficient. It will also prevent consumers being able to compare brands in the same store.

1.2.5.1.1 *Tying*

Another kind of foreclosure occurs when a supplier refuses to supply one product unless another be taken. The view of main stream economists, accepted by the Commission in Guideline 107(4), was that tying may force customers to pay a higher price for the tied product.

The answer from the Chicago school is that to the extent that customers would prefer not to take the tied product, they will pay less for the tying product, so suppliers are very unlikely to tie for this reason. There is only one monopoly profit to be made. Tying will not increase their profit overall. Tying, therefore, must occur for other reasons.

Where there are many other sources of both the tying and the tied product, there is no problem. No one objects to supermarket selling two or three chocolate products in a single pack, even if the total price is less than that for buying each item on its own, provided that all the items are easily available separately. The package serves as a quantity discount and may save time at the till.

The most common reason for tying where the market is concentrated is that a supplier may want to charge an intensive user of equipment or a facility more than it charges those to whom the tying product is worth less. No one objects to a royalty for a technology licence of X per cent although a licensee using the invention a lot will pay more than one who uses it less.

In theory tying could be avoided by charging a royalty, but in practice it may not be easy to monitor the amount of usage. It may be more reliable to arrange that

---

[107] See Warwick Rothnie's criticism of the Commission's decision in *ARD—Re Film Purchases by German TV Stations* OJ 1989, L284/36, [1990] 4 CMLR 841, [1990] 2 EIPR 72, 2.5.2 below.

some consumable be tied to the tying product, and the profit be made from sell-ing that rather than from a royalty. If the licensor sees the final product made from a different consumable, the licensor knows that it should investigate. The tie does not increase the aggregate cost of the two items to the buyer, but it may foreclose other suppliers of the tied product or its substitute. This matters only if there is a shortage of outlets for those products, which is seldom the case.

Another reason for tying is that the price of the tying product is limited by reg-ulation, and the supplier wants to avoid the effects of regulation by earning its monopoly profit on the tied product. Few price regulators would fail to object to such a strategy. There are many other innocent commercial reasons for tying.

Another form of tying is sometimes called "mixed bundling". A firm with some market power sells the complementary products separately, but sells two or more at less than the stand alone prices of each. Suppose that many customers want to buy products A, B and C. In deciding on the total price, the supplier takes into account the effects that the price of one will have on the sales of the others. Economists say that this involves internalisation of a pricing externality. It avoids "double marginalisation" (1.2.4.2 above). In Valentine's view, this is desirable as consumers obtain the package more cheaply, but competitors may complain that if they cannot sell the package, but only one item, they are at a competitive disad-vantage, especially if the bundler has significant market power.

1.2.5.2 Raising rivals' costs

A somewhat broader concern noted more in the United States than in Europe is that established firms may make it more expensive for new firms to enter, even if some outlets remain free.[108] Once many outlets are tied, it may become more expensive for others to tie further outlets or to persuade free outlets to stock their products. On this view, even if some free outlets remain, one should consider whether sup-plying them is as profitable as supplying those that are already foreclosed.

Krattenmaker and **Salop**, who developed this theory, think that such situations are rare. They presuppose market power and barriers to entry. Like Williamson, Scherer and others, they think that barriers are more prevalent than simplistic Chicago assumptions allow.

Kenneth Elzinga[109] agrees that the problem is rare, save when the government is persuaded to raise rivals' costs, for instance after a complaint about dumping. A complaint under the competition rules to the ED Commission may, sometimes,

---

[108] See **Krattenmaker** and **Salop**, "Anticompetitive Exclusion: Raising Rivals' Costs to Achieve Power over Price," 96 *Yale LJ* and **Salop** and **Scheffman**, "Raising Rivals' Cost," (1983) 73 *American Economic Review* 267.

For a resumé of more recent developments in the theory see, e.g., **Jonathan B. Baker**, "Recent Developments in Economics that Challenge Chicago School Views," (1989) 58 *Antitrust LJ* 645, 647 and the works cited at note 10 therein. An interesting recent contribution focussing on the European guidelines is by **S. Salop**, "Vertical restraints under EC law," in **Barry Hawk** (ed.) [2000] *Fordham Corporate Law Institute*, 177, 183.

[109] Speech at a conference organised by the Conference Board of New York, 6 March, 1991.

be a cheap way of raising the costs of a competitor, but it is seldom that tying retail outlets to raise the costs of competitors is worth the cost to the incumbent(s). Even if entry to retailing be not easy, only when most retailers have been persuaded or paid to give up their freedom will the price of further ties increase and significant foreclosure occur.

Nevertheless, where entry barriers downstream are high, non-compete clauses may raise rivals' costs. In the UK, planning rules interfere with the siting of petrol stations. Only if there is a stretch of new road of more than 12 miles without a garage will permission to build a new one normally be given, and then there must be a garage on both sides of the road, to avoid accidents caused by crossing to enter a garage.[110] Consequently, when AGIP attempted to enter the UK market it took so long for it to find acceptable sites for new garages that eventually it gave up the effort. The cost of tying free garages when Esso first did so was not high, but it became higher as fewer free stations remained and they realised their negotiating power.

Professor Salop argues that:

> The existence of input suppliers (e.g., distributors supplying the distribution service to suppliers) who are not tied up by the exclusive arrangements means that rivals have options and are not totally foreclosed. However, other input suppliers may not be sufficient to prevent rivals' costs from being raised. First the ability of remaining input suppliers to expand may be constrained by capacity limits. Second, their costs and prices may be higher than the suppliers who are parties to the exclusives. Third, if there are only a small number of unrestrained suppliers, they may have the incentive to raise their prices in response to the exclusives. This is because they no longer face competition from the input suppliers who now have been tied by the exclusives and can no longer sell to certain potential customers. In this sense, the exclusives may facilitate tacit or express collusion among the unrestrained suppliers still available to the rivals. This last condition sometimes is overlooked in vertical restraint analysis. Doing so creates a significant potential for error.[110a]

Professor Salop adds (183) that consumers are harmed only if raising rivals' costs leads to higher prices.

> The inquiry here focuses on the issue of whether output market prices will likely increase or whether rivals in the relevant output market, both the excluded firms and other firms that produce close substitutes, instead will maintain the ability and incentive to compete effectively. Because there may be close substitutes for the product the firm that achieves the exclusives and its competitors, injury to these competitors does not necessarily imply injury to consumers. Instead, competition among non-excluded firms may remain intense and there may be competition with other firms that have their own

---

[110] In the UK when branded petrol first started to be sold after the war Esso was able to obtain ties for £100 per station—a grant to enable the retailer to refurbish its stations and paint it in Esso colours. By the time Petrofina started to pay for ties they cost far more. *Report of the Monopolies Commission on the Supply of Petrol to Retailers in the United Kingdom*, 1965, HC 264. See p. 167 for the planning authority's practice.

[110a] "An Analysis of Foreclosure in the EC Guidelines on Vertical Restraints" in Barry Hawk (ed.) [2000] *Fordham Corporate Law Institute*, 177, 183.

exclusives. This last point means that multiple exclusives actually may cause less of an anticompetitive effect, a type of "reverse" cumulative effect. . . . Competition with substitute products may also prevent prices from rising.

Consumers are harmed only if single branding both raises rivals costs and leads to higher prices. In Europe, however, there have been traditional concerns about excluded competitors. So the second step of seeing whether prices have been raised may be omitted.

Unlike the holder of classical market power which raises prices by restricting its own production, the beneficiary of single branding raises prices by restricting the output of others.

1.2.5.3 Rigidity and facilitating actual or tacit collusion

Another objection to long term vertical single branding provisions, whereby the buyer agrees to handle mainly a single brand, is that the market may become rigid, even if there are many buyers and sellers within it. It may be harder for a more efficient supplier to expand its share of the market at the expense of less efficient competitors.

Moreover, long term single branding agreements may perpetuate a horizontal market allocation arrangement made before the application of the competition rules if adopted throughout a concentrated market where there are high barriers to entry at the dealer level, as noted by the Australian Trade Practices Tribunal in re Tooth & Co. Ltd.[111]

1.2.5.4 The protection of smaller firms and freedom

Nevertheless, the EC competition rules have not been concerned only to increase efficiency. The protection of small and medium-sized firms and liberty are also mentioned in the preamble to the Treaty. If these are also objectives of the competition rules, keeping out suppliers who want to enter a market may be perceived as anti-competitive, even if this does not lead to higher prices for the product.[112] To the extent that small firms are equally efficient, they need no special protection.[113] To the extent that they are not, protecting them may restrain larger firms

[111] (1979) ATPR 40-113, 18,174. See **Frances Hanks** and **Philip Williams**, "The Treatment of Vertical Restraints under the Australian Trade Practices Act," [1987] *Australian Business Law Review* 147,151. The article explains a wide range of economic literature in terms comprehensible to layers. The authors conclude that vertical restraints cannot restrict competition unless there is market power at both levels of trade and the restraints are long lasting.

[112] In *Metro II*, Case 75/84 [1986] ECR 3021, at 3064 and 3065, Advocate General VerLoren van Themaat described shortly the views in the national laws of member states about freedom of access, in a context of collective boycotts. Under only some of these laws was efficiency an important consideration.

[113] They may need exemption from some of the bureaucratic form filling requirements of member states, which is proportionately more expensive for them than for larger firms. For instance, firms with small turnover may choose to be exempt from the VAT regime, although they would pay less tax if they were not.

from operating as efficiently as possible. The costs in efficiency of protecting smaller firms may be significant.

As the Commission's guidelines accept, since important buyers are unlikely to agree to buy from a single source without some inducement, all suppliers are free to compete for such contracts. The freedom of the dealers exists at the moment it makes the agreement or when the tie comes up for renewal.

1.2.6 Justifications for Single Branding

1.2.6.1 Counterpart to exclusive supply obligation

At first, officials perceived exclusive purchasing obligations accepted by dealers as the counterpart of an exclusive territory,[114] but there are trades where exclusive territories are not balanced by exclusive purchasing obligations—the supplier may want consumers to be able to compare brands[115]—and there are other trades, such as the supply of beer, where exclusive purchasing by retailers is not balanced by an exclusive territory. The justification based on counterpart may be an example of the formalism which the Commission is beginning to abandon in favour of a more economic approach. Nevertheless, the Commission says in its guidelines:

> 158. Below the level of dominance the combination of non-compete with exclusive distribution may also justify the non-compete obligation lasting the full length of the agreement. In the latter case, the non-compete obligation is likely to improve the distribution efforts of the exclusive distributor in its territory (see paragraphs 161 to 177).

1.2.6.2 Counterpart to duty to supply dealer's full requirements

One economic justification for exclusive purchasing obligations arises where the dealer wants to be able to ensure continuing supplies, but is unable to estimate its requirements. Suppliers may not be prepared to agree to supply whatever quantity the dealer may choose to order if the dealer is free to buy unlimited amounts from third parties.

Exclusive purchasing seldom restricts competition. Few dealers need to persuade their supplier to agree to accept all their orders. Repeated small orders for specified quantities may be placed and, if one supplier is not prepared to supply, a supplier of another brand is likely to want to supply. Only if there is a paucity of competing suppliers and a shortage of the product is there likely to be a problem.

If, however, the dealer is going to have to invest heavily in specialised staff or equipment for handling the product of a specific supplier, it may need its supplier to be bound by a continuing duty to supply its requirements to make the

---

[114] Until in *de Norre* v. *Concordia*, Case 47/76 [1977] ECR 65, the ECJ held that a single branding agreement where the café owner enjoyed no exclusive territory, qualified under Regulation 67/67.

[115] As in *Villeroy and Boch*, OJ 1985, L376/15, [1988] 4 CMLR 461.

investment worthwhile.[116] Sometimes the problem is overcome by the supplier paying for all or part of the cost of the equipment etc. Recital 5 to Regulation 1984/83 (expired and replaced by Regulation 2790/99) refers to ensuring that the reseller's requirements will be met on a regular basis for the duration of the agreement.

1.2.6.3 May prevent retailer from taking a ride on the manufacturer's advertising by switching to other brands

The FTC obtained a court order restraining Coors from requiring bars and restaurants to buy only Coors' light coloured beer for sale in draught from it. Economists have suggested, however, that Coors' conduct might have been justified. Coors advertised its light coloured beer, and most customers ordering it, would not know if the local tavern or restaurant substituted another brand of draught.

Had the beer come in bottles or cans, or been dark the customer probably would have known.[117]

1.2.6.4 May help the supplier to plan its activities

Recital 5 of Regulation 1984/83 (now expired and replaced by Regulation 2790/99) refers to enabling the supplier to plan the sales of its goods with greater precision over longer periods. This may be important, but the supplier can usually achieve this objective by a less restrictive alternative.

It might enter into agreements to supply minimum quantities lasting for long enough to justify investment in production capacity and distribution facilities. This might foreclose somewhat less where the dealer's requirements cannot be anticipated accurately because, to the extent that the supplier under estimated the dealer's requirements, other suppliers would be able to make offers to it. Another less restrictive alternative is for the supplier to give quantity discounts. In *Delimitis*,[118] the ECJ said that a non-compete clause did not have the object of restricting competition as it helped the supplier to plan its distribution, but it then considered the criteria relevant to appraising its effect.

---

[116] This is an example of the "hold-up problem" considered at 1.2.4.1.1 above, where the sunk cost of building the pipeline in the context of an exclusive supply agreement was considered. See also Guidelines 116(4) and 155 where the Commission accepts the need to encourage specific investment, but only under Article 81(3), not under Article 81(1).

[117] Described in **Dennis W. Carlton** and **Jeffrey M. Perloff**, *Modern Industrial Organisation*, 3rd ed. p. 406, example 12.6.

See also 1.2.6.5 below where it is suggested that the single branding restriction might be supported by an exclusive territory to encourage a bar operator or restaurateur not to shirk on the cost of keeping draught beer properly.

[118] *Delimitis (Stergios)* v. *Henninger Bräu*, Case C-234/89 [1991] ECR I-935.

1.2.6.5 *Free rider justifications*

Another justification, mentioned in recital 6 of Regulation 1984/83 (expired and replaced by Regulation 2790/99) and Guideline 116, is inducing the supplier to provide benefits for its dealers. If a supplier of alcoholic drinks provides cafés with loans or equipment at less than an economic charge, or a brand owner invests in training a dealer's staff, it will want to ensure that these services do not inure to the benefit of its competitors.[119] It may be objected, however, that this problem could be, and often is, overcome by the supplier charging the dealers for these services rather than tying them.

Training services may be provided more cheaply by the supplier who can set up courses for the staff of several dealers. Moreover, it may be more efficient for the supplier than an outside lender to finance equipment or the modification of premises for the dealer because, for example, of its close connections with the dealer which results in the credit risk being smaller than in the case of an independent lender. It may, however, be easier to justify exclusive purchasing and the price paid for it on the European Community's desire to help small and medium sized firms than on efficiency.

Another free rider justification is that a dealer may gain a reputation for handling high quality products and use it to start handling rival products unless the first supplier is protected. Promotion by one supplier at the dealer's premises may also attract other suppliers to the premises to take a free ride on it.

A more sophisticated justification for Coors' single branding restraint (1.2.6.3 above) might be that the storage of draught beer must be carefully organised and the pipes kept clean. A retailer might shirk on these costs harming the reputation of the Coors brand. Customers might not know why the beer was not so good and switch to another tavern selling competing light beer.

Coors, however, might be able to make spot checks on the storage and hygiene from time to time and cut off shirking retailers. To make this an effective sanction, the retailer would have be persuaded that Coors was a profitable brand to sell and Coors might also give it an exclusive territory and not limit the retail prices by maximum rpm too tightly as to take away all monopoly profit.

1.2.7 Cumulation of Restrictions may Reduce Problems

The Commission accepts at paragraph 67 of *The Green Paper*[120] that the cumulation of restrictions may, or may not, aggravate the anticompetitive effects of an agreement. If a free rider problem is solved by giving the dealer an exclusive

---

[119] **Klein** and **Saft**, "The Law and Economics of Franchise Tying," (1985) 28 *JL & Econ* 345 argue also that the supplier is willing to invest in creating a common and uniform reputation amongst its dealers only if it can capture all the value of the reputation. It will not do so if its competitors can share in the benefit of its investment.

[120] On vertical restraints in EC Competition Policy, COM(96) 721 final, [1997] 4 CMLR 519.

territory, the dealer would gain any market power that the supplier might have. Imposing a maximum resale price might prevent the dealer taking advantage of this. Section III 2.2 of the *Follow up to the Green Paper on Vertical Restraints*[121] repeats the point with rather more examples each way.

1.3 BUYER POWER

Concern has been expressed in several countries about buyer power generally, and more particularly in relation to supermarket chains perceived as the gateway for producers to get their products to the public. Lobbying is intense. The concern about market power has arisen mainly in relation to the merger of large supermarket chains in national markets and with that a book on distribution is not directly concerned.

Buying power is often combined with some selling power downstream. If there were alternative retailers competing to supply consumers, small and medium-sized producers would be able to sell to them and the large multiple retailers would have little buying power.

The recent economic literature is extensive.[122]

1.3.1 Combinations of Small Firms to Match the Buying Power of their Competitors

The first question is what should be done to prevent buying power from arising. It may be that the problem of buyer power is best tackled structurally, through the control of mergers leading to a collective dominant position and of buying groups. With these horizontal aspects, this book on distribution is not directly concerned, but with the conduct of buyers who are already powerful towards their suppliers. Buyer power may be increased or exploited by various practices that concern distribution.

---

[121] OJ 1998, C365/3.

[122] In [2000] *Fordham Corporate Law Institute* a session was devoted to problems of buyer power, including **Margaret Bloom**, "Retailer Buying Power," **Philip G.H. Collins**, "Retailer Buyer Power: Abusive Behaviour and Mergers/Acquisitions," **Ulf Böge**, "Retailer Buyer Power in German Competition law," **Patrick Rey**, "Retailer Buying Power and Competition Policy," with a huge list of economic contributions, **Debra A. Valentine**, "Retailer Buyer Power: Abusive Behaviour and Mergers/Acquisitions, Roundtable, Prepared Remarks," **Joachim Lücking**, "Retailer Power in EC Competition Law."

See also **C.D. Ehlermann** and **L. Laudati** (eds.) *Proceedings of the European Competition Forum*, (Chichester, John Wiley & Sons Ltd., 1997) Part 3 "Economic Dependence", pp.183 *et seq.*, where many competition officials explained and criticised laws intended to reduce economic dependence.

The FTC held hearings on buyer power in May 2001. Transcripts are posted on the FTC website, http://www.ftc.gov.bc/slotting/index/htm.

Most of one issue of (2001) 15 *Antitrust* 69 was devoted to discussions of the proceedings of the FTC by leading economists.

See "Buyer Power", *Lexecon competition memo*, www.lexecon.co.uk.

The most obvious remedy is for antitrust authorities to minimise barriers to entry. They may advocate that planning controls to protect the environment do not unduly increase barriers to the entry or expansion of large retailers by making it unnecessarily difficult to open new stores out of town.

The ECJ has accepted that small independent firms may combine to increase their buying power against important suppliers. Buyers with small shares of the relevant market were allowed to combine into a cooperative in *H.G. Oude Luttikhuis and others* v. *Verenigde Cooperatiëve Melkindustrie Coberco*[123] and in *Gottrup Klim*,[124] but not in *Rennet*[125] where the cooperative had a virtual buying monopoly. The Commission has also accepted in *SPAR*[126] that joint buying by small grocers to reduce their disadvantage as against larger retailers may not appreciably restrict competition. The vertical agreements made by associations all of whose members are small may benefit from Regulation 2790/99 (3.4.7 below).

We think that this is basically the right approach. Small buyers need to obtain the economies of scale and scope and the negotiating strength enjoyed by their larger competitors. Combining to match their buying power may reduce the discrimination they suffer from suppliers, and increase competition. Unfortunately, however, the Commission and Court have not focused on the question how much buying power is needed for this purpose save to say it should be proportionate. Proportionate to what? It must vary from one market to another and over time. The minimum efficient scale for buying and selling and the levels of competition left in the market should be relevant.

1.3.2 Economic Dependence

In Europe, after the second world war, there was concern about the buying power of large multiple retailers and of buying groups, where independent firms combined their purchases to increase their buying power. Some suppliers complained that they suffered from discrimination. This was difficult to ascertain, because some suppliers and some buyers provided services not provided by others, such as storage, display services and analysis of demand trends. What price concessions in their favour were justifiable? Should they be based on the cost to the provider of the service or the benefit to the recipient when the system yielded efficiencies? Some very valuable services can be provided cheaply.

In Germany, France and Portugal there is legislation forbidding the abuse of economic dependence where the dependent firm had no equivalent alternative.[127]

---

[123] Case C-399/93 [1995] ECR I-4515.

[124] Case C-250/92 [1994] ECR I-5641.

[125] *Rennet* OJ 1980, L51/19, [1980] 2 CMLR 402, on appeal, *Stremsel* v. *Commission*, Case 61/80 [1981] ECR 851.

[126] *Re Intergroup Trading BV*, OJ 1975, L212/23, [1975] 2 CMLR D14.

[127] See e.g., **C.D. Ehlermann** and **L. Laudati**, *Proceedings of the European Competition Forum*, (Chichester, John Wiley & Sons Ltd., 1997) Part 3 "Economic Dependence", where experience under such legislation was described, analysed and criticised by competition officials in several member states.

Some countries have also banned discrimination by firms with buying or selling power. The application of the law has been of questionable utility. Even if there are only a few buyers, it is difficult to show that one of them applied unavoidable pressure on its suppliers, or that price differences were not due to differences in the services offered by suppliers or buyers. Suppliers hesitate to state in court that they are dependent on their customers for fear of harming their negotiating position.

In the *Proceedings of the European Competition Forum*, many of the contributors, competition experts from Member States, agreed with Professor Van Gerven[128] that the focus should now shift to protecting consumers rather than competitors. If, however, there is little competition downstream, economic dependence may become a competition concern.

If the object of competition law is to favour consumers, there should be little concern about the buying power of multiple retailers when they compete with each other downstream and competition forces them to pass on the benefits to shoppers.[129] Where there is competition downstream, however, there is unlikely to be much buyer power as there must be other middlemen to whom disfavoured producers can sell. So, where multiple retailers have buying power, competition downstream is unlikely to be very strong.

Rarely does a single supermarket chain enjoy a dominant position even within a regional market, but now that collective dominant positions are subject to control under Article 82[130] it is important that abuses are not found too easily. Some suppliers have more market power than others, so it is likely that supermarket

---

[128] **Ehlermann** and **Laudati**, above n. 127, p.183.

[129] See General Report of the UK Monopolies and Mergers Commission on Discounts to Retailers, 1981, HC 311, where the Commission concluded at 9.22 that:

> Consumers' interests are best safeguarded and promoted where competition flourishes. We have found that the practice has not in general had an adverse effect on competition among suppliers in the retail trade. On the contrary it has been widely associated with enhanced price competition among manufacturers. At the same time, the generally vigourous competition among retailers has so far ensured that the benefits of this competition among retailers has so far ensured that the benefits of this competition have in the main been passed on to the consumer in one form or another.
>
> 9.23 We conclude that the general effect of the practice on the public interest over recent years has not been harmful. Rather the practice has been part and parcel of developments which have been beneficial to competition and to the consumer. For the future, however, we recognise that this conclusion holds good only so long as there continues to be effective competition among suppliers and among retailers. We draw attention to the danger that the practice might encourage concentration in retailing to such an extent as to have harmful consequences.

Charles Baden Fuller, "Rising Concentration: The UK Grocery Trade 1970–1980," in *Firms and Markets, Essays in Honour of Basil Yamey*, K. Tucker and C. Baden Fuller (eds.) chapter 3, pp. 63, 76–79 was concerned that not only was concentration in the grocery trade still rising, laser check out systems were likely to impose a barrier to the entry of smaller firms. In the future the benefits of discriminatory prices may no longer be passed on.

The Competition Commission, *Supermarkets: a report on the supply of groceries from multiple stores in the UK*, 10 October 2000, CM 4842 found that various discriminatory buying practices by supermarket chains with market power should be controlled by a code of practice, although it found that the industry was still broadly competitive despite the barrier to entry caused by the difficulty of obtaining planning permission to open new large selling spaces out of town.

[130] *France* v. *Commission*, Cases C-68/94 and 30/95 [1998] ECR I-1375, (appeal from *Kali und Salz* (IV/M.308) OJ 1993, L395/1); *Compagnie Maritime Belge*, Case-395/96P [2000] ECR I-1365.

chains discriminate in their favour. A blanket prohibition of discrimination, however, is difficult to implement, since it is usually very difficult to quantify differential costs and benefits. Some brands attract consumers more than others and their
suppliers can negotiate higher prices than the holders of less popular brands.

The problems of farmers are particularly acute, because most of their produce
perishes rapidly, creating a hold-up problem. If one supermarket chain should
cease to deal with a particular producer or reduce the price it is prepared to pay,
there is unlikely to be time to arrange for another chain to do so. This may chill
their willingness to make relationship specific investments, such as packaging that
fits only the shelves of a specific retailer. We see no reason why retailers wanting
such investment should not make long term contracts to take a minimum quantity at a minimum price. This would reduce the scale of the problem, although it
would not remove it altogether.

There is concern also about sales below cost, but one should carefully examine
how "cost" is defined. In France the Galland law of 1996 forbids hypermarkets to
sell below the wholesale price that appears on the invoice, even if rebates later
amount to 20 or 40 per cent. This creates a price floor, which would be illegal if
agreed between producers.

1.3.3 Slotting Allowances

Concern is growing also in the USA about the practice of slotting allowances
required particularly in the grocery sector. The FTC held a workshop on slotting
allowances[131] and some of the practices and arguments are conveniently explained
by **Ronald W. Davis**.[132] A supermarket may require a fee from the supplier of a
new brand or even of a brand it already stocks, in order to obtain or retain space
on the buyer's shelves. Small suppliers complain that they cannot compete with
larger suppliers and that for many categories of products, supermarkets are stocking only a couple of independent brands and the house brand of the store.

One justification for requiring such payments is that even a supermarket cannot stock all the brands. To stock an extra one, it will probably have to throw out
old, reasonably successful, brands. This involves costs, burdens and risks. The
shelves will have to be emptied, old products disposed of, shelves restocked, products labelled and the scanners reprogrammed.

Large retailers would like new suppliers to cover some of these costs and risk.
One possibility is to require a "failure fee"—to charge a supplier if its brand does
not sell as well as expected; another is to require a slotting allowance. There are
many variations on the theme.

Some large manufacturers refuse to pay such fees. Other manufacturers and
growers pay under protest and complain to the antitrust agencies. Others pay

---

[131] Transcripts are posted on the FTC website, http://www.ftc.gov.bc/slotting/index.htm.
[132] On 31 May and 1 June 2000, "Developments in Distribution, A Mystery Wrapped in an Enigma:
Slotting Allowances and Antitrust," (2001) 15 *Antitrust* 69.

regularly and appear not to mind. Is that because they are considered reasonable and the amounts not too large, or because it helps to maintain the market share of the existing strong brands by raising the cost of introducing a new brand and protects shelf space from new entrants?

Practices vary: some retailers do not require slotting allowances, some require them only for new products, where there may be a cost justification, some also for old established products. There may also be other fees, such as a "presentation fee" in return for the opportunity for the brand owner to make a presentation, display fees, advertising allowances, fees to have one's brand displayed at eye level or at the end of a stack etc.

We use the term slotting allowances to refer to:

1) a sum payable in advance, unrelated to the amount sold,
2) contingent on the amount of shelf space, facings etc.,
3) not dependent on the retailer doing anything else, and
4) possibly, but not necessarily, contingent on the retailer agreeing not to sell other brands of similar products.

Even without an express commitment by the retailer not to promote or sell competing brands, the commitment of a specific amount of space forecloses that amount to other suppliers. Where several suppliers pay the slotting fee there may not be much space remaining for other brands of that product.

At the FTC's workshop there was substantial agreement that there is a wide range of such practices, and that since the payment is not proportional to turnover, the benefit is not always passed on to consumers. The fees would, however, make retailing more profitable and might result in more retailers competing.

It was also agreed that the fees for new products only were, by definition, barriers to entry[133] but they were the fees most likely to lead to efficiencies. Willard Tom, giving evidence for the FTC said:[134]

> Taking on a new product confronts the retailer with not only the actual costs of restocking shelves, changing labels, and reprogramming scanner equipment, but also the potential cost of product failure and being left with unsold inventory. Moreover, taking on a new product often means that some other product must be dropped from a store. The average supermarket stocks 30,000 items, but fully 100,000 grocery products are available from manufacturers, and another 10–15,000 new ones are offered each year. Supermarkets cannot stock all the available products, and when a new product comes in, that typically means an old product must go; under these circumstances it may be reasonable to ask the manufacturer, which has usually done the test marketing and has the best information about the potential of each individual product to bear some of the supermarket's risk if it wants to persuade the supermarket to try the product.

---

[133] If the incumbent had had to pay such fees when it first sold in the supermarket, it is unclear to Valentine that fees only for new products are an entry barrier.

[134] Now at Morgan Lewis and Bockius in Washington DC (2001) 15 *Antitrust* 69 at pp. 71 and 72.

Steven Salop perceived the main danger to competition as the fees being given in return for excluding new entrants.[135] He accepted, however, that slotting fees led to efficiencies and should not be condemned without the application of a full rule of reason. They should not be automatically treated as illegal, proof should be required that the effects were exclusionary.

Willard Tom said that relevant factors included:

What does the retailer offer in exchange for the payment?

—Is it a payment simply to be carried somewhere in the store?
—Is it for a fixed amount of shelf space?
—Is it for preferential display—the end-caps or eye-level shelves?
—Is it for the right to be the exclusive, or nearly exclusive, supplier in that product category?
—Is it for the right to control what other products in that category will be allowed on the shelves?
—Is it for a long or short time?

The answer to these questions can have a major effect on how much room is left for other suppliers in the market, and therefore on whether the allowances are harmful or innocuous, procompetitive or anticompetitive.[136]

The effect of slotting allowances on small manufacturers is controversial, as is the effect on consumers. Three sources of potential harm to consumers are:

1) reduced competition among manufacturers which may lead to higher wholesale prices passed on to consumers.
2) reduced competition among manufacturers which might lead to reduced variety or investment in quality.
3) buying power among retailers might be exercised in the form of slotting allowances, which improve the retailers' profits without being passed on to consumers.

All these possibilities are problematic. As to the first, brands usually become dominant because of superior quality or attractiveness and it would be hard to distinguish those effects from reduced competition. Some wonder whether consumers have more variety than they need, and some retailers pass on part of lump sum payments to consumers.

Not enough is known about the practices for the issuing of clear antitrust guidelines in the United States.

It is clear, in European law, that a promise by the retailer not to stock competing brands may foreclose, and infringes Article 81(1) when there are entry barriers at the retail level[137] and so many retailers tied to one or other of the suppliers,

---

[135] At p. 73.
[136] At p. 74.
[137] The most obvious barrier is the difficulty of obtaining planning consent for the creation of a new, large outlet.

that insufficient retailers remain to enable a new supplier to operate on an efficient scale.[138]

1.3.4 Category Management

In the same issue of *Antitrust*, **Robert Steiner** explained and analysed a pervasive new vertical/horizontal format—category management—which started in super-markets in the mid-1990s and rapidly swept across non-food categories in the US, Europe and elsewhere.[139]

The key insights are that supplier and customer each benefit if the other is more efficient and that many costs can be slashed by information sharing. As early as 1992, single suppliers and single retailers had achieved considerable savings, mainly in logistics.

This was carried further in the 1990s. The basic idea of category management is that a retail store decides to manage its business on the basis of categories of prod-ucts. For each, it appoints one of the leading manufacturers in the field as "Category Captain". The Category Captain and its team work with the retailer's "category manager."

The Captain collects detailed information on the recent performance of all the brands in the category and formulates a plan to the retailer for the whole category, not just the brands of the captain's firm. Some of the information can be bought from research firms such as IRI or Nielsen, but some might have to come from competing manufacturers, creating a horizontal problem. The retailer adds the output of its scanners and loyalty programmes. The plan specifies the stock keep-ing units the retailer should carry, the retail price of each, the layout of the retailer's "plan-o-gram" and often also a promotional plan for the retailer.

The retailer need not accept the Captain's plan, but frequently does. The verti-cal combination of information may lead to significant efficiencies, not only in logistics: such as demand led production and just in time delivery, but also elim-inating slow moving stock, reengineering store fittings, creating "store friendly" packaging etc. Nevertheless, there are competitive dangers in such cooperation. To control the Captain's tendency to promote its own firm's products, some retailers arrange for stocking decisions to be subject to a second opinion.

Cooperation is intense and loyalty is required. The retailer must be sure that the confidential information it provides is not passed on to its competitors and vice versa. Consequently, there may be a tendency not to compete for such margin as intensively as previously. The parties may be happy to increase the combined mar-gins of supplier and retailer, rather than compete for whatever margin there may be for the product.

---

[138] *Delimitis (Stergios)* v. *Henninger Bräu, Case* C-234/89, [1991] ECR I-935, 2.7.3 and 5.1.1.1.3 below.
[139] **R. Steiner**, "Category Management—a Pervasive, New Vertical/Horizontal Format," (2001) 15 *Antitrust* 77.

1.3.5 Conclusion on Buyer Power

From thinking in both Europe and the USA, it is clear that it is not easy to know what to do about buyer power. The focus depends in part on whether one is concerned about fair bargains for suppliers or on cheaper and better products for consumers. In both jurisdictions there is growing emphasis on the importance of protecting consumers, although the emphasis is stronger and better established in the USA.

If the emphasis is on protecting consumers, there should be concern only when there is insufficient competition downstream to ensure that the benefits of buyer power are passed on to buyers. Where there is insufficient competition downstream, the answers are not clear. There seems to be no room for *per se* rules. A prohibition on discrimination or on differential prices that do not reflect cost differences is arbitrary. Much produce is now branded and some brands are more attractive to consumers than others. Many services provided by only some buyers or sellers are very valuable to the other without being expensive to provide. Should price differences reflect differences in cost or in benefit?

1.4 THE LAW MAY BE BASED ON BROAD ECONOMIC PRINCIPLES OR ON SEPARATE CODES FOR EACH CATEGORY OF CONTRACT

How should competition law treat restrictions on conduct? Should it adopt broad principles, which require courts and Commission to analyse markets in the light of very general considerations based on the writings and depositions of economists as in the United States, or should there be separate codes of conduct for different types of agreement defined in formalistic terms, specifying the kinds of clauses that are acceptable in each? This is common in civil law systems.

Since the Supreme Court's judgment in *Continental TV* v. *GTE Sylvania*,[140] in the absence of substantial market power American courts have tended to treat as

---

[140] 433 US 36, (1977). Sylvania's share of the US market for television sets had declined to less than 2%, so it decided to encourage its dealers to provide better services. It reduced the number of retailers it supplied, requiring those that remained to sell only from a specified location. In this way it could restrain one dealer from poaching too near the premises of another. When one dealer started to sell from another location near to an existing dealer, Sylvania cut it off, and was sued for treble damages for infringing the antitrust laws.

The Supreme Court pointed out that a location clause was capable of increasing inter-brand competition. Indeed, Sylvania's market share had risen after it began to protect its dealers from each other from under 2% in 1962 to 5% in 1965. The Supreme Court expressly overruled its earlier case law and said that such a contract must be appraised under a rule of reason and was not necessarily illegal.

The case was referred back to the trial court which gave summary judgment in favour of Sylvania. On appeal, the 9th Circuit Court of Appeals held that a:

vertical restraint may be reasonable if it is likely to promote inter-brand competition without overly restricting intra-brand competition.

(694 F.2d 1132, 1982-2 Trade Cas (CCH) P64,962, 72,965.) It added that a restraint that may increase inter-brand competition should rarely be struck down for restraining intra-brand competition.

valid ancillary restraints necessary to make viable a transaction that increases inter-brand competition. They have looked to the causes for concern—concentrated markets,[141] entry barriers and horizontal restraints—and have approved agreements in which these were not involved. They have also accepted justifications for ancillary restraints likely to increase inter-brand competition.

When the US courts apply a rule of reason to most non-price vertical agreements, the onus of proving an anti-competitive effect on balance is on the party alleging it. Such trials take a long time and are very expensive. So the rule of reason almost amounts in practice to *per se* legality. This, however, may be due in part to the extensive discovery permitted under US law, and might not be so grave a problem in Europe.

Judge Easterbrook considers that practices should be condemned by courts only if it is established that the defendant enjoys market power and that the practices may enrich it at the cost of consumers. He suggests various filters that the courts might apply to dismiss most cases.[142]

First, in the absence of significant market power, there is no need to intervene: the market is a sufficient safeguard.

Secondly, if firms have the ability and incentive to behave in an anti-competitive way, then the court should see whether competitors use different methods of production and distribution, in which case, again, there will be sufficient competition.

Thirdly, if not, the court should ask whether the evidence is consistent with a reduction in output.

Fourthly, if the plaintiff is a competitor of the defendant, that is some evidence that the practice is beneficial to consumers.

This view has been criticised by **Oliver E. Williamson**.[143] He accepts Easterbrook's first filter—in the absence of market power there is no antitrust problem. He is, however, more likely than is Easterbrook to perceive market power in a given situation. He reduces the other filters to factors to be considered in a more extensive analysis.

Judge Easterbrook is concerned that, whereas there is a mechanism for correcting mistakes made in the market, the firm that makes bad decisions will not expand and may even cease to trade, there is no mechanism for correcting judicial mistakes. Unlike the market which punishes unsuccessful policies, the courts are not self correcting. So, it is very important not to forbid conduct, especially if it is novel, unless it is clearly anti-competitive.

Market analysis, and the assessment of whether investments would have been made if less protection were given, however, are not easy. Few European lawyers in the 1960s and 1970s, when the law was being developed, were familiar with price

[141] In *Jefferson Parish Hospital Dis. No 2* v. *Hyde*, 466 US 2, (1984) the Supreme Court held even tying, which a majority said was subject to a *per se* rule, was not illegal when only 30% of the tying product was supplied.
[142] "Vertical Aarrangements and Rule of Reason," (1984) 53 *Antitrust LJ* 135 and "The Limits of Antitrust," (1984) 3 *Texas L Rev* 1.
[143] (1987) 76 *Georgetown L Rev* 271.

theory, although this is changing and more are sufficiently educated to know when to call in economists to advise them.

The alternative form based approach, previously often adopted in the EC, is said to be based on the need to promote legal certainty. It is easier for a legal adviser, or official to go through the provisions in an agreement, ticking them off against check lists of permissible and prohibited clauses. Economists do not always agree with each other, although the extent of their disagreement is often exaggerated. Lawyers and officials may not be used to economic ways of thinking. So, simple rules based on economic factors have been suggested.

One disadvantage of this "checklist approach" is that the effect of many provisions in an agreement depends on the surrounding circumstances. In the absence of market power there may be no cause for concern.

A second disadvantage is that there are many kinds of provisions that may be used to overcome particular problems and it may be more efficient to permit the parties to choose the provision most convenient to them. Defining the relevant kinds of contract in different codes in group exemptions, without any economic reason for distinguishing one from another, may unduly limit the freedom of the parties to arrange their affairs. For this reason, the new far wider block group exemption is welcome.

A third problem is that the codes, or former group exemptions, have been adopted over a long period of time, and policies have changed meanwhile. Consequently, they are not always consistent. There used to be one block exemption for exclusive distribution agreements, where the dealer was given an exclusive territory, another for exclusive purchasing, where the buyer could be given only a principal sales area, a separate one for the distribution of vehicles, with which this book is only slightly concerned (7.6–7.6.3.6 below). Later, a group exemption for franchising was adopted permitting rather different clauses. The ECJ held that selective distribution sometimes fell outside the prohibition of Article 81(1).

Each group exemption applied only to a particular type of transaction narrowly defined by reference to typical transactions that had been frequently notified to the Commission rather than to the likely effects of the conduct to be encouraged or forbidden. This gave rise to the possibility of selecting the group exemption that enables one's client to distort its contracts as little as possible. Those who did not take legal advice sometimes found that an important transaction fell between two block exemptions and that important parts of their contract were void and illegal.

Even if, after taking legal advice, a business decided that it needed an agreement that did not fit into a group exemption and it notified it with a request for individual exemption, the Commission often tried to persuade the parties to alter their transactions to come within a group exemption[144] rather than assessing

---

[144] In its *20th Report on Competition Policy* the Commission stated that,

> In some cases, the Commission asked the parties to amend some of the provisions in their agreements so as to bring them into line with the conditions in the two regulations.

cont./

whether there was any real need to modify the agreement to avoid restricting competition.

After much agonising the Commission has decided to let the old group exemptions expire[145] and has replaced them with a single group exemption embracing many kinds of transaction, where restrictions are imposed on the conditions on which the parties may buy, sell or resell specified goods or services.

It was referring to the two regulations superseded by Regulation 2790/99. At p. 57, it stated that:

It sent some 30 letters to the firms concerned asking them to bring their agreements to an end.

[145] Commission Regulation 1475/95, the group exemption for motor vehicle distribution and servicing agreements, OJ 1995, L145/25, [1996] 4 CMLR 69, replacing Regulation 123/85, OJ 1985, L15/16, remains in force until the end of September 2002. Whether it will replaced is doubtful. Lobbying continues. See 7.6 *et seq* below.

2

The Law Before 2000—Article 81

Article 81(1) of the EC Treaty[1] prohibits as incompatible with the Common Market agreements between undertakings that may affect trade between Member States and have the object or effect of preventing, restricting or distorting competition within the Common Market. Article 81(3) provides for the possibility of exemption from the prohibition, while Article 81(2) renders void any contractual provisions in an infringing agreement that have the object or effect of restricting competition contrary to Article 81.[2]

Broadly speaking, infringement of Article 81(1) presupposes proof of three elements: 1) some form of concertation or collusion, 2) which restricts or inhibits (or is intended to restrict or inhibit) the competitive process and 3) which may affect trade between Member States. The onus of proving all three elements is on the person alleging infringement (7.4.5 below). Both European Court of Justice (ECJ) and Commission are particularly concerned about agreements that would not be sensible if the Common Market were more integrated. They attempt to ensure that goods and services that are sold at lower prices in some Member States are not kept out of Member States where prices are higher.

Until recently, the Commission, supported by the ECJ, has easily found collusion from unilateral conduct in the context of a long term distribution agreement.[3] In *Bayer* v. *Commission*,[4] however, the Court of First Instance, (the CFI) overruled the Commission's decision in *Adalat*.[5] It carefully distinguished the earlier case law of the ECJ and made it clear that for Article 81 to apply there must be

---

[1] The old EEC Treaty is now known as the EC Treaty and the articles were renumbered by the Treaty of Amsterdam. Article 85 has become Article 81. The new numbers will be used throughout this work, even in quotations.

[2] The ECJ has repeatedly held that only those provisions which restrict competition are void as a matter of Community law. It is for national courts to decide in accordance with national law whether the provisions that remain after deleting the terms that restrict competition are enforceable—*La Société Technique Minière* v. *Maschinenbau Ulm,* Case 56/65 [1966] ECR 235 and numerous judgments thereafter. The criterion of the effect on trade between Member States operates differently. The agreement is illegal if the agreement as a whole may affect trade between Member States, *Windsurfing,* Case 193/83 [1986] ECR 611, para. 96.

[3] *AEG—Allgemeine Elektricitäts-Gesellschaft AEG-Telefunken AG* v. *Commission,* Case 107/82, [1983] ECR 3151 and *Ford-Werke AG and Ford of Europe Inc.* v. *Commission,* Cases 25 & 26/84 [1985] ECR 2725.

[4] Case T-41/96, 26 October 2000, [2000] ECR I-0000. [2001] 4 CMLR 4. The Commission has appealed, Cases C-2 & 3/01 OJ 2001, C79/14.

[5] OJ 1996 L201/1, [1996] 5 CMLR 416.

a meeting of minds. It enquired very carefully whether the French and Spanish dealers had agreed with Bayer not to export to the UK (4.1.4 below).

On appeal, the Commission is challenging the finding that Bayer did not monitor from which dealers the parallel trade originated. Whether or not the appeal is successful, collusion may be found more easily from unilateral action under EC law than in the US.[6]

Moreover, the path which Bayer navigated is very narrow. The Commission fined Opel[7] for restricting the supply of cars to dealers who were exporting and treated this as a very serious infringement, but there were also other ways in which parallel trade was discouraged.

The concept of trade between Member States has been broadly construed and includes the freedom to set up business in another Member State,[8] as well as the freedom to supply goods and services across national frontiers. In our view, the concept embraces all the free movements that lie at the heart of the EC Treaty. If an agreement restricts competition appreciably it is likely also to "affect trade between Member States" contrary to Article 81(1).

Article 81(3) provides for exemptions from the prohibition of agreements, or categories of agreements, that contribute to improving the production or distribution of goods or to promoting technical or economic progress. For the agreement to be exempted, consumers must be allowed a fair share of the benefit and only restrictions of competition that are indispensable to the attainment of these objectives may be imposed. Moreover, the agreement must not afford the firms the possibility of eliminating competition in respect of a substantial part of the relevant products. The ECJ has allowed the Commission wide discretion in applying Article 81(3) and a party challenging a refusal to exempt must prove that all four conditions are fulfilled.[9]

By virtue of Article 9(1) of Regulation 17[10] the Commission alone has power to exempt individual agreements. As announced in its White Paper on Modernisation of the Rules Implementing Articles 81 and 82 of the EC Treaty,[11] the Commission has proposed that the Council replace Regulation 17 so as to enable national courts to apply Article 81(3) as well as the prohibition of Article 81(1).[12] If adopted by the Council as expected, this will be the most radical change in the law since 1962: Article 81(3) will have direct effect before national courts in the EC Member States. The Council is also being asked to empower the Commission to adopt regulations

---

[6] *Monsanto* v. *Spray-Rite Service Corp.*, 465 US 752 (1984).

[7] OJ 2001, 591/1.

[8] *Pronuptia de Paris GmbH* v. *Pronuptia de Paris Irmgard Schillgalis*, Case 161/84, [1986] ECR 353, para. 26.

[9] *Matra Hachette SA* v. *Commission*, Case T-17/93 15 July 1994, [1994] ECR-II 595, para. 104, but there are no kinds of agreement that are inherently incapable of exemption, *ibid.*, para. 85.

[10] Council Regulation 17/62 — Main implementing Regulation, OJ Spec Ed, 1959–62, 87; JO 1962, 204.

[11] *White Paper on Modernisation of the Rules Implementing Articles 81 and 82 of the EC Treaty.* Commission programme No 99/027, 2.12 below.

[12] Proposal of the Commission for a Council Regulation to replace Regulation 17/62, 2000/0243 (CNS); [1999] 5 CMLR 208, Commission Doc. Com (2000) 582 Final of 27.9.2000, 2.12 below.

exempting categories of agreement. The *vires* for Regulation 2790/99 exempting distribution agreements between non-competitors were, however, granted by Council Regulation 19/65.[13]

There are many books analysing the law generally under Article 81,[14] and this monograph will assume some familiarity with it. In this chapter, it is intended to deal rather shortly with matters of general interest for the application of Article 81, and in considerable detail with selective distribution, franchising and agency which are of direct relevance to distribution agreements that fall outside Regulation 2790/99.

2.2 EXCLUSIVE DISTRIBUTION AND *CONSTEN* & *GRUNDIG*

The law and practice relating to exclusive distribution was developed in the 1960s before any other aspect of competition law. The Commission's earliest decisions in 1964 related to exclusive distribution systems, most of which included export restraints to prevent poaching in other dealers' territories.

The Commission's early practice was to treat such export restraints as infringing Article 81, subject to the *de minimis* rule, which it applied first in *Grosfillex Sàrl*.[15] Nevertheless, the Commission exempted some territorial restraints, provided they did not lead to absolute territorial protection. The only two Member States with competition rules had conflicting attitudes: the French were most concerned about vertical restraints and the Germans with horizontal. By treating any export bans or deterrents as infringing Article 81(1), the Commission was able, through its exclusive right to exempt, to maintain control in the early days of competition policy,

Article 230 (ex Article 173) of the EC Treaty limits the jurisdiction of the ECJ to judicial review: to deciding whether the Commission has manifestly infringed the Treaty. The Court does not decide whether the Commission came to the correct conclusion. The ECJ has been reluctant to exercise the full jurisdiction of judicial review conferred on it.

The CFI which inherited the same jurisdiction subject to appeal on points of law to the ECJ, has progressively been annulling decisions because the Commission has not adequately spelled out its reasons, contrary to Article 253 (ex Article 190) or, very occasionally, for manifest error of assessment. In this way it has almost reheard the issues on their merits in some judgments and forced the Commission to adopt more cogent reasoning and has begun to control the Commission's policy. It may go further when the Commission ceases to have exclusive power to grant individual exemptions (2.12 below).

---

[13] OJ Spec Ed, 1965, 35, amended by Council Reg. 1215/99, OJ 1999, L148/1.

[14] There is a more general bibliography in **Valentine Korah**, *An Introductory Guide to EC Competition Law and Practice*, 7th edn (Oxford, Hart Publishing, 2000).

[15] JO 915/64, [1964] CMLR 237. In a contract to supply goods to an exclusive distributor for Switzerland, a restraint on selling back to the Common Market was not an appreciable restraint on competition, since the double customs barrier of the time made such reimport unprofitable.

The leading case on exclusive distribution (described at 1.2.2.2 above) is *Consten & Grundig*.[16] Shortly before the establishment of the Common Market, the German firm, Grundig, decided to start marketing its dictating machines, television sets and other products in France. It persuaded Consten to promote its brand there.

The agreement contained provisions that were then common. Grundig agreed not to supply the contract products within Consten's territory of the whole of France except to Consten; it isolated the territory further by restraining its wholesalers in Germany and distributors elsewhere from exporting to France. It reinforced these provisions by enabling Consten to register the mark "Gint" (Grundig International) that was stamped on its apparatus in those days.[17] Consten, in return, agreed not to handle competing apparatus and to promote the Grundig products, establishing a retail network, repair shops etc.

Consten's sunk costs[18] must have been significant and risky as perceived in 1957 before the ratification of the EC Treaty, when the agreement was made. Consten must have expected that French import quotas would limit its ability to import Grundig products for a decade although, as it happened, quotas were abolished in 1961. It would have to incur costs before knowing whether it would obtain any import licence. Consten must have feared that it would have to spread the costs of setting up a distribution system and obtaining import licences over limited turnover for the first decade.[19]

When quotas were abolished, parallel importers began to buy the apparatus in Germany and sell it in France at prices that, even allowing for discounts, were about 25 per cent lower than those of the Consten network. Grundig and Consten sued the parallel importers in the French courts for the French tort of unfair competition and for infringing the trade mark Gint. The Court of Appeal for the Paris region adjourned the proceedings to enable the parties to notify the agreement under Regulation 17 so that the Commission could decide whether it infringed Article 81.

In *Grundig*,[20] the Commission adopted a decision, alleging that four provisions had the object of restricting competition between dealers in Grundig products: 1) the exclusive territory granted to Consten, 2) the associated export bans on other dealers, 3) reinforced by the arrangement over the "Gint" mark and 4) Consten's duty to buy only from Grundig.

---

[16] The Commission's decision, JO 1964, 2545/64; [1964] CMLR 489; on appeal, *Consten & Grundig v. Commission*, Cases 56 & 58/64 [1966] ECR 299. The best comment on this case remains **René Joliet**, *The Rule of Reason in Antitrust Law* (Dordrecht, Nijhoff, 1967).

[17] This would enable Consten to sue for trademark infringement anyone who bought the apparatus in Germany for commercial sale in France. This kind of arrangement was less usual than the other three restrictions. It was a response to a Dutch judgment not letting Grundig use its Dutch registration of the Grundig mark to restrain imports of products it had put on the market in Germany, nor letting it assign its own mark to the Dutch dealer. The assignment was treated a sham.

[18] I.e., investments of less value for other purposes. Such investments are more risky than those that can more easily be resold. See 1.2.4.1.1 above.

[19] For an example of how risky such investment by a distributor can be see *Société La Technique Minière v. Maschinenbau Ulm*, Case 56/65 [1966] ECR 235.

[20] JO 2545/1964; [1964] CMLR 489.

The Commission did not address the questions whether Consten would have invested in building up Grundig's reputation in France and obtaining import licences without such protection, nor whether parallel importers would have wanted to import Grundig equipment had it not been promoted.

The Commission refused to exempt the exclusive territory as it considered that absolute territorial protection was not indispensable for obtaining any benefits that might result from the exclusive distribution agreement and condemned the agreement as a whole. The ECJ, however, quashed the decision, save for the parts condemning absolute territorial protection and the ancillary agreement relating to the GINT mark, for not giving reasons why the whole of the agreement and not just the restraints on parallel trade infringed Article 81(1).[21]

The Advocate General, Herr Roemer, advised the ECJ to quash the decision for failing to give sufficient reasons,[22] contrary to Article 253 (ex Article 190). Not only had the Commission failed to ask the key questions, it had not compared the situation after the agreement was made with that which would have developed without it. In other words, he rejected the Commission's analysis because it had not looked *ex ante* to the need in 1957 to provide incentives for Consten to invest. Nor had it examined the concrete effects of the agreement to see whether it had restricted competition appreciably. It had considered only competition between Grundig dealers and ignored the constraints caused by competition with other brands. The ECJ, however, perceived the matter *ex post*. Once Consten had established the reputation of the Grundig products, it would be more competitive to permit parallel imports of Grundig products. The Court denied the need to examine the concrete effects of an agreement when the Commission alleged that its *object* was to restrict competition between dealers in Grundig products. The ECJ added that:

> the exercise of the Commission's powers [to grant an exemption] necessarily implies complex evaluations on economic matters. A judicial review of these evaluations must take account of their nature by confining itself to an examination of the relevance of the facts and of the legal consequences which the Commission deduces therefrom. This review must in the first place be carried out in respect of the reasons given for the decisions which must set out the facts and considerations on which the evaluations are based.[23]

In *Grundig*, the ECJ limited its consideration to intra-brand competition and ignored the pro-competitive effect on the French market of a new brand being introduced.

[21] See Cases 56 & 58/64 [1966] ECR 299, 344 and the operative part of the judgment.
[22] *Ibid.*, 377.
[23] *Ibid.*, 347. This statement has been constantly repeated by the ECJ, but Judge Cooke of the CFI, speaking extra-judicially, suggested that the reason for review of decisions made under Article 81(3) being only marginal was that they related to matters of competition policy which were for the Commission, not the ECJ: "Changing Responsibilities and Relationships for Community and National Courts: The Implications of the White Paper," *The Modernisation of European Competition Law: The Next Ten Years*, CELS Occasional Paper No. 4, University of Cambridge, Centre for European Legal Studies, p. 58 at pp. 61 and 63.

On the limited arguments put forward for an exemption, the ECJ confirmed the Commission's refusal to apply Article 81(1).[24] Nevertheless, it quashed parts of the decision for not specifying adequately how much of the agreement infringed Article 81(1).

The judgment in *Consten & Grundig* had a profound effect on the subsequent law and practice of the courts and Commission for some 30 years. The Commission and ECJ frequently analysed agreements *ex post* and ignored the need for incentives to investment. To this day, the Commission has rarely cleared formally any exclusive agreement important in its market context as not infringing Article 81(1), although it has exempted exclusive agreements individually and by regulation, where parallel imports are possible.

The ECJ has occasionally cleared an agreement.[25] Perhaps, because the Common Market is not yet completely integrated, the Court and Commission are still hostile to absolute territorial protection which is thought to conflict with the fundamental principle of free movement within the Common Market.

Contrast *La Société Technique Minière* v. *Maschinenbau Ulm*,[26] where, two weeks before *Consten & Grundig*, the ECJ ruled that an exclusive distribution agreement not supported by export bans would not infringe Article 81(1) if it was necessary to enable a manufacturer to penetrate another member state. It added that an agreement should be appraised in its economic context before being found contrary to Article 81(1).

The drawback of looking to the symptom of price differentials between Member States rather than to the disease of different conditions in different Member States, especially when imposed by legislative or administrative measures of the States themselves, may have been to worsen the isolation of national markets.[27] Some time after the judgment, Grundig acquired Consten and many of its other exclusive dealers. This forward integration must have eliminated any intra-brand competition at that level of trade, although there may have been competition downstream: Grundig wholesalers and retailers may have competed with each other.

---

[24] Contrast *Pronuptia*, Case 161/84 [1984] ECR 353, where the Court stated (para. 24) that if the franchisee would not have been prepared to commit herself to payments and investment without an exclusive territory combined with location clauses, the Commission should consider the argument under Art. 81(3). The free rider argument was less well put to the Commission and ECJ in *Grundig*.

[25] See 2.7–2.7.3 below.

[26] Case 56/65 [1966] ECR 235.

See the cases described at 2.7–2.7.3 below and *Proceedings of the European Competition Forum*, C.D. Ehlermann and L. Laudati (eds.), (Chichester, Wiley, 1997) part 1. The forum considered and criticised the Commission's attitude to distribution agreements as being too interventionist and rigid, paying too little attention to market analysis. The question was also raised whether vertical restrictions that were currently being investigated under Article 81(3) should be treated as infringing Article 81(1). The whole book was a splendid precursor to the Commission's green paper on vertical restraints (2.10 below).

[27] See **Charles Baden Fuller**, "Economic Issues Relating to Property Rights in Trademarks: Export Bans, Differential Pricing, Restrictions on Resale and Repackaging," (1981) 6 *ELRev* 162.

2.3 EXHAUSTION OF INTELLECTUAL PROPERTY RIGHTS

At first, lawyers thought that if contractual export restraints were impermissible, clients could rely instead on the limited nature of intellectual property rights (which are mostly national) and could sue parallel traders for infringing patents, trademarks and so forth in the country of import. This was prevented in 1974 by the ECJ when it established a concept of Community exhaustion.[28]

Article 28 (ex Article 30) of the EC Treaty prohibits between Member States:

> Quantitative restrictions on exports and all measures having equivalent effect.

Article 30 (ex Article 36) provides a limited derogation from this fundamental principle:

> The provisions of Articles 28 and 29 shall not preclude prohibitions or restrictions on imports . . . of goods on grounds of . . . the protection of industrial and commercial property. Such prohibitions or restrictions shall not, however, constitute a means of arbitrary discrimination or a disguised restriction on trade between member states.

In *Centrafarm BV and de Peijper* v. *Sterling Drug Inc.*,[29] the ECJ held that where goods had been put on the market in the country of export by or with the consent of the holder of an intellectual property right, the holder could not exercise its rights in the country of import to restrain the commercial importation or sale of protected products into another member state. The patent was a measure of equivalent effect to a nil quota within the meaning of Article 28 and, since Article 30 derogates from one of the fundamental principles of the Common Market, it should be narrowly construed.

The doctrine of exhaustion has been widely applied to all sorts of intellectual property rights—patents in *Centrafarm* v. *Sterling*, trademarks in the companion case of *Centrafarm BV and de Peijper* v. *Winthrop*,[30] copyright in *Warner Bros. and Metronome* v. *Christiansen*,[31] although not performing rights in a film, which relate to services, *Coditel (SA Compagnie Générale pour la Diffusion de la Télévision)* v. *Ciné-Vog Films*.[32]

The doctrine applies to patents even when the holder was unable to obtain a patent in the country of export and there was no patent to exhaust.[33] Nevertheless, the doctrine prevents the exercise of the patent only when the goods were put on the market in the country of export by or with the consent of the holder. The words of the ECJ in *Centrafarm* v. *Sterling* have been construed like a statute.

---

[28] It is arguable that this was done even earlier in *Deutsche Grammophon* v. *Metro*, Case 78/70 [1971] ECR 487, but the ruling of the ECJ was less clear and might have applied only to rights analogous to copyright.

[29] Case 15/74 [1974] ECR 1147.

[30] Case 16/74 [1974] ECR 1183,

[31] Case 158/86 [1988] ECR 2605.

[32] Case 62/79 [1980] ECR 881.

[33] *Merck & Co. Inc.* v. *Stephar BV*, Case 187/80 [1981] ECR 2063, confirmed in *Merck & Co Inc.* v. *Primecrown Limited*, Cases C-267 & 268/95 [1996] ECR I-6285.

Consequently, if a licensee is not permitted to sell outside its territory, an intellectual property right may be exercised to restrain direct sales by a licensee outside its territory,[34] but if the licensee rightfully sells protected product where it is permitted and a purchaser exports to another member state, the rights are exhausted.

Where the product was put on the market by the holder or with its consent outside the EEA,[35] the doctrine of exhaustion does not apply, as Article 28 refers only to restraints on trade between Member States. Indeed if the trade mark law of a Member State includes a concept of exhaustion world wide that is irrelevant under the trade mark Directive.[36]

A trademark is exhausted as against an importer who repackages the product only if the repackaging was objectively necessary to penetrate a market,[37] and consent was given by the holder. In *Davidoff (Zino) SA & A & G Imports Ltd.* and *Levi Strauss & Co and another* v. *Tesco*,[38] the ECJ ruled that such consent cannot be implied from the failure of the holder to forbid subsequent traders to market within the EEA or place such a warning on the goods, nor from the transfer of ownership of the goods bearing the mark without imposing any contractual reservations. It is not relevant whether the importer of the goods bearing the mark is not aware that the holder objects to their being placed on the market within the EEA.

A supplier cannot avoid the illegality of export bans by exercising trademark and other rights to restrain sales between Member States. Nevertheless, the doctrine of exhaustion applies only between Member States of the EC and European Economic Area, so if a dealer in the US sells into a member state of the EC, there is no exhaustion, even if the country of import adopts a doctrine of international exhaustion.[39]

2.4   THE WIDE APPLICATION OF ARTICLE 81(1) BY THE COMMISSION IN THE EARLY YEARS

In the early years, the prohibition in Article 81(1) was widely interpreted by the Commission's Directorate General for Competition. Although Article 81(1) has

[34] Article 2(1)(14) of the Technology Transfer Regulation 240/96, OJ 1996, L31/2, [1996] 4 CMLR 405, [1996] 4 EIPR Supp. iv implies that patent rights remain to be exhausted and *Tiercé Ladbroke* v. *Commission*, Case T-504/93 [1997] ECR II-923 confirms this in relation to performing rights.

[35] Protocol 28 incorporates the doctrine of exhaustion throughout the EEA.

[36] *Silhouette Internationale Schmied GmbH & Co. KC* v. *Hartlauer Handellshaft mbh*, Case C-355/96 [1998] ECR I-4799. First Trade Mark Directive, OJ 1989, L40/1, CMR 5826.

[37] *Bristol-Myers Squibb & Ors* v. *Paranova* A/S, Cases C-427, 429 & 436/93, 11 July 1996 [1996] ECR I-3457, paras. 52–57. The concept of necessity was further considered in *Merck & Co Inc.* v. *Paranova* Case C-143/99 by Jacobs AG, 12 July 2001, paras. 104–119 as objectively necessary—not necessarily the only legal way of marketing, but something reasonably required for the parallel trader to have effective access to the market. Judgment had not been delivered by mid-January 2002. These cases were concerned with the First Council Directive on Trade Marks 89/104/EEC, OJ 1989, L40/1, CMR 5826. The Directive, however, should be construed in the light of Articles 28 and 30 of the Treaty so case law under the Directive may be relevant under the Treaty.

[38] Case C-414 & 415/99, 20 November 2001.

[39] *Silhouette Internationale Schmied GmbH & Co. KC* v. *Hartlauer Handellshaft mbh*, Case C355/96, [1998] ECR I 4799.

direct effect in the legal systems of Member States, Article 9(1) of Regulation 17 [40] reserves the application of Article 81(3) to the Commission. By interpreting Article 81(1) widely, it kept control over as many agreements as possible.

On occasion, both the Commission[41] and, more rarely the ECJ[42] have suggested that any restriction on conduct that is appreciable[43] has the object of restricting competition (2.7.1 below).

One of the arguments leading to the wide view of Article 81(1) is that since there is power to exempt deserving agreements in Article 81(3), there is no need to consider whether the agreement is justifiable under Article 81(1). Joliet answered this in 1967.[44] Article 81(3) permits non-competitive considerations to be brought in, but Article 81(1) forbids only agreements that have the object or effect of *restricting competition*. For the agreement to be forbidden, the object or effect must be to restrict competition and *not merely conduct.*

Fortunately, in relation to transactions other than horizontal or vertical price-fixing and absolute territorial protection the ECJ has only occasionally followed the Commission's line. More often, it has stated that if an ancillary restriction on conduct is necessary to make viable a transaction that has neither the object or effect of restricting competition it does not in itself infringe Article 81(1) (2.7–2.7.2 below). Moreover, it has stated that restrictions on conduct infringe only when seen in their economic context (2.7.3 below). This amounts to saying that apart from cartels, absolute territorial protection and resale price maintenance (rpm), a firm infringes Article 81(1) only if it has market power and there is no efficiency made possible by the restraint of conduct.

2.4.1 The *De Minimis* Rule

The ECJ has confirmed an implied condition introduced by the Commission[45] that both the restriction of competition and the possible effect on trade between member states should be appreciable. In *Völk* v. *Vervaecke*,[46] Völk made less than 1 per cent of the washing machines produced in Germany, and the ECJ ruled that

---

[40] OJ Spec Ed, 1959–62, 87, JO 1962, 204. The Commission has made a proposal to the Council, 2000/0243 (CNS), 27 September 2000, [2000] CMLR 1182, explanatory memorandum *ibid.* 1148, impact assessment form *Ibid.* 1205, to abandon its exclusive right, 2.2 and 2.12 below.

[41] See **Valentine Korah**, *An Introductory Guide to EC Competition Law and Practice*, 7th edn (Oxford, Hart Publishing, 2000) 2.4.4.

[42] E.g., *Société de Vente de Ciments et Bétons de l'Est SA* v. *Kerpen & Kerpen GmbH & Co. KG*, Case 319/82 [1983] ECR 4173 and *Windsurfing International Inc.* v. *Commission*, Case 193/83 [1986] ECR 611, which went rather further in treating restraints on conduct as having the object of restricting competition. Contrast the cases analysed at 2.7 and 2.8 below. See also **Helmuth R.B. Schröter**, "Antitrust Analysis under Article 85(1) and (3)", [1987] *Fordham Corporate Law Institute*. ch 27 and **Michel Waelbroeck**, "Antitrust Analysis under Article 85(1) and (3)," *Ibid.*, ch 28 and the ensuing discussion in ch 29.

[43] See 2.4.1–2.4.1.6 below.

[44] **René Joliet**, above n. 16, *passim.*

[45] *Grosfillex Sàrl*, JO 915/64, [1964] CMLR 237.

[46] Case 5/69 [1969] ECR 295, para. 3.

even absolute territorial protection granted to its exclusive distributor for Belgium and Luxembourg would not infringe Article 81(1) if it did not appreciably restrict competition and appreciably affect inter-State trade.

The Commission tried to reduce the uncertainty surrounding this *de minimis* rule by issuing a notice on Minor Agreements in 1970. The notice has been reissued with alterations several times, most recently in December 2001.[47]

2.4.1.1 Ceilings of market share

In the Commission's view,

7. . . . . agreements between undertakings which affect trade between member states do not appreciably restrict competition within the meaning of Article 81(1):

(a) if the aggregate market shares held by the parties to the agreement does not exceed 10% of any of the relevant markets affected by the agreement, where the agreement is made between undertakings which are actual or potential competitors on any of these markets (agreements between competitors),[48] or

(b) if the market share held by each of the parties to the agreement does not exceed 15% on any of the relevant markets affected by the agreement, where the agreement is made between undertakings which are not actual or potential competitors on any of these markets (agreements between non competitors).

In cases where it is difficult to classify the agreement as either an agreement between competitors or an agreement between non-competitors the 10% threshold is applicable.

8. Where in a relevant market competition is restricted by the cumulative effect of agreements for the sale of goods or services entered into by different suppliers or distributors (cumulative foreclosure effect of parallel networks of agreements having similar effects on the market), the market share thresholds under point 7 are reduced to 5% both for agreements between competitors and for agreements between non-competitors. . . . A cumulative foreclosure effect is unlikely to exist if less than 30% of the relative market is covered by parallel (networks of) agreements having similar effects.

There is some marginal relief (para. 9).

The ceiling used to be 5 per cent for both horizontal and vertical agreements. It was raised to 10 per cent for vertical agreements by the notice of 1997.[49] The higher ceiling for vertical agreements reflects the Commission's developing view that restrictions in vertical agreements are less serious than in horizontal agreements. In earlier decades many officials were more concerned about vertical restraints than horizontal ones because of their effect on trade between member states.

The safe harbour for firms with low market shares is reduced to 5 per cent where the cumulative effects of parallel networks of similar agreements established by dif-

---

[47] OJ 2001, C368/13.

[48] It refers to Guideline 9 on the applicability of Article 81 to horizontal co-operation, OJ 2001, C3/2, [2001] 4 CMLR 819. for the concept of actual or potential competitors.

[49] Notice on agreements of minor importance which do not fall within the meaning of Article 85(1) of the Treaty establishing the European Community, 1997 OJ, C372/13, [1998] 4 CMLR 192.

ferent suppliers or distributors restrict competition.[50] This is unlikely where the share of the market covered by parallel agreements is less than 30 per cent. Consequently, any firms participating in an agreement that qualifies under the notice are likely to be subject to competitive constraints.

Unlike its predecessors, the new notice deals only with the effect on competition not on trade between Member States (paras. 2 & 3). Consequently, some agreements outside the notice may be cleared on the ground that they do not affect trade between Member States. The exclusion of agreements with hard core restraints in para. 11 has been copied from Article 4 of Regulation 2790/99 (chapter 4 below). It should be remembered, however, that in *Völk*[51] the ECJ ruled that agreements infringe Article 81(1) only if both the effects on competition and on trade between Member States are appreciable. Although the notice purports to deal only with effects on competition, it adds at the end of para. 3 that agreements between small and medium sized undertakings are unlikely to affect trade between Member States (2.4.1.4 below).

2.4.1.2 *Relevant market*

The relevant market is defined by paras. 13–16 of the notice on the definition of the relevant market for the purposes of Community competition law,[52] to which the notice on minor agreements refers. The notice on the relevant market is, however, of general application and will become very important in view of the ceiling of market share imposed by Article 3 of Regulation 2790/99. The definition is in the concrete terms of substitutes on the demand side by reason of the product's characteristics, price and intended use. The notice on the relevant market, however, uses two tests—the second being that of the hypothetical monopolist.

> 15. The assessment of demand substitution entails a determination of the range of products which are viewed as substitutes by the consumer. One way of making this determination can be viewed as a speculative experiment postulating a hypothetical small, lasting change in relative prices and evaluating the likely reactions of customers to that increase. The exercise of market definition focuses on prices for operational and practical purposes, and more precisely on demand substitution arising from small permanent changes in relative prices. This concept can provide clear indications as to the evidence that is relevant in defining markets.

> 16. Conceptually, this approach means that starting from the type of products that the undertakings involved sell and the area in which they sell them, additional products and areas will be included in, or excluded from the market definition depending on whether competition from these other products and areas affect or restrain sufficiently the pricing of the parties' products in the short term.

---

[50] Para. 8. This follows the ruling of the ECJ in *Delimitis,* Case C-234/89 [1991] ECR I-935, since explained in *Neste Markkinointi Oy* v. *Yötuuli Ky, and others,* Case C-214/99 [2001] 4 CMLR 993 and *Greene King—Roberts & Roberts* v. *Commission,* Case T-25/99 [2001] CMLR 828, 2.7.3 and 7.2.6.5.1 below.

[51] Case 5/69 [1969] ECR 295, para. 3.

[52] OJ 1997, C372/5, [1998] 4 CMLR 177.

17. The question to be answered is whether the parties' customers would switch to read-ily available substitutes or to suppliers located elsewhere in response to a hypothetical small (in the range of 5 or 10%) but permanent relative price increase in the products and areas being considered. If substitution were enough to make the price increase unprofitable because of the resulting loss of sales, additional substitutes and areas are included in the relevant market. This would be done until the set of products and geo-graphical areas is such that prices would be profitable. The equivalent analysis is applic-able in cases concerning the concentration of buying power, where the starting point would then be the supplier and the price test serves to identify the alternative distribu-tion channels or outlets for the supplier's products. In the application of these principles, careful account should be taken of particular situations as described within paragraphs 56 and 58.

The test of the hypothetical monopolist was originally developed in the United States for appraising mergers, where the question is whether the merger will sub-stantially lessen competition. At para. 11 of its notice, however, the Commission states that the test is to apply also to appraisals under Articles 81 and 82.

If one takes the current market price as the basis of this exercise, one might ask why such a price rise had not been made if it would have been profitable. On policy grounds we should be as worried by practices that maintain high prices as by those that raise them.[53] At para. 19 of the notice on market definition the Commission implies that the price to be taken under Articles 81 and 82 is the price that would have been charged had the market been more competitive. Unfortunately, it is seldom possible to know what this is. There may be no better way of defining the relevant market but it is important to realise that the definition may produce unpredictable results.

Substitution on the supply side, or conditions of entry, are taken into account in defining the relevant market in Europe only if it is as immediate and effective as substitution on the demand side, although it may be taken into account when appraising market power within the market as defined (paras. 20–24). This leads to narrow markets being found relevant and often to under estimating the extent to which markets are volatile.

The test based on a small price rise is particularly inappropriate for new techno-logy markets where network externalities are important (1.2.1.2.3 above). In such markets, competition is primarily on innovation not on price. Other operating systems compete with Microsoft Windows not so much on price as on innova-tion. On the SSNIP test, the current winner of the technology race will inevitably be considered dominant, although its large market share is vulnerable to innova-tion by its competitors. It is likely to be so concerned to grow fast to obtain net-work efficiencies, that it is unlikely to be holding consumers to ransom.

It is often sensible to define markets in relation to the particular practice that is alleged to be anti-competitive. Usually both sides of the market should be rele-vant—those on both the input and output side. For instance, when judging a single

---

[53] See **S. Salop**, "Vertical Restraints under EC law," in **Barry Hawk** (ed.) [2000] *Fordham Corporate Law Institute*, 217, 235–36.

branding restraint, if there are sufficient other firms not foreclosed on the input side, there is no problem. If there are not enough free firms, then one should look to the output side and decide whether the foreclosure is likely to harm consumers,[54] but of this concept there is little trace in the guidelines on vertical restraints. It is also important, when applying the SSNIP test to consider practices that may prevent prices coming down as well as those that would raise them.

In the early 1990s, the Commission occasionally applied in individual cases a far higher threshold of appreciability than previously.[55] This had the advantage that the Commission was able to write a comfort letter clearing an agreement that was likely to be followed by a national court; but it conferred unbridled discretion on the Commission. This tendency seems to have ceased now that mergers and joint ventures between large firms often come to be treated formally under the more permissive test of the merger regulation, and not Article 81.

2.4.1.3 Hard core restraints

The notice on minor agreements goes on to state that the safe harbour may not always apply to horizontal agreements to fix prices, limit or allocate production or to vertical agreements to maintain resale prices or confer territorial protection. These are the provisions that are considered "by their very nature" to restrict competition and which are treated as having that "object" (2.7.1 below). Nevertheless, the Commission intends initially to leave such agreements to national authorities. It will itself intervene only when there is a Community interest to do so.

This is hard to reconcile with *Völk* v. *Vervaecke* (2.4.1 above), where markets were partitioned and territorial protection was absolute, but the ECJ confirmed that the agreement would infringe Article 81(1) only if the effects on competition and trade between member states were appreciable. It is also questionable on economic grounds since, with low market shares, competition will constrain suppliers not to restrict production to raise price. Below the 10 per cent ceiling for vertical agreements the parties are likely to be subject to competition since the safe harbour for firms with low market shares does not apply where the cumulative effects of parallel networks of similar agreements established by different manufacturers and dealers restrict competition.[56]

2.4.1.4 Small and medium-sized firms

The provisions about cumulative effect would have prevented many franchisees and dealers from relying on the notice, as they are often members of cumulative

---

[54] See **S. Salop**, above n. 53, 235–236.

[55] E.g., in the structural joint ventures in *Metaleurop* OJ 1990, L179/41; [1941] 4 CMLR 222, *GEC–Siemens/Plessey*, OJ 1990, C239/2; [1992] 4 CMLR 471 and in the joint sales organisation in *Finnpap*, notice under Article 19(3), OJ 1989, C45/4; [1989] 4 CMLR 413; and press release describing the comfort letter sent, IP(89)496.

[56] Para. 18. This follows the ruling of the ECJ in *Delimitis*, Case C-234/89 [1991] ECR I-935.

networks. In paragraph 3 of the new notice on minor agreements, therefore, the Commission went on to state that:

> It is however acknowledged that agreements between small and medium-sized under-takings, as defined in the annex to Commission recommendation 96/280/EC, are rarely capable of significantly affecting trade between Member States. Small and medium-sized undertakings are currently defined in that Recommendation as undertakings which have fewer than 250 employees and have either an annual turnover not exceeding 40 million euros or an annual balance-sheet total not exceeding 27 million euros.

A similar provision was introduced in 1997[57] as a new policy innovation. Small and medium-sized firms may not be in the habit of obtaining advice on EC competition law, but small firms in niche markets may have market shares exceeding the 5 and 10 per cent ceilings. So may firms that have developed new technology: their initial market share may be high if the innovation is radical. They may need to impose single branding restraints or protect dealers from others taking a free ride. Even small and medium-sized firms, however, should realise that they are likely to be punished for hard core restraints, such as agreements between competitors to fix prices or allocate markets.[58]

2.4.1.5 No limit of turnover

Formerly, there was a ceiling of turnover, at 300 million ecus since 1994. The ceiling on turnover has now been abrogated. Agreements made by large firms with small shares of particular markets may now come within the notice.

2.4.1.6 Commission notices are not binding

The Commission's notices on points of law are not binding on the Community or national courts (3.2 below): statements interpreting the law are matters for the ECJ and CFI but the notices may be persuasive. Statements of how the Commission intends to exercise its administrative discretion may give rise to legitimate expectations which should be honoured.

2.4.2 Decisions Preparatory to Group Exemption for Franchising

When the Commission intends to adopt a group exemption, it is required by the *vires* for each kind to adopt a number of individual decisions to gain experience.

In the past, the Commission has habitually exempted rather than cleared the agreements it selected for adopting formal decisions even when the market was

---

[57] Notice on agreements of minor importance which do not fall within the meaning of Article 85(1) of the Treaty establishing the European Community, OJ 1997, C372/13, [1998] 4 CMLR 192 at para. 12(3).

[58] E.g., *Britannia Alloys and Chemicals Ltd and others*—see the press release about the zinc phosphate cartel, IP/01/1799.

very competitive. For instance, in all the Commission's decisions relating to exclusive franchising agreements, the markets seem to have been highly competitive, but this was not taken into account when deciding that the grant of an exclusive territory infringed Article 81(1)—only when granting the exemption.[59] There is no reason for this practice to continue, since the Commission has requested the Council for power[60] to grant block exemptions even when it has not previously taken individual decisions in the area of concern.

2.5 INVALIDITY OF CONTRACTUAL PROVISIONS AND UNCERTAINTY

Unless and until the law is changed as a result of the Commission's proposal to the Council to replace Regulation 17 (2.12 below), only the Commission is empowered to exempt individual agreements[61] and, by virtue of Article 81(2), agreements that infringe Article 81 are void to the extent that their object or effect is to restrict competition within the Common Market. Consequently, until the Commission grants an exemption, there may be difficulty enforcing the restrictive provisions in a contract. The Commission has a very wide discretion whether to clear, exempt, ignore or forbid an agreement (2.2 above).[62] During the early 1990s the Commission seldom managed more than four or five exempting decisions.[63] Recently the number of individual exemptions has been erratic, none in 1998, 18 in 1999, but it is understood that the Commission is not currently monitoring notifications on a systematic basis as it expects notifications and even exemptions to cease to have any force when the Regulation to replace Regulation 17 comes into force.

The uncertainty as to whether individual contracts will be performed caused by the bifurcation of Article 81(1) and (3) can be serious. Where a firm is contemplating investing in something that has no alternative use—when costs are sunk (1.2.4.1.1 above)—it needs to know that it will be able to enforce the contractual provisions that make the investment viable. Otherwise, it may not undertake the activity at all and an investment that may be efficient from the point of view of the economy as a whole and of consumers downstream may not be made.

In broad terms, the dealer in the example at 1.2.4.1.1 above could not afford to invest in the pipeline unless it expected supplies of oil at the price which others were paying at the seller's end of the line. Without the absolute territorial protection promised would Consten have invested in promoting Grundig products

[59] See **Valentine Korah**, *Franchising and the EEC Competition Rules—Regulation 4087/88* (Oxford, ESC/Sweet & Maxwell, 1989) at 1.5.1–1.5.1.5. Similarly, before adopting a group exemption for know-how agreements, the Commission exempted several agreements that might well have been cleared.

[60] Article 28 of the Commission's proposal for a Council Regulation to replace Regulation 17/62, 2000/0243 (CNS).

[61] Council Regulation 17/62, OJ Spec Ed, 1959–62, 87; JO 1962, 204.

[62] **Valentine Korah**, *An Introductory Guide to EC Competition Law and Practice*, 7th edn (Oxford, Hart Publishing, 2000) ch 13.

[63] In its *27th Report on Competition Policy*, for 1997, p. 353, the Commission says it granted 3 exemptions. Later annual reports have been less specific, although the *28th Report* for 1998 at p. 363 lists no exemptions and the *29th Report* lists 18 for 1999.

when it still ran the risk of not obtaining an import licence (2.2 above)? The person making the investment must expect to be able to appropriate the agreed benefit from it if it is to be induced to invest. So it must expect to be able to rely on its contractual protection.

Hence, when negotiating a transaction it is important to the parties whether an agreement is outside the prohibition or merits exemption, since, if it merely merits exemption, the anti-competitive clauses in the agreement may not be enforceable unless and until the agreement be actually exempted.[64]

Whether the other parts of the contract should be enforced is a matter for national law. There may, however, be limits to this. For example, under English law, the rest of the contract may not be enforceable, as the agreement is illegal and not merely void. The plaintiff cannot rely on its own wrong.[65] In *Courage* v. *Crehan*,[66] however, following Mischo AG, the CFI considered that the English rule was not fully consistent with the direct effect of Article 81(2). Merely being party to an illegal agreement was not necessarily a wrong, if the party was not responsible for the distortion of competition. The full English rule made it too difficult for the plaintiff to enforce its Community rights to compensation, especially where the plaintiff was in too weak a bargaining position to choose the terms of its contract.

Those in whose favour restrictive clauses have been inserted should consider making express provision as to whether the other clauses should remain valid if the restrictive ones are held void. It is important, however, not to undermine the argument that without the restrictive clauses, the pro-competitive agreement would not have been made.

Group exemptions reduce the problem of invalidity. Although the Commission is usually given power to withdraw a group exemption from an individual agreement, it has only once exercised such a power.[67]

[64] The Commission may now exempt vertical distribution agreements retrospectively to before the date of notification. Council Regulation 1216/99 amending Reg. 17, enables the Commission to grant retrospective exemptions for vertical agreements, OJ 1999, L148/5. See 2.11 below. Meanwhile, the status of the agreement is anomalous—the restrictive provisions probably cannot be enforced, but are capable of being retrospectively validated. Unfortunately, the Commission does not have sufficient resources to make the system of notification work. Originally, the Court developed a concept of provisional validity for agreements made before Reg. 17 came into force and duly notified thereafter, *De Geus en Uitdenbogerd* v. *Robert Bosch GmbH* Case 13/61, [1962] ECR 45. Unfortunately, in *Brasserie de Haecht* v. *Wilkin Spouses (No. 2)*, Case 48/72 [1973] ECR 77, the ECJ refused to extend this doctrine to agreements made after Regulation 17 came into force. At one time the Commission considered that there might be provisional validity between the parties, but not as against third parties. This idea was absurd. "A" might be required by the other party, "B," to perform even if that would render him liable to damages as against a third party. Fortunately, the Court did not accept this view in either *Brasserie de Haecht (No. 2)* or in *Stergios Delimitis* v. *Henninger Bräu*, Case C-234/89, [1991] ECR I-935, paras. 43–55.
[65] *Gibbs Mew Plc and Gemmel* (CA) [1999] ECC 97, [1998] EuLR 588, paras. 39–45, *obiter*.
[66] Case C-453/99, [2001] 5 CMLR 1058.
[67] *Langnese-Iglo GmbH & Co. KG*, OJ 1993, L183/19, [1994] 4 CMLR 51. Usually when the Commission proposes to withdraw the group exemption, the parties are prepared to negotiate and waive their exclusive rights or whatever it may be that the Commission wants, as happened in *Tetra Pak Rausing SA* v. *Commission*, Case T-51/89, [1990] ECR II-309 and in many cases when the Commission first monitors a notification seriously, such as *Yves Saint Laurent Perfume*, 17 May 2001, IP/01/713. The agreement set up a system of selective distribution and the Commission stressed the importance of internet sales and Yves Saint Laurent amended its terms to permit its selected dealers to sell on the internet.

The former group exempting Regulations for exclusive distribution, purchasing and franchising tended to be drawn formalistically to meet a problem identified in notifications awaiting attention, and to exempt some agreements that were anti-competitive without exempting agreements for which the economic arguments were similar. The new group exemption[68] is more broadly based on economic principles, and subject to a ceiling of market share at 30 per cent. It is based on the idea that, in the absence of significant market power, vertical agreements are unlikely to restrict competition.

2.5.1 The Notification Procedure had Virtually Broken Down

To obtain an individual exemption, an agreement must be notified to the Commission. Its procedure is explained at (7.5.2 below). Since the Commission's competition department lacks adequate resources, however, it is able to have only a few formal decisions adopted each year by the members of the Commission (2.5 above). Recently the number fell to only 3 or 4 a year and the Commission is now not even monitoring notifications. Individual exemptions under Article 81(3) or negative clearances stating that the Commission sees no reason to intervene under Article 81(1) or Article 82 cannot be granted without a formal decision. The Commission terminates far more proceedings informally by sending an administrative letter.[69] Still more files are closed because the agreement has expired, or one party acquired the other.

A "comfort letter" saying that the agreement is not caught by the prohibition, for example, because of the firm's small market share, is helpful if one is enforcing the agreement in a national court, since the court is likely to take the Commission's view into account,[70] although it may be a Trojan horse a few years

---

[68] Regulation 2790/1999 on the application of Article 81(3) of the Treaty to vertical agreements and concerted practices, OJ 1999, L336/21, [2000] 4 CMLR 398, [2000] ECLR supp. to May issue.

[69] In its *19th Report on Competition Policy*, it stated (p.55)

In 1989, the Commission adopted fifteen decisions on substantive matters under Articles 85 and 86 of the EEC Treaty. The 13 decisions taken on the basis of Article 81 of the EEC Treaty are broken down as follows: 2 prohibition decisions accompanied by fines, 1 prohibition decision without fine, 1 negative clearance, 6 exemption decisions under Article 81(3) and 3 decisions rejecting complaints. The two decisions adopted under Article 82 of the EEC Treaty were decisions rejecting complaints.

In addition, 46 procedures were terminated by administrative letter. . .

In its *20th Report on Competition Policy*, point 90 at p. 73, (unfortunately switched with p. 111 by printer's error) it stated that in 1990 it took 9 decisions under Art. 85, of which 4 were exemptions. 158 procedures were terminated by sending comfort letters, 3 of them published under Art. 19(3). A further 710 cases were settled because the agreements were no longer in force, or their impact was too slight to warrant further considerations etc. The Commission's backlog was reduced to 2734 from 3239 cases, paras. 90–91 on p. 110.

[70] *Perfumes—Procureur de la République* v. *Giry and Guérlain*, Cases 253/78 & 1–3/79 [1980] ECR 2327, 2374, para. 13, *Lancôme*, Case 99/79 [1980] ECR 2511, 2533, para. 11; comment, **Valentine Korah**, "Comfort Letters—Reflections on the Perfume Cases," (1981) 6 *ELRev* 14. The system of notification and the informal procedure of sending of comfort letters is explained perceptively by:-

Michael Reynolds, "Practical Aspects of Notifying Agreements and the new form A/B", in Barry Hawk (ed.) [1985] *Fordham Corporate Law Institute*, ch. 32. See also the following two chapters; and

later when the parties have been successful in building up their share of the market. Unfortunately, the case law has developed by the Commission granting exemptions, with few clearances being granted.

If the parties receive an indication that they will get a positive formal decision, they may prefer an exemption, since it binds the parties and national courts, while a negative clearance does not. So there is no one to argue that the Commission should clear rather than exempt.

In *Stergios Delimitis* v. *Henninger Bräu*,[71] the ECJ stressed the central role of the Commission in the implementation and orientation of Community competition policy and stated that the Commission owes a duty to co-operate with national courts that enforce Article 81 by answering their questions as to the stage the Commission's procedure has reached, and the probable outcome, and providing legal and economic data.[72]

It is now arguable that a national court should follow the Commission's informal views until reversed by a formal decision of the Commission, unless clearly inconsistent with legislation or the case law of the Community Courts. The ECJ added at paragraph 47 that national courts should take care not to deliver judgments that conflict with the Commission's decisions, already adopted or envisaged. This emphasis on the avoidance of conflicting decisions may make the Commission's comfort letters binding on national courts notwithstanding the earlier judgments in the *Perfumes* cases of 1980,[73] where the ECJ stated that they were not binding although a national court might take them into account.

The judgment in *Delimitis*, however, did not spell this out nor was it directly concerned with the issue as it was in *Perfumes*. Moreover, it seems likely that in *Delimitis* the ECJ had in mind only formal decisions made or to be made under Regulation 17.[74] Once a comfort letter has been sent stating that the file has been closed, the Commission is seldom likely to take a formal decision.

Mario Siragusa, "Notification of Agreements in the EEC? to Notify or not to Notify", in Barry Hawk (ed.) [1986] *Fordham Corporate Law Institute*, ch. 11., and **Valentine Korah**, *An Introductory Guide to EC Competition Law and Practice*, 7th edn (Oxford, Hart Publishing, 2000) ch. 6.

[71] Case C-234/89, [1991] ECR I-935, para. 44.

[72] The ECJ observed that some agreements do not restrict competition and that old agreements enjoy provisional validity. At para. 53 it stated that the national court might:

> take advice from the Commission on the procedural position which this institution might engage and on the probability that the latter would pronounce officially on the contract in dispute pursuant to the provision of Reg. 17. The national jurisdiction may, under the same conditions, contact the Commission where the concrete application of Article 81, paragraph 1, or Article 82, raises particular difficulties, with a view to obtaining economic and legal data that this institution is in a position to provide it with. The Commission is indeed bound, pursuant to Article 10 (ex Article 5) of the Treaty, by an obligation of loyal cooperation with the judicial authorities of the member states charged with overseeing the application and observance of Community law in the national legal system. . . .

[73] *Procureur de la République* v. *Giry and Guérlain*, Cases 253/78 & 1–3/79, [1980] ECR 2327, 2374, para. 13, and *Lancôme—SA and Cosparfrance Nederland BV* v. *Etos BV and Albert Heijn Supermart BV*, Case 99/79 [1980] ECR 2511, 2533, para. 11.

[74] See Paul Lasok, "Assessing the Economic Consequences of Restrictive Agreements: A Comment on the Delimitis Case," [1991] 5 *ECLR* 194, 200.

This aspect of the *Delimitis* judgment combined with the Commission's practice of declaring that an agreement merits "favourable treatment" and then suspending further processing of the file leads to a particularly acute problem, whether or not the Commission's views be binding. The interests of legal certainty dictate that agreements in this state of "suspended animation" must be enforceable if they are to promote the harmonious development of economic activity in the Community. For a national court to enforce the agreement, however, seems tantamount to affording the agreement provisional validity for which there is no provision or granting it an exemption—which only the Commission is empowered to do.

If, however, the Commission's informal views do become binding, national judges may face a dilemma when the decision does not correspond with those of the ECJ or CFI.

In *Delimitis*, the ECJ stated at paragraphs 52–54 that the national court may decide to adjourn; either to enable the ECJ to make a preliminary ruling or for the Commission to resolve its position. The national court may take interim measures meanwhile in accordance with national procedural rules. The ECJ did not state that the national court may also take final measures.[75]

It could be argued in favour of the national court enforcing an agreement on which the Commission has pronounced favourably (if only provisionally) that there is little chance of conflict. The Commission is unlikely to take a formal decision. Apart from the conceptual difficulty of a national court enforcing an agreement which violates Article 81(1), however, paragraph 50 of the judgment in *Delimitis* implies that the national court can proceed only where there is not the slightest doubt about the Commission's future actions.

Moreover, procedural safeguards have been built into the formal decision making process, such as rights of third parties to express their views. These would be circumvented if a national court could make a final order. These legal difficulties would seem less where the Commission has clearly indicated that the agreement does not infringe Article 81(1) than when it has indicated that it merits exemption.

The problem may become less acute if the Commission's initiative on modernisation[76] is implemented. Not only will national courts be empowered to apply Article 81(3), the Commission is likely to take very few individual decisions relating to distribution.

It is clear that a national court may not give judgment contrary to a formal decision of the Commission. In *Masterfoods Ltd and HB Ice Cream* v. *Commission*,[77] the ECJ so ruled, even though the Commission's decision contradicted an earlier

---

[75] Moreover the statement about adjourning and taking interim measures came before the passage about seeking the Commission's advice. For an illustration of the uncertainty which the situation may lead to, see *Holleran* v. *Thwaites* [1989] 2 CMLR 917, 2.5.2 below.

[76] White Paper on Modernisation of the Rules Implementing Articles 81 and 82 of the EC Treaty. Commission programme No 99/027, OJ 1999, C132/1; [1999] 5 CMLR 208. This is being implemented by the Proposal of the Commission for a Council Regulation to replace Regulation 17/62, 2000/0243 (CNS), [2000] 5 CMLR 1148 (2.12 below).

[77] Case C-344/98 [2000] ECR I-1136.

judgment of a national court and was subject to an appeal to the CFI which had suspended the decision's operation until the CFI finally disposes of the case (3.2 below). A national court may adjourn until the CFI delivers judgment on appeal, probably more than two years after the decision, or it may request a preliminary ruling from the ECJ, but this is unlikely to be helpful when the issue is the application of the law to particular facts.

The uncertainty caused by *Masterfoods* is particularly unfortunate, as the Commission had earlier approved, informally, of revised conditions of sale, which enabled small retailers to buy the freezer cabinets of the dominant supplier of impulse ice creams on reasonable hire purchase terms and thereby obtain the right to sell competing brands in them.

2.5.2 Interference with Bargains

The Commission may attach conditions or obligations to an exemption or be prepared to grant a negative clearance or send a comfort letter only after the parties have modified their agreement. In either event, the balance of the bargain may be altered. Moreover, the party that has gained bargaining power, possibly through investment by the other party that cannot be used save in connection with the contract,[78] is in a position to renegotiate the whole agreement.

For instance, in *ARD*,[79] a German television station had agreed with MGM and United Artists to scrutinise a large library of old films and paid US $80 million for an exclusive licence to transmit any of them it wished over a period of years. After ARD had paid the fee and also invested resources scrutinising the library and dubbing or sub-titling many of the films, the Commission decided that the duration and extent of the exclusive licence was too great although the films represented less than 5 per cent of world production of feature films.[80]

The Commission was prepared to exempt the exclusive licence for West Germany only if MGM and United Artists were permitted freely to license third parties to transmit those films that ARD did not select and those which it did during specified periods, called windows. It even required ARD to provide the print copies and to pay part of the cost of dubbing or sub-titling the films that it had not already adapted.

When the Commission intervened, the copyright holders MGM and United Artists were not prepared to renegotiate the contract so that the terms could be modified in line with the Commission's requirements for an exemption. The

---

[78] "The hold-up problem" mentioned in Guidelines 116(4) as a justification for restrictive clauses. Sunk costs (1.2.4.1.1 above) may not be incurred, unless a contractual provision appropriating the agreed benefit appears enforceable.

[79] *Re Film Purchases by German TV Stations,* OJ 1989, L284/36; [1990] 4 CMLR 841; comment **Warwick A. Rothnie**, "Commission Re-runs Same Old Bill (Film Purchases by German Television Stations)" [1990] *EIPR* 72.

[80] This reasoning is *ex post* and unfortunate, but that is not the point that is being made here.

Commission avoided this problem by accepting an undertaking from ARD that it would not seek to rely on its contractual rights except to the extent that they were exempted.

German viewers benefited from the Commission's refusal to exempt the agreement as it was made by the chance to see more American films, and the popular ones more often. MGM and United Artists also gained a lucrative opportunity to grant further licences. The direct loser was ARD, which had paid and worked for long term exclusive rights. It is not clear that the cost would have been worthwhile had ARD known in advance that its rights would be reduced so substantially. Alternatively, it might have negotiated a smaller payment for more limited rights. The Commission's decision must make other television stations wary of agreeing to perform a similar service in adapting foreign films for Europe.

The lesson is, moreover, of wide application to other sectors of the economy. Novel arrangements in all economic sectors are at risk, although the most important competitive forces come from new ways of doing business (1.2.3.4 above). It seems that the Commission has not changed its practice: it issued a press release[81] stating that it had persuaded Philip Morris to shorten the licences it had granted to a joint venture with Tabacalera to produce and sell two brands of cigarettes in Spain. There was no formal decision because the parties gave in, so there is no discussion of whether the parties would have invested in production equipment without the expectation of longer licences. The parties' shares of the market, however, were far higher than ARD's—60 per cent of the demand for Marlboro cigarettes in Spain and the volume of L&M sufficient to supply the whole local market. It is surprising that a single brand was treated as the relevant market.

All firms do not behave opportunistically in this sort of situation. Many value their reputation for upright trading. When, however, things are going badly, a firm that has gained bargaining power might feel impelled to renegotiate or refuse to renegotiate when it received a windfall. Individual exemptions must be limited in time, so they expire and may have to be renewed, providing another occasion for renegotiation. The possibility of having to renegotiate the deal after relative bargaining power has shifted is very worrying indeed, both for a dealer who may have invested in building up the brand's reputation but finds it is no longer needed and for a supplier who may suffer disruption for months while it seeks another dealer after the failure of the first.

This scenario may be changing if and when the Commission's proposal in the White Paper on modernisation (2.12 below) is adopted and Article 81(3) has direct effect and can be applied by national courts.[82]

---

[81] IP/01/249, 23 February 2001.
[82] The onus of proof is on the person wanting an exemption *Matra Hachette SA* v. *Commission*, (T-17/93) [1994] ECR II-595 para. 105.

2.6 THE COMMISSION'S FORMER VIEWS

Despite the clear rulings by the ECJ (2.7.2 and 2.7.3 below), until recently the Commission rarely took into account under Article 81(1) the economic context of the agreement or whether, without the protection from competition agreed, the basic activity would have been commercially attractive. Often it has found that an agreement is caught by the prohibition of Article 81(1) and granted an exemption or sent a comfort letter on the ground that, without an exclusive territory, no dealer or licensee could have been found. Although if this were the case, one would have thought that the agreement should have been cleared rather than exempted.[83]

The Commission usually refused to analyse markets carefully under Article 81(1): it took the view that competition constitutes freedom from significant contractual restraints, even when these were necessary to induce investment. There were, however, occasional decisions taking a contrasting view, such as *Odin*,[84] where a joint venture was cleared despite significant restraints on the parties which were not considered by the Commission to be actual or potential competitors. During the "nineties" there have been several other decisions on joint ventures where the basic ancillary restraints were cleared, although some minor ones were exempted.[85]

The Commission is now abandoning its view that any significant restriction on conduct infringes Article 81(1) for many of its findings and limits the requirement of exemption to the instances where the ECJ has held that a practice "by its very nature" has the object of restricting competition—horizontal or vertical price fixing and absolute territorial protection (2.7.1 below). Even those practices may not have appreciable effects on trade between member states, and so may escape the prohibition.[86] It is dangerous to rely on old precedents and treat any important vertical restraint as contrary to Article 81(1).

In *Langnese*,[87] the Commission postponed its appraisal of the market until considering Article 81(3), but the CFI held that it should have done so under Article

---

[83] See, however, the narrow definition of ancillary restraints that do not infringe Article 81(1) given by the CFI in *Métropole Télévision SA and Others* v. *Commission,* Case T-112/99, 18 September 2001 [2001] 5 CMLR 1236, 2.7.2 below.

[84] *Odin—Elopak/Metal Box-Odin Developments Ltd.,* OJ 1990, L209/15; [1991] 4 CMLR 832. See also *Iridium,* OJ 1997, L18/87, [1997] 4 CMLR 1065.

See also *European Night Services (ENS) and others* v. *Commission,* Cases T-374, 375, 384 & 388/94, [1998] ECR II-3141, where the CFI quashed the Commission decision, OJ 1994, L259/20, [1995] 5 CMLR 76, for failing to give adequate economic reasons under Article 81(1) as well as under Article 81(3) for many of its findings. On one point the decision was quashed for manifest error of assessment. The CFI came close to adopting a rule of reason.

[85] E.g., *Olivetti/Digital* OJ 1994, L309/24, [1995] 1 CEC 2082.

[86] *Javico International and Javico AG* v. *Yves Saint Laurent Parfums SA,* Case C306/96 [1998] ECR I-1983.

[87] *Langnese-Iglo GmbH & Co. KG,* OJ 1993, L183/19; [1994] 4 CMLR 51, para. 68; on appeal, *Langnese-Iglo GmbH & Co. KG* v. *Commission,* Case T-7/93 [1995] ECR II-1533.

81(1).[88] More recently, In *Whitbread*,[89] the Commission appraised a single brand-ing restraint under Article 81(1) in the light of many market factors. Perhaps some officials have been influenced by the decisions of the CFI.

The Commission's practice of finding that exclusive territories and associated restrictions on poaching infringed Article 81(1) and required exemption was unfortunate. If one analyses a network of exclusive distribution agreements *ex post*—after the dealers have committed themselves to investing in premises and promotion—it is usually more competitive to let the more aggressive dealers poach in the territory of the others. If, however, one analyses the network *ex ante*—before the product had such a good reputation—it may be necessary to ensure that each dealer has some protection from the others or each will refuse to invest in creating demand for the network as a whole.[90] In several cases,[91] the ECJ has recognised under Article 81(1) the need for territorial protection when investment is required.

The Commission's old practice of applying Article 81(1) extensively and with-out market analysis has been extensively criticised,[92] although there are also apol-ogists for the Commission's views, and scholars[93] who take an intermediate or neutral position.

Officials have frequently stated, when speaking in their private capacity at confer-ences, that many files are closed with a comfort letter stating that the agreement is not forbidden by Article 81(1).[94] Some officials complain that decisions, originally

---

[88]   *Langnese-Iglo GmbH & Co. KG* v. *Commission*, Case T-7/93 [1995] ECR II-1533, paras. 94–113. The final appeal did not consider much of the substance, Case C-279/95P [1998] ECR I-5609.

[89]   OJ 1999 L88/26, [1999] 5 CMLR 118.

[90]   See 1.2.4.1–1.2.4.1.4 above.

[91]   Some of which are described at 2.7.2 below.

[92]   The following is a selection of writings on the subject. **C. Bright**, "Deregulations of EC Competition Policy: Rethinking Article 65(1)," [1994] *Fordham Corporate Law Institute* 505; **David Deacon**, "Vertical Restraints under EU Competition Law: New Directions," [1995] *Fordham Corporate Law Institute* 307; **J. Faull**, "Joint Ventures under the EEC Ccompetition Rules" (1984) 5 *ECLR* 358, 362; **I. Forrester** and **C. Norall**, "The Laicization of Community Law: Self Help and the Rule of Reason: How Competition Law is and Could be Applied," (1984) 21 *CMLRev* 11; **L. Gyselen**, "Vertical Restraints in the Distribution Process: Strength and Weakness of the Free Rider Rationale under EEC Competition Law," (1984) 21 *CMLRev* 648; **Barry Hawk**, "The American (Anti-trust) Revolution: Lessons for the EEC?" (1988) 9 *ECLR* 53; and **Hawk**, "System Failure, Vertical Restraints and EC Competition Law," (1995) 32 *CMLRev* 973; **René Joliet**, *The Rule of Reason in Antitrust Law* (The Hague, Martinus Nijhoff, 1967); also "Trademark Licensing Agreements under the EEC Law of Competition," (1984) 5 *Northwestern J of Int'l L & Bus* 755, from 773; **S. Kon**, "Article 85 para. 3: A Case for Application by National Courts," (1982) 19 *CMLRev* 541; **Valentine Korah**, "The Rise and Fall of Provisional Validity—the Need for a Rule of Reason in EEC Antitrust," (1981) 3 *Northwestern J of Int'l L & Bus* 320, at pp. 340 *et seq.*; and **Korah**, "EEC Competition Policy—Legal Form or Economic Efficiency", (1986) *Current Legal Problems* 85; and **Korah**, *An Introductory Guide to EC Competition Law and Practice*, 7th edn (Oxford, Hart Publishing, 2000) ch. 13; **M.C. Scheckter**, "The Rule of Reason in European Competition Law", (1982) 2 *LIEI* 1; **Rein Wesseling**, *The Modernisation of EC Antitrust Law*, (Oxford, Hart Publishing, 2000) pp. 78, 82–83.

[93]   **Michel Waelbroeck**, "Antitrust Analysis under Article 85(1) and (3)," [1987] *Fordham Corporate Law Institute*, ch. 28 and the ensuing discussion in ch. 29; **Richard Whish** and **Brenda Sufrin**, "Article 85 and the Rule of Reason," (1987) 7 *YEL* 1; **R. Whish**, *Competition Law*, 4th edn (London, Butterworths, 2001) 102

[94]   E.g., **J. Faull**, at a conference in Brussels in November 1988, organised by ESC. See also his article, "Joint Ventures under the EEC Competition Rules," [1984] 5 *ECLR* 358. Different views were expressed by **H. Schröter**, [1987] *Fordham Corporate Law Institute*, ch. 27. Not all officials think alike.

drafted as negative clearances, have ended up as exemptions after the file left DG Competition and went to the College of Commissioners for adoption. In future, if the officials concerned with individual decisions draft as clearances those of which they approve, the drafts are less likely to be altered to exemptions. The most frequent kind of comfort letter these days does not distinguish between agreements that are not contrary to Article 81(1) and those that merit exemption.

There were several signs in the franchising regulation and more in that on know-how licences, that the Commission had begun to analyse agreements *ex ante*,[95] but its recent practice when monitoring notified agreements has gone much further (2.8–2.8.2 below).

2.7 THE VIEWS OF THE ECJ AND CFI

The ECJ and CFI have no power to grant exemptions under Article 81(3) and, on judicial review, the CFI admits to only rather remote power to control the Commission's decisions on exemption.[96] It does not rehear a case, but decides whether the Commission has exceeded its discretionary powers or used them for an improper purpose.

From its earliest days, the ECJ has ruled that an agreement should be examined in its legal and economic context before deciding that it infringes Article 81(1) (2.7.3 below). Although restrictions on conduct have sometimes been equated with restrictions of competition,[97] in a series of cases, not all concerned with distribution, the ECJ and CFI have accepted that ancillary restrictions necessary to make a transaction viable do not, in themselves, restrict competition (2.7.2 below). It has several times ruled that the need to induce investment may take exclusive arrangements outside Article 81(1).

To start with, in *Société La Technique Minière* v. *Maschinenbau Ulm*,[98] the ECJ ruled, in effect, that if granting a French company an exclusive right to supply its graders (items of public works equipment) in France was necessary to enable a German manufacturer to penetrate the French market, reciprocal promises by the supplier to supply no other dealer in France and by the dealer not to handle com-

---

[95] For some examples taken from the know how Regulation, see **Valentine Korah**, *Know-How Licensing Agreements and the EEC Competition Rules—Regulation 556/89* (Oxford, ESC Publishing, 1989) p.10, note 6.

[96] See, e.g., **Francis G. Jacobs**, "Court of Justice Review of Competition Cases", in Barry Hawk (ed.) [1987] *Fordham Corporate Law Institute*, ch. 23. See also 2.2, above, the quotation from the ECJ's judgment in *Consten and Grundig* v. *Commission*. More recently, the CFI has used the requirement for the Commission to give reasons for its decisions to quash those where the reasoning is inadequate. It has almost taken power to rehear a case. See, e.g., *European Night Services (ENS) and others* v. *Commission*, Cases T-374, 375, 384 & 388/94, [1998] ECR II-3141.

[97] **Valentine Korah**, *An Introductory Guide to EC Competition Law and Practice*, 7th edn (Oxford, Hart Publishing, 2000) 13.1.2 and **Helmut Schröter** [1987] *Fordham Corporate Law Institute*, ch. 27.

[98] Case 56/65 [1966] ECR 235.

peting goods without consent would not have the effect of infringing Article 81(1). The national court should examine whether the restrictions were broader than necessary. The judgment can be reconciled with that in *Consten and Grundig* (2.2 above), only on the basis that there were export bans, supported by the arrangement for the Gint mark in the later case.

2.7.1 Object of Restricting Competition

The ECJ has been hostile to rpm and to absolute territorial protection. In *Erauw-Jacquery (Louis) SPRL* v. *La Hesbignonne SC*,[99] the ECJ condemned rpm between the licensor and licensee of plant breeders' rights in general terms as having the object and effect of restricting competition. It referred to the objectives of the single market and to the list of examples given in Article 81(1), which includes agreements to fix prices. It stated that vertical and horizontal price fixing have similar effects[100] and concluded that "the object and effect of such a provision is to restrict competition within the Common Market."

It is for the national court seeking guidance to decide whether a licence of plant breeders' rights maintaining sale prices might affect trade between member states. In view of the export ban on licensees of plant breeders' rights in basic seed, which it had virtually cleared, the ECJ suggested that the agreement might well have such an effect.

In *Miller International Schallplatten GmbH* v. *Commission*[101] the ECJ said:

7. In this connexion it must be held that, by its very nature, a clause prohibiting exports constitutes a restriction on competition, whether it is adopted at the instigation of the supplier or of the customer since the agreed purpose of the contracting parties is the endeavour to isolate a part of the market.

Thus the fact that the supplier is not strict in enforcing such prohibitions cannot establish that they had no effect since their very existence may create a "visual and psychological" background which satisfies customers and contributes to a more or less rigorous division of the markets.

It added at paragraph 15 that the Commission did not have to establish that the clause had appreciable effects on inter-state trade, only that it was capable of having them. The ECJ did not consider whether the effect on competition or cross border trade was appreciable, nor whether the practice was necessary to prevent free riding.

---

[99] Case 27/87 [1988] ECR 1919, paras. 12–15.
[100] Wrongly in our view: in a vertical relationship the supplier has an incentive to give to its dealer the minimum protection it thinks necessary to induce investment. It wants the dealer to sell on the minimum margin, whereas in a price fixing cartel between competitors, each has an interest in the others supplying less at higher prices (1.1 above).
[101] Case 19/77 [1978] ECR 131.

In *Erauw-Jacquery (Louis) SPRL* v. *La Hesbignonne SC*,[102] however, in view of
the substantial sunk costs incurred by the holder of plant breeders' rights in developing a plant variety and the need for careful handling of basic seed, the ECJ
cleared a restraint on the licensee selling and exporting basic seed although it conferred absolute territorial protection. The Commission applies the judgment only
in relation to basic seed.[103] It is generally agreed that the judgment creates a very
narrow exception and may be due to the fragility of plant breeders' rights which
expire once the variety ceases to be distinct, uniform, stable and useful. It may be
argued, however, that it applies to software licences, for which there is no group
exemption beyond what is allowed by Regulation 2790/99 (3.4.9– 3.4.9.2.5 below).

The Commission treats these cases as indicating that export bans and rpm have
at least the object of restricting competition and that it is not necessary to establish their effect.[104] In the *Green Paper*,[105] the Commission treated both rpm
and absolute territorial protection as automatically illegal and very unlikely ever to
be exempted.[106] Recently the Commission has been limiting the automatic application of Article 81(1) to export bans conferring absolute territorial protection
and rpm[107] (4.2–4.3.1.2 below).

---

[102] Case 27/87 [1988] ECR 1919, paras. 10 and 11.
[103] *SICASOV*, OJ 1999, L4/27, [1999] 4 CMLR 192, paras. 50 & 53.
[104] E.g., Guidelines 7 and 46–56. See also *Glaxo/Welcome*, 8 May 2001, OJ 2001, L302/1, 4.3 below.
[105] On vertical restraints in EC Competition Policy, COM(96) 721 final, [1997] 4 CMLR 519, para. 21.
[106] The rules on *de minimis* define categories of agreements that are too small to have an appreciable impact on trade or competition and are consequently outside the scope of Article 85(1) (now
Article 81(1). Above this level, Article 85(1) applies virtually automatically to certain vertical agreements which by their very nature can only distort competition, in particular to
—agreements which limit the freedom of distributors to set their resale prices (Resale Price
    Maintenance) and
—agreements which establish absolute territorial protection for exclusive distributors.
    This point is central to Commission policy. Not only is Article 85(1) applied, but an Article 85(3)
exemption is unlikely to be granted. Whilst a distributor may be allocated an exclusive territory in order
better to penetrate the market and make distribution more efficient and may be forbidden to sell or promote directly in the territory of other exclusive distributors, this protection must not be absolute. . . .

[107] **Giuliano Marenco**, in "La notion de restriction de concurrence dans le cadre de l'interdiction
des ententes," II *Mélanges en Hommage à Michel Waelbroeck*, 1217, 1237, was concerned about legal
certainty, and the time it takes to obtain an exemption. Without citing a single EC case, he confined the
concept of agreements which limit freedom of action to limitations on future transactions, such as
exclusive agreements. Even so, he considered that there should be some economic analysis before finding that agreements or concerted practices infringe Article 81(1). Signor Marenco heads the competition team in the Commission's legal service and his views are likely to be influential. See also J. Faull
and A. Nipkay (eds.), *The EC Law of Competition* (Oxford, OUP, 1998) pp. 81–82:

   2.53 In practice few types of agreement have as their object the restriction of competition. Typically
   those are agreements which, *prima facie*, do not appear to have significant beneficial effects and are
   entered into solely to restrict competition. For agreements between undertakings at the same level
   of the market (horizontal agreements), essentially only those which have the obvious consequence
   of price fixing or market sharing and likely to be held to be restrictive by object. For vertical agreements, only those which impede parallel trade within the Community or enforce resale price maintenance are likely to be considered restrictive by object. (footnotes omitted).

Chapter 2 was contributed by Faull and Nipkay, the general editors of the book. Jonathan Faull was
then a director in the competition department, particularly well respected and influential.

The ECJ has accepted limited restrictions on cross border trade as not infringing Article 81(1) in view of the investments made by both parties in *Nungesser (LG) KG and Kurt Eisele* v. *Commission.*[108]

Moreover, the ECJ has on two occasions accepted in relation to Article 81(1) that even absolute territorial protection was necessary to support investment. It permitted absolute territorial protection in relation to copyright in performing rights in *Coditel* v. *Ciné Vog Films (No 2)*[109] and in relation to a licence of plant breeders' rights in basic seed, in *Louis Erauw-Jacquery* v. *Hesbignonne.*[110] It is arguable that the rationale of encouraging investment is of general application, but the judgments in *Coditel* and *Louis Erauw-Jacquery* were carefully qualified, and it is doubtful whether they will be greatly extended beyond their special sectors.

2.7.2 Ancillary Restraints

In a series of cases, the ECJ held that where a transaction was not in itself anti-competitive, provisions needed to make it viable were not contrary to Article 81(1). In *Remia,*[111] for instance, a covenant not to compete with a business being sold was partially upheld as not infringing Article 81(1) on the ground that without such a covenant the sale could not take effect (para. 19). Nevertheless, the covenant must be limited to what is necessary (para. 20). It upheld the Commission's decision[112] reducing such a clause from 10 to 4 years.

The ECJ has adopted an ancillary restraint doctrine in clearing cases as not infringing Article 81(1) in many cases.[113] So has the CFI.[114]

A distinction has, however, sometimes been drawn between restraints necessary to make a particular transaction commercially viable, which may require exemption and those restraints without which a transaction of that class cannot be conceived. One cannot conceive of the transfer of a business without a covenant by the vendor not to compete. In *Métropole* v. *Commission,*[115] the CFI said, citing the Commission's notice on ancillary restraints,[116] that:

104. In Community law the concept of an "ancillary restriction" covers any restriction which is directly related and necessary to the implementation of a main operation.

---

[108] Case 258/78 [1982] ECR 2015.

[109] Case 262/81 [1982] ECR 3381.

[110] Case 27/87 [1988] ECR 1919.

[111] *Remia BV and Verenigde Bedrijven Nutricia* v. *Commission* Case 42/84 [1985] ECR 2545.

[112] *Nutricia,* OJ 1983, L376/22 [1984] 2 CMLR 165.

[113] E.g. the cases on selective distribution (2.8–2.8.1.6 below) such as *Lancôme* v. *Etos,* Case 99/79 [1980] ECR 2511; *Pronuptia* on franchising (2.8.2 below), the cases on agency (2.8.4 below), *Nungesser, Louis Erauw-Jacquerie* and *Coditel II* (2.7.1 above).

[114] *European Night Services (ENS) and Others* v. *Commission,* Cases T-374, 375, 384 & 388/94 [1998] ECR II-3141.

[115] *Métropole Télévision SA (M6) and Others* v. *Commission* Case T-112/99, 18 September 2001, paras. 104–127.

[116] Mergers Guidelines, 4 July 2001, OJ 2001, C118/5, [2001] 5 CMLR 787.

It had earlier held that there is no scope to balance the pro-competitive effects from those that are anti-competitive (para. 77) and in order to preserve the effectiveness of Article 81(3) and for the sake of consistency it concluded that:

> 109. . . . as the Commission has correctly asserted, examination of the objective necessity of a restriction in relation to the main operation cannot but be relatively abstract. It is not a question of analysing whether, in the light of the competitive situation on the relevant market, the restriction is indispensable to the commercial success of the main operation but of determining whether, in the specific context of the main operation the restriction is necessary to implement that operation. If, without the restriction the main operation is difficult or even impossible to implement, the restriction may be regarded as objectively necessary for its implication.

In our view, there has been tension between judgments that adopted the view expressed at para. 109 and others that accepted as outside Article 81(1) restraints required to make a particular transaction viable. The view in *Métropole* is compatible with some of the judgments of the ECJ, such as *Remia*[117], *Pronuptia* (2.8.2 below)[118] and much of the case law on selective distribution (2.8.1.1, but contrast 2.8.1.2.3 below), but is more difficult to reconcile with *Société La Technique Minière* v. *Maschinenbau Ulm GmbH*[119] or *Nungesser* where the ECJ looked to commercial viability.[120] An even stronger contrast was the judgment of the CFI in *European Night Services (ENS) and Others* v. *Commission.*[121] Currently, the narrow concept of ancillarity, which has been worked out by the Commission under the merger regulation, has the unfortunate result of making it more difficult to enforce restraints necessary to make viable a transaction, not in itself anticompetitive. If the regulation to replace Regulation 17 is adopted (2.12 below), it will be less serious as national courts and authorities will be able to adopt positive decisions taking Article 81(3) into account. Even then the onus will clearly be on the parties alleging legality[122]—the bifurcation of Article 81(1) and (3) will not entirely disappear (2.12 below).

2.7.3 The Relevance of Market Considerations

The ECJ and CFI have also stressed the need to assess an agreement in its legal and economic context.[123] In *Stergios Delimitis* v. *Henninger Bräu*,[124] the ECJ used this

---

[117] Case 42/84 [1985] ECR 2545.

[118] See **Enrique Gonzalez Diaz**, "Some Reflections on the Notion of Ancillary Restraints under EC Competition Law," [1995] *Fordham Corporate Law Institute* 325.

[119] Case 56/65 [1966] ECR 235.

[120] *Nungesser (LG) KG and Kurt Eisele* v. *Commission,* Case 258/78 [1982] ECR 2015.

[121] Cases T-374, 375, 384 & 388/94 [1998] ECR II-3141.

[122] *Matra Hachette SA* v. *Commission,* Case T-17/93 [1994] ECR-2 595, para. 104. Moreover, the Commission has wide discretion in applying Article 81(3), so the onus of challenging a refusal will be heavy.

[123] The first judgment was *La Société Technique Minière* (2.7 above). There are many more, such as *Brasserie de Haecht SA* v. *Wilkin,* Case 23/67 [1967] ECR 407 and *L'Oréal* v. *De Nieuwe AMCK,* Case 31/80 [1980] ECR 3775.

[124] Case C-234/89 [1991] ECR I-935, paras. 13–27, (5.1.1.1.3–5.1.1.1.7 below).

concept to rule that a single branding agreement[125] did not have the object of restricting competition and would not have that effect unless all the agreements tying dealers to one or other of the suppliers kept other suppliers out of the market. This would be the case only if there were entry barriers at the level downstream and so many outlets were tied for so long to one or other of the suppliers that a new one would not be able to enter the market on an efficient scale for advertising. Even then the effect on competition would be appreciable only if the particular brewer made a significant contribution to the foreclosure (1.2.5–1.2.5.4 above and 7.7 below).

Although the ECJ referred to the benefits to the parties of exclusive purchasing agreements as showing that the object was not anti-competitive, in my view, this is not an instance where the Court was invoking the ancillary restraint doctrine.[126] It required the national court to consider the agreement in its legal and economic context.

Since the CFI and ECJ are continuing with this line of argument generally[127] as well as with the ancillary restraint doctrine, many agreements that were difficult to enforce have become enforceable. *Delimitis* is clearly a precedent of major importance.

2.8 CASE LAW ON MARKETING UNDER ARTICLE 81(1)

The ECJ has held that Article 81 is not concerned with perfect competition but workable competition,[128] and it has applied the ancillary restraint doctrine as well as appraising agreements in their economic context.

2.8.1 Selective Distribution

Brand owners may want to control their retail outlets in order to compete on pre-sales service, location or ambience, for which it may be difficult to charge consumers, rather than on price. If so, they may well wish to limit the kinds of outlet selling their goods and to protect such expensive outlets from acute price competition. They may require the dealers to whom they sell their products to supply only the general public or authorised dealers.

---

[125] 1.2.2.1 above. The lessee of a beer house agreed to handle only Henninger Bräu beer and soft drinks on the premises, although it was allowed to buy beer from other Member States.

[126] Had it been applying the wider concept ancillary restraints it might have advised the national court to consider how long a tie was required for Henninger Bräu to plan its delivery schedule, or to amortize its investment in a brewery or depot. This it did not do. It may have accepted the "inherency" doctrine of German law, according to which, if the agreement is not inherently harmful, the normal attributes of it are not treated as anti-competitive. Most beer supply contracts include an exclusive purchasing obligation. It did not purport to be applying the more abstract concept of ancillary restraint adopted by the CFI in *Métropole* (2.7.1 above).

[127] See also *Neste Markkinointi Oy* v. *Yötuuli Ky, and Others*, Case C-214/99 [2001] 4 CMLR 993 and *Greene King—Roberts & Roberts* v. *Commission*, Case T25/99, 5 July 2001 [2001] CMLR 828 (7.2.6.5.1 below).

[128] *Metro* v. *Commission*, Case 26/76 [1977] ECR 1875, para. 20, quoted at 2.8.1.1 below.

It is still necessary to consider the case law on selective distribution as the case law of the ECJ proffers a safe harbour, available when the new group exemption does not apply for one reason or another. It should be remembered, however, that the definition of "selective distribution" in the Regulation differs from that used by the ECJ (2.8.1.4 below).

In the EC this is called "selective distribution."[129] A supplier which does not enjoy a dominant position may choose with whom to deal, although this may be limited by national law,[130] but a restriction on dealers who have bought goods restricts their conduct and in the 1960s and 1970s, when the law of selective distribution was being developed, any important restriction of conduct was usually treated as having the object of restricting competition.

A supplier may also want to provide for just in time delivery (1.1 above) and to instal scanning devices so that as a retailer sells each item a new one is ordered from depot or place of production. In that event the supplier will want to supply only chosen distributors, which it can include on its scanning system. This problem has arisen more recently, but Regulation 2790/99 allows for it by defining "selective distribution" more widely than the ECJ, although there is no case law under the new Regulation.

2.8.1.1 Not all restrictions of conduct have the object or effect of restricting competition

In *Metro*,[131] the ECJ first ruled that a restriction as to the dealers to whom an exclusive distributor may sell did not infringe Article 81(1) provided that the supplier specified objective, qualitative criteria for approval as to the premises and staff required and applied the criteria objectively without discrimination. At para. 20 the ECJ said that:

> The requirement contained in Articles 3 and 81 of the EEC Treaty that competition shall not be distorted implies the existence on the market of workable competition, that is to say the degree of competition necessary to ensure the observance of the basic requirements and the attainment of the objectives of the Treaty, in particular the creation of a single market achieving conditions similar to those of a domestic market.

[129] See, generally, C.D. Ehlermann and L. Laudati (eds.), *Proceedings of the European Competition Forum* (Chichester, Wiley, 1997) part 2. Jean Dubois, who was then in charge of distribution at the Competition Department of the Commission introduced the topic by describing the practice and case law of Commission and ECJ. There followed critical comments by officials from the competition authorities of Member States, many complaining of the formalistic rules and the paucity of economic analysis. This volume and the conference that produced the paper, must have been influential in the Commission's changed attitude to selective distribution, the definition in Article 1 of Regulation 2890/99 that does not limit the practice to systems based on qualitative and proportionate criteria.

[130] E.g., the French crime of *refus de vente* exists also in other countries. Both Commission and ECJ have sometimes inferred an agreement or concerted practice from a refusal to deal with former regular customers, but this has been limited by the judgment of the CFI in *Bayer* v. *Commission* Case T-41/96, 26 October 2000 [2001] 4 CMLR 4 (2.1 above). The Commission has appealed, C-2 & 3/01P OJ 2001, C79/14.

[131] Case 26/76 [1977] ECR 1875, appeal from *SABA—Schwarzwälder Apparate-Nau-Anstalt August Schwer & Söne GmbH*, Case 76/159/EEC, OJ 1976, L28/19, [1976] 1 CMLR D61.

In accordance with this requirement the nature and intensiveness of competition may vary to an extent dictated by the products or services in question and the economic structure of the relevant market sectors.

In the sector covering the production of high quality and technically advanced consumer durables, where a relatively small number of large- and medium-scale producers offer a varied range of items which, or so consumers may consider, are readily interchangeable, the structure of the market does not preclude the existence of a variety of channels of distribution adapted to the peculiar characteristics of the various producers and to the requirements of the various categories of consumers.

On this view the Commission was justified in recognizing that selective distribution systems constituted together with others, an aspect of competition which accords with Article 81(1), provided that resellers are chosen on the basis of objective criteria of a qualitative nature relating to the technical qualifications of the reseller and his staff and the suitability of his trading premises and that such conditions are laid down uniformly for all potential resellers and are not applied in a discriminatory fashion.

21. It is true that in such systems of distribution price competition is not generally emphasised either as an exclusive or indeed as a principal factor.

This is particularly so when, as in the present case, access to the distribution network is subject to conditions exceeding the requirements of an appropriate distribution of the products.

However, although price competition is so important that it can never be eliminated it does not constitute the only effective form of competition or that to which absolute priority must in all circumstances be accorded.

The ECJ stressed that there might be competition not only over price, but also over service—Article 81 was concerned not only with "perfect" but also "workable" competition. Nevertheless, where there were limitations on the number of dealers to be approved—quantitative criteria—the restraint on dealers selling to non-approved dealers would infringe Article 81(1).

The judgment was welcomed as being less formalistic than expected. It was one of the early cases in which the ECJ held that ancillary restrictions necessary to make a network successful did not necessarily restrict competition (2.7.2 above). The concept was abstract in that it provided a rule of law, rather than inquiring how far conduct had to be restrained to make the particular transaction viable.

2.8.1.2 The meaning of selective distribution

In *AEG Telefunken* v. *Commission*,[132] the ECJ confirmed its earlier judgment and stated that:

> . . . it has always been recognised in the case law of the Court that there are legitimate requirements, such as the maintenance of a specialist trade capable of providing specific

---

[132] *Allgemeine Elektricitäts-Gesellschaft AEG-Telefunken AG* v. *Commission*, Case 107/82 [1983] ECR 3151.

services as regards high-quality and high technology products, which may justify a
reduction of price competition in favour of competition relating to factors other than
price. Systems of selective distribution, in so far as they aim at the attainment of a legitimate goal capable of improving competition in relation to factors other than price,
therefore constitute an element of competition which is in conformity with Article 85(1),
(now Article 81(1)) . . . .

The Court specified in . . . [Metro I[133]] that such systems are permissible, provided that
resellers are chosen on the basis of objective criteria of a qualitative nature relating to the
technical qualifications of the reseller and his staff and the suitability of his trading
premises and that such conditions are laid down uniformly for all potential resellers and
are not applied in a discriminatory fashion.[134]

Four factors may be identified from these paragraphs as the key elements of the
concept of simple selective distribution.

First, a supplier may limit the sale of its products to the specialist trade.

Second, selective distribution is compatible with Article 81(1) where the products are of high quality and technically complex (2.8.1.2.1 below).

Third, selective distribution systems are compatible with Article 81(1) only
where the dealers are chosen on the basis of *qualitative* criteria relating to staff or
premises and not on the basis of *quantitative* criteria. Such limitations must, however, be proportionate: no more limiting than can be justified in the consumer
interest. Any attempt to protect the dealers (who may have to invest in order to
qualify) from others infringes Article 81(1) and will rarely be exempted (2.8.1.3
below). This is a very serious limitation to the case law of the ECJ, as it is usually
expensive for the dealer to qualify on the qualitative criteria and it may need protection to induce it to incur sunk costs.

A selective distribution system meeting these three conditions is called "simple."

Fourth, selective distribution systems that are not based solely on qualitative
criteria and include some other terms are not called "simple." They may need individual exemption to be enforceable. For example, in *Metro 1*,[135] requirements that
wholesalers should invest in setting up a retail network and achieve a target
turnover were treated as infringing Article 81(1) and as requiring exemption since
they excluded from the network wholesalers who were technically qualified, but
did not want to make such an investment (2.8.1.2.2 below).

Many of the commentators at the influential conference organised by
Dr. Ehlermann[136] thought that more emphasis should be placed on market analysis than on the nature of the product. What mattered was the strategy of the brand
owner.

---

[133] Case 26/76 [1977] ECR 1875.
[134] Case 107/82 [1983] ECR 3151, from ground 33 onwards. Compare its later judgment in *Metro
(II)* Case 75/84 [1986] ECR 3021, 2.8.1.2.3 below.
[135] Case 26/76 [1977] ECR 1875. Contrast *Villeroy & Boch*, OJ 1985, L376/15, The Commission
seems to have returned to its earlier views in *Yves Saint Laurent Parfums*, OJ 1991, C320/11; [1991] 4
CMLR 163.
[136] See, generally, C.D. Ehlermann and L. Laudati (eds.), *Proceedings of the European Competition
Forum*, (Chichester, Wiley, 1997) part 2.

2.8.1.2.1 *The nature of the products*

In *AEG Telefunken* v. *Commission* (2.8.1.2 above), the ECJ referred to the high quality or technical complexity of the products as justifying the need for specialist services which in turn justified the reduction of price competition.[137] The types of products for which such systems may be accepted is not closed. Nor, it seems, is the class of justifications.

The products considered there were hi-fi equipment and television sets.[138] In later cases, the Commission[139] and the CFI[140] have extended the justification to luxury products, such a jewellery and fine fragrances for the sale of which ambience is important and, in *Villeroy & Boch*,[141] to ceramic tableware although there was no need for specialised staff able to give technical advice for tableware. The Commission justified selective distribution because of the long life of the product and the need for retailers to hold stocks for customers to get replacements.[142] The group exemption for the selective distribution of motor vehicles with three or more wheels[143] is considered at (7.6–7.6.3.6 below).

In *Ideal-Standard's Distribution System*,[144] the Commission doubted whether DIY plumbing fittings are technically advanced products that justify selective distribution and whether limiting wholesalers rather than retailers to those technically qualified escapes the prohibition of Article 81(1).

In *Binon*, the ECJ ruled that a simple selective distribution system for newspapers did not infringe Article 81(1) owing to the need for speed in delivery.[145]

2.8.1.2.2 *Qualitative criteria*

In the second paragraph quoted from *AEG* (2.8.1.2 above), as in the *SABA/Metro* cases,[146] the ECJ distinguished "qualitative" from what it called "quantitative"

[137] The Commission has been concerned that specialist parts of department stores should qualify as well as specialist shops, as it considers that they may often sell on lower margins than specialist shops, *Junghans*, OJ 1977, L30/10, [1977] 1 CMLR D82, para. 18.
[138] As they were in *Metro (I)*, Case 26/76 [1977] ECR 1875 (2.8.1.1 above).
[139] *Murat*, OJ 1983, L348/10, [1984] 1 CMLR 219 concerned jewellery.
[140] *Parfums Yves Saint Laurent*, Case T-19/92 [1996] ECR II-1851, paras. 113–116. When the exemption expired, the Commission issued a press release IP/01/713 stating that the system now qualified under Regulation 2790/99. Yves Saint Laurent had had to modify its system to permit sales by department stores as required by the CFI and by selected dealers on the internet.
[141] OJ 1985, L376/15; [1988] 4 CMLR 461.
[142] *Ibid.*, para. 26. Keeping substantial stocks, even of out of date patterns, involves a sunk cost, of no value save for the sale of V & B tableware. In *Villeroy & Boch*, however, there seems to have been no protection of the dealer: the Commission was concerned whether the restriction on supplying unqualified dealers was valid in itself, not with an exclusive territory.
[143] Commission Regulation 1475/95—Group exemption for motor vehicle distribution and servicing agreements, OJ 1995, L145/25, [1996] 4 CMLR 69, replacing Regulation 123/85, OJ 1985, L15/16.
[144] OJ 1985, L20/24; [1988] 4 CMLR 627.
[145] Case 243/83 [1985] ECR 2015. This ruling is anomalous and formalistic. If speed in delivery is important, it is the number of drops that must be reduced, yet the Court ruled that quantitative criteria would bring the network within the prohibition of Art. 81(1) and require exemption.
[146] OJ 1976, L28/19; [1976] 1 CMLR D61, confirmed on appeal, Case 26/76 [1977] ECR 1875.
A later version of the same standard agreements was exempted in *SABA (II)*, OJ 1983, L376/41; [1984] 1 CMLR 676; confirmed on appeal *sub nom. Metro* v. *Commission*, Case 75/84 [1986] ECR 3021.

criteria. Qualitative criteria relate to the technical qualifications of the dealer's staff and the suitability of its premises. For the restriction to escape the prohibition of Article 81(1), the criteria must be objective in two senses: first, the supplier must specify the qualitative criteria that are sensible in the particular trade[147] and, secondly, it must apply them without discrimination, permitting any dealer who qualifies to be approved.

It is seldom possible to come within the ECJ's definition of a simple selective distribution system. Normally, it is expensive to comply with the criteria and the investment may have no other use.[148] Consequently, a manufacturer or trademark owner may also have to provide protection to induce such investment by adopting quantitative criteria, for example, promising not to select any other retailers within a given distance, or in an area with a specified population, or some such limitation.

The Commission has found that a selective distribution system may remain simple even if the dealer is protected by an exclusive territory.[149]

The Commission's hostility to the protection of existing dealers is exemplified by *Interlubke*,[150] where it objected informally to a network where dealers were permitted to sell only to end-users and not to any other dealers, whether authorised or not.

If the criteria be quantitative, the Commission is unlikely to grant an individual exemption. In *Hasselblad* v. *Commission*,[151] a maker of high quality cameras supplied a sole distributor in the UK. One of the practices condemned arose when the sole distributor restrained its dealers from selling to other dealers, authorised or not, without its consent. When there were a large number of dealers in the same area, the distributor refused to approve further dealers claiming that it needed to

---

[147] See 2.8.1.2.4 below. Compare *L'Oréal* v. *De Nieuwe AMCK*, Case 31/80 [1980] ECR 3775, para. 16:

> In order to determine the exact nature of such "qualitative" criteria for the selection of re-sellers, it is also necessary to consider whether the characteristics of the product in question necessitate a selective distribution system in order to preserve its quality and ensure its proper use, and whether those objectives are not already satisfied by national rules governing admission to the re-sale trade or the conditions of sale of the products are question.

In *Vichy*, OJ 1991, L75/57, the Commission withdrew the immunity from fines under Article 15(6) of Regulation 17 from a selective distribution system for beauty care products that was based partly on a quantitative criterion para. 18(a) and (b). One of the criteria was that there should be a pharmacist in each retail outlet, and the number of pharmacists licensed to operate in Belgium was limited by law. This was confirmed by the CFI, *Société d'Hygiène de Vichy* v. *Commission*, Case T-19/91 [1991] ECR II-265.

[148] See 1.2.4.1.1 above on sunk costs.

[149] *Junghans*, OJ 1977, L30/10, [1977] 1 CMLR D82, para. 31, where the Commission found that an exclusive distribution agreement came within an earlier group exemption granted by Reg. 67/67 despite a restriction on the dealer supplying unauthorised dealers.

[150] (1985) *Commission's 15th Report on Competition Policy*, p. 66. Dealers had been restrained from installing furniture in territories where other dealers were established and were required to respect the manufacturer's retail pricing policy. After the Commission's intervention, dealers were permitted to sell in other member states to other furniture dealers and to end-users. The short account in the annual report gives no indication of the manufacturer's market share, nor does it give any facts that support the Commission's view that other furniture dealers were foreclosed, as it alleged.

[151] Case 86/82 [1984] ECR 883, para. 50.

protect dealers who were required to make substantial minimum investments in stock, which it would take a turnover in Hasselblad products of £6,000 to finance.[152] Further, it disciplined dealers who supplied unauthorised traders, even in another member state, thereby protecting other authorised dealers.

At paragraph 51, the ECJ confirmed the Commission's[153] treatment of this protection as based in part on quantitative criteria, prohibited by Article 81(1) and not meriting exemption, although there were 110 authorised dealers in the UK and each must have been subject to considerable intra-brand competition as well as to competition from other brands.[154] The ECJ also confirmed the fine imposed on Hasselblad. Notwithstanding the other practices which the distributor engaged in, it is arguable that the mild territorial protection may have been an ancillary restraint necessary to make the selective distribution system viable.

In 1985, the Commission became less interventionist. Ivoclar made artificial teeth specifically tailored to the masticatory surfaces of the teeth of a particular patient and supplied them only to authorised exclusive distributors. It restrained these from supplying teeth to other distributors who might, in principle, meet the important and strict qualitative criteria Ivoclar applied. This was then a selective distribution system based in part on quantitative criteria.[155]

The Commission stated that this restriction of the dealers' rights to sell to whomever they wanted infringed Article 81(1) and prevented the application of Regulation 67/67. It granted an individual exemption, however, on the ground that Ivoclar provided training, education and advisory services to a manageable number of distribution depots.

The Commission was impressed by the cost saving in providing services to only a few depots. It might have been politically difficult for it to have stressed that any dealer required to invest in sunk costs needs to be induced by an element of protection from competition as this might have been contrary to the judgment of the ECJ in *Hasselblad*.[156]

In the New Zealand case of *Fisher & Peykell*,[157] the High Court[158] was also impressed by the pro-competitive effect of encouraging a brand owner to train its dealers. It balanced what it saw as the slightly anti-competitive effect of an exclusive purchasing agreement that could be terminated on either side by 90 days' notice against the competition in services it induced and found that single branding did not restrict competition.

---

[152] *Ibid.*, at 895.

[153] *Camera Care* OJ 1982; [1982] 2 CMLR 233.

[154] [1984] ECR 883, at p. 921, Sir Gordon Slynn explained the theory. Since not every dealer meeting Hasselblad's criteria was appointed, the selection was partially quantitative.

[155] OJ 1985, L369/1; [1988] 4 CMLR 781.

[156] The Commission had not granted an exemption in *Hasselblad*. The ECJ approved the imposition of a fine, which would hardly be appropriate if the agreement merited exemption.

[157] Judgment of Barker J., and R.G. Blunt; [1990] NZAR 241; (1990) 3 NZBLC 101,655, confirming the dissent by Mrs Karen Vautier to the Commerce Commission determination, *Re Fisher & Peykel Ltd (No. 2)* (1989), 2 NZBLC (Com) 104, 377.

[158] A court of first instance consisting of a judicial member and a lay member experienced in Australian competition law.

The decision in *Ivoclar* is difficult to reconcile with *Grundig (2)*,[159] decided only a few months earlier. In *Grundig (2)* the Commission exempted a selective distribution system for high-fi equipment only after the parties introduced a system whereby any dealer wishing to supply an unauthorised dealer who met Grundig's criteria was entitled to admit him to the network and dealers were also entitled to apply directly to Grundig and were treated as approved unless the application was dismissed within four weeks for good reason.

It was hoped that the decision in *Ivoclar* marked a change in view by the Commission because providing for automatic approval of qualified dealers may impose heavy administrative burdens on the brand-owner and this was not required in *Ivoclar*, where the Commission granted an exemption, nor in *Villeroy & Boch* (2.8.1.2.1 above) where the selective distribution system was found not to infringe Article 81(1).

The Commission later returned to intervention and reaffirmed the view that there should be an automatic right for qualifying dealers to be approved. In *Yves Saint Laurent Parfums*,[160] the Commission stated that it was in response to comments from the Commission that the brand owner was introducing a system, under which retailers wanting to be approved will be inspected and, if satisfying the qualitative criteria, admitted normally within a year. Previously, there had been a waiting list, and new accounts were approved only if there was sufficient local demand to warrant another outlet. In other words, the criteria used to be partly quantitative.

On appeal, the CFI in *Leclerc (Association des Centres Distributeurs Edouard)* v. *Commission*,[161] confirmed that the criteria must be applied without discrimination, but did not say anything about having to set up a system whereby dealers might seek approval.

2.8.1.2.3 *Market factors*

The earlier cases were largely concerned with the nature of the products for which selective distribution may not infringe Article 81(1). Later, as in the second *Metro* case,[162] the ECJ has increasingly stressed the relevance of inter-brand competition and required a more elaborate market analysis.

---

[159] OJ 1985, L233/1; [1988] 4 CMLR 865; paras. 20–21, referring to *SABA (2)*, OJ 1983, L376/41; [1984] 1 CMLR 676. See also *IBM (personal computers)* OJ 1984, L118/4; [1984] 2 CMLR 342.

[160] OJ 1991, C320/11; [1991] 4 CMLR 163. See also *Givenchy Parfums*, OJ 1991, C262/2.

[161] Case T-19/92 [1996] ECR II-1851, paras. 129 and 130. See also *Leclerc (Association des Centres Distributeurs Edouard)* v. *Commission* Case T-88/92, [1996] ECR II-1961, appeal from *Givenchy*.

[162] Case 75/84 [1986] ECR 3021.

In another case involving a selective distribution system, *Lancôme* v. *Etos*, Case 99/79 [1980] ECR 2511, after referring to the first *Metro* case, Case 26/76 [1977] ECR 1875, and to *Société La Technique Minière*, Case 56/65 [1966] ECR 235, the ECJ stressed the need for a market analysis:

> 24 ... in order to decide whether an agreement is to be considered as prohibited by reason of the distortion of competition which is its object or its effect, it is necessary to examine the competition within the actual context in which it would occur in the absence of the agreement in dispute. To that end, it is appropriate to take into account in particular the nature and quantity, limited or otherwise, of the products covered by the agreement, the position and importance of the parties on the market

In 1983, the Commission renewed the exemption it had granted in *SABA*.[163] On appeal, in *Metro* v. *Commission (No. 2)*,[164] the ECJ considered that the technology for colour television was sufficiently complex to justify specialised wholesalers and retailers and ruled that simple selective distribution systems based on objective criteria as to premises and staff are not necessarily incompatible with Article 81(1) and may need no exemption, even if many other brand owners of similar goods supply similar products in a similar way.

The judgment was interesting, first, because under Article 81(1) the ECJ looked more to the need for specialist dealers and to competition in the market than did the Commission. It stressed the competitive pressures on SABA. Secondly, it implied that even simple selective distribution agreements may infringe Article 81(1) where the market is concentrated, most brand owners adopt a selective distribution system and prices become rigid, or a specialist trade is not necessary.

In *Villeroy & Boch*, (2.8.1.2.1 above) in the light of inter-and intra-brand competition, the Commission went further and cleared a selective distribution agreement for dinner plates, which are not technically complex, despite a duty to promote which the ECJ has held is not qualitative. At last, it too, looked to economic factors—the need to induce dealers to invest by enabling them to appropriate the benefit of their sunk costs and the inability of dealers to conspire with each other when there were some 1700 of them.

In its three later cases, *Parfums Yves Saint Laurent, Parfums Givenchy* (2.8.1.2.2 above) and *Vichy*,[165] however, the Commission failed to analyse the market at all. The beauty care market involved in each case was very competitive. In *Parfums Yves Saint Laurent*,[166] the ECJ, however, instructed the national court that was seeking a preliminary ruling to consider whether many brand owners of fine fragrances adopted a selective distribution system, but added that even if they did, there would be no restriction of competition unless this resulted in price rigidity. It took considerable care to analyse the market and insisted that those alleging an infringement of Article 81(1) must establish price rigidity.

The importance of market analysis was stressed by most of the commentators in **Ehlermann** and **Laudati** (eds.) (2.8.1 above).

---

for the products concerned, and the isolated nature of the disputed agreement or, alternatively, its position in a series of agreements. In that regard the Court stated in its judgment of 12 December 1967 in Case 23/67, *Brasserie de Haecht I* [1967] ECR 407 that although not necessarily decisive the existence of similar contracts is a circumstance which, together with others, is capable of being a factor in the economic and legal context within which the contract must be judged.

[163] OJ 1983, L376/41; [1984] 1 CMLR 676, confirmed on appeal, Case 26/76 [1977] ECR 1875.
[164] Case 75/84 [1986] ECR 3021.
[165] OJ 1991, L75/57.
[166] Paras. 179–192.

2.8.1.2.4 *Proportionate*

The criteria must also be appropriate to the distribution of the particular kind of product. In *Vichy*,[167] the Commission added at paragraph 18(c) that even if the criteria had been objective, the agreement would have infringed Article 81(1) because the qualitative criteria were not necessary to maintain quality and ensure a proper use of the prestige brands of cosmetics involved. There were national and Community rules governing cosmetic products for the protection of consumers' health and the requirement that the prestige brands be sold through pharmacies was more stringent than necessary.

In two judgments in *Leclerc (Association des Centres Distributeurs Edouard)* v. *Commission*,[168] the CFI accepted:

> 122. . . . while it is in the interests of consumers to be able to obtain luxury cosmetics which are suitably presented for sale and to ensure that their luxury image is preserved in that way, it is also in their interest that distribution systems founded on that consideration are not applied too restrictively and in particular, that access to the products is not limited inordinately, . . . Also it is clear from the case law of the Court of Justice that Yves Saint Laurent's system cannot be regarded as pursuing a legitimate objective counterbalancing the restriction of competition inherent in that system unless it is open to all potential retailers who are capable of ensuring that the products will be well presented to consumers in an appropriate setting and of preserving the luxury image of the products concerned. A selective distribution system which resulted in the exclusion of certain forms of marketing capable of being used to sell products in enhancing conditions, for example in a space or area adapted for that purpose, would simply protect existing forms of trading from competition from new operators and would therefore be inconsistent with Article 81(1) of the Treaty (see *AEG*).

2.8.1.3 *Exemption where the criteria do not relate to premises and staff*

The Commission has been prepared to exempt selective distribution systems that include requirements that the dealers should stock, promote and repair the contract products.[169] These are treated as including quantitative criteria, as they exclude those dealers who are not prepared to perform these services.[170] If notification of agreements led to prompt exemptions, this might be a sufficient solution, but it rarely does.[171]

---

[167] OJ 1991, L75/57, on appeal, *Société d'Hygiène de Vichy* v. *Commission* Case T-19/91, [1991] ECR II-265. See also the informal compromise with the Commission by *the Belgian Association of Pharmacists*, IP/00/16.

[168] Case T-88/92, [1996] ECR II 1961, appeal from *Givenchy* and a virtually identical judgment under the same names on appeal from *Parfums Yves Saint Laurent*, Case T-19/92 [1996] ECR II-1851, paras. 120–123.

[169] *Grundig (2)*, OJ 1985, L233/1; [1988] 4 CMLR 865, paras. 20–25; *SABA (2)*, OJ 1983, L376/41; [1984] 1 CMLR 676; paras. 35–38; confirmed on appeal *sub nom. Metro* v. *Commission*, Case 75/84 [1986] ECR 3021. See also *IBM (personal computers)* OJ 1984, L118/4; [1984] 2 CMLR 342; where the brand owner had carefully refrained from imposing obligations to stock or promote.

[170] See AG Sir Gordon Slynn in *Hasselblad (GB) Ltd.* v. *Commission*, Case 86/82 [1984] ECR 883.

[171] 2.5–2.5.2 above.

Between 1985 and 1990, the Commission became more liberal as described at 2.8.1.2.3 above. Moreover, in *Villeroy & Boch*,[172] the Commission cleared a particular selective distribution system despite a duty on the dealers to maintain expensive stocks and the lack of provision for the automatic admission of new dealers. Collusion, either between producers or between dealers was not practicable in such a fragmented market and holding stocks would not restrain the dealers from promoting other brands since this was encouraged by Villeroy & Boch. The willingness of the Commission to consider the characteristics of the market was most welcome.

In *Yves Saint Laurent Parfums*,[173] the Commission persuaded the brand owner of luxury cosmetics to amend its arrangements in various ways before granting an exemption, but did not require the firm to delete the dealers' obligation to hold stock including any new products introduced to the market. Nor did it object to a requirement that the products be sold in their original packaging.[174]

In its early informal decisions, for instance in *Perfumes*[175] and some formal decisions,[176] the Commission insisted that dealers should be permitted to sell to dealers in other Member States even if they had been approved by a different distributor. This remains standard practice.[177] Franchisees must also be allowed to sell to other franchisees.[178]

The Commission is now also insisting that selected distributors be allowed to sell via the internet, as is stated in the guidelines on vertical restraints.[179]

The circumstances in which selective distribution has been justified in individual decisions as not restricting competition contrary to Article 81(1) are very narrow. Neither the ECJ nor the Commission has formally accepted the free market view that the market will punish suppliers that provide their dealers with more

---

[172] OJ 1985, L376/15; [1988] 4 CMLR 461.
The Commission stated in para. 30 that even if the obligation to promote sales:

cannot strictly be regarded as a qualitative selection criterion compatible with Art. 81(1), it is not to be considered in this case as giving rise to any appreciable restriction of competition.

[173] OJ 1992, L12/24, [1993] 4 CMLR 120. See also *Parfums Givenchy*, OJ 1992, L236/11 [1993] 5 CMLR 579 which is very similar.
[174] At 5(a)(v) the notice in *Parfums Yves Saint Laurent* states that retailers were required to sell only in the original packages, a provision forbidden in *Bayer Dental* OJ 1990, L351/46; [1991] 1 CEC 2003 in the context of what was seen as an attempt to isolate the German market, although prices were no higher there than elsewhere. Such an obligation was permitted in *Parfums Givenchy*, para. (a) (v).
[175] *Perfumes, 4th Report on Competition Policy*, (1974) p. 60, para. 94, and *5th Report on Competition Policy*, (1975) para. 24.
[176] E.g., *Omega*, OJ 1970, L242/22; [1970] CMLR D49; *Camera Care*, on appeal *Hasselblad* v. *Commission*, Case 86/82 [1984] ECR 883, para. 11; *SABA*, OJ 1976, L28/19; [1976] 1 CMLR D61; confirmed on appeal, *Metro* v. *Commission*, Case 26/76 [1977] ECR 1875. For a good, critical commentary, see **J.S. Chard**, "The Economics of the Application of Article 85 to Selective Distribution Systems," (1982) 7 *ELRev* 83, 89.
[177] In *Parfums Yves St Laurent*, para. 5(c) and *Parfums Givenchy*, the brand owner permitted this in response to suggestions from the Commission. In *Vichy*, OJ 1991, L75/57, para. 10, provision was made for cross-supplies within the network within the EC.
[178] *Pronuptia*, Case 161/84 [1986] ECR 353, para. 21.
[179] *Parfums Yves Saint Laurent*, IP/01/713. This is a press release about an informal proceedings leading to a settlement in 2001.

protection than is required to induce investment and that there is no need to intervene in the absence of a horizontal cartel. The refusal to clear obligations to stock may support the narrow view of ancillary restraints adopted by the CFI in *Metropole* (2.7.2 above) and the clearance in *Villeroy* v. *Boch* was an example of perceiving the agreement in its economic context (2.7.3 above).

2.8.1.4 *Selective distribution under Regulation 2790/99*

The new Regulation, 2790/99, however, exempts selective distribution in wider terms. Article 1 provides that:

For the purposes of this regulation:

(d) "Selective distribution system" means a distribution system where the supplier undertakes to sell the contract goods or services, either directly or indirectly, only to distributors selected on the basis of specified criteria and where these distributors undertake not to sell such goods or services to unauthorised distributors.

This is wider than the definition of the ECJ in that the criteria may be quantitative as well as qualitative. There is no requirement that the product being distributed should require specialised outlets, nor that the criteria should be proportionate. The first difference is very important as it is often costly to comply with the qualitative criteria, and some protection of dealers incurring sunk costs may be important.

Where the criteria of the ECJ and CFI are satisfied, the agreement does not infringe Article 81(1), and the limitations of market share described in chapter 3 and the lists in Articles 4 and 5 of Regulation 2790/99 of provisions that are not exempted do not make the whole agreement illegal and void, although the particular hard core restrictions listed in Article 4 may be invalid.

2.8.1.5 *Conclusion on selective distribution*

The Commission's views on selective distribution have varied over time. In 1985 the Commission became less formalistic and looked to economic considerations, but by 1990, again, it failed to analyse the market and was adopting very limiting rules of thumb in relation to competitive markets. These were limited by the CFI in *Parfums Yves Saint Laurent* and a requirement that markets be analysed was stressed.

The question arises whether the older case law will be interpreted more liberally in view of the terms of the new Regulation and its guidelines when, for some reason, the group exemption does not apply.

The Commission is unlikely to adopt more formal decisions on distribution as more and more of its resources are being devoted to horizontal cartels, the control of state aid and the activities of firms granted special and exclusive rights. The proposal to replace Regulation 17 (described at 2.12 below) is expected to be in force by 2004. Then the issues will move to national competition authorities and courts. The views of the Commission in Guidelines 184–189 will doubtless be influential, although they will not be binding (3.2 and 7.4.4.3.2 below).

2.8.1.6 Collective selective distribution systems

In *FEDETAB*,[180] the ECJ stated that its rulings that selective distribution based on qualitative criteria do not infringe Article 81(1) applies only to the conduct of an individual brand owner and not to collective agreements between competitors. Unfortunately, this qualification was forgotten in *Salonia v. Poidomani*,[181] where the ECJ ruled on a collective selective distribution system for distributing newspapers in Italy made between most of the Italian newspaper owners. The judgment in *FEDETAB* is more sensible.[182] *FEDETAB* is also a stronger precedent since the judgment was on an appeal from the Commission under Article 230 (ex Article 173) rather than a preliminary ruling under Article 234 (ex Article 177).

Unfortunately, the Commission used not always to realise the importance of the distinction between vertical and horizontal restraints.[183] Indeed, until recently, some officials were more concerned about vertical restraints, perceived as dividing the Common Market, than about horizontal relationships.

---

[180] Cases 209–215 & 218/78 [1980] ECR 3125.

[181] Case 126/80 [1981] ECR 1563.

[182] The Monopolies and Mergers Commission of the UK condemned collective discrimination in favour of selected dealers in goods in many reports between 1949 and 1956, when it ceased to be competent over the matter. It considered that such horizontal agreements were likely to lead to rigidity, higher prices and to delay innovation in distribution. The Restrictive Practices Court, which was given jurisdiction to make such decisions from 1957, continued to condemn the practice thereafter. In its *report on the Supply of Fire Insurance*, 2 August, 1972, HCP 396, the Monopolies Commission of the UK mentioned that it had been argued that the strict attitude it had taken earlier in relation to the supply of goods should not been carried over to services. It replied, however,

> 317. We accept that the distinction [between goods and services] exists and that we have to form a judgement on the effects of a particular collective restrictive system in the circumstances of a particular service industry. Nevertheless, in forming this judgement we think it right to take into account the fact that such restrictions have, when examined, generally been found to have some undesirable effects, though there may be cases where these effects are outweighed by advantages arising from the restrictions. It is to be expected that a collective arrangement, such as that adopted by the FOC [the service supply association, the Fire Offices Committee), which significantly limits the freedom of the parties in the conduct of their businesses, will tend to have some or all of the following effects—higher prices, less efficient use of resources, discouragement of new developments and rigidity in the structure and trading methods of the businesses. What we have to consider is whether there are, nevertheless, special features in this industry which should lead us to conclude that in this case removal of the restrictions would be likely, on balance, to produce effects more disadvantageous, or less advantageous than those which may be found to result from the restrictions.

Adopting this attitude, it is hardly surprising that the Monopolies Commission and Restrictive Practices Court condemned most of the collective agreements that came before them whether they related to goods or services.

[183] In *Vichy*, OJ 1991, L75/57, the Commission cited its decision in *Association de Pharmacistes Belges*, OJ 1990, L18/35; [1991] 4 CMLR 619, a case concerned with the organisation of a certification trade mark by a trade association of dealers, to explain its objections to what appears to be Vichy's vertical practice of refusing supplies to anyone other than dispensing chemists.

2.8.2 Franchising and *Pronuptia*

Since the new group exemption granted by Regulation 2790/99 will often not
apply to franchise agreements with long term single branding restraints (chapter 5
below), the ECJ's liberal treatment of franchising remains very important.

Pronuptia[184] concerned a franchising agreement for the distribution of wedding
clothes, which the ECJ said was so different from exclusive distribution that it did
not qualify for exemption under the original group exemption for limited
distribution, Regulation 67/67.[185] The reasons the ECJ gave for clearing most of
the restrictions are of general application. It held that since distribution franchising does not, in itself, restrict competition, any contractual provisions necessary to
make it viable do not do so either (paras. 16–22) (2.7 and 2.7.1 above).

On this ground it cleared provisions necessary to prevent the franchisor's assistance and know-how coming into the hands of competitors, such as a restriction
on the franchisee setting up a similar shop near any outlet in the network during
and for a reasonable time after the franchise is terminated, and the provisions necessary to establish the control necessary to maintain the reputation and uniformity
of the network.

Many restrictions on conduct were cleared on the second criterion:

—an obligation to sell the franchised goods only in premises laid out and decor-
  ated in accordance with instructions (para. 19),
—an obligation on the location of the shop (para. 19),
—the freedom of the franchisor to choose its franchisees (para. 20)
—an obligation to obtain the contract products only from a designated source
  when it is not possible to define the quality criteria, as in the case of fashion
  goods, or when there are too many franchisees to monitor, provided that cross
  supplies between franchisees are possible (para. 21).
—an obligation to obtain approval for the nature of any advertising, provided that
  this does not amount to rpm (paras. 22 and 25).

Nevertheless, the ECJ ruled that once the network is widespread,[186] the combination of provisions granting exclusive territories to each franchisee coupled
with a requirement that each should sell only from a specified location infringes
Article 81(1) even if the franchisees would not have been prepared to commit
themselves without such protection. In combination, those provisions confer
absolute territorial protection, although the ECJ did not use these words.

Even so the ECJ accepted that until the network was widespread even absolute
territorial protection may not infringe Article 81(1). It added that if such protection is needed to induce investment and commitments by the franchisee, this
should be considered in the context of Article 81(3). This is also more liberal than

[184] Case 161/84 [1986] ECR 35.
[185] Group exemption for exclusive dealing (expired), OJ Spec Ed 1967, 10.
[186] Valentine's translation of "répandu" in the French text that would have been the subject of the
judges' deliberations. The ECR uses the term "well known".

the judgment in *Consten & Grundig* v. *Commission*.[187] where the ECJ held that the Commission was not wrong[188] to refuse exemption to an agreement giving absolute territorial protection (2.7.1 and 2.7.2 above).

After the judgment in *Pronuptia*, there was concern that most franchisees required protection from other franchisees for at least a small territory, sometimes a regional town, sometimes only a few hundred yards. So, the Commission adopted Regulation 4087/88, the Group exemption for franchising agreements.[189]

In order to establish its power to adopt the regulation, the Commission adopted several individual decisions relating to various franchising networks (2.4.2 above). Each of the markets affected appears to have been competitive, but clearance would not have established the need to adopt a block exemption, so the Commission granted exemptions. Now that the block exemption of 2790/99 includes franchising, it is hoped that these old decisions are of little importance and may be ignored.

2.8.3 Information Technology Favours Franchising and Selective Distribution

Great cost savings have been generated by "just in time delivery." Multiple retailers, franchisors, and those organising selective distribution often put systems in place so that when the items the customer wants to buy are placed near the retailer's scanner, not only is an invoice prepared, but also the precise item of stock is re-ordered. Such a system saves costs because it is possible to operate with less stock, which reduces the capital tied up and the amount that has to be sold off cheaply as obsolescent or unfashionable at the end of the season (1.1 above).[190]

The imposition of such systems requires an agreement on how the system should work: bar codes, product codes, delivery and restocking methods plus a reliable system for exchanging information. The cost savings generated have made the Commission rethink the notion that any restriction of another's freedom is a restriction of competition. The group exemption granted by Regulation 2790/99 defines selective distribution more widely than the ECJ in that the criteria may be quantitative as well as qualitative. Moreover, there is no requirement that the product being distributed should require specialised outlets, nor that the criteria should be proportionate (2.8.1.4 above and 4.4 below).

---

[187] *Etablissements Consten SA and Grundig-Verkaufs-GmbH* v. *EEC Commission* Cases 56 & 58/64, [1966] ECR 299, paras. 58–84 (2.2 above).
[188] The Court does not substitute its view for that of the Commission in an appeal under Art. 230.
[189] OJ 1988, L359/46 [1989] 4 CMLR 387, now expired.
[190] See **David Deacon**, "Vertical Restraints under EU Competition Law: New Directions," [1995] *Fordham Corporate Law Institute* 307.

2.8.4 AGENCY

Some contracts made between a supplier and an agent that is closely integrated into the principal's organisation are also not caught by Article 81(1) (7.3.1.2 below). The Commission stated in 1962[191] that it:

> considers that contracts made with commercial agents, in which those agents undertake, for a specified part of the territory of the Common Market:
>
> —to negotiate transactions on behalf of an enterprise, or
> —to conclude transactions in the name and on behalf of an enterprise, or
> —to conclude transactions in their own name and on behalf of this enterprise,
>
> are not covered by the prohibition laid down in Article 81 paragraph (1) of the treaty.
>
> It is essential in this case that the contracting party, described as a commercial agent, should, in fact, be such, by the nature of his functions, and that he should neither undertake nor engage in activities proper to an independent trader in the course of commercial operations. The Commission regards as the decisive criterion, which distinguishes the commercial agent from the independent trader, the agreement—express or implied—which deals with responsibility for the financial risks bound up with the sale or with the performance of the contract. Thus the Commission's assessment is not governed by the way the "representative" is described. Except for the usual *del credere* guarantee, a commercial agent must not, by the nature of his functions, assume any risk resulting from the transaction. . . .

It was dangerous to rely on the Commission's notice on agency. It bound no one (3.2 below) and the Commission construed it very narrowly. It has been replaced by Vertical Guidelines 12–20, but the case law of the ECJ was based on the old notice. The Court applies Article 81(1) to agents unless they are tightly integrated into the organisation of a particular principal, so that it can be said that there is no agreement between undertakings independent of each other.

An agent acting for its employer is rarely an undertaking independent of it.[192] So agreements by a firm with its own employees are not subject to Article 81(1), but it is not clear how much further agreements between an agent and its principal escape the prohibition of Article 81(1). It is clear that attempting to turn a dealer into an agent by reserving title until property passes to a third party will not suffice to avoid the prohibition of Article 81(1). Both Commission and ECJ have relied heavily on the extent to which the agent is integrated into the organisation of the principal.

In *Suiker Unie*[193] the ECJ referred neither to the agent's outside activities nor to the large size of the group of companies to which it belonged, as the Commission

---

[191] Notice on Exclusive Dealing Contracts with Commercial Agents, JO 1962, 139/2921, since replaced by Vertical Guidelines 12–20.

[192] In *P. Pavlov and Another* v. *Stichting Pensioensfond Medische Specialisten*, Case C-180/98 [2001] 4 CMLR 30, paras. 57–71, the ECJ ruled that employed professionals might constitute undertakings, and a collective agreement between them might be subject to Article 81(1).

[193] *Suiker Unie and others* v. *Commission*, Cases 40–48, 50, 54–56, 111, 113 & 114/73 [1975] ECR 1663.

had done in *Pittsburgh Corning Europe*.[194] It stressed, rather, the economic integration of the agent into the principal's undertaking. Many independent dealers accept very detailed instructions, especially in relation to the preparation and maintenance of complex machinery. So integration is not a basis for the distinction that is easy to apply.

In the *Belgian Travel Agents* case,[195] the ECJ ruled that a legislative measure requiring compliance with an agreement made between travel agents to sell only at the prices fixed by their principals and not to share their commission with clients might infringe Article 10, (ex Article 5(2)), in combination with Articles 3(g) (ex Article 3(f)) and 81(1) of the EC treaty. It was for the national court to consider whether the agreements did so. At paragraph 19 the ECJ rejected the argument of the Belgian government that Article 81 could not apply to the relationship between travel agents and tour operators:

> 20. However, a travel agent of the kind referred to by the national court must be regarded as an independent agent who provides services on an entirely independent basis. He sells travel organised by a large number of different tour operators and a tour operator sells travel through a very large number of agents. Contrary to the Belgian Government's submissions, a travel agent cannot be treated as an auxiliary organ forming an integral part of the operator's undertaking.

The agreements in question were horizontal or collective although they related to charges fixed vertically between tour operator and each travel agent. So, the finding that Article 81(1) may have been infringed seems sensible whatever the situation may be as between a single principal and its agent.

The Commission's Guidelines 12–20 on vertical restraints (Appendix 4 below) have at last replaced the notice of 1962. They differ from the draft notice that circulated widely in 1990 in that qualifying agency agreements are regarded as entirely outside Article 81. Bans on even passive sales may be imposed on a "genuine" agent because the agent is treated as being part of the principal's undertaking and there is no agreement between undertaking independent of each other (Guideline 18).

Guideline 15 states that genuine agency agreements where significant commercial and financial risks are not borne by the agent escape Article 81(1).

Guideline 12 defines the concept of agency:[196]

[194] JO 1972, L272/35 [1973] CMLR D2.
[195] *Vereniging van Vlaamse Reisbureaus* v. *Sociale Dienst van de Plaatsselijke en Gewestelijke Overheidsdiensten*, Case 313/85 [1987] ECR 3801.
[196] The definition is slightly different from that in Article 1(2) of Council Directive (EEC) 86/653 on the coordination of the laws of Member States relating to self-employed commercial agents 18 December 1986, OJ 1986, L382/17, which defines a commercial agent as:

> a self employed intermediary who has continuing authority to negotiate the sale or the purchase of goods on behalf of another person, hereinafter called the principal, or to negotiate and conclude such transactions on behalf of another person, hereinafter called the principal, or to negotiate and conclude such transaction on behalf of and in the name of that principal.

This definition requires the relationship to be continuing, but the guidelines on vertical agreements do not. Yet Guideline 12 state that the Guidelines should be read in conjunction with the Directive.

(12) Paragraphs 12 to 20 replace the Notice on exclusive dealing contracts with commercial agents of 1962.[197] They must be read in conjunction with Council Directive
86/653/EEC.

Agency agreements cover the situation in which a legal or physical person (the agent) is
vested with the power to negotiate and/or conclude contracts on behalf of another person
(the principal), either in the agent's own name or in the name of the principal, for the:

—purchase of goods or services by the principal, or
—sale of goods or services supplied by the principal.

Guideline 13 explains the concept of a genuine agent.

(13) In the case of genuine agency agreements, the obligations imposed on the agent as
to the contracts negotiated and/or concluded on behalf of the principal do not fall within
the scope of application of Article 81(1). The determining factor in assessing whether
Article 81(1) is applicable is the financial or commercial risk borne by the agent in relation to the activities for which he has been appointed as an agent by the principal. In this
respect it is not material for the assessment whether the agent acts for one or several principals. Non-genuine agency agreements may be caught by Article 81(1), in which case the
Block Exemption Regulation and the other sections of these Guidelines will apply.

(14) There are two types of financial or commercial risk that are material to the assessment of the genuine nature of an agency agreement under Article 81(1). First there are
the risks which are directly related to the contracts concluded and/or negotiated by the
agent on behalf of the principal, such as financing of stocks. Secondly, there are the risks
related to market-specific investments. These are investments specifically required for
the type of activity for which the agent has been appointed by the principal, i.e. which are
required to enable the agent to conclude and/or negotiate this type of contract. Such
investments are usually sunk, if upon leaving that particular field of activity the investment cannot be used for other activities or sold other than at a significant loss.

It was widely thought that it was covering only the risk of unsold stocks that prevented the old notice from applying. This is the first kind of risk mentioned in
Guideline 14. The second kind of commercial risk now considered relevant is
investing in specialised equipment in order to market the products.[198]

It is not clear why an agent who bears sunk costs should not be treated as genuine. The Commission seems to be going back to its view in *Pittsburgh Corning
Europe* that an agent should be dependent on the principal, a view not expressed
by the ECJ in *Suiker Unie.*

In *Daimler/Chrysler*, the Commission found that Article 81(1) could apply to
agreements with its German agents because they bore substantial financial risk,
rather than applying the test of integration developed by the ECJ (7.3.1.2 below).

In suggesting in Guideline 13 that a genuine agent may work for several principals, the Commission rejects the view of the ECJ in *Belgian Travel Agents.*[199] A

---

[197] OJ 1962, 139/2921.
[198] "Sunk costs" are explained at 1.2.4.1.1 above.
[199] *Vereniging van Vlaamse Reisbureaus* v. *Sociale Dienst van de Plaatselijke en Gewestelijke
Overheidsdiensten,* Case 311/85 [1987] ECR 3801, para. 20 quoted in text below note 195 above.

travel agent who markets the tours of several operators is hardly integrated into the undertaking of any one of them. Is the Commission moving its focus from the integration of the parties to dependency? We believe that the judgment of the ECJ prevails.

The Commission states that risks will have to be appraised case-by-case but considers that Article 81 will rarely apply if the agent does not acquire property in the products and where the agent does not perform various functions specified in Guideline 16. A case-by-case development of the law leaves business with considerable uncertainty, especially as the Commission seems to be departing from the case law of the ECJ.

Limitations on the authority of a genuine agent are not subject to Article 81.

(18) If an agency agreement does not fall within the scope of application of Article 81(1), then all obligations imposed on the agent in relation to the contracts concluded and/or negotiated on behalf of the principal fall outside Article 81(1). The following obligations on the agent's part will generally be considered to form an inherent part of an agency agreement, as each of them relates to the ability of the principal to fix the scope of activity of the agent in relation to the contract goods or services, which is essential if the principal is to take the risks and therefore to be in a position to determine the commercial strategy:

—limitations on the territory in which the agent may sell these goods or services;
—limitations on the customers to whom the agent may sell these goods or services;
—the prices and conditions at which the agent must sell or purchase these goods or services.

An exclusive territory allocated to an agent affects only intra-brand competition and is unlikely to infringe Article 81(1), but a single branding restriction, whereby the agent agrees not to deal with competing products may well be anticompetitive:

(19) In addition to governing the conditions of sale or purchase of the contract goods or services by the agent on behalf of the principal, agency agreements often contain provisions which concern the relationship between the agent and the principal. In particular, they may contain a provision preventing the principal from appointing other agents in respect of a given type of transaction, customer or territory (exclusive agency provisions) and/or a provision preventing the agent from acting as an agent or distributor of undertakings which compete with the principal (non-compete provisions). Exclusive agency provisions concern only intra-brand competition and will in general not lead to anti-competitive effects. Non-compete provisions, including post-term non-compete provisions, concern inter-brand competition and may infringe Article 81(1) if they lead to foreclosure on the relevant market where the contract goods or services are sold or purchased (see Section VI.2.1).

Even if the agent bears no financial or commercial risks, the agreement may restrict competition when it facilitates collusion between the supplier and others. This may well be the case where the agent acts for several competing firms.

(20) An agency agreement may also fall within the scope of Article 81(1), even if the principal bears all the relevant financial and commercial risks, where it facilitates collusion.

This could for instance be the case when a number of principals use the same agents while collectively excluding others from using these agents, or when they use the agents to collude on marketing strategy or to exchange sensitive market information between the principals.

The main drawback of relying on agents to avoid the application of Article 81 is that they are often less entrepreneurial, and may use less initiative in marketing than an independent dealer. Another is that the directive on the coordination of the laws of Member States relating to self-employed commercial agents[200] applies and it becomes very expensive to terminate agency agreements even in accordance with the contract.

2.8.5 Resale Price Maintenance (RPM)

Economists have differed widely over time and between countries as to whether vertical rpm is anti-competitive. The practice may alleviate the free rider problem discussed at 1.2.4.1–1.2.4.1.5 above, in as much as a dealer providing the services will be protected from under-cutting by those that do not. It may restrain intra-brand competition less than an exclusive territory since competition on non-price items within the same area may be permitted.

On the other hand, in many trades the practice has originated in a horizontal cartel at the dealers' level.

Secondly, even in the absence of such a cartel, it may produce horizontal effects as described at 1.2.3.2 above.

Thirdly, there is no assurance that the dealer given a firm margin over the price it pays will use it to provide the services the supplier hopes to induce. The dealer may prefer to promote less, but keep the high margin, relying on other dealers to provide pre-sales services.

Fourthly, as described at 1.2.4, where it is only a few marginal consumers who desire the services, consumer welfare may not be increased by the increased demand.

Fifthly, resellers may compete away their assured margin by providing services that cost more than they are worth to customers; although if that be the case, one would expect the supplier to abrogate the practice.

Sixthly, where competition is not acute, it may enable the supplier to increase its share of the distribution margin in a way that increases the price to final buyers and reduces production.[201]

Seventhly, rpm may be used to maintain the status of a premium brand rather than to induce the provision of services.[202]

---

[200] Note 184 above.

[201] For elaboration of these ideas, see **F.M. Scherer** and **David Ross**, *Industrial Market Structure and Economic Performance*, 3rd edn (Houghton Mifflin, Boston, 1991) 541–8; **Robert L. Steiner**, "The Nature of Vertical Restraints," (1985) XXX *Antitrust Bulletin* 143; **B.S. Yamey**, *Resale Price Maintenance and Shoppers' Choice* (Hobart Paper I, 1960) and subsequent editions.

[202] See 1.2.4.1.5 above and Luc Gyselen, "Vertical Restraints in the Distribution Process: Strength and Weakness of the Free Rider Rationale under EEC Competition Law," (1984) 21 *CMLRev* 648, 652.

The Commission, however, has been concerned about market integration. It found that in many trades rpm was national and protected by export bans.[203]

Rpm may take different forms.[204] Sometimes an individual manufacturer imposed minimum prices on its dealers and enforced them by contract (vertical, individual rpm).

Frequently a trade association required its members to impose individual resale prices but enforced the agreements for its members (collective enforcement of individual rpm). Such a system was less likely to be justified by free rider arguments. Some trade associations whose members sold homogenous products went further and themselves imposed resale prices (collective rpm).

In France, the government required publishers of books to impose and maintain minimum prices and made it criminal for retailers to cut prices. Such a system may not be justified as inhibiting free riders, but as a system of price control to protect competitors. The government can control the prices of homogenous products like petrol directly by imposing a minimum or fixed price.[205] For heterogenous products, such as books or films, it has to rely on individual publishers or producers to set the minimum price.

2.8.5.1 Hostile attitude of the Commission and ECJ towards individual rpm

Article 81(1) of the EEC treaty provides a non-exhaustive list of the kinds of agreement that are likely to have the object or effect of restricting competition within the Common Market. These include those which:

(a) directly or indirectly fix purchase or selling prices or any other trading conditions.

The example is not expressly limited to horizontal agreements—those made between competitors or imposed by trade associations and applies equally to vertical agreements, although the latter are likely to be less anti-competitive (1.1 above).

The Commission considered from the beginning that even individual rpm was anti-competitive.[206] The practice was often confined to a single Member State and the Commission saw it as reinforcing the isolation of national markets.[207] In the

---

[203] See **Luc Gyselen**, [1983] *ELRev* Competition Checklist, CC 55, 65 para. XVI.

[204] See the opinion of Advocate General Verloren Van Themaat in *VBVB and CBBB* v. *Commission*, Cases 43 & 63/82 [1984] ECR 19, 74–5.

[205] In *Cullet and Another* v. *Centre Leclerc, Toulouse (SA Sodinord)*, Case 231/83 [1985] ECR 305, the government itself fixed the price of petrol, a homogenous product. See **Luc Gyselen**, [1983] *ELRev* Competition Checklist, CC 55, 65 and **Judge René Joliet**, "National, anti-competitive legislation and Community law," [1988] *Fordham Corporate Law Institute*, ch. 16 at p. 12.

[206] For the early history, see **René Joliet**, "Resale Price Maintenance under EEC Antitrust Law," XVI *The Antitrust Bulletin*, 589, being a translation of an article in French, published in (1971) *Cahiers de Droit* 16–52.

[207] The *Agfa Gevaert* case, discussed by **René Joliet**, above n. 206, never reached a formal decision, but the Commission persuaded the firm to alter its terms of supply. Previously, Agfa Gevaert had supplied dealers in each member state itself, subject to export bans and maintained different resale prices. The Commission stated that:

This restrictive scheme of distribution is thus designed to completely isolate the home markets, and especially the Belgo-Luxemburg and German markets, with respect to Agfa-Gevaert photographic

absence of export restrictions, however, it doubted whether systems of rpm confined to a single member state appreciably affected interstate trade. It took the view
that the practice usually escaped the prohibition of Article 81(1).

The Commission first attacked individual rpm indirectly. The practice was
often associated with exclusive distribution. When Regulation 17 first came into
force, the Commission enabled firms to notify exclusive distribution agreements
on form B1, provided that the applicant certified, *inter alia*, that there were no
impediments to exports and that resale prices were not maintained.[208] Since it was
clear that such forms would not be scrutinised,[209] this had the effect of persuading
businessmen to alter their standard forms of business to permit their dealers to set
their prices freely, although many continued to recommend resale prices.

Regulation 67/67, like Regulations 1983/83 and 1984/83, the successive group
exemptions for exclusive distribution and purchasing, permitted only specified
restrictions of competition to be imposed on the dealer. The Commission construed this to refer to restrictions on its conduct, so rpm took an exclusive dealing
agreement outside the earlier group exemptions.[210] Rpm is now a hard core
restraint that excludes an agreement from the current group exemption granted
by Regulation 2790/99 (4.2–4.2.6 below).

> supplies, and to maintain isolated national markets within the Community. It also makes it possible
> to apply to the products in question prices which, at the level of interstate commerce, are not sub-
> mitted to any effective competition at different stages of distribution.

[translation from a German text by **René Joliet**, "Resale Price Maintenance under EEC Antitrust Law,"
XVI *The Antitrust Bulletin* 589].

The Commission considered the isolation of the market far more important than any benefits
brought by the system to distribution. In that context, it dismissed the free rider argument on the
ground that the products were not new—they had been brought to the market many years before. Even
well known products may, however, require promotion. It did not mention the other arguments for or
against rpm.

In its *First Report on Competition Policy* (1971) p. 62, the Commission confirmed that although rpm
usually restricts competition, it was usually a matter for national law since it rarely affects trade between
member states.

[208] Reg. 153/62, JO 1962, 2918, amending Reg. 27.

[209] Only one copy was required of notifications made on the simpler form, Form B1. In the days
before plain paper copying was commercially available, this made it impossible for the Commission to
consult member states, so there was no way that it could process agreements notified on form B1.

[210] In *Hennessy/Henkell*, OJ 1980, L383/11, [1981] 1 CMLR 601, the supplier of cognac guaranteed
Henkell, its exclusive dealer for Germany, an 18% margin between the wholesale price charged to it and
the German domestic price with the intention of restraining parallel imports. The Commission found
that this clause and the maintenance of Henkell's prices prevented Regulation 67/67 from applying, as
they amounted to restrictions of a kind not expressly exempted by Article 2(1). Hennessy's consent was
required if Henkell wanted to sell more than 17% or at less than 12% above the price at which it bought,
although temporary price changes were permitted if Hennessy was informed as soon as possible (paras.
20, 29–30 and 33). The Commission did not state whether they were restrictions of conduct or of competition. Only if they restricted competition, however, should the provisions have prevented the application of the Regulation.

The Commission refused an individual exemption, although the prices of other brands were not
maintained, and there may have been inter-brand competition in the Federal Republic of Germany.
The only element of economic analysis in the published decision was the statement at paragraph 22 that
the restrictions of competition and the effect on trade between member states were appreciable because
Hennessy was one of the three major producers of cognac, Henkell's turnover was DM 330 million and
Germany was the third largest importer of cognac.

In the context of individual decisions on exclusive distribution agreements, too, the Commission has attacked rpm indirectly.[211]

The Commission has objected to rpm also in its decisions on selective distribution. In *SABA*,[212] it did not object to SABA being able to find out its dealers' gross income provided it did not enforce resale prices or offer incentives to dealers to sell only at recommended prices. The ECJ also has objected to measures taken by suppliers to maintain prices in judgments such as *Metro v. Commission*[213] and *Allgemeine Elektricitäts-Gesellschaft AEG-Telefunken AG v. Commission.*[214]

In *Pronuptia*,[215] the ECJ treated as contrary to Article 81(1) not only individual rpm, but also any control over the prices at which franchisees might advertise, but it treated recommended prices as outside the prohibition of Article 81(1).[216]

Per se treatment[217] may be expected in relation to rpm, since price agreements are given as examples of agreements that restrict competition in Article 81(1) itself (2.7.1 above), subject to finding a possible effect on trade between Member States (2.8.5.4 below).

In *Louis Erauw-Jacquery v. La Hesbignonne*,[218] the parties argued only that the maintenance of prices at which propagators might sell did not affect trade between Member States, not that it did not have the object or effect of restricting competition. The need to protect licensees of plant breeders' rights in basic seed against free riders was not raised and, on the basis of the first example given in Article 81(1), the ECJ assumed that the practice has the object of restricting competition without considering the possibility of free riders.

In the light of the arguments before it, the ECJ questioned only whether the maintenance of prices had a perceptible effect on trade between Member States when

---

[211] In *Brooke Bond Liebig*, OJ 1978, L53/20, [1978] 2 CMLR 116, where there do not seem to have been any export bans, the operative part of the decision prohibited only the restriction on the supermarkets selling spices other than Brooke Bond and own label brands, but the reasoning at para. 17 condemned the maintenance of resale prices with a big margin for retailers. Had it continued the practice, Brooke Bond Liebig would have risked substantial fines.

[212] *SABA (I)*, OJ 1976, L28/19, [1976]1 CMLR D61 and *SABA (II)*, OJ 1983, L376/41, [1984] 1 CMLR 676.

[213] Case 26/76 [1977] ECR 1875.

[214] Case 107/82 [1983] ECR 3151.

[215] Case 161/84 [1986] ECR 353, paras. 25 and 22.

[216] Although more control is permitted over franchisees than over exclusive distributors, the distinction from distribution may not be relevant to recommended prices. Often national advertising is organised by a brand owner for dealers who are not franchisees and is not very effective unless a rough guide of the prices to expect is provided to those to whom the advertisement is addressed. The maintenance of resale prices through a concerted practice was expressly treated by the Court in *Pronuptia* as contrary to Art. 81(1). The recommendation of resale prices would be dangerous if the brand owner refused to supply those operating on margins lower than those common in the trade. Even occasional refusals to supply were treated as systematic and as evidence of a concerted practice to maintain resale prices in *AEG*, Case 107/82 [1983] ECR 3151.

[217] In *Matra Hachette SA v. Commission*, Case T-17/93 [1994] ECR II-595 para. 85 the CFI held that no agreements are incapable of exemption, but the Commission is very unlikely to grant one.

[218] Case 27/87 [1988] ECR 1919, para. 20.
Speaking literally, the ruling was not about rpm, since the propagator grew the basic seed to produce certified seed and did not "resell". Economically, however, and in terms of competition policy there seems to be no reason to make this legalistic distinction.

both the breeder and propagator were in Belgium. It ruled that the maintenance of minimum resale prices would be unlawful if, in the context of other agreements concluded between the breeder and other licensees, the agreements might have an appreciable effect on trade between Member States[219] (2.8.5.4 below).

The Court has rarely considered that restrictions of competition did not affect trade between Member States. It has held that Article 81 applies if the agreement as a whole may affect trade between Member States even if the particular clause that restricts competition does not.[220] Large exclusive territories are likely to affect such trade. Resale prices are seldom maintained for an area smaller than a Member State, so the practice will often infringe Article 81(1) (2.8.5.4 below).

2.8.5.2 Collective rpm

Collective rpm where several sellers or their trade association agree to impose the same resale prices on their dealers amounts to a cartel and is illegal where there is an appreciable effect on trade between Member States. Collective rpm and other restraints[221] were condemned in *FEDETAB*.[222]

The collective enforcement of rpm was condemned in *VBVB and CBBB*.[223] An agreement between two trade associations of publishers, one in Belgium and the other in the Netherlands, and others was binding on the members of each. Members were forbidden to give discounts on retail prices except to recognised parties and required to abide by the retail prices. The Commission decided that the object and effect of the agreement was to restrict competition and the ECJ confirmed that various defences raised by the parties were not effective, such as the cultural interest accepted by governments in keeping specialised bookshops in business.

---

[219] See also *Groupement des Fabricants de Papiers Peints de Belgique*, OJ 1974, L237/3; [1974] 2 CMLR D102 where the arrangement was horizontal, not vertical. The Commission imposed fines on the members of a small trade association who had voted to boycott a firm that advertised prices below those it imposed. At para. 60, the Commission stated that even had resale prices not been imposed, but the parties had forbidden the advertisement of discounts, Art. 81 would have been infringed, because the recommendation of prices restricts competition. In Valentine Korah's view, a better argument is that it is of little use for a retailer to discount if it cannot advertise the fact.

The decision in *Papiers Peints* was quashed on appeal for reasoning insufficient to support the Commission's views on the effects on trade between member states, Case 73/74 [1975] ECR 1491.

In *Camera Care—Hasselblad*, OJ 1982, L161/18, [1982] 2 CMLR 233, the Commission objected in para. 60 to Hasselblad's control over the advertising of its dealers, which would enable it to prevent discounting, especially by those not importing through the locally authorised Hasselblad dealer. This was upheld by the Court in *Hasselblad v. Commission*, Case 86/82 [1984] ECR 883, para. 49, following the Advocate General [1984] ECR at 919–925.

[220] *Windsurfing International* v. *Commission*, Case 193/83 [1986] ECR 611, paras. 96 and 97.

[221] Each member of the trade association was allowed to buy only from the members at the level of trade immediately above it and to sell only at its own level of trade. Similar collective agreements were condemned by the Commission in numerous decisions, such as *VBVB and CBBB* v. *Commission* and *FEDETAB*, immediately below.

[222] *GB-Inno-BM SA* v. *Fédération Belgo-Luxembourgeoise des Industries du Tabac* OJ 1978, L224/29, [1978] 3 CMLR 524, confirmed on appeal—*Heintz van Landewyck Sàrl, Fédération Belgo-Luxembourgeoise des Industries du Tabac Asbl* v. *Commission*, Cases 209–215 & 218/78, [1980] ECR 3125.

[223] OJ 1982, L54/36, [1982] 2 CMLR 344, on appeal, Cases 43 & 63/82 [1984] ECR 19.

2.8.5.3 The imposition of resale prices by state measures[224]

The French government required publishers of books to impose a retail price on each and made it criminal for a dealer to sell at more than 5 per cent below that price. In *Association des Centres Distributeurs Edouard Leclerc* v. *Au Blé Vert Sàrl*,[225] the Leclerc low price outlet was prosecuted by various competitors for selling at more than 5 per cent below the maintained price. It was argued that the French legislation contravened Article 10 in combination with Articles 3(g) and 81 of the EC Treaty by making it unnecessary for publishers to make an agreement that would infringe Article 81. The ECJ rejected this argument on the ground that the Commission had not yet developed firm views about systems of rpm involving a single Member State.[226]

That state measures making it unnecessary to infringe Article 81(1) contravene Article 10 in combination with Article 3(g) and 81 seems to have been denied in a trilogy of cases: *Meng*,[227] *Ohra*[228] and *Reiff*.[229] **Luc Gyselen**,[230] however, argues

---

[224] For a general discussion of state measures, see **René Joliet**, "National, anti-competitive legislation and Community law," [1988] *Fordham Corporate Law Institute*, ch. 16 and the literature cited in note 2 thereof.

[225] Case 229/83, [1985] ECR 1.

[226] It said:

15. . . . the question arises as to whether national legislation which renders corporate behaviour of the type prohibited by Article 81(1) superfluous, by making the book publisher or importer responsible for freely fixing binding retail prices, detracts from the effectiveness of Article 81 and is therefore contrary to Article 10 of the Treaty. . . .

18. It may be observed that the Commission, which has publicly stated its intention to investigate all those systems and practices, has not yet succeeded in bringing that investigation to a conclusion or in determining what approach to adopt with regard to the exercise in this sphere of the powers conferred on it by the Treaty and by Regulation 17 . . . Moreover, it has so far failed to submit any proposal for action to the Council. Nor has it initiated any proceedings under Article 81 of the Treaty with a view to prohibiting national systems and practices for fixing book prices. . . .

20. It is thus apparent that the purely national systems and practices in the book trade have not yet been made subject to a Community competition policy with which the Member States would be required to comply by virtue of their duty to abstain from any measure which might jeopardize the attainment of the objectives of the Treaty. It follows that, as Community law stands, Member States" obligations under Article 5 (now Article 10) of the EEC Treaty, in conjunction with Articles 3(f) and 85 (now Articles 3(g) and 81), are not specific enough to preclude them from enacting legislation of the type at issue on competition in the retail prices of books, provided that such legislation is consonant with the other specific Treaty provisions, in particular those concerning the free movement of goods. It is therefore necessary to consider those provisions. . . .

At that time the only decision relating to the maintenance of retail prices for books was *VBVB* v. *VBBB* where publishers in both the Netherlands and Belgium participated. This made it easier to find that the agreement might affect trade between Member States.

See also **Judge Joliet**, "National, Anti-competitive Legislation and Community law," [1988] *Fordham Corporate Law Institute*, ch. 16, p. 11.

[227] *(Wolf W.)*, Case C-2/91, [1993] ECR I-5751.

[228] *Officiervan Justitie* v. *Ohra Shadeverzekeringen*, Case C-245/91 [1993] ECR I-5851.

[229] *Bundesanstalt für den Güterfernverkehr*, Case C-185/91 [1993] ECR I-5801.

[230] **Luc Gyselen**, [1983] *ELRev* Competition Checklist, CC 55, 65, paras XV and XVI. See also **Judge Joliet**, "National, Anti-competitive Legislation and Community Law," [1988] *Fordham Corporate Law Institute*, ch. 16 pp. 10 and 11.

that *Van Eycke Pascal* v. *ASPA NV*,[231] has established that where the State delegates discretion to individuals in the economic sphere, the Treaty may be infringed although in no case had the ECJ confirmed this. This might have led to reconsideration of *Leclerc* v. *Au Blé Vert Sàrl* but, in *Échirolles Distribution SA* v. *Association du Dauphin and others*,[232] on identical facts, *Van Eycke* was not cited and the issue was not raised. The ECJ ruled that since Articles 28, 30 and 81 had not been amended, there was no reason for it to depart from its earlier ruling. The ECJ has no jurisdiction to raise issues of substance not raised by the parties, so the point may yet be open.

2.8.5.4 Trade between Member States

In *Volkswagen*[233] the Commission imposed a fine of over 100 million Euros, at that time the highest ever, for having instructed its German dealers to show "price discipline" and not to sell far below the recommended prices. The effect on trade between Member States was created by dual pricing and various arrangments that discouraged Italian dealers from exporting to other Member States. The Commission did not have to establish that the recommendation on prices in Germany did so on its own.

In *Volkswagen Passat*,[234] the Commission concluded that it is not necessary to show an actual effect on trade between Member States, if rpm is capable of influencing the pattern of trade.

Given the ease with which the Commission finds that other restrictions may affect trade between Member States, Valentine has long thought it anomalous that it has been reluctant to do so in relation to rpm (2.8.5.1 above). It seems to be changing its mind. It was minded to clear the system of fixed book prices adopted by German publishers and booksellers on the ground that the agreements did not affect exports. It has now issued a statement of objections alleging that internet sales to countries outside Germany are regarded as infringing the system. The Commission also objects to refusals to sell to internet book sellers.[235]

The Commission states that it is aware that German state measures are envisaged to impose fixed prices for books, but considers that this is permitted as a result of the judgment in *Échirolles Distribution SA* v. *Association de Dauphiné and Others*,[236]

In a press release of 7 August, 2001,[237] the Commission started to investigate rpm by the major producers of CDs through contracts with retailers where cooperative advertising was linked to minimum advertised prices. Three of the majors

---

[231] Case 267/86 [1988] ECR 4769.

[232] 3 October 2000, C9/99, not yet reported save on the Court's web site.

[233] OJ 1998, L124/60, [1998] 5 CMLR 33, [1998] CEC 2189, on appeal, *Volkswagen* v. *Commission*, Case T-62/98, [2000] 5 CMLR 853 (7.6.3.1 below).

[234] OJ 2001, L 262/14, [2001] 5 CMLR 1309, paras. 82 & 88 (7.6.3.5 below).

[235] IP/01/1036. See also n 34 to 7.2.2 below.

[236] Case C-9/99 [2000] ECR I- 8207, criticised at 2.8.5.3 above.

[237] IP/01/1212.

abandoned the practice. The Commission also uncovered a limited practice by a major in Italy that could have the effect of maintaining retail prices. Since the possible infringements were confined to the territory of a single member state, the Commission terminated its investigations and infored the national competition authorities of the results of its enquiries.

2.9 TYING

Tying is the practice of refusing to supply the tying product without also supplying another, the tied product. It is not black listed by Article 4. This indicates "that when the ceiling of market share is exceeded, the Commission is prepared to weigh any benefits against the extension of market power from the tying product to the tied." This is helpful, because tying is one of the practices listed in Article 81 as having the object or effect of restricting competition.

Guideline 107 states that the objection to tying is that it enables the supplier to obtain a higher price from the tied product. Robert Bork has, however, demonstrated that tying is unlikely to be practiced in order to extend market power from the tying to the tied product. To the extent that customers dislike buying the tied product, they will be less willing to buy the tying product. Usually, there is only one monopoly rent to extract from the market (1.2.5.1.1 above). Tying is far more likely to be adopted to monitor usage.[238]

In the *Follow up to the Green Paper*,[239] the Commission said:

> Tying is in general considered as a somewhat less serious restriction (than resale price maintenance) and market partitioning). It concerns the possible extension of market power from one market into another. Possible efficiency arguments ("need to assure the buyer uses the right sort of input for a fragile machine we sold him as breakdowns may

---

[238] Common reasons for tying are:

—1) to ensure the quality of the product. This may be especially convincing when a complex new product is introduced and the supplier's reputation demands that it be technically satisfactory. In *Jerrold Electronics* v. *US* 187 F. Supp. 545 (ED Pa.) 1960, the Court of Appeals for Pennsylvania adopted this argument in relation to cable TV in the early days when the equipment was not robust. This justification must apply to many franchises and an obligation for the franchisee to obtain the products to be sold from a specific source was cleared by the ECJ in *Pronuptia de Paris GmbH* v. *Pronuptia de Paris Irmgard Schillgalis*, Case 161/84 [1986] ECR 353, para. 21, as long as it was not practical to monitor quality of fashion items.

—2) monitoring usage, so as to obtain greater compensation from intensive users, when counting devices are not reliable;

—3) where charges for the tying product are regulated, the regulatee may prefer to take part of its profits in an unregulated tied market. This should be controlled by the regulator;

—4) sometimes most customers want the package—is the sale of a vehicle a tied sale of all its components? Is it a tie for Microsoft to integrate more than word processing functions into Windows? The concept of tying is not clear cut, because it is not always clear when two products are separate;

—5) selling in bulk may reduce grading and transport costs,

—6) A tie may enable a firm to give a secret discount in an oligopolistic market.

[239] Section III. 4.

hurt our products image" or "joint delivery is cost saving") may be limited. Exclusive purchasing[240] is the least serious restriction within the group.

Under the earlier draft of the Regulation, tying was to be subject to the higher ceiling of a market share of 40 per cent, whereas other restrictions were subject to the lower ceiling of 20 per cent.

This marks a change from the 1970s when the Commission was very hostile to ties, which are listed in Article 81(1) as being likely to infringe the provision. Over time its views have softened. In the group exemption for patent licensing,[241] ties necessary to achieve a technically proper exploitation of the technology were treated as not infringing Article 81(1), but other ties were black listed. By the time the Commission adopted the Technology Transfer Regulation,[242] other ties were taken out of the black list and made subject only to the opposition procedure (Article 4(2)(a))[243]—if notified to the Commission they would be exempted by the Regulation unless the Commission opposed the exemption within four months.

In *Vaessen BV* v. *Moris and Alex Moris Pvba*,[244] an early decision, the Commission condemned tying in an individual decision. There, the tie of the sausage skins to a patented device for packing saussisons de Boulogne into them was probably a method of monitoring the use of the device and charging large users of the device more than those who used it only a little.[245] The use of cats' gut for making saussisons de Boulogne must have constituted only a small part of the demand for the gut. It can have foreclosed other suppliers from only a tiny part of the market.

In *Campari*,[246] a trademark licensee in an industrial franchise was required to buy the secret, dried, matted herbs from the licensor, and this was cleared on the ground that the tie was needed to ensure a uniform flavour and quality of the bitters produced with the herbs. The franchisor was not expected to disclose the identity and quantity of each herb,

---

[240] Exclusive purchasing should be distinguished from single branding. The latter is an obligation or incentive to handle mainly a single brand. Exclusive purchasing is an obligation to buy a particular product only from a designated source, leaving the buyer free to buy competing goods elsewhere. The two practices may, but need not, be combined.

[241] Commission Regulation 2349/84, OJ 1984, L219/15, corrections OJ 1985, C113/34, amended by Regulation 151/93, OJ 1993, L21/8.

In the draft published for comment in 1979, ties were black listed.

[242] Commission Regulation 240/96, OJ 1996, L31/2, [1996] 4 CMLR 405, [1996] 4 EIPR Supp. iv.

[243] The first item made subject to the opposition procedure was:

(a) the licensee is obliged at the time the agreement is entered into to accept quality specifications or further licences or to procure goods or services which are not necessary for a technically satisfactory exploitation of the licensed technology or for ensuring that the production of the licensee conforms to the quality standards that are respected by the licensor and other licensees.

The licensor may select any standard it wants: not only a middling kind of quality.

[244] OJ 1979, L19/32, [1979] 1 CMLR 511.

[245] **Lucio Zanon**, "Current Survey, 'Ties in Patent Licensing Agreements,'"(1980) 5 *ELRev* 391.

[246] *Re the Agreement of Davide Campari Milano SpA*, Case 78/253/EEC, OJ 1978, L70/69, [1978] 2 CMLR 397.

In *Rich Products/Jus-Rol*,[247] too, the Commission cleared an obligation to buy from the licensee a pre-mix whose composition was secret. This was a tie of the pre-mix to the licence to make and sell frozen yeast dough. The Commission did not require the licensor to disclose the confidential information to the licensee. It accepted the parties' statement that the pre-mix was necessary to a technically satisfactory exploitation of the licensed technology.

Some of the early decisons contained virtually no reasons for condemning ties. In *Velcro SA* v. *Aplix SA*,[248] an exclusive technology licensee was required to buy machinery from a particular manufacturer, Jacob Müller, who had developed it. The Decision says only:

> 53. . . . At least with effect from 1977, when it may be considered that substitute products were on the market. . . such an obligation prevents the licensee from obtaining the equipment from other manufacturers in the Common Market, possibly on more favourable terms.

> 54. Besides restricting the freedom of the licensee, this obligation also significantly affects the position of third parties, especially loom builders, who are thereby deprived of an important potential customer.

It added that the obligation:

> 71. . . . is a serious restriction on the licensee's freedom to choose his sources of supply. This restriction is not necessary to ensure a technically satisfactory exploitation of the invention. Furthermore, after 1977, there is no justification by way of legitimate recompense to Jacob Müller for the effort of developing the equipment necessary to exploit the invention as Jacob Müller was able to obtain such recompense from supplying Aplix and other licensees up to that date.

The licensor was a small firm that seems to have been unable to exploit the technology itself until the basic patents had expired and it had collected royalty revenue. It may well not have had the resources to pay for the development of the equipment, and had solved its problem by persuading the licensees to buy only from the designer. It was a way of making the licensee pay the cost of developing the euipment. Such matters were not considered in the published decision.

In the USA, in *Jefferson Parish Hospital Dis. (No. 2)* v. *Hyde*,[249] the Supreme Court split 5/4 and said that tying was still a *per se* offence but agreed that, with a market share no higher than 30 per cent in the tying product, there was a safe harbour even under the *per se* rule. There, it was argued that the tie of anesthesiologists to the other hospital services reduced costs and improved the quality of service.

Under Article 82, the ECJ and CFI have condemned tying and given little weight to the justifications.[250] It is hoped that when the undertaking that ties is not

---

[247] OJ 1988, L69/21 [1981] 4 CMLR 527.

[248] OJ 1985, L233/22, [1989] 4 CMLR 157.

[249] 446 US 2, 104 SCt 1551, 80 L Ed 2d 2 (1984).

[250] E.g., in *Hilti AG* v. *Commission,* Case T-30/89, [1991] ECR II-1439, *Tetra Pak Rausing SA* v. *Commission (No. 2),* Case T-83/91, 6 October 1994, [1994] ECR II-755, paras. 138–141 and *Télémarketing—Centre Belge d'Etudes du Marché-Télémarketing SA (CBEM)* v. *Compagnie Luxembourgeoise de Télédiffusion,* Case 311/84, [1985] ECR 3261, para. 27.

dominant, these cases will not be extended to situations where there is less market power.

It seems clear that when necessary to achieve a satisfactory application of technology, tying will not infringe Article 81(1). It would then be for the Commission to establish that the tie is not justified on that ground. On the other hand, it is feared that the Commission may treat tying for other reasons as infringing Article 81(1), leaving the parties to establish any efficiencies under Article 81(3).

Recently, there has been concern in merger decisions about "mixed bundling"—selling more than one product at less than their stand alone prices. In *Digital*,[251] under Article 86, the Commission alleged in a statement of objections that Digital abused its dominant position by supplying software services more cheaply as part of a package with hardware services. The Commission objected that this was part of a deliberate policy to restrict Digital's competitors in the market for hardware maintenance. Digital denied the allegations but undertook to end the practice until 2003.

Mixed bundling may reduce prices for the benefit of consumers when the supplier takes into consideration the profit from selling the other items when fixing the price of each (1.2.5.1.1 above). There is no reason why the total price should not remain cheaper than the aggregate stand alone prices. The practice may harm competitors who cannot supply some of the items, but it may help consumers in the long as well as the short term. Where, however, the market is concentrated, mixed bundling may raise rivals' costs and operate as a barrier to entry (1.2.5.2 above).

The omission of tying from the list of hard core restraints, seems to show that it is only when there is considerable market power that the Commission will object to mixed bundling. This limits the intervention of the Commission, but with very narrow definitions, firms exposed to potential competition may be deterred from practices that benefit competitors.

2.10 THE ADOPTION OF SUCCESSIVE REGULATIONS EXEMPTING DISTRIBUTION AGREEMENTS AND THE GREEN PAPER

Some 30,000 exclusive dealing agreements were notified to the Commission under Regulations 17[252] and 27/62[253] with requests for clearance or exemption in the 1960s, shortly after the Regulations introduced a system of notification for agreements which citizens wanted exempted.

---

[251] *Commission's Annual Report for 1977*, 153.

[252] Council Regulation 17/62—Main implementing regulation, OJ Spec Ed, 1959–62, 87; JO 1962, 204.

[253] Commission Regulation 27/62—Form, content and other details concerning applications and notification and complaints, OJ Spec Ed, 1962, 132, since replaced by Commission Regulation 3385/94, OJ 1994, L377/28; [1995] 5 CMLR 507.

The Commission might have dealt with the problem by deciding that agreements involving parties which did not have significant market power did not infringe Article 81(1) and needed no exemption, or that ancillary restrictions necessary to enable a firm to penetrate the market in another member state did not infringe the prohibition (2.7–2.7.3 above). Instead, it decided to reduce the number of pending files by granting group exemptions.[254] There was considerable doubt whether it had power to do so, and the Commission sought and received power from the Council in Regulation 19/65[255] to exempt exclusive dealing agreements and licences of intellectual property rights and know-how by regulation.

Regulation 19/65 dealt with the pressing problem of the time and the *vires* did not cover many types of agreement that are giving trouble nowadays. It was amended in 1999 to enable the Commission to adopt Regulation 2790/1999,[256]

Council Regulation 19/65 as amended, provides in part:

Article 1

1. Without prejudice to the application of Council Regulation No 17 and in accordance with Article 81(3) of the Treaty the Commission may by regulation declare that Article 81(1) shall not apply to

(a) categories of agreements which are entered into by two or more undertakings, each operating, for the purposes of the agreement, at a different level of the production or distribution chain, and which relate to the conditions under which the parties may purchase, sell or resell certain goods or services, ...

Article 1a

A Regulation pursuant to Article 1 may stipulate the conditions which may lead to the exclusion from its application of certain parallel networks of similar agreements or concerted practices operating on particular market; when these circumstances are fulfilled the Commission may establish this by means of Regulation and fix a period at the expiry of which the Regulation pursuant to Article 1 would no longer be applicable in respect of the relevant agreements or concerted practices on that market; such period must not be shorter than six months.

Already, by 1965 when proposing Regulation 19/65 to the Council, the Commission had decided not to operate through broad economic principles and to control only those agreements that might give cause for concern, but to treat all significant exclusive contracts as contrary to Article 81(1) and provide group exemptions for specified kinds of agreement into which Community businessmen are expected to distort their agreements.

---

[254] Largely, in order to avoid having to deal with so many agreements that were less anti-competitive than those between competitors limiting production to raise prices or collective boycotts. See the third recital to Regulation 19/65, OJ Spec Ed, 1965, 35, Appendix II below.

[255] Council Regulation 19/65—Vires for group exemptions for exclusive dealing and patent licences, OJ Spec Ed, 1965, 35.

[256] Council Regulation 1215/99, amending Reg. 19/65 on the application of Article 81(3) (ex Article 85(3)) of the Treaty to certain categories of agreements and concerted practices, OJ 1999, L148/1.

The Commission first exercised its power under Regulation 19/65 for distribution agreements in Regulation 67/67[257] which, after two renewals, expired at the end of June 1983. By Article 1(1) of that regulation it exempted from Article 81(1) agreements under which

(a) one party agrees with the other to supply only to that other certain goods for resale within a defined area of the Common Market; or

(b) one party agrees with the other to purchase only from that other certain goods for resale; or both.

This was replaced by two regulations. Commission Regulation 1983/83—Group exemption for exclusive dealing agreements[258]—I will sell only to you within a specified territory—and Commission Regulation 1984/83—Group exemption for exclusive purchasing agreements[259]—I will buy only from you, or only your brand of the contract products. There was a separate group exemption for franchising outlets for goods or services, but not for production.[260] Special treatment was given to exclusive distribution agreements for vehicles under Regulation 1475/95[261] and to beer and petrol under Regulation 1984/83. On these group exemption which were the subject matter of the second edition of **Korah and Rothnie**, *Exclusive Distribution and the EEC Competition Rules—Regulations 1983/83 and 1984/83*,[262] and **Korah**, *Franchising and the EEC Competition rules, Regulation 4087/88*[263] there will be no comment in this work. Apart from Regulation 1475/95[264] which will expire at the end of September 2002, they all finally expired at the end of May 2000, although agreements made before that date which qualified under one of them will continue to be exempt until the end of 2001.

In 1994, the Commission set in train a long internal and external consulting process including economic studies which led to the *Green Paper*[265] with radical ideas differing from its earlier view (2.6 above). The Commission was concerned that monitoring notifications was a waste of resources both its own and those of business. Moreover, thinking had been transformed by the experience of the merger task force. This included officials, many seconded from member states and other departments of the Commission, who were educated in economics or had worked closely with economists. An economist, David Deacon, was appointed to

---

[257] Commission Regulation 67/67 (expired), OJ Spec Ed, 1967, 10.

[258] OJ 1983, L173/1, corrections OJ 1984, C101/2, [1983] 2 CLE 255.

[259] OJ 1983, L173/7, corrections OJ 1984, C101/2, [1983] 2 CLE 262.

[260] Commission Regulation 4087/88—Group Exemption for Franchising Agreements, OJ 1988, L359/46, [1989] 4 CMLR 387.

[261] 28 June 1995, OJ L145/25, replacing Regulation 123/85, OJ 1985, L15/16.

[262] See also **Joanna Goyder**, *EU Distribution Law*, 3rd edn. (London, Palladian Law Publishing, 2001) and the earlier editions.

[263] (Oxford, ESC/Sweet & Maxwell, 1989).

[264] OJ 1995, L145/25, [1996] 4 CMLR 69, replacing Regulation 123/85, OJ 1985, L15/16.

[265] Green Paper on Vertical Restraints in EC Competition Policy, COM(96) 721 final, [1997] 4 CMLR 519.

head the policy directorate of the competition department and he was in charge of the team producing the *Green Paper*.[266]

In the *Green Paper*, the Commission analysed the drawbacks of the current system; made it clear that vertical restraints were less harmful than horizontal ones, that vertical restraints had anti-competitive effects, but also solved some possible causes of market failure. It added:

> the fiercer is interbrand competition the more likely are the pro-competitive and efficiency effects to outweigh any anti-competitive effects of vertical restraints. The inverse is true when interbrand competition is weak and there are significant barriers to entry.
>
> To further the interest of the consumer is at the heart of competition policy. Effective competition is the best guarantee for consumers to be able to buy good quality products at the lowest possible prices. Whenever in this green paper the introduction of protection of effective competition is mentioned, the protection of the consumer's interest by ensuring low prices is implied. (para. 54)

It went on to consider various economic arguments and proposed four options for discussion.

After holding a two-day hearing in Brussels, the Commission published the *Follow up to the Green Paper*.[267] This analysed the competitive harms and benefits that might be attributed to vertical restraints more systematically than in the Green Paper.[268] It criticised the former group exemptions for not taking account of market power. It claimed[269] that its views were based more on economic considerations than formerly.

The Commission's policy conclusions were that vertical restraints were less harmful than horizontal restraints (III.1), that in the absence of market power, vertical restraints can be assumed to be legal (IV.2), except for certain hard core restraints: rpm and absolute territorial protection. It was unable to pinpoint the level of market power that raised concern—certainly less than that evidenced by a market share of about 40 per cent which is required for a dominant position under Article 82, and probably more than the 10 per cent ceiling in the *de minimis* notice current at the time (2.4.1–2.4.1.5 above).[270]

It accepted (IV.3) that market shares are not a reliable indicator of market power, but a market analysis appropriate in infringement proceedings is too complex to be used generally. No one has suggested a better test. Later, it decided that it would grant a group exemption with a ceiling of market share at 30 per cent. In return for such a ceiling, the Commission was prepared to grant a group

---

[266] He has been succeeded by Dr Kirtikumar Mehta, also an economist by education. The later detailed work on consultation and preparing a draft regulation was performed by another economist, Luc Peeperkorn.

[267] Draft communication on the application of the EC Competition rules to vertical restraints—Follow-up to the Green Paper on Vertical Restraints—OJ 1998, C365/3; comments by Economic and Social Committee—OJ 1999, C116/22.

[268] Also more systematically and with more arguments based on policy than the later Guidelines on Vertical Restraints, OJ 2000, C2291/1, Appendix V below.

[269] *Follow up to the Green Paper*, section IV.2.

[270] Now raised to 15% by the new notice on agreements of minor importance, OJ 2001, C149/18.

exemption to a wider class of agreements than had formerly been exempt. This has replaced the old form-based group exemptions with one requiring some analysis of market structure.

The Commission added (*Follow up to the Green Paper*, IV.5) that there would be no presumption when the market share exceeded the ceiling that the agreement was illegal: the Commission would still bear the burden of proof and should also consider whether an individual exemption was appropriate. It promised to issue guidelines explaining the Commission's policy.

2.11 RETROSPECTIVE EXEMPTION—REGULATION 1216/99

In the hope of reducing the number of notifications before the implementation of the Green Paper, the Commission proposed and the Council adopted Regulation 1216/99.[271] This extended the list of agreements that the Commission may exempt retrospectively to a period before notification to include

> . . . agreements or concerted practices . . . entered into by two or more undertakings, each operating, for the purposes of the agreement, at a different level of the production or distribution chain, and relat[ing] to the conditions under which the parties may purchase, sell or resell certain goods or services. (Article 2(a)).[272]

The possibility of retrospective exemption mitigates the consequences of the uncertainty caused by the impossibility of being sure of the relevant market definition on which the application of the new group exemption depends. If the parties thought their agreement qualified for the group exemption because they misdefined the relevant market, they can notify later. Retrospective exemption was thought likely to reduce the number of notifications. It takes much time and expert advice to notify, and there is now less need to do so soon after signing an agreement.

Some firms will wait to notify until they have fallen out with the other party and are considering enforcing the agreement. Notification will then become a preliminary step to proceedings in court. By the time the parties have fallen out, a party likely to be sued in contract may well point out to the Commission the anticompetitive effects of the agreement and, by then, if the transaction was successful, the market share of the parties may have risen. So, it may be less likely that an exemption will be granted than if the agreement had been notified early. There still remain some incentives for notifying early, but the balance between the cost and the benefits of doing so has changed: the Regulation is likely to reduce the number of notifications (7.5–7.5.7.5.5 below).

---

[271] Council Regulation 1216/99 amending Reg. 17—retrospective exemption for vertical agreements, OJ 1999, L148/5, Article 1. The Commission feared a mass of notifications by firms that would be excluded from the new block exemption by the ceiling of market share and from those who were not sure what the relevant market was.

[272] The provisions providing for retrospective exemption of limited licences and assignments in Article 2(b) of Reg. 17 have not changed in substance and are seldom invoked.

If the notification procedure is withdrawn with the implementation of the White Paper (2.12 below), this Regulation will cease to be significant. Meanwhile it seems that the Commission is not monitoring notifications systematically and that both notifications and individual exemptions will cease to have any effect if the proposed regulation to replace Regulation 17 (Appendix IV below) is adopted without amendment (Article 35).

Professor Whish,[273] has raised the question whether Regulation 1216/99 operates retrospectively to enable agreements entered into before 17 June 1999 when the Regulation came into force to be exempted retrospectively. The language is retrospective—Regulation 17 is amended without any reference to time. The contrary argument is the general principle of law not to interpret legislation retrospectively.[274] A similar question arose several times when former group exemptions were extended some months after their expiry,[275] but there is no case law.

Notification, however is to be abrogated by the new regulation to replace Regulation 17, and individual exemptions already granted are to expire according to Article 35, a controversial provision. The recent initiatives resulting in the Green and White Papers came from different parts of DG Competition and their inter-relationship is now being considered. Regulation 1216/99 is likely to have effect for only a few years.

2.12 THE WHITE PAPER ON MODERNISATION

The Commission is making a U-turn. It now accepts that its policy used to be too formalistic and that a more economic approach is appropriate. The radical proposal suggested in its white paper on modernisation[276] is to end its exclusive rights

---

[273] "Regulation 2790/99: the Commission's 'New Style' Block Exemption for Vertical agreements," (2000) *CMLRev* 1074. The same question arises as to the retrospective effect of Regulation 1215/99 (Appendix III below) empowering a national authority to withdraw the benefit of group exemptions granted under Article 1 of Regulation 19/65. The technology transfer Regulation 240/96, OJ 1996, L31/2; [1996] 4 CMLR 405; [1996] 4 EIPR Supp. iv, was made under Article 1 before it was amended (6.1.2 below).

[274] **T.C. Hartley,** *The Foundations of European Community Law,* 4th edn. (Oxford, OUP, 1998) pp. 143–5.

[275] See **C.S. Kerse,** "Block exemptions under Article 85(30): the Technology Transfer Regulation— Procedural Issues," (1996) 17 *ECLR* 10, at 11.

[276] White Paper on Modernisation of the Rules Implementing Articles 81 and 82 of the EC Treaty. Commission programme No 99/027, [1999] 5 CMLR 208.

There have been many excellent comments on the White Paper. Taken chronologically, they include: **José Rivas** and **Margot Horspool** (eds.), *Modernisation and Decentralisation of EC Competition Law,* (Kluwer Law International, The Hague, 2000) vii + 134 pp. House of Lords, Select Committee on the European Community, Session 1999–2000, Reforming EC Competition Procedures, with Evidence, 4th Report, HL Paper 33, 38 + 163 large pp. The report is on the WWW but the minutes of evidence, which are fascinating, are published only by HMSO. *The Modernisation of European Competition Law: The Next 10 Years,* (University of Cambridge, Centre of European Legal Studies Occasional Paper No. 4, June 2000). **Rein Wesseling,** *The Modernisation of EC Antitrust Law* (Oxford, Hart Publishing, 2001). **Dr C.D. Ehlermann,** "The Modernisation of EC Antitrust Policy: A Legal and Cultural Revolution," [2000] 37 *CMLRev* 537; Barry Hawk (ed.) [2000] *Fordham Corporate Law Institute,*

to grant exemptions. It has proposed that the Council should revise Regulation 17 radically.[277] The Commission will no longer have exclusive competence to grant individual exemptions: Article 81(3) will have direct effect in national courts, which will be able to make positive decisions in the light of Article 81 as a whole. The bifurcation of Articles 81(1) and (3) will matter less once the same bodies are competent to apply both provisions.[278] Indeed the Commission also envisages itself taking either positive or negative decisions, and the positive ones would not distinguish between clearance and exemption.

Moreover, the Commission proposes that national authorities may adopt positive decisions taking into account the whole of Article 81 as well as negative ones when there is a distinct market within its territory, although these will be effective only within the territory (Article 5). Such decisions will not be constitutive (they will not last for a set number of years) but merely declare that as a whole Article 81 is not infringed at that moment.

The Commission will also provide some safe harbours for firms lacking market power by granting more broadly drafted group exemptions. They will be based economically on the kind of agreement where any harm to competition is likely to be outweighed by benefits to consumers. To compensate for the broader coverage, they will probably be subject to ceilings of market share.[279] Market shares may not be a perfect indicator of market power, but no one has suggested any better test, and the Commission thinks it is easier to quantify market shares than market power.

Market share caps have been greatly criticised in the past, for instance when a maximum market share of 40 per cent for a competing licensee was proposed for the group exemption for technology transfer.[280] Business claimed that it was difficult to

International Antitrust Law and Policy, chaps 10–17, pp 2.133–346; **Wouter P.J. Wils**, "Notification, Clearance and Exemption in EC Competition Law: an Economic Analysis," (1999) 24 ELRev 139; "The Modernisation of the Enforcement of Articles 81 and 82 EC: A Legal and Economic Analysis of the Commission's proposal for a new Council Regulation Replacing Regulation No. 17, in Barry Hawk (ed.) [2000] Fordham Corporate Law Institute 279–394; **C.D. Ehlermann** and **I. Atanasiu** (eds.), European Competition Law Annual 2000: The Modernisation of EC Antitrust Policy (Oxford, Hart Publishing, 2001).

[277] Proposal of the Commission for a Council regulation to replace Regulation 17/62, 2000/0243 (CNS), [2000] 5 CMLR 1148.

[278] Article 2 provides that the onus of establishing an infringement of Article 81(1) will remain on the party alleging illegality, but the onus of establishing that an agreement merits exemption will be on the party invoking Article 81(3). The bifurcation of Article 81 will remain but be less important.

[279] The new group exemptions of general application adopted after Regulation 2790/99 all have ceilings of market share. They are:

—Commission Regulation 2658/2000, on the application of Article 81(3) of the Treaty to categories of specialisation agreements, OJ 2000, L304/3, [2001] 4 CMLR 800 and

—Commission Regulation 2659/2000, on the application of Article 81(3) of the Treaty to categories of research and development agreements, OJ 2000, L304/7, [2001] 4 CMLR 808. Theyare subject to ceilings of 20 and 25% respectively.

The Commission has proposed in Article 28 of the new Regulation to replace Regulation 17 that the Council should grant it broader vires to adopt group exemptions without requiring it to have had prior experience in the area.

[280] It became Commission Regulation 240/96, OJ 1996, L31/2; [1996] 4 CMLR 405; [1996] 4 EIPR Supp. iv with no ceiling of market share, although one of the instances when the Commission may withdraw the benefit of the regulation for individual agreements is where the licensee's market share exceeds 40%.

identify what market would be found to be relevant by the Commission or a court. The difficulty is particularly great for new technology when markets may be rapidly changing, and the market share cap was largely abandoned for Regulation 240/96.[281]

When consulting on the group exemption for distribution agreements, however, the Commission made it clear that there must be a ceiling of market share. Originally there were to be two caps, 40 per cent for the least harmful restraints, and 20 per cent for those considered more harmful. This was thought to be too complex, and finally a single cap at 30 per cent was selected.

Notification is to end. Pending notifications will lapse when the new regulation comes into force and so will existing individual exemptions (Article 35). These provisions are controversial and will lead to uncertainty where the 30 per cent market share is exceeded.

There will still be problems advising firms as to the relevant market but we now have many precedents of the Commission's findings in its merger decisions,[282] and the notice on the definition of the relevant market (2.4.1.2 above) is helpful although in merger cases for many products, there are often two or three possible definitions that comply with the notice. Since the Commission intends to abrogate the notification system, and there is no word of notification in the new draft Regulation to replace Regulation 17, firms unsure of the relevant market and consequently of their market share, will not be able to avoid uncertainty through notification, although Commission officials may give non-binding advice.

2.13 FEW VERTICAL AGREEMENTS INFRINGE ARTICLE 81(1)

When perusing the group exemption in Regulation 2790/99, it is important to keep in mind that few vertical agreements infringe Article 81(1) in the absence of hard core restraints unless there is substantial market power. Even then there may not be a significant effect on trade between member states. Old decisions of the Commission that exclusive vertical agreements infringed Article 81(1) in the absence of rpm or territorial restraints are suspect, now that officials are being so much more influenced by economic considerations. Moreover, the CFI is

---

[281] The Commission was required by Art. 12 of Reg. 240/96 to draw up a report on the operation of the Regulation by the end of March 2000.The report appeared on DG Competition's home page, (http://comm/competition/antitrust/technology_transfer/) on 21 December 2001. Doubtless it will soon be published in the OJ. The Commission contemplates revising Regulation 240/96 before its expiry in 2006. It may extend its scope to include copyright, design rights and trade marks and will consult on the possibility of imposing a ceiling of market share. Many other important issues are raised in a paper of 42 pages with small print. Comments are requested by 26 March, 2002.

[282] The CFI has held that the relevant market must be selected at the time a merger takes place and that old precedents will not be binding. *The Coca-Cola Company and Coca-Cola Enterprises Inc.* v. *Commission*, Cases T-125 & 127/97 [2000] ECR II 1733. Nevertheless, the precedents give an indication of the Commission's thinking and are likely to be followed in the absence of significant changes in the patterns of substitution.

requiring the Commission to give better reasons for its decisions.[283] There has been a radical change of view by both the CFI and Commission in the last decade.

[283] E.g., *Langnese-Iglo GmbH & Co. KG* v. *Commission*, Case T-7/93 [1995] ECR II-1533, para. 98. In *European Night Services (ENS) and others* v. *Commission*, Cases T-374, 375, 384 & 388/94 [1998] ECR II-3141, the CFI annulled a Commission decision about a joint venture on many grounds, mainly for failing to consider economic arguments and in one instance for manifest error of assessment.

3

The Group Exemption

3.1 INTRODUCTION

There are significant advantages in bringing an agreement within a group exemption. There will be no competition problems when suing to enforce it, or persuading the other party to perform. It is strongly arguable that national competition law cannot override a group exemption.[1] There will be no danger of being fined except for infringements of Article 82.[2]

Under the former regulations, where the firm protected from competition had market power short of a dominant position, anti-competitive agreements were legal *per se*, at least until the block exemption was withdrawn from an individual agreement. On the other hand, harmless agreements had to be modified so as to fit into the strait jacket prescribed by a particular regulation.

The new group exemption granted by Regulation 2790/99[3] is said to be more firmly based on economic principles and market structure. It is far less formalistic. It exempts a wider class of agreements with similar economic justifications than did its predecessors, but it imposes a ceiling of market share as well as a list of hard core provisions that prevent the Regulation from applying. If the supplier supplies more than 30 per cent of the relevant market, the Regulation will not apply. The parties may have difficulty in identifying the relevant market, and the safe harbour will not be safe if they get the answer wrong. The ceiling of market share follows the view expressed in the *Green Paper*[4] that the more inter-brand competition there is the more likely it is that the benefit to consumers will outweigh any reduction of competition.

Even if the supplier's turnover exceeds the 30 per cent cap, and its agreement fails to qualify for the exemption, however, there is no presumption that the agreement infringes Article 81(1) and anyone alleging that it does will bear the burden of proof (Guideline 62, 7.4.5 below).

---

[1] Tesauro AG in *BMW* v. *ALD*, Case C-70/93 [1995] ECR I-3441 paras. 32–42, The ECJ did not address the question, which remains open.

[2] *Tetra Pak Rausing SA* v. *Commission*, Case T-51/89 [1990] ECR II-309.

[3] On the application of Article 81(3) of the Treaty to vertical agreements and concerted practices, OJ 1999, L336/21, [2000] 4 CMLR 398.

[4] On vertical restraints in EC Competition Policy, COM(96) 721 final, [1997] 4 CMLR 519, paras. 54, 65 and 85 (2.10 above).

3.2 STATUS OF RECITALS AND GUIDELINES[5]

On 26 May 2000, the Commission published extensive guidelines on vertical restraints,[6] giving its view not only on the meaning of the Regulation, but also on agreements that are outside its scope. Unfortunately, most of them give the Commission's conclusions and few give its reasoning. More reasoning is to be found in the Green Paper and its follow up[7] (2.10 above) but policy was reconsidered in the consultation period that followed their publications, so they are not a reliable guide to interpretation. As is habitual in Community regulations, it also adopted recitals explaining the construction of the Regulation.

There is controversy over the status of recitals. One view is that they form part of the instrument adopted by the Commission and are vital under Community law since the Articles are sometimes construed so as to give effect to them, even when this is contrary to the clear meaning of the operative part.[8] The ECJ, however, has also decided that recitals cannot override clear wording.[9] Valentine is told, how-

[5] We would like to thank Paul Lasok QC, for a most helpful note on the status of guidelines. We have plagiarised it, but incorporated some of our own ideas. He cannot be blamed for any resulting errors.

[6] OJ 2000, C291/1, Appendix IV below.

[7] Green Paper on vertical restraints in EC Competition Policy, COM(96) 721 final, [1997] 4 CMLR 519. *Communication on the Application of the EC Competition Rules to Vertical Restraints—Follow-up to the Green Paper on Vertical Restraints*—OJ 1998, C365/3.

[8] For instance, in *Fonderies Roubaix* v. *Fonderies Roux*, Case 63/75 [1976] ECR 111; in the light of unclear recitals, the ECJ virtually read Article 1(2) out of Reg. 67/67 because it led to anomalous results that would, otherwise, have required amendment. This was confirmed in *de Norre* v. *Concordia*, Case 47/76 [1977] ECR 65; paras. 16–20. For the effect of recitals, see generally, Paul Lasok QC in David Vaughan QC (ed.) 51 *Halsbury's Laws of England*, 2.268. A court may use recitals to confirm the interpretation in the regulation, *Stauder* v. *Ulm*, Case 29/69 [1969] ECR 419, 425; *Adorno* v. *EC Commission* [1981] ECR 1469 at 1484 & 5; *Effer* v. *Kantner*, Case 38/81 [1982] ECR 825 at 834.

[9] *Joseph Hoche and Roomboterfabriek "De Bester Boter"* v. *Bundesanstalt für landwirtschaftliche Marktordnung*, Cases 154 and 155/83 [1985] ECR 1232, para. 13. The recitals mentioned a smaller class than the articles of the Regulation. The ECJ concluded that

> 13 . . . as [the defendant] and the Commission rightly argued, the decisive factor in the interpretation of Article 6(a) on that point is not the preamble of the regulation which introduced it, which merely sets out the general aims of the regulation, but the wording of the Article itself, which makes it clear that Article 6(a) is not restricted to products falling under the heading 19.08 of the Common Customs Tariff but applies to all products referred to in Article 6(i)(c)."

In this, the Court followed AG Lenz, [1985] ECR 1215, 1223 "because the statement of reasons such preambles contain are not always comprehensive."

In *Criminal proceedings against Gunnery Nilsson and others*, Case C162/97 [1988] ECR I-7477, an argument was based on a recital to a directive. AG Mischo said:

> 92. As the Commission rightly points out, the preamble is not a rule of law. It cannot therefore be invoked to derogate from the rules laid down in the directive. The recitals in the preamble state the reasons for the contents of the rule and can sometimes help with its interpretation, but they cannot form the basis of a derogation from one of the directive's express provisions.

> 93. Moreover, I see no contradiction between the preamble and Article 2 of the directive.

The ECJ agreed:

> 54. On this point, it must be stated that the preamble to a Community act has no binding force and cannot be relied on as a ground for derogating from the actual provisions of the act in question.

ever, that in the directives on intellectual property, the official who loses an argument and finds the Article drafted contrary to his wishes, may be compensated by a recital that contradicts the Article, making interpretation difficult for those not involved in the drafting process.

Guidelines are not listed amongst the sources of Community law in Article 249. They are sometimes referred to as "soft law," but may be persuasive.

The third and fourth Guidelines on Vertical Restraints state:

> 3. By issuing these Guidelines the Commission aims to help companies to make their own assessment of vertical agreements under the EC competition rules. The standards set forth in these guidelines must be applied in circumstances specific to each case. This rules out a mechanical application. Each case must be evaluated in the light of its own facts. The Commission will apply the Guidelines reasonably and flexibly.

> 4. These Guidelines are without prejudice to the interpretation that may be given by the Court of First Instance and the Court of Justice of the European Communities in relation to the application of Article 81 to vertical agreements.

Guidelines are of two sorts. Those that give the Commission's view of the law have no binding legal effect, although they may persuade national and Community courts. They may also bind the institution issuing them, at least to the extent that it should not punish an undertaking that has acted on them before they were withdrawn.[10]

Guidelines relating to how the Commission intends to exercise its discretionary powers (for instance its policy on fines or the approval of state aids) may well bind the Commission to the extent that they create legitimate expectations.[11]

> 55. Besides, a reading of the fourth recital in the preamble to Directive 87/328, in which the expressions used in the question appear, does not show any contradiction between that recital and the actual provisions of the directive.

The fact that both Advocate General and Court observed that there was no contradiction between the recital and the actual provisions of the directive does not reduce the cogency of the preceding paragraphs. A court that allows no dissents or separate opinions often gives more than one reason.

[10] In the *Sugar Cartel*, Cases 40–48/73, 50/73, 54–56/73, 111/73, 113–114/73 [1975] ECR 1663, para. 555, the Court reduced a fine on the ground that undertakings might have relied on a Commission notice. One infringement was not taken into account by the Court when fixing the amount of the fine because the parties might have been misled by the Commission's notice on agency, since replaced by Guidelines 12–20 on Vertical Restraints. If a guideline giving the Commission's view is mistaken, but acted upon by an undertaking, the consequences in a court might be different from those before the Commission. The court would not be bound by the guideline and might find that, on a proper construction of Article 81, the contractual term sought to be enforced was void *ab initio*. The firm might argue, however, that it should not be fined by the Commission for past conduct based on legitimate expectations, although the Commission might order it to terminate the infringement in future.

[11] Not all statements give rise to legitimate expectations. In *Evelyne Delauche* v. *Commission*, Case 111/86 [1987] ECR 5345, the ECJ said:

> 23. As regards breach of the principle of protection of legitimate expectations, Mrs. Delauche refers to the many declarations made by the Commission concerning the need to increase the number of women in positions of responsibility. She maintains that, as a result of those declarations, she could legitimately expect that her application would be successful.

> 24. It must be pointed out that Mrs. Delauche did not receive any personal assurance which could have led her to hope that she would be promoted. Accordingly she is not in any event entitled to

To avoid the latter, the Commission would have to withdraw the guideline generally, or give specific undertakings notice before they act on the basis of them.[12] In *Dijkstra*,[13] the ECJ stated that in order to avoid decisions inconsistent with those envisaged by the Commission (para. 28) in interpreting a Council Regulation "it is necessary to take into account its genesis and the reasons on which Regulation 26 is based" (para. 17). It added at para. 32 that a national court should also take

> into account the criteria established by the case-law of the Court and the practice of the Commission, which is apparent not only from the decisions adopted by it but also, in particular, from its reports on competition policy and its communications.

Most of the Guidelines on Vertical Restraints indicate the Commission's construction of the Regulation or the application of Article 81. These are not binding on courts or national competition authorities although experts study them closely and they are likely to be persuasive.

The Commission's notices on the construction of the competition rules in the treaty have frequently been mentioned by Advocates General, who have advised the Court to ignore them.[14] This it has consistently done, except in the *Sugar Cartel*,[15] where the Court reduced a fine on the ground that undertakings might have relied on a Commission notice. In *European Night Services*,[16] the CFI refused to follow blindly the notice on minor agreements and in *Langnese-Iglo GmbH & Co. KG v. Commission*,[17] the CFI refused to follow the notice on minor agree-

---

maintain that the contested decisions are in breach of the principle of protection of legitimate expectations.

See also *World Wide Fund for Nature* v. *Commission*, Case T-105/95 [1997] ECR II-313, paras. 55 & 56, where the CFI stated that the Commission was bound to comply with a series of obligations it had voluntarily accepted and apply the exceptions strictly.

[12] In *CIRFS—Comité International de la Rayonne et des Fibres Synthétiques and Others* v. *Commission*, Case C-313/90 [1993] ECR 1125, the Commission had changed its policy in relation to state aids for synthetic fibres of which there was already excess production capacity (para. 39). The ECJ stated:

44. A measure of general application cannot be impliedly amended by an individual decision.

45. Furthermore, neither the principle of equal treatment nor that of the protection of legitimate expectations may be relied upon in order to justify the repetition of an incorrect interpretation of a measure.

[13] *Hendrik Evert Dijkstra and Others* v. *Friesland (Frico Domo) Coöperatie BA and Others*, Case C-319/93, 40 & 224/94 [1995] ECR I-4471.

[14] E.g., AG Warner in *Miller* v. *Commission*, Case 19/77 [1978] ECR 154, 157 *et seq.* and AG Dutheillet de Lamothe in *Cadillon* v. *Höss*, Case 1/71 [1971] ECR 358, 361, and in *Beguelin*, [1971] ECR 964, 968.

[15] See *The Sugar Cartel*, Cases 40–48/73, 50/73, 54–56/73, 111/73, 113–114/73 [1975] ECR 1663, para. 555. One infringement was not taken into account by the Court when fixing the amount of the fine because the parties might have been misled by the Commission's notice on agency, since replaced.

[16] Cases T-374, 375, 384 & 388/94 [1998] ECR II-3141, para. 102. See also *Greene King—Roberts and Roberts* v. *Commission*, Case T-25/911 [2001] CMLR 828, paras. 90 & 120.

[17] Case T-7/93, [1995] ECR II-1533, para. 98.

ments, which it thought was inconsistent with the judgment of the ECJ in *Delimitis (Stergios)* v. *Henninger Bräu.*[18]

The Commission has also issued explanatory notes on the interpretation of the Common Customs Tariff, which is a regulation passed by the Council on the proposal of the Commission. In *Witt* v. *Hauptzollamt Hamburg-Ericus*,[19] the Court followed the opinion of Advocate General Trabucchi and stated that,

> The Explanatory Notes to the Common Customs Tariff, although an important factor as regards interpretation in all cases where the provisions of the tariff provoke uncertainty, cannot amend those provisions, the meaning and scope of which are sufficiently clear.

In *Hauptzollamt Bremen-Freihafen* v. *Waren-Import-Gesellschaft Krohn & Co.*[20] the ECJ said:

> [a]n interpretation of a regulation by an informal document of the Commission is not enough to confer on that interpretation an authentic Community character. Such documents, which no doubt have their value for the purpose of applying certain regulations, have, however, no binding effect, and thus cannot ensure that the descriptions of the goods to which they refer have the same scope in all the Member States. The uniform application of Community law is only guaranteed if it is the subject of formal measures taken in the context of the Treaty.

The interpretation was contained in a communication from the Commission to the German government. Officials have suggested that the Commission's views on one of its own regulations and published in the Official Journal might be more persuasive, but the guidelines do not form part of the regulation, or take legislative form.

Nevertheless, the guidelines are likely to be taken into account by national courts or competition authorities when interpreting the Regulation. They are very important in practice. There are various points at which the guidelines take a position that is not made clear in the Regulation itself or arguably conflicts with the words of the Regulation[21] and it will be argued that it is the Regulation that governs, and that the guidelines should be invoked only when the Regulation is unclear.

In *Delimitis*,[22] when the Commission had exclusive power to grant individual exemptions,[23] the ECJ stressed that the Commission was responsible for the implementation and orientation of Community competition policy. Consequently,

---

[18] Case C-234/89, [1991] ECR I-935. In *Métropole Télévision (M6)* v. *Commission*, Case T-112/99 [2001] 5 CMLR 1236, para. 104 (7.2 above), however, the CFI based the concept of ancillary restraint on notices of the Commission that are hard to reconcile with *European Night Services* v. *Commission*, Cases T-374, 375, 384 and 388/94 [1998] ECR II-3141.

[19] Case 149/73 [1973] ECR 1587, para 3.

[20] Case 74/69 [1970] ECR 451, para. 9.

[21] See, e.g., 3.4.9.2 below in relation to intellectual property rights.

[22] *Delimitis (Stergios)* v. *Henninger Bräu*, Case C-234/89 [1991] ECR I-935.

[23] If the Regulation to replace Regulation 17 (2.12 above) is adopted, it will lose this exclusive power early in 2004.

national courts were required not to adopt decisions that conflict with Commission decisions actual or envisaged. It seemed to follow that national courts were virtually bound to follow guidelines in order to avoid such conflict.

In the earlier *Perfumes* judgments,[24] the ECJ had stated that national courts were not bound to follow the views expressed by the Commission in comfort letters, but they were entitled to take them into account and this was not expressly overruled in *Delimitis*, although if a national court were to take an independent line, its judgment might well contradict a subsequent formal decision of the Commission, which the ECJ said it should not do.

In *Masterfoods Ltd and HB Ice Cream* v. *Commission,*[25] the ECJ ruled that:

> Where a national court is ruling on an agreement or practice the compatibility of which with Articles 85(1) and 86 of the EC Treaty . . . is already the subject of a Commission decision, it cannot take a decision running counter to that of the Commission, even if the latter's decision conflicts with a decision given by a national court of first instance. If the addressee of the Commission decision has, within the period prescribed . . ., brought an action for annulment of that decision, it is for the national court decide whether to stay proceedings pending a final judgment in that action for annulment or in order to refer a question to the Court for a preliminary ruling.

The ruling was strong in that there was already an appeal from the Commission's decision pending before the CFI which had suspended the operation of the decision pending its final decision.

According to the *White Paper on Modernisation,*[26] however, the power to grant exemptions is to be shared with national courts and national authorities and, if that be adopted by the Council, the position will be less clear. The Commission may no longer be uniquely responsible for the implementation and orientation of Community competition policy, although only it will be empowered to grant group exemptions. Moreover, when the Commission's staff have been taken from monitoring agreements to detecting international cartels, monitoring state aids and appraising the activities of undertakings given special or exclusive rights, it is unlikely that the Commission will make subsequent conflicting decisions in other fields. The strength of guidelines may decline over time.

Moreover, the guidelines are stated not to bind the ECJ or CFI and it would be unfortunate if those courts applied a different test from national courts or competition authorities.

---

[24] E.g., in *Guérlain—Procureur de la République* v. *Giry and Guérlain,* Cases 253/78 & 1–3/79 [1980] ECR 2327 and *Lancôme—SA Lancôme and Cosparfrance Nederland BV* v. *Etos BV and Albert Heijn Supermart BV,* Case 99/79 [1980] ECR 2511, the ECJ ruled that an individual comfort letter may be taken into account by a national court, but does not bind it.

[25] Case C-344/98 [2000] ECR I-1136,

[26] Commission programme No 99/027, OJ C 132/1, (2.12 above), implemented by the proposal for a Council Regulation on the implementation of the rules on competition laid down in Articles 81 and 82 of the Treaty . . . 2000/0243(CNS), recitals 4–7 and Articles 1, 2 & 6.

3.3 JOINT DOMINANT POSITION

Group exemptions apply only to Article 81 not to Article 82.[27] The ECJ accepted in *Compagnie Maritime Belge Transports SA* v. *Commission*[28] that undertakings may be collectively dominant when they act as a unit, whether or not as a result of links between them (3.4.7 below).

Suppose there are only two or three dealers within a relevant market and they all demand slotting allowances and all pay smaller suppliers less (1.3.3 above).[29] If there is an agreement between them so to act, clearly the Regulation would not apply to it and they would be acting as a single entity and jointly dominant.

Suppose, however, that they act in similar ways as a result of individual decisions in the context of the market structure. We hope that this would not be treated as abusive. It is important that parallel conduct without actual collusion should not be treated as illegal. Competition, even between firms with market power, must not be chilled.[30] At 1.3.2 above, the efficiencies of such practices were explained.

Nevertheless, undertakings with a market share of less than 30 per cent may be treated as jointly dominant, and should consider Article 82 before competing too aggressively. The trauma of an investigation under Article 82 might outweigh the gain from vigourous competition. The application of the rule against abuse of a collective dominant position has not yet been worked out. Valentine hopes that the Commission will intervene little.

3.4 REGULATION 2790/99—ARTICLE 2 RECITALS 3–6, GUIDELINES 23–27

The former group exemptions for distribution are described at 2.10 above. They were form based, drafted to exempt the kinds of agreement of which the Commission had received many notifications. Classes of agreement with similar economic effects were excluded and the market context of the agreement was relevant only when the Commission was considering whether to withdraw the benefit of the group exemption to an individual agreement.

---

[27] *Tetra Pak Rausing SA* v. *Commission,* Case T-51/89 [1990] ECR II-309.

[28] Case C-395/96P [2000] ECR I-1365.

[29] It may be more expensive to take supplies from smaller firms that cannot provide some of the services supplied by larger suppliers, and cost justified discounts would not amount to discrimination, but it is often not possible to quantify savings. No firm wants to get involved in the effort.

[30] In *Compagnie Maritime Belge,* Case C-395/96P, 16 March 2000, [2000] ECR I-1365, at para 132, Fennelly AG stressed the importance of permitting even dominant firms to compete, especially when they are not super-dominant. As explained at 1.3.2–1.3.5 above, there should be no *per se* prohibition of discrimination by firms with buying power. Slotting allowances and similar practices may reflect efficiencies.

After much consideration, in Regulation 2790/99,[31] the Commission granted a single exemption for vertical agreements "relating to the conditions under which the parties may purchase, sell or resell certain goods and services" (Article 2) but limited its application by imposing a ceiling of market share (Article 3). Where the supplier supplies more than 30 per cent of the relevant market, the group exemption does not apply, although the agreement will not necessarily infringe Article 81(1) and require exemption.

Unlike the earlier block exemptions, there is no limiting "white list" of provisions that are exempted. All provisions are exempted unless of the kind included in the lists of hard-core restraints in Articles 4 and 5. So the exemption operates less as a strait jacket. There are two hard-core lists. The inclusion of a restraint of the kind listed in Article 4 prevents the application of the Regulation even to other provisions, while the presence of any of the provisions listed in Article 5 prevents the Regulation applying to that provision, but not to others. Since it may be argued that the single branding restraints (1.2.2.1 above) listed in Article 5 seldom restrict competition, and they may not affect trade between member states, it is thought that Article 5 will rarely be important.

The single Regulation applies to exclusive distribution, exclusive purchasing, franchising and selective distribution. It may even apply to other transactions (3.4.9–3.4.9.2 below). For the first time in decades one chapter of a book on EC competition law can be shortened, although there are some differences between the different categories of contract resulting from the lists of Articles 4 and 5.

Franchising is not specifically mentioned in the Regulation, but the application of the Regulation to franchising is considered in Guidelines 42–44 and franchise agreements outside the regulation are considered generally in Guidelines 199–201. The Commission considers that franchising comes within the definition of Article 2(1). Since the word is not used in the Regulation, it is not defined there, nor is it defined in the guidelines. Since usage is not uniform, this may give rise to problems of construction and of the compatibility of the Guidelines with the Regulation.

Article 1 consists of various definitions, but the important definitions of "vertical agreements" and "vertical restraints" are in Article 2(1). It is proposed to pick up the definitions in Article 1 when discussing the provisions using the words defined.

Article 2(1) exempts "vertical agreements":

> 1. Pursuant to Article 81(3) of the Treaty and subject to the provisions of this Regulation, it is hereby declared that Article 81(1) shall not apply to agreements or concerted practices entered into between two or more undertakings each of which operates

---

[31] OJ 1999, L336/21, set out in Appendix I below. See Richard Whish, "Regulation 2790/99: The Commission's 'New Style' Block Exemption for Vertical Agreements," (2000) *CMLRev* 1074. The sufficiency of the consultation process has been challenged before the CFI, and the failure of the Commission to exclude agreement with economically dependent parties from the exemption. whether such an important amendment can be made without amending the Treaty has also been called in question. *Conseil National des Professions de l'Automobile (CNPA) and others* v. *Commission*, Case T-45/00 and *Bond van de Fegarbel-Beroepsverenigingen* v. *Commission*, Case T-58/00, OJ 2000, C149/20 and 37, [2000] 5 CMLR 270 and 271. In fact, the consultation by publication in the OJ and through organisations was more thorough than for any previous group exemption. On the other hand, the change of approach was more radical.

for the purposes of the agreement, at a different level of the production or distribution chain, and relating to the conditions under which the parties may purchase, sell or resell certain goods or services ("vertical agreements"). This exemption shall apply to the extent that such agreements contain restrictions of competition falling within the scope of Article 81(1) ("vertical restraints").

3.4.1 Agreements or Concerted Practices Between Two or More Undertakings

To come within the group exemption and, indeed, to infringe Article 81(1), there must be collusion between "undertakings." Vertical agreements with final purchasers are subject to the competition rules only when the purchaser constitutes an undertaking (Guideline 24). A vertical agreement to buy a television set for the home is unlikely to be an agreement between undertakings, but an agreement whereby a hotel buys identical television sets for guests' bedrooms would amount to an agreement between undertakings within the meaning of Article 81, although it would be unlikely to have appreciable effects on competition or trade between member states.

Unlike the position under the earlier group exemptions, an agreement to which more than two undertakings are party may be exempt. For instance, a single contract may be made between the holder of a trademark, the supplier of the product and the customer, or between a supplier, a distributor for a single member state and a wholesaler for a smaller region.

3.4.2 "Each Operating for the Purpose of the Agreement, at a Different Level of the Production or Distribution Chain"

Even if a supermarket chain manufactures its own brand of chocolate biscuits and arranges to buy a brand of plain biscuits to sell in its stores, the agreement on plain biscuits qualifies as vertical: "for the purpose of the agreement, the parties operate at different level of trade". Whether the supermarket's own brand of chocolate biscuits competes with the plain biscuits would be relevant under Article 2(4) (3.4.4 below).

3.4.3 "Relating to Conditions Under Which the Parties may Purchase, Sell or Resell Certain Goods or Services"—Art. 2(1), Guideline 24

The exemption is not expressly limited to distribution: it applies to agreements and concerted practices

relating to the conditions under which the parties may purchase, sell or resell certain goods or services ("vertical agreements").

It is arguable that there is a very important difference between Article 2(1) and the third indent of Guideline 24 which states that:

This reflects the purpose of the Block Exemption Regulation to cover purchase and distribution agreements.

The words quoted from the Regulation seem to Valentine to relate to terms under which the parties are restrained from further purchases and sales. There is no reason expressed why this should be done only in a contract of sale made between one party, "A" to the other party, "B."

B may agree in a contract not of sale but a copyright or trade mark licence under which B agrees to duplicate disks and sell them under A's mark, not to sell brands other than A's, or A may promise not to make any direct sales within a territory in which B is interested. If the phrase were intended to relate only to the transaction of sale there would be no need to refer to "the conditions under which the parties may . . ." On this view, the Regulation may apply to a pure trade mark or copyright licence under which the parties limit their rights to buy from or sell to other parties.

Confining the Regulation to agreements for the distribution of goods or services may have been the purpose of some officials, but Article 2(1) does not limit such conditions to products that have been sold by A to B, nor do the recitals.

The possible exclusion of licences of intellectual property rights does not appear in the words of Article 2(1). Many licences are excluded from the group exemption by Article 2(5) (3.4.8 below), which excludes agreements, the subject matter of which is covered by another group exemption. A pure copyright or trade mark licence, however, cannot be brought within the Technology Transfer Regulation[32] which applies only if patents and/or know-how are licensed and the copyright or mark is ancillary. The controversial issue, which is very important in practice, will be further discussed at 3.4.9–3.4.9.2 below.

It is clear, however, that the conditions must relate to purchase or sale, although Guideline 24 seems to ensure that all distribution agreements may qualify (subject to Articles 3, 4 and 5).

If B, an internet service provider, were to need inter-connection not to the local loop of a telecoms operator whose share of the wires market would probably exceed 30 per cent, but to the wires of a cable company with a share of wires in the locality of less than 30 per cent, would the agreement relate to the conditions on which B might buy interconnection services or sell internet services? The agreement would have to specify the terms on which B could inter-connect and whether he might take unbundled services. Those conditions would relate to the purchase or sale of services.

Article 2(1) uses the term "parties" in the plural. Is it enough that one party should accept conditions as to purchase or sale? Or does the Regulation apply only if A also accepted conditions as to the licences it might grant others: for instance, that it would not grant any other licences that would interfere technically with B's exploitation of its licence. Would it suffice that such a term would be implied by national law?

---

[32] Regulation 240/96, OJ 1996, L31/2, [1996] 4 CMLR 405.

The Regulation is said to be less formalistic than its predecessors (recitals 6 and 7), and there is no economic reason for requiring both to accept conditions as to sale or purchase.

A buyer may operate as the agent of another firm, and if the agreement with its supplier infringes Article 81(1) it may benefit from the block exemption.[33]

3.4.4 Vertical Agreements—Article 2(1) & (4) and Guidelines 26 & 7

"Vertical agreements" are not included in the list of definitions in Article 1, but in Article 2(1). After describing the agreements to which the Regulation applies, the Commission adds the words "('vertical agreements')." This inelegant drafting results in its becoming the definition of "vertical agreements" where the term is used elsewhere in the Regulation (Guideline 23).

The definition, which is identical to that in the empowering Regulation, no. 1215/99,[34] is misleading. Some agreements that economists or lawyers practising non-Community law would call "vertical" are excluded from the term. Article 2(5) prevents the Regulation from including vertical patent and/or know-how licences, the subject matter of which may come within Regulation 240/96 on Technology Transfer,[35] or the distribution of motor vehicles, the subject matter of which may fall within Regulation 1475/95,[36] at least until that Regulation expires in September 2002 (3.4.8 and 7.6–7.6.2.2.1 below).

The definition of "vertical agreements" is, in other ways, broader than that used by the US agencies. They treat an agreement as vertical only if the parties did not and could not easily have competed at either level without the agreement.

Article 2(4) largely removes the difference by excluding from the exemption agreements between "actual or potential suppliers in the same product market"[37] unless the agreement is not reciprocal and the buyer is small or the supplier is a manufacturer and distributor of goods while the buyer does not manufacture goods competing with the contract goods.

Article 2(4) provides:

> 4. The exemption provided for in paragraph I shall not apply to vertical agreements entered into between competing undertakings; however, it shall apply where competing undertakings enter into a nonreciprocal vertical agreement and:

---

[33] Art. 1(g). For agency, see Guidelines 12–20 (2.8.4 above).

[34] Council Regulation, amending Reg. 19/65 on the application of Article 81(3) (ex Article 85(3)) of the Treaty to certain categories of agreements and concerted practices, OJ 1999, L148/1, Appendix II below.

[35] Article 2(1) might apply to provisions in a licence of patents or know-how, were it not for Article 2(5).

[36] OJ 1985, L145/25, due to expire in September 2002. Whether it be abrogated or amended is subject to intense lobbying and the outcome is unknown. The Commission published a report on the options on 10 December 2001 on the DG Comp website (7.6.2.2 below). If it be allowed to expire, agreements between suppliers and dealers of automobiles will have to be renegotiated with Regulation 2790/99 in mind.

(a) the buyer has a total annual turnover not exceeding EURO 100 million, or

(b) the supplier is a manufacturer and a distributor of goods, while the buyer is a distributor not manufacturing goods competing with the contract goods, or

(c) the supplier is a provider of services at several levels of trade, while the buyer does not provide competing services at the level of trade where it purchases the contract services.

Paragraph (a) is similar to Article 3(b) of the old Regulation 1983/83,[38] save that thereunder, either party might have a turnover under €100 million, whereas now, only if the buyer's turnover is small does the Regulation apply. With inflation the limit is effectively lower now. The calculation of turnover is prescribed in Article 10:

1. For the purpose of calculating total annual turnover within the meaning of Article 2(2) and (4), the turnover achieved during the previous financial year by the relevant party to the vertical agreement and the turnover achieved by its connected undertakings in respect of all goods and services, excluding all taxes and other duties, shall be added together. For this purpose, no account shall be taken of dealings between the party to the vertical agreement and its connected undertakings or between its connected undertakings.

2. The exemption provided for in Article 2 shall remain applicable where, for any period of two consecutive financial years, the total annual turnover threshold is exceeded by no more than 10%.

Sub-paragraphs (b) and (c) of Article 2(4) were inserted during the period of consultation on the Green Paper. It was objected that some manufacturers supply at more than one level of trade ("dual distribution") and that this might be discouraged if the Regulation did not apply to their agreements. Consequently, there is no restriction of turnover. Sub-paragraph (b) relates to goods and (c) to services.

Article 2(4) brings the law close to that in the US, but the drafting is more complex with exceptions to the exception to the exemption. This complication also leads to confusion when interpreting the term "vertical agreement" in contexts other than the group exemption, such as guidelines, which contain no similar definition.

For the purposes of this Regulation, the definition of "competing undertakings" in Article 1(a) includes "actual or potential suppliers in the same product market."

(a) "competing undertakings" means actual or potential suppliers in the same product market; the, product market includes goods or services which are regarded by the buyer as interchangeable with or substitutable for the contract goods or services, by reason of the products' characteristics, their prices and their intended use;

---

[37] See the definition of "competing undertakings" in Article 1(a).
[38] The former group exemption for exclusive dealing agreements, OJ 1983, L173/1, corrections OJ 1984, C101/2, [1983] 2 CLE 255 (2.10 above).

Guideline 26 states that the definition applies whether or not the parties supply to the same geographic market. This follows the wording of the definition, which expressly refer to "the product market".[39]

In other respects, "competing undertakings" should be identified on the basis of the Commission's notice on the relevant market (2.4.1.2 above): A and B, who are suppliers, compete in the same market if they supply substitutes in terms of the characteristics, price and intended use of their products; or if, in response to a small but significant price increase by A, so many customers would buy from B that A's price rise would not be profitable. Nevertheless, the second test is not the same as the definition in Article 1(a). Where they differ in result, it may be that the concrete test derived from judgments of the ECR should be used. Nevertheless, the kinds of evidence to which the notice refers should be considered.

The exclusion of agreements between "competing undertakings" is wide and may be unclear in application. Article 9 defines the relevant market for the purpose of ascertaining the market share limitation to the application of the Regulation in the concrete terms (3.4.13.1 below), but does not refer either to the definition in Article 1, or to the exclusion in Article 2(4), so is probably not relevant.

Guideline 27 states that a distributor which has its own brand of products made to its specifications by a manufacturer is not to be treated as their manufacturer.

An agreement between two manufacturers may be vertical if they operate for the purposes of the agreement at a different level of the production chain (3.4.2 below). An agreement between a component manufacturer and the maker of a final product of which the component will form part, about the conditions under which the parties may sell the components to others may come within Article 2(1), provided that the buyer does not manufacture that particular component. Limitations on this have been imposed by Article 4(e) discussed at 4.5 below.

It is clear that a tripartite agreement between supplier and two competing dealers is excluded from the Regulation, but that if separate agreements, not dependent on each other,[40] are made between the supplier and each dealer, the Regulation may apply.

Agreements between competitors have also been considered by the Commission recently. At the end of 2000, it adopted Regulations granting group exemptions for

---

[39] It is doubted whether Guideline 91 applies to this provision. The heading refers to "the relevant market for calculating the 30% market share threshold under the BER," but Guideline 91 starts "For the application of the BER." It refers, however, to the product and geographic market, and the latter is irrelevant to this provision. It is not clear why the geographic market should not be relevant. Often it depends on whether it is sensible to transport the products. Perhaps the Commission expects geographic markets to expand as the Common Market becomes more integrated.

[40] The term "agreement" may embrace more than one contract. In *BP Kemi*, Case 79/934/EEC, OJ 1979, L286/32, two contracts made between the same parties on the same day each dependent on the other, were treated as a single agreement by the Commission. Where one is dependent on the other, but not vice versa, such as an option and its exercise, the contracts might be treated as separate agreements.

specialisation[41] and research and development[42] to replace Regulations 417 and 418/85[43] and guidelines about horizontal agreements whether or not exempted by the new group exemptions.[44] The group exemption for r & d will seldom apply as most of the ways that each can ensure that it benefits from its investment are black listed, but the guidelines on the application of Article 81 are more liberal.

3.4.5 Goods and Services for Sale or Incorporation—Article 2(1)

The former group exemptions for exclusive distribution and purchasing[45] applied only to agreements for "the supply of goods for resale." The new exemption is far wider. It applies to the supply of goods, such as components or raw materials, for incorporation in other products as well as to the supply of services. There is no need to consider whether goods are supplied for resale when the final stage of production takes place at the retail level. The "bottling" problem has been avoided.

Nor is there any need to decide whether the dealer is providing services that prevent the agreement being for the "resale of goods", or whether the supply of a car to be rented out amounts to "resale."

For the agreement to qualify, there must be a restraint relating to the conditions under which the parties may buy, sell or resell goods or services. Guideline 25 states:

> The BER also applies to goods sold and purchased for renting to third parties. However, rent and lease agreements as such are not covered, as no good or service is being sold by the supplier to the buyer. More generally, the BER does not cover restrictions or obligations that do not relate to the conditions of purchase, sale and resale, such as an obligation preventing parties from carrying out independent research and development which the parties may have included in an otherwise vertical agreement. In addition, Article 2(2) to (5) directly or indirectly exclude certain vertical agreements from the application of the BER.

The second sentence seems to Valentine to contradict Article 2(1): a renting agreement may impose conditions about the sale or purchase of goods or services, in which event, on one view, the last phrase in Article 2(1) applies (3.4.9–3.4.9.2 below). The Commission also takes the view that Article 2(1) does not apply to licences of intellectual property rights save in so far as Article 2(3) permits, another conclusion that Valentine doubts for the same reasons where the licence imposes conditions as to purchase, sale or resale of goods or services.

---

[41] Commission Regulation 2658/2000, on the application of Article 81(3) of the Treaty to categories of specialisation agreements, 29 Nov. 2000, OJ 2000, L304/3, [2001] 4 CMLR 800.

[42] Commission Regulation 2659/2000, on the application of Article 81(3) of the Treaty to categories of research and development agreements, 29 Nov. 2000, OJ 2000, L304/7, [2001] 4 CMLR 808.

[43] Group exemptions for specialisation agreements, OJ 1985, L53/1, CMR 2743 and for research and development agreements, OJ 1985, L53/5, both amended by Regulation 151/93, OJ 1993, L21/8.

[44] Guidelines on the applicability of Article 81 to horizontal co-operation, OJ 2001, C 3/2, [2001] 4 CMLR 819.

[45] Commission Regulations 1983 and 1984/83, 22 June 1983, OJ L 173/1 and 5.

3.4.6 Two or More Undertakings

Also, unlike its predecessors, the new Regulation applies whether or not there are more than two undertakings, provided that none of them competes with any of the others (3.4.4 above). It is often sensible to have tripartite registered user agreements between a brand owner, a manufacturer and a distributor. Additional parties no longer prevent the application of the exemption. As long as none of the parties are actual or potential competitors at any level of trade, there is no reason of policy to exclude multipartite agreements.

For the supplier to make a single agreement with two distributors, who each agree not to make active sales into the other's territory, however, would be excluded by Article 2(4). Two contracts independent of each other, one with each dealer, would not be excluded.

3.4.7 Retailer Associations—Article 2(2)

Article 2(2) extends the Regulation to agreements made between a retailer and its trade association or between the retailer association and its supplier, provided that all the members are small retailers of goods, not services (7.2.1.2 below).

> 2. The exemption provided for in paragraph 1 shall apply to vertical agreements entered into between an association of undertakings and its members, or between such an association and its suppliers, only if all its members are retailers of goods and if no individual member of the association, together with its connected undertakings, has a total annual turnover exceeding EUR 50 million; vertical agreements entered into by such associations shall be covered by this Regulation without prejudice to the application of Article 81 to horizontal agreements concluded between the members of the association or decisions adopted by the association.

"Retailer" is not defined in Regulation 2790/99 or the empowering Regulation, but Guideline 28 states:

> Retailers are distributors reselling goods to final consumers.

The Guideline seems to include small multiple retailers, such as supermarkets if they buy through their trade association, but not farmer's cooperatives, whose members produce rather than buy.

The horizontal agreements by which the retailers joined the association, however, are not exempted[46] (7.2.1.3 below). Guideline 29 states that the horizontal aspects should be assessed according to the principles set out in the guidelines on horizontal cooperation[47] and that only if acceptable are the vertical aspects exempted under Regulation 2790/99, although this is not expressly stated in the

---

[46] There were no *vires* to exempt horizontal agreements. Where the association has a modest market share, the horizontal agreement is unlikely to infringe 81(1).

[47] OJ 2001, C3/2, [2001] CMLR 819.

Regulation and we doubt whether the validity of the validity of the vertical agreement depends on whether the horizontal agreement is valid.

It might have been simpler to have relied on existing case law[48] ruling that small cooperatives and retailers may combine their buying power in order to compete with supermarkets and other chains or with very large farmers without infringing Article 81(1). Such agreements, provided that the restrictions are no stricter than necessary, do not have the object or effect of restricting competition, but of enabling small firms to compete with larger ones. Many are not caught by Article 81(1).

An exemption is given for vertical agreements made by retailers' associations, so it is not immediately obvious why none is provided for farmers' co-operatives which are common on the continent.[49] Probably the reason was that small retailers competing with supermarket chains lobbied successfully in the Economic and Social Committee. The Commission probably considers that farmers' co-operatives buying seed or fertiliser are not retailers, but their agreements may contain conditions as to sale or purchase by the parties. The membership agreement in *Oude Luttikhuis* imposed conditions as to the persons to whom members might sell their milk. So, we believe that their contracts to buy seed, fertiliser or equipment may well qualify under Article 2(1).

Article 2(2) of the Regulation requires every member to be a retailer of goods, but may they also provide services? Guideline 28 implies that if they do the exemption does not apply. Nevertheless, where the association's members have little market power, Article 81(1) is unlikely to be infringed.

The size of each member may vary with time, and the Regulation will suddenly cease to apply if one of the member's turnover grows over the ceiling. The CFI has held that the relevant market changes with time, and should be reassessed each time it becomes relevant.[50] Presumably, the same applies to ceilings of turnover. The association may not immediately know a member's turnover has grown over

---

[48] *SPAR—Re Intergroup Trading BV*, OJ 1975, L212/23, [1975] 2 CMLR D14 in relation to small grocers; *H.G. Oude Luttikhuis and others* v. *Verenigde Cooperatiëve Melkindustrie Coberco*, Case C-399/93, [1995] ECR I-4515 in relation to agricultural cooperatives. The members of Coberco agreed to sell all their output of milk to the cooperative and there were penalties for leaving it. A bench of 11 judges in the ECJ held that such agreements did not have the object of restricting competition (para. 12). Provided that the measures to ensure their loyalty were no stricter than necessary to achieve a wide enough commercial base (para. 14) and were not of such a long duration as to make the market too rigid, the agreement would not have the effect of restricting competition contrary to Article 81(1). Nothing specific was said about the maximum market share but the economic context and structure of the market were stressed. In *Rennet*, OJ 1980, L51/19, [1980] 2 CMLR 402, the Commission, confirmed by the ECJ in *Stremsel* v. *Commission*, Case 61/80 [1981] ECR 851, condemned an agreement whereby a trade association required its members to buy their total requirements of rennet from it. The association was virtually a monopolist in the Netherlands.

[49] The empowering Council Regulation no. 1215/99—amending Regulation 19/65 on the application of Article 81(3) (ex Article 85(3)) of the Treaty to certain categories of agreements and concerted practices, OJ 1999, L148/1, provided power to exempt only retailers' agreements, but it might have been drawn more widely.

[50] *The Coca-Cola Company and Coca-Cola Enterprises Inc.* v. *Commission*, Cases T-125 & 127/97, [2000] 5 CMLR 467, paras. 81–83.

€50 million. Thought should be given to altering the constitution of retailers' associations automatically to exclude members whose turnover exceeds the limit.
Articles 10 and 11 deal with the calculation of turnover and connected undertakings.

Guideline 28, however, states that:

> Where only a limited number of the members of the association have a turnover not sig-
> nificantly exceeding the EUR 50 million threshold, this will normally not change the
> assessment under Article 81.

The Commission does not explain the legal basis for this view which seems to conflict with the wording of the Regulation. It may imply only that the agreement may
not infringe Article 81(1). From judgments such as *Oude Luttikhuis*, this depends on
the market power of the association rather than on that of particular members.

When assessing the market share cap in Article 3, it is the share of the association rather than that of each retailer that is relevant. This seems sensible. If an individual association's market share is below 30 per cent neither it nor its members
are likely to be able to exercise disproportionate market power.

Where, however, the market is generally concentrated, it is possible that there
might be joint dominance between undertakings with a market share below 30 per
cent (3.3 above). Joint buying and selling might be treated as abusive. There is little case law on the abuse of joint dominance. It is important that the Community
and national institutions should not automatically apply to joint dominance the
abuses found in relation to single firm dominance. Already, dominant positions
have been found under Article 82, where the market power is well below that
required for monopolisation under the US Sherman Act. In our view, to go further under the concept of joint dominance would be unduly interventionist.

3.4.8 Other Group Exemptions—Article 2(5)

It is easier to analyse Article 2(3), after Article 2(5) is understood. It ensures that
one cannot avoid the lists of hard core restraints in the group exemptions for other
kinds of agreements by invoking Regulation 2790/99 which has a far shorter list.
Article 2(5) provides:

> This Regulation shall not apply to vertical agreements the subject matter of which falls
> within the scope of any other block exemption regulation.

If the provision had provided that the Regulation does not apply where the
agreement is already exempt under another group exemption, it would have had
no effect. Once the agreement is exempt, it does not matter whether or not it falls
within this Regulation. Article 2(5), however, refers to "the subject matter" of the
agreement falling within another group exemption, such as technology transfer,[51]

---

[51] Commission Regulation 240/96, OJ 1996, L31/2.

motor vehicles[52] or vertical agreement connected to horizontal agreements.[53] Guideline 45 adds nothing to what is said in the Regulation. The group exemptions relating to transport all relate to horizontal arrangements, so there is no need to exclude those.

Most experts take the view that agreements, such as pure copyright licences, which could not be brought within any other group exemption, are not excluded by Article 2(5), but that they must qualify also under Article 2(3) (3.4.9–3.4.9.2 below).

If there is a patent or know-how licence, the subject matter will fall within Regulation 240/96, even if there are hard core provisions which prevent the application of Regulation 240/96. If there are provisions relating to trade marks or copyright that are ancillary, the subject matter of the agreement will also fall within Regulation 240/96. So, the agreement cannot come within Regulation 2790/99. If, however, provisions relating to copyright or trade marks are not ancillary to a patent or know-how licence, they will not be prevented from qualifying under Regulation 2790/99 by Article 2(5), but may be excluded by Article 2(3) (3.4.9.2 below).

Industrial franchising, or what lawyers call a "trade mark license," has never clearly been the subject matter of any group exemption. In *Moosehead/ Whitbread*,[54] the Commission found that the licence of a trade mark virtually unknown in Europe coupled with a recipe was not ancillary to the know-how in the recipe and did not qualify as ancillary within the meaning of the group exemption for know-how licensing agreements,[55] since the mark was crucial to the transaction. It is arguable, however, that provided that there is a licence of a patent or of secret substantial and recorded know-how, such a licence might be exempt under the more recent Regulation 240/96.[56] That Regulation contains a surprising definition of "ancillary provisions" in Article 10(15):

(15) "ancillary provisions" are provisions relating to the exploitation of intellectual property rights other than patents, which contain no obligations restrictive of competition other than those also attached to the licensed know-how or patents and exempted under this Regulation.

[52] Commission Regulation 1475/95—group exemption for motor vehicle distribution and servicing agreements, OJ 1995, L145/25. The Regulation will expire on September 30, 2002 and may or may not be renewed. Lobbying is intense. DG Comp published a report on the possible options—for the distribution of motor vehicles, see 7.6–7.6.2.2.1 below.

[53] Recital 10 of Commission Regulation 2658/2000, on the application of Article 81(3) of the Treaty to categories of specialisation agreements, 29 Nov. 2000, OJ 2000, L304/3, [2001] 4 CMLR 800, states that Regulation 2790/99 may apply. See also para. 11 of the guidelines on the applicability of Article 81 to horizontal co-operation, OJ 2001, C 3/2, [2001] 4 CMLR 819, which states that the horizontal guidelines do not apply to vertical agreements, save where the parties are actual or potential competitors. In that event, the guidelines on horizontal cooperation may apply. Where the parties are operating only at different levels of trade and there are no conditions about sale, resale or purchase, none of the group exemptions apply, but the agreement may not infringe Article 81(1) (2.7–2.7.3 above).

[54] OJ 1990, L100/32, [1991] 4 CMLR 391.

[55] Commission Regulation 556/89, OJ 1989, L61/1, [1989] 4 CMLR 774, since expired.

[56] On technology transfer, OJ 1996, L31/2. See **Valentine Korah**, *Technology Transfer Agreements and the EC Competition Rules*, (Oxford, OUP, 1996) 117–20.

That definition does not expressly require that the trade mark or copyright be less important than the know-how or patent, and may have reversed the decision in *Moosehead/Whitbread*. The law is controversial. If such a licence can qualify under Regulation 240/96, it cannot qualify under Regulation 2790/99. If it cannot qualify under Regulation 240/96, it will not be excluded from Regulation 2790/99 by Article 2(5). Firms with low shares of the relevant market may well be arguing that it does not qualify as technology transfer,[57] so as to benefit from the narrower list of hard core provisions; while firms with larger market shares which cannot qualify under Regulation 2790/99 may argue for the opposite view.

It is clear, however, that where there is no patent or know-how licence, but only the licence of a trade mark or copyright, Regulation 240/96 cannot apply and Article 2(5) is irrelevant.

In the paper adopted by the Commission at the end of 2001 and published on 21 December (on the home page of DG Competition) the Commission raised the question whether there should be a group exemption for other kinds of intellectual property licences, such as trade mark (industrial franchising), design rights and copyright. Article 2(5) would also apply to agreements "the subject matter of which falls within the scope" of such a new group exemption. It is possible that Regulation 240/96[58] may be replaced before it is due to expire in 2006 by a broader group exemption to include licences of other kinds of intellectual property, whether or not ancillary to a patent and/or knowhow licence.[59]

If the group exemption for motor vehicles, Regulation 1475/95,[60] is allowed to expire on 30 September 2002 (7.6.2 below), the distribution of vehicles may qualify under Regulation 2790/99, but until then it does not. Previously distribution agreements for vehicles might be exempt under either Regulation 1475/95 or 1983/83. Now there is no choice. Those who previously relied on Regulation 1983/83 will have to amend their agreements, even though this may make them more restrictive. This could be postponed until the end of 2001 under the transitional provisions where an agreement exempt under Regulation 1983/83 was in force at the end of May 2000.

3.4.9 Intellectual Property Rights—Article 2(3)

As explained at 3.4.8 above, there have been problems in arranging for industrial franchising and the distribution of software. Where there is no licence of a patent or know-how, or the copyright or trade mark licence is not ancillary to qualifying knowhow or to a patent, the application of Regulation 2790/99 is not excluded by

---

[57] Valentine assumes that the agreement is not excluded from Regulation 2790/99 by Article 2(3).

[58] OJ 1996, L31/2, [1996] 4 CMLR 405, [1996] 4 *EIPR* Supp. iv.

[59] Evaluation Report on the Transfer of Technology Regulation No 240/96, Technology Transfer Agreeents under Article 81, 20 December 2001.

[60] OJ 1995, L145/25, [1996] 4 CMLR 69. Its provisions are analysed by **Denis O'Sullivan** and others in the chapter on distribution in **Valentine Korah** (ed.), *EC Competition Law* (New York, Bender, looseleaf).

Article 2(5) because the Technology Transfer Regulation cannot apply to such an agreement.

Can a supplier of pure software or an industrial franchisor take advantage of Regulation 2790/99? Article 2(3) provides that

> [t]he exemption . . . shall apply to vertical agreements containing provisions which relate to the assignment to the buyer or use by the buyer of intellectual property rights, provided that those provisions do not constitute the primary object of such agreements and are directly related to the use, sale or resale of goods or services by the buyer or its customers. The exemption applies on condition that, in relation to the contract goods or services, those provisions do not contain restrictions of competition having the same object or effect as vertical restraints which are not exempted under this regulation.

This provision was intended to bring franchising agreements within the block exemption. The Commission is treating know-how as an intellectual property right (7.2.4.1 below). The assignment of domain rights or a special home page design, logo or trademark may qualify as well as the older fashioned kinds of iprs.

"Vertical agreements" are defined in Article 2(1) (3.4.4 above) which, on a literal interpretation, does not limit the Regulation to the distribution of goods and services. Article 2(1) requires that conditions relating to the purchase or sale of goods by the parties must be imposed. A copyright licence or industrial franchise might impose such provisions.

Article 2(3) is drafted narrowly. So, it is important to decide whether it extends or limits Article 2(1).

3.4.9.1 Permissive view

On one view, there is no reason why technology licences that are not excluded by Article 2(5) (3.4.8 above) should not qualify under Article 2(1) if the agreement is vertical within the meaning of Article 2(1) and (4). Denis doubts the validity of this argument.

After stating that vertical agreements are exempted, recital 3 adds that the group exemption: "also *includes* agreements containing ancillary provisions on the assignment or use of intellectual property rights."[61] That seems to suggest that two kinds of agreement qualify—vertical agreements as defined in Article 2(1) and also those described in Article 2(3).

The introductory words of Article 2(3) "The exemption provided for in paragraph 1 shall apply to . . ." are the same as those in Article 2(2), which the Commission accepts extend Article 2(1) and do not limit it.

Recital 10 of Regulation 2658/2000, which provides a group exemption for specialisation agreements, states that unilateral specialisation agreements do not qualify under that group exemption, but may qualify under Regulation 2790/99. This implies that Regulation 2790/99 is not confined to agreements under which

---

[61] Emphasis added.

products are bought or sold. Since specialisation agreements must, however, include provisions for sale to the other parties, this argument is less robust.

The main reason for invoking this view is that the Commission has for decades delayed providing a group exemption for software licences and industrial franchising which are common. Moreover, the refusal of the CFI in *Métropole Télévision SA and Others* v. *Commission*[62] to adopt an ancillary restraint doctrine that would enable parties to encourage investment by restraining free riding (2.7.2 above) reinforces the need for a group exemption. If, however, the Commission does revise Regulation 240/96 to cover copyright and trademark licences, there will be less need to use this controversial argument.

3.4.9.2 Narrower view

The contrary view is that Article 2(1) and (3) should be interpreted together. Article 2(3) is a *lex specialis* for intellectual property rights and overrides any general provisions relating to them.[63] A similar argument is that Article 2(3) limits the scope of Article 2(1).

This conclusion may, possibly, be supported by the judgment of the ECJ in *Pronuptia*,[64] where the ECJ held that franchising did not come within the first exemption for exclusive distribution agreements, Regulation 67/67,[65] because franchising is different from distribution, even though the franchisee agreed to buy goods for resale from the franchisor and the agreement seemed to come within the wording of the Regulation. The support from *Pronuptia* is also not robust in as much as franchising is mentioned in the guidelines for vertical restraints more than once as being capable of exemption under Regulation 2790/99, although it is not mentioned in the Regulation itself.

Guideline 30 clearly treats Article 2(3) as limiting the definition of Article 2(1), although there are no words in the Regulation expressly producing this result.

Is there sufficient ambiguity in the Regulation to enable the guidelines to establish the true position? Most experts follow the guidelines. The issue is most likely to come before national courts, but may have to be considered also by national competition authorities.

3.4.9.2.1 *Contract to purchase or distribute goods or services*

Guidelines 30 and the following ones give the Commission's conclusions about the interpretation of Article 2(1) and 2(3) without explaining its reasoning:

> [t]he IPR provision must be part of a vertical agreement, i.e., an agreement with conditions under which the parties may purchase, sell or resell certain goods or services; . . .

---

[62] Case T-112/99, 18 September 2001, [2001] 5 CMLR 1236.

[63] This argument was suggested by Christoph Huetteroth when acting as Valentine's research assistant at Fordham law school. He graduated for the LL.M. magnum cum laude and has qualified as a New York attorney.

[64] *Pronuptia de Paris GmbH* v. *Pronuptia de Paris Irmgard Schillgalis,* Case 161/84 [1986] ECR 353, para. 33, discussed at 3.4.10.2 below.

[65] OJ Spec Ed 1967, 10.

32. The first condition makes clear that the context in which the IPRs are provided is an agreement to purchase or distribute goods or an agreement to purchase or provide services and not an agreement concerning the assignment or licensing of IPRs for the manufacture of goods, nor a pure licensing agreement. The BER does not cover, for instance:

—agreements where a party provides another party with a recipe and licenses the other party to produce a drink with this recipe;
—agreements under which one party provides another party with a mould or master copy and licenses the other party to produce or distribute copies;
—the pure licence of a trade mark or sign for the purposes of merchandising;
—sponsorship contracts concerning the right to advertise oneself as being an official sponsor of an event;
—copyright licensing such as broadcasting contracts concerning the right to record and/or the right to broadcast an event.

On the wider view, Article 2(1) may apply to the transfer of property provided there are provisions relating to the conditions under which the parties may buy or sell goods or services. If Article 2(1) covers the transaction, there is no need to progress to Article 2(3). On this view, Guideline 32 conflicts with the Regulation.

Article 2(5) excludes licences the subject matter of which comes within another group exemption. By 1996 the Commission had completed a mammoth effort to exempt some intellectual property licences. Pure copyright or trade mark licences however were not covered: they remained to be dealt with. Is there any reason of policy why those that qualify under Article 2(1) should not be included in Regulation 2790/99, despite the guidelines to the contrary?

3.4.9.2.2 *IPRs for use of the buyer*

Guideline 30 continues to deal with the converse situation: where the buyer provides the intellectual property rights: "The IPRs must be assigned to, or for use by the buyer;" and concludes in Guideline 33 that:

The second condition makes clear that the BER does not apply when the IPRs are provided by the buyer to the supplier, no matter whether the IPRs concern the manner of manufacture or of distribution. An agreement relating to the transfer of IPRs to the supplier and containing possible restrictions on the sales made by the supplier is not covered by the BER. This means in particular that subcontracting involving the transfer of know-how to a subcontractor does not fall within the scope of the BER. However, vertical agreements under which the buyer provides only specifications to the supplier which describe the goods or services to be supplied are covered by the BER (Footnotes omitted.)

The Commission's conclusion here is also based on the view that Article 2(1) does not apply to agreements relating to the transfer of property, contrary to the first view expressed at 3.4.9 above, but the Commission's reasoning is not spelled out.

If Article 2(1) does apply to contracts for the transfer of property, it is not necessary to rely on Article 2(3), unless 2(3) limits the scope of Article 2(1). An agreement under which the sub-contractor (i.e. the supplier) is given some know-how in order to enable it to make components for the contractor would, on the first view, come within Article 2(1) of the Regulation, provided that the parties accept conditions as to the goods or services that may be bought or sold. Frequently, sub-contractors agree not to use the contractor's technology to supply goods or services to the contractor's competitors, and the contractor agrees to buy the contract goods only or largely from the sub-contractor.

If, however, the Commission's guideline is correct about the construction of Article 2(1) and if Article 2(3) limits Article 2(1), many sub-contracting agreements will be excluded from the group exemption, although the buyer may specify to the seller the characteristics of the components to be supplied without losing the benefit of the group exemption. There may be problems also for e-commerce where new products are developed almost daily. The developer may transfer secret know-how to the potential supplier of an intermediate product. If not covered by the group exemption the launch of new products may be chilled. Where the new development is important even the initial market share may exceed the ceiling of the notice on minor agreements (2.4.1.1 above).

Know-how is not usually included in the phrase "intellectual property rights." Article 1(e) does not give a definition of the phrase, but states that it includes industrial property rights. The heading to the guidelines on franchising starting at number 42 is "know-how," suggesting that the Commission treats know-how as an intellectual property right. It is arguable, therefore, that licences of marketing know-how fall entirely outside the Regulation on the narrow view.

Whether the Regulation applies may not matter often in relation to sub-contracting agreements which are the subject of a well drafted and flexible notice of the Commission[66] stating that often the sub-contractor is not to be treated as a separate undertaking from the contractor, and that the agreements do not infringe Article 81(1). The provisions cleared by the notice might be described as ancillary restraints reasonably necessary to make viable a transaction that is not anti-competitive. The view implied by the notice is that the sub-contractor is not a separate undertaking from the contractor. Both views can be argued.

3.4.9.2.3 *Primary object*

The third indent of Guideline 30 states:

> The IPR provisions must not constitute the primary object of the agreement;

This repeats part of Article 2(3) and is explained in Guideline 34:

> 34. The third condition makes clear that in order to be covered by the BER the primary object of the agreement must not be the assignment or licensing of IPRs. The primary object must be the purchase or distribution of goods or services and the IPR provisions must serve the implementation of the vertical agreement.

---

[66] Notice on sub-contracting agreements 1978, OJ 1979, C1/2, CMR 2701.

It is hoped that this qualification will not create as much difficulty as did the exclusion of software and trade marks that were not ancillary to a patent or know-how licence under the old know-how Regulation (2.4.8 above).[67]

The Guideline follows the language of Article 2(3) which provides that the intellectual property rights must not be the primary object of the agreement, but the Guideline adds that the sale or purchase must be. The Regulation does not address the situation where neither the intellectual property rights nor the sale or purchase is the primary object of the agreement. If one needs the recipe and the trade mark licence, they are complementary: neither is the primary object of the agreement because neither is much use without the other. It is hoped that, even if Article 2(3) limits the scope of Article 2(1), this condition will seldom restrict the application of the Regulation.

Nevertheless, we fear that the Guideline requiring the sale or purchase of goods or services to be the primary object of the agreement may exclude the common situation where trade mark licence and purchase of goods or services are complementary—where neither constitutes the primary object of the agreement. There is no guidance in Regulation or Guidelines.

On whom is the burden of establishing that the IPR is not the primary object of the agreement? If Article 2(3) is treated as limiting Article 2(1), it may be argued that it should be interpreted narrowly as a limitation of Article 2(1). On the other hand, Article 2(1) provides an exemption from Article 81, and it may be cogently argued that it should be narrowly construed. The position is uncertain.

3.4.9.2.4 *Directly related to use or sale*

The fourth indent to Guideline 30 states:

> The IPR provisions must be directly related to the use, sale or resale of goods or services by the buyer or its customers. In the case of franchising where marketing forms the object of the exploitation of the IPRs, the goods and services are distributed by the master franchisee or the franchisees;

Many franchisees agree to buy most of the goods or services they handle from their franchisor or a designated source and obtain the right to use the franchisor's trade marks, get-up and so forth as well as marketing know-how.[68] So the trade mark usually is directly related to the use, sale or resale of goods or services. The franchising Regulation expired at the end of May 2000, so Article 2(5) does not prevent the application of Regulation 2790/99. Few franchising agreements will be excluded by this condition.

In relation to those that are excluded, the question arises whether it is enough for the agreement to come within Article 2(1) or whether the narrower view explained at 3.4.9.2 above is correct and the addition of a trade mark licence takes the agreement outside the group exemption unless it qualifies under Article 2(3).

---

[67] Regulation 556/89, OJ 1989, L61/1, [1989] 4 CMLR 774. See *Whitbread/Moosehead*, OJ 1990, L100/32, [1991] 4 CMLR 391.
[68] See Guideline 42, 3.4.10.2 below.

Valentine sees in the Regulation no words that do that, but the doctrine of *lex specialis* may do so. Her view clearly conflicts with the conclusion of the Commission. Guideline 35 explains:

> The fourth condition requires that the IPR provisions facilitate the use, sale or resale of goods or services by the buyer or his customers. The goods or services for use or resale are usually supplied by the licensor but may also be purchased by the licensee from a third supplier. The IPR provisions will normally concern the marketing of goods or services. This is for instance the case in a franchise agreement where the franchisor sells to the franchisee goods for resale and in addition licenses the franchisee to use its trade mark and know-how to market the goods. Also covered is the case where the supplier of a concentrated extract licenses the buyer to dilute and bottle the extract before selling it as a drink.

3.4.9.2.5 *Hard core restraints and conditions*

The final indent of Guideline 30 states:

> The IPR provisions, in relation to the contract goods or services, must not contain restrictions of competition having the same object or effect as vertical restraints which are not exempted under the BER.

Guideline 36 states:

> The fifth condition signifies in particular that the IPR provisions should not have the same object or effect as any of the hardcore restrictions listed in Article 4 of the BER or any of the restrictions excluded from the coverage of the BER by Article 5 (see paragraphs 46–61).

The last sentence of Article 2(3) takes this position. One anomaly may result from the wording of Article 2(3). If the IPRs have the object or effect of foreclosing competing suppliers—it seems that the Regulation will not apply to the other provisions that would otherwise be exempt. Whereas, if there is a contractual provision that the buyer will buy mainly from the supplier that exceeds the limitation of Article 5, the rest of the agreement may be exempt.

3.4.10 Other Guidelines Relating to IPRs

Guideline 37 states that:

> Intellectual property rights which may be considered to serve the implementation of vertical agreements within the meaning of Article 2(3) of the BER generally concern three main areas: trade marks, copyright and know-how.

This may be true and serves to introduce the next topic.

Guidelines 38–44 are expressed to deal separately with trade marks, copyright and know-how. It might have been better to substitute "franchising" for the heading "know-how" above Guidelines 42–44. They deal with franchising and there is nothing other than Guideline 38 expressed to deal with trade marks. Guideline 38 points out that if a trade mark licence is exclusive, so will be the vertical agreement.

3.4.10.1 Copyright

The next three Guidelines on copyright are more important.

> 39. Resellers of goods covered by copyright (books, software, etc.) may be obliged by the copyright holder only to resell under the condition that the buyer, whether another reseller or the end user, shall not infringe the copyright. Such obligations on the reseller, to the extent that they fall under Article 81(1) at all, are covered by the BER.

Usually there is no need for a contractual restriction on infringing copyright. Subject to the doctrine of exhaustion within the EEA, which does not apply to performing rights[69] or to direct sales by a licensee outside its territory,[70] the holder can rely on the copyright and does not need a consensual agreement contrary to Article 81(1).[71] Consequently, even an express contractual provision would be unlikely to have significant effects on competition or trade between member states.

Paragraph 40 resolves the problems of a dealer in cassettes or tapes without it being necessary to decide which view of Article 2(3) is correct: whether it extends or limits Article 2(1) (3.4.9.1–3.4.9.2 above).

> 40. Agreements under which hard copies of software are supplied for resale and where the reseller does not acquire a licence to any rights over the software but only has the right to resell the hard copies, are to be regarded as agreements for the supply of goods for resale for the purpose of the BER. Under this form of distribution the licence of the software only takes place between the copyright owner and the user of the software. This may take the form of a "shrink wrap" licence, i.e. a set of conditions included in the package of the hard copy which the end user is deemed to accept by opening the package.

The disk or cassette is of no use without a licence to duplicate it. Even getting a disk up on the screen without saving it on a hard or floppy disk amounts to copyright infringement. Many experts advised that the former Regulations relating to the supply of goods for resale did not apply since a copyright licence to the dealer was also required and was not "ancillary".

The reasoning underlying the contrary view in Guideline 40 is based on the narrower view of Article 2(3) and not on the idea that the copyright licence is a service, differentiating Regulation 2790/99 from its predecessors. The Guideline

---

[69] *Coditel (SA Compagnie Générale pour la Diffusion de la Télévision)* v. *Ciné-Vog Films,* Case 62/79 [1980] ECR 881, because there are no goods, the freedom of whose movement is restrained, or because the film industry is special. The judgment does not distinguish.

[70] *Tiercé Ladbroke* v. *Commission,* Case T-504/93 [1997] ECR II-923 and Article 2(1)(14) of Regulation 240/96.

[71] Although such an agreement might be easier to enforce when the holder does not know what has happened to the "grey goods."

assumes that no licence is given to the reseller, but that a "shrink wrap" licence will automatically arise in favour of a consumer who opens the packaging.

The analysis of shrink-wrap licences under national law is unclear. In the US, the Supreme Court has held that the copyright statute applies only to the first sale of a protected work.[72] Whether a transaction amounts to a sale or a licence (not subject to the first sale rule) depends on the substance of the transaction and not on whether it is called a licence. Assent to a licence will not be implied easily. Where customers agree to the terms of a licence on installing a programme, the terms do not bind those who have not installed it.[73]

One might have thought that the question was one for national law. The Commission's argument does not apply when the distributor is sent an electronic message and duplicates the discs or cassettes as, then, he does require a licence. Traces of formalism remain under the Guidelines. Nor can the argument be extended to trade marks where the reseller needs a licence. So the question which view of Article 2(3) is correct remains important.

The next Guideline states that:

> 41. Buyers of hardware incorporating software protected by copyright may be obliged by the copyright holder not to infringe the copyright, for example not to make copies and resell the software or not to make copies and use the software in combination with other hardware. Such use-restrictions, to the extent that they fall within Article 81(1) at all, are covered by the BER.

Officials have long taken the view that an obligation to make only one back-up copy and to use the software on only an identified computer is justified by the rulings of the ECJ in *Coditel (SA Compagnie Générale pour la Diffusion de la Télévision)* v. *Ciné-Vog Films*[74] and does not require exemption.[75]

> 12. . . . The right of a copyright owner and his assigns to require fees for any showing of a film is part of the essential function of copyright in this type of literary and artistic work.

It seems that the ECJ in referring to "this type of literary and artistic work" is not to be understood as relating only to performing rights, but also to works in electronic form. Technological development leading to many computers in a workplace sharing the same software has bypassed this view, but the principle remains. The Commission has published very few decisions on copyright licensing.

The problem on the second view of Article 2(3) is that the group exemption will not apply to other terms, such as an exclusive territory or limited single branding restriction.

---

[72] *Bobbs-Merrill Co* v. *Straus*, 210 US 339 (1908).

[73] There is a particularly clear analysis of the issues by Judge Pregarson, when vacating an interim injunction in *Softman Products Co. LLC* v. *Adobe Systems Inc. et al*, Case No. CV 00-04161 DPP (AJWx)

[74] Case 62/79 [1980] ECR 881, para.14, confirmed by the ECJ in *Coditel SA* v. *Ciné-Vog Films SA (No. 2)*, Case 262/81, [1982] ECR 3381, para. 12.

[75] Colin Overbury, then the official in charge of computer problems in the competition department, said at the Law Society in London that an arrangement to use a disk only on an identified machine did not infringe Article 81(1) for this reason.

3.4.10.2 Franchising

Turning to a heading: "know-how" the Commission deals with both trade marks and marketing know-how in franchising agreements.

> 42. Franchise agreements, with the exception of industrial franchise agreements,[76] are the most obvious example where know-how for marketing purposes is communicated to the buyer. Franchise agreements contain licences of intellectual property rights relating to trade marks or signs and know-how for the use and distribution of goods or the provision of services. In addition to the licence of IPR, the franchisor usually provides the franchisee during the life of the agreement with commercial or technical assistance, such as procurement services, training, advice on real estate, financial planning etc. The licence and the assistance are integral components of the business method being franchised.

Industrial franchising is probably not exempted by any other group exemptions,[77] so is not excluded by Article 2(5). The exclusion of industrial franchising is supported only by Guidelines 42–44, not by the Regulation itself. It is arguable that an industrial franchise may qualify under Article 2(1) and that Article 2(3) does not limit Article 2(1) (3.4.9.1 above). That is, at best, controversial.

Article 2(3) implies that there is a buyer. It may be that the franchisee buys the use of the marketing know-how from the franchisor. The trade mark licence may well be important, but it is arguable that it and the recipe are complementary and neither is the primary object of the agreement as required by the Regulation (3.4.9.2.3 above). The mark may well be related to the sale of goods to be produced by the franchisee. The controversial argument that industrial franchises are covered by the technology transfer Regulation[78] may be stronger than the argument that it is covered by Article 2(1) or (3). If the technology transfer Regulation be amended to include trade mark licences both controversial arguments become less strong, since they are based on the policy that trade mark licences should enjoy a group exemption.

Why is the Commission unwilling to exempt industrial franchises? Does it fear that the franchisee may already be a potential competitor of the franchisor? If so, Article 2(4) will prevent the Regulation applying.

---

[76] Industrial franchise agreements probably refers to trade mark licence combined with a recipe or other secret, substantial and recorded technical know-how, according to which the licensee produces something, as in *Moosehead/Whitbread*, OJ 1990, L100/32, [1991] 4 CMLR 391. Since the franchisee will have to market that product it could be argued that the trade mark is related to the sale of goods by the buyer. It is not clear, however, that the trade mark does "not constitute the primary object of such agreements and are directly related to the . . . sale . . . of goods or services by the buyer or its customers' within the meaning of Article 2(3). Valentine's view conflicts with that expressed in the guidelines.

[77] There is a possible view that owing to the unusual definition of "ancillary provisions" in Article 10(15) of the Regulation for technology transfer, industrial franchising qualifies under Regulation 240/96, OJ 1996, L31/2, [1996] 4 CMLR 405, [1996] 4 EIPR Supp. iv, even if the trade mark is crucial (3.4.8 above).

[78] See **Valentine Korah**, *Technology Transfer Agreements and the EC Competition Rules* (Oxford, OUP, 1996) 5.1.4, pp. 117–20.

Guideline 43 continues:

Licensing contained in franchise agreements is covered by the BER if all five conditions listed in point 30 are fulfilled. This is usually the case, as under most franchise agreements, including master franchise agreements,[79] the franchisor provides goods and/or services, in particular commercial or technical assistance services, to the franchisee. The IPRs help the franchisee to resell the products supplied by the franchisor or by a supplier designated by the franchisor or to use those products and sell the resulting goods or services. Where the franchise agreement only or primarily concerns licensing of IPRs, such an agreement is not covered by the BER, but it will be treated in a way similar to those franchise agreements which are covered by the BER.

The final situation is unclear. Does the Commission intend to grant individual exemptions or a comfort letter stating that Article 81(1) is not infringed? When it ceases to have exclusive power to grant individual exemptions as a result of the proposed substitute for Regulation 17,[80] it may not matter so much that an exemption is required.

Franchisors are concerned that the Commission's view is also difficult to reconcile with its decision in *Moosehead/ Whitbread* (3.4.8 above)[81] that even a trade mark virtually unknown in Europe at the time of the transaction was crucial. Is the guideline sufficient to indicate that a trade mark licence "crucial" to a transaction does "not constitute the primary object" of the franchise within the meaning of Guideline 34? If not, they may have to rely on the first view described at 3.4.9.1.

From the judgment of the ECJ in *Pronuptia de Paris GmbH* v. *Pronuptia de Paris Irmgard Schillgalis*,[82] it seems that many franchising agreements will infringe Article 81(1) once the franchise is widespread, since most franchisees enjoy an exclusive territory, even if only for a few hundred meters, and must be protected by location clauses imposed on other members of the same franchised network.

If the agreement infringes Article 81 because the franchise is widespread and there is absolute territorial protection, at least within a small area, and the Regulation does not apply, the agreement will need individual exemption and, at

---

[79] These are defined by Article 1(3) of the former group exemption for franchising and for the purposes of that Regulation, as "an agreement whereby one undertaking, the franchisor, grants the other, the master franchisee, in exchange of direct or indirect financial consideration, the right to exploit a franchise for the purposes of concluding franchise agreements with their parties, the franchisees." Under UK law, it was almost impossible to bring master franchise agreements within the former franchising group exemption, OJ 1988, L359/46, [1989] 4 CMLR 387, because usually a tripartite agreement was required between franchisor, master franchisee and each franchisee acknowledging that the reputation in the mark belonged to the franchisor. This is no longer a problem, as multipartite agreements may qualify under Article 2(1) of Reg. 2790/99.

[80] Proposal of the Commission for a Council Regulation to replace Regulation 17/62, 2000/0243 (CNS) (2.12 above). If this is adopted and implemented, the Commission intends to adopt positive decisions that do not distinguish Article 81(1) and (3). The validity of this procedure will doubtless be raised in the ECJ or CFI

[81] OJ 1990, L100/32.

[82] Case 161/84, [1986] ECR 353, para. 24, (2.8.2 above).

least until the White Paper is implemented, only the Commission has power to grant one. Perhaps the Commission contemplates granting a retrospective exemption under Regulation 1216/99 where the franchisor's market share is under 30 per cent[83] and there is no hard core restraint. This possibility, however, may not survive the implementation of the White Paper.

The application of the block exemption to franchises is not as clear as would be desirable, although this may not be as serious as some franchisors and franchisees fear, as few franchise agreements are likely to infringe Article 81(1).

There is a helpful list in Guideline 44 of clauses that may be inserted in a trade mark license to a franchisee on the ground that they are necessary to protect the franchisor's intellectual property rights:

(a) an obligation on the franchisee not to engage, directly or indirectly, in any similar business;

(b) an obligation on the franchisee not to acquire financial interests in the capital of a competing undertaking such as would give the franchisee the power to influence the economic conduct of such an undertaking;

(c) an obligation on the franchisee not to disclose to third parties the know-how provided by the franchisor as long as this know-how is not in the public domain;

(d) an obligation on the franchisee to communicate to the franchisor any experience gained in exploiting the franchise and to grant it, and other franchisees, a non-exclusive licence for the know-how resulting from that experience;

(e) an obligation on the franchisee to inform the franchisor of infringements of licensed industrial or intellectual property rights, to take legal action against infringers or to assist the franchisor in any legal actions against infringers;

(f) an obligation on the franchisee not to use know-how licensed by the franchisor for purposes other than the exploitation of the franchise;

(g) an obligation on the franchisee not to assign the rights and obligations under the franchise agreement without the franchisor's consent.

The first three and last of these obligations were cleared by the ECJ in *Pronuptia* as necessary ancillary restraints. Confidentiality has always been considered by the Commission as the specific object of know-how and outside Article 81(1). The other obligations are similar to those expressly cleared in *Pronuptia.*

Many of these provisions may also be required in trade mark licences that do not involve the provision of marketing know-how and do not amount to franchises. There seems to be no reason why such provisions should not be outside Article 81(1) even in an industrial franchise.

---

[83] Guideline 95 states that where a business method is franchised, it is the supplier's market share on the market where the business method is to be exploited by the franchisees (in the plural) that is relevant under Article 3.

These guidelines give the Commission's conclusions on complementary intellectual property rights on the basis that Article 2(3) limits Article 2(1). At several points the Commission observes that the inclusion of the intellectual property rights may not infringe Article 81(1), but that is little solace if the rights prevent the Regulation applying to other contractual provisions that are not hard core restraints. With a market share for the licensor of under 30 per cent it may often be argued that the agreement does not infringe Article 81(1) and need an exemption, but the safe harbour is removed.

3.4.11 Conclusion on Article 2

The wide coverage of Article 2(1) embracing agreements between two or more parties containing conditions relating to the purchase or sale of goods or services, whether for resale or incorporation in other products, is most welcome. The question whether the exempt agreement must itself constitute a contract of sale of goods or services is important, especially when trade mark licences are granted. Valentine sees nothing in the Regulation requiring this, but the guidelines clearly do.

On the permissive view, the exempted agreement can be about anything, the sale of land or the licensing of intellectual property rights, provided that it imposes conditions under which the parties may sell or buy goods or services. This is not the view of the Commission. The proper construction will have to be decided by the ECJ under Article 234 (ex Article 177), or by the CFI on appeal from the Commission.[84]

Valentine would be prepared to argue that the Regulation is sufficiently clear: Article 2(1) includes an agreement that is not one of sale or purchase, provided that conditions relate to sales or purchases to be made by the parties. Article 2(3) is expressed to extend Article 2(1) and, consequently, the grant of complementary intellectual property rights does not exclude the application of the Regulation even if they are crucial. Alternatively, she would argue that Guideline 34 goes beyond the wording of Article 2(3) in providing that sale and purchase must be the primary object of the transaction—complementary intellectual property rights do not prevent the exemption applying even if Article 2(3) limits the application of Article 2(1). She sees no reason for excluding such licences from the safe harbour of the Regulation.

It is possible, however, that a new group exemption including intellectual property rights other than patents may be adopted even before 2006, when Regulation 240/96 expires, in which case there may be no need for such an argument which at best is controversial.

---

[84] If and when the Treaty of Nice is ratified, it is possible that the CFI will obtain jurisdiction to make preliminary rulings on competition cases.

3.4.12 No White List

Contrary to the Commission's earlier practice when drafting block exemptions, there is no limiting white list to this Regulation. Any clause is permitted in a vertical agreement as defined in Article 2 provided that there is no hard core restriction (chapter 4 below) or condition (chapter 5 below) and provided that the ceiling of market share (3.4.13–3.4.13.7 below) is not exceeded.[85]

Note, however, that the introductory words to Article 4 listing the "hard core" restraints are broad and cover the direct or indirect object of fixing resale prices, etc. More restrictions are treated as hard core than might be thought at first glance. The conditions in Article 5 are also broadly defined.

Since there is no limiting white list, there is no need for an opposition procedure for restrictions of competition not expressly exempted. They will automatically come within the group exemption in the absence of a hard core restraint if the market share is not excessive, as will provisions of the same type but more limited scope.[86]

The absence of a white list was followed in the recent group exemptions for horizontal agreements[87] and is likely to be followed in any others that may be adopted. The Commission takes the view that the white lists, at least those of the kind before the group exemptions for technology transfer were adopted, when the permissible clauses were limited, acted as "strait jackets".

3.4.13 30 Per Cent Ceiling of Market Share—Articles 3 & 9, Recital 8 and Guidelines 21, 22, 88–99 (7.2.5–7.2.5.4 below)

The Commission has been concerned that where there is market power, vertical agreements should not be legal *per se* even when neither party has a dominant position within the meaning of Article 82. In its *Green Paper on Vertical Restraints in EC Competition Policy*,[88] the Commission stated:

> 10. . . . Vertical restraints are no longer regarded as *per se* suspicious or per se pro-competitive. Economists are less willing to make sweeping statements. Rather, they rely more on the analysis of the facts of a case in question. However, one element stands out: the importance of market structure in determining the impact of vertical restraints. The fiercer is interbrand competition, the more likely are the pro-competitive and efficiency effects to outweigh any anti-competitive effects of vertical restraints. Anti-competitive

---

[85] *The Communication on the Application of the EC Competition Rules to Vertical Restraints—Follow-up to the Green Paper on Vertical Restraints*—OJ 1998, C365/3, p. 24.

[86] Expressly exempted by Article 1(5) of the Technology Transfer Regulation, 140/1996 and earlier group exemptions for IP licensing, although not those for distribution.

[87] Commission Regulation 2658/2000, on the application of Article 81(3) of the Treaty to categories of specialisation agreements, OJ 2000, L304/3, [2001] 4 CMLR 800 and Commission Regulation 2659/2000, on the application of Article 81(3) of the Treaty to categories of research and development agreements, OJ 2000, L304/7, [2001] 4 CMLR 808.

[88] COM(96) 721 final, [1997] 4 CMLR 519.

effects are only likely where interbrand competition is weak and there are barriers to entry at either producer or distributor level. In addition it is recognised that contracts in the distribution chain reduce transaction costs, and can allow the potential efficiencies in distribution to be realised. In contrast there are cases where vertical restraints raise barriers to entry or further dampen horizontal competition in oligopolistic markets.

In recital 8 to the Regulation, the Commission stated rather more precisely:

8. It can be presumed that, where the share of the relevant market accounted for by the supplier does not exceed 30%, vertical agreements which do not contain certain types of severely anticompetitive restraints generally lead to an improvement in production or distribution and allow consumers a fair share of the resulting benefits; in the case of vertical agreements containing exclusive supply obligations, it is the market share of the buyer which is relevant in determining the overall effects of such vertical agreements on the market.[89]

9. Above the market share threshold of 30%, there can be no presumption that vertical agreements falling within the scope of Article 81(1) will usually give rise to objective advantages of such a character and size as to compensate for the disadvantages which they create for competition.

The Commission was determined to impose a ceiling of market share to the application of the group exemptions as part of its current policy, according to which the structure of markets is more important than formalistic rules as to what is permitted, based on the need to reduce the mass of notifications.

The Commission recognises that market shares are not a precise indicator of market power,[90] but it is difficult to quantify market power in any other way so, as early as the publication of the *Green Paper*,[91] it considered imposing a ceiling of market share.

The Commission's views as to the height of the ceiling have varied since the publication of the *Green Paper*. There the Commission suggested two ceilings: below 20 per cent there would be a rebuttable presumption that Article 81 did not apply, and between 20 and 40 per cent the group exemption would apply (paras. 294–299). The *Follow up to the Green Paper*[92] also provided for two ceilings: 20 per cent for restrictions it considered more serious and 40 per cent for others.

During the consulting process it was decided that a double ceiling was too complex, although the notice on agreements of minor importance[93] has been extended

---

[89] In the *Communication on the Application of the EC Competition Rules to Vertical Restraints— Follow-up to the Green Paper on Vertical Restraints*—OJ 1998, C365/3, p. 23, the Commission rejected the view that vertical agreements even below the thresholds were harmless, and provided for the withdrawal of the group exemption (6.1–6.1.3 below).

[90] *Ibid.*, paras. 12 and 42.

[91] Green Paper on Vertical Restraints in EC Competition Policy, COM(96) 721 final, [1997] 4 CMLR 519, paras. 12 and 42.

[92] OJ 1998, C365/3. Section V. 3.

[93] Notice on agreements of minor importance which do not fall within the meaning of Article 85(1) of the Treaty establishing the European Community, 1997 OJ, C372/13, [1998] 4 CMLR 192, Notice relating to the revision of the 1997 notice on agreements of minor importance which do not fall under Article 81(10 of the EC Treaty, OJ 2001, C149/18.

to higher market shares: 10 per cent for agreements between competitors and 15 per cent for those between non-competitors. In effect this will provide a second ceiling. Single firm dominance under Article 82 provides a third and joint dominant positions a fourth, although the last two are based only indirectly on market share.

A 30 per cent ceiling to limit the block exemption has eventually been chosen. Law reform groups and industry have objected that with such a low ceiling, more provisions should be allowed. Article 5 limiting non-compete provisions (now called "single branding") seems unnecessary. Not only is 30 per cent somewhat lower than the market share at which lawyers become concerned in the US,[94] markets are defined narrowly under EC law, often leading to higher market shares being perceived. Nevertheless, the vertical agreements of most suppliers will come below the threshold.

It has been objected that the test of market share may operate to discriminate against suppliers in the smaller member states. Mario Monti, the member of the Commission responsible for competition, has replied that antitrust markets are not always defined by reference to the territory of a member state and that agreements by suppliers above the ceiling may not infringe Article 81(1).[95] In cases involving distribution under the Merger Regulation, the Commission has often treated geographic markets for distributors as national, resulting in large supermarket chains being treated as having market power. The vertical agreement between undertakings, however, is likely to be that where the supplier sells to the supermarket chain,[96] and at that level of trade, fewer markets are national.

3.4.13.1 Problems of defining markets

Calculating market shares presupposes a definition of the relevant market and often this is difficult to predict. Nevertheless, lawyers have become more used to coping with these problems over the last decade. There are now some 300 formal decisions on merger cases a year, and the analysis in those has depended on market definitions. In the context of mergers, it is not always necessary to consider the exact boundaries—in many decisions the Commission has said that the geographic market embraced at least the whole of the EEA without deciding whether it was worldwide. This avoidance of the issue will sometimes be possible under the group exemption.

The Commission tried to insert a ceiling of market share of licensees when preparing the group exemption for technology transfer, but was deterred by an outcry from business which claimed that it seldom knew what market would be

---

[94] Even after deciding in *Jefferson Parish Hospital Dist. No. 2* v. *Hyde*, 466 US 2, 104 SCt 1551, 80 L Ed 2d 2 (1984) that tying should still be called a *per se* offence, the Supreme Court held that with a market share as low as 30 per cent there was a safe haven. For rule of reason analysis, the ceiling is usually put a little higher.

[95] Answer to Parliamentary questions, E-1995/99, [2000] 5 CMLR 409.

[96] Usually it is the supplier's market share that is relevant, 3.3.13.2 below.

found relevant and that a ceiling of market share would deprive contracting parties of legal certainty. In technologically developing markets, the identification of the relevant markets is particularly difficult.

Since then, however, the Commission's notice on the relevant market[97] has clarified the position considerably, especially as it sets out its views on the kinds of evidence appropriate.

In Guideline 88 on vertical restraints, the Commission states:

> The Commission Notice on definition of the relevant market . . . provides guidance on the rules, criteria and evidence which the Commission uses when considering market definition issues. That Notice will not be further explained in these Guidelines and should serve as the basis for market definition issues. These Guidelines will only deal with specific issues that arise in the context of vertical restraints and that are not dealt with in the general notice on market definition.

Article 9 and Vertical Guideline 90 provide criteria for defining the relevant market in the concrete terms used by the ECJ—substitution on the demand side "by reason of the products' characteristics, their prices and their intended use", rather than in the abstract SSNIP test,[98] also used in the notice on market definition.[99] Guideline 90 also refers to the geographic market being homogenous. Although the reason for that limitation escapes us, it is mentioned in several judgments. Usually it is the supplier's share of market, where it sells, that is relevant (3.4.13.2 below).

Guideline 95 provides that where there are provisions relating not only to the supply of goods but also to intellectual property rights, for instance if the dealer is allowed to use its supplier's trade mark, the relevant market share is that of the supplier on the markets where it sells the contract goods.

Where a franchisor does not supply goods for resale, but provides a bundle of services combined with provisions relating to intellectual property, the franchisor's share of the market as a provider of business methods is relevant—the market on which the business method is exploited. This is to be based on the value of the goods or services supplied by the franchisees on this market.

---

[97] Notice on the definition of the relevant market for the purposes of Community competition law, OJ C372/5, [1998] 4 CMLR 177, 2.4.1.2 above.

[98] Small but significant non-transitory increase in prices, sometimes called the "hypothetical monopolist" test. Take the obvious product, A, and hypothesise a small increase in its price relative to other products of about 5 or 10% that is expected to last. Then consider whether so many buyers would switch to other products as to make the increase unprofitable and whether so many suppliers would start making or expanding production of A as to make the initial price increase unprofitable. In either case, the possibilities of substitution constrain the market conduct of A suppliers.

[99] Notice on the definition of the relevant market for the purposes of Community competition law, OJ 1997, C372/5, [1998] 4 CMLR 177, paras. 15–23 (2.4.1.2 above). It has also issued guidelines in relation to telecoms and electronic communications which may help to analyse other sectors too: 1) notice on the application of the competition rules to access agreements in the telecommunications sector-framework, relevant markets and principles, OJ 1998, C265/28, 2) Commission working document on proposed new regulatory framework for electronic communications network services www.europa. eu.int/comm/competition/antitrust/others. and 3) draft guidelines on market analysis and the calculation of significant market power under Article 14 of the proposed directive, Com 2001 175 final, 28.3.2001.

As electronic marketing develops, will the share be taken from the electronic market or include the more traditional ways of disposing of products? The advent of B2B markets might be looked at as changing competitive structures.

Another major problem is that businesspeople often do not know their share of the relevant market, even if they know how to define it. Recent turnover figures of competitors are usually confidential, and their disclosure to each other would be illegal as a facilitative cartel. Sometimes trade associations can give some help, but they can relate only to information that is over a year old.[100]

When appraising supply agreements to traders, product markets may be wide, since peas or fish fingers compete with ice cream for space in a trader's freezer cabinet, display shelf, container or vehicle. In Guideline 91, the Commission suggests that an entire portfolio from a single supplier may constitute the relevant market.

Where the same distribution agreement is used for a variety of goods or services and the market share is exceeded for some of them only, the group exemption may apply to the others (Guideline 68). Moreover, there is no presumption that Article 81(1) is infringed where the Regulation does not apply. If the market share differs from product to product, the parties will have to consider how to avoid falling outside the Regulation or infringing Article 81, possibly by making distribution agreements with different terms for different products or geographic markets.

Since it is the supplier's share of the market where it sells that is usually relevant, the geographic market may well be the whole Common Market, and fewer agreements will exceed the 30 per cent ceiling than might be expected at first glance at the Regulation. Where the geographic market is national, however, there may be gaps in the coverage of the Regulation. The member states where the market share exceeds 30 per cent may be excluded. This has the anomalous result that active sales from those markets to countries where the market share is below 30 per cent may not be restrained, whereas active sales from the countries with lower shares to protect dealers in the markets where there is a higher market share can be.

Officials sometimes allege that the uncertainty as to the application of a group exemption is less important nowadays, since agreements that are excluded can be notified late and exempted retrospectively,[101] but notification is to be abolished by the proposed Regulation to replace Regulation 17 (2.12 above). In Guideline 65, the Commission promises not to impose fines when the parties assumed in good faith that there agreement came within the group exemption, but this is little help to a party that finds the agreement in reliance on which investments have been made is void.

---

[100]   *UK Agricultural Registration Exchange,* 17 February 1992, OJ 1992, L68/19, [1993] 4 CMLR 358, [1992] 1 CEC 2126; affirmed in *Fiatagri UK Ltd and New Holland Ford Ltd* v. *Commission,* Case T34/92, 27 Oct 1994, [1994] ECR II 904; and *New Holland Ford Ltd.* v. *Commission,* Case C-7/95P, 28 May 1998, [1998] ECR I-3111, [1998] 5 CMLR 311, [1998] CEC 611—that agreement to pool information about the number and models of tractor sold in each of many small areas did not include information about prices. There are many decisions and judgment treating agreements to exchange prices as illegal.

[101]   Council Regulation 1216 amending Reg. 17 Article 4(2) and providing for retrospective exemption of vertical agreements, OJ 1999, L148/5, (2.13 above).

Where a manufacturer of original equipment supplies both original equipment and spares, Guideline 94 leaves it unclear whether the OE and RE markets should be appraised separately. It depends on

> the circumstances of the case, such as the effects of the restrictions involved, the lifetime of the equipment and importance of the repair or replacement costs. (Footnote omitted.)

A footnote refers to several cases, mostly merger decisions. The earlier draft of the guidelines stated that only the original equipment market share was relevant.

3.4.13.2 Whose market share?

Usually it is the market share of the supplier that is relevant, but where the dealer is protected by a promise of an exclusive territory for the whole common market, the dealer's share of the market on which it buys the contract products is relevant. Article 3 provides:

> 1. Subject to paragraph 2 of this Article, the exemption provided for in Article 2 shall apply on condition that the market share held by the supplier does not exceed 30% of the relevant market on which it sells the contract goods or services.

> 2. In the case of vertical agreements containing exclusive supply obligations, the exemption provided for in Article 2 shall apply on condition that the market share held by the buyer does not exceed 30% of the relevant market on which it purchases the contract goods or services.

"Exclusive supply obligation" is defined in Article 1(c) of the regulation to mean

> any direct or indirect obligation causing the supplier to sell the goods or services specified in the agreement only to one buyer inside the Community for the purpose of a specific use or for resale.

The definition is broad in that it includes indirect obligations, such as dual pricing systems that encourage the supplier to use only one dealer, but it is narrow in that the exclusive territory must extend to the whole Common Market.

When applying Article 3(2) it is the share of the market on which the buyer buys that is relevant (3.4.13.4 below). The Article seems to distinguish between buyers in the Common Market, whose market share is relevant, and those buying outside to sell within. In their case it will be the supplier's market share that is relevant.[102] In this, Article 3 may be anomalous generally, but particularly in relation to electronic commerce.

The reason for looking to the dealer's market share when it is the only one to buy within the Common Market is that the restraint affects the competitors of the dealer, but if so, it is hard to see why the definition should be limited to contracts under which the territory embraces *the whole of the Common Market*. Perhaps the Commission accepts that where geographic markets are smaller, parallel trade will

---

[102] **Jochen B. Burrichter**, "Vertical Restraints and E-Commerce," Barry Hawk (ed.) *Fordham Corporate Law Institute*, ch. 10, p.142.

enable other dealers to obtain supplies, but some products do not pass through more than one level of dealer.

3.4.13.3 Which level of trade? Guidelines 22, 91–93

Guideline 22 recognises that vertical agreements at one level of trade may affect those downstream but, for the sake of simplicity and certainty, the group exemption takes into account the share of the market in which the parties are making a contract. If there are significant problems in related markets, the group exemption may be withdrawn under Articles 6–8 (6.1–6.1.3 below).

Guideline 91 states that:

> For the application of the BER, the market share of the supplier is his share on the relevant product and geographic market on which he sells to his buyers. . . . The product market depends in the first place on substitutability from the buyers' perspective. When the supplied product is used as an input to produce other products and is generally not recognisable in the final product, the product market is normally defined by the direct buyer's preferences.

Where buyers of the final product will not recognise the input, the market will be the intermediate one—the sale to the maker of the product of which it forms part. Where, however, final goods are supplied to a distributor, what amounts to a substitute may be influenced by the preferences of consumers.

A producer may supply supermarket chains direct, but use wholesalers to distribute to smaller buyers (dual distribution). Are these to be treated as separate markets? Guideline 91 suggests that such distribution formats usually compete with each other, so are usually in the same market.

If a supplier, A, appoints B, an exclusive distributor for a whole member state and, in turn, B appoints C as an exclusive wholesaler for a region, the relevant market for the first agreement is that on which A sells, but that relevant to the second agreement is that on which B sells. Geographic markets for sales to professional buyers are often wider than those for sales to consumers.

Guideline 92 states that in the case of exclusive supply, the buyer's market share is its share of all purchases on the relevant purchase market. "Exclusive supply obligation" is defined in Article 1(c) for the purposes of the Regulation to refer to a dealer's exclusive territory for the whole Common Market. The diagram in Guideline 92 assumes however, that the supplier is supplying more than one dealer, so, perhaps, it is referring to smaller exclusive territories. It is confusing that the guidelines seem not to be using the same definitions as are used in the Regulation.

Guideline 93 states that:

> Where a vertical distribution agreement involves three parties, each operating at a different level of trade, their market shares will have to be below the market share threshold of 30% at both levels in order to benefit from the BER. If for instance, in an agreement between a manufacturer, a wholesaler (or association of retailers) and a retailer, a non-compete obligation is agreed, then the market share of both the manu-

facturer and the wholesaler (or association of retailers) must not exceed 30% in order to benefit from the BER.

When a buyer, B, agrees to buy mainly from the same supplier A, the relevant market is that on which B purchases the contract goods, although it is A's market share that is relevant. If A sells direct to supermarket chains, but uses wholesalers to supply smaller retailers, the market for testing the agreements with the wholesalers may exclude sales to supermarkets, because the wholesalers are unlikely to buy from them. This is dubious on policy grounds, as the wholesalers' prices will often be constrained by the prices charged by supermarkets. The matter is not explained very clearly in the guidelines.

3.4.13.4 Original and replacement equipment—Guideline 94

Where a subcontractor or others supply both original equipment and spare parts, Guideline 94 states that:

> ... The relevant market for application of the BER may be the original equipment market including the spare parts or a separate original equipment market and after-market depending on the circumstances of the case, such as the effects of the restrictions involved, the lifetime of the equipment and importance of the repair or replacement costs. (Footnote omitted).

This paragraph does not specify a test. The price of each replacement part often exceeds the price of the same part supplied as original equipment, at least where it is specific to a single brand. The market for original equipment is usually acutely price sensitive, and that for a replacement part is not. Consequently, many suppliers of components recover much of their design costs and other overheads from the replacement market.

There should be no objection to this on competition grounds, since it maximises supply. Prices in the market that is most price sensitive are lower than under a uniform price system. So, more is likely to be demanded and supplied. Nevertheless, the Community institutions are less sympathetic to discrimination that enables a firm with significant sunk costs and low variable costs to recover its overhead costs than are economists, and the SSNIP test adopted in the notice on market definition might lead to the spare part being treated as being in a separate market.[103]

Under Article 82, it has been argued by manufacturers that spare parts should be treated as part of the market for original equipment. The cost of replacements

---

[103] The SSNIP test is fallacious when applied to Articles 81 and 82, as is recognised by the Commission in its notice on the definition of the relevant market for the purposes of Community competition law, OJ 1997, C372/5, [1998] 4 CMLR 177 at para. 19 (2.4.1.2 above). Where there is market power, the holder is likely already to have raised the price above the competitive level and it is usually impossible to tell what this would have been had the market been more competitive.

It should not apply to markets where competition takes the form of innovation rather than price. A price rise of 5 or 10% is unlikely to cause customers for new or improved products to switch, but the innovator may be subject to considerable competition to develop the next new product.

may be taken into account by consumers when they buy the original equipment.[104]

In *Eastman Kodak Co.* v. *Image Technical Services Inc*,[105] evidence was given that
customers could not all consider the lifetime costs of using equipment,[106] especially if the policy of the brand owner as to the availability of spare parts changed.
The US Supreme Court decided that Kodak could be dominant over the supply of
spare parts even if it was not dominant over the original equipment and remanded
the case for further fact finding.

The Commission's hostility to discrimination makes it difficult for suppliers of
spare parts to recover their overheads mainly from the replacement market. It
results from trying to define markets before analysing them rather than considering the optimal way for charging to compensate for overhead costs.

3.4.13.5 Franchisors' market shares—Guideline 95

Guideline 95 states that the market share of a franchisor that provides a package of
IPRs and business method services, should be calculated on the basis of the market for those services, measured by the turnover of its franchisees in exploiting
them. The market will include suppliers of substitutable goods or services that are
not franchised. This is hard to reconcile with Article 3(1) of Regulation 2790/99.[107]
One might have thought that the royalties paid by the franchisees should be the
correct test, but there should be a second relevant market, that for the products
sold by the franchisees.

3.4.13.6 Calculation of market share—Article 9 and Guidelines 97–99

The mechanics for calculating market share are prescribed in Article 9:

1. The market share of 30% provided for in Article 3(1) shall be calculated on the basis
of the market sales value of the contract goods or services and other goods or services
sold by the supplier, which are regarded as interchangeable or substitutable by the buyer,
by reason of the products' characteristics, their prices and their intended use; if market
sales value data are not available, estimates based on other reliable market information,
including market sales volumes, may be used to establish the market share of the undertaking concerned. For the purposes of Article 3(2), it is either the market purchase value
or estimates thereof which shall be used to calculate the market share.

---

[104] E.g., in *Volvo AB* v. *Erik Veng (UK) Ltd.*, Case 238/87, [1988] ECR 6211, see AG Mischo, paras.
6–8. Nevertheless, he thought that the time a part required replacement, a motorist was tied to spare
parts that would fit and if these could be obtained only from the brand owner, he might be in a dominant position. The ECJ did not address the question whether Volvo was dominant over front wing pan-
els for its vehicles.

[105] 504 US 451, (1992).

[106] Much was procured by hospitals, and often the initial cost of buying the equipment came from
a different budget from the one used for repair and maintenance.

[107] **Raymond Hill** and **Kassie Smith**, chapter 7 of **Bellamy** and **Child**, *European Community Law of
Competition*, 5th edn. (London, Sweet & Maxwell) p.504, note 68.

2. For the purposes of applying the market share, threshold provided for in Article 3 the following rules shall apply:

(a) the market share shall be calculated on the basis of data relating to the preceding cal-
     endar year;
(b) the market share shall include any goods or services supplied to integrated distribu-
     tors for the purposes of sale;
(c) if the market share is initially not more than 30% but subsequently rises above that
     level without exceeding 35%, the exemption provided for in Article 2 shall continue
     to apply for a period of two consecutive calendar years following the year in which
     the 30% market share threshold was first exceeded;
(d) if the market share is initially not more than 30% but subsequently rises above 35%,
     the exemption provided for in Article 2 shall continue to apply for one calendar year
     following the year in which the level of 35% was first exceeded;
(e) the benefit of points (c) and (d) may not be combined so as to exceed a period of two
     calendar years.

If possible, the calculation of market shares should be prepared on the basis of value. Where this is not possible, for instance because the prices of competitors at the relevant level of trade are unknown, estimates based, for instance, on volume may have to suffice. Much evidence about the retail level of trade can be obtained by firms that collect from retailers and classify information obtained by bar coding. There may be greater difficulty appraising upstream markets. In-house production may be important and reduce the part of the demand curve supplied that way but according to Guideline 98 is not included in the calculation of market shares.

The relevant period for calculating the market share is the preceding calendar year, rather than the preceding accounting year, which it might have been more convenient to ascertain. The marginal relief in Article 9(2)(c) & (d) will sometimes accommodate this.

Where there is dual distribution of final goods, Guideline 99 provides that

. . . the market definition and market share calculation need to include the goods sold by
the producer and competing producers through their integrated distributors and agents.
. . . "Integrated distributors" are connected undertakings within the meaning of Article
11 of the BER.

An undertaking cannot reduce its market share at the wholesale level by doing its own wholesaling.

3.4.13.7 Conclusion on the market share cap

There is much criticism of the market share cap on the ground that it leads to uncertainty. Where there is inadequate inter-brand competition, however, verti-cal agreements may have serious anti-competitive effects and should not be auto-matically legal until a firm is dominant.

There is a trade off between legal certainty and a more economic approach to block exemptions. The former formalistic block exemptions covered some anti-competitive agreements. Nevertheless, many experts argue that there is no need for a cap of market share because Regulation 2790/99 exempts agreements only from the application of Article 81(1), not from Article 82[108] and the threshold for finding a dominant position is low under EC law. There is a rebuttable presumption of dominance if there is a stable market share of 50 per cent,[109] it has been found at lower market shares and, with the new concept of joint dominance, there is concern that it may be found at lower levels in oligopolistic markets.[110]

Firms with market shares exceeding 30 per cent in some geographic markets may find that their agreements for those areas do not infringe Article 81(1), because the restraints are ancillary to an agreement not in itself anticompetitive (2.7.2 above and 7.2.5.4 below), or they may obtain a retrospective individual exemption, but there will be no safe harbour for the markets where their market share exceeds 30 per cent (Guideline 68). They may, however, have taken advantage of the transitional provision and ensured that agreements exempt under the old regulations were in force before 1 June 2000 and enjoy a safe harbour until the end of 2001. Multipartite agreements where the parties operate at different levels of trade will have to satisfy the 30 per cent ceiling at all levels (3.4.13.3 above). Where there is doubt whether some of the other parties have excessive market shares, care should be devoted to deciding whether the other parts of the agreement should remain valid.

Some firms with low turnover serving niche markets, such as specialised machinery, may find that their market share exceeds 30 per cent. In Europe narrow markets have been treated as relevant. The ECJ has considered substitutes on the supply side only when new entry is likely to take place fast—it takes too long to build a new factory.[111] According to Article 3 of the notice on Agreements of Minor importance, there is a fairly safe harbour for small and medium-sized firms[112] but firms too large to qualify may not have been used to seeking advice on competition law.

---

[108] Recital 16 and *Tetra Pak Rausing SA* v. *Commission,* Case T-51/89 [1990] ECR II-309.

[109] *AKZO Chemie BV* v. *Commission,* Case 62/86 [1991] ECR I-3359, para. 59.

[110] *Compagnie Maritime Belge* v. *Commission,* Case C-395/96P [2000] 4 CMLR 1076 (ECJ) and *Gencor Ltd.* v. *Commission,* Case T-102/96 [1999] ECR II-753. A market share of 60%, divided 23/37 does not of itself conclusively establish joint dominance, *France* v. *Commission,* Cases C-68/94 & 30/95 [1998] ECR I-1375, para. 226 (3.3 above). There would be considerable concern if the Commission were to invoke the concept of joint dominance and treat the conduct of an oligopolist as forbidden by Article 82 where it would be treated as abusive if committed by a single dominant firm, **Enrique González-Dias**, "Recent Developments in EC Merger Control law — The *Gencor* Judgment," [1999] *World Competition Law and Economics Review* 3 and **Valentine Korah**, "*Gencor* v. *Commission*: Collective Dominance," (1999) 20 *ECLR* 337.

[111] *Michelin—Nederlandsche Banden-Industrie Michelin* v. *Commission,* Case 322/81 [1983] ECR 3461, para. 41.

[112] Small and medium-sized undertakings are defined in Small and Medium-Sized Enterprises (Definition) Recommendation, and are cleared by the Notice on Minor agreements. Annex, Article 1

1. Small and medium-sized enterprises, hereinafter referred to as "SMEs", are defined as enterprises which:

—have fewer than 250 employees and
—have either an annual turnover not exceeding 40 million ECUs or an annual balance sheet total not exceeding 27 million ECUs,   *cont./*

Valentine would prefer vertical restraints to be subject to a rule of reason, where conditions of entry would be more relevant, than enjoy the benefit of group exemptions with a market share cap. Supply substitution is hardly considered under the Commission's notice on the definition of the relevant market for the purposes of Community competition law and firms subject to serious non-price competition may have no safe harbour.

Market power rather than market share should be the relevant basis of appraisal, but market power is hard to quantify for a group exemption and no one has suggested a better surrogate than market share. Business wanted what it conceived as the greater certainty of a group exemption. Having advocated a more economic approach for 30 years, Valentine welcomes the ceiling of market power.

Firms will still be able to argue that ancillary restraints do not infringe Article 81(1), but since *Métropole Télévision SA and Others* v. *Commission*[113] restraints required to induce investment by obviating the risk of free riding may infringe Article 81(1). Where a narrow market is accepted by an institution enforcing competition law, the firms are free to appeal on the ground that the institution has not given adequate reasons for denying that it still faces competition from other products in neighbouring markets and could not raise its prices above a competitive level. Proof, however, may be difficult and judicial review is limited.[114] The problem caused by the wide treatment of the prohibition is that justifications have to be established for agreements that may not restrict competition significantly.

Markets do not all have sharp edges, and it is formalistic to treat everything within the defined market as relevant and nothing outside it. More remote substitutes may constrain market behaviour even if to a lesser extent than those within a defined market. The Commission has said there is no presumption that firms with market shares above the ceiling have infringed Article 81(1). The burden of proof is on those alleging that Article 81 is infringed (7.2.5.2 below).

—conform to the criterion of independence as defined in paragraph 3.

These limitations are low.

[113] Case T-112/99 [2001] 12 CMLR 1236 (2.7.2 above).
[114] Although less narrowly after *European Night Services (ENS) and others* v. *Commission,* Cases T-374, 375, 384 & 388/94, [1998] ECR II-3141.

4

Hard Core Restraints

4.1 INTRODUCTION

Article 4 lists the hard core restraints: resale price maintenance (rpm) and absolute territorial protection as well as some other post-sales restraints. These prevent the application of the Regulation to the agreement, even to the provisions that are not hard core restraints. Moreover, the Commission has been imposing substantial fines for these practices, even when adopted indirectly.

The ECJ has treated both rpm and absolute territorial protection as practices which "by their very nature" have the object of restricting competition (2.7.1 and 2.8.5–2.8.5.4 above).

As repeated in Vertical Guideline 10, in its notice on agreements of minor importance[1] the Commission said that vertical agreements between parties whose aggregate market share does not exceed 15 per cent (para. 7(b)) seldom restrict competition, but it added in para. 11 the exclusion from the Regulation does not apply to the full list of practices taken from Article 4 of Regulation 2790/99.

The Commission remains hostile to rpm and absolute territorial protection although these are both intra-brand restraints and at Guideline 102 the Commission states that in general:

> In the assessment of individual cases, the Commission will adopt an economic approach in the application of Article 81 to vertical restraints. This will limit the scope of application of Article 81 to undertakings holding a certain degree of market power where inter-brand competition may be insufficient. In those cases, the protection of inter-brand and intra-brand competition is important to ensure efficiencies and benefits for consumers.

It is difficult to envisage much market power if the parties' aggregate market share does not exceed 15 per cent.[2]

Now that the block exemption has a ceiling as low as a 30 per cent share of the market, some hard core restraints may not have appreciable effects on inter-state trade or competition but, even so, if the agreement as a whole has such effects, they prevent the Regulation applying to other provisions in the same agreement—a term that is wider than contract.[3] Moreover, the Commission states that they are unlikely to be exempted individually.

---

[1] Published on DG Competition's home page on 21 Dec. 2001, OJ 2001, C368/13.
[2] See, however, Steiner's arguments against rpm of "must stock" brands, 1.2.3.4 above. It does not apply to less important brands.
[3] *BP Kemi—Atka A/S* v. *BP Kemi A/S and A/S de Danske Spritfabrikker*, OJ 1979, L286/32, [1979] 3 CMLR 684, paras. 50–55.

4.1.1 Not Severable

There are two lists of non-exempt restraints in Regulation 2790/99. Article 4 lists the hard core restraints: the maintenance of fixed or minimum resale prices, territorial and customer restraints and some other post sales restraints with specified exceptions. It prevents the exemption applying even to other provisions of the agreement if any of the hard core restraints is included (Guideline 66).

The single branding provisions listed in Article 5,[4] however, are severable. They are not exempted, but do not prevent the application of the group exemption to other provisions. This is important, as single branding restraints have the object or effect of restricting competition only in narrowly-defined circumstances (2.7.3 above).

We regret the lack of severability in Article 4: it may harm smaller firms who do not regularly take antitrust advice. The sophisticated will avoid the hard core restraints and others, even with modest market shares, may lose their exemption. Unless and until the hard core restraints have been removed, the agreement may be illegal and unenforceable.[5]

Providing in a contract that any provision that is found to restrict competition shall have no effect will not save the other provisions. The ECJ held in *Miller*[6] that even provisions that are not enforced infringe Article 81, because they may still influence conduct. The Commission has ignored provisions depriving anti-competitive clauses of legal effect on the same ground.[7]

---

[4] Whereby the dealer agrees to handle only a single brand, or to obtain at least 80% of its requirements from a designated source.

[5] In *Gibbs Mew Plc and Gemmel* (CA) [1999] ECC 97, paras. 39–45, *obiter*, the English Court of Appeal held that the party to an illegal contract cannot obtain any relief. It assumed that this would be the position in other member states. In *Courage* v. *Crehan*, Case C-453/99, 20 September 2001, [2001] 5 CMLR 1058, however, following the opinion of AG Mischo, the ECJ considered that so wide a doctrine of illegality was inconsistent with the direct effect of Community law. A small firm which had no choice but to accept a contract of adhesion might not be *in pari delicto* and should be able to sue the other party for infringing Article 81(1) (2.5–2.5.1 above).

[6] *Miller International Schallplatten GmbH* v. *Commission*, Case 19/77 [1978] ECR 131 (2.7.1 above).

[7] In *John Deere Ltd.* v. *Commission*, OJ 1985, L35/58, [1985] 2 CMLR 554, para. 27, the export ban in the contract was qualified by the words "as far as no contrary legal regulation exists." The Commission dismissed such a qualification by a large firm that had legal advice in a letter to small dealers that were less likely to know the law. At para. 26, it was argued that the instructions to penalise parallel trading were ineffective. The Commission replied that the instructions had the object of preventing such trade and that the burden of proof was on Deere to show that the instructions were never obeyed, but invariably ignored. In *IFTRA rules for producers of virgin aluminium*, OJ 1975, L228/3, [1975] CMLR D20, the parties argued that the rules had never operated, but were introduced at the end of a period of recession and maintained thereafter as a safety net (para. 8). The Commission went further than onus of proof, referring to the object of the rules, and that they were ready drafted and could be rapidly put into effect (para. 11) The rules were said to restrain unfair competition, but that did not prevent the Commission examining them in detail and finding that they infringed Article 81.

In *IFTRA rules on glass containers—Re European Glass Manufacturers*, OJ 1974, L160/1, [1974] 2 CMLR D50, the Commission added at para. 34 that the mere labelling of the rules as "fair trading rules" does not suffice to remove the agreement from the ambit of Art. 81. It condemned many of them as restraining price competition. See also *De Laval/Stork VOF (Re) (No. 2)*, OJ 1988, L59/32, [1988] 4 CMLR 715, para. 8.

4.1.2 Hard Core Restraints may not Affect Trade Between Member States

Although Guideline 46 refers to the practices listed in Article 4 as "hard core restrictions" which are unlikely to receive an individual exemption, rpm, territorial restraints and the other provisions listed do not infringe Article 81(1) and need no exemption unless they may have an appreciable effect on trade between member states.[8] Problems arise, however, if the agreement infringes Article 81(1) because of other provisions even if these are not hard core restraints.

4.1.3 Broad Definition of Restraints

The introductory words of Article 4 are broad:

> The exemption provided for in Article 2 shall not apply to vertical agreements which, directly or indirectly, in isolation or in combination with other factors under the control of the parties, have as their object: . . .

The new notice on minor agreements[9] states that vertical agreements containing any of the restraints listed in Article 4 or Regulation 2790/99 may infringe Article 81(1) even when the market share held by each of the parties does not exceed 15 per cent.

Guidelines 47 (4.2 below) and 49 (4.3 below) make it clear that not only do contractual prohibitions prevent the application of the exemption, deterrents and incentives, rebates or refusal to supply may do so too. At 3.4.9.2.5 it was explained that Article 2(3) prevents an undertaking from indirectly imposing hard core restraints by attaching them to a trademark licence or other intellectual property rights.

No guidance is given as to how the object of a restraint is to be established. It may well be that the object will be inferred from the likely effects of an agreement. In the light of *Métropole Télévision SA and Others* v. *Commission*[10] (2.7.2 above), it may well be not so much to the actual effects that one should look, as to the nature of the restriction.

The introductory words refer only to the object of the agreement, not to the effect. It is, however, difficult to envisage provisions that have the effect, but not even the indirect object prohibited: perhaps the sale of a business, where the buyer agrees not to compete within an area smaller than the Common Market might have a different object. The provision would amount to a condition as to where products may be sold, and may have the effect of dividing the Common Market.[11] On

---

[8] *Javico International and Javico AG* v. *Yves Saint Laurent Parfums SA*, Case C-306/96, [1998] ECR I-1983 and *Louis Erauw Jacquerie*, Case 27/87, [1988] ECR 1919, paras. 12–20. See also 2.8.5.4. above.

[9] Published on DG Competition's home page on 21 Dec. 2001, OJ 2001, C368/13.

[10] Case T-112/99, 18 September 2001, [2001] 12 CMLR 1236.

[11] The ECJ seemed not to notice that the covenant not to compete in *Remia BV and Verenigde Bedrijven Nutricia* v. *Commission*, Case 42/84 [1985] ECR 2545, was limited to the area where the vendor had established a reputation, the Netherlands. Consequently, the vendor and its successors in title were entitled to carry on the trade in other Member States but not in the Netherlands.

the more permissive view of Article 2(1) explained at 3.4.9.1 above, such a covenant might qualify for the group exemption. If limited in time and space to what is necessary, it would not infringe Article 81(1), but other provisions might do so.

The agreement must be looked at in the context of other factors "within the control of the parties." It will be interesting to see what this limitation means. The cumulative effect of similar practices by others seems to be excluded.

There is considerable case law on indirect effects that have been condemned under Article 81(1), which may be applied to the construction of Article 4. The fines for vertical agreements imposed since the Regulation came into force have been for indirect ways of deterring low prices or export bans (4.2.3 and 7.6.3–7.6.3.6 below). Failure to provide a Community wide guarantee in the original agreement may prevent the application of the Regulation.[12] Charging more for exported product than for that sold locally was condemned in *Glaxo Wellcome*.[13] A prohibition on charging substantially less than a recommended price was condemned in *Volkswagen Passat*[14] (7.6.3.5 below).

The Commission fined Opel €43 million for blocking parallel exports from the Netherlands in various ways[15] (7.6.3.3 below). It alleged first that Opel had restricted the supply of cars to dealers who were exporting on the basis of the agreed sales target for its territory; secondly, dealers" bonuses were conditional on a sales target in which car registrations in the Netherlands only were included; thirdly there had been specific interventions to stop dealers exporting (7.6.3.3 below). Opel"s intervention was justified when the vehicles were sold to non-authorised dealers, but its measures did not clarify this and targeted all exports in general, including exports to other Opel dealers and consumers based abroad.

4.1.4 Agreement or Concerted Practice

In the US, a supplier is free to refuse supplies, and may even state a policy of not supplying those failing to supply services or operating on unspecified low margins, unless a dealer who has been terminated can prove a common understanding between its supplier and its legitimate dealers as to specific resale prices, price levels or some other restraint.[16] The onus of proving collusion is heavy.

Much less evidence is required to find a concerted practice in the EC. In *AEG*,[17] the ECJ confirmed that the Commission was entitled to find a concerted practice,

---

[12] *Hasselblad* v. *Commission*, Case 86/82 [1984] ECR 883, paras. 32–35.

[13] OJ 2001, L302/1. No fine was imposed on an agreement that had been notified to the Commission. This method of playing safe may cease to be possible if and when the new Regulation 17 is adopted (2.12 above).

[14] OJ 2001, L 262/14, [2001] 5 CMLR 1309.

[15] OJ 2001, L591/1.

[16] *Monsanto Co.* v. *Spray-Rite Service Corp.*, 465 US 752, (1984) and *Business Electronics Corp.* v. *Sharp Electronics Corp.*, 485 US 717, (1988).

[17] *AEG—Allgemeine Elektrizitäts-Gesellschaft AEG-Telefunken AG* v. *Commission*, Case 107/82 [1983] ECR 3151, paras. 38 & 39. See also *Ford-Werke AG and Ford of Europe Inc.* v. *Commission*, Cases 25 & 26/84 [1985] ECR 2725, paras. 20–22.

in the context of a long term dealership relationship, from systematically but uni-laterally cutting off low-price dealers. The refusals to deal in *AEG* consisted of 26 incidents out of thousands of agreements, and half of those incidents had not been adequately established according to the ECJ. Yet the ECJ treated the conduct as systematic.

Nevertheless, even in the EC, to establish an infringement of Article 81 it must be possible to spell out acquiescence by both parties. Purely unilateral action by a supplier does not amount to a concerted practice. This case law might be applied to decide whether there is collusion within the meaning of the introductory words to Article 4 of the Regulation.

In *Bayer AG* v. *Commission*,[18] the Commission had condemned Bayer for imposing an export ban on its dealers in member states where prices were lower than in the UK. Bayer admitted that it wanted to inhibit parallel trade, but claimed that it had never asked its dealers not to export nor discouraged them from doing so. It had supplied them with insufficient quantities of its best selling drug to enable them to export as much Adalat as they wanted to the UK. The dealers had done everything they could to obtain additional supplies, and had freely exported any they could get. The CFI set out the law carefully:

66. The case-law shows that, where a decision on the part of a manufacturer constitutes unilateral conduct of the undertaking, that decision escapes the prohibition in Article 81(1) of the Treaty (Case 107/82 *AEG* v *Commission* [1983] ECR 3151, paragraph 38; Joined Cases 25/84 and 26/84 *Ford and Ford Europe* v *Commission* [1985] ECR 2725, paragraph 21; Case T-43/92 *Dunlop Slazenger* v *Commission* [1994] ECR II-441, paragraph 56).

67. It is also clear from the case-law in that in order for there to be an agreement within the meaning of Article 81(1) of the Treaty it is sufficient that the undertakings in question should have expressed their joint intention to conduct themselves on the market in a specific way (Case 41/69 *ACF Chemiefarma* v *Commission* [1970] ECR 661, paragraph 112; Joined Cases 209/78 to 215/78 and 218/78 *Van Landewyck and Others* v *Commission* [1980] ECR 3125, paragraph 86; Case T-7/89 *Hercules Chemicals* v *Commission* [1991] ECR II-1711, paragraph 256).

68. As regards the form in which that common intention is expressed, it is sufficient for a stipulation to be the expression of the parties" intention to behave on the market in accordance with its terms (see, in particular, *ACF Chemiefarma*, paragraph 112, and *Van Landewyck*, paragraph 86), without its having to constitute a valid and binding contract under national law (*Sandoz*, paragraph 13).

69. It follows that the concept of an agreement within the meaning of Article 81(1) of the Treaty, as interpreted by the case-law, centres around the existence of a concurrence of wills between at least two parties, the form in which it is manifested being unimportant so long as it constitutes the faithful expression of the parties" intention.

---

[18]   Case T-41/96, [2001] 4 CMLR 4, appeal from *Adalat*, OJ 1996 L201/1, [1996] 5 CMLR 416 (2.1 above).

See also *Micro Leader Business*, Case T-198/98 [1999] ECR I-3989 and *Davidoff (Zino) SA & A & G Imports Ltd.*, Case C-414/99 and *Levi Strauss & Co and another* v. *Tesco*, Case C-415/99, 20 November 2001 in relation to the consent required for exhaustion (2.2 above).

70. In certain circumstances, measures adopted or imposed in an apparently unilateral manner by a manufacturer in the context of his continuing relations with his distributors have been regarded as constituting an agreement within the meaning of Article 81(1) of the Treaty (Joined Cases 32/78, 36/78 to 82/78 *BMW Belgium and Others* v *Commission* [1979] ECR 2435, paragraphs 28 to 30; *AEG*, paragraph 38; *Ford and Ford Europe*, paragraph 21; Case 75/84 *Metro* v *Commission* ("*Metro II* [1986] ECR 3021, paragraphs 72 and 73; *Sandoz*, paragraphs 7 to 12; Case C-70/93 *BMW* v *ALD* [1995] ECR I-3439, paragraphs 16 and 17).

71. That case-law shows that a distinction should be drawn between cases in which an undertaking has adopted a genuinely unilateral measure, and thus without the express or implied participation of another undertaking, and those in which the unilateral character of the measure is merely apparent. Whilst the former do not fall within Article 81(1) of the Treaty, the latter must be regarded as revealing an agreement between undertakings and may therefore fall within the scope of that Article. That is the case, in particular, with practices and measures in restraint of competition which, though apparently adopted unilaterally by the manufacturer in the context of its contractual relations with its dealers, nevertheless receive at least the tacit acquiescence of those dealers.

72. It is also clear from that case-law that the Commission cannot hold that apparently unilateral conduct on the part of a manufacturer, adopted in the context of the contractual relations which he maintains with his dealers, in reality forms the basis of an agreement between undertakings within the meaning of Article 81(1) of the Treaty if it does not establish the existence of an acquiescence by the other partners, express or implied, in the attitude adopted by the manufacturer (*BMW Belgium*, paragraphs 28 to 30; *AEG*, paragraph 38; *Ford and Ford Europe*, paragraph 21; *Metro II*, paragraphs 72 and 73; *Sandoz*, paragraphs 7 to 12; *BMW* v *ALD*, paragraphs 16 and 17)."

The CFI then went very carefully through the evidence relating to Bayer's dealing with each of its dealers in Spain and France and the way the latter had reacted and found no acquiescence by its dealers in Bayer's policy. The Commission had not established that Bayer monitored the final destination of the Adalat supplied to each dealer, nor that it had forbidden exports. The Commission had not established that the dealers had conformed to any export ban. They had tried to get all the Adalat they could and exported what was not required locally. Bayer's requirement that dealers should satisfy the local demand in combination with the limitation of supply was not treated as an export ban or deterrent, perhaps because it was required by national law.

From paragraph 158 the CFI went through the precedents cited by the Commission and distinguished each of them. Any firm trying to restrain dealers without action constituting a concerted practice must draw the distinction between unilateral action and tacit acquiescence very carefully.

In our view, the earlier judgment of the CFI finding that a circular was not unilateral in *Volkswagen* v. *Commission*,[19] cannot satisfactorily be distinguished from *Bayer*. It had been decided too recently for the Commission to have invoked it and it

---

[19] Case T-62/98 [2000] 5 CMLR 853, para. 126: appeal from Commission decision in *Volkswagen*, OJ 1998, L124/60, [1998] 5 CMLR 33.

was not discussed in *Bayer*. By a chamber of five judges, the CFI in *Volkswagen* merely followed cases like *Ford* in a single paragraph without any discussion. We believe that *Bayer* is the precedent to follow because the issue was so carefully considered.

Since the judgment of the CFI is under appeal, we can expect a judgment from the ECJ, perhaps, in 2003. Meanwhile, caution is required especially from pharmaceutical suppliers.[20] Commissioner Monti and officials of DG Competition have said they will invoke Article 82 if a dominant firm claims to have restrained parallel trade unilaterally.

4.2 RESALE PRICE MAINTENANCE (RPM)—ARTICLE 4(A) AND GUIDELINES 47 & 48

The first hard core restraint is

(a) the restriction of the buyer's ability to determine its sale price, without prejudice to the possibility of the supplier's imposing a maximum sale price or recommending a sale price provided that they do not amount to a fixed or minimum resale price as a result of pressure from, or incentives offered by, any of the parties;

4.2.1 Minimum and Fixed RPM

Vertical agreements imposing minimum and fixed resale prices on the buyer are hard core restraints listed in Article 4(a). The imposition of sales prices on the supplier, however, is not black listed, so most favoured customer clauses are not black listed. Undertakings that have large market shares in concentrated markets, however, should beware that promising many customers most favoured treatment may be a facilitating device discouraging each oligopolist from offering discounts. The Commission has not yet developed its theories about facilitating devices other than agreements to exchange information about detailed bargains. It could however try to control facilitating devices as an abuse of joint dominance.

The treatment of rpm under Article 81 and the former Regulations was considered at 2.8.5–2.8.5.4 above. The Commission has been hostile to the practice from the beginning,[21] although it has seldom found that a purely national system may affect trade between member states (2.8.5.4). Whether or not it does so, minimum or fixed price maintenance prevents the Regulation applying to other restraints.

---

[20] Discrimination in this industry is accepted as pro-competitive by most economists. Where there are high overhead costs and low marginal costs, more is likely to be produced and sold if those who cannot pay the average cost of the product are able to acquire it at a price that makes even a small contribution to the overheads. The arguments were unsuccessful on the facts in *Glaxo Wellcome*, 8 May 2001, OJ 2001, L302/1.

[21] In *Volkswagen Passat*, OJ 2001, L 262/14, [2001] 5 CMLR 1309, the Commission imposed a fine of 30.96 million euros on Volkswagen for taking measures to restrain dealers in Germany from discounting the recommended resale price of a new model for nearly three years. It did, however, also find that there were various practices discouraging dealers in Italy from exporting to Germany.

A restraint on publishing prices in advertisements or the internet is not black listed. National law should, however, be watched on this issue.

The Regulation does not exempt most agreements between competitors, so collective rpm does not have to be included as a hard core restraint (2.8.5.2 above).

4.2.2 Maximum RPM

The imposition of minimum and fixed rpm are hard core restraints listed in Article 4(a), but imposing maximum resale prices is not. In *Kahn v State Oil*,[22] the US Supreme Court expressly reversed its earlier case law treating maximum rpm as illegal. It observed that if the vendor had any market power it would be passed on to an exclusive dealer, which might raise prices to a level that harmed both consumers and the supplier, neither of which had an incentive to increase the dealers' margins. Maximum rpm may prevent double marginalisation, explained at 1.2.4.2 above. Recommendations as to price are hard core only if they "amount to" fixed or minimum prices "as a result of pressure from or incentives offered by any of the parties."

4.2.3 Indirectly Affecting Resale Prices

Following the introductory words of Article 4, Guideline 47 makes it clear that not only is the setting of a minimum resale price a hard core restraint, but so are many indirect ways of maintaining prices. It seems, however, from the introductory words of Article 4(b) that there must be collusion to bring the provision into play.

Guideline 47 states:

> . . . However, RPM can also be achieved through indirect means. Examples of the latter are an agreement fixing the distribution margin, fixing the maximum level of discount the distributor can grant from a prescribed price level, making the grant of rebates or reimbursement of promotional costs by the supplier subject to the observance of a given price level, linking the prescribed resale price to the resale prices of competitors, threats, intimidation, warnings, penalties, delay or suspension of deliveries[23] or contract terminations in relation to observance of a given price level.
>
> Direct or indirect means of achieving price fixing can be made more effective when combined with measures to identify price-cutting distributors, such as the implementation of a price monitoring system, or the obligation on retailers to report other members of the distribution network who deviate from the standard price level.

---

[22] 522 US 3 (1997).

[23] Delay or suspension might amount to a vertical agreement if intended as a penalty, to induce dealers not to undercut. Even when such a measure does not amount to a vertical agreement in the light of *Bayer* v. *Commission* (4.1.4 above), however, it might be argued that delay prevents the application of the Regulation to the dealership agreement. In Valentine's view, however, the agreement would not have the restriction of the buyer's pricing as its object, although the supplier might.

Similarly, direct or indirect price fixing can be made more effective when combined with measures which may reduce the buyer's incentive to lower the resale price, such as the supplier printing a recommended resale price on the product or the supplier obliging the buyer to apply a most-favoured-customer clause.

The same indirect means and the same "supportive" measures can be used to make maximum or recommended prices work as RPM. However, the provision of a list of recommended prices or maximum prices by the supplier to the buyer is not considered in itself as leading to RPM. . . . [We have divided part a very long paragraph into four to make it easier to follow.]

Problems may arise when franchisees or other retailers rarely sell below a recommended price. Their agreements may have been saved by a late addition at the end of Article 4(a) which excludes recommended prices from the list of hard core restraints if they do not amount to a fixed or minimum price,

as a result of pressure from, or incentives offered by, any of the parties.

Few franchisees are likely to depart from a recommended price which is indicated in advertising, but the franchisor does not have to provide sanctions or incentives. Guideline 47 states that the provision of a list of recommended prices is not in itself to be treated as rpm, although printing a recommended price on the product may be.

It is hoped that the provision of promotional material, whether on national or regional television, in the press or for the retailers' premises, stating a recommended price is not treated as pressure or an incentive to abide by it. Otherwise, franchising would not often be exempted. Nor would cooperative buying schemes organised by trade associations of small retailers which frequently achieve scale economies by providing their members with advertising material.[24]

Moreover, in the absence of absolute territorial protection, one may argue that franchising rarely infringes Article 81(1) because 1) most franchised systems have little market power and 2) the provision of advertising material is a reasonable ancillary restraint.[25]

Guideline 48 adds that restraining an agent from sharing its commission with clients is to be treated as a hard core restraint. Agency agreements seldom infringe Article 81(1) when the agent is integrated into the organisation of its principle and incurs little financial or commercial risk (2.8.4 above), in which case even limits on sharing commission do not infringe Article 81(1).

[24] Expressly allowed by Article 2(2). Note that such arrangements may not infringe Article 81(1) when the network has little market power, 3.4.7 above. Nevertheless, there may sometimes be other provisions requiring exemption.

[25] *Pronuptia de Paris GmbH* v. *Pronuptia de Paris Irmgard Schillgalis*, Case 161/84) [1986] ECR 353 (2.7.2 above), paras. 15, 24, 25 and 27.

4.2.4 National Legislation Imposing RPM

For some products, national legislation has required producers to impose minimum prices and made it illegal for dealers to sell far below the retail prices set (2.8.5.3 above). Such legislation protects the traditional trade from low cost competition from supermarkets and other discounters. Its object is to raise prices.

On the other hand, the Community institutions have not objected to national laws intended to set retail prices. Where the product is homogenous, such as petrol of a specified grade, it is clear that laws setting prices are not contrary to Article 81 combined with Articles 3(g) and 10.[26] Should the position be different for heterogenous products, where the state has to delegate to the supplier the fixing of the actual resale price? *Van Eycke Pascal* v. *ASPA NV*[27] seems to have been ignored in *Echirolles Distribution SA* v. *Association de Dauphiné and Others*[28] (2.8.5.3 above).

4.2.5 Policy and RPM

From the earliest days, the Commission has opposed rpm (2.8.5.1 above), originally because price fixing is one of the kinds of agreement expressly prohibited by Article 81(1) and national systems supported by export restraints are particularly likely to partition the Common Market and recently for the reasons given in 1.2.2.3 above. The ECJ has repeatedly ruled that rpm restricts competition, but requires a possible effect on trade between member states to be established.

Economists have varied over time as to the appropriate policy. They are agreed that where there are horizontal elements, or even when rpm facilitates tacit collusion between competitors, it should be forbidden (1.2.3.2 above). In other circumstances, any disadvantages may be outweighed by providing inducements to dealers to provide opportunities for browsing and other services.

4.2.6 Conclusion on RPM

Unless an effect of the agreement as a whole on inter-state trade can be avoided, rpm whether imposed directly or indirectly, is clearly dangerous and difficult to justify. Little territorial protection can be granted to protect one dealer from others taking a free ride (4.3–4.3.1.2 below). It is anomalous that for competition reasons, for the supplier itself to provide services at the point of sale enables it to maintain the retail price, although that is likely to be less efficient than encouraging dealers to do so.

---

[26] *Cullet and Another* v. *Centre Leclerc, Toulouse (SA Sodinord)*, Case 231/83 [1985] ECR 305.
[27] Case 267/86 [1988] ECR 4769.
[28] 2 October 2000, Case C-9/99.

4.3 TERRITORIAL AND CUSTOMER PROTECTION—ARTICLE 4(B) & GUIDELINES 49–51

The other black listed provisions are various other categories of post-sales restraints.[29] Article 4(b) lists as a hard core restraint territorial and customer protection:

> (b) the restriction of the territory into which, or the customers to whom, the buyer may sell the contract goods or services, except: . . .

Absolute territorial protection has long been a "no-no" under EC competition law (2.2 and 2.7.1 above) although, as was argued in *Nungesser*,[30] the doctrine of exhaustion of intellectual property rights prevents contractual protection being extended to subsequent traders through the exercise of intellectual property rights. Consequently, any territorial protection is not absolute.

Following the introductory words of Article 4 (4.1.3 above), Guideline 49 states that indirect restraints, incentives and deterrents are relevant as well as outright prohibitions. The case law under Article 81 may be invoked to establish export deterrents.

In *Glaxo Wellcome*,[31] the Commission condemned as contrary to article 81 a dual pricing system according to which more was charged to Spanish wholesalers for medicines exported to other Member States than for those sold to the home trade. This had the object of reducing the incentives for the wholesalers to export (para. 116) and was analogous to an export ban (para. 118). The Commission cited its decision in *Distillers*[32] (para. 118). It went on to cite other decisions where dual pricing had been treated as a restriction by object (paras. 119 & 124–125). It stated clearly that there is no need for the Commission to establish the effects of restrictions by object although, for the sake of completeness, it went on to appraise the effects of the practice.

The interest of the case is that the Commission did not accept the arguments that the pharmaceutical industry should be treated differently. It spends more on r & d than any other industry not supported by research contracts, so has high overheads and low average variable costs.[33] Economists are in favour of price discrimination in such a market as it leads to larger sales. This presupposes that arbitrage can be controlled. The distortion is due to the price control exercised by

---

[29] Contrast *US* v. *Arnold Schwinn & Co*, 388 US 365, (1967), since reversed by the Supreme Court in *Continental TV Inc.* v. *GTE Sylvania Inc.*, 433 US 36, (1977) after cogent criticism. Market integration was never a major goal of US antitrust law.

[30] *Nungesser (LG) KG and Kurt Eisele* v. *Commission,* Case 258/78 [1982] ECR 2015, para. 62.

[31] 8 May 2001, OJ 2001, L302/1.

[32] *The Distillers Company Ltd.,* Case 78/163/EEC, OJ 1978, L50/16 [1978] 1 CMLR 400. On appeal, *The Distillers Co. Ltd.* v. *Commission,* Case (30/78, [1980] ECR 2229.

[33] See Derek Ridyard and D. Lewis, "Parallel Trade in Patented Medicines—Economics in Defence of Market Segmentation," [1988] *Int Trade LR* 14, and "What Price is Right? Lessons from the UK Calls to Mobile Inquiry, Lexecon Competition Memo, 12 Mar. 1999, www.lexecon.co.uk.

member states not to Glaxo's policy. Moreover, as argued in *Organon*,[34] the price reductions that parallel trade would induce would benefit only the parallel traders, not consumers.

The Commission found that the existence of divergent national price legislation does not exclude the principle of free movement of goods, nor the application of the EC competition rules. It argued that Spanish price control does not fully determine prices, the level of the regulatory maximum price caps can be negotiated and was negotiated for the four products that are the main candidates for parallel trade. Parallel trade is affected more by currency fluctuations than price controls.[35]

Glaxo has appealed, arguing also that its conditions of sale do not amount to an agreement.[36]

The question arises whether rationing dealers to the amount likely to be demanded in their area or by their customer group is caught. There is no definition of "agreement" in the Regulation, although Article 2(1) calls an agreement or concerted practice a "vertical agreement", but the CFI in cartel cases has not distinguished sharply between the two concepts. Guideline 49 clearly mentions "agreements or concerted practices," but Article 4 does not.

It is thought that in the light of *Bayer* v. *Commission*[37] (2.1 and 4.1.4 above) there must be a meeting of minds between the supplier and its dealers to constitute even a concerted practice. Otherwise, there is no vertical agreement having the object of restraining sales within the meaning of the introductory words of Article 4. If the dealer is persuaded not to export by the threat of withholding supplies, there may well be an agreement, but if it is made impossible for the dealer to export, without any persuasion or threats, there seems to be no agreement or concerted practice. The Commission has appealed against the judgment of the CFI and meanwhile it will try to condemn unilateral conduct under Article 82 where the firm is dominant. There is the danger that it may allege collective dominance when the suppliers of substitute medicines each adopt unilateral practices to reduce parallel trade.

As for rpm,[38] monitoring systems aggravate the risk of indirect methods of partitioning markets being treated as hard core. Guideline 49 adds that obligations on the reseller relating to the display of the supplier's brand name is not classified as hard core, probably as a result of the judgment of the ECJ in *Pronuptia de Paris GmbH* v. *Pronuptia de Paris Irmgard Schillgalis*.[39]

---

[34] See "Comment" by John Ratliff (1997) *ICCLR* 44–45.
[35] See the perceptive annual review of recent developments in EC Competition Law by John Ratliff to be published in *International Company and Commercial Law Review* in Jan./Feb. 2002.
[36] OJ 2001, C275/17.
[37] Case T-41/96, 26 October 2000, [2001] 4 CMLR 4, appeal pending.
[38] Guideline 47.
[39] Case 161/84 [1986] ECR 353, (2.8.2 above).

4.3.1 First Exception—Exclusive Territory or Customer Group—Article 4(b) first indent

The four exceptions to Article 4(b) are explained in Guideline 50. The first indent of Article 4(b) excepts from the list of hard core restraints,

> —the restriction of active sales into the exclusive territory or to an exclusive customer group reserved to the supplier or allocated by the supplier to another buyer, where such a restriction does not limit sales by the customers of the buyer, . . .

To restrain active sales under the Regulation, a supplier must reserve an exclusive territory or customer group either for itself or its other dealers. It was not clear whether a sole dealer can be protected from active sales by other dealers when the supplier is free to sell within the dealer's territory as well.[40] From Guideline 50, it now seems that he can. A dealer with prime responsibility for a particular territory or customer group, however, cannot be protected under the Regulation from even active sales by other dealers. There is a perverse incentive encouraging suppliers to provide more protection by granting an exclusive territory if they want to protect a dealer from even active sales.

In the *Follow up to the Green Paper*[41] the Commission said at 2.2 that some combinations of restraints should be viewed positively. For instance, a combination of exclusive distribution and a ban on active sales may overcome a free rider problem, an exclusive territory and maximum resale price maintenance may prevent double marginalisation (1.2.4.2 above).

The Regulation does not specifically mention that passive sales cannot be restricted, but the guidelines do. It is also implied by the Regulation which lists no-poaching clauses as hard core and excepts from that only active sales. Guidelines 50 and 51 explain the first exception:

> 50. . . . A territory or customer group is exclusively allocated when the supplier agrees to sell its product only to one distributor for distribution in a particular territory or to a particular customer group and the exclusive distributor is protected against active selling into his territory or to his customer group by the supplier and all other buyers of the supplier inside the Community.

The specific exception of exclusive customer groups is new in this Regulation[42] and very welcome. Nevertheless, the protection is limited to active sales and with the advent of the internet the protection in many markets is minimal. Where different customer groups buy through different trade channels providing different services, the only way of encouraging a distributor to invest in attracting each

---

[40] **Romano Subiotto** and **Filippo Amato** "Preliminary Analysis of the Commission's Reform Concerning Vertical Restraints," [2000] June, *World Competition Law and Economics Review* 5, 18.

[41] *Communication on the Application of the EC Competition rules to Vertical Restraints Follow-up to the Green Paper on Vertical Restraints*, OJ 1998, C365/3 (2.10 above).

[42] Under earlier regulations, however, the reseller could be restrained from selling to anyone outside its territory, whether or not to protect an exclusive territory.

group of customers may be to isolate the channels. Field of use restrictions in licences of intellectual property may have this function and are permitted under the technology licensing regulation.[43]

Where a staggered launch is planned for a new product, the territories and customer groups to be exploited later may initially be reserved for the supplier. As it appoints an exclusive distributor for another territory, active sales thither may still be banned. The exclusive status of a territory may change over time. "Exclusive territory" is not defined in the Regulation, only in Guideline 50.

Guideline 50 continues:

> The supplier is allowed to combine the allocation of an exclusive territory and an exclusive customer group by for instance appointing an exclusive distributor for a particular customer group in a certain territory. This protection of exclusively allocated territories or customer groups must, however, permit passive sale to such territories or customer groups.

The exceptions to the list of hard core restraints resemble the white lists of the earlier Regulations,[44] but there is no provision that terms of the same kind but more limited scope are included in the exceptions. The supplier may promise in three separate agreements to supply a product only to A for sale to hospitals in Belgium, to supply it only to B for sale to pharmacists there and to C for sale to the veterinary outlets in Belgium and protect each dealer by imposing a ban on active sales on the other two. A single arrangement to sell to A, B and C for resale to anyone in Belgium appears not to be included by the Guideline, even if there is a promise not to supply any further dealers if A, B and C compete. A and B might be potential competitors in which event their agreement would not qualify for the group exemption under Article 2(4), but C probably would not.

The terms "active" and "passive" are not defined in the regulation, but are in Guidelines 50 and 51. Posting an offer on a web site must be permitted in the languages of any member states. Unsolicited emails to specific firms or customer groups may, however, be restricted.

> For the application of Article 4(b) of the BER, the Commission interprets "active" and "passive" sales as follows:
>
> — "active sales" mean
>
>> [1] actively approaching individual customers inside another distributor's exclusive territory or exclusive customer group by for instance direct mail or visits; or
>>
>> [2] actively approaching a specific customer group or customers in a specific territory allocated exclusively to another distributor through advertisement in media or other promotions specifically targeted at that customer group or targeted at customers in that territory; or

---

[43] OJ 1996, L31/2, [1996] 4 CMLR 405, Art. 2(1)(8).
[44] See, e.g., Article 2(1) of the Technology Transfer Regulation, OJ 1996, L31/2, [1996] 4 CMLR 405, [1996] 4 EIPR Supp. iv.

[3] establishing a warehouse or distribution outlet in another distributor's exclusive territory.

— "Passive" sales mean responding to unsolicited requests from individual customers including delivery of goods or services to such customers. General advertising or promotion in media or on the Internet that reaches customers in other distributors' exclusive territories or customer groups but which is a reasonable way to reach customers outside those territories or customer groups, for instance to reach customers in non-exclusive territories or in one's own territory, are passive sales.
[We have divided a long paragraph to make it easier to digest.]

Other questions remain undecided. For instance, is paying a fee to a search engine to have one's advertisements come up first an active or passive sale?

Now that it is so easy for customers to click on to advertisements on the internet and order products with their credit cards, protection from active sales is of little value for products which can conveniently be mailed and which few customers want to inspect.

51. Every distributor must be free to use the Internet to advertise or to sell products. A restriction on the use of the Internet by distributors could only be compatible with the BER to the extent that promotion on the Internet or sales over the Internet would lead to active selling into other distributors' exclusive territories or customer groups.

In general, the use of the Internet is not considered to be a form of active sales into such territories or customer groups, since it is a reasonable way to reach every customer. The fact that it may have effects outside one's own territory or customer group results from the technology, i.e. the easy access from everywhere. . . .

This Guideline suggests that a prohibition of advertisements on the internet is not allowed. There is no mention of justification save for the exceptions to Article 4(b). In *Yves Saint Laurent*,[45] the Commission closed its file against the company, only when it arranged to end its prohibition on selective distributors using the internet. Provided dealers already have a physical shop, they may now use the internet.

The reason for treating sales on the internet as not being active does not allow for any of the reasons usually given in favour of permitting vertical restraints. It is a return to formalism. If a market analysis were being applied, one would want to know how much protection the dealer required to induce the optimal amount and kind of investment and how much protection the cost of freight would provide.[46] The resulting uncertainty has been avoided.

51. . . . If a customer visits the web site of a distributor and contacts the distributor and if such contact leads to a sale, including delivery, then that is considered passive selling.

The language used on the web site or in the communication plays normally no role in that respect. . . .

[45] IP/01/713, 17 May 2001.
[46] Alternatively, the Chicago view might be that the supplier has no interest in giving more protection than is needed to induce investment by the dealer, although in chapter 1, some limitations to this view were described.

The Commission treats this like a telephone call to a different language area, answered in the language of the caller. This goes very far. If the exclusive distributor for the UK maintains a web site in German, that is not treated as actively selling in Germany even if it can have no object other than to solicit orders from the territories of the German or Austrian exclusive distributors. Jochen Burrichter[47] suggests, however, that this might be treated as active selling into the territory of an exclusive distributor and exempted.

He does not, however, go as far as to suggest that internet buyers constitute a specific customer group reserved to the supplier or allocated to another buyer.[48] Buyers on the internet are neither a specific nor fixed group of customers.

Guideline 51 continues:

> 51. . . . Insofar as a web site is not specifically targeted at reaching customers primarily inside the territory or customer group exclusively allocated to another distributor, for instance with the use of banners or links in pages of providers specifically available to these exclusively allocated customers, the website is not considered a form of active selling.
>
> However, unsolicited e-mails sent to individual customers or specific customer groups are considered active selling.
>
> The same considerations apply to selling by catalogue.
>
> Notwithstanding what has been said before, the supplier may require quality standards for the use of the Internet site to resell its goods, just as the supplier may require quality standards for a shop or for advertising and promotion in general. The latter may be relevant in particular for selective distribution.
>
> An outright ban on Internet or catalogue selling is only possible if there is an objective justification.
>
> In any case, the supplier cannot reserve to itself sales and/or advertising over the Internet. [We have divided this guideline too.]

Sometimes a dealer on the internet requires little margin on which to operate because of the chance to advertise. So the supplier can no longer avoid the provisions by selling to the customers it wants at a price nearly as low as those it charges its dealers.

The territorial protection permitted under this Regulation is narrower than under the former Regulation, no. 1983/83, in that only the supplier or exclusive dealers may be protected from even active sales. In the old days, an exclusive distributor could be restrained from active sales anywhere outside its territory. Now any distributor, exclusive or otherwise, may be restrained from selling into an exclusive sales territory or customer group. Those without an exclusive sales territory or customer group, however, cannot be protected.

An exclusive technology licensee can no longer be protected from dealers, although he may have to bear the risky sunk cost of establishing a production line as well as of developing a market—the triumph of formalistic theology over

---

[47] **Burrichter** "Vertical Restraints and E-Commerce," [2000] *Fordham Corporate Law Institute*, 131, 145.
    [48] *Ibid.*

common sense.[49] Agreements in force at the end of May 2000 remained exempt until the end of 2001 if they qualified under Regulation 1983/83, but undertakings granting technology licences to supply parts of Europe and using distributors in other parts should reconsider their distribution agreements and may even be discouraged from producing anywhere unless they can raise sufficient capital to produce for the whole Common Market: a thoroughly perverse disincentive.

Protection even of exclusive dealers may not be easy to organise. Need each dealer be told which other territories are exclusive and advised of changes as they occur, or is it enough for the supplier to reserve exclusively for itself all territories and customer groups that are not currently being supplied, until exclusive dealers are appointed? Since the protection against active sales is so slight for products that can be sold on the net, organising the restraint may not be worth while at all. This may make it even more difficult for brand owners of complex or prestigious brands to compete in ambience or by encouraging dealers or licensees to provide services.

In no case can the supplier rely on its trade marks or other intellectual property rights to prevent parallel trade, once goods have been sold in the EEA[50] by it or with its consent. The rights will be exhausted. Nor can the supplier require the main distributor to restrain its dealers from selling, even actively outside its exclusive territory into that of another exclusive dealer.

> 50. . . . However, a prohibition imposed on all distributors to sell to certain end users is not classified as a hardcore restriction if there is an objective justification related to the product, such as a general ban on selling dangerous substances to certain customers for reasons of safety or health. It implies that also the supplier himself does not sell to those customers. Nor are obligations on the reseller relating to the display of the supplier's brand name classified as hardcore.

This exception is justifiable in a vertical agreement as long as the market is not concentrated. It would be worrying if it enabled all the suppliers to maintain a similar dealers' list when this was not really necessary.[51] Even if it were, in most markets it might be safer to control the outlets by national or regional legislation. If the market is concentrated, or a similar list is maintained by all the manufacturers, there might be good cause to withdraw the exemption pursuant to Article 6 or 7 for fear that the list is unduly narrow.

The exception from Article 4(b) of the Regulation by guideline 50 is of dubious validity (3.2 above). Restrictions justified on grounds of safety may not themselves infringe Article 81(1), but Article 4 prevents the application of the Regulation to

---

[49] Valentine made this objection to those in charge of preparing the Regulation eleven months before it was adopted.

[50] Protocol 28 of the EEA Treaty. The European Economic Area includes all the member states of the EC and also Norway, Iceland and Liechtenstein.

[51] In the UK the Monopolies Commission condemned lists of legitimate traders in goods or services drawn up by trade associations in wide term in the 1950s and when this competence was transferred to the Restrictive Practices Court it also condemned them save for the judgment in ABTA.

other provisions in the agreement, such as the exclusive territory or consumer group allocated to a dealer.

One problem that arose under the earlier Regulations with limited white lists does not exist under Regulation 2790/99: one may now promise each distributor that the permissible restraint on active sale will be imposed on all the others. It is not forbidden, so is exempt.

4.3.1.1 Protection between distributors and technology licensees

The lack of protection possible under Regulation 2790/99 for technology licensees makes no sense. Small brand owners may not be able to invest in a plant large enough to supply the whole Common Market, and may have to find a licensee to supply part of it if their innovations are to be exploited.

Technology licensees can be restrained under Regulation 240/96[52] from selling actively or passively into a territory reserved to the licensor, for ten years where substantial, secret know-how remains, or, where patents are licensed, for the life of the patent in both the territory licensed and that being protected, Article 1(1)(3). The licensor can reserve to itself all territories where it has not granted a technology licence. Where the holder of technology treats the whole Common Market in the same way, the different amount of protection allowed may not seem absurd, but when the holder produces for some parts of the common market and licenses for the rest, the situation is anomalous.

One might complain further on policy grounds that the first exception to Article 4(b) encourages firms to grant exclusive territories to dealers. A brand owner might prefer to grant less protection to each dealer, imposing an area of prime responsibility or supplying directly only a few dealers, but then it cannot restrain other dealers from even active sales into the territory.[53]

4.3.1.2 Permitted protection narrowly construed

The permissible restraint on active sales under Article 2(2)(c) of Regulation 1983/83 (since expired) was narrowly construed by the Commission. Dealers might be restrained from making sales into the reserved territories, but the Commission took the view in *La Maison des Bibliotheques* that a supplier could not be restrained from itself selling passively to end users.[54] Under that Regulation there was a limited white list. Under the new Regulation, anything not excluded by Article 4 or 5 is included. Article 4(b) does not list as hard core any restraints on the supplier. So, for the future, we can forget the informal decision in *La Maison des Bibliotheques.*

---

[52] Commission Regulation 240/96 for Technology Transfer, OJ 1996, L31/2, [1996] 4 CMLR 405, Art. 1.

[53] See discussion of the question asked by **Mark Patterson**, "Vertical restraints under EC law," in **Barry Hawk** (ed.) [2000] *Fordham Corporate Law Institute*, 217, 243–45.

[54] *La Maison des Bibliotheques*, [1984] 1 CMLR 261; IP(84)16; *14th Report on Competition Policy*, para. 68. This informal decision was controversial.

In *Tipp-ex,*[55] Clause 14 restrained each dealer from selling within its territory to other dealers who might sell into the territory of another exclusive dealer. The Commission condemned this at paragraph 62 because the restraint was aimed at conferring absolute territorial protection on the distributors in their allotted territories. It added that it prevented Regulation 67/67 (now expired), which in this respect was the same as Regulation 1983/83, from applying.

This precedent probably applies to Regulation 2790/99. The provision comes within Article 4(b) and not within any of the limited exceptions.

4.3.2 Second Exception—Protection of Retailers from Wholesalers—Article 4(b) second indent and Guideline 52

The next three indents allow restraints on passive as well as active sales. They are not further explained in the guidelines.

The second exception to the list of hard core restraints in Article 4(b) is:

—the restriction of sales to end users by a buyer operating at the wholesale level of trade,
. . .

It may be intended to preserve the German distinction between different levels of trade. A wholesaler may be restrained from selling by retail as it is considered unfair to earn a double margin and use it to undercut a retailer. In *Metro I,*[56] the ECJ cleared such a restriction. This is hard for common lawyers to understand. Huge cost savings resulted from the confusion of wholesaling and retailing by multiple retailers that perform both functions. There is, however, no need to take advantage of the exception to the black list. The German law of unfair competition does not override EC Competition law.[57] Only if German law applies to the contract will it be relevant.

4.3.3 Third Exception—Selective Distribution—Article 4(b) third indent

Suppliers of branded complex or prestigious products often want to ensure control over the retail outlets where their goods are sold, to ensure an appropriate ambience or the availability of skilled advice or other services.

---

[55] OJ 1987, L222/1; [1989] 4 CMLR 425; confirmed by the ECJ in (279/87) [1990] ECR 261. The inconsistency between the text of the Regulation on the one hand and the guideline and the decision in *Tipp-ex* on the other may create difficulties for national courts. At para. 46 of its judgment in *Delimitis,* (2.7.3 above) the Court warned national courts not to modify the scope of group exemptions, yet in the next paragraph, it stressed the importance of avoiding conflicting decisions. If the Commission is not interpreting the Regulations according to their terms, there will be conflicting decisions when a national court follows their terms.

[56] Case 26/76 [1977] ECR 1875, para. 34.

[57] *IFTRA Rules for Producers of Virgin Aluminium (Re),* OJ 1975, L228/3, [1975] 2 CMLR D20 and *IFTRA rules on glass containers—Re European Glass Manufacturers,* OJ 1974, L160/1, [1974] 2 CMLR D50.

The third indent excepts from the list of hard core restraints:

—the restriction of sales to unauthorized distributors by the members of a selective distribution system, . . .

This exception is broader than the case law of the ECJ under Article 81(1) that started with *Metro* v. *Commission I*[58] (2.8.1–2.8.1.5 above). An undertaking that is not dominant is under no Community duty to supply third parties[59] but, according to many Commission decisions and the ECJ, to instruct one dealer not to supply non-approved dealers does infringe Article 81(1) unless the criteria for approval are specified, qualitative, proportionate and applied without discrimination. They must be appropriate to the products being distributed and no stricter than is reasonably necessary. Misleadingly, this is called selective distribution. It remains a safe harbour for those outside the group exemption, at least unless too much of the market is controlled by selective distribution systems (2.8.1.2.3 above).

To qualify under the doctrine of the ECJ, there must be no quantitative criteria, such as a limitation on the number of retailers. The Court's exclusion from Article 81(1) was, therefore of limited value, because usually investment is required to qualify under the specified criteria. A brand owner could not induce promotion by an approved dealer by requiring a promise from its other approved dealers not to appoint more than the local demand would warrant.

The definition of "selective distribution system" in Article 1(d) of the Regulation "for the purposes of the Regulation", however, differs from that used hitherto by the Court. It reads:

"Selective distribution system" means a distribution system where the supplier undertakes to sell the contract goods or services, either directly or indirectly, only to distributors selected on the basis of specified criteria and where these distributors undertake not to sell such goods or services to unauthorised distributors;

Selective distribution networks based on quantitative criteria are not excluded from the group exemption provided that the criteria are specified. The criteria need not be proportionate though there may be no incentive for suppliers to impose criteria that are not reasonably necessary. If the criteria are specified, resale to non-approved dealers can be restrained under the Regulation, but Article 4(c) and (d) prevents the Regulation applying to selective distribution unless cross sales between distributors are permitted as well as active and passive sales to end users. It is not easy to maintain different price levels in different member states through selective distribution.

While restraints on sales to unauthorised distributors are permitted, active or passive sales to approved dealers and consumers cannot be restrained even to protect the supplier or its exclusive dealers (Guideline 53 and 4.4 below). This pre-

---

[58] Case 26/76 [1977] ECR 1875.
[59] There may be duties to supply under national law, for instance to avoid the crime in France of *refus de vente*. Moreover, the Commission may infer collusion from refusals to supply parallel traders.

vents selective distribution being combined with exclusive territories or customer groups at the same level of trade because any approved dealer must be allowed to deal with the others. At least any exclusivity will be fragile unless products do not pass through further traders.

4.3.4 Fourth Exception—Protection of Component Suppliers—Article 4(b) Fourth indent

The final exception from Article 4(b) is:

—the restriction of the buyer's ability to sell components, supplied for the purposes of incorporation, to customers who would use them to manufacture the same type of goods as those produced by the supplier;

Guideline 52 states that "component" includes any intermediate goods and "incorporation" refers to the use of any input to produce goods. Raw materials are included as well as specially designed goods, but services are not.

The protection is limited as the buyer must be allowed to sell the components to traders, who may sell on a large scale to the competitors of the supplier in the replacement market on a narrow margin.

The reason for this exception is not stated. It may be because component makers often discriminate in favour of original equipment which tends to be more elastic to price than replacement parts. The component maker would not want the components he may sell at little more than average variable cost to compete with him in the more lucrative replacement market where it hopes to recover the overheads in designing and marketing the component.

4.4 SELECTIVE DISTRIBUTION—ARTICLE 4(C) & (D), GUIDELINES 53 AND 54

Article 4(c) lists as hard core restraints:

the restriction of active or passive sales to end users by members of a selective distribution system operating at the retail level of trade, without prejudice to the possibility of prohibiting a member of the system from operating out of an unauthorised place of establishment.

Selective distribution, as defined in Article 1(d) (4.3.3 above), includes most franchises, since the franchisor usually permits sale only to retail customers or other franchisees. It is usually adopted at the retail level. Unlike the Commission's decision in *Givenchy*,[60] a requirement that specific brands be sold by retailers was deleted from the draft Regulation. Guideline 53 says that Article 4(c)

---

[60] OJ 1992, L236/11, [1993] 5 CMLR 579 at p. 13 of OJ, where an exemption was granted only when the requirement that retailers should sell specific brands was deleted from the conditions for approval.

means that dealers in a selective distribution system, as defined in Article 1(d) of the BER, cannot be restricted in the users or purchasing agents acting on behalf of these users to whom they may sell. For instance, also in a selective distribution system the dealer should be free to advertise and sell with the help of the Internet. Selective distribution may be combined with exclusive distribution provided that active and passive selling is not restricted anywhere.[61] The supplier may therefore commit itself to supplying only one dealer or a limited number of dealers in a given territory.

54. In addition, in the case of selective distribution, restrictions can be imposed on the dealer's ability to determine the location of its business premises. Selected dealers may be prevented from running their[62] business from different premises or from opening a new outlet in a different location. If the dealer's outlet is mobile ("shop on wheels"), an area may be defined outside which the mobile outlet cannot be operated.

The location clauses expressly allowed by Guideline 54 do not infringe Article 81(1) unless, in combination with an exclusive territory, they provide absolute territorial protection.[63] If they provide absolute territorial protection, it is thought that Article 4(b) applies, subject to the exceptions in the four indents thereto. The Articles of the Regulation must prevail over an incomplete guideline. It is understood that the Commission considers that a location clause cannot be used to restrain a dealer from opening in another member state an outlet that meets the specified criteria without losing the benefit of the group exemption.

Will the block exemption apply if a selective dealer is forbidden to sell save on a specific internet address? The Regulation speaks of a restraint on "operating out of an unauthorised place of establishment." Guideline 54 of "running their business from different premises." Is one internet address a different place of establishment from another? If a German dealer is required to operate from an address in Barcelona, it can be restrained from opening a shop on Berlin. It should be permitted to restrain it from setting up a website in German.

Article 4(d) lists as hard core:

the restriction of cross-supplies between distributors within a selective distribution system, including between distributors operating at different levels of trade.

Restrictions on cross-supplies between dealers were allowed under the old Regulation 1983/83. They helped a brand owner to benefit from different prices in different member states, as dealers in the higher priced area were not allowed to buy from dealers where prices were lower. To qualify under the new group exemption, an approved retailer in territory A must be able to sell to an approved dealer, even a wholesaler, in territory B where prices may be higher.

---

[61] The exclusive distribution permitted, without any restriction on active or passive sales, does not give much protection, unless freight or some other natural barrier operates to restrain sales through more than one dealer.

[62] **Jochen Burrichter**, "Vertical Restraints and E-Commerce," in **Barry Hawk** (ed.), [2000] *Fordham Corporate Law Institute* 146.

[63] *Pronuptia de Paris GmbH* v. *Pronuptia de Paris Irmgard Schillgalis*, Case 161/84, [1986] ECR 353, paras. 19, 23 and 24.

The question arises whether an approved dealer may be restrained from making active sales into the territory of an exclusive dealer when a system of selective distribution is in place. Does the first indent to Article 4(b) or Article 4(d) take priority? Since the indent is an exception only to Article 4(b), it does not except from Article 4(d). The answer must be negative.

In many decisions the Commission has refused an individual exemption to selective distribution systems with qualitative criteria unless the parties permit cross-sales. In *Pronuptia de Paris GmbH* v. *Pronuptia de Paris Irmgard Schillgalis*,[64] the ECJ's clearance of most provisions in franchising agreements was subject to each franchisee being free to sell to or buy from the others.

Both Article 4(c) and (d) can be avoided by not specifying the criteria on which authorised dealers are selected.[65] If, however, the criteria are not specified, the ECJ's clearance of simple selective distribution systems cannot apply. Nor can the third indent to Article 4(b). So it will not be possible to restrain approved dealers from supplying non-approved dealers. The supplier may select its dealers, but in the absence of specified criteria it may not restrain sale to non-approved dealers.

Most franchise systems will involve only selected retailers, so advice will have to be given on whether to specify the criteria for approval. Where the franchisees are small, they may be unlikely to want to sell to non-approved dealers. If so, there may be no need to specify the criteria in order to take advantage of the third indent to Article 4(b). It is sufficient to select only suitable franchisees. If the criteria are not specified, Article 4(c) and (d) do not apply. There is no need to permit active and passive sales to consumers anywhere or to permit cross sales between franchisees. In that event, however, it is unlikely that they would want to export.

In the absence of absolute territorial protection, franchising will escape the prohibition of Article 81(1) whether or not the criteria are specified, because franchisors are entitled to choose with whom to deal without infringing Article 81(1).[66] Provided the provisions of the contract go no further than was permitted in *Pronuptia*, there may be no need to bring the agreement within the group exemption.

4.5 COMPONENTS—ARTICLE 4(E), GUIDELINES 56 & 95

Article 4(e) prevents the application of the Regulation where a restriction is:

> agreed between a supplier of components and a buyer who incorporates those components, which limits the supplier to selling the components as spare parts to end-users or to repairers or other service providers not entrusted by the buyer with the repair or servicing of its goods.

---

[64] Case 161/84 [1986] ECR 353, para. 21 (2.8.2 above).
[65] See the definition of "selective distribution" in Article 1(d).
[66] *Pronuptia de Paris GmbH* v. *Pronuptia de Paris Irmgard Schillgalis*, Case 161/84 [1986] ECR 353, para. 20.

The French text of the second line reads "when the supplier is restrained from selling as spare parts. . ." "*lorsque le fournisseur est restreint dans la vente de ces composants . . .*" This is confirmed by Guideline 56. The English and German[67] texts are the other way round from the French. The French texts indicates concern that repairers should be able to obtain the parts, the English and German texts that other firms should be able to do so. All three texts are equally authoritative, so the matter must be left to the CFI or ECJ to decide.

Guideline 52 defines "component" broadly to include "any intermediate goods" including unprocessed materials. There is no definition in the Regulation. Guideline 56 makes it clear that firms buying components from independent suppliers, may not restrict the latter from supplying end users or repairers, confirming the French text.[68] Component producers must be allowed to supply repairers or end users. The maker of the component may, however, require its own dealers to acquire spares only from it.

Guideline 56 also makes it clear that indirect restrictions are also hard core restraints, as is also made clear by the introductory words of Article 4 (4.1.3 above).

4.6 CONCLUSION ON ARTICLE 4

4.6.1 All Hard Core Restraints Affect only Intra-Brand Competition

The strongest objection to Article 4 is that the provisions listed as hard core are all restraints on intra-brand competition, which the Commission said in the Green Paper and in Guideline 119(1) were less important where there is sufficient interbrand competition now that it is applying a more economic approach. With the 30 per cent ceiling of market share, is there any need for Article 4?

A possible answer to this criticism is that both the limitation of price cutting and the number of dealers handling a product may go further than is necessary to prevent free riding, and may delay the achievement of scale economies for new low price forms of retailing (1.2.3.4 above).

Since the ECJ treats rpm and export bans as "by their very nature" having the object of restricting competition, the onus to justify these seems to be on the person enforcing the agreement. In the US, under the rule of reason, there is no need to justify a vertical restraint unless there is significant market power and the onus is on the plaintiff. Vertical price restrictions (other than maximum prices), however, are currently being considered as *per se* illegal under US law.

---

[67] We are grateful to Christoph Huetteroth for checking the German text.

[68] Compare *Hugin—Liptons Cash Registers and Business Equipment Ltd.* v. *Hugin Kassaregister AB* OJ 1978, L22/23, [1978] 1 CMLR D19, On appeal, *Hugin Kassaregister AB* v. *Commission*, Case 22/78, [1979] ECR 1869. See also the US Supreme Court in *Eastman Kodak Co.* v. *Image Technical Services, Inc.*, 504 US 451 (1992).

4.6.2 Tying and Quantitative Criteria for Selective Distribution Allowed

A major advantage of Article 4 is that it treats very few restraints as hard core. Provided that the supplier's market share is below 30 per cent, tying (1.2.5.1.1 above) is not excluded from the exemption, despite the Commission's earlier hostile attitude. Nor is quantitative selective distribution.

Valentine is particularly delighted that tying does not prevent the application of the Regulation. The practice is seldom adopted to extend market power from one product to another because usually there is only one monopoly profit to be taken.[69] To the extent that buyers do not want to take the tied product, they will pay less for the tying product. The practice is commonly adopted for many other reasons and often benefits consumers (2.9 above).

As argued at 4.3.3 above, selective distribution on the basis of quantitative criteria and combined with an exclusive territory enables the supplier to encourage dealers to invest in providing an elegant ambience or technical and other services at the point of retail sale. The obvious incompatibility with the Common Market of a restriction on cross sales between approved dealers is listed as hard core.

4.6.3 RPM

Rpm (1.2.2.3, 2.8.5–2.8.5.4, 4.1.3 and 4.2–4.2.6 above) has raised concern in Europe as it is often based on national boundaries, with different prices in different member states. Moreover, in the 1960s, the Commission rejected Chicago views (1.1 above) that firms at different levels of trade provide complementary products and neither has an incentive to restrict the production of the other except when this is necessary to induce investment in sunk costs.

There is now concern that one cannot rely on the supplier not giving more protection than benefits consumers, because he might want to induce investments and services that are wanted only by marginal consumers. Moreover, rpm may delay the introduction of new low cost ways of distributing, by preventing stores like Walmart from taking advantage of its economies of scale to reduce prices (1.2.3.4 above).

The most easily justifiable kind of rpm is the imposition of a maximum price and this is not listed as hard core. Nor is the recommendation of fixed or minimum prices,

> provided that they do not amount to a fixed or minimum sale price as a result of pressure from, or incentives offered by, any of the parties.

---

[69] Sometimes the profits or prices of a monopolist are regulated, and tying may enable it to take the profit on a non-regulated product (1.2.5.1.1 above). Sometimes, mixed bundling may lead to incentives to sell each product at a lower price in order to reap the benefit of more sales of the other product (1.2.5.1.1 above).

There is concern that if all dealers, especially if all franchisees charge the recommended price, this might be treated as a fixed price. It is hoped, however, that even if the recommended price is advertised on television or on the premises, this would not be treated as pressure or an incentive by the supplier to abide by the recommended price. Otherwise franchising or sales by an association of small retailers would be difficult to arrange to fit the Regulation although, in the absence of market power, few franchises will infringe Article 81(1).

4.6.4 Territorial and Customer Restrictions

Territorial restraints (2.7.1, 4.1.3 and 4.3–4.3.4 above) have been treated by Commission and ECJ as infringing article 81(1) "by their very nature:" no market analysis is required. The doctrine of exhaustion once products have been sold within the EEA by or with the consent of the holder prevents the use of intellectual property rights to divide the market (2.3 above).

Why a supplier should be able to protect itself or a dealer with an exclusive territory but not an exclusive technology licensee from active sales is unclear. Moreover, the distinction between active and passive sales is arbitrary. The problem of grey goods will become far greater as the internet reduces the margin on which parallel traders can operate. Websites on which products can be ordered are cutting out middlemen in some sectors of the economy. Manufacturers or wholesalers are beginning to sell directly to consumers. It will become even more difficult to persuade retailers to supply services for technically complex products at their own expense. The problem cannot be avoided by the use of agents, as if they bear significant sunk costs, they will not be treated as genuine or their contract as outside Article 81(1).

Territorial protection is treated rather more favourably than rpm in that there are four exceptions to Article 4(b). Yet, it is widely agreed by economists that rpm is less inefficient than exclusive territories as firms can compete in other ways (1.2.3.4 above).

5

Single Branding

Article 5 prevents the Regulation applying to various provisions requiring dealers to handle mainly products obtained from a single supplier or brand owner (single branding 1.2.2.1 above). Unlike the hard core restraints listed in Article 4, however, Article 5 does not prevent other provisions in the same agreement from benefiting from the group exemption. The single branding provisions may be severed. It is important that if there are other provisions that require the exemption, a contract that may be caught by Article 5 be drafted in such a way as to be severable under national law.

The *Follow up to the Green Paper*,[1] ranked the four groups of restraints (1.2.2–1.2.2.4 above) in order of their likely harm to competition. Resale price maintenance and market partitioning headed the list, then came single branding and limited distribution.[2]

> [N]on-compete obligations [single branding] are likely to have more net negative effects than exclusive distribution. The former, by foreclosing other brands, may prevent these brands from reaching the market. The latter, while foreclosing certain buyers, does not, in general, prevent the good from reaching the final consumer.[3]

Single branding affects inter-brand competition, while exclusive distribution affects competition between dealers in the same brand. Recital 11 to the Regulation gives only two reasons for objecting to single branding without much explanation:

---

[1] *Communication on the Application of the EC Competition Rules to Vertical Restraints—Follow-up to the Green Paper on Vertical Restraints*—OJ 1998, C365/3 at 13 (2.10 above) (beginning of section III 4).

[2] Limited distribution is exempted from the black list of Article 4 when used to protect the supplier or a dealer with an exclusive territory or customer group from active sales by other dealers.

[3] Section III, 4, second para. Over the years, the Commission has attacked single branding restrictions in favour of firms with considerable market power. In its *Seventh Report on Competition Policy* for 1977, it observed that single branding, then called exclusive purchasing, enabled both supplier and buyer to plan ahead and expressed its mild objections to the practice: such agreements limit the buyer's freedom of choice and foreclose other suppliers (point 9). Valentine is glad that the limitation of choice is no longer stressed—the buyer's loyalty has usually to be paid for by granting rebates, or other bonuses. The buyer has choice when it enters into the commitment.

The Commission observed at point 12 that in *Vitamins—Hoffmann-La Roche & Co. AG* v. *Commission*, Case 85/76 [1979] ECR 461, the ECJ had condemned loyalty rebates offered by a dominant firm to customers for taking less than all their requirements from it. It had also condemned rebates given for *de facto* loyalty, even when not promised.

In order to ensure access to or to prevent collusion on the relevant market, certain conditions are to be attached to the block exemption; to this end, the exemption of non-compete obligations should be limited to obligations which do not exceed a definite duration; for the same reasons, any direct or indirect obligation causing the members of a selective distribution system not to sell the brands of particular competing suppliers should be excluded from the benefit of this Regulation.

Guideline 138 is more helpful: it repeats the objections to collusion between suppliers and foreclosure, but adds a third.

138. A non-compete arrangement is based on an obligation or incentive scheme which makes the buyer purchase practically all his requirements on a particular market from only one supplier. It does not mean that the buyer can only buy directly from the supplier, but that the buyer will not buy and resell or incorporate competing goods or services. The possible competition risks are foreclosure of the market to competing suppliers and potential suppliers, facilitation of collusion between suppliers in case of cumulative use and, where the buyers is a retailer selling to final consumers, a loss of in-store inter-brand competition. All three restrictive effects have a direct impact on inter-brand competition.

Guideline 148 adds in relation to agreements when the supplier has more than 30 per cent of the relevant market:

148. For final products, foreclosure is in general more likely to occur at the retail level, given the significant entry barriers for most manufacturers to start retail outlets just for their own products. In addition, it is at the retail level that non-compete agreements may lead to reduced in-store inter-brand competition. It is for these reasons that for final products at the retail level, significant anticompetitive effects may start to arise. . . .

When in Guideline 138 it refers to "collusion" it seems that the Commission is concerned that suppliers might collude together to encourage their dealers to boycott particular competitors (5.2.3 below).

5.1.1 "Non-Compete Obligations" for more than Five Years not Exempt

Article 5 replaces with rather more precision the provisions of Article 3(d) of the former regulation 1984/83.[4] Article 5 provides that the exemption shall not apply to various single branding restrictions:

The exemption provided for in Article 2 shall not apply to any of the following obligations contained in vertical agreements:

(a) any direct or indirect non-compete obligation, the duration of which is indefinite or exceeds five years. A noncompete obligation which is tacitly renewable beyond a period of five years is to be deemed to have been concluded for an indefinite duration. . . .

---

[4] OJ 1983, L173/7, [1983] 2 CLE 262. The most important difference is that it is only the non-compete provision that is not exempt, the other provisions in the contract may be (5.1.2 below).

The reference to direct or indirect obligations, which is found in the introductory words to Article 4 (4.1.3 and 4.2.3 above), occurs in each lettered paragraph of Article 5.

Article 1(b) defines a "non compete obligation" widely as requiring a buyer not to make, buy or sell competing goods or services or to take 80 per cent or more of its total requirements of the contract goods and their substitutes from a designated source. It also repeats the reference to "direct or indirect."

> "non-compete obligation" means any direct or indirect obligation causing the buyer not to manufacture, purchase, sell or resell goods or services which compete with the contract goods or services, or
>
> any direct or indirect obligation on the buyer to purchase from the supplier or from another undertaking designated by the supplier more than 80% of the buyer's total purchases of the contract goods or services and their substitutes on the relevant market, calculated on the basis of the value of its purchases in the preceding calendar year; [*A single sentence has been divided for ease of comprehension.*]

Lesser foreclosure, such as a restraint on selling competing goods on the internet or by catalogue seems, however, not to be forbidden.[5]

5.1.1.1 *"Direct or indirect obligation"*

The definitions in each paragraph of Article 5 and in Article 1(b) include obligations indirectly "causing the buyer not to manufacture, purchase, sell or resell goods or services which compete with the contract goods or services," as well as a direct or indirect obligation to take more than 80 per cent of the contract goods from a designated supplier. Since indirect inducements are included in the definition, granting loyalty rebates for more than five years is also outside the exemption Regulation 2790/99.[6]

5.1.1.1.1 *Guidelines on indirect foreclosure*

Guideline 58 does not far explore the concept of indirectly "causing the buyer not to" handle competing products. It does, however, end with the words:

> 58. . . . If for instance the agreement provides for a five-year non-compete obligation and the supplier provides a loan to the buyer, the repayment of that loan should not hinder the buyer from effectively terminating the non-compete obligation at the end of the 5 year period; the repayment needs to be structured in equal or decreasing instalments and not increase over time.[7] The buyer must have the possibility to repay the remaining debt where there is still an outstanding debt at the end of the non-compete obligation.

---

[5] **Jochen Burrichter**, "Vertical Restraints and E-Commerce," in **Barry Hawk**, (ed.) [2000] *Fordham Corporate Law Institute* 131, 147.

[6] As explained in n. 3 above, under Article 82, the ECJ has objected to obligations to take more than 70% of requirements from a firm in a dominant position, rebates given when a large part of requirements is in fact taken from a dominant firm and other attenuated exclusive purchasing obligations or incentives. For other examples, see 5.1.1.1.5 below.

[7] "This is without prejudice to the possibility, in the case for instance of a new distribution outlet, to delay repayment for the first one or two years until sales have reached a certain level."

Where a dealer agrees to supply mainly the products of a single supplier, it is often more efficient for the supplier than a bank to finance the development of retail premises. The supplier will have more information than a bank about how business at the outlet continues to fare and be in a better position to call in the debt before it is too late. Consequently, the risk is less and lower interest may be charged.

Article 1(b) seems to Valentine to treat an irredeemable loan as an obstacle to handling competing products. To comply with the guidelines, if the non-compete clause is to be exempt, a right to terminate a non-compete obligation after five years by repaying a loan should be provided for. This is likely to be inserted in contracts governed by English law to comply with the law relating to restraint of trade.

In *Remia*,[8] however, the ECJ confirmed the Commission's limitation of a non-compete clause to a shorter period rather than striking out a clause of excessive length as illegal.[9] So, it can be argued that a clause of excessive length is contrary to Article 81(1) only in respect of the excess. This is important because one can sever a single branding provision, and other restraints may be exempted under the Regulation.

Guideline 58, however goes further than the Regulation in suggesting that the single branding obligation is outside the Regulation even if repayment of the loan discharges the non-compete obligations at any time on reasonable notice after the five years. We would argue that to this extent the guideline cannot alter the terms of the Regulation.[10]

The Commission ignores the possibility of a new supplier financing repayment of the debt if the duty to repay discourages the buyer from switching suppliers in part or in whole. A non-compete obligation is allowed beyond five years when the reseller operates from premises provided by the supplier (Article 5(b)). The identical economic argument applies where the premises are financed by the supplier. Guideline 58 encourages the loan to be structured as a grant of the buyer's land to the supplier, leased back for 999 years subject to the loan to take advantage of the last few lines of Article 5(a). This seems unnecessarily formalistic.

Where the loan is small in relation to the business, five years may suffice for repayment but, where major reconstruction is required, it may take the dealer more than five years to repay. Given that the Regulation applies only if the supplier has a market share of under 30 per cent, the clause in qualifying agreements may well not infringe Article 81(1), so the limitation to five years may not be too serious.

---

[8] *BV and Verenigde Bedrijven Nutricia and Remia v. Commission*, Case 42/84 [1985] ECR 2545. paras. 25–36, appeal from *the Agreements of Verenigde Bedrijven Nutricia NV*, OJ 1983, L376/22, [1984] 2 CMLR 165.

[9] That case concerned a covenant not to compete with a business sold as a going concern, rather than a single branding restraint, but the issues of foreclosure are the same.

[10] See the view of the ECJ in *Neste* (5.1.1.1.3 below) that a single branding obligation lasting for a fixed period of years forecloses more than one of indefinite duration that can be abrogated by the buyer at any time on giving short notice. See also *Greene King—Roberts & Roberts v. Commission*, Case T-25/99, [2001] 5 CMLR 828, para. 77, (5.1.1.1.3 and 7.7 below)

Guideline 58 continues:

58. . . . Similarly, when the supplier provides the buyer with equipment which is not relationship-specific, the buyer should have the possibility to take over the equipment at its market asset value at the end of the non-compete obligation.

What is meant by "relationship-specific"? Often oil companies install petrol tanks and pumps on and under the retailer's forecourt. Are these relationship-specific within the meaning of Guideline 58 when they could be used for another brand of petrol? The term is not defined. A new potential supplier might be expected to provide equipment, but this is not addressed in the Regulation or guidelines. If someone else will pay for the equipment, not much of the cost would be sunk (1.2.4.1.1 above).

The application of the Regulation, however, will seldom be important since it is only when there is a barrier to entry downstream and so many dealers tied to one or other of the suppliers that a new or expanding supplier will be foreclosed and Article 81(1) will apply, and even then, only to suppliers who have contributed significantly to the foreclosure,[11] (2.7.3 above and 5.1.1.1.3 below).

5.1.1.1.2 *Commission's earlier decisions on foreclosure under Article 81*

The Commission's formal and informal interventions under Article 81 help to indicate some of the indirect ways of foreclosing competitors. In *Liebig*,[12] Liebig sold nearly 40 per cent of the spices in Belgium and three other firms sold 45 per cent between them leaving 15 per cent to a fringe of small firms. Impulse buying and sales promotion account for a large part of consumer purchases of the many spices available. Liebig's price per gram for spices was higher than that of other suppliers.

Liebig had agreements with the three largest supermarket chains and some 80 other dealers. These supermarkets agreed to sell only Liebig spices plus their own brands. One supermarket chain was also allowed to sell other brands of spices not in the Liebig range. They were required to sell Liebig's spices above items with a rapid turnover in cabinets provided with five trays, three for Liebig spices and two for the stores' own brands. Resale prices were also maintained at a level allowing a wide margin. There were rebates depending on how far sales had increased over the previous year.

McCormick complained that it had not been able to penetrate the Belgian market as a result of these practices. Single branding was condemned in the context of the other provisions, which illustrate indirect efforts to achieve dual branding.

17. The obligation in all the agreements with GB, Delhaize Frères and Sarma to sell only Liebig products, apart from spices under their own brands, is likely to prevent the purchase and sale of brands other than Liebig by the distributors concerned.

This obligation is reinforced by significant financial benefits that the rebate referred to paragraph 13 and the system of resale price maintenance afford a minimum gross profit

---

[11] *Delimitis*, Case C-234/89 [1991] ECR I-935.
[12] *Brooke Bond Liebig Limited*, OJ 1978 L53/20 [1978] 2 CMLR 116.

of 35 per cent on the resale price which may amount to almost 60 per cent of the purchase price paid by the distributor. Furthermore, a certain profit is expressly guaranteed in the contracts.

The major part of this high financial return is primarily intended to compensate these undertakings for excluding sales of spices competing with those of Liebig. This financial return therefore also restricts competition.

The market was concentrated, and Liebig supplied nearly half of it. The Commission found that the agreements restricted competition contrary to Article 81, although it might have invoked Article 82.

At points 13 and 131 of its 7th *Annual Report on Competition Policy* for 1997, the Commission described the informal proceedings in *Billiton and Metal Thermit Chemicals* and observed that

> 14. The applicability of Article 81(1) to exclusive purchasing and other such arrangements depends on whether or not the arrangement, either alone or in conjunction with other similar arrangements between the same or different firms, may appreciably affect entry to the market and sales by third parties.

5.1.1.1.3 *Judgments under Article 81*

The ECJ and CFI cannot grant an exemption, but in making a preliminary ruling the ECJ can imply that an agreement does not infringe Article 81(1). In that event, the non-application of the Regulation does not matter provided that the clause is severable from other restraints under national law. Any other provisions that may be caught by the prohibition of Article 81(1) will be exempt under the Regulation. The CFI can exercise judicial review of both Article 81(1) and (3), but refrains from interfering frequently with decisions of exemption, because it considers that they involve decisions of policy which should be made mainly by the Commission, which is in charge of the orientation of Competition policy.[13]

In *Delimitis (Stergios)* v. *Henninger Bräu*[14] the ECJ ruled that single branding provisions do not have the object of restricting competition because they enable the supplier to plan supplies and the dealer can usually negotiate some benefit in return.

Such provisions have the effect of restricting competition only when the supplier's competitors lack real and concrete opportunities to enter the market on a viable scale. This is so only if there are entry barriers downstream and so many dealers are tied to one or other of the suppliers for so long that a new supplier cannot enter the market or existing ones grow to a minimum efficient size. Moreover, the agreements of only those suppliers making a substantial contribution to the

---

[13] The ECJ normally speaks of the complex economic appraisal required under article 81(3), but John Cooke, a judge of the CFI, gave a different view. See "Changing Responsibilities and Relationships for Community and National Courts: The Implications of the White Paper," in *The Modernisation of European Competition Law: the Next Ten Years* (University of Cambridge Centre for European Legal Studies) Occasional Paper No. 4, 58, 61–63.

[14] Case C-234/89 [1991] ECR I-935 (2.7.3 above). See also *Greene King—Roberts & Roberts* v. *Commission*, Case T25/99 [2001] CMLR 828 (7.2.6.5.1 below).

"the cumulative effect produced in that respect by the totality of similar agree-ments[15] found on that market" infringe Article 81(1). There is seldom need for an exemption of a single branding clause (2.7.3 above).

In *Neste Markkinointi Oy* v. *Yötuuli Ky, and others*,[16] the question arose under Article 81(1) in respect of what characteristic must the contracts be similar when considering whether the contribution to foreclosure is substantial. The Commission argued that all agreements tying buyers to one or other of the suppliers were "similar".

Neste had many tying agreements that were for fixed terms of no more than five years and exempt under Regulation 1984/83,[17] but a few were for fixed terms that could be terminated at any time after the first 10 years by the buyer on giving a year's notice.[18] Neste sought to enforce one of these, and the question arose whether it infringed Article 81(1).

The ECJ observed that suppliers placed equipment on the premises of their dealers and that changing supplier was a technically complex matter. Consequently, one year's notice was short. It said:

> 33. . . . it must be recognised that, as the national court has suggested, fixed term con-tracts concluded for a number of years are more likely to restrict access to the market than those which may be terminated upon short notice at any time.

This contrasts with the view taken by Commission officials when drafting the group exemptions for exclusive purchasing, Regulation 1984/83 and Article 5 of Regulation 2790/99. The group exemptions do not apply to contracts of indefinite duration even if they are terminable by the dealer. The Commission has not hith-erto accepted the argument that dealers would realise that they could escape the tie by giving notice. The Court's ruling on the interpretation of Article 81(1) com-bined with the severability of single branding restraints makes the application of the group exemption unimportant.

In *Neste* the ECJ concluded that:

> 36. In those circumstances, when, as in the case before the national court, the contracts which may be terminated upon one year's notice at any time represent only a very small proportion of all the exclusive purchasing agreements entered into by a particular sup-plier, they must be regarded as making no significant contribution to the cumulative effect, for the purposes of the judgment in *Delimitis*, and therefore as not being caught by the prohibition laid down by Article 81(1) of the Treaty.

> 37. The fact of subdividing, exceptionally, a supplier's network is not arbitrary nor does it undermine the principle of legal certainty. Subdividing the network in that way results

---

[15] The ECJ used the term "similar agreements" many times, paras. 14, 19, 20, 23 and 24. without specifying in what respect the agreements are similar.

[16] Case C-214/99 7 December 2000, [2000] ECR-I 11,121 [2001] 4 CMLR 993 (7.2.6.5.1 below).

[17] Commission Regulation 1984/83—Group exemption for exclusive purchasing agreements, OJ 1983, L173/7, corrections OJ 1984, C101/2, [1983] 2 CLE 262, now expired.

[18] The failure of the Court to consider the first ten years, which had expired may slightly confirm the view taken in *Remia* that a single branding clause of excessive duration if forbidden only as to the excess.

from a factual assessment of the position held by the operator concerned on the relevant market, the aim of the assessment being, on the basis of an objective criterion of particular relevance in that it takes into account the market's distinctive features, to limit the number of cases in which a supplier's contracts are declared void to those which, together, contribute significantly to the cumulative effect of sealing off the market.

In *Greene King*,[19] the CFI went further in confirming the decision of the Commission clearing the standard leases and tied house agreements used by a small brewer supplying less than 2 per cent of the English market. Moreover, only some of its agreements, with a duration of 5 years and affecting less than 20 per cent of the beer it sold had an exclusive purchasing obligation and three other agreements had stocking requirements (para. 135).

The CFI confirmed that the relevant market was all outlets with a licence to sell alcohol for consumption on the premises and not only pubs. The exclusion of retailers followed the view of the ECJ in *Delimitis (Stergios)* v. *Henninger Bräu*,[20] but is wrong in Valentine's view. A brewer trying to attain a minimum economic scale would be able to sell in both places where the beer can be consumed on the premises and in supermarkets and other retail stores.[21]

It then found that the average duration of Greene King's leases was nine years: less than that of the major brewers. Valentine originally regretted that the CFI looked to the custom of the trade. That may be helpful in deciding the validity of commercial contracts which tend to improve with experience as problems arise in an industry which standard form contracts come address. When judging foreclosure, however, the longer the duration of the other contracts, the worse the foreclosure. The CFI was, however, judging the contribution made by Greene King to the foreclosure, so the relative duration was relevant to the formulation by the ECJ, although not to its basic reasoning about foreclosure. Any criticism must be levied against the ECJ in *Delimitis*. The test should be not so much the contribution to foreclosure as the extent by which it is increased.

Valentine is happy that the CFI looked only to those contracts of supply by Greene King that contained single branding restraints, defined widely (paras. 106 & 137). The other sales, even if substantial, do not contribute to the foreclosure or increase the foreclosing effect.

5.1.1.1.4 *The ice cream cases*

Several cases concerned major manufacturers of ice cream, most of them subsidiaries of Unilever, that supplied freezers free of charge to small retail outlets in return for an obligation to place in them only the supplier's brand of single unit ice cream, "freezer exclusivity." Sometimes retailers agreed to sell only the manufacturer's ice cream in the outlet, "outlet exclusivity." The narrow product definition by the Commission—single unit ice cream—excluded the supermarket trade

---

[19] *Roberts & Roberts* v. *Commission*, Case T25/99 [2001] 5 CMLR 828 (7.7 below).
[20] Case C-234/89 [1991] ECR I-935, para. 16.
[21] See Roemer AG in *Brasserie de Haecht SA* v. *Wilkin*, Case 23/67 [1967] ECR 407.

in blocks of ice cream to be divided by consumers and resulted in high market shares.

Mars, which was trying to introduce its brand of single unit ice cream in various countries, made several complaints to the Commission that as the result of these agreements it could not expand sales rapidly.

In *Schöller Lebensmittel GmbH & Co KG*.[22] the Commission found that "outlet exclusivity" infringed Article 81(1) and refused an exemption. The operative part of the decision did not deal with freezer exclusivity, although the reasoning was hostile. Schöller (SLG) supplied freezers to many small retailers and petrol stations in Germany and required that all "single item ice cream" sold in those outlets be acquired only from it. The Commission found that the agreements restrained each retailer from stocking other single item ice creams. It said:

> 68. The retailer undertakes to purchase contract goods only from SLG. Because of the contractual prohibition, offers of contract goods from other suppliers cannot be entertained by the retailer. Competition for the retailer between SLG and other suppliers of contract goods is precluded (restriction of inter-brand competition).

> 69. Exclusive purchasing obligations also have an indirect effect on competition between suppliers of goods throughout the relevant market (inter-brand competition). They make it more difficult or impossible to set up independent distribution structures such as are necessary if new entrants are to gain access to the relevant market or if an existing market is to be consolidated.

The Commission then devoted several pages to defining the relevant market as single item ice creams in Germany and concluded that SLG supplied over 20 per cent of these, although not all of it through outlets subject to a single branding restraint. So the agreement had appreciable effects. It did not consider what other outlets existed for competing makers of single item ice creams until deciding to refuse an exemption. It merely cited its notice on minor agreements to show that with a market share exceeding 20 per cent the agreements had appreciable effects (paras. 103–107). It followed its notice (2.4.1–2.4.1.6 above) rather than the judgment of the ECJ in *Delimitis*.

In an almost identical case involving *Langnese*,[23] which had a slightly larger share of the German market, the Commission adopted a virtually identical decision and also withdrew the benefit of the group exemption under Regulation 1984/83.[24] In *Langnese v. Commission*,[25] the CFI confirmed the decision. Langnese had an important position on the market and more than 15 per cent of the relevant product passed through its tied outlets. Moreover, more than 10 per cent passed through Schöller's tied outlets. The CFI's analysis seems to Valentine to be more appropriate than the Commission's concern with the total amounts sold by

---

[22] (93/405) OJ 1993, L183/1, [1994] 4 CMLR 51.

[23] *Langnese-Iglo GmbH & Co. KG*, OJ 1993, L183/19, [1994] 4 CMLR 51.

[24] Commission Regulation 1984/83—Group exemption for exclusive purchasing agreements, OJ 1983, L173/7, corrections OJ 1984, C101/2, [1983] 2 CLE 262.

[25] *Langnese-Iglo GmbH & Co. KG v. Commission*, Case T-7/93 [1995] ECR II-1533. The final appeal did not consider much of the substance, Case C-279/95P [1998] ECR I-5609.

the two large suppliers.[26] In view of many factors about the market, which the Commission had considered only under Article 81(3), the CFI confirmed that there was sufficient foreclosure to infringe Article 81(1).

The judgment confirmed the importance of making a market analysis under Article 81(1) and not only when deciding about exemptions.

In *HB Ice cream*, the Commission issued a statement of objections under both Articles 81 and 82 against the conduct of HB, another Unilever subsidiary and the largest maker of ice cream in Ireland. HB provided freezers to small retailers in Ireland, responsible for about 40 per cent of the sales of single unit ice cream in that country in return for an obligation that the retailer would stock only HB ice cream therein. The Commission accepted that providing freezers had brought some improvement to distribution but condemned HB under Articles 81 and 82 for excluding competing suppliers from retailers that had room for only one freezer.

HB then changed its policy and permitted retailers to whom it had lent a freezer to buy the cabinets outright or on hire purchase terms and thereby terminate the tie. After investigating further complaints, the Commission published a notice in the OJ stating that it intended to take a favourable view of this compromise.[27] HB obtained an injunction from the Irish High Court restraining Mars from persuading retailers to stock its ice cream in HB cabinets.[28]

Mars, which wished to enter the market by having its ices stocked in HB's cabinets complained to the Commission that few retailers were prepared to take advantage of the possibility of terminating the tie. So, the Commission reopened proceedings in *Van den Bergh Foods Ltd*[29] and condemned freezer exclusivity. An appeal has been taken again that decision to the CFI.

The Irish judgment granting an injunction against Mars came before the Irish Supreme Court, which requested a preliminary ruling from the ECJ. Consequently, the CFI suspended its proceedings on the appeal from the Commission's decision save in respect of ties of petrol stations. In the event the ECJ dealt only with the procedural issue whether an Irish court could maintain an injunction despite a contrary decision of the Commission that was subject to appeal to the CFI when the operation of the decision had been suspended by its President.[30]

The Commission accepted that supplying the freezers had contributed to an improvement of distribution by overcoming the lack of capital of many small retailers. Nevertheless, the first mover advantage was considerable. Many small retailers lacked the space for a second freezer, and if they entered into an alternative arrangement with Mars, they would have to give up the sale of their existing supplier's product. Moreover, Mars produced only one kind of impulse ice

---

[26] In *Greene King—Roberts & Roberts* v. *Commission*, Case T-25/99 [2001] 5 CMLR 828, paras. 106 and 137 (5.1.1.1.3 below), the CFI looked only to the amounts where there was a single branding obligation and not to the total bought from the same firm.

[27] OJ 1995, C 211/4 notice under Article 19(3) of Regulation 17 and 18th *Annual Report on Competition Policy*, 1998.

[28] *Masterfoods Ltd.* v. *HB Ice Cream Ltd*, [1992] 3 CMLR 830.

[29] OJ 1998, L246/1, [1998] 5 CMLR 530.

[30] *Masterfoods Ltd and HB Ice Cream* v. *Commission*, Case C-344/98, [2000] ECR I-1136.

cream, which might discourage retailers from giving up the wide range supplied by Van den Bergh. It would be harder for Mars to persuade small retailers to carry its brands than it had been for the first mover.[31]

5.1.1.1.5 *Judgments under Article 82*

There is much case law under Article 82 about rebate systems that exclude third parties. The supplier, instead of requiring customers to buy only its product may promise rebates to those who take most of their requirements from it, or a specified large percentage. These amount to attenuated single branding obligations. Care must be taken when invoking judgments under Article 82, as they presuppose a dominant position. The more trade affected by single branding restraints imposed by suppliers, the more they foreclose.

Moreover, many of the judgments have referred to Article 82(c), which lists discrimination as an example of an abuse, whereas under Article 81(1) it is only collusion to discriminate that is listed. It should also be remembered that the group exemption applies only to Article 81 and not Article 82 (3.3 above). Nevertheless, reference to the cases on Article 82 may be useful to indicate what amounts to an indirect single branding restriction.

Loyalty rebates were held to be abusive in *Vitamins*[32] and many other cases. Roche supplied very large shares of the markets for some vitamins, and about half over all. It granted discounts to 22 large customers out of some 5,000 for taking or promising to take 70 per cent or a large proportion of requirements. The 22 favoured customers accounted for about a quarter of Roche's sales of vitamins in the Common Market. Each of the contracts was worded differently, and the percentages required to earn the discount and other terms varied.

In *Michelin*,[33] condemnaton of rebates given to large buyers and on a somewhat *ad hoc* basis to buyers who sold more than in the previous year was confirmed by the ECJ. The rebates were based on the number of tyres sold, not on a percentage basis, but the ECJ observed that they had the same foreclosing effect (paras. 80–82).[34] The foreclosure was aggravated by Michelin's failure to put each dealer's target in writing, as the dealers did not always know when they were achieving their target and free to buy elsewhere (para. 83). The Commission has recently imposed a fine of nearly €20 million on the French subsidiary of Michelin for

---

[31] For a fuller economic analysis, see **Aidan Robertson** and **Mark Williams**, "An Ice Cream War: the Law and Economics of Freezer Exclusivity," (1995) 16 *ECLR* 7, 12–15. The sequel to the article that was promised in that one was delayed in the hope that the ECJ would deal with the substance in *Masterfoods Ltd and HB Ice Cream* v. *Commission*, Case C-344/98, [2000] ECR I-000. It will now be further delayed until the CFI gives judgment.

See also **Julian Maitland-Walker**, "Ice-cream Wars: An Honourable Peace or the Beginning of a Greater Conflict? (1995) 16 *ECLR* 451.

[32] *Hoffmann-La Roche & Co. AG* v. *Commission*, Case 85/76 [1979] ECR 461, paras. 89–91. See also the earlier judgment in the *Sugar cartel—Cooperatieve Vereniging Suiker Unie' UA and others* v. *Commission*, Cases 40–48, 50, 54–56, 111 & 113–114/73 [1975] ECR 1663, paras. 517–528.

[33] *Nederlandsche Banden-Industrie Michelin* v. *Commission*, Case 322/81 [1983] ECR 3461.

[34] A customer who expects nearly to reach the agreed quantity is under considerable pressure to order extra to reach that quantity.

again operating a complex system of quantitative rebates, bonuses and commercial agreements which constitute a loyalty inducing and unfair system vis-à-vis its
dealers.[35] Since this is the second time Michelin has engaged in similar behaviour
the fine has been increased for recidivism. The Commission is strongly rejecting
the argument that such inducements by a dominant firm amount to competition
on the merits.

Following precedents from Germany,[36] target discounts have been permitted by
the Commission when the reference period has been only three months.[37] This
forecloses less as a dealer about to fail to reach its target can order extra quantities,
sell them in the next quarter and qualify again for discount in the third quarter. It
also encourages a dealer to run the last mile far less.

In *Soda Ash*,[38] the Commission treated as abusive "top slicing" rebates granted
by ICI and Solvay. The two firms, each dominant in part of the Community, tried
to ascertain their customers' anticipated requirements each year and gave discounts for any excess above these figures. This discouraged their customers from
buying from competitors. ICI sometimes also encouraged customers to enter into
requirements contracts.

Many of these precedents were followed by the Commission and CFI in *Irish
Sugar*,[39] in condemning fidelity, target and selective discounts. The Commission
relied in part on evidence of an intention to exclude, although abuse is said in case
after case to be an objective concept. Article 81(1) prohibits agreements with an
anti-competitive object as well as effect and Article 1(b) of Regulation 2790/99 to
"direct or indirect" obligations. Intent may well be relevant under the Regulation.

Discounts in respect to individual orders, in so far as they can be justified on the
ground of cost savings, foreclose but encourage buyers to operate in ways that
enable the seller to save costs. Since they are based on objective criteria, they may be
treated as not discriminatory by the Commission.[40] It is doubted whether this can
bring them within the group exemptions, but they may be outside Article 81(1).

---

[35] IP/01/873.

[36] *Fertigfutter* (Pet Foods), WuW (OLG) 2463 (Berlin Court of Appeal 1980).

[37] In *Coca Cola/Amalgamated Beverages*, M 794, OJ 1997 L218/15, [1997] CEC 2226, the
Commission cleared a merger only when Coca Cola gave various commitments, one of which was that
it would use reference periods lasting no more than 3 months. The commitments were no part of the
decision, as at that time, the Commission lacked power to accept binding commitments in a stage 1
merger decision. The decision was confirmed by the CFI in *The Coca-Cola Company and Coca-Cola
Enterprises Inc.* v. *Commission*, Case T-125 & 127/97 [2000] ECR II 1733.

[38] *Solvay et Cie.* v. *Commission* and *ICI* v. *Commission*, OJ 1991, L152/21 and 40, [1994] 4 CMLR
645, The appeals from these decisions were on formal grounds.

[39] OJ 1997, L258/1, [1997] 5 CMLR 666 (Commission), Case T-228/97 [1999] ECR–II 2969 (CFI),
C497/99R, [2001] 5 CMLR 1082 (ECJ).

[40] *Irish Sugar*, OJ 1997, L 258/1 para. 150, referring to *Michelin*, without indicating where. The ECJ
in *Nederlandsche Banden-Industrie Michelin* v. *Commission*, Case 322/81 [1983] ECR 3461, para. 73,
said:

> In deciding whether Michelin NV abused its dominant position in applying its discount system it is
> therefore necessary to consider all the circumstances, particularly the criteria and rules for the grant
> of the discount, and to investigate whether, in providing *an advantage not based on any economic ser-
> vice* justifying it, the discount tends to remove or restrict the buyer's freedom to choose his sources

5.1.1.1.6 *Agreements to take a fixed quantity likely to amount to most of requirements*

The Commission has been less concerned by obligations to take a fixed quantity of products from a single supplier, as it is difficult to estimate in advance how much the purchaser may require and there is likely to be some scope for buying from other suppliers to the extent requirements are underestimated. In *BP Kemi*,[41] where there was significant market power, the Commission said:

> 68. When on such a market, which already displays a weak competitive structure, one of the most important suppliers enters into long-term contracts with one of the most important purchasers, which induce the purchaser to take all his requirement or the major part of his requirements from the same supplier, there exists an appreciable disadvantage for the supplier's competitors and for purchasers, and there is thus a restriction of competition for the purposes of Article 81(1). A six year agreement certainly goes beyond what is appropriate under EEC rules of competition to the nature of the legal and economic relationship between the parties. Certainly DDSF's (the buyer's) interest in a regular guaranteed supply is to be recognised, as is BPCL's (the supplier's) interest in lasting and steady sales of its output. But these interests could be met by concluding purchasing agreements stipulating fixed quantities, without reference to the purchaser's unspecified or not precisely specified requirements and without the restriction resulting from an English clause; such agreements could be regularly renewed after negotiating to adopt them to changing interests and the shifting competitive balance.

This thinking is *ex post.* A common reason for imposing a single branding restraint is that the supplier has to incur sunk costs to enable it to produce the product to be sold.

Agreements to take fixed quantities may be treated as indirect non-compete provisions in the context of other agreements with major buyers containing a single branding restriction.[42] They are, however, somewhat less likely than fidelity obligations to infringe Article 81(1).

In *Nutra Sweet*,[43] the Commission reported that it had persuaded Coca-Cola and Pepsico, the two largest users of the artificial sweetener Aspartame, to abandon an obligation to buy Aspartame exclusively from Nutrasweet, but they were allowed to agree to buy fixed quantities from Nutrasweet, the largest producer in the world for two further years. We are not told whether the Commission intervened under Article 81 or 82, nor whether the fixed quantities were a large part of requirements.

of supply, to bar competitors from access to the market, to apply dissimilar conditions to equivalent transactions with other trading parties or to strengthen the dominant position by distorting competition. (*Emphasis added*)

For the buyer to organise its purchases so as to minimise transport or other costs of the supplier would amount to an economic service.

[41] *Atka A/S* v. *BP Kemi A/S and A/S de Danske Spritfabrikker* OJ 1979, L286/32, [1979] 3 CMLR 684, paras. 59–61 & 68. See also informal pressure by the Commission in *Nutra Sweet*, and *Shotton* below.

[42] As was decided in the first *Michelin* case.

[43] *18th Annual Report on Competition Policy*, 1988, point 53.

The Commission announced its intention to take a favourable decision in *Shotton Paper Co.*[44] Originally, Shotton agreed to buy its total requirement of a certain kind of paper for recycling from two suppliers but, although the amount foreclosed was only between 10 and 20 per cent and barriers to entry were low, the Commission persuaded the parties to alter the agreement so that Shotton was bound to buy only 85 per cent of its expected requirements from the two suppliers. It preferred the obligation to be expressed in terms of quantity rather than requirements. The market shares were not very large and entry barriers low, so the foreclosure might not have sufficed to meet the tests of the judgment in *Delimitis* (2.7.3 above). Cases settled informally are not subject to the same checks as those that are investigated up to a formal decision.

5.1.1.1.7 *Other ways of foreclosing*

There are other indirect ways of encouraging a customer to take more from the designated supplier, such as a two part tariff—paying a fixed price up front plus a lower price per item—which reduces the customer's marginal cost and encourages expansion of its demand. The foreclosure may be justified economically for reducing the risk of incurring sunk costs to enable the supplier to produce, but this has never been accepted by the Commission.

5.1.1.2 *Not to handle competing goods etc.*

The non-compete provision may be expressed in either of two ways, but they do not differ greatly in substance. The first is not to handle competing goods:

> any direct or indirect obligation causing the buyer not to manufacture, purchase, sell or resell goods or services which compete with the contract goods or services . . .

This is the core concept of a single branding restraint.

The problem of identifying what goods compete with the contract goods is the same as under the second kind of non-compete clause (5.1.1.3 below.) An example of such a provision was condemned by the Commission under Article 81 in *Liebig.*[45]

The second kind of non-compete clause excluded from the exemption by Article 5(a) is a requirements provision:

> any direct or indirect obligation on the buyer to purchase from the supplier or from another undertaking designated by the supplier more than 80% of the buyer's total purchases of the contract goods or services and their substitutes on the relevant market.

BP Kemi[46] was an example of a requirements provisions provision.

---

[44] OJ 1990, C106/3, [1990] 4 CMLR 596, *20th Competition Report* of the Commission for 1990. para. 93.

[45] *Brooke Bond Liebig Limited,* OJ 1978 L53/20, [1978] 2 CMLR 116, 5.1.1.1.2 above.

[46] *Atka A/S v. BP Kemi A/S and A/S de Danske Spritfabrikker,* OJ 1979, L286/32, [1979] 3 CMLR 684, paras. 59–61 and 68. See quotation at 5.1.1.2 above.

From the limitation of the black listed restriction to 80 per cent of the market, can one infer that restraints on handling competing goods is also limited to 80 per cent of requirements?

On both definitions, there will be problems identifying the relevant market. At Guidelines 89–95 the Commission explains the relevant market for the purpose of calculating the 30 per cent market share under Article 3, and from Guideline 96 for individual assessment for agreements not covered by the group exemption. We are given little help by the Regulation in calculating the 80 per cent share of "the buyer's total purchases of the contract products and their substitutes" in the second definition in Article 2(b) or of "the goods or services which compete with the contract goods" in the first. Guideline 88 is, however, general.

> 88. The Commission notice on definition of the relevant market . . . provides guidance on the rules, criteria and evidence which the Commission uses when considering market definition issues. This notice will not be further explained in these Guidelines and should serve as the basis of market definition issues. These guidelines will only deal with specific issues that arise in the context of vertical restraints and that are not dealt with in the general notice on market definition.

The notice was considered shortly at 2.4.1.2 and 3.4.13.1 above[47] and receives major consideration in all the recent practitioners' books. It starts with the test developed by the ECJ based on substitutes, mainly on the demand side, by reason of the product's "characteristics, price and intended use." Later it uses the "hypothetical monopolist" test adopted in merger cases, but said to apply also to Articles 81 and 82: would there be so large a shift of customers or suppliers as to make a hypothetical increase in price of 5 or 10 per cent unprofitable? Substitution on the supply side has been little used under Article 81 since the publication of the notice.

One problem that arises in appraising distribution agreements is that many things that would not be substitutes for consumers are substitutable by dealers. While a supermarket must stock milk and butter, there is considerable flexibility as to how much cabinet space or how many brands need be devoted to each. It might be more profitable to reduce the space given to them and allow more radios to be displayed at another part of the shop.

The contract goods may include more than one group of products. Where several product groups come from the same supplier, an obligation to take all of a new and untried product from it might come within the exemption, provided that other products, for which the supplier has a stronger reputation and less difficulty in making sales, may be bought elsewhere. This has the anomalous result that firms that produce a wide range of products are less constrained than smaller firms which make only one or two product groups.

As the Commission recognises in the *Follow up to the Green Paper* (2.10 above), however, there is competition between suppliers to persuade the dealer to agree not to handle competing goods (1.1 above).

---

[47] See also 1.2.1–1.2.1.2.6 above for economists' ideas on market power.

5.1.1.3 Basis of calculation

Guideline 58 is flexible:

> 58. . . . Where for the year preceding the conclusion of the contract no relevant purchasing data for the buyer are available, the buyer's best estimate of its annual total requirements may be used. . . .

5.1.2 Provisions Severable

The introductory words to Article 5 provide that the obligations listed in the Article are not exempted, but the other provisions in an agreement may qualify for exemption.

The concept of severance is not further addressed in the Regulation. In Guideline 67 it is stated that it is only the obligation listed in Article 5 that is excluded from the Regulation. Presumably it is for national law to determine whether enough remains of the contract to be enforceable, as in the case of particular provisions that infringe Article 81 and are void under Article 81(2).[48] This severability is extremely important because single branding forecloses only in exceptional circumstances (2.7.3 and 5.1.1.1.3 above).

5.2 OBLIGATIONS IN VERTICAL AGREEMENTS THAT ARE NOT EXEMPT— ARTICLE 5, RECITAL 11, GUIDELINES 57–61

Article 5(a) prevents the exemption applying to non-compete clauses imposed on buyers that may last for more than 5 years. The introductory words of Article 5 are:

> The exemption provided for in Article 2 shall not apply to any of the following obligations contained in vertical agreements:

> The inclusion of indirect obligations comes in each of the three listed obligations as well as the definition of "non-compete obligation in Article 1(b) (5.1.1.1 above).

5.2.1 Article 5(a) Non-Compete Obligations for over 5 years—Guidelines 58 & 59

The first obligation that is excluded from exemption is:

> (a) any direct or indirect non-compete obligation, the duration of which is indefinite or exceeds five years. A non-compete obligation which is tacitly renewable beyond a period of five years is to be deemed to have been concluded for an indefinite duration. . . .

---

[48] *Société La Technique Minière* v. *Maschinenbau Ulm GmbH*, Case 56/65 [1966] ECR 235, *Société de Vente de Ciments et Bétons de l'Est SA* v. *Kerpen & Kerpen GmbH & Co. KG*, Case 319/82 [1983] ECR 4173 and many other cases.

Recital 11 states:

> In order to ensure access to or to prevent collusion on the relevant market, certain conditions are to be attached to the block exemption; to this end, the exemption of non-compete obligations should be limited to obligations which do not exceed a definite duration;
>
> for the same reasons, any direct or indirect obligation causing the members of a selective distribution system not to sell the brands of particular competing suppliers should be excluded from the benefit of this Regulation. [The paragraph has been split for ease of reference.]

The first objective: ensuring access is what concerned the ECJ in *Delimitis (Stergios)* v. *Henninger Bräu*[49] (2.7.3 above). The objective of avoiding collusion is stated by the second paragraph—directed at collective boycotts—and implemented by Article 5(c) (5.2.3 below): the fear that several suppliers would collude to prevent their dealers handling the goods of a specific competitor.

5.2.1.1 Duration

The Commission still assumes that tacitly renewable contracts last too long even when the dealer can terminate the contract unilaterally at short notice. In *Langnese-Iglo GmbH & Co. KG* v. *Commission*,[50] the CFI held that the Commission was entitled to find that an agreement subject to tacit renewal should be considered as made for an indefinite period.

The Guideline is somewhat stricter than Article 5(a) in making it clear that even if each party can escape the non-compete clause by giving notice without incurring penalties, the exemption cannot apply. Nevertheless, in *Neste*[51] (5.1.1.1.3 above) the ECJ, following Fennelly AG, ruled that where the buyer could escape the obligation by giving short notice at any time, a single branding clause would make little contribution to foreclosure and would escape Article 81(1). Consequently, exclusion of the provision from the group exemption is not material.

Five years is rather longer than the period of 2 or 3 years often permitted by the Commission for agreements outside Article 81(1).

> 58. . . . However, non-compete obligations are covered when their duration is limited to five years or less, or when renewal beyond five years requires explicit consent of both parties and no obstacles exist that hinder the buyer from effectively terminating the non-compete obligation at the end of the five year period. . . .

To qualify under the Regulation, renewable contracts will have to provide that the non-compete clause will not be renewed beyond five years. Alternatively the supplier may provide for termination of the whole agreement after five years to allow for a new agreement to be entered into with a new non-compete clause.

[49] Case C-234/89 [1991] ECR I-935.
[50] Case T-7/93 [1995] ECR II-1533, paras. 137 & 8.
[51] 5.1.1.1.3. See also *Greene King* 5.1.1.1.1 & 5.1.1.1.4 above.

Where the dealer has gained reputation or marketing know-how by carrying the supplier's product for five years, its bargaining power may have increased and it may be less willing to sign up. So the possibility of entering into successive contracts of five years may be somewhat theoretical. Under the former regulations, some suppliers annually entered into a new five-year contract with each dealer to replace the existing contract.

5.2.1.2 Non-compete clauses excepted while buyer occupies seller's premises

Where the buyer is operating from premises provided by the supplier, non-compete provisions are permitted for as long as the premises are occupied.[52] The guidelines do not state that the buyer should be able to escape the obligation by giving up the premises. Nevertheless the non-compete obligation may well extend only to a specified outlet in which event it will be ineffective once that outlet is abandoned.

Article 5(a) continues:

> (a) . . . However, the time limitation of five years shall not apply where the contract goods or services are sold by the buyer from premises and land owned by the supplier or leased by the supplier from third parties not connected with the buyer, provided that the duration of the non-compete obligation does not exceed the period of occupancy of the premises and land by the buyer;

Guideline 59 explains that:

> 59. The five-year duration limit does not apply when the goods or services are resold by the buyer "from premises and land owned by the supplier or leased by the supplier from third parties not connected with the buyer." In such cases the non-compete obligation may be of the same duration as the period of occupancy of the point of sale by the buyer (Article 5(a) of the BER).
>
>   The reason for this exception is that it is normally unreasonable to expect a supplier to allow competing products to be sold from premises and land owned by the supplier without its permission. Artificial ownership constructions intended to avoid the five-year limit cannot benefit from this exception. [We have divided this paragraph.]

This reason seems to based on ideas of fair competition, rather than on free competition for the benefit of consumers. It might have been more helpful to base the rule on the need to induce the investment by the supplier in the premises. That would then cover all forms of help, the supply of finance, equipment or premises. It might even cover the supply of marketing know-how, which is dealt with in Article 5(b). These arguments can be used to establish that the agreement does not infringe Article 81(1).

Sometimes a firm about to open a petrol station faces costs in preparing a forecourt and installing tanks and pumps. It sells the land to an oil company, which

---

[52] Article 5(b) second indent. Non-compete provisions are also permitted where indispensibe to protect know-how transferred by the supplier, provided that the provision cannot last more than a year after the expiry of the agreement (Article 5(b) third indent).

grants a long lease back subject to a mortgage and a non-compete clause. Does this convenient method of financing the retailer amount to an artificial ownership construction? The practice was widespread in the UK before it joined the Common Market. The non-compete clause is a sensible way of inducing the investment which may be cheaper for an oil company making many such contracts. This, however, is not the reason given by Guideline 59. There are other ways the supplier can finance the investment in the retailer's premises. It may install the equipment itself or grant a loan to cover the cost, but these alternatives are subject to limitations (5.1.1.1 above).

5.2.2 Article 5(b) Obligation not to Compete After the Term of the Agreement—Guideline 60

Article 5(b) prevents the application of the group exemption when the non-compete obligation outlasts the agreement:

> (b) any direct or indirect obligation causing the buyer, after termination of the agreement, not to manufacture, purchase, sell or resell goods or services, unless such obligation:
>
> —relates to goods or services which compete with the contract goods or services, and
> —is limited to the premises and land from which the buyer has operated during the contract period, and
> —is indispensable to protect know-how transferred by the supplier to the buyer,
> and provided that the duration of such non-compete obligation is limited to a period of one year after termination of the agreement; this obligation is without prejudice to the possibility of imposing a restriction which is unlimited in time on the use and disclosure of know-how which has not entered the public domain;

These four conditions are cumulative. "Know-how" is defined in Article 1(f):

> (f) "know-how" means a package of non-patented practical information, resulting from experience and testing by the supplier, which is secret, substantial and identified: in this context, "secret" means that the know-how, as a body or in the precise configuration and assembly of its components, is not generally known or easily accessible; "substantial" means that the know-how includes information which is indispensable to the buyer for the use, sale or resale of the contract goods or services; "identified" means that the know-how must be described in a sufficiently comprehensive manner so as to make it possible to verify that it fulfils the criteria of secrecy and substantiality;

The definition was devised for the Regulation granting a group exemption for know-how agreements[53] and, after confining its application to marketing know-how, inserted into the Regulation for franchising,[54] which was being prepared at that time. The definition[55] is broad, but when there are some thousands of franchisees

---

[53] Commission Regulation 556/89, OJ 1989, L61/1, [1989] 4 CMLR 774.
[54] Commission Regulation 4087/88, OJ 1988, L359/46, [1989] 4 CMLR 387.
[55] The same definition as in Reg. 2790/99 is used in the group exemption for r & d, Commission Regulation 2659/2000, on the application of Article 81(3) of the Treaty to categories of research and development agreements, OJ 2000, L304/7.

each with copies of the franchisor's manual, can the marketing formula still be described as secret know-how which as "a body or in the precise configuration and assembly of its components, . . . is not generally known or easily accessible?" These concerns were voiced[56] when the franchising Regulation was going through its consultation phase, but Valentine has not heard of problems arising.

Many franchisors are concerned by Article 5(a) and (b). Five years may be too short a period for a single branding provision where the buyer gains experience and a reputation through dealing with the products of the franchisor and wants to use it to promote competing products. The franchisee cannot be prevented under the Regulation from setting up a competing business on other land nearby after the five years and it is free of the non-compete provision when the original contract has expired or a year thereafter if the cumulative conditions of Article 5(b) have expired.

In *Pronuptia de Paris GmbH* v. *Pronuptia de Paris Irmgard Schillgalis*,[57] however, the ECJ held that in the absence of absolute territorial protection, which would prevent the Regulation from applying anyway, a non-compete clause was required to protect the franchisor's know-how and might continue throughout the franchise relationship and for *a reasonable time after the termination of the contract* without infringing Article 81(1). Since the conditions listed in Article 5 do not affect other provisions in the agreement and non-compete provisions rarely have the effect of restricting competition, the Commission's limitations are not as important as those under Article 4.

Given the ceiling of the buyer's market share at 30 per cent and the possibility of the Commission or a national authority withdrawing the exemption, one might ask why Article 5 is necessary or whether it will have much effect. Nevertheless, the Commission stated in its Green Paper on vertical agreements and Guideline 119(1) that it was more concerned by restraints on inter-brand than on intra-brand competition and non-compete obligations may reduce inter-brand competition.

5.2.3 Article 5(c) Boycott Through Parallel Selective Distribution Systems—Recital 11 and Guideline 61

Article 5(c) excludes from the block exemption:

> (c) any direct or indirect obligation causing the members of a selective distribution system not to sell the brands of particular competing suppliers.

Recital 11 merely states that such obligations should be excluded from the Regulation (5.2.1 above). Guideline 61 is more helpful and states that Article 5(c) is intended to prevent competing suppliers from each approving the same dealers and preventing other suppliers from supplying them.

---

[56] By Maitre Jacques Steenbergen.
[57] Case 161/84 [1986] ECR 353.

61. . . . The BER covers the combination of selective distribution with a non-compete obligation, obliging the dealers not to resell competing brands in general. However, if the supplier prevents its appointed dealers, either directly or indirectly, from buying products for resale from specific competing suppliers, such an obligation cannot enjoy the benefit of the BER.

The objective of the exclusion of this obligation is to avoid a situation whereby a number of suppliers using the same selective distribution outlets prevent one specific competitor or certain specific competitors from using these outlets to distribute their products (foreclosure of a competing supplier which would be a form of collective boycott).[58]

This is an example of the Commission's more economic approach: it is concerned about the horizontal effects of vertical agreements (1.2.3.2 above). If there actually is a collective boycott, that would not be exempt under the Regulation even without Article 5(c) because the agreement would not be vertical, but it might not be easy to discover the collective agreement or any collusion may be tacit.

The suppliers might act as if there were an agreement, without there actually being any collusion. Economists often use the words "tacit collusion" to embrace such a situation. Is this caught by the words of Article 5(c) which refer to any *direct or indirect* obligation. It is thought not, in the absence of any meeting of the minds of the parties.[59] The oligopolists are giving each other no incentives to boycott.

As under Article 5(a), it is thought that a restraint on selling competing goods by certain methods is not included in the severable black list.[60] On the other hand, the Commission wants to ensure that dealers may use the internet. It will be interesting to see on what legal ground it tries to ensure this.[61]

Where there is no need to restrain dealers or franchisees from selling to non-approved dealers, Article 5(c) may be avoided by not specifying the criteria on the basis of which dealers are approved (4.3.3 above) or by a location clause which, in the absence of absolute territorial protection, does not infringe Article 81(1).[62] Again, the non-compete provision would have the effect of restricting competition only in the circumstances specified in *Delimitis* (2.7.3 above).

5.2.4 Conclusion on Article 5

Those who long for the security of a harbour safe from the gales of competition law may be concerned that Article 5 allows non-compete provisions only for 5

---

[58] An example of indirect measures having such exclusionary effects can be found in the Commission Decision *Givenchy*, (OJ L236/11, [1993] 5 CMLR 579.

[59] *Bayer* v. *Commission*, Case T-41/96, 26 October 2000, [2000] ECR I-000. [2001] 4 CMLR 4. The Commission has appealed, Case C-2 & 3/01, OJ 2001, C79/14 (2.1 above).

[60] **Jochen Burrichter**, "Vertical Restraints and E-Commerce," in **Barry Hawk** (ed.), [2000] *Fordham Corporate Law Institute* 131, 147.

[61] *Yves Saint Laurent*, IP/01/713, 17 May 2001 (2.5 above) Since Yves Saint Laurent gave in, the Commission did not have to state the legal basis.

[62] *Pronuptia*, Case 161/84 [1986] ECR 353, para. 19.

years. This may be extended to the period while a dealer occupies the supplier's premises (5.2.1.2 above). Moreover, the dealer may use the marketing know-how imparted by the supplier, and the reputation gained from him, to compete from other premises.

Such agreements will seldom infringe Article 81(1), however, when the supplier's market share does not exceed 30 per cent. Article 4(b) and the doctrine of exhaustion of intellectual property rights prevents dealers being given absolute territorial protection, so the case law developed in *Pronuptia de Paris GmbH* v. *Pronuptia de Paris Irmgard Schillgalis*[63] (2.7.2 above) and *Delimitis (Stergios)* v. *Henninger Bräu*[64] (2.7.3 above) remains helpful. Ancillary restraints to make franchising viable do not infringe Article 81(1).[65] Many of the same arguments can be made for other kinds of distribution. So, non-compete provisions needed by the supplier to appropriate the marketing know-how imparted to dealers do not infringe Article 81(1).

Moreover, single branding agreements foreclose competitors appreciably only when there are barriers to entry downstream and so many dealers are tied to the same or other suppliers, that new suppliers or those wanting to expand lack real and concrete opportunities to reach a minimum efficient scale. In those circumstances, in the absence of Article 5, one might expect the Commission or a national authority to withdraw the benefit of the group exemption under Articles 6–8 (6.1–6.1.3 below).

Where there are wholesalers dealing in many brands and the foreclosure upstream is limited, new entrants can gain access more easily. In *Greene King*,[66] the CFI observed that

> 108. If the restrictive effect of the "upstream" agreements is limited other breweries are able to conclude supply agreements with the wholesaling brewery and so enter the latter's network of "downstream" agreements. They are thus in a position to have access to all the establishment in that network without it being necessary to conclude separate agreements with each outlet. The existence of a network of "downstream" agreements thus constitutes a factor which can promote penetration of the market by other brewers.

Non-compete restraints were automatically exempted under titles II and III of Regulation 1984/83.[67] By the end of 2001, when the transitional provisions expire, suppliers of beer and petrol may have to renegotiate their contracts where the non-compete provision makes a significant contribution to foreclosure (Article 2(5), 3.4.8 above).

---

[63]   Case 161/84 [1986] ECR 353.

[64]   Case C-234/89 [1991] ECR I-935.

[65]   *Métropole Télévision SA (M6) and Others* v. *Commission*, Case T-112/99 (2.7.2 above) however, gives rise to concern. It seems to narrow the doctrine of ancillary restraint to what is necessary from the nature of the transaction, to the exclusion of restraints that make the particular transaction viable (2.7.2 above).

[66]   *Roberts & Roberts* v. *Commission*, Case T25/99 [2001] 5 CMLR 828, para. 108.

[67]   OJ 1983, L173/7, corrections OJ 1984, C101/2 [1983] 2 CLE 262.

6

Miscellaneous Provisions

6.1 WITHDRAWAL OF EXEMPTION—ARTICLES 6–8, RECITALS 12–13, GUIDELINES 71, 77, 103–114, 142, 189, 198, 224

The group exemption applies whatever the dealer's market share, save for an exclusive distribution territory covering the whole Common Market. Where the dealer has market power in a market downstream, single anti-competitive agreements may qualify or a very important distributor may agree to handle only a single brand and confer market power on a supplier that does not currently have much. Moreover, even when each contract is not in itself anticompetitive, the aggregate effect of many similar contracts may foreclose. Such restraints are not always justified by the free rider or any other argument (Guideline 71).

Consequently, the Commission has been granted power to withdraw the benefit of the group exemption[1] in Articles 6–8 of Regulation 2790/99, even when there are no hard core provisions and the ceiling of market share is not exceeded. The Commission has no general duty to exercise these powers, but a discretion to do so if the negative effects exceed the positive ones.

The provisions for withdrawal are complex. Article 6 provides for the Commission to withdraw the benefit of the exemptions where the agreement does not merit it. National authorities also have power under Article 7 to withdraw it where the agreement does not merit exemption and there is a distinct geographic market within its territory. If the agreement restricts competition in more than one member state, only the Commission can terminate the benefit of the group exemption.[2] The Commission may also withdraw the benefit by regulation under paragraph 1 of Article 8 where parallel networks of similar vertical agreements cover more than 50 per cent of a relevant market.

Regulation 19/65, which empowered the Commission to adopt Regulation 2970/99, requires the Commission to provide for withdrawing group exemptions. In only one reported case has a group exemption been withdrawn[3] and, with the low ceiling of market share compatible with Regulation 2970/99, one might expect few individual withdrawals in future. Nevertheless, the possibility of withdrawal is important. Before adopting a decision of withdrawal, the Commission is required

---

[1] The empowering Regulation, 19/65, OJ Spec Ed, 1965, 35 was amended by Council Reg. 1215/99, OJ 1999, L148/1.

[2] Guideline 77 and the wording of Article 7.

[3] *Langnese-Iglo GmbH & Co. KG* v. *Mars GmbH* Case 93/406/EEC, OJ 1993, L183/19, [1994] 4 CMLR 51, 2123; confirmed by CFI *Langnese-Iglo GmbH & Co. KG* v. *Commission*, Case T-7/93, [1995] ECR II-1533, paras. 208–9.

to talk to the parties, and at that point they are under considerable pressure to satisfy the Commission by amending their agreement or waiving rights. The only reported cases where this happened are *Tetra Pak I*[4] and *ARD*[5] but there may well be others that have not been publicised by a decision on the substance. There is no duty to publish such decisions in the OJ.

The benefit of the exemption can be withdrawn from existing agreements for the future where an agreement infringes Article 81(1) and does not merit exemption, although the same supplier may continue to benefit from the group exemption in the future.[6] Guideline 71 states that:

> 71. The presumption of legality conferred by the BER may be withdrawn if a vertical agreement, considered either in isolation or in conjunction with similar agreements enforced by competing suppliers or buyers, comes within the scope of Article 81(1) and does not fulfil all the conditions of Article 81(3). This may occur when a supplier, or a buyer in the case of exclusive supply agreements,[7] holding a market share not exceeding 30%, enters into a vertical agreement which does not give rise to objective advantages such as to compensate for the damage which it causes to competition. This may particularly be the case with respect to the distribution of goods to final consumers, who are often in a much weaker position than professional buyers of intermediate goods. In the case of sales to final consumers, the disadvantages caused by a vertical agreement may have a stronger impact than in a case concerning the sale and purchase of intermediate goods. . . .

> 72. Where the withdrawal procedure is applied, the Commission bears the burden of proof that the agreement falls within the scope of application of Article 81(1) and that the agreement does not fulfil all four conditions of Article 81(1).

In *Langnese*,[8] the CFI said:

> 179. It is also settled law that, where an exemption is being applied for under Article 81(3) it is in the first place for the undertakings concerned to present to the Commission the evidence intended to establish that the agreement fulfil the conditions laid down by Article 81(3) of the Treaty.

[4] OJ 1988, L272/27, [1990] 4 CMLR 47. Appeal, *Tetra Pak Rausing SA* v. *Commission*, Case T-51/89, [1990] ECR II-309.

[5] *Re Film Purchases by German TV Stations*, OJ 1989, L284/36, [1990] 4 CMLR 841—not a group exemption.

[6] Guideline 75 and *Langnese-Iglo GmbH & Co. KG* v. *Mars GmbH* OJ 1993, L183/19, [1994] 4 CMLR 51, On appeal, *Langnese-Iglo GmbH & Co. KG* v. *Commission*, Case T-7/93, [1995] ECR II-1533, paras. 205–211. The final appeal did not consider much of the substance, Case C-279/95P, [1998] ECR I-5609. Where more than half a relevant market is covered by similar vertical restraints, the Commission may terminate the group exemption by regulation, and then parties would not be able to continue to take advantage of it (6.1.3 below). If the proposed Regulation to replace Regulation 17 is adopted by the Council without amendment, Article 30 will enable the Commission, by regulation, to exclude from the scope of a group exemption specified classes of agreements.

[7] Exclusive supply obligation is defined in Article 1(c) to mean

> any direct or indirect obligation causing the supplier to sell the goods or services specified in the agreement only to one buyer inside the Community for the purposes of a specific use or resale.

It does not include exclusive territories granted for less than the whole Common Market.

[8] *Langnese-Iglo GmbH & Co. KG* v. *Commission*, Case T-7/93, [1995] ECR II-1533, citing *Remia BV and Verenigde Bedrijven Nutricia* v. *Commission*, Case 42/84, [1985] ECR 2545, and *VBVB and CBBB* v. *Commission*, [1984] ECR 19.

It added (para. 193) that the same is true when the Commission withdraws a group exemption. Is this consistent with Guideline 72? It may be that it is still for the parties to produce the arguments and evidence warranting an exemption, but that at that point the burden moves to the Commission. It is also arguable that when the Commission states how it will exercise its discretion, the CFI will hold that it should keep its promise, as it did in relation to access to the file.[9]

Would the courts also keep national authorities to the Commission's Guidelines on the ground that it would be unfortunate if different rules apply? Recital 14 states:

> Member States should ensure that the exercise of this power of withdrawal does not prejudice the uniform application throughout the Common Market of the Community competition rules or the full effect of the measures adopted in implementation of those rules.[10]

Withdrawal cannot date from a period before a decision is made (Guidelines 75 and 87).

When appraising whether the exemption should be withdrawn in a particular case, it may be helpful to consider all the factors that are of interest for agreements that are outside the group exemption, with the qualification that if the market share is below 30 per cent, the detrimental effects on the economy may be less.

6.1.1 Withdrawal by the Commission—Article 6, Recital 13 and Guidelines 71–75

Article 6 provides:

> The Commission may withdraw the benefit of this Regulation, pursuant to Article 7(1) of Regulation No 19/65/EEC, where it finds in any particular case that vertical agreements to which this Regulation applies nevertheless have effects which are incompatible with the conditions laid down in Article 81(3) of the Treaty, and in particular where access to the relevant market or competition therein is significantly restricted by the cumulative effect of parallel networks of similar vertical restraints implemented by competing suppliers or buyers.

Recital 13 explains:

> In particular cases in which the agreements falling under this regulation nevertheless have effects incompatible with Article 81(3), the Commission may withdraw the benefit

---

[9] In *Hercules* v. *Commission*, Case T-7/89 [1991] ECR II-1711, the CFI, after stating how narrow were the Commission's obligations to give access to its files according to the case law of the ECJ, added:

53. It must be observed, however, that in establishing a procedure for providing access to the file in competition cases, the Commission imposed on itself rules exceeding the requirements laid down by the Court of Justice.

It held the Commission bound to apply the rules which it explained in the *12th Report on Competition Policy* (pages 40 and 41).
[10] See also Guideline 78, the relevant part of which is quoted at 6.1.1 below.

of the block exemption; this may occur in particular where the buyer has significant market power in the relevant market in which it resells the goods or provides the services or where parallel networks of vertical agreements have similar effects which significantly restrict access to a relevant market or competition therein; such cumulative effects may for example arise in the case of selective distribution or non-compete obligations.

Guideline 73 repeats this and adds:

> 73. . . . Similar effects will normally occur when vertical restraints practised by competing suppliers or buyers come within one of the four groups listed in paragraphs 104–114.[11]

While the cumulative effect of parallel networks is the obvious reason for withdrawing the group exemption, given the 30 per cent ceiling of market share for each supplier, it would seem more appropriate for the Commission to invoke Article 8 and withdraw the benefit of the exemption by Regulation from the market as a whole, provided that half the market is covered by the parallel restraints. At Guideline 84, the Commission says the choice of an individual decision or a Regulation:

> may depend, in particular, on the number of competing undertakings contributing to a cumulative effect on the market or the number of affected geographic markets within the Community.

Where an individual decision to withdraw is used, the parties can invoke the group exemption to enter into further agreements as in *Langnese*,[12] but this is not so when the exemption is withdrawn by Regulation (6.1.3 below).

Since it is the supplier's market power that is relevant under Article 3, except in the case of exclusive supply—an exclusive dealer territory covering the whole of the Common Market[13]—the regulation may apply when a dealer with market power is protected by being given an exclusive territory or customer group. It is understandable that the Commission might wish to terminate such an agreement if there was little intra-brand competition especially if inter-brand competition is also weak.

The Commission recognises the importance of the judgment in *Delimitis*:[14] to be caught by Article 81(1) it must be shown not only that competitors of the supplier lack real and concrete opportunities of entering the market or expanding on an efficient scale, but also that the agreements of a particular brewer contributed significantly to the foreclosure. The Commission has extended the concept of cumulative effects in the judgment in *Delimitis* from single branding restraints to all four categories, in so far as they are not excluded by Article 4, and applies the need for a substantial contribution to all four.

---

[11] "Such a situation may arise for example when, on a given market, certain suppliers practise purely qualitative selective distribution while other suppliers practise quantitative selective distribution. In such circumstances, the assessment must take account of the anti-competitive effects attributable to each individual network of agreements. Where appropriate, withdrawal may concern only the quantitative limitations imposed on the number of authorised distributors." Guidelines 103–114 describe the four kinds of vertical restraints that may have negative effects on the market (1.2.2–1.2.2.4).

[12] *Langnese-Iglo GmbH & Co. KG* v. *Commission*, Case T-7/93 [1995] ECR II-1533, paras. 205–210.

[13] See the definition in Article 1(c).

[14] *Delimitis (Stergios)* v. *Henninger Bräu*, Case C-234/89 [1991] ECR I-935, paras. 24–26 (2.7.3 above).

74. Responsibility for an anti-competitive cumulative effect can only be attributed to those undertakings which make an appreciable contribution to it. Agreements entered into by undertakings whose contribution to the cumulative effect is insignificant do not fall under the prohibition provided for Article 81(1) and are therefore not subject to the withdrawal mechanism. The assessment of such a contribution will be made in accordance with the criteria set out in paragraphs 137 to 229.[15]

6.1.2 Withdrawal by National Authorities—Article 7, Recital 14 and Guideline 76

Where there is a distinct geographic market within a national territory, the national authority there has power to withdraw the group exemption in respect of that territory.

Article 7 provides:

> Where in any particular case vertical agreements to which the exemption provided for in Article 2 applies have effects incompatible with the conditions laid down in Article 81(3) of the Treaty in the territory of a Member State, or in a part thereof, which has all the characteristics of a distinct geographic market, the competent authority of that Member State may withdraw the benefit of application of this regulation in respect of that territory, under the same conditions as provided in Article 6.

Recital 14: explains:

> Regulation No 19/65/EEC empowers the competent authorities of Member States to withdraw the benefit of the block exemption in respect of vertical agreements having effects incompatible with the conditions laid down in Article 81(3), where such effects are felt in their respective territory, or in a part thereof, and where such territory has the characteristics of a distinct geographic market; Member States should ensure that the exercise of this power of withdrawal does not prejudice the uniform application throughout the Common Market of the Community competition rules or the full effect of the measures adopted in implementation of those rules.

In Article 1(4) of Regulation 1215/99,[16] the Council amended Regulation 19/65 (6.1 above) to enable national authorities to withdraw a group exemption in those circumstances:

> 4. In Article 7 [of Regulation 19/65] . . . the following paragraph shall be added:
>
> 2. When in any particular case agreements or concerted practices to which a regulation adopted pursuant to Article 1 applies[17] have certain effects which are incompatible with

---

[15] Section VI 1.2 starts at Guideline 115 and describes the possible positive effects of vertical restraints.

[16] OJ 1999, L148/1.

[17] This now applies to regulations relating to technology transfer. The question arises whether it is retrospective and applies to Commission Regulation 240/96, OJ 1996, L31/2, [1996] 4 CMLR 405, [1996] 4 EIPR Supp. iv. It was adopted under Article 1 of Regulation 19/65 before it was amended. Linguistically, there is no reason why it should not. See the arguments at 2.11 above in relation to the retrospective operation of Regulation 1216/99 enabling the Commission to grant individual exemptions retrospective to the date of the agreement.

the conditions laid down in Article 81(3) of the Treaty in the territory of a Member State, or in part thereof, which has all the characteristics of a distinct market, the competent authority in that Member State may on its own initiative or at the request of the Commission or of natural or legal persons claiming a legitimate interest withdraw the benefit of application of that regulation."

Article 81(1) is infringed only if the agreement may affect trade between member states. So, the question arises how distinct the geographic market must be for national authorities to intervene.

The concept of a "distinct market" is not defined anywhere in relation to the withdrawal of the block exemption. The wording, however, is the same as that used in Article 9(2) and (3) of the Merger Regulation[18] to which reference may well be made. There have not, however, been many precedents under that provision. It is widely considered that a separate market as defined in the notice on the definition of the relevant market for the purposes of Community competition law,[19] amounts to a distinct market.[20]

National authorities must use the procedures provided by national law and the withdrawal will have no effect outside that country.[21] Where the national authority has not been empowered to enforce the Community competition rules by its national law,[22] there may be no such procedures available, but Guideline 76 states that the national authority may ask the Commission to withdraw the exemption.

Community rules may have direct effect in the laws of those countries, and be enforceable in their courts, but the Commission has not pressed the national authorities to enforce the Community rules. Most national authorities have been enforcing their national competition rules, most of which are virtually identical with Articles 81 and 82, although this will be ended by Article 3 of the proposed replacement for Regulation 17.[23]

National authorities must respect the priority of Community law (recital 17 of Regulation 2790/99 and Guideline 78). Consequently an agreement cannot be attacked under national competition law until the group exemption has been withdrawn.[24]

78. . . . Such national decisions must not prejudice the uniform application of the Community competition rules and the full effect of the measures adopted in implemen-

---

[18] Council Regulation 4064/89, OJ 1990, L257/14, [1990] 4 CMLR 859, as amended by Council Regulation 1301/97, OJ 1997, L180/1.

[19] OJ 1997, C372/5, [1998] 4 CMLR 177.

[20] See, e.g., **Nicholas Levy**, "The Control of Concentrations between Undertakings," in Valentine Korah (general ed.) *Competition Law of the European Community*, 8.05[2][a] (Bender, looseleaf).

[21] Wording of Article 7 and Guideline 78.

[22] This is the general position in the UK, save for sectors like air transport between one member state and a non-member state, where there is no Community implementing regulation. It may well change under The Enterprise Bill expected to implement the white paper of the DTI.

[23] Proposal of the Commission for a Council Regulation to replace Regulation 17/62, 2000/0243 (CNS), [2000] 5 CMLR 1148 (2.12 above). The Commission hopes this may be adopted in 2002 and come into effect in 2004. Article 3 is highly controversial and may be amended.

[24] Advocate General Tesauro in *BMW v. ALD-Bayerische Motorenwerke AG and VAG v. ALD Autoleasing D GmbH*, Case C-70/93 [1995] ECR I-3459. The judgment did not address the issue.

tation of those rules.[25] Compliance with this principle implies that national competition authorities must carry out their assessment under Article 81 in the light of the relevant criteria developed by the Court of Justice and the Court of First Instance and in the light of notices and previous decisions adopted by the Commission."

Guideline 79 adds that:

79. The Commission considers that the consultation mechanisms provided for in the Notice on cooperation between national competition authorities and the Commission[26] should be used to avert the risk of conflicting decisions and duplication of procedures.

The notice may be revised as part of the implementation of the White Paper on Modernisation (2.12 above). In particular, the Commission wants to reserve to itself important cases and those involving new points. Article 11 of the Proposal of the Commission for a Council Regulation to replace Regulation 17/62[27] provides for consultation between the Commission on the one hand, and authorities and courts of member states on the other.

The safe harbour of the Regulation, when the relevant market share is below 30 per cent, is not entirely safe even if there are no hard core provisions in a contract. The exemption may be withdrawn by national authorities as well as the Commission and some national authorities, such as the Italian, are becoming very active. Nevertheless, if withdrawal proceedings are commenced, the parties are entitled to be given a chance to put their views, because a decision of withdrawal would affect their rights.[28]

6.1.3 Withdrawal by Regulation—Article 8, Recital 15 & Guidelines 80–87, 142, 189, 198 and 224

Power was obtained from the Council for the Commission to enable itself to withdraw group exemptions from an entire market by regulation. Article 1a of Regulation 19/65 was inserted by regulation 1215/99. It provides:

A regulation pursuant to Article 1 may stipulate the conditions which may lead to the exclusion from its application of certain parallel networks of similar agreements or concerted practices operating on [a] particular market; when these circumstances are fulfilled the Commission may establish this by means of regulation and fix a period at the expiry of which the regulation pursuant to article 1 would no longer be applicable in respect of the relevant agreements or concerted practices on that market; such period must not be shorter than six months.

---

[25] *Walt Wilhelm and others* v. *Bundeskartellamt*, Case 14/68 [1969] ECR 1, point 4, and *Delimitis* Case 234/89 [1991] ECR I-935.

[26] See OJ 1997, C 313/3, points 49–53.

[27] 2000/0243 (CNS), [2000] 5 CMLR 1148.

[28] *Cimenteries—Re Noordwijks Cement Accoord: Cimenteries CBR Cementbedrijven NV* v. *EEC Commission*, Cases 8–11/66, [1967] ECR 75. The decision in that case involved an application of Article 15(6) of Regulation 17 withdrawing the immunity from fines.

Article 8 provides for the Commission to withdraw the exemption from a particular market by regulation where parallel networks of similar vertical restraints cover over half the relevant market (Guidelines 80–87):

1. Pursuant to Article 1a of Regulation No 19/65/EEC, the Commission may by regulation declare that, where parallel networks of similar vertical restraints cover more than 50% of a relevant market, this Regulation shall not apply to vertical agreements containing specific restraints relating to that market.

2. A Regulation pursuant to paragraph 1 shall not become applicable earlier than six months following its adoption.

Recital 15 explains:

In order to strengthen supervision of parallel networks of vertical agreements which have similar restrictive effects and which cover more than 50% of a given market, the Commission may declare this Regulation inapplicable to vertical agreements containing specific restraints relating to the market concerned, thereby restoring the full application of article 81 to such agreements.

This provision avoids the difficulty faced by the Commission after the judgment of the CFI in *Langnese*[29] from its decisions on ice creams in Germany. It said that the Commission could condemn existing agreements, but had no power to restrain the parties from taking advantage of the group exemption for the future. Now it has been expressly given such power.

The Commission may take a decision under Article 6 which may guide all the undertakings operating on the market before adopting a regulation (Guideline 81).

---

[29] *Langnese-Iglo GmbH & Co. KG* v. *Commission*, Case T-7/93 [1995] ECR II-1533, paras. 205–210.

208. Regulation 1984/83, being a measure of general application makes available to undertakings a block exemption for certain exclusive purchasing agreements which satisfy in principle the conditions laid down by Article 81(3). According to the hierarchy of legal rules, the Commission is not empowered, by means of an individual decision, to restrict or limit the legal effects of a legislative measure, unless the latter expressly provides a legal basis for that purpose. Although Article 14 of Regulation 1984/83 (empowering the Commission to withdraw the block exemption) confers on the Commission power to withdraw the benefit of the Regulation if it finds that, in a particular case, an exempted agreement nevertheless has certain effects which are incompatible with the conditions set out in Article 81(3) of the Treaty, Article 14 does not provide any legal basis for the benefit of a block exemption to be withheld from future agreements.

209. The Court also considers that it would be contrary to the principle of equal treatment, one of the fundamental principles of Community law, to exclude for certain undertakings the benefit of a block exemption regulation as regards the future whilst other undertakings, such as the intervener in this case, could continue to conclude exclusive purchasing agreements such as those prohibited by the decision. Such a prohibition would therefore be liable to undermine the economic freedom of certain undertakings and create distortions of competition on the market, contrary to the objectives of the Treaty.

The objection on ground of discrimination is avoided by withdrawing the exemption from a whole sector.

Guideline 82 states:

82. For the purpose of calculating the 50% market coverage ratio, account must be taken of each individual network of vertical agreements containing restraints, or combinations of restraints, producing similar effects on the market. Similar effects normally result when the restraints come within one of the four groups listed in paragraphs 104–114.[30]

The Commission has a discretion whether to adopt a regulation under Article 8 or a decision under Article 6. It may choose its own priorities and do nothing beyond dismissing a complaint after sending a letter under Article 6 of Regulation 99/62. Guideline 83 states that it is likely to adopt a regulation:

83. . . . in particular when parallel networks of selective distribution covering more than 50% of a market make use of selection criteria which are not required by the nature of the relevant goods or discriminate against certain forms of distribution capable of selling such goods.

This complements the case law of the ECJ and CFI on selective distribution, according to which the criteria for selection must be appropriate to the goods in question, no more restrictive than required and applied without discrimination. Even supermarkets should be supplied with fine fragrances if they can provide the elegant ambience, as may be possible when there are individual shops at the side of the grocery.[31] Note that the definition of "selective distribution" in Article 1(d) is not limited to qualitative and proportionate criteria. The Commission has long been concerned that not only specialist shops, but also department stores and other cheaper outlets should be able to get supplies.[32]

Guideline 85 states that:

85. Any regulation adopted under Article 8 must clearly set out its scope of application. This means, first, that the Commission must define the relevant product and geographic markets, that it must identify the type of vertical restraint in respect of which the BER will not longer apply.

As regards the latter aspect, the Commission may modulate the scope of its regulation according to the competition concern which it intends to address.

For instance while all parallel networks of single-branding type arrangements shall be taken into account in view of establishing the 50% market coverage ratio, the Commission may nevertheless restrict the scope of the disapplication regulation only to non-compete obligations exceeding a certain duration. Thus agreements of shorter duration or of a less restrictive nature might be left unaffected, in consideration of the lesser degree of foreclosure attributable to such restraints.

Similarly, when on a particular market selective distribution is practised in combination with additional restraints such as non-compete or quantity—forcing on the buyer, the disapplication regulation may concern only such additional restraints.

---

[30] The four groups are discussed shortly at 1.2.2–1.2.2.4 above.
[31] *Leclerc (Association des Centres Distributeurs Edouard)* v. *Commission*, Case T-88/92 [1996] ECR II 1851–1861, appeals from *Givenchy* and *Yves Saint Laurent* (2.8.1.2.4 above).
[32] *Junghans*, OJ 1977, L30/10, paras. 6 & 18, [1977] 1 CMLR D82, para. 17(c). An exemption was granted to some provisions only after the parties had been persuaded to enable specialised departments in department stores, supermarkets and similar stores to stock Junghans clocks.

Where appropriate, the Commission may also provide guidance by specifying the market share level which, in the specific market context, may be regarded as insufficient to bring about a significant contribution by an individual undertaking to the cumulative effect. [We have divided a long paragraph.]

86. The transitional period of not less than six months that the Commission will have to set under Article 8(2) should allow the undertakings concerned to adapt their agreements to take account of the regulation disapplying the BER.

Guideline 86 is optimistic. Many standard distribution agreements are revised only occasionally, and consultations with, for instance, a trade association of dealers or franchisees may have to be held before the agreements can be modified in accordance with their terms. Where premises are made available, for instance to public houses, there may be legal requirements to serve notice on individual tenants and negotiate. If such problems arise, the parties should bring them to the attention of the Commission before it adopts a regulation. It is entitled to give the parties longer to adapt their agreements. Whether it does so may depend on how serious it considers the problems and effects on competition to be.

The institution withdrawing the exemption from an individual agreement bears the onus of proof to show that the agreement infringes Article 81(1) and does not merit exemption (Guideline 71, 6.1 above).

6.2 CALCULATING MARKET SHARE AND TURNOVER—ARTICLES 9 AND 10

Article 9 provides that the market share of 30 per cent under Article 3 shall be calculated on the basis of the sales value of the contract products and their substitutes. This was considered at 3.4.13.6 above. Article 10 continues:

1. For the purpose of calculating total annual turnover within the meaning of Article 2(2) and (4), the turnover achieved during the previous financial year by the relevant party to the vertical agreement and the turnover achieved by its connected undertakings in respect of all goods and services, excluding all taxes and other duties, shall be added together. For this purpose, no account shall be taken of dealings between the party to the vertical agreement and its connected undertakings or between its connected undertakings.

2. The exemption provided for in Article 2 shall remain applicable where, for any period of two consecutive financial years, the total annual turnover threshold is exceeded by no more than 10%.

The calculation of annual turnover for deciding when agreements between competing suppliers qualify under Article 2(1) and (4) when the buyer is small (3.4.7 above) is prescribed in Article 10. One takes the aggregate turnover for the previous financial year[33] achieved by its connected undertakings (6.3 below) in

---

[33] A more convenient basis of calculation than the previous calendar year in Article 9(2)(a) applicable to the calculation of the 30% market share.

respect of all goods and services, excluding taxes and other duties. Dealings between any of the connected undertakings, however, are excluded. This is much the same definition as in Article 5 of Regulations 1983/83 and 1984/83 except that the old 10 per cent marginal relief has gone. There has, however, been inflation since 1983, so the definition of small now covers less.

6.3 "CONNECTED UNDERTAKINGS"

Article 11 provides a definition of connected undertakings for the purpose of the Regulation to cover undertakings in which a party to the agreement has more than half the control. 50–50 joint ventures are not included. This is the definition of "connected undertakings" habitually given for the last 20 years in Commission group exemption regulations, and is more precise than the definition of "undertaking" given by the ECJ in *Viho* v. *Commission*, where a parent and the wholly owned subsidiary it controlled were treated as a single undertaking, so that instructions given did not constitute an agreement between undertakings.[34]

The definition of "connected undertakings" in Article 11 is used when considering the market share or turnover of an undertaking, supplier or buyer: subject to paragraph 3, the market share of its parent, subsidiaries and fellow subsidiaries should be included. In the case of a joint venture, its market share should be allocated between its parents even when one has *de facto* control.

1. For the purposes of this Regulation, the terms "undertaking", "supplier" and "buyer" shall include their respective connected undertakings.

2. "Connected undertakings" are:
   (a) undertakings in which a party to the agreement, directly or indirectly:
   —has the power to exercise more than half the voting rights, or
   —has the power to appoint more than half the members of the supervisory board, board of management or bodies legally representing the undertaking, or
   —has the right to manage the undertaking's affairs;
   (b) undertakings which directly or indirectly have, over a party to the agreement, the rights or powers listed in (a);
   (c) undertakings in which an undertaking referred to in (b) has, directly or indirectly, the rights or powers listed in (a);
   (d) undertakings in which a party to the agreement together with one or more of the undertakings referred to in (a), (b) or (c), or in which two or more of the latter undertakings, jointly have the rights or powers listed in (a);
   (e) undertakings in which the rights or the powers listed in (a) are jointly held by:
   —parties to the agreement or their respective connected undertakings referred to in (a) to (d), or

---

[34] Case C-73/95P, [1996] ECR I-5457. In *Viho*, the ECJ did not have to consider how strong the control had to be. When attributing the acts of an affiliate to its parent, the ECJ took into account the acts of a jointly owned subsidiary, where the parent had a second or casting vote in the board of the joint venture which it had never used, *Istituto Chemioterapico Italiano SpA and Commercial Solvents Corp.* v. *Commission*, Cases 6 & 7/73 [1974] ECR 223.

—one or more of the parties to the agreement or one or more of their connected undertakings referred to in (a) to (d) and one or more third parties.

3. For the purposes of Article 3, the market share held by the undertakings referred to in paragraph 2(e) of this Article shall be apportioned equally to each undertaking having the rights or the powers listed in paragraph 2(a).

This is not very different from the definition in Article 4 of Regulation 1983/83 and of Regulation 1984/83, but Article 11(3) is new. There was no equivalent in the former Regulation.

6.4 TRANSITIONAL PROVISIONS—ARTICLE 12, GUIDELINE 70

The Regulation came into effect at the beginning of 2000 to extend the life of the former group exemptions, but the new regime started from 1 June 2000. Article 12 provides:

1. The exemptions provided for in Commission Regulations (EEC) No 1983/83[35], (EEC) No 1984/83[36] and (EEC) No 4087/88[37] shall continue to apply until 31 May 2000.

2. The prohibition laid down in Article 81(1) of the EC Treaty shall not apply during the period from 1 June 2000 to 31 December 2001 in respect of agreements already in force on 31 May 2000 which do not satisfy the conditions for exemption provided for in this Regulation but which satisfy the conditions for exemption provided for in Regulations (EEC) No 1983/83, (EEC) No 1984/83 or (EEC) No 4087/88.

Old agreements, for example, by manufacturers with large market shares, made before June 2000 were exempt until the end of 2001 if they complied with one of the former Regulations. It is thought that this applies also to new agreements made on forms no more restrictive than those used before June 2000.[38] A non-compete provision in such an "old agreement" will remain exempt if there are no more than five years to run at the end of 2001 (Guideline 70).

6.5 ENTRY INTO FORCE—ARTICLE 13

Article 13 provides:

This Regulation shall enter into force on I January 2000.

It shall apply from I June 2000, except for Article 12(1) which shall apply from I January 2000.

This Regulation shall expire on 31 May 2010.

[35] OJ 1983, L 173/1.
[36] Ibid., 5.
[37] OJ 1988, L 359/46.
[38] *Parfums Marcel Rochas Vertriebs-GmbH* v. *Bitsch*, Case 1/70 [1970] ECR 515.

7

Distribution Agreements Outside the Block Exemption

This chapter is concerned with those distribution agreements which, for some reason, do not benefit from the exemption conferred by Regulation 2790/99. In it we consider the arrangements that fall outside the "safe harbour" of the BER, and we examine what options are open to parties to such agreements to fulfil their distribution requirements with as little exposure as possible to risks under the EC competition law rules.

In general, undertakings whose distribution systems cannot benefit from the BER are now in a difficult situation. Although the Commission insists that agreements outside the "safe harbour" are not presumed to infringe Article 81(1), and encourages self-assessment,[1] this is cold comfort for businesses and their advisors, especially if they are risk-averse. The Commission's plans for doing away with the centralised notification system, and its reluctance to deal with those notifications which might still be made,[2] leave some managers in the unenviable position of suspecting that a particular arrangement may technically infringe Article 81(1), but being unable to confirm or dispel that suspicion by recourse to the Commission. Unless nullity under Article 81(2) has already been pleaded in litigation before a national court, it is no longer practicable to get an administrative, or "comfort" letter which could allay the firm's worries or help persuade a national judge. Even if national courts and competition authorities will be granted power to apply Article 81(3) in the future,[3] this is an uncertain and largely untested avenue, the exploration of which may prove time-consuming and costly, especially if the distribution system in question extends across several jurisdictions. Moreover, the NAs will not have power under the new Regulation 17 to do more than declare that an agreement was, as a whole, lawful on a certain date.

---

[1] Commission *Guidelines on Vertical Restraints* OJ 2000, C291/1. [2000] 5 CMLR 1074. Guideline 62. See Appendix V. The *Guidelines* do not take into account that the information necessary to carry out a proper self-assessment of market conditions may not be available to individual undertakings.

[2] See 2.12 above, and Guideline 65.

[3] The modernisation plans are not yet certain to go ahead. It has been reported that the German Monopolies Commission doubts their compatibility with the Treaty, and that it has recommended that the German Government challenge any changes before the ECJ. *Frankfurter Allgemeine Zeitung*, 31 October 2001, p.15.

7.2 DISTRIBUTION ARRANGEMENTS WHICH FALL OUTSIDE REGULATION 2790/99

Recital 5 of Regulation 2790/99 declares that "the benefit of the block exemption should be limited to vertical agreements for which it can be assumed with sufficient certainty that they satisfy the conditions of Article 81(3)". The Regulation prevents a number of distribution arrangements from benefiting from the block exemption on the ground, presumably, that the Commission regards them as possibly falling within the prohibition in Article 81(1),[4] and as not meriting exemption under Article 81(3).

The category of distribution arrangements which do not come within the "safe harbour" of Regulation 2790/99 includes: certain agreements between competitors;[5] agreements which contain hard-core restrictions of competition;[6] certain non-compete restraints of more than five years' duration;[7] agreements of a type the subject-matter of which is covered by a group exemption other than Regulation 2790/99;[8] agreements which fall outside the scope of the exemption entirely,[9] including those which do not conform to the definition of "vertical agreements" in Article 2;[10] agreements between parties whose relevant market share exceeds the thirty per cent ceiling of Article 3;[11] and, agreements in respect of which the European Commission or a competent national authority is contemplating withdrawing (or has withdrawn) the benefit of an exemption.[12]

---

[4] Article 81(1) does not apply to agreements with final consumers, unless they are acting as undertakings. Regulation 2790/99 is therefore only applicable to distribution arrangements between business undertakings acting as such, as noted by the Commission in Guideline 24. However, it may be difficult to decide when a business is acting as a final consumer or as an undertaking, since both Court and Commission have tended towards a broad concept of "undertaking", in order to justify applying the competition rules in certain borderline cases. Artists and members of the liberal professions have been regarded as "undertakings". See, for example, Commission Decision 78/516 *RAI/Unitel* OJ 1978, L175/39 (Opera Singers); also *Commission* v. *Italy*, Case C-35/96 [1998] ECR-I 3851, (CNSD—Customs Agents) at paras. 36 *et seq.*

[5] On "competing undertakings", See 3.4.4 above.

[6] On hardcore restraints identified by Article 4 of Regulation 2790/99, see chapter 4 above.

[7] On non-compete obligations under Article 5 of Regulation 2790/99, see chapter 5 above.

[8] On the other exemptions in force, see 3.4.8 above.

[9] On the scope of exemption under Article 2 of Regulation 2790/99, see chapter 3 above.

[10] In Guideline 24, the Commission says that the purpose of the Regulation is "to cover purchase and distribution agreements", although it would probably be more correct to say that it applies to such agreements only when they have a particular type of vertical dimension. The wording of the exemption provided for in Article 2 of the Regulation is arguably wider-reaching than Guideline 24, since it makes no mention of "distribution" at all. See 3.4.9 above. Note also that the other terms of Article 2 may exclude certain agreements which are clearly vertical in nature, such as vertical licenses of intellectual property rights, or distribution agreements the subject-matter of which comes under another block exemption.

[11] On the 30% market share ceiling, see 3.4.13–3.4.13.7 above.

[12] On withdrawal of the exemption, see 6.1.1–6.1.3 above.

7.2.1   Agreements Between Actual or Potential Competitors

7.2.1.1   Competing undertakings

Article 2(4) excepts from the exemption a number of distribution agreements entered into between "competing undertakings" as defined in Article 1(a), which includes potential competitors.[13] However, if the agreement is non-reciprocal, if the buyer's turnover is below €100 million, or if the agreement concerns so-called "dual distribution" of goods or services,[14] then the block exemption will still apply. These conditions exclude most distribution agreements between telecoms (and other utilities) operators, for example, since even where the agreement for the supply of services is non-reciprocal, the buyer is usually also a provider of services at the same level as the supplier.

7.2.1.2   Retailers' associations

Article 2(2) of Regulation 2790/99 exempts certain distribution agreements entered into between an association of retailers and its members or suppliers. This exemption is provided for without prejudice to the question of whether the association's horizontal activities are compatible with Article 81(1).[15]

7.2.1.3   Horizontal agreements

In November 2000, the Commission adopted two block exemption Regulations for horizontal co-operation agreements,[16] and a set of general guidelines on horizontal co-operation agreements.[17] Specialisation and research and development arrangements,[18] and all distribution agreements between competitors, other than those special cases mentioned in Articles 2(2) and 2(4) of Regulation 2790/99, therefore fall outside the safe harbour of Regulation 2790/99, by virtue of Article 2(5) of that provision. Parties to such agreements should consider modifying their arrangements in order to conform with and benefit from the available block exemptions.

---

[13] See 3.4.4 *et seq.* above.

[14] On dual distribution, see Guideline 27 and 3.4.4 above.

[15] On Article 2(2) and the status of retailers' associations and agricultural co-operatives, see 3.4.7 above.

[16] Commission Regulation (EC) No 2659/2000 of 29 November 2000 on the application of Article 81(3) of the Treaty to categories of research and development agreements, OJ 2000, L 304/7, [2001] 4 CMLR 808. Commission Regulation (EC) No 2658/2000 of 29 November 2000 on the application of Article 81(3) of the Treaty to categories of specialisation agreements OJ 2000, L 304/3, [2001] 4 CMLR 800.

[17] Guidelines on the applicability of Article 81 to horizontal co-operation agreements, OJ 2001, C03/2 6 January 2001 [2001] CMLR 819.

[18] Note that Article 2(5) of Regulation 2790/99 excludes from exemption agreements the subject-matter of which comes under another block exemption Regulation.

Guideline 26 on vertical restraints says that the horizontal aspects of agreements between competitors fall to be considered under the horizontal co-operation guidelines, while the vertical aspects are dealt with in the guidelines on vertical restraints. Guideline 29 on vertical restraints indicates the order in which the respective horizontal and vertical elements of agreements concerning a retailers' association should be assessed. In the Commission's opinion, one should first consider any horizontal elements, under the horizontal co-operation guidelines.[19] If this assessment indicates that the co-operation as such is permissible, then the association's vertical agreements must be considered in the light of Regulation 2790/99 and of the vertical restraints *Guidelines*. The Commission takes the view that "only if this [first] assessment is [*sic.*] positive[20] does it become relevant to assess the vertical agreements between the association and individual members or between the association and suppliers".

We think that Article 2(2) provides no legal basis for this interpretation, and that there is no reason why, when considering agreements between competitors— be they retailers or otherwise—an analysis of the horizontal aspects can displace the need also to consider the vertical aspects. For example, the compatibility of an association's vertical agreements with Article 81(1) or Article 81(3) does not necessarily depend on that association's horizontal behaviour. Even in the case of a distribution agreement between only two competitors, the extent of any putative nullity under Article 81(2) is a matter for national law,[21] and there may well be vertical arrangements which are validly subsisting. Indeed, even a hard-core cartel can engage in distribution, without the distribution contracts—at least those between the individual participants and their buyers or suppliers—thereby being void. However, many, if not most, agreements by co-operatives of small firms are not caught by the prohibition in Article 81(1).[22]

7.2.2 Agreements Containing "Hardcore" Restrictions of Competition

In Guidelines 46–56, the Commission sets out the practices which it regards as "hardcore" restrictions of competition under Regulation 2790/99. These consist of resale price maintenance (RPM), and certain restrictions with respect to the territory into which, or the customers to whom, the buyer may re-sell the contract

---

[19] Guidelines on the applicability of Article 81 to horizontal co-operation agreements, OJ C03 OJ 2001, C03/2, [2001] CMLR 819.

[20] For "positive", read "favourable".

[21] See, for example, *Cabour SA* v. *Arnor "SOCO"*, Case C-230/96 [1998] ECR-I 2055, at para. 51: "the consequences, for all other parts of the agreement or for other obligations flowing from it, of the fact that those contractual provisions which are incompatible with Article 81(1) are automatically void are not a matter for Community law. It is therefore also for the national court to determine, in accordance with the relevant national law, the extent and consequences, for the contractual relation as a whole, of the nullity of certain contractual provisions by virtue of Article 81(2)."

[22] See 3.4.7 above. On whether Article 81(1) applies to agricultural co-operatives, see also *Dijkstra, Roessel, de Bie* v. *Friesland Cooperatie, Campina*, Cases C-319/93, C-40/94, C-224/94 [1995] ECR-I 4471 [1996] 5 CMLR 178, at paras. 10 and 24.

goods or services.[23] There are limited exemptions under Article 4 of the BER for a number of territorial or customer restraints,[24] but other "hardcore" measures attract opprobrium from Commission and Courts.

The Guidelines have made the Commission's negative attitude to RPM and territorial or customer restraints quite clear. The presence of so-called "hardcore" restrictions is enough to disqualify any agreement for an automatic exemption. In the *Matra Hachette* case, however, the Court of First Instance considered that:

> in principle, no anti-competitive practice can exist which, whatever the extent of its effects on a given market, cannot be exempted, provided that all the conditions laid down in Article 81(3) of the Treaty are satisfied and the practice in question has been properly notified to the Commission.[25]

In theory, therefore, it is possible for *any* infringement of the prohibition in Article 81(1) to be notified and exempted. However, in Guideline 46, the Commission says that "individual exemption of vertical agreements containing such hardcore restrictions is . . . unlikely".

In its recent Decision on Glaxo Wellcome's Spanish distribution system, the Commission rejected novel economic arguments adduced to justify a dual pricing system for pharmaceuticals.[26] Because Spanish regulations maintain the prices of drugs at an artificially low level, and in order to protect the profitability of its operations in other countries, Glaxo had notified to the Commission a system under which Spanish wholesalers were obliged to buy supplies destined for parallel export at a higher price than those destined for domestic consumption. Although there are compelling arguments to be made in favour of the proposition that such State measures distort the Common Market far more than any pricing restraint implemented by a particular manufacturer, the Commission took the

---

[23] Moreover, certain clauses in distribution contracts which have the object of restricting competition are regarded as attracting the Treaty prohibition by their very nature, without the need for further economic analysis. In *Miller*, the Court found that "by its very nature, a clause prohibiting exports constitutes a restriction on competition, whether it is adopted at the instigation of the supplier or of the customer since the agreed purpose of the contracting parties is the endeavour to isolate a part of the market". *Miller International Schallplatten GmbH* v. *Commission,* Case 19/77 [1978] ECR– I 131, para 7, at p.148. [1978] 2 CMLR 334, CMR 8439 (See 2.7.1 above). Finally, distribution practices may also be shown to have the effect of restricting competition, in which case they too fall foul of Article 81(1). In *Erauw-Jacquery*, the Court quoted from *Consten and Grundig* and indicated that an agreement has this anticompetitive effect where it is "possible to foresee, on the basis of all the objective factors of law or of fact, with a sufficient degree of probability that it may have an influence, direct or indirect, actual or potential, on the pattern of trade between Member States in such a way that it might hinder the attainment of the objectives of a single market between Member States". *SPRL Louis Erauw-Jacquery* v. *La Hesbignonne SC,* Case 27/87 [1988] ECR 1919, at para. 14, [1988] 4 CMLR 576, [1989] 2 CEC 637. For comment on the meaning of "restrictive effect" under Article 81(1), see **Okeoghene Odudu** "Interpreting Article 81(1): Demonstrating Restrictive Effect" (2001) 26 *ELRev* 261.

[24] See chapter 4 above.

[25] *Matra Hachette SA* v. *Commission,* Case T-17/93 [1994] ECR-II 595, at para. 85.

[26] Commission Decision of 8 May 2001, OJ 2001, L302 of 17 November 2001. Also Commission Press Release IP/01/661 of 8 May 2001, available on the internet at http://www.europa.eu.int/rapid/start/welcome.htm The Decision is under appeal as *Glaxo Wellcome plc* v. *Commission,* Case T-168/01 (see the notice in OJ 2001, C275/17), but has been publicly defended by Commissioner Monti—see SPEECH/01/450 of 11 October 2001.

position that protecting the possibility of arbitrage by parallel traders is para-mount, and dismissed the economic arguments as unfounded.[27] Since the system had been notified, the Commission could not impose a fine, but it ordered Glaxo to bring the dual-pricing system to an immediate end.[28]

The European Courts have adopted a somewhat less trenchant position on RPM and customer restrictions.[29] Although they have not yet used the Commission's pejorative expression "hardcore restraints", the Courts have long regarded such clauses in distribution contracts as having the object of restricting competition and therefore attracting the Treaty prohibition by their very nature, without the need for further economic analysis.[30]

Even though there are cogent economic arguments to suggest that RPM and cus-tomer or territorial restraints may be competition-neutral or even preferable to pro-viding for long exclusive territories in certain circumstances,[31] it is most unlikely that the Commission or European Courts will treat such behaviour as anything other than an infringement of Article 81(1). This is a dogma of Community law.[32] The Glaxo Wellcome Decision re-emphasises that undertakings and their advisors must consider their business activities carefully, to be sure that they are not main-taining prices either directly or indirectly and, moreover, to ensure that they are not seen so to be doing. Furthermore, caution should be exercised even in operating the recommended-price and maximum-price restrictions permitted by Article 4(a), in order to avoid arousing suspicion of clandestine or *de facto* price-fixing,[33] since the

---

[27] It is interesting that the Commission relied by analogy on the ruling in *Merck et. al. v. Primecrown et. al. and Beecham Group v. Europharm*, Joined Cases C-267 & 268/95 [1996] ECR-I 6285, [1997] 1 CMLR 83, [1997] 1 CEC 261 as establishing that a divergence in national price regulations does not exclude the application of the Treaty's competition provisions. Although the Court of Justice ulti-mately preferred to uphold the principle of unrestrained parallel trade, Advocate-General Fennelly's opinion in *Merck* made a cogent case for allowing manufacturers to take restrictive measures to com-pensate for the market distortions caused by State regulation. We think that the A-G's opinion reflected the economic reality of the situation better than the rather poorly reasoned judgment of the Court.

[28] Although it is not directly mentioned in the Commission press release, Glaxo presumably could not rely on the CFI's new *Bayer/Adalat* doctrine that unilateral restrictions of competition imposed by a supplier escape the prohibition in Article 81(1), since the Spanish wholesalers had "signed the new sales conditions". See 2.1 above.

[29] See 2.4.1.3 above.

[30] See 2.7.1 and 4.2–4.2.6 above. In *Miller*, the Court found that "by its very nature, a clause pro-hibiting exports constitutes a restriction on competition, whether it is adopted at the instigation of the supplier or of the customer since the agreed purpose of the contracting parties is the endeavour to iso-late a part of the market". *Miller International Schallplatten GmbH v. Commission*, Case 19/77 [1978] ECR I 131, para. 7, at p.148.

[31] See 1.2.2.3 and 2.8.5 *et seq.* above.

[32] Valentine recalls that the Commission has been averse to retail price maintenance since the 1960's. Short-form notification for example, was only available in cases where the parties certified that their distribution measures contain no rpm. Only after representations from the American Bar Association did the Commission agree to permit maximum and recommended retail prices. See 2.8.5 above.

[33] See Guideline 47. It would be prudent, in cases where such a suspicion might arise, to document the parties' intention that no part of the distribution arrangement should be construed as, or as having the effect of, RPM or a territorial or customer restriction, other than any clause covered by the limited exceptions to Article 4.

Commission seems intent on applying a very broad interpretation of what behaviour amounts to price maintenance.[34]

In brief, although *Matra Hachette* suggests that no restriction of competition is beyond exemption, there appears to be no real possibility of redeeming the so-called "hardcore" restraints, and their inclusion in any distribution arrangement—even one which would otherwise satisfy the conditions for exemption under Regulation 2790/99—exposes the parties to serious risk of fines and nullity. Businesses would be well advised simply to avoid such restraints entirely.[35]

7.2.3 Non-Compete Obligations of Long Duration

Article 5 of Regulation 2790/99 refers to certain obligations which, if they appear in vertical agreements otherwise covered by the BER, will not benefit from exemption.[36] These are non-compete obligations,[37] whether during the lifetime of the agreement or post-term,[38] and selective distribution arrangements amounting to

[34] Paradoxically, in June 2000 the Commission proposed clearing an agreement between publishers and booksellers in Germany the sole purpose of which was to fix book prices. The agreements were structured in such a way as to confine their effect to national markets only, thus neutralising their Community dimension, and effectively taking the agreements out of the sphere of Commission control. We find it strange that the net book agreement was not thought to affect trade between the Member States (normally a notoriously low hurdle in the Community jurisprudence), but the Commission claims that the judgment of the ECJ in *Echirolles Distribution SA* v. *Association du Dauphiné*, Case C-9/99 of 3 October 2000 permits State measures fixing the price of books. Compare *Publishers' Association* v. *Commission*, Case C-360/92 P [1995] ECR-I 23, at para.34, where it was not disputed that net book agreements infringed Article 81(1). See 2.8.5.4 above. In July 2001, the Commission announced it had re-opened its investigation into the German net-price agreements. "Dawn-raids" were carried out in August 2000, following complaints from two internet bookstores, *Libro* of Austria, and *Proxis* of Belgium. The searches disclosed that the German system was not being operated in a manner consistent with the Commission's clearance. Several German wholesalers had refused to supply the internet sellers with books unless they agreed to abide by the German system of fixed prices. The wholesalers systematically treated discount internet sales as a circumvention of the net-price system, which the Commission regarded as illegal collusion, contrary to Article 81(1). A formal statement of objections has been issued, and it is now likely that fines will be imposed in due course. Commission Press Release IP/01/1035.

[35] In the—probably unlikely—event that the parties regard such restraints as indispensable, they must be notified to the Commission, in order to preclude the imposition of fines, as was the case in the Glaxo Decision. The notification procedure is considered at 7.5 below.

[36] Under the *Delimitis* and *Pronuptia* lines of case law, some such obligations can, in certain circumstances escape the prohibition in Article 81(1) entirely, because they are either of limited anti-competitive effect on the market, or because they are necessary for the operation of a pro-competitive distribution system. See 2.7.2 and 2.7.3 above.

[37] A "non-compete obligation" is defined in Article 1(b), and means a provision which restricts the buyer from manufacturing, purchasing, selling or reselling products competing with those of the supplier, or which requires the buyer to purchase more than 80% of its annual requirements of the contract products and their substitutes from the seller or from his nominee. The 80% test is applied to the buyer's requirements in the year preceding conclusion of the contract. According to Guideline 58, if no relevant data is available for that period, the buyer's best estimate of its annual total requirements may be used.

[38] Article 5(c) withholds exemption from post-term non-compete obligations on the buyer. See 5.2.2 above. However, there is a derogation under which indispensable obligations aimed at protecting the supplier's know-how may be exempted under the BER where their duration does not exceed one year, where they relate to the contract products or their substitutes, and where they are limited to the location in which

a boycott of particular suppliers.[39] They are referred to collectively as "single branding".[40] Unlike the list of hardcore restraints in Article 4, it is not the entire agreement which loses exemption, but only the specific obligation.[41] This raises the issue of whether grey-listed obligations are severable from the other provisions of an agreement. If not, and if the single-branding is not saved by the *Delimitis* or *Pronuptia* doctrines,[42] then the whole agreement will be deprived of exemption under the BER. Since these obligations are considered incompatible with an automatic exemption under Article 81(3), it can be assumed that they are also capable of infringing Article 81(1) when they appear in agreements which otherwise fall outside Regulation 2790/99, although the onus of proving any suspected infringement falls upon the person alleging an illegality.[43]

Parties to agreements which contain such single-branding obligations can consider the following options:

i) Reducing the intensity of the obligation, so that it does not amount to a non-compete clause, within the meaning of Article 1(b) of Regulation 2790/99. The

---

the buyer operated under the contract. Know-how is defined in Article 1(f), as non-patented practical information, which is secret, substantial and identified. See also Guideline 60. This does not, however, prevent the supplier from taking measures to protect the confidentiality of know-how for an indefinite period. Note that in *Pronuptia*, the Court of Justice indicated that post-term non-compete obligations would not infringe Article 81(1) if imposed for a reasonable period after expiry of a franchise agreement. *Pronuptia*, Case 161/84 [1986] ECR 353, at para. 16. [1986] 1 CMLR 414, CMR 14245. What is a reasonable period will depend on the individual case. There is no reason why, in appropriate circumstances, this reasonable period may not be longer than the one year mentioned in Article 5(b) of the BER.

[39] Article 5(c) expressly denies exemption for practices by which a supplier singles out the products of specific competitors, and prevents its authorised dealers from selling those products. See 5.2.3 above. In Guideline 61, the Commission says that this is intended to prevent the situation where several (perhaps leading) suppliers connive at foreclosing access to their common selected outlets vis-à-vis a common competitor. The Commission mentions its *Givenchy*, Decision OJ 1992, L236/11, [1993] 5 CMLR 579, [1992] 2 CEC 208 as an instance where indirect measures were used to effect a boycott. This seems to be an error in the Guidelines, as the Commission in fact exempted the Givenchy system, saying (in para. II.B.5) that the contracts did not contain any no-competition clauses. Perhaps there were originally such clauses, but they were deleted by the parties in order to satisfy the Commission.

[40] On the economics of single branding see 1.2.2.1 and 1.2.5–1.2.6.5 above. Article 5(a) withholds exemption from a blanket obligation not to manufacture or sell competing goods or services, referred to in the Guidelines as "Single Branding". This covers an obligation which *directly or indirectly* requires the buyer to meets more than 80% of its needs from the supplier or from the supplier's nominee. It also covers any *indirect* restriction which prevents or discourages the buyer from purchasing products competing with those of the supplier entirely, or which limits such purchases to 20% or less of the buyer's needs. Note that expressing purchases as a percentage of the buyer's needs is not required. If the seller specifies a minimum purchase requirement, by reference to value or numbers of units for instance, and this exceeds four-fifths of the buyers' relevant purchases, the obligation will still fall foul of Article 5(a), as it amounts to quantity-forcing. The definition of non-compete obligation covers in large part what was formerly known as exclusive purchasing. Single branding is discussed in Guidelines 106–108 and Guidelines 138–160, and exclusive purchasing in Guideline 113.

[41] Guideline 57. See 5.1.2 above.

[42] Under *Delimitis*, single branding will only infringe Article 81(1) if, having regard to its economic and legal context, it hinders access to the market or renders it difficult to increase existing market share. Under *Pronuptia*, certain restraints on competition may fall outside the prohibition in Article 81(1) where they are ancillary to a pro-competitive transaction. Note, however the narrow meaning of "ancillary" in *Métropole Télévision SA & Others* v. *Commission*, Case T-112/99 judgment of 18 September 2001, [2001] 12 CMLR 1236. See 2.7.3 and 2.7.2 above.

[43] See 2.7.2 above.

arrangement should not account for more than four-fifths of the buyer's total needs for the contract goods or services. This reduction may bring the obligation, in an otherwise qualifying agreement, back within the block exemption. Even where the overall agreement does not come within the terms of the BER, limiting the exclusivity still reduces the risk that the obligation will be regarded as infringing Article 81(1).

ii) Shortening the duration of the non-compete obligation, to conform to the model in Article 5 of Regulation 2790/99. The BER does not exclude non-compete obligations of five years' duration or less, provided they are not tacitly renewable beyond the five-year period. Even in the case of agreements which do not otherwise qualify for exemption under the BER, the Commission is likely to regard short non-compete obligations as qualifying for exemption under Article 81(3). Indeed, the *Delimitis* and *Pronuptia* doctrines indicate that many, if not most, such arrangements do not infringe Article 81(1) at all. The *Delimitis* doctrine has been refined in the recent *Neste* and *Roberts* cases.[44] Limiting the duration of the obligations to the five-year model in Article 5 minimises the risk that the Treaty prohibition might still be thought to apply.

Note that according to Guideline 58, obstacles under the seller's control which effectively hinder the buyer from terminating the obligation after the five-year period, such as a tied loan or equipment, may take the non-compete obligation outside the Article 81(3) exemption. Such obstacles to termination should be avoided in distribution agreements, or an alternative mechanism should be used where possible,[45] and the termination provisions (including any notice periods) should be drafted so as to avoid any appearance of unreasonableness which would amount to an unjustified exit barrier.

7.2.3.1 Supplier boycotts

In Guideline 192, the Commission takes the view that a boycott clause of the kind referred to in Article 5(c) falls outside the scope of exemption under Regulation 2790/99 and it would also be unlikely to benefit from individual exemption under Article 81(3) in circumstances where the aggregate market share of the five leading market players exceeds 50 per cent, unless the supplier in question is not one of the top five. In other words, it may be risky to attempt to boycott competing suppliers where they are small, and/or where the market is concentrated. A more elegant solution might be to require selected dealers to stock a particular

---

[44] *Neste Markkinointi Oy* v. *Yötuuli Ky and Others*, Case C-214/99, ECJ Judgment of 7 December 2000, [2001] 4 CMLR 27. *Roberts & Roberts* v. *Commission*, Case T-25/99 CFI Judgment of 5 July 2001. See also 2.5.2 and 5.1.1.1.3 above.

[45] In the case of a loan, this might mean permitting the buyer to repay it on normal commercial terms following termination of the distribution agreement. See 5.2.1.2 above. In the case of equipment, the supplier may agree to buy it back at current market value, where the buyer cannot otherwise dispose of it.

competing brand, the display of which would show the supplier's own brand in a positive light—in effect a form of comparative advertising/selling, combined with inter-brand competition.[46]

7.2.3.2 Premises owned or leased by the supplier

There is a derogation from the five-year rule in the specific case where the supplier owns or leases out the premises used by the buyer.[47] This is particularly important in the case of beer-supply agreements between breweries and their tenant public-ans,[48] and petrol filling-station "solus" agreements,[49] which normally include exclusive or semi-exclusive supply provisions of long duration.[50] Since a tenancy held from the supplier can usually justify non-compete arrangements for its dura-tion, there is little risk in providing for long-term non-compete obligations in such circumstances. Most such arrangements certainly fall under the BER. Similar pro-visions in agreements which fall outside the BER for other reasons arguably do not infringe Article 81(1) in circumstances where the level of restriction on the tenant is not disproportionate to the landlord's investment in the premises.[51] In the case of an important distribution partnership, for which the parties require long-term single-branding to recoup or protect their investments, it may be worthwhile for the supplier to lease premises to or for the buyer, since the Commission is unlikely to intervene, unless the supplier enjoys a dominant position.

7.2.4 Agreements Falling Outside the Definition of Vertical Agreements

Article 2 of Regulation 2790/99 sets out the various agreements which can benefit from the block exemption.[52] By definition, other distribution arrangements fall outside the "safe harbour" of this Regulation. Of these distribution arrangements which do not involve "vertical agreements" as defined in the BER, two types in

---

[46] An earlier draft of the BER would also have denied exemption to a positive obligation on selected distributors to sell certain brands, but this restriction has been dropped. However, if it became com-mon practice on a particular market, the Commission might consider a general withdrawal of the exemption under Article 8. See 6.1.3 above.

[47] Discussed in Guidelines 59 and 150.

[48] For recent cases concerning Article 81(1) and tied public houses, see *Courage Ltd.* v. *Bernhard Crehan.* Case C-453/99 ECJ Judgment of 20 September 2001, and *Roberts & Roberts* v. *Commission* Case T-25/99, CFI's Judgment of 5 July 2001. See also 7.7 below.

[49] See, for example, the *Neste Markkinointi Oy* v. *Yötuuli Ky and Others,* Case C-214/99 ECJ Judgment of 7 December 2000 [2001] 4 CMLR 27.

[50] The former Regulation 1984/83 block exempted beer-supply and filling-station agreements. These exemptions remained in force until the end of 2001 by virtue of the transitional provisions of Regulation 2790/99. Such agreements should be reviewed, and if necessary amended, to ensure that they come within the exemption under Regulation 2790/99.

[51] Regulation 1984/83, for example, allowed the landlord to tie beer sales, but afforded the tenant some freedom as to purchases of soft-drinks.

[52] The scope of the exemption is analysed in chapter 3, above.

particular give cause for concern: agreements in which intellectual property rights are an important element, and the (industrial) franchising of well-known brands.

7.2.4.1 IPR Agreements[53]

Article 2(3) of Regulation 2790/99 exempts certain vertical agreements containing provisions as to intellectual property rights (IPRs) assigned to or used by the buyer.[54] This applies where those provisions are not the "primary object" of the agreement, and where they relate to the use, sale, or resale of goods or services by the buyer or its customers.[55] The provisions are exempted only in so far as they do not have the same object or effect as other vertical restraints not exempted by the BER. There are thus five grounds why an agreement with provisions concerning IPRs may fall outside the "safe harbour": the IPR provisions are part of an agreement which is not "vertical"; the IPRs are not assigned or licensed to the buyer; the IPR provisions are the "primary object" of the agreement; the IPR provisions do not relate to the use, sale or resale of goods or services; and, the agreement contains other non-exempted restrictions of competition.

The Commission appears to contemplate introducing a new block exemption regulation to deal with industrial franchising, copyright and trade mark licenses. This would extend the scope of the current technology transfer block exemption, a report on which was published late in December 2001 on the internet.[56] See also 7.2.4.3 below.

7.2.4.2 Franchising with territorial restraints where the brand is "répandu"[57]

Distribution through franchising has been the subject of only one case before the European Court of Justice, but that case raises some concerns for parties to franchise agreements. In *Pronuptia*, the ECJ held that the compatibility of franchising arrangements with Article 81(1) depends upon their economic context, and also on whether the restrictive clauses in the franchise could be said to be restraints ancillary to an otherwise pro-competitive transaction.[58] The Court considered that proportionate restrictions necessary to avoid undertakings outside the franchise network benefiting from the franchisor's know-how are compatible with Article 81(1),[59] as are clauses which protect the identity and reputation of the franchise.[60] Although it

---

[53] See the detailed treatment in chapter 3 above, especially sections 3.4.9–3.4.9.2.

[54] On Article 2 generally, see chapter 3 above. "Intellectual property rights" are defined in Article 1(e), and "know-how" in Article 1(f). Note that Article 2(3) applies only to intellectual property rights as defined, and not to know-how, which is referred to only in respect of the duration of non-compete obligations under Article 5.

[55] See 3.4.9 above.

[56] http://europa.eu.int/comm/competition/antitrust/technology_transfer/.

[57] On franchising arrangements generally, see 1.1.5, 2.7.2, 2.8.2 and 3.4.10.2 above.

[58] *Pronuptia de Paris* v. *Schillgalis*, Case 161/84 [1986] ECR 353 at para. 27. *Pronuptia* is discussed in detail at 2.8.2 above.

[59] *Ibid.*, at para. 16.

[60] *Ibid.*, at para. 17.

cleared many clauses which form part of standard franchise agreements, the Court, notably, also made the point that absolute territorial protection conferred on a franchisee through a combination of exclusive territory and a location clause *could* constitute a restriction of competition prohibited by Article 81(1) in circumstances where the franchised name or symbol is already well-known.[61] The French text of the judgment uses the term "*répandu*" in this context, which suggests that the franchise be geographically widespread, rather than a well-known brand.

After *Pronuptia,* the Commission was under pressure to introduce a group exemption for franchising agreements, because of their great commercial importance. Probably in order to demonstrate that it had legal grounds for adopting such a general measure,[62] the Commission issued a series of Article 81(3) exemption decisions (rather than negative clearances) concerning franchise agreements in 1987.[63] The fact that exemptions were deemed necessary in these cases (although the restrictions of competition in question were arguably either ancillary to the franchises, or were of insignificant effect on highly competitive markets) has reinforced the conclusion in *Pronuptia* that franchises are capable of infringing Article 81(1).[64]

In so far as franchising agreements require exemption under Article 81(3) at all, many now come within the protection of Regulation 2790/99. Guidelines 42–44 list a number of common clauses in franchise agreements which can benefit from protection under the BER. However, not all franchise agreements can come within the so-called "safe harbour". Franchises, the principal subject-matter of which is intellectual property rights, agreements in relation to which the 30 per cent market share ceiling is exceeded, and obligations incompatible with Article 5 can all require an individual exemption if there is provision for territorial protection and the brand is widespread or well-known.

The principal risk in such agreements is that the allocation of an exclusive territory by the franchisor may, if coupled with a location clause, confer absolute territorial protection where the franchise is already widespread. This problem is more than theoretical, as the better-known a brand, the more important it is for franchisees to secure a degree of territorial protection, even if the allocated territory is small.[65] Franchised fast-food outlets in cities, for instance, may be numerous, but location clauses normally ensure that two restaurants in the same chain are not

---

[61] *Pronuptia de Paris* v. *Schillgalis* Case 161/84 [1986] ECR 353 at para 24. See also **Korah**, *Franchising and the EEC Competition Rules* (London, Sweet & Maxwell, 1989).

[62] As required by Recital 4 of Regulation 19/65.

[63] [1987] *Yves Rocher* OJ 1988, L8/49 [1988] 4 CMLR 592, CMR 10855; *Pronuptia,* OJ L13/39; *Computerland* OJ 1989, L222/12 [1989] 4 CMLR 259, CMR 10906. Also *Charles Jourdan,* OJ 1989, L35/31 [1989] 4 CMLR 591, [1989] 1 CEC 2119.

[64] The franchising block exemption Regulation was adopted in 1988. Commission Regulation 4087/88 of 30 November 1988. OJ 1989 L359/46. [1989] 4 CMLR 387, CMR 2767. Article 12 of Regulation 2790/99 provides that exemptions under Regulation 4087/88 continued to apply until 31 May 2000, with marginal relief until the end of 2001 for those arrangements exempted by the former franchising Regulation, but which fall outside the current BER.

[65] When the franchised brand is strong, the various franchised outlets are—from the consumer's point of view—largely interchangeable. In the case of weaker brands, the individual franchisee's goodwill plays a greater role. See 1.1.5 above.

situated within sight of each other. This is territorial protection, although the territory may be a small one.[66]

Despite the problem posed by the Court's judgment in *Pronuptia*, franchising agreements do not seem to the Commission to raise serious competition concerns. Even those franchise/licensing agreements falling outside the BER seem to benefit from a quasi-exemption by analogy to that provision.[67] In the Guidelines on Vertical Restraints, the Commission more or less glosses over the problem, saying only that the more important the transfer of know-how under the franchise, the more likely it is that Article 81(3) *could* apply to exempt restrictive clauses.[68] This raises the question of whether industrial franchising (in the sense of a trademark license combined with some know-how) which involves the transmission of only a limited amount of know-how can actually justify clauses restrictive of territory. Arguably, the know-how attached to the trademark license for a fast-food outlet is neither particularly considerable,[69] nor very secret, but many such outlets nevertheless benefit from territorial protection to some extent.

7.2.4.3 Industrial franchising and technology transfer

Just before Christmas 2001, the Commission published on the internet a preliminary report and call for comments concerning the revision of Regulation 240/96, the technology transfer block exemption, which is due to expire in 2006.[70] The report notes that trademark licensing for the purposes of manufacturing accounted for 19 per cent of the Commission's cases involving IPRs between 1996 and 2000, roughly half of which amount concerned a combination of licensing and know-how provisions.[71] Although the report assumes that franchising is covered by Regulation 2790/99,[72] it nevertheless seems to suggest that the Commission contemplates exempting IPR licensing agreements between non-competitors which include territorial exclusivity up to the level of market dominance.[73] It may well be that this will resolve the current difficulty with regard to common industrial franchises which provide for small exclusive territories.

7.2.5 Agreements Where the Relevant Market Share Exceeds the 30 per cent Ceiling

This is likely to be the largest, and is also the most problematic, category of agreements which cannot benefit from exemption under Regulation 2790/99. The

---

[66] In many cases, widespread franchises with pervasive, but small, territories, may fall to be considered under national competition law rules, since the territorial provisions have little or no effect on trade between Member States, except perhaps in so far as there are large-scale network effects.
[67] Guideline 43.
[68] See Guidelines 199–201.
[69] The definition of "know-how" in Article 1(f) of Regulation 2790/99 does not require much.
[70] OJ 1996, L31/2–13. The new Report is available at www.europa.eu.int/comm/.
[71] At para. 88.
[72] Para. 158.
[73] Para. 186.

difficulties of dealing with market share and "relevant markets", determining whether the ceiling has been exceeded, and if so, for how long and to what extent, are legion.[74]

Assuming that an undertaking has determined that the 30 per cent ceiling has been reached, or is soon going to be reached, it is faced with a number of options:

7.2.5.1 Marginal relief under Article 10

If the 30 per cent ceiling is not exceeded by more than a further 5 per cent, Article 10(2)(c) provides that any existing exemption shall continue for two calendar years following the year in which the 30 per cent level was first exceeded. Similarly, Article 10(2)(d) extends the exemption for one year following that in which the 35 per cent level was exceeded. The reliefs cannot be relied upon in combination with one another, so the maximum extension possible is two years.

Under Article 10(2)(a), market shares are to be calculated by reference to dates covering the preceding calendar year. There is thus no advantage by way of extension to be gained from carrying out the market share assessment at a particular time of year. However, the annual assessment should not be neglected, and should be carried out as early in the calendar year as possible (provided the necessary data are available) because, if it should transpire that the various ceilings (30 or 35 per cent) have been exceeded, the time available for management and their advisors to consider the best course of future action is maximised.

The options available where the market share ceiling has been exceeded, and the marginal reliefs under Article 10 are either inapplicable, or have been exhausted are:

7.2.5.2 Take no action

In many cases, if the parties' relevant market share(s) do not exceed the 30 per cent level by much, and the agreements in question otherwise fulfil the conditions of Regulation 2790/99, there is in practice little or no likelihood that they will be considered to have sufficient market power to bring their agreement within the prohibition in Article 81(1). There is, as the Commission says in Guideline 62, no presumption that agreements which fall outside the block exemption actually infringe the competition rules. There are various assessments to be carried out to

---

[74] See 3.4.13.7 above. One of the principal difficulties in practice is the frequent inability of undertakings to determine their market share accurately. They may have a general idea that their share is between 25 and 35%, but be unable to say on which side of the 30% ceiling they find themselves. Given the complexity of the market share and market definition issue, and the numerous traps for the unwary, it is important to note that in Guideline 65, the Commission says that it will not fine undertakings which have failed to notify an agreement because they assumed, in good faith, that they had not exceeded the 30% market share ceiling. Presumably, the Commission will adhere to this policy even if the notification procedure is abolished, as is currently planned. In borderline cases, firms and their advisors should therefore be aware of the need to generate sufficient and appropriate documentation to evidence a good faith mis-assessment. This does not, however, reduce the risk that the agreement in question may still have been rendered (at least partly) unenforceable by Article 81(2).

determine whether Article 81(1) applies. If it does, then further examination can
determine whether an exemption under Article 81(3) would be possible.

By how much the 30 per cent level can be exceeded without raising serious concerns for the undertakings involved in the distribution agreement will also depend
on the market in question, and on how well that market can be defined. On a
lively, competitive market, with several active competitors, and easy entry and exit,
even a large market share may be no cause for concern.[75] The Commission says in
Guideline 119:

> Where there are many firms competing in an unconcentrated market, it can be assumed
> that non-hardcore vertical restraints will not have appreciable negative effects. A market
> is deemed unconcentrated when the HHI index, i.e. the sum of the squares of the indi-
> vidual market shares of all companies in the relevant market, is below 1000.

On the other hand, if the market is concentrated, or the conditions of competition
on it are rigid, then even the market power associated with a share not much more
than 30 per cent may attract unwelcome attention from competition authorities
or complaints from competitors.[76] Note that a market share of 50 per cent may
give rise to a rebuttable presumption of dominance, and that the Commission may
regard companies as having "market power" even below that level.[77]

Additionally, if the parties take no immediate action, new entrants may join the
market, thus diluting the parties' market share. This may often happen on new
markets for emerging technologies, when a "first-mover" is quickly joined by
many competitors. However, it is less likely on established, static markets, or
where there are barriers to entry, such as patents or regulatory requirements.[78]

7.2.5.3 Shedding market share through divestitures

Divesting product lines is, at first sight, hardly a pro-competitive option, but one
which may be appropriate if the parties place a high value on the certainty afforded

---

[75] This is a question of the contestability of the market. In the *Cigarette Filter Rods* case (HC 335,
1968–69, 23.7.1969), the UK Monopolies Commission found that Cigarette Components Ltd. (a subsidiary of another public company, Bunzl) had nearly a 100% share of the market for filter rods, and yet
had no market power at all, because it was small in relation to its three big customers, the tobacco companies, each of which could have entered the market and made its own cigarette filter rods at any time
it so wished. The MC found that Cigarette Components was able to survive and thrive only because it
was efficient, and the firm's 44% return on capital was not a bare monopoly profit, but rather an indication that it was an effective competitor. Conversely, a firm may have a low market share, but nevertheless enjoy real market power if, for example, its competitors lack the production or distribution
capacity to meet market demand. (Denis would like to thank Lara Levis of the Office of Fair Trading for
generously providing him with a summary of the *Filter Rods* case, which is rather hard to find.)

[76] The new *de minimis* notice indicates that certain agreements which do not contain "hardcore"
restraints will not normally be regarded as appreciably restricting competition within the meaning of
Article 81(1): agreements between competitors whose aggregate market share does not exceed 10%;
and, agreements between non-competitors whose aggregate market share does not exceed 15%. OJ
2001, C 368/13–15.

[77] *AKZO* v. *Commission* Case C-62/86 [1991] ECR I 3359 para. 60. [1993] 5 CMLR 215, [1993] 2
CEC 115. See also Guidelines 119 & 135.

[78] On barriers to entry, see 1.2.1.2–1.2.1.2.6 above.

by bringing a particular distribution arrangement within the terms of Regulation 2790/99. It may be possible to shed or hive-off distribution of a related (i.e. substitutable) product in order to bring the market share in respect of the principal product under the 30 per cent ceiling,[79] or to lower it to a level above the ceiling which nevertheless raises no competition-law concerns. This is the converse of integrating into the distribution channel for one's own products.

7.2.5.4 Agreements where there is uneven market share across several Member States

Suppliers which operate distribution systems spanning several EU or EEA States may find that their arrangements concern more than one relevant market (in the sense of Article 3 BER), and that their market share may be uneven as across these markets.[80] In some markets the supplier may have low market shares for a product, clearly coming under the ceiling for exemption, while in others, its share may reach or exceed the 30 per cent ceiling. This "hole" causes a problem, not only in respect of those States in which the 30 per cent level is exceeded,[81] but also for the effectiveness of the distribution system generally. On the markets where the 30 per cent ceiling is exceeded, the supplier may not wish or be able to apply its standard-form contractual restrictions, for fear that they may infringe Article 81(1), and that they might not be capable of exemption.

Where the supplier restricts its buyers' active sales as allowed by the first indent of Article 4(b) of Regulation 2790/99, such a "hole" in the distribution system has the rather absurd consequence that the supplier can benefit from the automatic exemption and protect buyers within areas where the market share is high from those without, but not *vice-versa*. Moreover, if a particular distribution contract extends to an area greater than that of the "hole", that entire agreement may lose the benefit of the exemption, because of nullity under Article 81(2).

---

[79] Note the definition in Article 11 of "connected undertakings" whose market share is taken into account. See 3.4.13.1 above.

[80] In Guideline 90, the Commission repeats the formula used by the ECJ in *United Brands*, Case 27/76 [1978] ECR 207 [1978] 1 CMLR 429, CMR 8429 at paras. 10 & 11, and defines the relevant geographic market as

the area in which the undertakings concerned are involved in the supply and demand of relevant goods or services, in which the conditions of competition are sufficiently homogeneous, and which can be distinguished from neighbouring geographic areas because, in particular, conditions of competition are appreciably different in those areas.

Valentine notes that the Commission has usually treated downstream markets in distribution cases as being national, although they are frequently treated as extending across borders in cases under Article 82 and the Merger Regulation. We think that the introduction of the Euro from 1 January 2002 will make it more likely for future distribution markets to be supranational.

[81] Such a "hole" in the system can also come about when a national competition authority withdraws the benefit of exemption under Article 7 in respect of its jurisdiction. Guidelines 76–79. See 6.1.2 above.

However, on the basis of Guidelines 68–69 and *78*, it can be argued that this loss should extend to the agreement only in so far as it relates to distribution within the geographical market upon which the 30 per cent ceiling is exceeded. This would be consistent with the Commission's treatment where a product falls within several product markets, on only some of which the supplier's market share exceeds the ceiling.

A supplier whose market share is uneven may try to bring those shares exceeding 30 per cent under the ceiling of the BER using the options outlined at 7.2.5 *et seq.* above in order to ensure that the whole distribution system benefits from Regulation 2790/99. However, this may not be possible in every case, since it may be too costly to renounce a large share of a profitable market, in order to protect weaker or developing markets from imports. In these circumstances, Denis suggests that if the supplier still wishes to protect the weak markets from the strong, it may be possible to use contractual restrictions analogous to those in the first subparagraph of Article 4(b), on the controversial argument that the subparagraphs are references to lawful practices unlikely to infringe Article 81(1). A further measure would be to ensure that distribution for markets on which the 30 per cent ceiling is exceeded be organised using contracts separate from those for markets where the share is lower. This may, in practice, lead to situations where the supplier has several contracts with one and the same buyer, in respect of different markets. This may increase negotiation and management costs, and partition the Common Market, but such compartmentalisation isolates those distribution agreements exempted under the BER from contamination by any possible nullity of those agreements relating to areas where the market share is high.

7.2.6 Agreements Affected by Withdrawal of the Exemption

As discussed in detail in chapter 6 above, Regulation 2790/99 includes provisions under which the benefit of an automatic exemption may be withdrawn from distribution agreements. The European Commission can withdraw the exemption in particular cases where the requirements of Article 81(3) are not fulfilled,[82] as can national competition authorities,[83] acting in respect of their own jurisdictions.[84]

---

[82] Article 6. According to Guideline 71, the Commission will be particularly vigilant in respect of agreements which fail to ensure that final consumers share in the benefits brought about by restraints on competition.

[83] The provision of a withdrawal mechanism for national competition authorities is a novel feature of Regulation 2790/99. It is in line with the Commission's general policy of modernising and decentralising the enforcement of competition law, and of transferring as much of the enforcement procedure as possible to the respective national agencies, in order to free up Commission resources for dealing with cross-border restrictions of competition.

[84] Where a national authority does not have legal powers to effect a withdrawal itself, it may ask the Commission to do so on its behalf. (Guideline 76.) In either case, the withdrawal will be limited in effect to the territory of the Member State concerned. (Guideline 78.)

In addition, the Commission can adopt a Regulation withdrawing the exemption from an entire market if it is affected by parallel networks of similar restraints.[85]

7.2.6.1 Pre-withdrawal contacts with officials

The power to withdraw exemptions has long been a feature of block exemption regulations, but it is very seldom used, and then only in a serious case, where there is a clear infringement.[86] There is one reported instance where the Commission has actually withdrawn the benefit of a block exemption,[87] since in most cases where a withdrawal is contemplated, the parties will negotiate with the Commission and amend their agreement in order to allay its concerns.[88]

An undertaking which enters into frank negotiations with the responsible officials as soon as possible may be able to forestall or pre-empt formal measures.[89] Officials frequently act on the basis of pressure or complaints from competitors of the undertakings concerned or from interest-groups in the industry, with the result that they have an incomplete or one-sided picture of actual market conditions. In these circumstances, a visit by a sufficiently senior business-person, who can explain the commercial justifications for the restraints in question, may be enough to persuade the authorities not to interfere with the *status quo*, provided

---

[85] See 6.1 and 6.1.3 above. The Commission's power under Article 8 of Regulation 2790/99 to dis-apply a block exemption in relation to a particular market or industry blocks a legal loophole which was exposed by the "ice-cream wars" cases. In the past, the Commission could withdraw the benefit of an exemption from a particular agreement, but it could not prevent the parties to that agreement making new arrangements which would again benefit from the general exemption. *Langnese-Iglo GmbH & Co. KG* v. *Mars GmbH*. Commission Decision 93/406/EEC [1993] OJ 1993, L183/9, at paras. 208–9. The CFI upheld the legality of the Commission's withdrawal of exemption under Article 14(1) of Regulation 1984/83 in *Langnese-Iglo GmbH* v. *Commission*, Case T-7/93 [1995] ECR II-1533. The ECJ did not disturb the CFI's ruling on appeal in Case C-279/95 P [1998] ECR I-5609. The Commission had found that the existing freezer-exclusivity agreements could not be exempted, but it had no power to prevent the parties simply setting up further agreements which, at least at face value, fell under the block exemption regulation then in force. *Langnese-Iglo GmbH & Co. KG*, (93/406/EEC), 23 December 1992, OJ 1993, L183/19, [1994] 4 CMLR 51, [1993] 2 CEC 2123. On appeal, *Langnese-Iglo GmbH & Co. KG* v. *Commission*, Case T-7/93, 8 June 1995, [1995] ECR II-1533, [1995] 5 CMLR 602, [1995] 2 CEC 217. The final appeal did not consider much of the substance, Case C-279/95P, 1 October 1998, [1998] ECR I-5609, [1998] 5 CMLR 933. For an interesting discussion of the ice-cream wars, see **Aidan Robertson** and **Mark Williams**, "An Ice Cream War: The law and economics of freezer exclusivity" in [1995] 1 *ECLR* 7. The sequel to this article is expected after the CFI renders judgment in *Van den Bergh Foods* v. *Commission*, Case T-65/98 R. For the facts of that case, see the Order of the President of the Court of First Instance of 7 July 1998 in OJ 1998, C312/12.

[86] Because the market share ceiling for application of the BER is now set quite low, it is now unlikely that the Commission will find many cases which have sufficiently serious effects on competition to warrant an individual withdrawal.

[87] The *Langnese-Iglo* case. See 6.1.3 above.

[88] *Tetra Pak*, Commission Decision 88/501/EEC, OJ 1988, L272/27, [1990] 4 CMLR 47, CMR 11015. On appeal, *Tetra Pak Rausing SA* v. *Commission*, Case T-51/89, 10 July 1990, [1990] ECR II-309, [1991] 4 CMLR 334, [1990] 2 CEC 409. See 6.1 above.

[89] Of course, such negotiations may be hampered if the parties to the agreement in question are no longer on good terms, and are not prepared to co-operate with one another in order to lobby effectively. In these circumstances, the beneficiary of a restriction may be able to avoid a withdrawal of the exemption by waiving part of the restriction, as in the *ARD* case. See 2.5.2 above.

the arrangements otherwise appear to come squarely within the terms of Regulation 2790/99. If the arrangements are necessary, but overly restrictive of competition, officials may be able to suggest equivalent measures which would be acceptable to the authorities.

7.2.6.2 Notice periods for withdrawals

Where the Commission, under Article 8, withdraws the BER from certain markets, the affected parties have six months' grace before a disapplying Regulation can take effect. It is therefore extremely important for distributors, their advisors, and any trade or industry associations to monitor whether the Commission acts under Article 8, in order to have as much leeway as possible, in case agreements covering affected markets will need to be individually notified, renegotiated or amended. Where an individual withdrawal is contemplated under Articles 6 or 7, no notice period is stipulated. However, Community law recognises the principle of *audi alteram partem*,[90] which would suggest that the authorities must indicate to the parties concerned that a withdrawal is being contemplated, and give them an opportunity to make known their views. If the Commission intends to withdraw the exemption and simultaneously issue a Decision declaring that the arrangement in question is prohibited by Article 81(1), it must respect the normal procedural rules under Regulation 17 as to the issuing of a statement of objections *etc.*. Denis thinks that, in any case, the effective notice period before an individual withdrawal should, by analogy with Article 8, not be less than six months. This should give the parties an opportunity to negotiate alternatives.

7.2.6.3 Withdrawal procedure

As a matter of procedure, and because there is a presumption that agreements complying with the block exemption Regulation come under Article 81(3), the Commission (or the national competition authority) bears the burden of proving that at least one of the four conditions for exemption is not being met.[91]

Individual withdrawal of an exemption may be coupled with a finding that the agreement in question is prohibited by Article 81(1). However, the Commission takes the view that such a withdrawal is effective only from the date it enters into

---

[90] *Audi alteram partem* (literally "hear the other side"): A rule of natural justice, recognised by the Community Courts, which states that a decision cannot stand unless the person directly affected by it was given a fair opportunity both to state his case and to know and answer the other side's case. See, for example, the Order of the Court of First Instance of 19 June 1996 in *Commission* v. *NMH Stahlwerke* Case T-134/94 [1996] ECR-II 537 at paras 73–74.

[91] Guideline 72. The use of "all" in the English wording of the Guideline is somewhat misleading, as it seems to suggest that the Commission must show that the agreement from which the exemption is to be withdrawn fulfils *none* of the conditions of Article 81(3). This reading would be incorrect. The Community Courts have consistently held that the conditions for exemption are cumulative, and that an applicant for individual exemption must show that all four conditions are met. See, for example, *Stichting Certificatie Kraanverhuurbedrijf (SCK) and Federatie van Nederlandse Kraanbedrijven (FNK)* v. *Commission*, Joined Cases T-213/95 and T-18/96 [1997] ECR II-1739, at para. 206.

force, and that it does not retroactively render void an agreement since its inception.[92] In the event that the Commission issues a formal Decision of withdrawal and prohibition, the affected undertakings may be able to preserve the validity of their distribution agreement for a considerable part, if not the entirety, of the original term of the contract: if the parties can have the Decision suspended as an interim measure in an action for its annulment, the delay before the Court of First Instance delivers judgement may afford a considerable period of respite.

7.2.6.4 Withdrawal by national authorities

The ability of national competition authorities to withdraw exemptions is likely to prove increasingly important in the future, as some countries pursue more assertive antitrust enforcement policies.[93] Although the Member States' authorities are bound to co-operate in ensuring the efficacy of Community law,[94] it remains to be seen what effect Article 7 will have on the overall harmony of the application of EC competition rules. The Commission is taking no chances and, in Guideline 77, has reserved to itself the right to "take on certain cases displaying a particular Community interest" from the national authorities, in the event that the existing co-operation and consultation mechanisms prove insufficient.[95]

As a practical matter, it may be advantageous for undertakings threatened with withdrawal of the exemption in a particular Member State to ask the European Commission to take on the case on grounds of Community interest. Large companies and their advisors, in particular, may already have experience in dealing with the Commission officials responsible for their industry, while the authorities at national level may be an unknown quantity. The language of the proceedings may be a

---

[92] Guideline 75.

[93] This view is not shared by all commentators. **Ritter**, **Braun** and **Rawlinson** make the following argument as to why national authorities cannot withdraw an exemption: (i) under Article 2(1) the BER applies only to agreements which "contain restrictions of competition falling within the scope of Article 81(1)"; (ii) agreements whose effect is solely on a distinct national or regional market may not appreciably affect trade between Member States, in which case they are (iii) outside Article 81(1) and (iv) therefore not covered by the block exemption, which therefore (v) could not be withdrawn. *European Competition Law: A Practitioner's Guide—Supplement, January 2001* (available to download from the internet at http://www.wkap.nl/kapis/appendices/ritter.pdf). This argument, however, is based on a mis-reading of Article 7. The agreement must have anticompetitive effects in the territory of the Member State in question, but the power to withdraw the exemption does not require that those effects be felt "solely" in that Member State. It is sufficient that there be some Community dimension to the agreement's effects, a test which is a notoriously low hurdle in the Community case-law. The authors do however, raise an interesting question of what practical effect a purported withdrawal could have upon an agreement which never required exemption in the first place.

[94] Article 10 of the EC Treaty and Guideline 78. The Commission refers to the ECJ judgment in *Walt Wilhelm v. Bundeskartellamt*, Case 14/68, [1969] ECR 1 [1969] CMLR 100, CMR 8056. 21 ELR Dec. 1996, at para. 4. For comment on national courts' duty of sincere co-operation with the Commission, see **Siún O'Keeffe**, "First among equals: the Commission and the national courts as enforcers of EC competition law", in (2001) 1 *ELRev* 301.

[95] Guideline 79 refers to the consultation mechanisms provided for in the Notice on cooperation between national competition authorities and the Commission OJ 1997, C313/3 [1997] 5 CMLR 884, points 49 to 53.

hindrance,[96] as may be the need to retain local counsel. It may be possible to convince the Commission to take the "bigger picture" into account, whereas a national authority will not necessarily be swayed by arguments as to how the distribution arrangements in its jurisdiction fit into a system extending across several Member States, the EU or EEA. Moreover, hostile interest-groups or competitors may be able to lobby their local authorities more effectively than they can lobby Commission officials. Since the national authorities' power to withdraw exemptions is new, they may be more eager to assert it than would be the Commission, for reasons of national or institutional prestige or politics. Regulation 2790/99 is silent on this point, as are the *Guidelines*, but it would seem that once "taken on" by the Commission, a particular case cannot revert to the national authority concerned, even if the local officials later disagree with the Commission's handling of the matter. The influence of political factors on the Article 7 procedure is difficult to gauge.

7.2.6.5 Withdrawal on "cumulative effects" grounds

Articles 6 and 8 refer explicitly to the presence of "parallel networks of similar vertical restraints" as being a ground for withdrawal of the exemption. The same consideration also seems, albeit implicitly, to be a ground upon which national competition authorities could rely when exercising their powers under Article 7.

A doctrine of cumulative effect has been recognised in Community competition law since the judgments in *Brasserie de Haecht I* and *Delimitis*.[97] Certain restrictions of competition which, if they are operated by only one or a few market actors, would either not be caught by Article 81(1) at all, or would normally be capable of exemption under Article 81(3), can have the effect of foreclosing a particular market if the same or similar restraints are operated by many or the leading market actors.[98] This situation could arise, for instance, where all the suppliers on a given market practise selective distribution, with the result that other forms of distribution are excluded. In Guideline 73, the Commission indicates the kind of restraints which it would expect to give rise to such network effects.[99]

---

[96] Undertakings can require the European Commission to communicate with them in the official language of their choice. There are 11 official languages of the Community: Danish, Dutch, English, Finnish, French, German, Greek, Italian, Portuguese, Spanish, Swedish. See EEC Council Regulation No 1 determining the languages to be used by the European Economic Community OJ 1958, 17/385, as amended by Council Decision of the European Communities of 1 January 1973 adjusting the documents concerning the accession of the new Member States to the European Communities OJ 1973, L002/1. Irish is also a working language of the Community, but there is no record of competition law matters ever having been dealt with through Irish. It is not usually possible to have national competition authorities use languages other than those recognised in their own jurisdiction.

[97] Respectively, Case 23/67 [1967] ECR 407, at 415, and Case *Delimitis (Stergios)* v. *Henninger Bräu*, Case C-234/89, 28 February 1991 [1991] ECR I-935, [1992] 5 CMLR 210, [1992] 2 CEC 530. See 7.3.3 above.

[98] Note Guideline 143, in which the Commission says there is unlikely to be a cumulative foreclosure effect where the market share of the largest supplier is below 30%, and the market share of the five largest suppliers together is below 50%.

[99] Single branding (exclusive dealing or non-compete obligations), exclusive distribution, exclusive customer allocation, selective distribution, franchising, exclusive supply, tying, recommended and maximum resale prices.

7.2.6.5.1   *Defences where cumulative effects are claimed*—Delimitis, Neste & Roberts

Undertakings which are faced with a withdrawal of their exemption on grounds of network effects are not entirely helpless. Following the Court of Justice's decision in *Delimitis*,[100] the Commission can only attribute responsibility for network effects to those undertakings whose contribution to the overall foreclosure is "appreciable".[101] Therefore, if a market is covered and foreclosed by many agreements, and a particular undertaking is a party to only a few of them, that undertaking and those few agreements may be unaffected by the purported withdrawal of the block exemption, since the agreements might never have been subject to the prohibition in Article 81(1) at all.

The *Delimitis* judgment has been further refined by the judgements in the *Neste* and *Roberts* cases.[102] In *Neste*, a buyer (the operator of a filling station) sought to avoid an action for damages for breach of contract on the ground that its exclusive-purchasing agreement for motor fuels was contrary to Article 81(1), and therefore void. In its reference, the national court called for clarification of *Delimitis*. The buyer's agreement was only one out of several exclusive-supply agreements entered into by the supplier. Most of these agreements however, were of a long fixed duration, while that of the buyer was terminable upon one year's notice by the retailer.[103] In these circumstances, the agreement in question accounted only for a small proportion of the overall market-partitioning effect. The national court asked whether the individual agreement could therefore be regarded as making only an insignificant contribution to the cumulative market foreclosure, and thus not affected by the prohibition in Article 81(1).

The Court of Justice found that exclusive purchasing agreements for fuel are different from agreements relating to other goods, because service-stations stock only one brand of fuel,[104] and because of the considerable investment necessary on the part of the supplier to adapt sales points to the image of the brand to be sold.[105] The duration of such contracts is, therefore, of more fundamental importance than the exclusivity which they confer, and this duration is the decisive factor in foreclosing the market.[106] The Court held that a one-year notice period for termination of the supply agreement sufficiently protects the respective parties' interests and limits restrictive effects on the market for fuel distribution.[107]

---

[100] *Delimitis* v. *Henniger Bräu*, Case C-234/89, ECJ Judgment of 28 February 1991 [1991] ECR I-935, [1992] 5 CMLR 210, [1992] 2 CEC 530 paragraphs 19 to 27. See 5.1.1.1.3 above.

[101] Guideline 74.

[102] *Neste Markkinointi Oy* v. *Yötuuli Ky and Others*, Case C-214/99, ECJ Judgment of 7 December 2000 [2001] 4 CMLR 27. *Roberts & Roberts* v. *Commission*, Case T-25/99 CFI Judgment of 5 July 2001.

[103] In fact, Neste's contract seems to have been for ten years certain, renewable annually thereafter. At the time the litigation arose, the ten-year term had already expired.

[104] Case C-214/99, ECJ Judgment of 7 December 2000, at point 30.

[105] *Ibid.*, at point 34.

[106] *Ibid.*, at point 32.

[107] *Ibid.*, at point 35.

The novel element of the Court's judgment lies in its acceptance of the proposition (also accepted by Advocate-General Fennelly) that the economic market assessment required under *Delimitis* can, exceptionally, be carried out selectively according to the *various categories* of contract entered into by a particular supplier.[108] Where the exclusive-supply agreement in question is terminable by the retailer upon a year's notice and where exclusive-supply agreements (whether involving the same or other suppliers) have an appreciable market-foreclosing effect, but most other agreements of this kind are concluded for a fixed term of more than one year, the individual agreement in question *will not be caught by the prohibition* in Article 81(1).[109]

The *Neste* ruling suggests that certain contracts, even within a network of parallel agreements the overall effect of which is to foreclose a market, can be economically distinguished from the suppliers' other agreements by having regard to their insignificant impact on competition. Such agreements, which are less harmful than the "average" contract, can escape the prohibition in Article 81(1) entirely. In *Delimitis*, the Court ruled that the agreement would infringe Article 81(1) only if two conditions, including that of appreciable effect were met. The *Neste* agreement fell outside that prohibition altogether. Therefore, the agreement in question would not be affected by any purported withdrawal of the exemption under Regulation 2790/99.

In July 2001, the Court of First Instance upheld the Commission's decision to reject a complaint concerning the Greene King pub lease.[110] The CFI applied the Court of Justice's rulings in the *Delimitis* and *Neste* cases,[111] and held that the Commission was correct in its finding that the licence did not foreclose the UK beer market. The case thus restates the doctrine that individual supply contracts forming part of a distribution network can fall outside the prohibition in Article 81(1) entirely where they contribute only insignificantly to market foreclosure, and dispels the lingering doubt that the *Neste* precedent may have been applicable only to service-station agreements.

Mr and Mrs Roberts operated, as tenants, a public house belonging to the Greene King brewery ("GK"). Under the terms of their lease, they were obliged to purchase beer from GK. They complained to the European Commission that this obligation infringed Article 81(1), but the Commission rejected their complaint, on the ground that the standard Greene King lease did not fall within the prohibition in Article 81(1) at all. The complainants appealed this decision to the CFI.

The Court of First Instance, after upholding the Commission's definition of the relevant product market as the distribution of beer in establishments selling alcoholic beverages for consumption on the premises, considered whether the fact that Greene King operates a network of "tied houses" made a significant contribution to the foreclosure of the market as defined. It noted that in order to assess the

---

[108] *Ibid.*, at points 36 & 38.
[109] *Ibid.*, at point 39.
[110] *Roberts & Roberts* v. *Commission*, Case T-25/99, CFI Judgment of 5 July 2001.
[111] *Delimitis* v. *Henniger Bräu*, Case C-234/89 [1991] ECR I-935. *Neste Markkinointi*, Case C-214/99.

extent to which the beer supply agreements concluded by a brewery contribute to the cumulative effect of closing off the market produced by all such agreements, the position of the contracting parties in the market must be taken into consideration.

The agreements' contribution to market foreclosure also depends on their *duration*. If it is manifestly excessive in relation to the average duration of agreements generally concluded in the relevant market, the individual agreement falls under the prohibition in Article 81(1).[112] In this regard, a brewery holding a relatively small share of the market which ties its sales outlets for many years may contribute to foreclosure of the market as significantly as a brewery with a comparatively strong position in the market which regularly frees its outlets at frequent intervals. Since Greene King's standard nine-year leases were not manifestly excessive, and indeed, were considerably shorter than those of its competitors (often 20 years or more), there was no significant foreclosure.

The CFI found that Greene King's share of the beer distribution market in the UK was less than 2 per cent, on the basis of either the volume of sales, or the number of licensed establishments. GK had concluded upstream supply agreements with the major national breweries, in which it effectively acted as a wholesaler for the national brewers *vis-à-vis* its own tenants. The Court rejected the complainants' argument that Greene King's tied-house agreements should therefore be regarded as in some way intertwined with the national brewers' tied-house or other supply agreements, thus leading to market foreclosure over and above the level normally indicated by Greene King's own 2 per cent market penetration.

The Court found that GK's wholesaling arrangements could only be regarded as part of the national brewers' networks of agreements if they a) contained a purchasing obligation, and b) were so restrictive as to make access for other brewers to GK's downstream network difficult or impossible.[113] These conditions were not fulfilled on the facts, and the CFI even added that where access to the wholesaling brewer's network is not foreclosed by the upstream contracts, the wholesaler can actually promote other brewers' market penetration by allowing them access to the downstream network.[114]

Clearly, where the Commission, or a national competition authority, purports to withdraw the exemption under Regulation 2790/99, those undertakings whose agreements did not contribute appreciably to any network effect cannot be affected, because the agreements anyway fell outside the prohibition in Article 81(1). However, there is some practical difficulty with relying on this defence, as there is no way, short of litigation, for firms who believe that they come within the *Delimitis/Neste/Roberts* case-law to verify that belief. Especially where the Commission exercises its power under Article 8 of the BER to withdraw the

---

[112] *Roberts & Roberts* v. *Commission*, Case T-25/99, at para. 76. This is a reference to *Neste Markkinointi*, Case C-214/99 at para. 27 and to *Delimitis* v. *Henniger Bräu*, Case C-234/89 [1991] ECR I-935 at para. 19.

[113] *Roberts & Roberts* v. *Commission*, Case T-25/99, CFI judgment of 5 July 2001, paras. 106–7.

[114] *Ibid.*, para. 108.

exemption by Regulation, undertakings can probably not challenge the Regulation without thereby conceding that their agreements indeed required exemption.

7.3 GENERAL OPTIONS FOR PARTIES TO AGREEMENTS OUTSIDE THE BER

Most experts agree that, where the parties do not enjoy market power,[115] few vertical agreements actually infringe the prohibition in Article 81(1), unless they contain so-called "hardcore" restrictions of competition—resale price maintenance and exclusive territorial protection.[116] This is still true in respect of many agreements which cannot benefit from automatic exemption under Regulation 2790/99.

Agreements between competitors are mostly excluded from the BER, but many do not infringe Article 81(1). Agreements which contain black-listed or so-called "hardcore" restrictions of competition are, according to the Commission, unlikely to be exempted under Article 81(3).[117] Such restrictions bring the spectre of nullity under Article 81(2) upon the agreements in which they feature, and should, as a matter of prudence, probably be avoided entirely.[118] Where agreements which have an appreciable effect on trade between the Community Member States[119] contain non-compete obligations analogous to those listed in Article 5 of Regulation 2790/99, it is thought that limiting their duration to five years—unless there are particular circumstances justifying a longer restriction—should avoid problems in most circumstances.[120] Diluting the intensity of the non-compete

---

[115] Market power is a somewhat nebulous concept. See 1.2.1–1.2.1.2.6 above. However, most experts accept the Commission's pragmatic policy of using market share as an indicator of market power, albeit an imprecise one. The Commission has issued Draft Guidelines in the telecommunications field, some of the reasoning in which may be useful in other areas. Commission Working Document on Proposed New Regulatory Framework for Electronic Communications Networks and Services Draft Guidelines on market analysis and the calculation of significant market power under Article 14 of the proposed Directive on a common regulatory framework for electronic communications networks and services Document COM (2001) 175 of 28 March 2001. Available on the internet at http://europa.eu.int/comm/competition/liberalization/legislation/#telecom_regulations.

[116] See 2.13 above.

[117] Guideline 46.

[118] This is a management decision. In certain circumstances, hardcore restraints of competition may not infringe Article 81(1) because they have no, or no appreciable, effect on trade between the Member States. See *Franz Völk v. SPRL Ets J. Vervaecke*, Case 5/69 [1969] ECR 295, [1969] CMLR 273, CMR 8074. National competition rules may still apply.

[119] Many industrial franchising agreements, for example, fall outside Article 2 of Regulation 2790/99, (according to Guidelines 42–43), but still have no effect on trade between the Member States.

[120] Non-compete obligations are considered in some detail in Guidelines 138 to 159. Note especially Guideline 141: "non-compete obligations exceeding five years are for most types of investments not considered necessary to achieve the claimed efficiencies or the efficiencies are not sufficient to outweigh their foreclosure effect." However, the provision of substantial relationship-specific investments, premises or know-how by the seller may justify longer restrictions. See Guidelines 155, 150 and 157, respectively. In *European Night Services (ENS) and others v. Commission*, Cases T-374, 375, 384 & 388/94, 15 September 1998, [1998] ECR II-3141, [1998] 5 CMLR 718, [1998] CEC 955, appeal from Commission decision, 21 September 1994, OJ 1994, L259/20, [1995] 5 CMLR 76, [1998] CEC 955., the Commission in its disputed decision had granted an exemption for only eight years, since it could not foresee a more distant future. (OJ 1994, L259/26 paras. 72–78.). This was quashed by the CFI, which recognised that there had been a huge investment to protect, which had been funded over a 25 year period. (See paras. 225–234 of the CFI's judgment.)

obligation may also be an option. In the case of other arrangements which fall outside the available block exemptions, the parties' practical options are often limited to amending and/or notifying their agreements,[121] or to carrying on business under agreements the notification of which has been postponed, perhaps indefinitely.[122] In the following sections, we examine these options in more detail.

7.3.1 Avoiding the Prohibition in Article 81(1)

Before considering the options available to parties whose distribution agreements cannot benefit from exemption under Regulation 2790/99, it is worth recalling that an undertaking's distribution needs can sometimes be met through arrangements other than variations on the common theme of manufacturer–wholesaler–retailer supply chains.[123] These arrangements may avoid the actual or supposed competition law risks associated with "classical" distribution systems which come under the prohibition in Article 81(1), but which cannot be automatically exempted, and in respect of which no individual exemption is forthcoming.

Since practitioners are concerned to ensure that distribution arrangements will be legally, as well as functionally effective, avoiding non-exemptible infringements of Article 81(1) is a priority in drafting. A practical rule of thumb for agreements which do not benefit from a block exemption is to assume that any restrictive provisions which would be listed under Articles 4 and 5 of Regulation 2790/99 as not exempted would also be unlikely to receive an individual exemption if (they could be) notified to the Commission.[124] Since the availability of exemptions under Article 81(3) is increasingly uncertain, other restrictions of competition, if not clearly falling outside the prohibition in Article 81(1), should be as limited in scope and duration as possible. Where several restraints could achieve the same justifiable purpose, then the least competition-restrictive option should be employed.

---

[121] Note that if the proposals in the Commission's White Paper on Modernisation take effect, [see 2.12 above] the notification system will be abolished altogether, and the power to apply Article 81(3) will devolve upon national courts and competition authorities. White Paper on Modernisation of the Rules Implementing Articles 81 and 82 of the EC Treaty. Commission programme No. 99/027, OJ 1999, C132/1; [1999] 5 CMLR 208.

[122] On notification under Regulation 17/62, see 7.5 below.

[123] See 1.1.1–1.1.8 above. Distribution may be perceived as a service bought by the supplier. Arrangements of the kind covered by—or excluded from—Regulation 2790/99 may not be the only practical way for the supplier to secure the desired distribution services.

[124] The readiness and competence of national competition authorities and courts to grant exemptions, if the Commission's modernisation plans go through, is still an unknown quantity. Some practitioners report that since the BER came into force, certain national authorities are inclined to treat any restriction of competition not within the scope of exemption under Regulation 2790/99 as *prima facie* prohibited by Article 81(1), although this interpretation is clearly contrary to Guideline 62. This has the effect, at national level, of reversing the burden of proof, with businesses being called on to adduce reasons why their arrangements should not be prohibited. It is to be hoped that this is an aberration, which will pass away when national officials gain more experience of arrangements falling outside the BER.

7.3.1.1 Integrated distribution

A manufacturer of goods may integrate downstream[125] into the distribution channel for its own products without giving rise to any agreement or concerted practice between undertakings which is amenable to Article 81. Therefore, provided it
does not amount to the abuse of a dominant position under Article 82, and is not
blocked or modified as a result of procedures under the EC Merger Regulation, the
acquisition of up- or down-stream firms normally triggers no intervention on the
part of Community competition law.[126]

This may account for the increasing trend towards downstream integration in
certain distribution fields where the Article 81(1) prohibition was traditionally
problematic. For example, the cinema industry, which, being a supplier of services
rather than goods, did not qualify for exemption under the previous regime of
block exemptions, has been a fertile ground for the downstream expansion of film-
distribution undertakings into the ownership of cinema complexes.[127]

On the negative side, although downstream integration into the distribution
chain certainly avoids difficulties with Article 81, it is usually an option only for
larger companies, which have the necessary financial and logistic resources.[128]
Even large manufacturers may be unable to integrate downstream into retailing,
unless they have a portfolio of goods. Moreover, it may be extremely difficult for

---

[125] Upstream integration is also possible—a distributor may integrate upstream into production,
but this is rarer.

[126] See *Centrafarm BV and de Peijper* v. *Sterling Drug Inc.*, Case 15/74, 31 October 1974, [1974] ECR
1147, [1974] 2 CMLR 480, CMR 8246, applied in *Bodson* v. *Pompes Funèbres des Régions Libérées SA*,
Case 30/87, 4 May 1988, [1988] ECR 2479, [1989] 4 CMLR 984, [1990] 1 CEC 3. In *Viho*, the Court of
Justice upheld a judgment of the Court of First Instance, and confirmed that where the supply or sale
of goods takes place between companies which are integrated in the same corporate group, competition law may treat the group as a single "undertaking", so that the Article 81 prohibition does not apply
to distribution agreements made between those companies. *Viho* v. *Commission*, Case C-73/95 P, 24
October 1996, [1996] ECR I-5457, [1997] 4 CMLR 419, at para. 51. Whether related companies can
indeed be treated as a single undertaking does not depend on the form or degree of integration of the
companies (wholly-owned, or with a 51% shareholding, and so on). Decisive is whether the two companies enjoy real autonomy from each other in determining their course of action on the market. If the
"daughter" company simply carries out instructions issued to it by the parent company, then there is
no real autonomy, and the companies will be regarded as a single economic unit. If there is a single unit,
then there cannot be a concordance of economically independent wills which could constitute an
agreement or concerted practice subject to the competition rules. On the activities of a "single economic unit" see also *Shell* v. *Commission* (*Polypropylene*), Case T-11/89 [1992] ECR II-757, paragraph
311. See also **Wouter Wils** "The undertaking as subject of EC competition law and the imputation of
infringements to natural or legal persons", (2000) 25 *ELRev* 99. The author argues that even if the parent firm does not specifically dictate the behaviour of the daughter, there is still only a single undertaking, the subsidiary acting as it does only because the parent permits it.

[127] On the application of Article 81(1) to distribution arrangements in the cinema industry, see the
Commission's Notice published pursuant to Article 19(3) of Council Regulation No. 17 concerning an
application for a renewal of the Commission decision of 12 July 1989, OJ 1989 L 226/25, to grant an
exemption pursuant to Article 81(3) of the EC Treaty (Case No IV/C.2/30.566—*UIP Cinema*) OJ 1999,
C205/6. *UIP—Re the Application of United International Pictures BV* (89/467/EEC), 12 July 1989, OJ
1989, L226/25, [1990] 4 CMLR 749, [1989] 2 CEC 2019. The undertakings given by UIP are available on
the internet: http://europa.eu.int/comm/competition/antitrust/undertakings/ 30566.pdf.

[128] See the discussion of the reasons for vertical integration in **Level** and **Neubauer** "Vertical
Restraints: Their Motivation and Justification" [2000] 21 *ECLR* 7.

dominant undertakings to integrate vertically without triggering Article 82. Integration may also require compliance with the requirements of the Merger Regulation, which can be burdensome, but which may nonetheless be better than remaining in a position of uncertainty outside the safe harbour of the BER, especially as the merger procedure guarantees a "one-stop-shop"[129] and a fixed timetable, neither of which will be certain if the application of Article 81(3) devolves to the national level. However, it is arguable that integration undertaken only to remedy an otherwise precarious position under Article 81(1) may in fact be inefficient, and can reduce competition overall.[130]

7.3.1.2 Agency agreements[131]

A producer of goods or services may choose to distribute its products through an agent. In appropriate circumstances—where the agent is sufficiently integrated into the undertaking of the principal,[132] there is no agreement or concerted practice between undertakings within the meaning of Article 81(1), so no competition law risk.

The Commission considers that "genuine" agency agreements fall outside Article 81(1) if the agent does not bear any, or bears only insignificant, risks in relation to the contracts concluded and/or negotiated on behalf of the principal, and in relation to market-specific investments for that field of activity. Risks related to the activity of providing agency services in general, such as the risk of the

---

[129] "One-stop-shop": the Procedure under the Merger Regulation enables the Commission to (a) clear a concentration in relation to the entire territory of the EEA, and (b) to exempt or clear restrictions of competition which are ancillary to the concentration, without the need for a separate notification. The recent Commission Notice on restrictions directly related and necessary to concentrations (OJ 2001, C 188/5–11 at para. 2) indicates that the Commission no longer intends to assess ancillary restraints in future decisions under the Merger Regulation, and asserts that prior such assessments are "only of a declaratory nature".

[130] In Guideline 127 on Vertical Restraints, the Commission itself points out that vertical integration may operate as a barrier to market entry against competitors.

[131] On the competition law status of agents generally, see the detailed treatment at 2.8.4 above. Note especially the effect of the latest notice on agency agreements, included in the Commission's Guidelines on Vertical Restraints, at points 12–20.

[132] What amounts to sufficient integration has been treated differently by the Commission and the European Courts. In the 1962 Agency Notice, (OJ 1962, Eng Spec Ed 139/2921 CMR 2697) the Commission recognised that distribution carried on through a tied agent could be functionally equivalent to distribution through an integrated entity, and that agency agreements may provide an alternative option for firms unwilling or unable to integrate downstream into the distribution chain. The Commission then treated the *allocation of financial risk* as the decisive criterion which distinguished the commercial agent from the independent trader, and it has largely repeated this assessment in the latest Agency Notice—in Guidelines on Vertical Restraints 12–20. On the other hand, the ECJ has applied the test of the level of integration of the agent into the principal, rather than the allocation of risk. In *Flemish Travel Agents*, it held that travel agents who concluded contracts with clients on behalf of a principal—the tour operator—could not be treated as auxiliary organs forming an integral part of that tour operator's undertaking, since the agents sold travel organised by a large number of different tour operators and the operators sold travel through a very large number of agents. *ASBL Vereniging van Vlaamse Reisbureaus* v. *ASBL Sociale Dienst van de Plaatselijke en Gewestelijke Overheidsdiensten*, Case 311/85 [1987] ECR 3801, [1989] 4 CMLR 213, CMR 14499, paras. 19 & 20 (2.8.4 above).

agent's income being dependent upon his success as an agent or general investments in premises or personnel, are not material to the assessment.[133]

The current agency notice lists a number of examples of agency-type obligations
which the Commission regards as unlikely to attract the Article 81(1) prohibition
in the context of goods and services distribution.[134] Where an agency agreement
falls outside the terms of Article 81(1),[135] then there is no bar to the principal
imposing customer, territorial or pricing restrictions on the agent as regards the
principal's business, features which may be attractive for a producer seeking distribution services, especially since it is precisely such restrictions which may be problematic if Regulation 2790/99 does not apply.[136] The Commission also takes the
position that exclusive agency agreements—by which the principal refrains from
appointing multiple agents in relation to a given territory or customer group—
concern intra-brand competition only, and do not lead to anti-competitive effects.

Not all "genuine" agency arrangements escape from the prohibition in
Article 81(1), however. Provisions under which the agent agrees not to distribute
goods or services competing with those of the principal may be unlawful if they
lead to inter-brand foreclosure, especially where they have effect after the term of
the agency agreement.[137] Agency agreements which, although "genuine" as to the
allocation of risk, nevertheless facilitate collusion are also regarded as falling under
Article 81(1).[138]

7.3.1.3 Concentrative joint ventures and horizontal co-operation agreements

A further option which might be considered, if a distribution project with a particular partner is sufficiently important, is to establish an autonomous concentrative joint-venture company to be responsible for developing, producing
and marketing the product. This is particularly apt in the case of intermediate

---

[133] Guideline 15.

[134] Guideline 16. However, it indicates that market-specific investments in infrastructure (by petrol
or insurance retail agents for instance), and *del credere* obligations in general, are assumptions of risk
tending to negate "genuine" agency status.

[135] On the status of agents as "genuine" or otherwise, note the Commission's recent Decision fining
DaimlerChrysler for restricting cross-border trade in motor vehicles. The Commission took the view
that Article 81(1) could apply to the instructions given by DC to its German agents to restrict sales of
new Mercedes cars: *"The application of Article 81 to the restrictions agreed between DaimlerChrysler and
its German agents results from the fact that these agents have to bear a considerable commercial risk linked
to their activity. From the point of view of EC competition law, they must therefore be treated as dealers."*
(Press Release IP/01/1394 of 10 October 2001)

[136] Guideline 18. This is a logical consequence of the Court's judgments in *Belgian Travel Agents* and
in *Viho.*

[137] Guideline 19. See also *Bundeskartellamt* v. *Volkswagen,* Case C-266/93 [1995] ECR I 3477 at
paras. 22–24 & 27.

[138] Guideline 20. The Commission cites the case of principals using the same agent or agents in order
to exclude competitors from access to those agents, or to exchange information as between the principals. The legal basis for this opinion is not clear, as the Court's case-law on integrated agents is unam-
biguous—any arrangements between an integrated agent and its principal are not amenable to
Article 81(1). Presumably, the Commission means that collusion facilitated under the auspices of an
agent amounts to a prohibited concerted practice as between the respective principals. See the discussion
of Fertilizer Sales Agencies in the Commission's *4th Report on Competition Policy,* 1974, at para. 145.

products, whose incorporation into finished goods by the buyer requires some degree of reciprocal exchange of know-how, and for the distribution of which the parties would otherwise want a level of mutual exclusivity (normally exclusive supply coupled with exclusive purchasing) which would be incompatible with an exemption under Article 81(3) due to foreclosure of other market actors. Provided the threshold turnover values under the EC Merger Regulation are met—as may frequently be the case in respect of parties which enjoy more than a 30 per cent market share (and which therefore cannot benefit from the BER)—such an arrangement could be notified to the Commission under the Merger Regulation. If the joint venture is truly autonomous and concentrative, a clearance under the merger rules could extend to the exclusive supply and exclusive purchasing with the parents for an indefinite period.[139]

The block exemption regulations for horizontal co-operation agreements (specialisation and research and development arrangements[140]) adopted in November 2000, where they apply, may also extend to joint distribution of products resulting from the co-operation.[141] However, exemption under the co-operation regulations is limited, and does not extend to restrictions of competition which would be regarded as "hard-core" under Regulation 2790/99.

7.3.2 A "Wait and See" Approach

In many cases, distribution agreements which do not fall squarely within the terms of Regulation 2790/99 will nevertheless not infringe Article 81(1).[142] Indeed, there is, as the Commission says in Guideline 62, no presumption that agreements which fall outside the block exemption actually infringe the competition rules. In addition, even agreements which technically infringe Article 81(1) may never be the subject of enforcement action or litigation. The Commission's policy is now one of minimal intervention in the field of vertical agreements and, provided a particular agreement does not contain "hardcore" restrictions of competition, give rise to perverse results on the market, or provoke complaints from consumers or competitors, there is probably no reason to suppose that the Treaty prohibition applies or will be enforced, at least below the level of dominance. This may be cold comfort for businesses or their advisors if they are risk-averse, and concerned about the residual possibility of latent nullity under Article 81(2), but there is, in practice, little alternative to the wait and

---

[139] Joint production agreements with exclusive supply and purchasing are possible under Regulation 2658/2000 on specialisation agreements, but there is a 20% market share ceiling for exemption.

[140] Commission Regulation (EC) No 2659/2000 of 29 November 2000 on the application of Article 81(3) of the Treaty to categories of research and development agreements, (OJ 2000, L 304/7 [2001] 4 CMLR 808) Commission Regulation (EC) No 2658/2000 of 29 November 2000 on the application of Article 81(3) of the Treaty to categories of specialisation agreements (OJ 2000 L 304/3 [2001] 4 CMLR 800).

[141] Guidelines on the applicability of Article 81 of the EC Treaty to horizontal co-operation agreements. OJ 2001, C 3/2 [2001] CMLR 819, paras. 144 et seq.

[142] See 22.1.3 above.

see approach in most cases falling outside the BER, except notification, while that procedure is still available. Informal contacts with Commission officials may provide some reassurance, but comfort letters will normally not be forthcoming.

7.3.3 Bringing the Agreement into Conformity with Regulation 2790/99

If a serious risk is identified, it may be possible for the parties to amend their arrangements in some respect which will suffice to bring them within the scope of the exemption under Regulation 2790/99. This may take the form of alterations which make the agreement "vertical"; reducing the relevant market share to come under the 30 per cent ceiling; avoiding hardcore restraints; or, reducing the duration of any non-compete obligations.[143]

7.3.4 Enforcement Actions under the Brussels and Lugano Conventions

If the Commission's plans for allowing national courts to grant exemptions under Article 81(3) are implemented, Denis thinks that it may be possible to rely on the Brussels and/or Lugano conventions to secure the cross-border enforcement of such judgements.[144] In circumstances where an undertaking obtains a "blessing" under Article 81(3) for particular distribution arrangements in one European jurisdiction, it may then be able to enforce that judgement in other jurisdictions in respect of the same parties, and the same or possibly also closely related arrangements. Although it may sound far-fetched, this is the situation which arose in the "ice-cream wars" case in Ireland.[145] There, the High Court found that freezer-exclusivity arrangements did not infringe the competition rules in Ireland. Had the High Court been empowered to apply Article 81(3), it might instead have granted an exemption. The same parties litigated the same issue in other European jurisdictions. Since the Brussels Convention does not mention competition law in the list of subject-matter to which it does not apply,[146] it would have been open to the

---

[143] The Conditions for the application of Regulation 2790/99 are discussed in detail in chapter 3 above.
[144] Respectively: 1968 Brussels Convention on jurisdiction and the enforcement of judgments in civil and commercial matters (consolidated version) OJ 1998, C27/1. Council Regulation (EC) No 44/2001 of 22 December 2000 on jurisdiction and the recognition and enforcement of judgements in civil and commercial matters OJ 2001, L12/1.
[145] See 5.1.1.4, 6.1.3 and 7.2.6 above
[146] The Brussels Convention provides:

Article 1
This Convention shall apply in civil and commercial matters whatever the nature of the court or tribunal. It shall not extend, in particular, to revenue, customs or administrative matters.
The Convention shall not apply to:
1. the status or legal capacity of natural persons, rights in property arising out of a matrimonial relationship, wills and succession
2. bankruptcy, proceedings relating to the winding-up of insolvent companies or other legal persons, judicial arrangements, compositions and analogous proceedings
3. social security
4. arbitration.

successful party in Ireland to obtain the enforcement of that judgement elsewhere. Speaking in public, Commission officials have confirmed that there are no plans to amend the Conventions to exclude competition law matters from their ambit.

7.4 SELF ASSESSMENT AND THE GUIDELINES ON VERTICAL RESTRAINTS

7.4.1 The Commission's New Approach

The Commission's plans for modernising the enforcement of Community competition law centre around allowing undertakings to organise their distribution arrangements after their own lights, and in the way which bests suits their commercial needs, provided these arrangements do not severely interfere with the conditions of competition. It is moving away from the prior form-based analysis, which was motivated by the desire to centralise and control the development of principles of competition law, but which had the unfortunate effect of forcing businesses to bring their distribution arrangements within rigidly defined categories in order to benefit from a block exemption. Most of the vertical restraints normally found in distribution agreements no longer give the Commission serious cause for concern, and it is diverting its attention and resources to more pressing problems, such as detecting and bringing to an end unmeritorious horizontal cartels, dealing with abuses prohibited under Article 82, and applying the State aids and public monopolies rules.

The Commission now acknowledges that "the protection of competition is the primary objective of EC competition policy, as this enhances consumer welfare, and creates an efficient allocation of resources".[147] It also acknowledges that there is no presumption that agreements which fall outside the safe harbour of Regulation 2790/99 actually infringe Article 81(1). In those particular cases where it intervenes, the Commission still has to show that an agreement outside Regulation 2790/99 actually infringes the competition rules.[148]

7.4.2 Assessment of Restraints under the Guidelines

The approach for assessing the effect of distribution agreements on competition is set out in the *Guidelines on Vertical Restraints*. The Commission's basic premises are that vertical restraints[149] are generally less harmful to competition than horizontal

---

[147] Guideline 7.

[148] See 2.7.2 and 2.7.3 above.

[149] In Guidelines 106–114, the Commission identifies four main groups of vertical restraints, and sets out why they have anti-competitive effects. See 1.2.2–1.2.2.4 above. The groups are "single branding" (those which constrain a buyer to purchase mainly from a particular supplier); "limited distribution" (the seller supplies only a limited group of buyers); "resale price maintenance"; and, "market partitioning" restraints. Interestingly, Guideline 115 acknowledges that vertical restraints can have positive effects on competition, especially by promoting competition on service and on aspects other than price.

restraints,[150] and that "for most vertical restraints competition concerns can arise only if there is insufficient inter-brand competition".[151] The insufficiency of inter-brand competition is identified by considering whether the parties enjoy market power. Only undertakings which have such market power are likely to be found to be infringing Article 81(1) through the use of vertical restraints.[152]

Guideline 62 encourages companies to assess their agreements independently without notifying them to the competition authorities, whether European or national. Even if a competent authority later finds that the agreement has "appreciable anti-competitive effects", it is still open to the parties to the agreement to adduce efficiency claims in order to ground an exemption under Article 81(3).[153]

The Guidelines offer a framework for analysing vertical agreements generally, and for assessing whether a particular agreement not covered by a block exemption requires to be notified to the Commission for exemption under Article 81(3) while that is still possible.[154] It is important to (be seen to) review any agreement which falls outside the block exemption regulations in the light of the Commission's advice in the Guidelines, and adequately to document this process. If the market share of parties to an agreement has been honestly mis-assessed, and the agreement therefore not notified while following the Commission's paradigm, fines will not be imposed.[155] It is also the settled practice of the European Court to give undertakings the benefit of any doubt or ambiguity in Commission notices upon which they have relied in good faith.[156]

7.4.3 Methodology of Analysis

In Guideline 120, the Commission sets out the four steps in analysing a vertical restraint:

(1) First, the undertakings involved need to define the relevant market in order to establish the market share of the supplier or the buyer, depending on the vertical restraint involved.[157]

---

[150] Guideline 100. This is an insight of the Chicago school of economists. See 1.1 above.
[151] I.e. if there exists a certain degree of market power at the level of the supplier or the buyer or both, Guideline 119.
[152] The meaning of Guideline 102 is opaque. The Commission seems to be saying that it will only find infringements of Article 81 on the part of undertakings with market power, because market power is the touchstone for insufficient inter-brand competition.
[153] If the Commission's modernisation plans go ahead, the power to apply Article 81(3) will devolve on national courts and competition authorities. However, it is not clear whether the national authorities will be able to grant full exemptions, or merely record positive decisions which would not be constitutive.
[154] On notification, see 7.5 below.
[155] Guideline 65.
[156] *Suiker Unie* v. *Commission,* Joined Cases 40–48/73 [1975] ECR 1663 [1976] 1 CMLR 295, CMR 8334. On the legal value and status of Commission notices, see 3.2 above.
[157] See 3.4.13–3.4.13.7 above.

(2) If the relevant market share does not exceed the 30 per cent threshold, the vertical agreement is covered by the Block Exemption Regulation, subject to the hardcore restrictions and conditions set out in that Regulation.[158]

(3) If the relevant market share is above the 30 per cent threshold, it is necessary to assess whether the vertical agreement falls within Article 81(1).[159]

(4) If the vertical agreement falls within Article 81(1), it is necessary to examine whether it fulfils the conditions for exemption under Article 81(3).

Since this chapter is concerned with those distribution agreements which fall within Article 81(1), but outside the exemption provided for in Regulation 2790/99, we will consider the possible justifications for vertical restraints, and how they can be applied in practice.

7.4.4 Justifications for Vertical Restraints

Note that Guideline 103 indicates four negative effects of vertical restraints which it is the Commission's policy to prevent. They are:

—foreclosure of other suppliers or other buyers by raising barriers to entry;[160]

—reduction of inter-brand competition between the companies operating on a market, including facilitation of collusion amongst suppliers or buyers; by collusion is meant both explicit collusion and tacit collusion (conscious parallel behaviour);[161]

—reduction of intra-brand competition between distributors of the same brand;

—the creation of obstacles to market integration, including, above all, limitations on the freedom of consumers to purchase goods or services in any Member State they may choose.[162]

Therefore, to ensure the viability of distribution agreements falling outside the exemption provided by Regulation 2790/99, but raising competition concerns under Article 81(1),[163] these four undesirable effects should be avoided. If, for commercial reasons, they cannot be avoided entirely, they should be limited as far as possible. Where some feature of the distribution system in question necessarily entails an appreciable level of one of the four anti-competitive effects, the parties should identify and document economic factors, efficiencies or ancillary restraints justifying the restraint on competition. The justification should be such that, if the arrangement had to be (or could be) notified, the restrictions would escape the prohibition in Article 81(1) entirely, or Article 81(3) could be applied. The

---

[158] On hardcore restrictions and the conditions, see chapter 4 above.
[159] See chapter 2 above for the case-law on the application of Article 81(1).
[160] On foreclosure, see 1.2.5.1 above.
[161] On reduction of inter-brand competition, see 1.2.3 *et seq.* above.
[162] On market integration, see 1.2.3.1 above.
[163] Guideline 121 indicates factors relevant to the Article 81(1) assessment.

Commission identifies reasons justifying the application of certain vertical restraints in Guidelines 116 to 136, but prefers to treat most as grounds for exemption under Article 81(3), rather than as restraints ancillary to a pro-competitive transaction.[164]

A distribution agreement falling outside the BER, but which does not contain hardcore restrictions of competition, or other practices which the case-law indicates cannot be exempted, and in relation to which any relevant justifying efficiencies have been identified in accordance with the Guidelines, is very unlikely to be found invalid or to attract fines, and should not be a cause for concern for the parties. Where there is no manifestly anti-competitive behaviour to complain of, and where the party relying on the distribution agreement can adduce *prima facie* economic justifications for any lower-level contractual restrictions of competition, the burden upon a complainant before national courts or competition authorities is very likely to be insurmountable. The judges in national commercial courts, and the officials of national competition authorities, often approach restraint-of-competition arguments with a healthy scepticism, especially where the issue is raised either by a competitor of the distributor, or by a party seeking to resile from an agreement.

The Commission gives a useful, but not exhaustive, list of justifications for vertical restraints in Guideline 116; these are examined from an economic point of view in chapter one above. In Guideline 136 it sets out to what extent efficiencies claims must be substantiated.

7.4.4.1 Absolute territorial protection

In the *Consten & Grundig* case,[165] the European Court of Justice confirmed the Commission's decision that the distribution arrangements in question infringed Article 81(1). Moreover, they could not be exempted under Article 81(3) because they operated in such a way as to afford Consten "absolute territorial protection" on the French market for hi-fi goods. This (somewhat misleading) expression indicates that the distribution system in question forecloses all intra-brand competition in relation to the contract goods within the buyer's allocated territory. In Consten's case, the intra-brand protection was absolute since the French distributor faced competition neither from other appointed dealers within the allocated

---

[164] The Commission seems to take the view that efficiencies go only to the consideration of an exemption under Article 81(3). This is clearly not necessarily the case, as the Court of Justice has held that the nature of certain vertical restraints takes them outside the prohibition in Article 81(1) entirely. See 2.7.2 and 2.7.3 above. Consider the cases of purely qualitative selective distribution (see 1.1.6 and 2.8.1 above), or "*Pronuptia*" franchising [see 2.8.2 above], for example. In *Remia*, the Court accepted that a non-compete clause ancillary to the transfer of a business was compatible with Article 81(1). Case 42/84 [1985] ECR 2545, at paras. 17–20. In *Coditel II* the Court cleared even restrictions amounting to absolute territorial protection. Case 262/81 [1982] ECR 3381, [1981] 2 CMLR 362, CMR 8662, at para. 20. Compare Guideline 135.

[165] See 2.2 above.

territory, nor (because of the use of the "GINT" trade mark) from parallel importers of the contract goods into France.[166]

Measures, including oral agreements,[167] which confer absolute territorial protection on the buyer and which thereby affect intra-Community trade infringe Article 81(1). They are not normally capable of exemption under Article 81(3), because they exclude competition between the various distributors of a particular brand, foreclose entry by potential new distributors, and because they are an obstacle to the integration of the Common Market.[168] They are difficult to justify and thus best avoided in distribution arrangements.

7.4.4.2 Export bans and measures restricting parallel trade

By an export ban, a supplier seeks to protect the value of its buyers' respective operating territories (and, indirectly, its own profit margins). By insulating each buyer from potential intra-brand competition arising from parallel importation of contract goods supplied to other buyers, the supplier offers a more or less guaranteed share of the market. From the supplier's point of view, this guarantee may induce the buyer to bear sunk costs and to make investments in providing services connected with the contract goods.

Except in the very special (and somewhat disputed) case of products which are supplied to territories outside the EEA, and whose re-importation into the Area is contractually forbidden,[169] the operation of an export ban will almost certainly

---

[166] The "absolute" nature of such territorial protection is of course mitigated by the possibility of inter-brand competition, and in circumstances where the supplier's trade mark right has been "exhausted" in relation to the protected territory. According to the case-law of the Court of Justice, the function of a trade mark is to allow its proprietor to chose the conditions under which the marked product is first marketed in the EEA. Any subsequent reliance on the mark in order to prevent the free circulation of goods legitimately marketed with the rightholder's permission is an abuse of the national-law right, since it seeks to re-partition the internal market. See, for example, *Centrafarm* v. *Sterling Drug*, Case 15/74 [1974] ECR 1147 [1974] 2 CMLR 480, CMR 8246. This doctrine was developed after the judgment in *Consten*. See 2.3 above.

[167] *Tepea BV* v. *Commission*, Case 28/77 [1978] ECR 1391 [1978] 3 CMLR 392, CMR 8467, at para 41.

[168] In *Erauw-Jacquery*, the Court indicated that an agreement has this anticompetitive effect where it is "possible to foresee, on the basis of all the objective factors of law or of fact, with a sufficient degree of probability that it may have an influence, direct or indirect, actual or potential, on the pattern of trade between Member States in such a way that it might hinder the attainment of the objectives of a single market between Member States". *SPRL Louis Erauw-Jacquery* v. *La Hesbignonne SC*, Case 27/87 [1988] ECR 1919 [1988] 4 CMLR 576, [1989] 2 CEC 637, at para. 14.

[169] In the *Silhouette* and *Sebago* cases (concerning Article 7 of Directive 89/104) the Court held that, even where goods are circulating in the Community with the consent of the trade mark proprietor, the right to oppose unauthorised imports from outside the Community is not exhausted. Respectively, *Silhouette International Schmied GmbH & Co. KG* v. *Hartlauer Handelsgesellschaft mbH*, Case C-355/96 [1998] ECR I, 4799 [1998] 2 CMLR 953, and *Sebago Inc. and Ancienne Maison Dubois & Fils SA* v. *G-B Unic SA*, Case C-137/98 [1999] ECR I, 4103. In *Javico*, it held that that a ban on non-EEA buyers re-importing the contract goods into the Area did not have the object of restricting intra-Community trade. However, the Court of Justice left it open to national courts to determine whether, on the facts, the ban produced effects contrary to Article 81(1). *Javico International and Javico AG* v. *Yves Saint Laurent Parfums SA*, Case C-306/96 [1998] ECR I-1983, [1998] 5 CMLR 172, [1998] CEC 813 paras. 20–22. *Silhouette* and *Sebago* were approved in the ECJ's Judgment of 20 November 2001 in *Zino*

amount to a hardcore restriction of competition.[170] The European Courts and the Commission object to intra-EEA export restrictions on two grounds: they may result in an artificial re-partitioning of the Common Market; and, they prevent entrepreneurs from engaging in parallel trade based on price arbitrage. Parallel traders are thought to have an important price-levelling effect across the Common Market (at least in respect of products for which search and transport costs are not prohibitive).

Export bans and measures limiting parallel trade have consistently been found to infringe Article 81(1) in the case-law.[171] In *Miller*, the Court of Justice held that if the parties included an export ban in their agreement, it must have been intended by them to have some appreciable market-partitioning effect, and it was therefore capable of infringing Article 81(1).[172]

In the case-law, many and various practices have been found to interfere either directly or indirectly with parallel trade and thereby to infringe the Treaty prohibition. Contractual clauses which deprive distributors of rebates in respect of products purchased for re-export are prohibited, as are pricing structures which differentiate between domestic and export sales.[173] Even an export ban which takes effect within the territory of one and the same Member State has been struck down.[174] Manufacturers who refuse warranty or after-sales cover to customers

---

Davidoff SA v. *A&G Imports Ltd, Levi Strauss* v. *Tesco Stores Ltd., Levi Strauss* v. *Costco Wholesale UK Ltd.*, Joined Cases C-414/99 to C-416/99. Not yet reported in the ECR, but available on the ECJ website: http://www.curia.eu.int. Note that in *Micro Leader Business* v. *Commission*, Case T-198/98 [1999] ECR II-3989, [2000] 4 CMLR 886, [2000] CEC 540 at para. 56, the Court of First Instance pointed out that a supplier's promise to its dealers that it would exercise national law rights to prevent grey imports into the Community may, in exceptional circumstances, amount to abusive conduct under Article 82. This doctrine may be of interest in connection with the Commission's recently announced investigation into the pricing of movie DVDs. Films on DVD, for which the distributors hold copyright licences, are released in a staggered fashion depending on region, and discs from different regions are not interchangeable on standard player hardware. (The US, Canada, and US Territories make up "Region 1", and Japan, Europe, South Africa, and Middle East including Egypt are in "Region 2".) This is arguably a case where the copyright is being used in a spill-over fashion to curtail parallel imports into the Community. See Commissioner Monti's SPEECH/01/275 and Commission Press Release IP/01/815 of 11 June 2001, both available at www.europa.eu.int/rapid/start/welcome.htm.

[170] In some early decisions, the Commission held that otherwise hardcore restrictions, such as export bans, did not come within the prohibition in Article 81(1) in cases where the agreement in question only regulated trade with a buyer outside the Community. See, for example, the *Grosfillex* decision—OJ 915/64 [1964] CMLR 237. Valentine has suggested that it is no longer safe to rely upon this old precedent, now that customs duties and quotas have been abolished or reduced as between the EC and many countries.

[171] See 1.2.1 above. However, in *Völk* v. *Ets. Vervaecke Sprl*, Case 5/69, 9 July 1969, [1969] ECR 295, [1969] CMLR 273, CMR 8074, there was an export ban, but it had no appreciable effect on intra-Community trade.

[172] *Miller International Schallplatten GmbH* v. *Commission*, Case 19/77 [1978] ECR I-131, [1978] 2 CMLR 334, CMR 8439 para. 12. See 2.7.1 above.

[173] *Distillers* v. *Commission*, Case 30/78 [1980] ECR 2229 [1980] 3 CMLR 121, CMR 8613, paras. 6 & 26. Also Commission Decision 91/335 *Gosmé/Martel*, OJ 1991, L185/23 [1992] 5 CMLR 586, [1991] 2 CEC 2110, points 31–2.

[174] *Société de Vente de Ciments et Bétons de l'Est SA* v. *Kerpen & Kerpen GmbH und Co. KG*, Case 319/82 [1983] ECR 4173, CMR 14043, at para. 9.

purchasing through parallel traders also infringe Article 81(1).[175] The exercise of industrial property and other rights under national law may amount to a measure hindering exports or parallel trade, as the Court of Justice found in connection with Grundig's use of the "GINT" mark to give Consten territorial protection.[176] Practices which indirectly support this market-partitioning behaviour are also caught by the prohibition, especially those by which the parties seek to identify or sanction parallel exporters.[177]

Since the *Miller* case, the European Courts and the Commission have consistently treated practices restricting parallel trade as having the object of restricting competition.[178] The Commission recently rejected Glaxo Wellcome's attempts to adduce economic justifications for measures curbing parallel imports. Commenting on the decision, Mr Monti underlined the Commission's policy:

> Pharmaceutical companies or other companies cannot put in place distribution arrangements which perpetuate the partitioning of the Single Market into national markets. In principle market partitioning arrangements do not qualify for an exemption . . .[179]

Market-partitioning behaviour and restraints on parallel trade operate to take even otherwise qualifying distribution agreements outside the protective ambit of Regulation 2790/99. Moreover, distribution systems in connection with which market partitioning is practised on a large scale cannot normally benefit from exemption under Article 81(3), and are quite likely to attract fines in the event of

---

[175] See *"Swatch watches"*, *ETA Fabriques d'ébauches* v. *SA DK Investment and others*, Case 31/85 [1985] ECR 3933, at para. 14. In *Hasselblad* v. *Commission* Case 86/82 [1984] ECR 883, [1984] 1 CMLR 559, CMR 14014 at paras. 34–5, the Court found that general discrimination against parallel-imported products in the provision of guarantee services would amount to an infringement of Article 81(1), but that there is no infringement where an authorised dealer provides services to its own customers over and above the level assured by the manufacturer's guarantee to all customers. More recently, the Commission required *Saeco* to implement a non-discriminatory warranty system for its coffee machines. See Press Release IP/00/684 of 29 June 2000, available online at http://www.europa.eu.int/rapid/start/welcome.htm.

[176] *Consten & Grundig* v. *Commission*, Joined Cases 56 & 58/64 [1966] ECR 299, at 343. [1966] CMLR 418, CMR 8046. There is an important body of law concerning the exercise of national law rights, much of which is outside the scope of this chapter. For an introduction, see for example, **Inge Govaere**, *The Use and Abuse of Intellectual Property Rights in EC Law*, (London, Sweet & Maxwell, 1996). Chapter 5 deals with the interaction of IP rights with the competition rules.

[177] See *Van Megen Sports Group BV* v. *Commission*, Case T-49/95 [1996] ECR II-1799, at paras. 34–5. There, the parties tracked parallel exports of tennis balls by printing special identifying date-stamps on their products.

[178] See, for example *Herlitz AG* v. *Commission*, Case T-66/92 [1994] ECR II-531, at paras. 29–30.

[179] Commission Press Release IP/01/661 of 8 May 2001. Mr Monti's statement is not consistent with the judgement of the CFI in *Matra Hachette SA* v. *Commission*, Case T-17/93 [1994] ECR-II 595, at para. 85, where it was held that *any* restriction of competition can be exempted if it fulfils the requirements of Article 81(3). See 2.1 above.

complaints from customers or consumers.[180] Such practices should therefore be avoided entirely.[181]

7.4.4.3 Non-absolute territorial protection

Under this heading fall those arrangements by which a supplier provides a buyer some measure of territorial exclusivity as against the supplier himself and other buyers, but without necessarily infringing Article 81(1). This includes exclusive and selective distribution systems and franchising.

7.4.4.3.1 Exclusive distribution agreements

The Commission, for policy reasons which Denis believes were sound in the early years of the Community,[182] has often found that distribution agreements which confer commercial exclusivity on the parties have either the object or (more frequently) the effect of infringing the prohibition in Article 81(1).[183] In contrast, the Court of Justice, in two distinct lines of case-law, has been somewhat more open to clearing exclusivity.

In its early cases, starting with *Technique Minière*,[184] the Court doubted whether an "exclusive right of sale" interfered with competition in circumstances where the distribution agreement was necessary in order to enable the parties to penetrate a new area, and it held that agreements containing such a clause do not of their very nature contain elements incompatible with Article 81(1). In the *Consten* case

---

[180] Speaking at European competition day, in June 2000, Commissioner Monti announced that the Commission, acting on the basis of "a significant number of complaints from private citizens" had issued Article 11 letters to major film production companies in connection with the regional pricing structure of DVDs. The complaints centred around the fact that DVD prices in the EU are significantly higher than in the US. DVD player hardware is inhibited from playing imported disks by a worldwide regional coding system, which is the subject of a second Article 11 questionnaire. See SPEECH/01/275 and Press Release IP/01/815 of 11 June 2001, both available at www.europa.eu.int/rapid/start/welcome.htm.

[181] The situation is less clear where the territory conferred on the buyer by the seller (or on the franchisee by the franchisor) is small. Recall that, in *Pronuptia*, the ECJ thought that territorial exclusivity conferred on the franchisee could restrict competition if the franchised brand is well-known.

[182] Not all commentators agree that the Commission's policy of banning restraints on parallel trade was sound. See, for example, **Van Bael**, "Heretical Reflections on the Basic dogma of EC Antitrust Single Market Integration", [1980] 10 *RSDIC* 39; **Korah** "Goodbye Red Label: Condemnation of Dual Pricing by Distillers," (1978) 3 *ELRev* 62; also **Charles Baden Fuller**, [1981] 6 *ELRev* 162, who suggests that the ban actually delayed European integration.

[183] The Commission did clear a small number of early exclusive distribution cases. These often involved a manufacturer within the EC which had appointed an exclusive distributor in some non-EC territory, before the abolition of customs duties. See *Grosfillex*, decision of 11 March 1964, OJ 915, [1964] CMLR 237; and *Rieckerman*, decision of 6 November OJ 1968 L276/25. See also *Béguelin Import Co.* v. *GL Import Export SA*, Case 22/71, 25 November 1971, [1971] ECR 949, [1972] CMLR 81, CMR 8149. See the *SOCEMAS* decision, OJ 1968, L201/4, for example. Also *SPAR—Re Intergroup Trading BV* (75/482/EEC), 14 July 1975, OJ 1975, L212/23, [1975] 2 CMLR D14, CMR 9759. There, small traders combined their buying power to compete with supermarket chains.

[184] *Société Technique Minière* v. *Maschinenbau Ulm* Case 56/65, [1966] ECR 235, at 250–51, [1966] CMLR 357, CMR 8047.

shortly thereafter,[185] the Court condemned restrictions of competition which gave rise to absolute territorial protection. However, it held that the infringement did not stem from Grundig's undertaking not to make direct deliveries in France except to Consten, but rather from other clauses which, when added to the exclusivity, were intended to impede parallel imports.[186] In subsequent cases, such as *Brasserie de Haecht I*, and the important *Delimitis* judgment,[187] the Court re-emphasised that it is the economic context of an agreement which determines whether particular clauses attract the prohibition in Article 81(1).[188] In another line of cases, the Court enunciated a doctrine of competitive restraints, including buyer exclusivity, which are "ancillary" to a competition-neutral or pro-competitive business transaction, and which therefore fall outside Article 81(1).[189] This approach was taken by the Court in the *Nungesser*, *Remia* and *Pronuptia* cases, for example.[190]

Guidelines 161–177 deal with exclusive distribution systems. Where the agreement falls outside Regulation 2790/99, the Commission perceives a "risk of a significant reduction of inter-brand competition", which should be balanced by efficiencies. Unfortunately, the Guidelines do not make it clear that this justification is necessary only in the relatively few cases where the agreement in question is not such as to benefit from the *Technique Minière* doctrine of benign economic context or from the *Pronuptia* doctrine of ancillary restraints. Although the Guidelines refer to a number of competition risks raised by exclusivity, market foreclosure is perhaps the most serious. In BP Kemi, the Commission pointed out that distribution agreements which provide for exclusivity, if concluded for long periods, could effectively freeze competition on the market. Even where the supplier included a so-called

---

[185] *Consten and Grunding* v. *Commission*, Joined Cases 56 & 58/64 [1966] ECR 299, [1966] CMLR 418, CMR 8046 (see 2.2 above).

[186] The other clauses in question were those by which Grundig granted Consten exclusive rights to use the GINT mark in France. *Consten and Grundig* v. *Commission*, Joined Cases 56 & 58/64 [1966] ECR 299, at 344, second paragraph. [1966] CMLR 418, CMR 8046. See 2.2 above.

[187] Respectively, *Brasserie De Haecht* v. *Wilkin*, Case 23/67 [1967] ECR 407, [1973] CMLR 287, CMR 8170, and *Delimitis* v. *Henninger Bräu*, Case C-234/89 [1991] ECR I-935 [1992] 5 CMLR 210, [1992] 2 CEC 530.

[188] See 2.7.3 above.

[189] See 2.7.2 above.

[190] Respectively, *Nungesser (LG) KG and Kurt Eisele* v. *Commission*, Case 258/78, 8 June 1982, [1982] ECR 2015, [1983] 1 CMLR 278, CMR 8805, *Remia BV and Verenigde Bedrijven Nutricia* v. *Commission*, Case 42/84, 11 July 1985, [1985] ECR 2545, [1987] 1 CMLR 1, CMR 14217, at paras. 17–20, and *Pronuptia*, Case 161/84 [1986] ECR 353, [1986] 1 CMLR 414, CMR 14245 at paras. 15–22. Note the narrow view of ancillary restraint in *Métropole Télévision SA and Others* v. *Commission*, Case T-112/99, 18 September 2001, [2001] 12 CMLR 1236, para. 109:

> examination of the objective necessity of a restriction in relation to the main operation cannot but be relatively abstract. It is not a question of analysing whether, in the light of the competitive situation on the relevant market, the restriction is indispensable to the commercial success of the main operation but of determining whether, in the specific context of the main operation, the restriction is necessary to implement that operation. If, without the restriction, the main operation is difficult or even impossible to implement, the restriction may be regarded as objectively necessary for its implementation.

"English clause" in the agreement,[191] its effect—rather than guaranteeing the best deal to the buyer—was to allow the supplier to exclude his competitors at the competitive edge of the market. An "English clause" attenuates single branding, but also allows a dominant firm to discover exact details of offers made by its competitors. Similarly, in the *Ice-Cream* cases, freezer exclusivity effectively foreclosed the market to alternative suppliers, because it was a combination of exclusive distribution with single branding.[192] In the *Liebig Spices* decision, both the supplier and the buyers of the contract goods enjoyed strong positions on their respective markets, with the effect that 35 per cent of the market for spices was foreclosed.[193]

In the cases where single branding raises problems, including that of market foreclosure, the Commission has identified a number of counterbalancing efficiencies.[194] These include encouraging distributors to invest in promoting and protecting a brand image, and the logistical savings to be realised due to economies of scale.

7.4.4.3.2 *Selective distribution agreements*

Selective distribution agreements falling outside Article 81 under the *Metro* doctrine are discussed at 2.8.1.6 above. Arrangements whereby the supplier applies selection criteria which go beyond those recognised in *Metro* as being objectively justified on qualitative grounds are normally treated as infringing Article 81(1), and therefore requiring to be exempted. In many—if not most—of these cases, the system in question will benefit from a general exemption under Regulation 2790/99,[195] even where the supplier applies quantitative selection criteria.[196] Note, however, that agreements which prevent authorised distributors from carrying out active or passive sales in any territory, or which prevent cross-supplies between authorised distributors at any level cannot benefit from Regulation 2790/99.

Where a selective distribution system requires exemption (because it applies conditions not recognised in *Metro*), but does not benefit from a group exemption, the Commission is principally concerned with three possible effects on competition:

---

[191] An English clause is a contractual provision by which the buyer is bound not to purchase from suppliers other than the seller, unless the seller is first given an opportunity to match his competitors' best offer on prices for the contract goods or their substitutes.

[192] *Langnese-Iglo GmbH & Co. KG* v. *Mars GmbH.* Commission Decision 93/406/EEC, OJ 1993, L183/19, at paras. 208–9. The CFI upheld the legality of the Commission's withdrawal of exemption under Article 14(1) of Regulation 1984/83 in *Langnese-Iglo GmbH* v. *Commission,* Case T-7/93 [1995] ECR II-1533. The ECJ did not disturb the CFI's ruling on appeal in Case C-279/95 P [1998] ECR I 5609. Compare Guideline 165.

[193] OJ 1978, L53/20. Compare Guidelines 166–7. See 2.6 above.

[194] Guideline 174.

[195] Note press release IP/01/713 of 17 May 2001, in which the Commission announced that the selective distribution system for *Yves Saint Laurent Perfumes* could benefit from an exemption under Regulation 2790/99, which came into force since the system was notified. The former YSL distribution system was exempted by the Commission between 1991 and 1997. In 1996, the Court of First Instance partially annulled the exemption decision, in so far as it allowed YSL to raise indirect obstacles to sales through supermarkets which met the system's qualitative criteria. *Groupement d'achat Edouard Leclerc* v. *Commission,* Case T-88/92 [1996] ECR II-1961.

[196] Guideline 186. Regulation 1475/95 provides an exemption in the case of certain selective distribution systems for motor vehicles. See 7.6 *et seq.* below.

reduction in inter-brand competition,[197] foreclosure of the market to other suppliers or buyers, and the cumulative effect of parallel networks of selective distribution networks.[198] These risks may be balanced in practice by logistical savings due to economies of scale, and a system of selective distribution can be justified in circumstances where it is necessary to establish a brand image (especially for new or complex products), or to counteract free-riding between distributors.[199] Note that the Commission expects that the combination of selective and exclusive distribution can only "exceptionally" fulfil the conditions of Article 81(3) if operated by a supplier with more than 30 per cent market share, or if the market is foreclosed by cumulative effects of parallel networks of such systems.[200]

7.4.4.4 Tying

Tying is the practice of refusing to supply a certain product (the "tying" product) without also supplying another (the "tied" product). Tying is one of the practices listed in Article 81 of the Treaty as having the object or effect of restricting competition. However, it is not listed in Article 4 of Regulation 2790/99 as a clause which automatically takes agreements outside the block exemption. (See 4.6.2 above.) This indicates that, in the case of agreements which fall outside the exemption, the pro- and anti-competitive effects of tying are to be balanced against each other in order to determine whether the tie would be exempted under Article 81(3). The various justifications for tying are analysed at 2.9 above. The arrangement know as a "tied-house" for beer, or a "tied" service-station for motor fuel, is actually a particular type of exclusive-purchasing agreement between the tenant of premises and its landlord, and does not concern "tying" as described above.

7.4.5 Burden of Proof

In Guideline 62, the Commission says:

> Vertical agreements falling outside the Block Exemption Regulation will not be presumed to be illegal but may need individual examination. Companies are encouraged to do their own assessment without notification. In the case of an individual examination

---

[197] In *BMW*, the Commission exempted a ban on selected dealers' selling other makes of car, OJ 1975, L29/1. However, selectivity in respect of motor vehicle distribution is a special case, and has since been made the subject of a separate block exemption regulation. On motor vehicle distribution, see 7.6 *et seq.* below.

[198] See Guidelines 184–198. According to Guideline 189, cumulative effect problems are unlikely to arise where the share of the market covered by selective distribution systems is less than 50%, or where the market coverage is higher, but the aggregate market share of the five largest suppliers is less than 50%.

[199] Guideline 195. The Commission expects logistical efficiencies to be marginal.

[200] Guideline 195. The combination of exclusivity and selectivity should be "indispensable to protect substantial and relationship-specific investments made by the authorised dealers".

by the Commission, the latter will bear the burden of proof that the agreement in question infringes Article 81(1). When appreciable anti-competitive effects are demonstrated, undertakings may substantiate efficiency claims and explain why a certain distribution system is likely to bring about benefits which are relevant to the conditions for exemption under Article 81(3).

This position is reflected in Article 2 of the Commission's proposal for a regulation to replace Regulation 17/62:

> In any national or Community proceedings for the application of Article 81 and Article 82 of the Treaty, the burden of proving an infringement of Article 81(1) or of Article 82 shall rest on the party alleging the infringement. A party claiming the benefit of Article 81(3) shall bear the burden of proving that the conditions of that paragraph are fulfilled.[201]

There is, therefore, no presumption that distribution agreements which do not qualify for automatic exemption under Regulation 2790/99 actually infringe Article 81(1), or are tainted with nullity under Article 82. However, the fact that an agreement falls outside the BER indicates that there is at least some doubt as to whether its terms meet the requirement for exemption under Article 81(3). If the arrangement does not obviously fall outside Article 81(1) entirely, then there remains a concern for the parties that it is indeed caught by that prohibition.

Where this concern remains, the case-law of the European Courts indicates that it is for the person or authority alleging an illegality to prove it. Where a party to an agreement claims that some feature of it is a restraint on competition ancillary to a pro-competitive transaction, and therefore falling outside Article 81(1), that party bears the burden of proof. Where the party does not prove otherwise, the Commission's assessment that the restraint infringes the Treaty prohibition cannot be displaced. In the recent *Métropole* case,[202] the Court of First Instance held:

> It is clear from point 101 of the contested decision that the main reason why the Commission refused to classify the clause as an ancillary restriction was that it had a negative impact on the situation of third parties over quite a long period.
>
> The applicants, despite having the burden of proof in that regard, have not adduced any evidence to invalidate that assessment.

---

[201] In its explanatory memorandum to the proposal, the Commission says:

This Article clarifies which party bears the burden of proving the facts pertaining to the fulfilment of the conditions of Article 81. It is based on the division in the Treaty between the prohibition in Article 81(1) and the conditions under which it may be declared inapplicable set out in Article 81(3). It is also in line with the principle, widely observed in the laws of the Member States, that each party to litigation has to prove the facts on which it relies.

The rule proposed ensures a fair balance between the parties. In particular, the party invoking the benefit of Article 81(3) is generally best placed to supply the information required to demonstrate that the conditions of Article 81(3) are satisfied (e.g. regarding efficiencies). It is therefore appropriate that that party should bear the burden of proof as regards Article 81(3).

[202] *Métropole Télévision SA & Others* v. *Commission*, Case T-112/99, Judgment of 18 September 2001 [2001] 12 CMLR 1236, at paras. 130–131.

Moreover, if the agreement in question has been demonstrated to infringe the prohibition in Article 81(1), it is for the party then seeking an exemption to show that all four conditions under Article 81(3) have been met, by adducing the relevant evidence.[203] There is, according to the Courts, an onus which falls on the applicant to provide information to challenge the Commission's appraisal.[204]

This case-law presupposes that it is open to the parties to the agreement to notify it for exemption under Article 81(3).[205] In such circumstances, the Courts are reluctant to replace the Commission's assessment of complex economic matters with an evaluation of their own, unless there is a manifest error.[206] However, if the Commission's modernisation plans go ahead in their current form, it is not clear that it will be possible to obtain individual exemptions in the future.

This begs the question of where the burden of proof will lie if the exemption procedure is discontinued. Extrapolating from the case-law, one would expect that national competition authorities which claim the illegality of an agreement must substantiate that position, as must third-party complainants or litigants. The situation is more complex with regard to litigation between the parties to an agreement, in which one seeks to resile from it on grounds of illegality. In *Courage* v. *Crehan*,[207] the Court of Justice held that national procedural rules which prevent one party to an unlawful agreement seeking damages from the other party are incompatible with Community law. There would thus seem to be no bar to litigants claiming the illegality of their erstwhile agreements, provided they also raise a claim (or counterclaim) in damages and, indeed, this is commonly known as the "Euro" defence.

The burden of proof in litigation between the erstwhile business partners is still on the party claiming the illegality. It may therefore be prudent for parties to agreements which raise concerns under Article 81(1), but which can no longer be notified, together to produce documentation at the time of entering into the agreement (and before business relations turn sour) to show that the conditions for exemption under Article 81(3) are met. Although retrospective notification and exemption is now provided for, it may be impossible in practice to meet the burden of proving entitlement to an exemption in circumstances where the parties are in dispute.[208]

---

[203] See *Matra Hachette s.a.* v. *Commission,* Case T-17/93 [1994] ECR-II 595 at para 104: "It must first be borne in mind that the Commission may only grant an individual exemption decision if, in particular, the four conditions laid down by Article 85(3) of the Treaty are all met by the agreement, with the result that an exemption must be refused if any of the four conditions is not met".

[204] *Métropole Télévision SA & Others* v. *Commission,* Case T-112/99, judgment of 18 September 2001 [2001] 12 CMLR 1236, at para 158, referring to *Matra Hachette* v. *Commission,* Case T-17/93 and *VBVB and VBBB* v. *Commission,* Joined Cases 43/82 and 63/82.

[205] On notification, see 7.5 *et seq.* below.

[206] See, for example, *Consten and Grundig* v. *Commission,* Cases 56/64 and 58/64 [1966] ECR 382 at para. 59.

[207] *Courage Ltd* v. *Bernard Crehan and Bernard Crehan* v. *Courage Ltd and Others.* Case C-453/99 Judgment of the Court of 20 September 2001. See paras. 26–28.

[208] See also 7.5.3 below.

7.5.1 Provision for Retroactive Notification

The Council's amendment to Regulation 17 in 1999 provides that vertical agreements may now be exempted under Article 81(3) with retroactive effect to a date
prior to their notification.[209] So, even if an assessment reveals that a particular
agreement requires exemption,[210] the considerable trouble and expense of a notification can be forestalled indefinitely, or at least until the need to have an exemption decision crystallises. In practice, it may be easier to notify an agreement at its
inception—with the co-operation of the other party—than at some future time
when disagreements have taken root and litigation may be pending, or when the
other party may already have complained of anti-competitive behaviour to the
Commission or a national authority. Note that immunity from fines is still triggered only by notification,[211] and that any nullity under Article 81(2) has direct
effect from the outset, and may be a factor in litigation before national courts.[212]

7.5.2 Notification Procedure

Under the current notification system,[213] if the Commission intends formally to
clear or exempt an agreement, it must publish a call for third parties' comments.[214] After examining the arrangements, and considering any comments, the

[209] See 2.11 above, Article 4(2) and Article 6(2) of Regulation 17 and Guidelines 63–65. The Council
amended Regulation 17 by way of Regulation 1216/99, OJ 1999, L148. This empowered the
Commission to grant Article 81(3) exemptions with effect from the date upon which the agreement in
question came into being, rather than from the date of its notification. In practice, this means that
agreements need not be notified as a precautionary measure.

[210] Note that since there is no presumption that agreements falling outside the scope of Regulation
2790/99 infringe Article 81(1) [see Guideline 62], parties to agreements which fall outside that article—
such as purely qualitative selective distribution, or "genuine" agency agreements—are still entitled to
apply to the Commission for a negative clearance. This may be necessary in order to forestall pleadings
before a national court, based on putative nullity under Article 81(2), for example.

[211] Article 15(5) of Regulation 17.

[212] The modernisation plans beg the question whether it might not be better to notify certain agreements to the Commission as a "one-stop-shop" before the application of Article 81(3) devolves to
numerous national authorities and, perhaps, loses its uniformity thereby. In Guideline 65, however, the
Commission says that notifications will not be given priority, unless the agreement in question is the
subject of litigation or complaints. Article 35 of the Commission's current proposal for a new regulation implementing the competition rules, if enacted, would do away with the notification process and
with any pre-existing notifications and exemptions. See Article 35 of the Commission's proposal; document (2000) 582 final of 27 September 2000.

[213] The precise terminology is that one "applies" for negative clearance, or "notifies" an agreement
for exemption under Article 81(3). In practice, both occur together, and are generally referred to as
notification.

[214] Article 21 of Regulation 17. The call for comments may be published in abridged form. The
Commission is not required to call for comments before issuing a comfort letter (although the bare fact
of having issued the letter is made known on the Commission website), so the notifying parties may in
fact prefer to ask for a comfort letter if they wish their arrangements to remain low-key.

Commission may issue a negative clearance either by formal decision or by comfort letter,[215] it may issue an exemption (perhaps subject to conditions or obligations), or it may reject the application outright. Usually an outright rejection can be avoided if the parties amend their arrangements to address the Commission's competition concerns, or if they can agree to an exemption subject to conditions.[216]

7.5.3 Effect of Modernisation on Notification

The current plans for modernising implementation of the competition law rules will probably do away with the notification system at the level of the European Commission. If the Council adopts unchanged the Commission's proposal of September 2000 proposal for a Regulation to replace Regulation 17/62,[217] no further notification to the Commission will be possible, and existing applications and notifications will lapse.

It is expected that a new implementing Regulation will enter into force in January 2004,[218] and that power to grant exemptions under Article 81(3) will then devolve upon national courts and competition authorities.[219] From the point of view of undertakings who wish to distribute in several EEA countries, but whose agreements may fall outside the scope of Regulation 2790/99, this is regrettable, as the Commission's "one-stop-shop" for clearance or exemption will no longer be

---

[215] It is rare for the Commission to issue formal decisions under Article 81(3). In most cases it "closes" the matter with a comfort letter. See 2.5.1 above. The Commission may accede to the parties request for a formal decision where it is necessary to create legal certainty, or to resolve a point of law or practice which is of general application. In the recent *Inntrepreneur/Spring* notification, a formal decision was taken even though the Commission had already issued a comfort letter, because a possible buy-out of the parties' share capital depended on having formal evidence that their distribution agreements were exempted. Commission decision of 29 June 2000 (Cases IV/36.456/F3—*Inntrepreneur* and IV/36.492/F3—*Spring*), OJ 2000, L195/49.

[216] It is rare for the Commission fully to reject an application. There is a flexible informal procedure for meetings and consultations between Commission officials and the notifying parties, and it is usually the case that some agreement can be reached.

[217] Commission's proposal—Document COM (2000) 582 final of 27 September 2000.

[218] See 2.12 above. On 6 September 2001, MEPs voted 409 to 54 with 25 abstentions in favour of the Commission's proposal as part of the consultation procedure. However, the MEPs declared that they were are concerned about the possibility of the changes leading to legal uncertainty, and approved several non-binding amendments seeking to avoid this. Other non-binding amendments approved by the Parliament seek to introduce an element of harmonisation as far as fines are concerned, and a clearer definition of public interest. A further amendment aims to limit the Commission's power to interview company staff during an investigation, so as to protect individual employees' positions. MEPs also voted to delete the Commission's proposal for a registration system to replace the current notification and authorisation system on the grounds that the value of the proposed new system had not been demonstrated.

[219] It is not yet clear whether national competition authorities will have constitutive, or merely declaratory powers under the proposed new Article 5. On the modernisation plans, see **R. Whish** and **B. Sufrin** "Community Competition Law: Notification and Individual Exemption—Goodbye to all that" in **D. Hayton** (ed.) *Law's Future(s)* (Hart Publishing, Oxford, 2000); also **C.D. Ehlermann**, "The Modernization of EC Antitrust Policy: A Legal and Cultural Revolution", 37 *CMLRev*, 537–90; and **Moschel**, "Guest Editorial", 37 *CMLRev.*, 495–99.

available. The need, in complicated or borderline cases, to deal with multiple competition authorities will constitute a considerable financial and administrative burden, and there is a not-inconsiderable risk that the application of Article 81(3) may vary as between the respective competences, despite the Commission's reminders of the importance of uniform application of Community law, and the need for co-operation between national authorities.[220]

7.5.4 Commission Attitude to Notification

As a result of the modernisation plans, officials are no longer dealing with routine notifications concerning distribution arrangements. In Guideline 65, the Commission says:

> Unless there is litigation in national courts or complaints, notifications of vertical agreements will not be given priority in the Commission's enforcement policy. Notifications as such do not provide provisional validity for the execution of agreements. Where undertakings have not notified an agreement because they assumed in good faith that the market share threshold under the Block Exemption Regulation was not exceeded, the Commission will not impose fines.

In the *Inntrepreneur/Spring* case,[221] the parties were able to convince the Commission to re-open a notification in respect of which it had issued a comfort letter, in circumstances where the validity of the agreements in question was central to a third party's offer to buy out the share capital of the companies which had originally notified. The Commission issued a formal negative clearance Decision. However, it is now the exception, rather than the rule, that the Commission react at all to notifications, and most experts doubt that officials are processing notifications any more.

The Commission has assumed that existing notifications, and any individual exemptions still in force, will lapse in the event that the proposed Regulation replacing Regulation 17 enters into force. Parties affected will therefore need to monitor the situation, in order to be able to avert any risks which would arise from the effective withdrawal of an individual exemption.

---

[220] See, for instance, Guidelines 78 and 79. Recently, Sir Christopher Bellamy (President of the Competition Commission Appeals Tribunal in the UK) has pointed out that successful devolution of powers under Article 81(3) to national courts will require a substantial investment in training national judges to deal with competition law issues, and will necessitate closer contacts between judges in the respective Member States. [Speech to the *Studienvereinigung Kartellrecht Nineteenth International Forum on EC Competition Law*, Brussels, 27 June 2001, proceedings not yet published.]

[221] Case 2000/484/EC: Commission Decision of 29 June 2000 relating to a proceeding pursuant to Article 81 of the EC Treaty (Cases IV/36.456/F3—*Inntrepreneur* and IV/36.492/F3—*Spring*, OJ 2000, L195/49.

7.5.5 Immunity from Fines

While the notification procedure is still available, so is immunity from fines for undertakings which have notified agreements. Indeed, despite the Commission's insistence that agreements outside the BER are not presumed to infringe Article 81(1), immunity is still triggered only by notification.[222] Note that in its Decision on Glaxo Wellcome's dual-pricing scheme for pharmaceuticals sold in Spain,[223] the Commission expressly referred to the fact that no fine was imposed on Glaxo because the arrangements had been notified. In cases where the application of Article 81(1) to the distribution arrangements is not clear, or where the parties are particularly risk-averse, notification is still a prudent option, and remains the only certain protection from fines.

In a borderline case, the Commission's policy of not processing notifications may work to the notifying parties' advantage. A cursory form A/B can be submitted, thus triggering immunity from fines, at least until such time as the Commission reacts to declare the notification incomplete, which is now unlikely to happen.

7.6 DISTRIBUTION OF MOTOR VEHICLES[224]

The Commission has recognised that motor vehicle distribution is a special case. This is not only because of the great importance of the vehicle manufacturing and distribution industry to the European economy as a whole, but also because buying a new car is one of the most important and expensive purchases that many consumers make. The Commission has therefore been concerned to ensure that vehicles are distributed through systems which encourage the economic development of the sector, while ensuring that customers get proper access, choice and a share of the benefits. Since 1985, the Commission has given effect to this concern by means of block exemption regulations applying specifically to motor vehicle distribution and servicing.

7.6.1 Regulation 1475/95—Overview

Until September 2002, there is still a special sectoral block exemption in force, covering the combined selective and exclusive distributorship/dealership system

---

[222] Regulation 17, Art. 15(5).

[223] Commission Decision of 8 May 2001, OJ 2001, L302. Also Commission Press Release IP/01/661 of 8 May 2001, available on the internet at http://www.europa.eu.int/rapid/ start/welcome.htm. The Decision is under appeal as *Glaxo Wellcome plc* v. *Commission*, Case T-168/01 (see the notice in OJ 2001, C275/17), but has been publicly defended by Commissioner Monti—see SPEECH/01/450 of 11 October 2001.

[224] There is a great deal of useful information concerning the motor vehicles sector available on the DG Competition website: http://europa.eu.int/comm/competition/car_sector/.

commonly employed in the distribution and servicing of new motor vehicles. The current Regulation 1475/95 replaces a broadly similar provision from 1984.[225] It is at present the object of a major review process by the Commission.[226] While Regulation 1475/95 is in force, agreements the subject-matter of which concern vehicle distribution and servicing cannot benefit from exemption under Regulation 2790/99.[227]

The Commission adopted the exemption regulation for vehicle distribution based on the assumption that the sector had special needs. It was thought necessary to preserve the possibility for vehicle manufacturers to operate networks of selected exclusive dealers through which new vehicles could be sold under controlled conditions appropriate to the cost and complexity of such goods. In addition, competent under-warranty and post-warranty servicing and repairs could be assured through these networks. Since the Commission took the view that such exclusivity combined with selectivity would infringe Article 81(1), it made provision for a relatively restricted exemption which, it intended, would: make the dividing line between acceptable and unacceptable agreements clear, while giving car dealers greater commercial independence vis-à-vis manufacturers; give independent spare-part manufacturers easier access to the car manufacturers' networks; and improve the position of final consumers.[228]

7.6.1.1 Regulation 1475/95—scope

Regulation 1475/95 exempts certain vehicle distribution and servicing agreements from the prohibition in Article 81(1). It applies to arrangements for the supply of new motor vehicles for resale (including hire-purchase or leasing sales), together with spare parts for such vehicles.[229] The vehicles must be intended for use on public roads and have three or more road wheels.[230] The distribution of vehicle accessories, used or second-hand motor vehicles and motorcycles is not covered. Neither is the distribution of "consumables" such as oils, lubricants and tyres.

---

[225] Commission Regulation (EC) No. 1475/95 of June 1995 on the application of Article 85(3) of the Treaty to certain categories of motor vehicle distribution and servicing agreements, OJ 1995, L145/25, [1996] 4 CMLR 69. This replaces Commission Regulation (EEC) 123/85 of 12 December 1984, OJ 1985, L015/16, 18 January 1985.

[226] See http://www.europa.eu.int/comm/competition/car_sector/distribution/.

[227] Pursuant to Article 2(5) of Regulation 2790/99.

[228] See the Commission's *Explanatory Brochure* on Regulation 1475/95. Document IV/9509/95. Valentine points out that the Commission's explanation for the regime under Regulation 1475/95 displays some *ex-post* reasoning. The provisions protecting dealers do not necessarily give them more independence. The efficient aggressive ones might like less protection and lower prices.

[229] Regulation 1475/95 does not apply to pure servicing agreements for motor vehicles. See *Ford Service Outlet Agreement* in the Commission's Twenty-Seventh Report on Competition Policy, at p.147. Such pure servicing agreements now fall to be considered under Regulation 2790/99.

[230] The distribution of industrial and agricultural vehicles (such as forklifts and tractors) is therefore not subject to the Regulation, if their main use is not on public roads.

7.6.1.2 *Regulation 1475/95—exclusivity and selectivity*

The Regulation applies to exempt a manufacturer's granting an exclusive territory to a distributor, or to a distributor and a specified number of dealers within a selective distribution system.[231] It also provides protection for a ban on active sales outside the allocated territories. Without losing the benefit of the exemption, the supplier (normally the vehicle manufacturer or a principal distributor) may forbid its exclusive distributors or dealers to maintain branches or depots for the distribution of vehicles or spare parts outside their respective exclusive territories, to entrust any third party with such distribution, or to solicit customers by personalised advertising. Passive sales by the distributor or dealer may not, however, be restricted. The dealer may also be restrained from selling another manufacturer's vehicles, except through a separate sales premises, and from selling the supplier's vehicles or spare parts to resellers outside the authorised distribution network.[232]

In addition to providing for exclusivity, Regulation 1475/95 allows the supplier to set certain objective requirements and certain minimum standards for the distributor or dealer. The objective requirements may relate to the equipment of the business premises and the technical facilities for servicing, the specialised technical training of staff, advertising, the collection, storage and delivery of motor vehicles and sales and after-sales servicing, the repair and maintenance of motor vehicles (especially as regards their safety).[233] However, the supplier may not apply these requirements in a discriminatory manner. Therefore, those candidates who meet the objective requirements as to quality and service should normally be allowed to become authorised dealers.[234] The minimum standards may take the form of a "best endeavours" sales target,[235] minimum stocking obligations, and a commitment to honour the manufacturer's guarantee and any vehicle recall actions.

7.6.1.3 *Regulation 1475/95—obligations imposed on the parties by the Commission*

In Article 5, the Commission imposed a number of obligations on the parties to vehicle distribution agreements, non-fulfilment of which will take the agreement

---

[231] Regulation 1475/95, Article 1.

[232] Regulation 1475/95, Article 3. The Regulation allows for a restriction on sales to unauthorised resellers (Article 3(10)), but provides that dealers may not be prevented from making sales to intermediaries authorised in writing by final consumers (Article 3(11)).

[233] Regulation 1475/95, Article 4.

[234] Regulation 1475/95, Article 5(2)(a).

[235] The manufacturer may require from the distributor, and the distributor from the dealer to sell, with the exclusive territory and during a specific period, a minimum annual quantity of motor vehicles or spare parts to be determined by the parties by common agreement or, in the event of disagreement by an expert third party, taking account of sales previously achieved in the territory and of forecast sales for the territory and at national level. Recourse to a third party expert may also be had to resolve disagreement on levels of stock and necessary demonstration vehicles. The manufacturer may not unilaterally set stocking levels. See *Cabour*, Case C-230/96 [1998] ECR-I 2055, at paragraph 38.

outside the protection afforded by the Regulation. In this way, the Commission has effectively forced the motor vehicle sector to conform to the Commission's vision of an acceptable distribution system. Note that all the major vehicle manufacturers currently operate distribution systems compatible with Regulation 1475/95.

The Commission requires the dealer to undertake to honour the supplier's guarantees and to carry out repair and maintenance work, and to pass on this obligation to any sub-dealer. The supplier, on the other hand, is forbidden unreasonably to withhold its consent to sub-dealerships, to discriminate between members of the distribution network, or to aggregate sales figures in a way which discriminates between spare parts and other goods. Particularly important, from the point of view of both the Commission and the consumer, is the requirement on the supplier to provide any authorised dealer with any passenger car put on the Community market in a potential customer's home country. This provision is aimed at ensuring that the consumer may purchase his car of choice in any country, and is not confined only to buying in the country where he intends to register the vehicle. This allows the buyer to take advantage of price differences as between the EEA countries, which may be very considerable.[236] In fact, since the Regulation has been in force, the Commission has required the major vehicle manufacturers each to set up a telephone "hotline" system to advise customers on how to effect cross-border purchases.[237]

The Commission also obliges the suppliers of motor vehicles to adopt certain provisions as to the duration and termination of distribution agreements. The parties may conclude an agreement for a definite or for an indefinite period. The duration of the former must be at least five years, and termination may take place upon six months' notice. If the parties prefer to conclude an agreement of indefinite duration, then they are deemed to agree on a two year period of notice for termination. This notwithstanding, such agreements can be terminated on one year's notice if the manufacturer undertakes to pay damages, if the agreement is concluded with a newcomer to the network, or if there is a need to restructure the whole or a substantial part of the network.

---

[236] List prices of new vehicles may vary by as much as 30% as between Member States. The Commission seems to take the view that a price differential of 12% or more provides sufficient incentive to engage in parallel trade. The existing differentials are probably due in large part to the peculiarities of the system whereby motor vehicles are taxed, which has not yet been harmonised. In some Member States (especially the Nordic countries) the tax may amount to double the net list price. This forces distributors there to adopt very low net list prices, because the vehicles would otherwise be prohibitively expensive for the local consumer. Because new vehicles are taxed only in the country of first registration however, it is possible to buy a vehicle net of tax in a high-tax country, and register it in a low-tax country, and to make a considerable saving in the process. The Commission regularly publishes information on car price differentials, but does not seem to be so active in pushing for harmonisation of the Member States' tax systems. See http://www.europa.eu.int/comm/competition/car_sector/price_diffs/.

[237] http://www.europa.eu.int/comm/competition/car_sector/car_hotlines_en.html.

7.6.1.4 Regulation 1475/95—forbidden obligations

Article 6 of the Regulation effectively forbids a number of restrictions which the parties might agree,[238] including the tying of vehicle distribution and servicing agreements to the supply of other goods or services; the operation of restrictions of competition either not contemplated by Regulation 1745/95 or falling under the former exclusive distribution or exclusive purchasing exemptions; and, the operation of "closed" dealer selectivity by the supplier. In addition, the Article renders void certain restrictions which might be operated by the vehicle manufacturer or distributor, such as: interfering with the dealer's freedom to set prices; restricting final customers in their choice of dealer; and, linking dealer discounts to the country of residence of the purchaser.

Article 6 also contains a number of unique provisions regarding market access for independent repairers and the manufacturers of spare parts, which were not present in the corresponding 1985 Regulation. It renders void any practice which prevents authorised dealers from obtaining spare parts from third parties, or which prevents such third parties selling spare parts to authorised dealers, or which restricts their use of identifying trade marks,[239] provided the goods are of comparable quality with those of the vehicle manufacturer. Article 6 also grants independent repairers specific rights to obtain from vehicle manufacturers or distributors the technical information necessary for their maintenance and repair, and even information which is subject to know-how or other intellectual property rights may not be withheld "improperly".

7.6.1.5 Regulation 1475/95—withdrawal of the exemption

Article 8 empowers the Commission to withdraw the benefit of the exemption under Regulation 1475/95 in individual cases where agreements have effects incompatible with Article 81(3) of the Treaty. The provision specifically refers to certain circumstances which may trigger a withdrawal, including a finding that motor vehicles are not subject to effective competition, that prices as between the Member States differ substantially as a result of practices exempted by the Regulation, or that the parties are unjustifiably applying discriminatory prices or sales conditions.

---

[238] Strictly speaking, the Regulation does not forbid the listed restraints, but their inclusion takes vehicles distribution agreements outside the scope of the block exemption. Since all the major motor manufactures operate distribution systems tailored to benefit from the exemption, Article 6 can be regarded as prohibiting the restraints listed.

[239] This corresponds to a non-infringing use of a trade mark for the purposes of identification under Article 12 of the Community Trade Mark Regulation: "A Community trade mark shall not entitle the proprietor to prohibit a third party from using in the course of trade . . . the trade mark where it is necessary to indicate the intended purpose of a product or service, in particular as accessories or spare parts, provided he uses them in accordance with honest practices in industrial or commercial matters." Council Regulation 40/94 of 20 December 1993, OJ 1994, L011/1, as amended by Council Regulation 3288/94, and subsequently implemented by Commission Regulation 2868/95, OJ 1995, L303/1. Interestingly, the Commission did not stipulate in Regulation 1475/95 that the use of a mark by the supplier of vehicle spare parts need be "in accordance with honest practices".

Since the Regulation is due to expire in 2002, and is already under review, it is unlikely that the Commission will now formally exercise its power to withdraw the exemption.[240] However, it has long used this threat as a sword of Damocles over the heads of vehicle manufacturers, in order informally to encourage compliance with the Commission's vision of a vehicle market which should be transparent and benefit the European consumer.

7.6.2   Review of Regulation 1475/95

Regulation 1475/95 entered into force in July 1995 and it is due to expire in September 2002. Article 11 requires the Commission regularly to evaluate its application, and to consider the effect of the exempted distribution system on price differentials between Member States and on the quality of service to final users. During 1999 and 2000, the Commission carried out a major review, and sent questionnaires to various interested parties—car manufacturers, dealer associations, consumers' associations, independent repairers, spare-parts suppliers, internet car-sales companies, intermediaries and independent distributors. In March 2002, the Commission published a new draft regulation to replace Regulation 1475/95.[241] (See 7.6.2.2.1 below.)

7.6.2.1 Commissioner Monti in the Driver's Seat

In May 2000, Commissioner Monti gave a speech entitled "who will be in the driver's seat?"[242] in which he discussed his department's evaluation of the current vehicle distribution regime. He likened Regulation 1475/95 to a "highway code" for vehicle manufacturers who, metaphorically taking the back seat, dictate to their "chauffeur" (the dealer) how to drive new vehicles down the "distribution highway" to the customer. According to the Commissioner, the distribution route manufacturers choose to travel is not the fastest, most economical or smoothest available. Moreover, the back-seat driver "all too often" instructs the dealer-driver to do things which are outside the highway code of the Regulation. Mr Monti concluded that since the consumer is not yet in the driver's seat, the current exemption regime "seems not in all respects the best-possible solution".

[240] Note the discussion of the withdrawal mechanism under Article 8 of Regulation 2790/99 at 7.2.6 above. Regulation 1475/95 contains no provision for the withdrawal of the exemption from an entire market segment.
[241] The draft Regulation and explanatory memorandum thereto were published in OJ 2002, C67/2. It is also available on the internet: http://www.europa.eu.int/comm.competition/car_sector.
[242] SPEECH/00/177 of 11 May 2000 delivered to the Forum Europe Conference. Available on the Internet in the Commission's "rapid" database: http://www.europa.eu.int/rapid/start/welcome.htm.

7.6.2.2 Reports evaluating Regulation 1475/95

The "driver's seat" speech clearly set the tone for the Commission's Report evaluating the distribution system under Regulation 1475/95, which was published in November 2000.[243] The thrust of the Report was that current market conditions justify neither the combination of exclusive and selective distribution nor a link between sales and servicing. The Report of November 2000 was followed by a hearing at the Commission offices in Brussels during February 2001, at which most of those who had submitted responses to the questionnaire were represented, along with several other interested parties.[244] In December 2001, the Commission made available on the internet two further reports by external consultants, considering the various possible future legislative options, and consumers' preferences.[245]

7.6.2.2.1 New draft Regulation

In March 2002, the Commission published a new draft block exemption Regulation to cover the distribution and after-sales servicing of new motor vehicles.[246] It is to enter into force on 1 October 2002. The new Regulation will bring distribution arrangements in the motor vehicle sector largely into line with the general regime for vertical agreements under Regulation 2790/99, on which it is based. It is somewhat stricter from the viewpoint of vehicle manufacturers than Regulation 1475/95, while promising greater competitive freedom to vehicle distributors, repairers and intermediaries. Predictably, the draft received a mixed reception from stakeholders: the vehicle manufacturers complained that it is too broad and too restrictive,[247] while the European Consumers' Organisation welcomed the introduction of multibranding, the general removal of location clauses and the softening of the link between sales and services.[248]

Under the new Regulation, carmakers may choose either a territorially exclusive distribution system for authorised dealers and repairers, or a selective distribution system. Selective systems may be based on a combination of qualitative and quantitative selection criteria, or may apply purely qualitative criteria. Purely qualitative selective systems are not subject to a market share ceiling on the supplier, but the supplier is then obliged to authorise all prospective members which meet the qualitative standard. The Regulation will allow manufacturers to require dealers to

---

[243] See Commission Press Release IP/00/1306 of 15 November 2000. The Report is document COM(2000) 743 final, and is available on the internet: http://europa.eu.int/comm/competition/car_sector/distribution/eval_reg_1475_95/report/.

[244] Commission Press Release No. IP/01/204 of 14 February 2001. Available through the Commission's "Rapid" database: www.europa.eu.int/rapid/start/welcome.htm.

[245] Commission Press Release IP/01/1781. Also http://www.europa.eu.int/comm.competition/car_sector/.

[246] OJ 2002, C67/2. See also Commission Press Release IP/02/380.

[247] Association of European Car Manufacturers (ACEA). Press Release and Position Paper of 16 April 2002, available at http://www.acea.be.

[248] European Consumers' Organisation. Press Release of 16 April 2002, and Position Paper BEUC/X/017/2002 of 17 April 2002, both available at http://www.beuc.org.

sell competing brands in separate premises or sales areas, probably through a separate company, with separate management and a separate sales force, and in practice this may make multi-brand sales uneconomic, although internet advertising
and sales by qualified dealers, which cannot be prevented (recital 15), may open
up new economic possibilities. Manufacturers will not be allowed to impose
restrictions on the activities of intermediaries, and can only impose a requirement
that the intermediary must produce a mandate from the consumer. The
Regulation also seeks to open up the follow-on market for vehicle spare parts, both
original and competing parts of matching quality, and the market for independent
servicing and repairs. Some provisions as to the status of the vehicle manufacturers' intellectual property rights are novel, and may be fertile ground for future
litigation.

Article 1 of the draft Regulation contains definitions, several of which are similar or identical to those used in the vertical restraints block exemption
(Regulation 2790/99, the BER).[249] There are some new definitions which are
specific to the motor vehicles sector: "non-compete obligation" covers obligations
on the buyer to purchase more than 50 per cent of its needs from the supplier or
the latter's nominee, rather than the 80 per cent referred to in the BER; the draft
alludes to "repairers", whether "authorised", "unauthorised" or "independent";
the definition of a "selective distribution system" is made without prejudice to the
legitimate activities of unauthorised repairers; and, "quantitative selective distribution system" is now defined.[250] The draft Regulation also defines the product
range coming under the sectoral regime in more detail than under the previous
Regulation, with more specific references to contract vehicles, their corresponding
models, and to spare parts, whether "original" or competing "spare parts of
matching quality". In addition, the draft defines "end users" (including leasing
companies) and "independent operators".

The exemption provided for in Article 2 applies to vertical restraints occurring
in vertical agreements relating to the conditions under which the parties may purchase, sell or resell motor vehicles, spare parts for motor vehicles, or repair and
maintenance services for motor vehicles. Agreements involving retailers' associations are covered, provided no individual member has a turnover exceeding €50
million. The exemption extends to provisions dealing with intellectual property
rights, and to situations of dual distribution. Article 2 is largely analogous with its
counterpart in Regulation 2790/99.

---

[249] On the definitions used in Regulation 2790/99, see chapter 3 above, *passim*. The Commission has
not indicated whether it will adopt separate Guidelines on the new regime for motor vehicles (although
it produced a memorandum explaining the draft regulation). Since certain definitions are common to
Regulation 2790/99 and the draft vehicles regulation, the general Guidelines on Vertical Restraints and
the discussion of the BER and the Guidelines in preceding chapters are relevant to an understanding of
the new system for vehicles. See above, *passim*.

[250] "Quantitative selective distribution system" is not defined in the general BER, probably because
such arrangements are exempted up to the 30% market share ceiling, all other conditions being
satisfied. The Guidelines refer several times to quantitative selective distribution, and the new
definition in the draft motor vehicles regulation is consistent with the sense used in the Guidelines.

Article 3 indicates the conditions under which the exemption granted in Article 2 will apply, principal among which is a market share ceiling on the supplier of 30 per cent, increasing to 40 per cent where the agreement establishes a quantitative selective distribution system. Purely qualitative selective distribution systems are exempted without reference to market share. Agreements containing exclusive supply obligations are subject to a further market share ceiling on the buyer of 30 per cent. In addition, Article 3 requires that agreements provide for reasoned notices of termination by the supplier (to avoid dealers' being terminated for behaviour permitted by the Regulation), with minimum regular notice periods of up to two years. Article 3 also requires the parties to make provision for referring disputes to an independent third party or arbitrator.

Article 4 sets out the "hardcore restrictions" on competition, the inclusion of which will deprive an entire agreement of exemption. Some of these are analogous with the hardcore restrictions set out in the BER, while others are specific to the motor vehicles sector. Familiar hard-core restrictions are curbs on the distributor's or repairer's ability freely to set retail prices (RPM), although maximum or recommended prices are allowed. Also forbidden are restrictions as to customers or territory, except those whose object is: to protect exclusively allocated territories or customer groups; to maintain the wholesale level of trade; to prevent members of a selective distribution system selling to unauthorised distributors; and, to prevent the sale of components to competing manufacturers.

Article 4 also treats as hard-core: restrictions on cross-supplies between selected distributors; restrictions on active *or* passive sales to end users by selected distributors (although confining selected dealers to authorised places of establishment is permitted); restrictions on selected dealers' or distributors' sales of spare parts to independent repairers; restrictions on the distributor's ability to sell all vehicles corresponding to the contract range;[251] restrictions on the distributor against subcontracting repair and maintenance services, provided the consumer is informed in advance of the subcontractor's location; and, restrictions against repairers who provide only maintenance and spare parts. Also regarded as hard-core are restrictions agreed between vehicle manufacturers and their suppliers which limit the suppliers' ability to sell into the independent market downstream of the manufacturer. Similarly, manufacturers may not agree with their suppliers of original vehicle components to limit the latter's ability to place its logo or trademark on components or spare parts. Moreover, distributors and repairers may not be restricted in their ability to source original spare parts, or competing parts of matching quality, except where the vehicle manufacturer insists upon the use of original spare parts in warranty, free-servicing and vehicle-recall work.

Article 4(2) provides that the exemption shall not apply where the supplier of motor vehicles refuses to give independent operators non-discriminatory and

---

[251] This hard-core restraint refers to previous practices of certain manufacturers which made it difficult for dealers in continental Europe to obtain right-hand-drive versions of vehicles in their normal contract range for subsequent sale to customers in the UK and Ireland. The Commission refers to Article 5(b) as the "availability clause".

proportionate access to any technical information, diagnostic and other equipment, tools, including any relevant software, and training required for the repair and maintenance of these motor vehicles or for the implementation of environmental protection measures. Moreover, information covered by an intellectual property right or constituting know-how is not to be withheld in an abusive manner.

Article 5 of the draft Regulation lists obligations which, if they appear in an agreement to which the Regulation otherwise applies, will not benefit from the exemption. These include: direct or indirect non-compete obligations relating to the sale of motor vehicles;[252] post-term non-compete obligations; obligations not to sell leasing services; obligations limiting the provision of repair or maintenance service for brands of competing suppliers; obligations limiting selected dealers from selling the brands of particular competing suppliers; obligations limiting the ability of members of a selective distribution system to operate elsewhere in the Common Market;[253] obligations of more than five years' duration limiting the location from which members of a selective distribution system sell vehicles other than passenger cars; and, obligations as to the place of establishment of authorised repairers.

Article 6 provides that the Commission may withdraw the benefit of the exemption from particular agreements, in particular where there are cumulative effects of parallel networks of similar agreements, where a supplier is not exposed to effective competition, where prices for corresponding goods differ substantially between geographic markets, or where discriminatory prices are applied within a geographic market. Article 7 empowers national authorities to withdraw the exemption under the same conditions, where distinct geographic markets in the territory of a Member State are affected, and Article 8 provides that the Commission may, by regulation with at least one year's notice, disapply the Regulation where parallel networks of vertical restraints cover more than 50 per cent of a relevant market.

The remainder of the draft Regulation is analogous with the BER. Article 9 indicates how market share is to be calculated, for the purposes of applying the 30 per cent and 40 per cent ceilings, and provides for marginal relief for up to two years. Article 10 indicates how turnover is to be calculated. Article 11 defines "connected undertakings". Article 12 provides for a transitional period of exemption from 1 October 2002 to 30 September 2003 for agreements which were exempted under Regulation 1475/95, but which do not satisfy the requirements of the new

---

[252] Article 1(b) provides that an obligation on the distributor to sell motor vehicles from other suppliers in a separate area of the showroom in order to avoid confusion between the makes is not to be regarded as a non-compete obligation.

[253] How this condition interacts with Article 4(d) is not clear. Article 4(d) provides that a restriction on a selected dealer against operating from an unauthorised place of establishment is not a restriction on active or passive sales. Article 5 refers to individual conditions which are not exemptible, rather than to hard-core restrictions which deprive the whole agreement of exemption. Denis thinks Article 5(f) probably means that suppliers operating a selective distribution system must, on request, authorise qualitatively suitable places of establishment in other Member States.

Regulation. Article 13 requires the Commission to draw up a report on the evaluation of the Regulation by 31 May 2002, and Article 14 provides that the Regulation will enter into force on 1 October 2002, and expire on 31 May 2010.

7.6.3 Cases Concerning Motor Vehicle Distribution

The motor vehicle distribution sector regularly attracts the attention of the European Commission's antitrust enforcement officials, often acting on the basis of complaints from consumers who find that they are unable to shop around in order to purchase new vehicles in the country of their choice and/or in the country where prices are lowest. In 1998, the Commission imposed a (then) record fine of €102 million on the Volkswagen group, for having taken measures to prevent its Italian dealers from selling new cars to customers from elsewhere in Europe, and in 2000, it fined Opel Netherlands €43 million for a similar infringement of the competition rules. Most recently, in May 2001, the Commission again fined Volkswagen for practising retail price maintenance on the German market.[254]

The Commission has taken several decisions fining vehicle manufacturers for making it difficult for consumers to obtain vehicles in the Member States where they are cheapest net of tax. As long ago as the *BMW* case in 1979,[255] the European Court held that a national distributor's behaviour discouraging dealers from exporting vehicles was incompatible with a distribution system which benefited from an exemption decision under Article 81(3). In 1985, the Court upheld the Commission's decision that *Ford*, by preventing its German dealers from selling right-hand drive cars for export to the UK and Ireland, was artificially partitioning the Common Market.[256] Despite the Commission's consistent practice of fining vehicle manufacturers whose distribution systems deliberately hinder trade between the Member States, and the Court's support for that policy,[257] such cases have recurred with surprising regularity. The most recent are discussed below.

[254] Commission Press Release IP/01/760, of 30 May 2001. Available on the internet at http://www.europa.eu.int/rapid/start/welcome.htm. The Commission fined VW €30.96 million for enforcing "price discipline" among German dealers of its Passat model in 1996 and 1997.

[255] *BMW Belgium and Others* v. *Commission,* Joined Cases 32/78, 36/78 to 82/78 [1979] ECR 2435 [1980] 1 CMLR 370, CMR 8548. The Commission's exemption decision on BMW's selective distribution system is published in OJ 1975, L29/1. The exemption was granted only after BMW agreed to remove export bans from its new dealer agreements.

[256] *Ford—Werke AG and Ford of Europe Inc.* v. *Commission of the European Communities*, Joined Cases 25 and 26/84 [1985] ECR 2725, at para. 33.

[257] The Commission's attitude on restraints to parallel trade in vehicles is still not rigorous enough for all interested parties. In February 2000, *Services pour le Groupement d'Acquisitions* ("SGA"), an intermediary in the automobile distribution sector, lodged an appeal against the Court of First Instance's ruling in 1999 which upheld the Commission's decision not to investigate a complaint by SGA concerning Peugeot's vehicle distribution practices. (Appeal to the ECJ, *Services pour le Groupement d'Acquisitions* v. *Commission*, Case C-39/00, appealing CFI Judgment of 13 December 1999 in Joined Cases T-189/95, T-39/96 and T-123/96 [1999] ECR II-3587.) In 1994, SGA alleged to the Commission that Peugeot was pressurising Peugeot and Citroën dealers outside France not to sell Peugeot vehicles to French customers. In 1996, the Commission, (which was by this time already busy

7.6.3.1 CFI reduces record fine on Volkswagen, but upholds finding of infringement

In July 2000, the Court of First Instance partially annulled the Commission's Decision which had imposed a record fine of €102 million on Volkswagen in 1998. In the contested Decision the Commission had found that the VW group took measures to curb exports of new vehicles from Italy to other Member States, including tying dealer bonuses to the subsequent registration of vehicles in Italy, rigorous investigations of and penalties applied to Italian dealerships—which were carried out by a special "task force"—and restrictions on supplies.

The Court of First Instance held that the Commission's evidence showing a policy of partitioning off the Italian market was both relevant and consistent,[258] and that the policy was an obstacle to consumers and VW dealers in other Member States who wished to purchase cars in Italy. This entitled the Commission to find that Volkswagen had infringed Article 81(1). However, the Commission did not properly prove that the infringement which began in 1993 extended beyond 1996. The Court therefore annulled the decision in as much as it related to the period after October 1996.[259] The Court also found that since the object of VW's policy was to isolate the Italian market, it was necessarily capable of affecting trade between the Member States, so the Commission was not required to define a geographic market when applying Article 81.[260] In this regard, the Court pointedly observed that although the block exemption regime for motor vehicle distribution provides manufacturers with substantial means of protecting their distributor networks, it does not entitle them to partition the Common Market.[261] Interestingly, in contrast to the *Bayer* case,[262] the Court regarded as a settled proposition of law that a call by a motor vehicle manufacturer to its authorised dealers is *not* a unilateral act which falls outside the scope of Article 81(1), but is an agreement within the meaning of

---

investigating the Volkswagen group's export-restricting measures, in relation to which it subsequently imposed a record fine) decided that SGA's allegations, even if substantiated, did not disclose a sufficient community interest, took no action against Peugeot, and did not impose the interim measures sought by SGA. SGA claimed that the Court of Justice should set aside the CFI judgment, particularly upon the grounds that the Commission took too long in deciding whether to take action on foot of SGA's complaint, that it erred in finding insufficient Community interest, and that it incorrectly assessed the probative value of the evidence adduced in support of SGA's allegations. In December 2000, the President of the Sixth Chamber dismissed SGA's appeal. (Order of the Court (Sixth Chamber) of 13 December 2000 in *Services pour le Groupement d'Acquisitions SARL (SGA)* v. *Commission,* Case C-39/00 P, OJ 2001, C200/26).

[258] *Volkswagen AG* v. *Commission,* Case T-62/98, CFI Judgment of 6 July 2000, [2000] ECR-II 2713, [2000] 5 CMLR 853 at paragraph 162.

[259] *Ibid.,* at paragraph 192.

[260] *Ibid.,* at paragraph 231.

[261] *Volkswagen AG* v. *Commission,* Case T-62/98, at paragraph 49.

[262] Commission Decision 96/478/EEC, OJ 1996, L201/1. Appealed as *Bayer AG* v. *Commission* Case T-41/96 [2001] 4 CMLR 4. The CFI judgement of 26 October 2000 is not yet reported in the ECR, but is available online at www.curia.eu.int. *Volkswagen,* although it was handed down after the hearing in *Bayer* took place, *and* is probably inconsistent with the final judgment in that case. In *Volkswagen,* the Court relied heavily on the cases cited by the Commission, and did not make as thorough an analysis as in the *Adalat* appeal.

that provision if it forms part of a set of continuous business relations governed by a general agreement drawn up in advance.[263]

The Court accepted Volkswagen's argument that the Commission, by leaking details of its decision to the press prior to formally adopting the measure, had failed to comply with the principle that competition law investigations are confidential. Although the Court admonished the Commission for this breach of the principle of good administration, it found that the irregularity had not altered the amount of the fine or the substance of the decision.[264]

In exercising its unlimited jurisdiction to consider the amount of the fine, the Court of First Instance demonstrated that it, just as much as the Commission, is prepared to take a hard line against distribution practices which intentionally seek to re-partition the Community market. Despite its partial annulment of the original Commission decision, the Court found that Volkswagen had carried out a "highly grave" infringement with "intensity".[265] It decided that such activity merited a fine which would be a "real deterrent",[266] particularly because Volkswagen had "jointly with its subsidiaries, prevented consumers from enjoying without impediment freedoms of the Common Market laid down by the Treaty, thus detracting from one of the most important achievements in the building of the Community."[267] The Court regarded the size of the VW Group and the fact that it had disregarded the warning constituted by the settled case-law on parallel imports in the motor vehicle industry as aggravating factors.[268] It reduced the fine from €102 million to €90 million (still a record amount), and ordered VW to pay its own costs of the appeal plus 90 per cent of the Commission's costs. Volkswagen has appealed to the Court of Justice.

7.6.3.2 Commission fines VW again in May 2001

After the judgment of the Court of First Instance upholding the Volkswagen decision, the Commission issued a press release in which it stressed its preparedness to take action against car manufacturers who do not comply with the distribution rules.[269] Mr. Monti's language is worth noting:

> This ruling is good news for European consumers. The possibility to buy goods at better prices in other Member States is indeed one of the key advantages of the Single Market. Carmakers have some latitude in the way they choose to organise their distribution networks, but the rules also give consumers the unalterable right to buy, either directly or

---

[263] *Volkswagen AG* v. *Commission*, Case T-62/98, CFI Judgment of 6 July 2000, at paragraph 236, referring to *Ford* v. *Commission*, Joined Cases 25/84 and 26/84 [1985] ECR 2725, paragraph 21 and *Bayerische Motorenwerke*, Case C-70/93 [1995] ECR I-3439, paragraphs 15 and 16.

[264] *Ibid.*, at paragraphs 279 to 284.

[265] *Ibid.*, at paragraph 347.

[266] *Ibid.*, at paragraph 347.

[267] *Ibid.*, at paragraph 336.

[268] *Ibid.*

[269] Commission Press Release No. IP/00/725 of 6 July 2000. Available on the Internet through the Commission's "Rapid" database: www.europa.eu.int/rapid/start/welcome.htm.

through an authorised intermediary, a car in the Member State of their choice. By upholding such rights, competition policy directly serves citizens.

7.6.3.3 Commission fines Opel Netherlands €43 million

In September 2000, the Commission imposed a fine on Opel in the Netherlands for obstructing exports of new cars to end users in other Member States.[270] Acting on complaints from customers, the Commission carried out investigations at Opel premises in 1996, and found evidence of practices intended to restrict sales to purchasers abroad. These included instructions to dealers to stop export sales, to concentrate their sales generally within the Netherlands, and a sales campaign in which dealers were refused bonuses on sales to customers abroad.

The Commission found evidence of at least three practices intended to restrict sales to purchasers abroad: (a) restrictions on supplies to dealers who exported (based on the dealers' agreed sales targets for their Dutch territories; (b) instructions to dealers to stop export sales and to concentrate their sales generally within the Netherlands; and, (c) a sales promotion campaign in which dealers were refused bonuses on sales made to customers abroad.

The Commission considered that Opel's measures, accepted by Dutch dealers, were caught by the prohibition in Article 81(1), and that they were also in breach of the block exemption regulation for motor vehicle distribution (Regulation 1475/95). There was evidence that some restrictions might have been justified, as some sales were being made to resellers who were not part of Opel's authorised distribution network. However, Opel did not target only those dealers selling outside the network, but took measures which restricted exports in general.

Although the Commission described the infringement as comparable to that of Volkswagen, and referred to the scathing judgment of the Court of First Instance in that case, it imposed a lower fine on Opel Netherlands (€43 million), after taking the duration and the intensity of the infringement into account. The Commission described the infringement as "very serious", and imposed a basic fine of €40 million, which it increased by 7.5 per cent, to take the "medium" duration into account. It did not accept Opel's claim that it had "retroactively" removed export restrictions, since those earlier restrictions had already had an effect.

Interestingly—or perhaps alarmingly—the Commission refused to treat as privileged a document internal to Opel which summarised written and oral advice from outside legal advisors. The Commission did not treat the legal opinions expressed in the document as evidence that Opel's infringement was intentional, although Commissioner Monti is reported to have said that such documents might in future be relied on to show the existence of an infringement, rather than the intention of the infringing party.

---

[270] Commission Press Release No. IP/00/1028 of 20 September 2000. Available through the Commission's "Rapid" database: www.europa.eu.int/rapid/start/welcome.htm. The Commission's full Decision is published in OJ 2001, L059/1.

7.6.3.4 Commission intervenes to end Triumph motorcycle export ban

Also in September 2000, the Commission announced that it had closed its proceedings against the UK motorcycle manufacturer Triumph, because the company
stopped prohibiting its dealers in the Benelux region from selling to customers in
the United Kingdom.[271] Again acting on complaints from disgruntled customers,
the Commission had carried out so-called "dawn raids" on Triumph, its Benelux
importer and on certain dealers. Confronted with the results of the investigation,
Triumph admitted to having imposed an export ban in 1997–1998 when faced
with price differentials of up to 30 per cent between the UK and continental
Europe, as a result of the strong Pound.

The Commission's intervention in this case is largely of symbolic value only,
since Triumph's market share in the EU is less than 5 per cent, except in the UK,
where it has up to 10 per cent of the market, indicating that the actual number of
exports blocked was not great. Given the minor importance of the matter, and
Triumph's public co-operation in bringing the restrictions to an end, the
Commission closed its file without imposing a fine. It is interesting however, to
note that the Commission has pointedly used the Triumph case to fire a
metaphorical "warning shot" across the bows of the motorcycle industry. In its
press release, it stressed that motorcycle distribution does not benefit from the
block exemption for selective and exclusive distribution of motor-vehicles
(Regulation 1475/95), and that it regards export restrictions as one of the "most
serious" restrictions of competition. Also of interest is the Commission's adoption
of a category of "motorcycles of large engine capacity", being those of 750cc and
above. It remains to be seen whether the Commission will abide by this categori-
sation in the future when it calculates market shares in the motorcycle industry.

7.6.3.5 VW Passat—€30.96 million fine

In June 2001, the Commission again fined Volkswagen, this time for practising
resale price maintenance (rpm) in relation to sales of its *Passat* model in
Germany.[272] Investigations revealed that, when the new model was introduced in
1997, VW issued circulars warning dealers not to sell the car at a discount exceeding 10 per cent of the recommended retail price, as this would be "extremely damaging to the brand". They were also asked to report other dealers who advertised
large discounts. At least one dealer was individually disciplined for offering excessive discounts.

The Commission found that this behaviour, in the context of its business relations with the dealers, effectively made its price recommendations binding.
Although there was no evidence that VW had practised rpm outside Germany, the

---

[271] Commission Press Release No. IP/00/1014 of 15 September 2000. Available through the
Commission's "Rapid" database: www.europa.eu.int/rapid/start/welcome.htm.
[272] Decision 2001/711/EC of 29 June 2001 *Volkswagen Passat*, OJ 2001, L262/14. [2001] 5 CMLR
1309.

Commission found that trade between the EU Member States was affected, because high prices in Germany created an incentive for parallel trade into Germany, and a disincentive for exports from Germany to the UK, where prices were higher still. VW had argued, without success, that an "effect on trade" within the meaning of Article 81(1) required there to be a market-partitioning effect, of which there was no direct evidence.

The Commission found that the infringement was "very serious", and increased the basic fine of €20 million by 29 per cent to take account of the "medium" duration (three years) and of aggravating factors, including threats to dealers, and the fact that dealers had to "spy" on each other.

7.6.3.6 DaimlerChrysler fined €71.8 million

In October 2001 the Commission announced that it had fined DaimlerChrysler (DC) for behaviour restraining parallel trade in cars, and for restraining competition on the leasing market.[273]

The Commission identified three infringements of the competition rules:

i) Measures constituting obstacles to parallel trade in Mercedes cars. DC issued circular letters to its authorised dealers and agents in Germany, forbidding them to sell outside their territories, and instructing them to require non-German customers to pay a 15 per cent advance deposit, which was not required of local buyers.
ii) Measures limiting sales to independent leasing companies by Mercedes agents and dealers in Spain. Dealers were instructed not to sell cars to leasing companies unless a lessee for the vehicle had already been found. This prevented independent leasing companies from keeping cars in stock, and from buying in bulk, which would have earned rebates.
iii) A price-fixing arrangement in Belgium, which limited the rebates which could be granted to consumers. A "ghost shopper" investigated the rebates offered, and supplies were restricted to dealers offering more than 3 per cent.

The Commission found that the arrangements not only infringed Article 81(1), but that they were also clearly incompatible with the provisions of the block exemption regulation for motor vehicle distribution (Regulation 1475/95). Manufacturers which wish to benefit from the Regulation in order to operate distribution systems combining selectivity and exclusivity are forbidden from restricting parallel trade between the EU Member States, or from fixing the prices charged by dealers to end consumers. The Regulation specifically provides that leasing companies are to be treated as end consumers for this purpose.

The Commission found that the first infringement was "very serious" and of long duration. The others were "serious" and of medium duration.

---

[273] Commission Press Release IP/01/1394.

The DaimlerChrysler decision is particularly interesting, because the Commission has, for the first time, applied its latest notice on Agents, as embodied in the Guidelines on vertical restraints.[274] The Commission took the view that Article 81(1) could apply to the instructions given by DC to its German agents, because these latter bore "a considerable commercial risk linked to their activity" and should, therefore be regarded as separate business undertakings, capable of entering into an anti-competitive agreement.

7.7 BEER SUPPLY AGREEMENTS

Arrangements for the supply of beer have previously been the object of a great deal of attention under the competition rules. Many beer-supply agreements were notified to the Commission for exemption[275] until Title II of Regulation 1984/83 on exclusive purchasing provided a block exemption for long-term purchasing agreements entered into for the resale of beer in premises used for sale and consumption.[276]

Article 6 of Regulation 1984/83 provided:

> Article 81(1) of the Treaty shall not apply to agreements to which only two undertakings are party and whereby one party, the reseller, agrees with the other, the supplier, in consideration for according special commercial or financial advantages, to purchase only from the supplier, an undertaking connected with the supplier or another undertaking entrusted by the supplier with the distribution of his goods, certain beers, or certain beers and certain other drinks, specified in the Agreement for resale in premises used for the sale and consumption of drinks and designated in the Agreement.[277]

The exemption for beer-supply agreements under Regulation 1984/83 remained in force until the end of 2001 by virtue of the transitional provisions of Regulation 2790/99. Such agreements should have been reviewed, and if necessary amended, to ensure that they now come within the exemption under the BER, or have been notified for exemption, while that is still possible. A number of standard beer-supply agreements were granted individual exemptions by the Commission in 1999, on the basis that, where they were not used to force tied customers to pay

---

[274] OJ 2000, C291/1.

[275] See, for example, *Brasserie de Haecht SA* v. *Wilkin (No. 2)*, Case 48/72, 6 February 1973, [1973] ECR 77, [1973] CMLR 287, CMR 8170.

[276] Commission Regulation 1984/83—Group exemption for exclusive purchasing agreements, OJ 1983, L173/7, corrections OJ 1984, C101/2, CMR 2733, [1983] 2 CLE 262.

[277] Article 6(2) continued: "The Declaration in paragraph 1 shall also apply where exclusive purchasing obligations of the kind described in paragraph 1 are imposed on the reseller in favour of the supplier by another undertaking which is itself not a supplier." See the detailed treatment of Regulation 1984/83 in **Korah** & **Rothnie**, *Exclusive Distribution and the EEC Competition rules—Regulations 1983/83 and 1984/83*m 2nd edn. (Oxford, ESC, 1986).

more for beer than non-tied customers, the efficiency of the tying arrangements outweighed their anti-competitive effect.[278]

Although there is no special mention of beer-supply agreements in Regulation 2790/99, so-called "tied-house" supply arrangements between breweries and their tenants can, where the other conditions of the BER are met, benefit from Article 5(a), in respect of non-compete obligations (under Article 1(b), a requirement on the tenant to purchase 80 per cent or more of its requirements from the landlord or its designee) which last for the duration of the tenancy.

Tied-house agreements which fall outside Regulation 2790/99, perhaps because the market-share of the supplier exceeds 30 per cent, do not necessarily infringe Article 81(1) at all. At least some provisions of most such arrangements can benefit from the doctrine in *Delimitis*,[279] a case which concerned beer-supply. According to the Court in that case, single branding will only infringe Article 81(1) if, having regard to its economic and legal context, it hinders access to the market or renders it difficult for other suppliers to increase existing market share. The *Delimitis* doctrine has been refined in the *Neste* case,[280] and more recently, in *Roberts* v. *Commission*, the Court of First Instance upheld the Commission's decision to reject a complaint concerning the Greene King pub lease.[281]

The CFI applied the Court of Justice's rulings in the earlier *Delimitis* and *Neste* cases,[282] and held that the Commission was correct in its finding that the lease did not foreclose the UK beer market. The case thus restates the doctrine that individual supply contracts forming part of a distribution network can fall outside the prohibition in Article 81(1) where they contribute only insignificantly to market foreclosure.[283]

The Court found that GK's wholesaling arrangements could only be regarded as part of the national brewers' networks of agreements if they a) contained a purchasing obligation, and b) were so restrictive as to make access for other brewers to GK's downstream network difficult or impossible.[284] These conditions were not fulfilled on the facts, and the CFI even added that where access to the wholesaling brewer's network is not foreclosed by the upstream contracts, the wholesaler can

---

[278] See, for example: *Whitbread* [1999] OJ L 88/28 [1999] 5 CMLR 118 on appeal as *Shaw et al.* v. *Commission*, Case T-131/99. Action brought on 27 May 1999 by Michael Hamilton Shaw, Timothy John Falla and WPP Luxembourg Appeal Group Limited against the Commission of the European Communities OJ 1999, C246/36; *Bass* OJ 1999, L186/1 [1999] 5 CMLR 782; *Scottish & Newcastle* [1999] OJ 1999, L186/26 [1999] 5 CMLR 831.

[279] *Delimitis (Stergios)* v. *Henninger Bräu*, Case C-234/89, 28 February 1991, [1991] ECR I-935, [1992] 5 CMLR 210, [1992] 2 CEC 530.

[280] *Neste Markkinointi Oy* v. *Yötuuli Ky, and others*, Case C-214/99, 7 December 2000, [2000] ECR-I 11, 121 [2001] 4 CMLR 27, [2001] CEC 54.

[281] *Roberts & Roberts* v. *Commission,*. Case T-25/99, CFI judgment of 5 July 2001. See 5.1.1.1.3 above.

[282] *Delimitis* v. *Henniger Bräu*, Case C-234/89 [1991] ECR I-935, *Neste Markkinointi Oy* v. *Yötuuli Ky, and others*, Case C-214/99, 7 December 2000, [2000] ECR I-11, 121 [2001] 4 CMLR 27, [2001] CEC 54.

[283] *Roberts* v. *Commission* is discussed in more detail at 7.2.6.5.1 above.

[284] *Roberts & Roberts* v. *Commission*, Case T-25/99 CFI judgment of 5 July 2001, paras. 106–7.

actually promote other brewers' market penetration by allowing them access to the downstream network.[285]

In August 2000, the Commission published its decision clearing the *Inntrepreneur* and *Spring* pub tenancy agreements.[286] These had already been cleared by comfort letter covering the period up to March 1998, but a formal decision relating to the period thereafter was sought because the original parties' share capital was then bought by The Grand Pub Company, a subsidiary of Nomura investment bank.

The Commission noted that the market concerned was that of the whole UK on-trade (i.e. sale and consumption on the premises). It also considered the degree of concentration on that market and, notably, referred to Herfindahl-Hirschmann index figures.[287] The pub leases provided for exclusive purchasing coupled with explicit and implicit non-compete obligations on the part of the publican.[288] However, the Commission pointed out that the lessor undertakings were "free-standing" pub companies, which in effect act as exclusive wholesalers for their many tenants and are not, as is often the case, integrated with any one brewery. Inntrepreneur and Spring source a diversified portfolio of beers from multiple national and regional brewers through periodic short-term tendering, with the effect that in a five-year period, practically all their sales volume would be subject to an opportunity for third parties to tender. Interestingly, the Commission therefore found that, rather than the tied leases' restricting competition, the parties' independent distribution structure would actually reduce market foreclosure by offering a "gateway" to the market for both British and international brewers.[289]

After *Delimitis, Roberts* and *Inntrepreneur/Spring*, it seems that many, if not most, beer-supply agreements which do not qualify for automatic exemption under Regulation 2790/99 either fall outside Article 81(1) altogether, or would qualify for exemption under Article 81(3) if they could be notified. The Commission's several exemption decisions in 1999 are of use, by way of guidance for the parties to any agreements still unaccounted for. The Commission seems adamant that the tie should not raise prices for tenants in real terms, as compared with the prices charged to their non-tied counterparts. In addition, the former Regulation 1983/84 gives some indication as to the types of contractual restrictions which may be appropriate (Article 7) or which may be likely to raise competition concerns (Article 8).

---

[285] *Ibid.*, para. 108.

[286] Commission Decisions of 29 June 2000 relating to a proceeding pursuant to Article 81 of the EC Treaty *Inntrepreneur and Spring,* OJ 2000, L195/49.

[287] The Herfindahl-Hirschmann index (HHI) is a statistical measure of the degree of market concentration, to which increasing importance is being attached in recent Commission practice. Here, it is interesting to see HHIs being applied in the context of a distribution market, rather than (as is more usual) in connection with a merger notification.

[288] *Ibid.*, paragraphs 47–50.

[289] *Ibid.*, paragraphs 60–62.

8

Conclusion on the Regulation and Guidelines

The Commission's ambitious exercise on vertical restraints took many years, and came close to failure before the publication of the Green Paper. There is much to praise. Economists now accept that vertical restraints may have both pro- and anti-competitive effects.[1] The guidelines are right to balance these.

The Commission now accepts that restraining competition between dealers in the same brand is not anticompetitive unless there is insufficient interbrand competition (Guidelines 6 and 119(1)). Its stress on the importance of protecting consumers rather than competitors (Guideline 7, 1.2.2 above) is also welcome, although the Commission rather easily assumes that excluding competitors will harm consumers in the long run. Consequently, it imposes a high burden of proof under Article 81(3) that a practice is indispensable to achieve efficiencies and that part of the benefit will be passed on to consumers if those efficiencies will make business harder for competitors[2] (7.4.5 above). One of the objectives of competition law is to ensure that those firms good at providing what customers want to buy thrive at the expense of those less good, but there are still traces in Europe of ideas of fair competition, which may mean protecting less efficient competitors, especially if they are of small or medium size.

Despite the ancillary restraint doctrine (2.7.2 above) the Commission treats restraints as outside Article 81(1) only if one could not conceive such a transaction without them.[3] We regret that efficiencies are not considered under Article 81(1) where the burden of proof is on the person alleging illegality. It is only when invoking Article 81(3) that the Treaty requires the restraints to be indispensable and for it to be established that a fair share of the benefit is passed on to ultimate buyers. Some of the judgments considered at 2.7.2 above, such as *Société La Technique Minière v. Maschinenbau Ulm GmbH*,[4] *Nungesser (L.G.) KG and Kurt Eisele v.*

---

[1] 1.2.2 above). See **S. Salop**, "Vertical restraints under EC law," in **Barry Hawk** (ed.) [2000] *Fordham Corporate Law Institute* 217, 229.

[2] In *Consten and Grundig v. Commission*, paras. 54–59, the ECJ said that the Commission was not entitled to confine itself to requiring the parties to prove that the conditions for exemption were met, but it went on to observe that the restraint must be indispensable to obtaining the benefits claimed.

[3] Following *Métropole Télévision SA and Others v. Commission*, Case T-112/99, 18 September 2001, [2001] 12 CMLR 1236, but contrary to *European Night Services (ENS) and others v. Commission*, Cases T-374, 375, 384 & 388/94, [1998] ECR II-3141, para. 136.

[4] Case 56/65, [1966] ECR 235.

Commission,[5] and *European Night Services (ENS) and others* v. *Commission*,[6] go further and accept as not infringing Article 81(1) restraints that make commercially viable transactions not in themselves anti-competitive. The case law on ancillary restraints and Article 81(1) is unclear.

8.1 WIDE COVERAGE

Regulation 2790/99 will be widely welcomed for its wider coverage; distribution of services as well as goods, and sale for incorporation into something else as well as for resale. The economic considerations are similar. The new Regulation also covers vertical agreements between two or more undertakings, which enable agreements between, for instance a trade mark holder, the manufacturer of products bearing the mark and distributors to be exempt. This is also welcome.

Some complain that technology licences are largely excluded by Article 2(3) and (5), but the Commission gave birth to its group exemption for technology transfer only in 1996 after difficult labour. It is understandable that it did not want to reopen Pandora's box. It was argued at 3.3.9.1 above that on one view technology licences imposing conditions as to the sale or purchase of goods or services may be exempt, but the Commission denies this.

The Commission adopted a document at the end of 2001[7] seeking comments, inter alia, on the extension of the exemption for technology transfer to pure copyright, design and trade mark agreements. If such an exemption is adopted, the argument for a wide interpretation of Regulation 2790/99 to cover them will become weaker.

8.2 CEILING OF MARKET SHARE

The ceiling of market share is widely criticised as creating uncertainty. Many lawyers in Europe expect to be able to give reliable advice to their clients, and training in economics in most European university law schools lagged behind that in North American and even British universities, although many post-graduates of the last decade have been introduced to the economic concept of markets.

The concern about legal certainty may be over done. Expert competition lawyers have been advising on relevant markets under Article 82 from the beginning, and under the Merger Regulation for over a decade. They have learned from the economists they have hired for individual cases. The ECJ has stressed the importance of appraising agreements under article 81 in their "legal and economic context" since 1966.[8]

---

[5] Case 258/78, [1982] ECR 2015, paras 56–59.

[6] Cases T-374, 375, 384 & 388/94, [1998] ECR II-3141.

[7] Published on its website on December 21.

[8] *Société La Technique Minière* v. *Maschinenbau Ulm GmbH*, Case 56/65, [1966] ECR 235 and many cases since (2.7.3 above).

Often, however, there are at least two market definitions that comply with the Guidelines and precedents, but if a more economic approach is to be adopted, we cannot rely on formalistic definitions which may yield legal certainty, but are often irrelevant to the economic detriments and benefits of restraints. We are going to have to live with a measure of uncertainty.

At the moment, if we define the market wrongly, and later there is an objection, we can notify the agreement late, and the Commission can grant an individual exemption retrospectively. This will, however, cease to be true if the Regulation to replace Regulation 17 is adopted (2.12 above). A reasonable mistake is mitigation against fines but invalidity and illegality may be more serious sanctions.

8.2.1 Geographic markets

Also in relation to the market share ceiling for the application of Regulation 2790/99, practitioners would like to see guidance from the Commission on geographic markets. It could be presumed, rebuttably, that geographic markets are Europe-wide for the purposes of applying the 30 per cent ceiling, unless there is *prima facie* evidence that they are smaller.[9] Where the market is actually smaller, any competition problems which arise could reasonably be dealt with by one or more of the national competition authorities. This approach would, in many cases, avoid the situation where a distribution system which otherwise fulfils the requirements of the BER is denied automatic exemption because the supplier enjoys a high market share in one Member State, and the problem of "holes" in otherwise effective distribution arrangements.[10]

8.3 NO LIMITING WHITE LIST

Subject to the ceiling of market share, anything that is not black listed is exempt, at least until the benefit is withdrawn by formal decision or regulation. The objection that group exemptions act as strait jackets has gone. This seems to be universally welcomed.

8.4 LIST OF HARDCORE RESTRAINTS INAPPROPRIATE

Many complain that every restraint listed in Article 4 relates to intra-brand competition, which the Commission says is less anticompetitive than restraints on

---

[9] Arguably, such a presumption would require a change in legislation or, perhaps, in the Treaties, since the ECJ has rendered judgments on the meaning of the geographic market. See, for example *Europemballage Corporation and Continental Can Co. Inc.* v. *Commission*, Case 6/72 [1973] ECR 215, [1973] CMLR 199, CMR 8171; also *United Brands* v. *Commission*, Case 27/76 [1978] ECR 207, [1978] 1 CMLR 429, CMR 8429. However, informal guidance from the Commission on such a presumption would be helpful.

[10] See 7.2.5.4 above on the effects of uneven market share.

inter-brand competition. Nevertheless, the ECJ has more than once held that resale price maintenance and absolute territorial protection "by their very nature" restrict competition and has examined only the question of affecting trade between Member States.

The list of provisions in Article 4 that prevent the application of the exemption to the contract as a whole do not include tying or selective distribution based on quantitative criteria (2.9, 4.6.2, 7.4.4.3.2 and 7.4.4.4 above). There are many commercial reasons for tying that do not restrict competition, so this is welcome. It is usually expensive to qualify under qualitative criteria for selective distribution, so quantitative criteria are often important commercially. This change is also welcome. Black lists have been more comprehensive in other Regulations.

The possibility of appointing separate excusive dealers for different customer groups is very welcome. It used not to be possible, although it may be hard to find a dealer to service a particular customer group unless given exclusive rights.

Article 5, preventing single branding restraints from qualifying may not cause as many problems as feared. It is only the particular obligation that is not exempted, the rest of the agreement may be exempt. In the absence of absolute territorial protection,[11] many single branding restraints do not infringe Article 81(1), in which case they need no exemption.

On the other hand, in *Pronuptia*,[12] the Court stated that once a franchised network was widespread, the combination of a location clause with an exclusive territory would infringe Article 81(1). Would the same be true where the exclusive territory is very small? Around Piccadilly in London there are many McDonalds' outlets, but one can never see more than one at once. Is paragraph 24 concerned with absolute territorial protection, and is that to be appraised formalistically from reading the agreement, or realistically, taking account of the size of the territory and the proximity of other outlets in the network?

We hope that there are so many other fast food shops in the area that in the light of *Delimitis* (2.7.3 above) there is no appreciable foreclosure of other suppliers of snacks.

8.5 WITHDRAWAL OF BENEFIT BY REGULATION

The Commission's new power to withdraw the benefit of the Regulation from a whole market seems very sensible. It was absurd that when the benefit of Regulation 1984/83 had been withdrawn from Langnese by individual decision (6.1.3 above), it was free to make other agreements under the same Regulation.

---

[11] It is hoped that the combination of an exclusive territory with a location clause will not be treated as absolute territorial protection when the territory is so small that customers can easily visit another franchisee. The three territories in *Pronuptia de Paris GmbH* v. *Pronuptia de Paris Irmgard Schillgalis*, Case 161/84, [1986] ECR 353 covered regional towns with their surrounding countryside. The issue has not been addressed.

[12] *Pronuptia de Paris GmbH* v. *Pronuptia de Paris Irmgard Schillgalis*, Case 161/84, [1986] ECR 353, para. 24 (2.8.2 above).

Moreover, new firms entering the market may be subject to similar constraints to those already operating in it. The Commission has the flexibility to limit the Regulation to those contributing significantly to the anti-competitive effects, and new entrants may be let out on the basis of market share, turnover in the relevant market and so on.

8.6 RULE OF REASON?

We would prefer a full economic appraisal of each agreement to be made. We believe that this would lead to fewer errors.[13] We would like conditions of entry to be treated as being as important as substitutes on the demand side even if they take time to work. Indeed the consideration of substitutes on the demand side should embrace more than a very few years. The hypothetical monopolist or SSNIP test should be modified to consider non-price competition, especially in markets where new technology is being continually developed and exploited (2.4.1.2 above).

We wonder whether such an economic appraisal would lead to greater uncertainty than a ceiling of market share, when it is often difficult to identify the relevant market that will be picked by the authority making decisions, whether national courts or competition authorities. Civil lawyers, however, seem to be very loathe to carry out economic analysis and the introduction of a full rule of reason or a wider economic appraisal under Article 81(1) is unlikely to be introduced by legislation any time soon, despite some helpful indications by both the CFI and ECJ (2.7.2 and 2.7.3 above).

8.7 CONCLUSION

The Regulation and Guidelines are a great improvement on what existed previously. It is hoped, however, that they do not remain carved in stone. We would like to see the Guidelines revised every few years in the light of experience and continuing economic research.

---

[13] See **S. Salop**, "Vertical restraints under EC law," in **Barry Hawk** (ed.) [2000] *Fordham Corporate Law Institute* 217, 236.

Appendix I

COMMISSION REGULATION (EC) No 2790/1999*
of 22 December 1999
on the application of Article 81(3) of the Treaty to categories of vertical
agreements and concerted practices
(Text with EEA relevance)

HEADINGS AND CROSS REFERENCES BY VALENTINE KORAH**

THE COMMISSION OF THE
EUROPEAN COMMUNITIES,
Having regard to the Treaty establish-
ing the European Community,

Empowering Regulation

Having regard to Council Regulation
No 19/65/EEC of 2 March 1965 on the
application of Article 85(3) of the
Treaty to certain categories of agreements and concerted practices, as last
amended by Regulation (EC) No
1215/1999[1], and in particular Article I
thereof,

Having published a draft of this
Regulation[2],

Having consulted the Advisory Committee on Restrictive Practices and
Dominant Positions,

Whereas:

Empowering Regulation

(1) Regulation No. 19/65/EEC
empowers the Commission to
apply Article 81(3) of the Treaty
(formerly Article 85(3)) by regulation to certain categories of vertical
agreements and corresponding
concerted practices falling within
Article 81(1).

(2) Experience acquired to date makes
it possible to define a category of
vertical agreements which can be
regarded as normally satisfying the
conditions laid down in Article
81(3).

Vertical Agreements Art. 2(1) & (3)

(3) This category includes vertical
agreements for the purchase or sale
of goods or services where these
agreements are concluded between

---

* OJ 1999, L336/21.
** © 2000. The text was downloaded from the
net, and the annotations added in bold. The
Arts. after the headings to the recitals indicate
the Articles they govern, and *vice versa*. The
Arts. referred to at the end of a provision indicate related provisions which should be consulted before giving advice. I have also added,
at the top of provisions the numbers of the relevant guidelines, OJ 2000, C 000
[1] OJ L 148, 15.6.1999, p. 1.
[2] OJ C 270, 24.9.1999, p. 7.

non-competing undertakings, between certain competitors or by certain associations of retailers of goods; it also includes vertical agreements containing ancillary provisions on the assignment or use of intellectual property rights; for the purposes of this Regulation, the term 'vertical agreements' includes the corresponding concerted practices. **Arts. 1(a) and 1(e).**

May be Outside Art. 81(1)

(4) For the application of Article 81(3) by regulation, it is not necessary to define those vertical agreements which are capable of falling within Article 81 (1); in the individual assessment of agreements under Article 8 1 (1), account has to be taken of several factors, and in particular the market structure on the supply and purchase side.

Vertical Agreements Art. 2(1) & (4)

(5) The benefit of the block exemption should be limited to vertical agreements for which it can be assumed with sufficient certainty that they satisfy the conditions of Article 81(3).

Efficiency Art. 2

(6) Vertical agreements of the category defined in this Regulation can improve economic efficiency within a chain of production or distribution by facilitating better coordination between the participating undertakings; in particular, they can lead to a reduction in the transaction and distribution costs of the parties and to an optimisation of their sales and investment levels.

Market Power Art. 3

(7) The likelihood that such efficiencyenhancing effects will outweigh any anti-competitive effects due to restrictions contained in vertical agreements depends on the degree of market power of the undertakings concerned and, therefore, on the extent to which those undertakings face competition from other suppliers of goods or services regarded by the buyer as interchangeable or substitutable for one another, by reason of the products' characteristics, their prices and their intended use. **Art 1(g).**

Fair Share to Consumers up to 30% Art. 3

(8) It can be presumed that, where the share of the relevant market accounted-for by the supplier does not exceed 30%, vertical agreements which do not contain certain types of severely anticompetitive restraints generally lead to an improvement in production or distribution and allow consumers a fair share of the resulting benefits; in the case of vertical agreements containing exclusive supply obligations, it is the market share of the buyer which is relevant in determining the overall effects of such vertical agreements on the market. **Art. 1(c).**

Above 30% Art. 3

(9) Above the market share threshold of 30%, there can be no presumption that vertical agreements falling within the scope of Article 8 1 (1) will usually give rise to objective advantages of such a character and size as to compensate for the disadvantages which they create for competition.

Black List Art. 4

(10) This Regulation should not exempt vertical agreements containing restrictions which are not indispensable to the attainment of the positive effects mentioned above; in particular, vertical agreements containing certain types of severely anti-competitive restraints such as minimum and fixed resale-prices, as well as certain types of territorial protection, should be excluded from the benefit of the block exemption established by this Regulation irrespective of the market share of the undertakings concerned.

Conditions Art. 5

(11) In order to ensure access to or to prevent collusion on the relevant market, certain conditions are to be attached to the block exemption; to this end, the exemption of non-compete obligations should be limited to obligations which do not exceed a definite duration; for the same reasons, any direct or indirect obligation causing the members of a selective distribution system not to sell the brands

of particular competing suppliers should be excluded from the benefit of this Regulation. **Art. 1(d)**.

Not Eliminate Competition Rec. 9, Arts. 3–5

(12) The market-share limitation, the nonexemption of certain vertical agreements and the conditions provided for in this Regulation normally ensure that the agreements to which the block exemption applies do not enable the participating undertakings to eliminate competition in respect of a substantial part of the products in question.

Commission May Withdraw Art. 6, Guidelines 71–75

(13) In particular cases in which the agreements falling under this Regulation nevertheless have effects incompatible with Article 81(3), the Commission may withdraw the benefit of the block exemption; this may occur in particular where the buyer has significant market power in the relevant market in which it resells the goods or provides the services or where parallel networks of vertical agreements have similar effects which significantly restrict access to a relevant market or competition therein; such cumulative effects may for example arise in the case of selective distribution or non-compete obligations. **Art. 1(b)**.

NAs May Withdraw Art. 7

(14) Regulation No 19/65/EEC empowers the competent authorities of Member States to withdraw the benefit of the block exemption in respect of vertical agreements having effects incompatible with the conditions laid down in Article 81(3), where such effects are felt in their respective territory, or in a part thereof, and where such territory has the characteristics of a distinct geographic market; Member States should ensure that the exercise of this power of withdrawal does not prejudice the uniform application throughout the common market of the Community competition rules or the full effect of the measures adopted in implementation of those rules.

Commission May Withdraw by Reg. Art 8

(15) In order to strengthen supervision of parallel networks of vertical agreements which have similar restrictive effects and which cover more than 50% of a given market, the Commission may declare this Regulation inapplicable to vertical agreements containing specific restraints relating to the market concerned, thereby restoring the full application of Article 81 to such agreements.

Art. 82

(16) This Regulation is without prejudice to the application of Article 82.

Primacy of Community Law

(17) In accordance with the principle of the primacy of Community law, no measure taken pursuant to national laws on competition should prejudice the uniform application throughout the common market of the Community competition rules or the full effect of any measures adopted in implementation of those rules, including this Regulation.

HAS ADOPTED THIS
REGULATION:

Article 1

For the purposes of this Regulation:

Arts. 2(4),

(a) '*competing undertakings*' means actual or potential suppliers in the same product market;. the, product market includes goods or services which are regarded by the buyer as interchangeable with or substitutable for the contract goods or services, by reason of the products' characteristics, their prices and their intended use;

Art. 5(a) and (b)

(b) '*non-compete obligation*' means any direct or indirect obligation causing the buyer not to manufacture, purchase, sell or resell goods or services which compete with the contract goods or services, or any direct or indirect obligation on the buyer to purchase from the supplier or from another undertaking designated by the supplier more than 80 % of the buyer's total purchases of the contract goods or services and their substitutes on the relevant market, calculated on the basis of the value of its purchases in the preceding calendar year;

Art. 3(2)

(c) '*exclusive supply obligation*' means any direct or indirect obligation causing the supplier to sell the goods or services specified in the agreement only to one buyer inside the Community for the purposes of a specific use or for resale;

Arts. 4(b), 4(c), 4(d) and 5(c)

(d) '*Selective distribution system*' means a distribution system where the supplier undertakes to sell the contract goods or services, either directly or indirectly, only to distributors selected on the basis of specified criteria and where these distributors undertake not to sell such goods or services to unauthorised distributors;

Rec. 3 and Art. 2(3)

(e) '*intellectual property rights*' includes industrial property rights, copyright and neighbouring rights;

Art. 5(b)

(f) '*know-how*' means a package of nonpatented practical information, resulting from experience and testing by the supplier, which is secret, substantial and identified: in this context, 'secret' means that the know-how, as a body or in the precise configuration and assembly of its components, is not generally known or easily accessible; 'substantial' means that the know-how includes information which is indispensable to the buyer for the use, sale or resale of the contract goods or services; 'identified' means that the know-how must be described in a sufficiently comprehensive manner so as to make it possible to verify that it fulfils the criteria of secrecy and substantiality;

Arts. 2(3), 2(4), 3(2) and 5(b)

(g) '*buyer*' includes an undertaking which, under an agreement falling within Article 81(l) of the Treaty, sells goods or services on behalf of another undertaking.

Article 2

Exemption Recs. 3 and 5–8, Gs. 23–27

1. Pursuant to Article 81(3) of the Treaty and subject to the provisions of this Regulation, it is hereby declared that Article 8 1 (1) shall not apply to agreements or concerted practices entered into between two or more undertakings each of which operates, for the purposes of the agreement, at a different level of the production or distribution chain, and relating to the conditions under which the parties may purchase, sell or resell certain goods or services ('vertical agreements'). This exemption shall apply to the extent that such agreements contain restrictions of

competition falling within the scope of Article 8 1 (1) ('vertical restraints').

Associations of Retailers Rec 3 Gs. 28 & 29

2. The exemption provided for in paragraph 1 shall apply to vertical agreements entered into between an association of undertakings and its members, or between such an association and its suppliers, only if all its members are retailers of goods and if no individual member of the association, together with its connected undertakings, has a total annual turnover exceeding EUR 50 million; vertical agreements entered into by such associations shall be covered by this Regulation without prejudice to the application of Article 81 to horizontal agreements concluded between the members of the association or decisions adopted by the association.

IPRs Rec. 3 and Gs. 30–44 & 95

3. The exemption provided for in paragraph I shall apply to vertical agreements containing provisions which relate to the assignment to the buyer or use by the buyer of intellectual property rights, provided that those provisions do not constitute the primary object of such agreements and are directly related to the use, sale or resale of goods or services by the buyer or its customers. The exemption applies on condition that, in relation to the contract goods or services, those provisions do not contain restric-

tions of competition having the same object or effect as vertical restraints which are not exempted under this Regulation. **Art. 1(e).**

Competing Undertakings Gs. 26 & 27

4. The exemption provided for in paragraph I shall not apply to vertical agreements entered into between competing undertakings; however, it shall apply where competing undertakings enter into a nonreciprocal vertical agreement and: **Art. 1(a)**

   (a) the buyer has a total annual turnover not exceeding EUR 100 million, or

   (b) the supplier is a manufacturer and a distributor of goods, while the buyer is a distributor not manufacturing goods competing with the contract goods, or

   (c) the supplier is a provider of services at several levels of trade, while the buyer does not provide competing services at the level of trade where it purchases the contract services.

Other b.e.s G. 45

5. This Regulation shall not apply to vertical agreements the subject matter of which falls within the scope of any other block exemption regulation.

Article 3

**Up to 30% Recs. 8 and 9 and Art. 9
Gs. 21, 88–99**

1. Subject to paragraph 2 of this Article, the exemption provided for in Article 2 shall apply on condition that the market share held by the supplier does not exceed 30 % of the relevant market on which it sells the contract goods or services.

2. In the case of vertical agreements containing exclusive supply obligations, the exemption provided for in Article 2 shall apply on condition that the market share held by the buyer does not exceed 30% of the relevant market on which it purchases the contract goods or services. **Art. 1(c)**

Article 4

Black List Rec. 10, Gs. 46–56

The exemption provided for in Article 2 shall not apply to vertical agreements which, directly or indirectly, in isolation or in combination with other factors under the control of the parties, have as their object:

R.P.M. Gs. 47 & 48

(a) the restriction of the buyer's ability to determine its sale price, without prejudice to the possibility of the supplier's imposing a maximum sale price or recommending a sale price, provided that they do not amount to a fixed or minimum sale price as a result of pressure from, or incentives offered by, any of the parties;

Territorial and Customer Protection Gs. 49–51

(b) the restriction of the territory into which, or of the customers to whom, the buyer may sell the contract goods or services, except:

To Protect Supplier or Exclusive Dealer

— the restriction of active sales into the exclusive territory or to an exclusive customer group reserved to the supplier or allocated by the supplier to another buyer, where such a restriction does not limit sales by the customers of the buyer,

To Protect Retailers G. 52

— the restriction of sales to end users by a buyer operating at the wholesale level of trade,

Selective Distribution

— the restriction of sales to unauthorised distributors by the members of a selective distribution system, and, **Art. 1(d)**

To Protect Component Manufacturer

— the restriction of the buyer's ability to sell components, supplied for the purposes of incorporation, to customers who would use them to manufacture the same type of goods as those produced by the supplier;

Selective Distribution Gs. 53 & 54

(c) the restriction of active or passive sales to end users by members of a selective distribution system operating at the retail level of trade, without prejudice to the possibility of prohibiting a member of the system from operating out of an unauthorised place of establishment; **Art.1(d)**

Cross Supplies G. 55

(d) the restriction of cross-supplies between distributors within a selective distribution system, including between distributors operating at different level of trade; **Art. 1(d)**

Components G. 56 & 95

(e) the restriction agreed between a supplier of components and a buyer who incorporates those components, which limits the supplier to selling the components as spare parts to end-users or to repairers or other service providers not entrusted by the buyer with the repair or servicing of its goods.

Article 5

Conditions Rec. 11, Gs. 57–61

The exemption provided for in Article 2 shall not apply to any of the following obligations contained in vertical agreements:

Non-compete Over 5 Years, Gs. 58 & 59

(a) any direct or indirect non-compete obligation, the duration of which is indefinite or exceeds five years. A noncompete obligation which is tacitly renewable beyond a period of five years is to be deemed to have been concluded for an indefinite duration. However, the time limitation of five years shall not apply where the contract goods or services are sold by the buyer from premises and land owned by the supplier or leased, by the supplier from third parties not connected with the buyer, provided that the duration of the noncompete obligation does not exceed the period of occupancy of the premises and land by the buyer; **Art. 1(b)**

Non-compete After Term, G. 60

(b) any direct or indirect obligation causing the buyer, after termination of the agreement, not to manufacture, purchase, sell or resell goods or services, unless such obligation:

— relates to goods or services which compete with the contract goods or services, and

— is limited to the premises and land from which the buyer has operated during the contract period, and

— is indispensable to protect knowhow transferred by the supplier to the buyer, and provided that the duration' of such non-compete obligation is limited to a period of one year after termination of the agreement; this obligation is without prejudice to the possibility of imposing a restriction which is unlimited in time on the use and disclosure of know-how which has not entered the public domain; **Arts. 1(b), 1(f).**

Selective Distribution, Art. 1(d). G. 61

(c) any direct or indirect obligation causing the members of a selective distribution system not to sell the brands of particular competing suppliers. **Art. 1(d)**

Article 6

Commission May Withdraw Rec. 13 and G. 192

The Commission may withdraw the benefit of this Regulation, pursuant to Article 7(1) of Regulation No 19/65/EEC, where it finds in any particular case that vertical agreements to which this Regulation applies nevertheless have effects which are incompatible with the conditions laid down in Article 81(3) of the Treaty, and in particular where access to the relevant market or competition therein is significantly restricted by the cumulative effect of parallel networks of similar vertical restraints implemented by competing suppliers or buyers.

Article 7

NAs May Withdraw BE, Rec. 14

Where in any particular case vertical agreements to which the exemption provided for in Article 2 applies have effects incompatible with the conditions laid down in Article 81(3) of the Treaty in the territory of a Member State, or in a part thereof, which has all the characteristics of a distinct geographic market, the competent author-

ity of that Member State may withdraw the benefit of application of this Regulation in respect of that territory, under the same conditions as provided in Article 6.

Article 8

Commission May Disapply BE by Reg. Rec. 15 & Gs. 80–87, 142, 189, 198 and 224

1. Pursuant to Article I a of Regulation No 19/65/EEC, the Commission may by regulation declare that, where parallel networks of similar vertical restraints cover more than 50 % of a relevant market, this Regulation shall not apply to vertical agre ements containing specific restraints relating to that market.

2. A regulation pursuant to paragraph I shall not become applicable earlier than six months following its adoption.

Article 9

Calculating Market Share Art. 3, Gs. 88–99

1. The market share of 30 % provided for in Article 3(1) shall be calculated on the basis of the market sales value of the contract goods or services and other goods or services sold by the supplier, which are regarded as interchangeable or substitutable by the buyer, by reason of the products' characteristics, their prices and their intended use; if market sales value data are not available, estimates based on

other reliable market information, including market sales volumes, may be used to establish the market share of the undertaking concerned. For the purposes of Article 3(2), it is either the market purchase value or estimates thereof which shall be used to calculate the market share.

2. For the purposes of applying the market share, threshold provided for in Article 3 the following rules shall apply:

(a) the market share shall be calculated on the basis of data relating to the preceding calendar year;

(b) the market share shall include any goods or services supplied to integrated distributors for the purposes of sale;

(c) if the market share is initially not more than 30 % but subsequently rises above that level without exceeding 35 %, the exemption provided for in Article 2 shall continue to apply for a period of two consecutive calendar years following the year in which the 30% market share threshold was first exceeded;

(d) if the market share is initially not more than 30 % but subsequently rises above 35 %, the exemption provided for in Article 2 shall continue to apply for one calendar year following the year in which the level of 35% was first exceeded;

(e) the benefit of points (c) and (d) may not be combined so as to

exceed a period of two calendar years.

Article 10

Calculating Turnover Art. 1 (a)

1. For the purpose of calculating total annual turnover within the meaning of Article 2(2) and (4), the turnover achieved during the previous financial year by the relevant party to the vertical agreement and the turnover achieved by its connected undertakings in respect of all goods and services, excluding all taxes and other duties, shall be added together. For this purpose, no account shall be taken of dealings between the party to the vertical agreement and its connected undertakings or between its connected undertakings.

2. The exemption provided for in Article 2 shall remain applicable where, for any period of two consecutive financial years, the total annual turnover threshold is exceeded by no more than 10%.

Article 11

Connected Undertakings

1. For the purposes of this Regulation, the terms 'undertaking', 'supplier' and 'buyer' shall include their respective connected undertakings.

2. 'Connected undertakings' are:

(a) undertakings in which a party to the agreement, directly or indirectly:

— has the power to exercise more than half the voting rights, or

— has the power to appoint more than half the members of the supervisory board, board of management or bodies legally representing the undertaking, or

— has the right to manage the undertaking's affairs;

(b) undertakings which directly or indirectly have, over a party to the agreement, the rights or powers listed in (a);

(c) undertakings in which an undertaking referred to in (b) has, directly or indirectly, the rights or powers listed in (a);

(d) undertakings in which a party to the agreement together with one or more of the undertakings referred to in (a), (b) or (c), or in which two or more of the latter undertakings, jointly have the rights or powers listed in (a);

(e) undertakings in which the rights or the powers listed in (a) are jointly held by:

— parties to the agreement or their respective connected undertakings referred to in (a) to (d), or

— one or more of the parties to the agreement or one or more of their connected undertakings referred to in (a) to (d) and one or more third parties.

3. For the purposes of Article 3, the market share held by the undertakings referred to in paragraph 2(e) of this Article shall be apportioned equally to each undertaking having the rights or the powers listed in paragraph 2(a).

Article 12

Transitional Provisions

1. The exemptions provided for in Commission Regulations (EEC) No 1983/83[3], (EEC) No 1984/83[4] and (EEC) No 4087/88[5] shall continue to apply until 31 May 2000.

2. The prohibition laid down in Article 8 1 (1) of the EC Treaty shall not apply during the period from I June 2000 to 31 December 2001 in respect of agreements already in force on 31 May 2000 which do not satisfy the conditions for exemption provided for in this Regulation but which satisfy the conditions for exemption provided for in Regulations (EEC) No 1983/83, (EEC) No 1984/83 or (EEC) No 4087/88.

Article 13

Entry into Force

This Regulation shall enter into force on I January 2000.

It shall apply from I June 2000, except for Article 12(1) which shall apply from I January 2000.

---

[3] OJ L 173, 30.6.1983, P. 1.
[4] OJ L 173, 30.6.1983, p. 5.
[5] OJ L 359, 28.12.1988, p. 46.

This Regulation shall expire on 31 May 2010.

This Regulation shall be binding in its entirety and directly applicable in all Member States.

Done at Brussels, 22 December 1999.

For the Commission

Mario MONTI

Member of the Commission

Appendix II

REGULATION No 19/65/EEC OF THE COUNCIL
of 2 March 1965
on application of Article 85 (3) of the Treaty to certain categories
of agreements and concerted practices (OJ 36, 6.3.1965 p. 533)
as amended by Council Regulation (EC) No 1215/1999 of
10 June 1999 (OJ L 148, 15.6.1999 p. 1)

THE COUNCIL OF THE EUROPEAN ECONOMIC COMMUNITY,

Having regard to the Treaty establishing the European Economic Community, and in particular Article 87 thereof;

Having regard to the proposal from the Commission;

Having regard to the Opinion of the European Parliament[1];

Having regard to the Opinion of the Economic and Social Committee[2];

Whereas Article 85 (1) of the Treaty may in accordance with Article 85 (3) be declared inapplicable to certain categories of agreements, decisions and concerted practices which fulfil the conditions contained in Article 85 (3);

Whereas the provisions for implementation of Article 85 (3) must be adopted by way of regulation pursuant to Article 87;

Whereas in view of the large number of notifications submitted in pursuance of Regulation No 17[3] it is desirable that in order to facilitate the task of the Commission it should be enabled to declare by way of regulation that the provisions of Article 85 (1) do not apply to certain categories of agreements and concerted practices;

Whereas it should be laid down under what conditions the Commission, in close and constant liaison with the competent authorities of the Member States, may exercise such powers after sufficient experience has been gained in the light of individual decisions and it becomes possible to define categories of agreements and concerted practices in respect of which the conditions of Article 85 (3) may be considered as being fulfilled;

Whereas the Commission has indicated by the action it has taken, in particular by Regulation No 153,[4] that there can be no easing of the procedures prescribed by Regulation No 17 in respect

[1] OJ No 81, 27.5.1964, p. 1275/64.
[2] OJ No 197, 30.11.1964, p. 3320/64.

[3] OJ No 13, 21.2.1962, p. 204/62 (Regulation No 17 as amended by Regulation No 59 – OJ No 58, 10.7.1962, p. 1655/62 – and Regulation No 118/63/EEC – OJ No 162, 7.11.1963, p. 2696/63.
[4] OJ No 139, 24.12.1962, p. 2918/62.

of certain types of agreements and concerted practices that are particularly liable to distort competition in the common market;

Whereas under Article 6 of Regulation No 17 the Commission may provide that a decision taken pursuant to Article 85 (3) of the Treaty shall apply with retroactive effect; whereas it is desirable that the Commission be also empowered to adopt, by regulation, provisions to the like effect;

Whereas under Article 7 of Regulation No 17 agreements, decisions and concerted practices may, by decision of the Commission, be exempted from prohibition in particular if they are modified in such manner that they satisfy the requirements of Article 85 (3); whereas it is desirable that the Commission be enabled to grant like exemption by regulation to such agreements and concerted practices if they are modified in such manner as to fall within a category defined in an exempting regulation;

Whereas, since there can be no exemption if the conditions set out in Article 85 (3) are not satisfied, the Commission must have power to lay down by decision the conditions that must be satisfied by an agreement or concerted practice which owing to special circumstances has certain effects incompatible with Article 85 (3);

HAS ADOPTED THIS REGULATION:

Article 1

1. Without prejudice to the application of Regulation No 17 and in accordance with Article 81(3) of the Treaty the Commission may by regulation declare that Article 81(1) shall not apply to:

(a) categories of agreements which are entered into by two or more undertakings, each operating, for the purposes of the agreement, at a different level of the production or distribution chain, and which relate to the conditions under which the parties may purchase, sell or resell certain goods or services,

(b) categories of agreements to which only two undertakings are party and which include restrictions imposed in relation to the acquisition or use of industrial property rights, in particular of patents, utility models, designs or trade marks, or to the rights arising out of contracts for assignment of, or the right to use, a method of manufacture or knowledge relating to the use or to the application of indu[s]trial processes

2. The regulation shall define the categories of agreements to which it applies and shall specify in particular:

(a) the restrictions or clauses which must not be contained in the agreements;

(b) the other conditions which must be satisfied.

3. Paragraphs 1 and 2 shall apply by analogy to categories of concerted practices.

Article 1a

A regulation pursuant to Article 1 may stipulate the conditions which may lead to the exclusion from its application of certain parallel networks of similar agreements or concerted practices operating on particular market; when these circumstances are fulfilled the Commission may establish this by means of regulation and fix a period at the expiry of which the Regulation pursuant to Article 1 would no longer be applicable in respect of the relevant agreements or concerted practices on that market; such period must not be shorter than six months.

Article 2

1. A regulation pursuant to Article 1 shall be made for a specified period.

2. It may be repealed or amended where circumstances have changed with respect to any factor which was basic to its being made; in such case, a period shall be fixed for modification of the agreements and concerted practices to which the earlier regulation applies.

Article 3

A regulation pursuant to Article 1 may stipulate that it shall apply with retroactive effect to agreements and concerted practices to which, at the date of entry into force of that regulation, a decision issued with retroactive effect in pursuance of Article 6 of Regulation No 17 would have applied.

Article 4

1. A regulation pursuant to Article 1 may stipulate that the prohibition

contained in Article 85 (1) of the Treaty shall not apply, for such period as shall be fixed by that regulation, to agreements and concerted practices already in existence on 13 March 1962 which do not satisfy the conditions of Article 85 (3), where:

— within three months from the entry into force of the Regulation, they are so modified as to satisfy the said conditions in accordance with the provisions of the regulation; and

— the modifications are brought to the notice of the Commission within the time limit fixed by the regulation.

2. Paragraph 1 shall apply to agreements and concerted practices which had to be notified before 1 February 1963, in accordance with Article 5 of Regulation No 17, only where they have been so notified before that date.

3. The benefit of the provisions laid down pursuant to paragraph 1 may not be claimed in actions pending at the date of entry into force of a regulation adopted pursuant to Article 1 ; neither may it be relied on as grounds for claims for damages against third parties.

Article 5

Before adopting a regulation, the Commission shall publish a draft thereof and invite all persons concerned to submit their comments within such time limit, being not less than one month, as the Commission shall fix.

Article 6

1. The Commission shall consult the Advisory Committee on Restrictive Practices and Monopolies:

    (a) with regard to a regulation pursuant to Article 1 before publishing a draft regulation and before adopting a regulation;

    (b) with regard to a regulation pursuant to Article 1a before publishing a draft regulation if requested by a Member State, and before adopting a regulation.

2. Article 10 (5) and (6) of Regulation No 17, relating to consultation with the Advisory Committee, shall apply by analogy, it being understood that joint meetings with the Commission shall take place not earlier than one month after dispatch of the notice convening them.

Article 7

1. Where the Commission, either on its own initiative or at the request of a Member State or of natural or legal persons claiming a legitimate interest, finds that in any particular case agreements or concerted practices to which a regulation adopted

pursuant to Article 1 of this Regulation applies have nevertheless certain effects which are incompatible with the conditions laid down in Article 85 (3) of the Treaty, it may withdraw the benefit of application of that regulation and issue a decision in accordance with Articles 6 and 8 of Regulation No 17, without any notification under Article 4 (1) of Regulation No 17 being required.

2. When in any particular case agreements or concerted practices to which a regulation adopted pursuant to Article 1 applies have certain effects which are incompatible with the conditions laid down in Article 81(3) of the Treaty in the territory of a Member State, or in part thereof, which has all the characteristics of a distinct market, the competent authority in that Member State may on its own initiative or at the request of the Commission or of natural or legal persons claiming a legitimate interest withdraw the benefit of application of that regulation.

Article 8

The Commission shall, before 1 January 1970, submit to the Council a proposal for a Regulation for such amendment of this Regulation as may prove necessary in the light of experience.

This Regulation shall be binding in its entirety and directly applicable in all Member States.

Done at Brussels, 2 March 1965.

For the Council
The President
M. COUVE DE MURVILLE

Appendix III

COUNCIL REGULATION (EC) No 1215/1999
of 10 June 1999
amending Regulation No 19/65/EEC on the application of Article 81(3) of the Treaty to certain categories of agreements and concerted practices(*)

THE COUNCIL OF THE EUROPEAN UNION,

Having regard to the Treaty establishing the European Community, and in particular Article 83 thereof,

Having regard to the proposal from the Commission[1],

Having regard to the opinion of the European Parliament[2],

Having regard to the opinion of the Economic and Social Committee[3],

(1) Whereas by Regulation No 19/65/EEC[4], the Council empowered the Commission, without prejudice to the application of Council Regulation No 17: first Regulation implementing Articles 81 and 82 of the Treaty[5], and in accordance with Article 81(3) of the Treaty, to adopt regulations declaring that Article 81(1) does not apply to certain categories of agreements, and in particular to categories of agreements to which only two undertakings are party and whereby one party agrees with the other to supply only to that other certain goods for resale within a defined area of the common market, or whereby one party agrees with the other to purchase only from that other certain goods for resale, or whereby the two undertakings enter into into such obligations with each other in respect of exclusive supply and purchase for resale;

(2) Whereas, pursuant to Regulation No 19/65/EEC, the Commission has in particular adopted Regulation (EEC) No 1983/83 of 22 June 1983 on the application of Article 81(3) of the Treaty to categories of exclusive distribution agree-

(*) Editorial Note: The title of Regulation No 19/65/EEC has been adjusted to take account of the renumbering of the Articles of the Treaty establishing the European Community in accordance with Article 12 of the Treaty of Amsterdam; the original reference was to Article 85(3) of the Treaty.

[1] OJ C 365, 26.11.1998, p. 27.
[2] Opinion delivered on 15 April 1999 (not yet published in the Official Journal).
[3] OJ C 116, 28.4.1999.
[4] OJ 36, 6.3.1965, p. 533/65. Regulation as last amended by the 1994 Act of Accession.
[5] OJ 13, 21.2.1962, p. 204/62. Regulation as last amended by the 1994 Act of Accession.

ments[6], Regulation (EEC) No 1984/83 of 22 June 1983 on the application of Article 81(3) of the Treaty to categories of exclusive purchasing agreements[7] and Regulation (EEC) No 4087/88 of 30 November 1988 on the application of Article 81(3) of the Treaty to categories of franchise agreements[8] (exemption regulations);

(3) Whereas on 22 January 1997 the Commission published a Green Paper on Vertical Restraints in EC Competition Policy, which generated a wide-ranging public debate on the application of Article 81(1) and (3) of the Treaty to vertical agreements or concerted practices;

(4) Whereas the response to the Green Paper from the Member States, the European Parliament, the Economic and Social Committee, the Committee of the Regions and interested parties has been generally in favour of reform of Community competition policy on vertical agreements; whereas the block exemption regulations already referred to should accordingly be revised;

(5) Whereas any such reform must meet the two requirements of ensuring effective protection of competition and providing ade-

quate legal certainty for firms; whereas the pursuit of those objectives should take account of the need as far as possible to simplify administrative supervision and the legislative framework; whereas at the same level of market power vertical restraints are generally considered less harmful to competition than horizontal restraints;

(6) Whereas the exemption regulations referred to do not confine themselves to defining the categories of agreements to which they apply and to specifying the restrictions or clauses which are not to be contained in the agreements, but they also list the exempted clauses; whereas this legislative approach to contractual relations is generally perceived to be over rigid in an economic context where distribution structures and techniques are rapidly changing;

(7) Whereas the said exemption regulations cover only those categories of bilateral exclusive agreements entered into with a view to resale which are concerned with the exclusive distribution or purchase of goods, or both, or which include restrictions imposed in relation to the assignment or use of industrial property rights; whereas they exclude from their scope, inter alia, vertical agreements between more thn two undertakings, selective distribution agreements, agreements concerning services, and agreements concerning the supply or purchase, or both, of goods or services intended for processing or

---

[6] OJ L 173, 30.6.1983, p. 1. Regulation as last amended by Regulation (EC) No 1582/97 (OJ L 214, 6.8.1997, p. 27).

[7] OJ L 173, 30.6.1983, p. 5. Regulation as last amended by Regulation (EC) No 1582/97.

[8] OJ L 359, 28.12.1988, p. 46. Regulation as amended by the 1994 Act of Accession.

incorporation; whereas a substantial number of vertical agreements consequently cannot qualify for exemption under Article 81(3) of the Treaty until they have been examined individually by the Commission, which may reduce the legal certainty available to the undertakings concerned and make administrative supervision unnecessarily burdensome;

(8) Whereas the debate which followed the publication of the Green Paper also drew attention to the fact that in determining the manner in which Article 81(1) and (3) are to apply proper account needs to be taken of the economic effects of vertical agreements; whereas any economic criteria limiting the scope of a block exemption by reason of the anticompetitive effects which an agreement may produce should take into account the share of the relevant market accounted for by the undertaking concerned;

(9) Whereas, therefore, the Commission should be empowered to replace the existing legislation with legislation which is simpler, more flexible and better targeted, and which may cover all types of vertical agreements; whereas if the scope of the exemption regulation covering such agreements is to be broadened in this way, there should be criteria such as market-share thresholds to specify the circumstances where, in view of the possible economic effects of the agreements, the regulation ceases to be applicable;

whereas the setting of such market share thresholds should take account of the market power of the undertaking concerned; whereas certain severe anticompetitive vertical restraints like minium and fixed resale prices and certain types of territorial protection should be excluded from the application of the regulation irrespective of the market share of the undertaking concerned;

(10) Whereas the powers conferred on the Commission by Regulation No 19/65/EEC do not allow it to conduct a reform of the rules currently in force which would cover all types of vertical agreements; whereas the scope of Article 1(1)(a) and (2)(b) thereof should consequently be broadened to cover all agreements caught by Article 81(1) of the Treaty which are entered into by two or more undertakings, each operating, for the purposes of the agreement, at a different level of the production or distribution chain and which relate to the conditions under which the parties may purchase, sell or resell certain goods or services (vertical agreements), including exclusive distribution agreements, exclusive purchasing agreements, franchising agreements and selective distribution agreements, or any combination of these, and certain non-reciprocal vertical agreements entered into between competing undertakings, as well as vertical agreements between an association of

small and medium-sized retailers and its members or between such an association and its suppliers;

(11) Whereas the exemption regulations referred to empower the Commission, in accordance with Article 7 of Regulation No 19/65/EEC, to withdraw the benefit of application of those regulations wherever, in a particular case, an agreement or a network of similar agreements has certain effects which are incompatible with the conditions laid down in Article 81(3); whereas in order to ensure effective supervision of markets and greater decentralisation in the application of the Community competition rules, it is appropriate to provide that where the effects of such an agreement are felt in the territory of a Member State, or in a part thereof, which has all the characteristics of a distinct market the competent authority in that Member State may withdraw the benefit of the block exemption in its territory and adopt a decision aime at eliminating those effects; whereas the said Article 7 should accordingly be supplemented so as to specify the circumstances in which the competent authorities in the Member States can withdraw the benefit of application of the block-exemption regulation;

(12) Whereas, in order to guarantee an effective control of the effects arising in a given market from the existence of parallel networks of similar agreements, a block-exemption regulation may establish the conditions under which those networks of agreements may be excluded from its application by means of regulation; whereas such conditions may be based on criteria such as the market coverage rate of these networks of agreements; whereas the Commission will accordingly be empowered to establish by means of regulation that in a given market the relevant agreements fulfil the said conditions; whereas in such a case, the Commission will have to fix a transitional period of not less than six months, at the expiry of which the block exemption will cease to be applicable to the relevant agreements on that market; whereas this regulation establishing the non-application of the block-exemption regulation for the relevant agreements on a particular market has as effect the application of Article 81 of the Treaty by individual examination; whereas the Commission will consult the Advisory Committee before the adoption of such a regulation and, on request of a Member State, also before the publication of the draft regulation,

HAS ADOPTED THIS REGULATION:

Article 1

Regulation No 19/65/EEC is hereby amended as follows:

1. Article 1 shall be amended as follows:

   (a) paragraph 1 shall be replaced by the following:

   "1. Without prejudice to the application of Regulation No 17 and in accordance with Article 81(3) of the Treaty the Commission may by regulation declare that Article 81(1) shall not apply to:

   (a) categories of agreements which are entered into by two or more undertakings, each operating, for the purposes of the agreement, at a different level of the production or distribution chain, and which relate to the conditions under which the parties may purchase, sell or resell certain goods or services,

   (b) categories of agreements to which only two undertakings are party and which include restrictions imposed in relation to the acquisition or use of industrial property rights, in particular of patents, utility models, designs or trade marks, or to the rights arising out of contracts for assignment of, or the right to use, a method of manufacture or knowledge relating to the use or to the application of indutrial processes";

   (b) in paragraph 2(b), the words "the clauses which must be contained in the agreements, or" shall be deleted;

   (c) paragraph 3 shall be replace by the following:

   "3. Paragraphs 1 and 2 shall apply by analogy to categories of concerted practices".

2. The following Article shall be inserted:

   "*Article 1a*

   A regulation pursuant to Article 1 may stipulate the conditions which may lead to the exclusion from its application of certain parallel networks of similar agreements or concerted practices operating on particular market; when these circumstances are fulfilled the Commission may establish this by means of regulation and fix a period at the expiry of which the Regulation pursuant to Article 1 would no longer be applicable in respect of the relevant agreements or concerted practices on that market; such period must not be shorter than six months".

3. Article 6(1) shall be replaced by the following:

   "1. The Commission shall consult the Advisory Committee on Restrictive Practices and Monopolies:

   (a) with regard to a regulation pursuant to Article 1 before publishing a draft regulation and before adopting a regulation;

   (b) with regard to a regulation pursuant to Article 1a before publishing a draft regulation if requested by a Member State, and before adopting a regulation".

4. In Article 7 the existing paragraph shall become paragraph 1 and the following paragraph shall be added:

"2. When in any particular case agreements or concerted practices to which a regulation adopted pursuant to Article 1 applies have certain effects which are incompatible with the conditions laid down in Article 81(3) of the Treaty in the territory of a Member State, or in part thereof, which has all the characteristics of a distinct market, the competent authority in that Member State may on its own initiative or at the request of the Commission or of natural or legal persons claiming a legitimate interest withdraw the benefit of application of that regulation".

Article 2

This Regulation shall enter into force on the third day following its publication in the *Official Journal of the European Communities.*

This Regulation shall be binding in its entirety and directly applicable in all Member States.

Done at Luxembourg, 10 June 1999.

For the Council
The President
K.-H. FUNKE

Appendix IV

COUNCIL REGULATION (EC) No 1216/1999
of 10 June 1999
amending Regulation No 17: first Regulation implementing
Articles 81 and 82 of the Treaty[*] (OJ L 148, 15.6.1999 p. 5)

THE COUNCIL OF THE
EUROPEAN UNION,

Having regard to the Treaty establishing the European Community, and in particular Article 83 thereof,

Having regard to the proposal from the Commission[1],

Having regard to the opinion of the European Parliament[2],

Having regard to the opinion of the Economic and Social Committee[3],

(1) Whereas Article 4(2) of Regulation No 17[4] dispenses a number of agreements, decisions and concerted practices from the requirement of notification prior to exemption under Article 4(1);

(*) Editorial Note: The title of Regulation No 17 has been adjusted to take account of the renumbering of the Articles of the Treaty establishing the European Community in accordance with Article 12 of the Treaty of Amsterdam; the original reference was to Articles 85 and 86 of the Treaty.

(1) OJ C 365, 26.11.1998, p. 30.

(2) Opinion delivered on 15 April 1999 (not yet published in the Official Journal).

(3) OJ C 116, 28.4.1999.

(4) OJ 13, 21.2.1962, p. 204/62. Regulation as last amended by the 1994 Act of Accession.

(2) Whereas this dispensation relates in particular to agreements, decisions and concerted practices where the only parties thereto are undertakings from one Member State and the agreements, decisions or practices do not relate either to imports or exports between Member States, or where not more than two undertakings are party thereto and the agreements only restrict the freedom of one party to the contract in determining the prices or conditions of business on which the goods he has obtained from the other party to the contract may be resold; whereas this dispensation does not cover mot agreements caught by Articles 81(1) of the Treaty which are entered into by two or more undertakings, each operating, for the purposes of the agreement, at a different level of the production or distribution chain, and which relate to the conditions under which the parties may purchase, sell or resell certain goods or services ('vertical agreements');

(3) Whereas on 22 January 1997 the Commission published a Green

Paper on Vertical Restraints in EC Competition Policy which generated a wide-ranging public debate on the application of Article 81(1) and (3) of the Treaty to vertical agreements; whereas the response from Member States, the European Parliament, the Economic and Social Committee, the Committee of the Regions and interested parties has been generally in favour of reform of Community competition policy in this area;

(4) Whereas any such reform must meet the two requirements of ensuring effective protection of competition and providing adequate legal certainty for firms; whereas, in order to achieve these objectives, the Commission has been empowered by the Council to declare, by regulation and in accordance with Article 81(3) of the Treaty, that Article 81(1) is not applicable to categories of vertical agreements;

(5) Whereas reform of the regulatory framework applicable to vertical agreements must in addition take account of the need to simplify administrative supervision which would result in a reduction of the number of notifications of vertical agreements; whereas thee should be a reduction of the incentive to notify vertical agreements which are in compliance with the policy of the Commission and the case-law of the Court of Justice and the Court of first instance; whereas, to achieve that objective, the Com-

mission should be empowered to grant individual exemption for vertical agreements caught by Article 81(1) of the Treaty from the date on which they were entered into;

(6) Whereas the requirement of notification prior to exemption imposes on firms which are party to vertical agreements an unnecessary administrative burden;

(7) Whereas the agreements referred to in Article 4(2) of Regulation No 17 are dispensed from the requirement of notification prior to exemption; whereas the purpose of this dispensation is to reduce the number of notifications, which enables the Commission to concentrate its efforts on supervising those restrictive agreements which are the most damaging to competition; whereas, therefore, this amendment does not entail any relaxation in the supervision which the Commission has a duty to exercise under Article 81(1);

(8) Whereas the scope of Article 4(2) of Regulation No 17 should therefore be extended, and all vertical agreements should be dispensed from the requirement of notification prior to exemption,

HAS ADOPTED THIS
REGULATION:

Article 1

Point 2 of Article 4(2) of Regulation No 17 shall be replaced by the following:

"2. (a) the agreements or concerted practices are entered into by two or more undertakings, each operating, for the purposes of the agreement, at a different level of the production or distribution chain, and relate to the conditions under which the parties may purchase, sell or resell certain goods or services;

(b) not more than two undertakings are party thereto, and the agreements only impose restrictions on the exercise of the rights of the assignee or user of industrial property rights, in particular patents, utility models, designs or trade marks, or of the person entitled under a contract to the assignment, or grant, of the right to use a method of manufacture or knowledge relating to the use and to the application of industrial processes".

Article 2

This Regulation shall enter into force on the third day following its publication in the *Official Journal of the European Communities.*

This Regulation shall be binding in its entirety and directly applicable in all Member States.

Done at Luxembourg, 10 June 1999.

For the Council
The President
K.-H. FUNKE

Appendix V

COMMISSION NOTICE
Guidelines on Vertical Restraints (2000/C 291/01)
(Text with EEA relevance)

I. INTRODUCTION

1. Purpose of the Guidelines

(1)   These Guidelines set out the principles for the assessment of vertical agreements under Article 81 of the EC Treaty. What are considered vertical agreements is defined in Article 2(1) of Commission Regulation (EC) No 2790/1999 of 22 December 1999 on the application of Article 81(3) of the Treaty to categories of vertical agreements and concerted practices[1] (Block Exemption Regulation) (see paragraphs 23 to 45). These Guidelines are without prejudice to the possible parallel application of Article 82 of the Treaty to vertical agreements. The Guidelines are structured in the following way:

— Section II (paragraphs 8 to 20) describes vertical agreements which generally fall outside Article 81(1);

— Section III (paragraphs 21 to 70) comments on the application of the Block Exemption Regulation;

— Section IV (paragraphs 71 to 87) describes the principles concerning the withdrawal of the block exemption and the disapplication of the Block Exemption Regulation;

— Section V (paragraphs 88 to 99) addresses market definition and market share calculation issues;

— Section VI (paragraphs 100 to 229) describes the general framework of analysis and the

---

[1] (1) OJ L 336, 29.12.1999, p. 21.

enforcement policy of the Commission in individual cases concerning vertical agreements.

(2) Throughout these Guidelines the analysis applies to both goods and services, although certain vertical restraints are mainly used in the distribution of goods. Similarly, vertical agreements can be concluded for intermediate and final goods and services. Unless otherwise stated, the analysis and arguments in the text apply to all types of goods and services and to all levels of trade. The term 'products' includes both goods and services. The terms 'supplier' and 'buyer' are used for all levels of trade.

(3) By issuing these Guidelines the Commission aims to help companies to make their own assessment of vertical agreements under the EC competition rules. The standards set forth in these Guidelines must be applied in circumstances specific to each case. This rules out a mechanical application. Each case must be evaluated in the light of its own facts. The Commission will apply the Guidelines reasonably and flexibly.

(4) These Guidelines are without prejudice to the interpretation that may be given by the Court of First Instance and the Court of Justice of the European Communities in relation to the application of Article 81 to vertical agreements.

2. Applicability of Article 81 to vertical agreements

(5) Article 81 of the EC Treaty applies to vertical agreements that may affect trade between Member States and that prevent, restrict or distort competition (hereinafter referred to as 'vertical restraints'[2]. For vertical restraints, Article 81 provides an appropriate legal framework for assessment, recognising the distinction between anti-competitive and pro-competitive effects: Article 81(1) prohibits those agreements which appreciably restrict or distort competition, while Article 81(3) allows for exemption of those agreements which confer sufficient benefits to outweigh the anti-competitive effects.

(6) For most vertical restraints, competition concerns can only arise if there is insufficient inter-brand competition, i.e. if there is some degree of market power at the level of the supplier or the buyer or at both levels. If there is insufficient inter-brand competition, the protection of inter- and intra-brand competition becomes important.

(7) The protection of competition is the primary objective of EC competition policy, as this enhances consumer welfare and creates an

---

[2] See inter alia judgment of the Court of Justice of the European Communities in Joined Cases 56/64 and 58/64 *Grundig-Consten* v. *Commission* [1966] ECR 299; Case 56/65 *Technique Minière* v. *Machinenbau Ulm* [1966] ECR 235; and of the Court of First Instance of the European Communities in Case T-77/92 *Parker Pen* v. *Commission* [1994] ECR II 549.

efficient allocation of resources. In applying the EC competition rules, the Commission will adopt an economic approach which is based on the effects on the market; vertical agreements have to be analysed in their legal and economic context. However, in the case of restrictions by object as listed in Article 4 of the Block Exemption Regulation, the Commission is not required to assess the actual effects on the market. Market integration is an additional goal of EC competition policy. Market integration enhances competition in the Community. Companies should not be allowed to recreate private barriers between Member States where State barriers have been successfully abolished.

II. VERTICAL AGREEMENTS WHICH GENERALLY FALL OUTSIDE ARTICLE 81(1)

1. Agreements of minor importance and SMEs

(8) Agreements which are not capable of appreciably affecting trade between Member States or capable of appreciably restricting competition by object or effect are not caught by Article 81(1). The Block Exemption Regulation applies only to agreements falling within the scope of application of Article 81(1). These Guidelines are without prejudice to the application of the present or any future 'de minimis' notice.[3]

(9) Subject to the conditions set out in points 11, 18 and 20 of the 'de minimis' notice concerning hardcore restrictions and cumulative effect issues, vertical agreements entered into by undertakings whose market share on the relevant market does not exceed 10% are generally considered to fall outside the scope of Article 81(1). There is no presumption that vertical agreements concluded by undertakings having more than 10% market share automatically infringe Article 81(1). Agreements between undertakings whose market share exceeds the 10 % threshold may still not have an appreciable effect on trade between Member States or may not constitute an appreciable restriction of competition[4]. Such agreements need to be assessed in their legal and economic context. The criteria for the assessment of individual agreements are set out in paragraphs 100 to 229.

(10) As regards hardcore restrictions defined in the 'de minimis' notice, Article 81(1) may apply below the 10% threshold, provided that there is an appreciable effect on trade between Member States and on competition. The applicable case-law of the Court of Justice and the Court of First Instance is relevant in this respect[5].

---

[3] See Notice on agreements of minor importance of 9 December 1997, OJ C 372, 9.12.1997, p. 13.

[4] See judgment of the Court of First Instance in Case T-7/93 Langnese-Iglo v. Commission [1995] ECR II-1533, paragraph 98.

[5] See judgment of the Court of Justice in Case 5/69 Volk v. Vervaecke [1969] ECR 295; Case 1/71 Cadillon v. Hoss [1971] ECR 351 and Case C-306/96 Javico v. Yves Saint Laurent [1998] ECR I-1983, paragraphs 16 and 17.

Reference is also made to the particular situation of launching a new product or entering a new market which is dealt with in these Guidelines (paragraph 119, point 10).

(11) In addition, the Commission considers that, subject to cumulative effect and hardcore restrictions, agreements between small and medium-sized undertakings as defined in the Annex to Commission Recommendation 96/280/EC[6] are rarely capable of appreciably affecting trade between Member States or of appreciably restricting competition within the meaning of Article 81(1), and therefore generally fall outside the scope of Article 81(1). In cases where such agreements nonetheless meet the conditions for the application of Article 81(1), the Commission will normally refrain from opening proceedings for lack of sufficient Community interest unless those undertakings collectively or individually hold a dominant position in a substantial part of the common market.

2. Agency agreements

(12) Paragraphs 12 to 20 replace the Notice on exclusive dealing contracts with commercial agents of 1962[7]. They must be read in conjunction with Council Directive 86/653/EEC[8].

---

[6] OJ L 107, 30.4.1996, p. 4.
[7] OJ 139, 24.12.1962, p. 2921/62.
[8] OJ L 382, 31.12.1986, p. 17.

Agency agreements cover the situation in which a legal or physical person (the agent) is vested with the power to negotiate and/or conclude contracts on behalf of another person (the principal), either in the agent's own name or in the name of the principal, for the:

— purchase of goods or services by the principal, or

— sale of goods or services supplied by the principal.

(13) In the case of genuine agency agreements, the obligations imposed on the agent as to the contracts negotiated and/or concluded on behalf of the principal do not fall within the scope of application of Article 81(1). The determining factor in assessing whether Article 81(1) is applicable is the financial or commercial risk borne by the agent in relation to the activities for which he has been appointed as an agent by the principal. In this respect it is not material for the assessment whether the agent acts for one or several principals. Non-genuine agency agreements may be caught by Article 81(1), in which case the Block Exemption Regulation and the other sections of these Guidelines will apply.

(14) There are two types of financial or commercial risk that are material to the assessment of the genuine nature of an agency agreement under Article 81(1). First there are

the risks which are directly related to the contracts concluded and/or negotiated by the agent on behalf of the principal, such as financing of stocks. Secondly, there are the risks related to market-specific investments. These are investments specifically required for the type of activity for which the agent has been appointed by the principal, i.e. which are required to enable the agent to conclude and/or negotiate this type of contract. Such investments are usually sunk, if upon leaving that particular field of activity the investment cannot be used for other activities or sold other than at a significant loss.

(15) The agency agreement is considered a genuine agency agreement and consequently falls outside Article 81(1) if the agent does not bear any, or bears only insignificant, risks in relation to the contracts concluded and/or negotiated on behalf of the principal and in relation to market-specific investments for that field of activity. In such a situation, the selling or purchasing function forms part of the principal's activities, despite the fact that the agent is a separate undertaking. The principal thus bears the related financial and commercial risks and the agent does not exercise an independent economic activity in relation to the activities for which he has been appointed as an agent by the principal. In the opposite situation the agency agreement is considered a non-genuine agency

agreement and may fall under Article 81(1). In that case the agent does bear such risks and will be treated as an independent dealer who must remain free in determining his marketing strategy in order to be able to recover his contract- or market-specific investments. Risks that are related to the activity of providing agency services in general, such as the risk of the agent's income being dependent upon his success as an agent or general investments in for instance premises or personnel, are not material to this assessment.

(16) The question of risk must be assessed on a case-by-case basis, and with regard to the economic reality of the situation rather than the legal form. Nonetheless, the Commission considers that Article 81(1) will generally not be applicable to the obligations imposed on the agent as to the contracts negotiated and/or concluded on behalf of the principal where property in the contract goods bought or sold does not vest in the agent, or the agent does not himself supply the contract services and where the agent:

— does not contribute to the costs relating to the supply/purchase of the contract goods or services, including the costs of transporting the goods. This does not preclude the agent from carrying out the transport service, provided that the costs are covered by the principal;

— is not, directly or indirectly, obliged to invest in sales promotion, such as contributions to the advertising budgets of the principal;

— does not maintain at his own cost or risk stocks of the contract goods, including the costs of financing the stocks and the costs of loss of stocks and can return unsold goods to the principal without charge, unless the agent is liable for fault (for example, by failing to comply with reasonable security measures to avoid loss of stocks);

— does not create and/or operate an after-sales service, repair service or a warranty service unless it is fully reimbursed by the principal;

— does not make market-specific investments in equipment, premises or training of personnel, such as for example the petrol storage tank in the case of petrol retailing or specific software to sell insurance policies in case of insurance agents;

— does not undertake responsibility towards third parties for damage caused by the product sold (product liability), unless, as agent, he is liable for fault in this respect;

— does not take responsibility for customers' non-performance of the contract, with the exception of the loss of the agent's commission, unless the agent is liable for fault (for example, by failing to comply with reasonable security or anti-theft measures or failing to comply with reasonable measures to report theft to the principal or police or to communicate to the principal all necessary information available to him on the customer's financial reliability).

(17) This list is not exhaustive. However, where the agent incurs one or more of the above risks or costs, then Article 81(1) may apply as with any other vertical agreement.

(18) If an agency agreement does not fall within the scope of application of Article 81(1), then all obligations imposed on the agent in relation to the contracts concluded and/or negotiated on behalf of the principal fall outside Article 81(1). The following obligations on the agent's part will generally be considered to form an inherent part of an agency agreement, as each of them relates to the ability of the principal to fix the scope of activity of the agent in relation to the contract goods or services, which is essential if the principal is to take the risks and therefore to be in a position to determine the commercial strategy:

— limitations on the territory in which the agent may sell these goods or services;

— limitations on the customers to whom the agent may sell these goods or services;

— the prices and conditions at which the agent must sell or purchase these goods or services.

(19) In addition to governing the conditions of sale or purchase of the contract goods or services by the agent on behalf of the principal, agency agreements often contain provisions which concern the relationship between the agent and the principal. In particular, they may contain a provision preventing the principal from appointing other agents in respect of a given type of transaction, customer or territory (exclusive agency provisions) and/or a provision preventing the agent from acting as an agent or distributor of undertakings which compete with the principal (non-compete provisions). Exclusive agency provisions concern only intra-brand competition and will in general not lead to anti-competitive effects. Non-compete provisions, including post-term non-compete provisions, concern inter-brand competition and may infringe Article 81(1) if they lead to foreclosure on the relevant market where the contract goods or services are sold or purchased (see Section VI.2.1).

(20) An agency agreement may also fall within the scope of Article 81(1), even if the principal bears all the relevant financial and commercial risks, where it facilitates collusion. This could for instance be the case when a number of principals use the same agents while collectively excluding others from using these agents, or when they use the agents to collude on marketing strategy or to exchange sensitive market information between the principals.

III. APPLICATION OF THE BLOCK EXEMPTION REGULATION

1. Safe harbour created by the Block Exemption Regulation

(21) The Block Exemption Regulation creates a presumption of legality for vertical agreements depending on the market share of the supplier or the buyer. Pursuant to Article 3 of the Block Exemption Regulation, it is in general the market share of the supplier on the market where it sells the contract goods or services which determines the applicability of the block exemption. This market share may not exceed the threshold of 30 % in order for the block exemption to apply. Only where the agreement containsan exclusive supply obligation, as defined in Article 1(c) of the Block Exemption Regulation, is it the buyer's market share on the market where it purchases the contract goods or services which may not exceed the threshold of 30% in order for the block exemption to apply. For market share issues see Section V (paragraphs 88 to 99).

(22) From an economic point of view, a vertical agreement may have effects not only on the market between supplier and buyer but also on markets downstream of the buyer. The simplified approach of the Block Exemption Regulation, which only takes into account the market share of the supplier or the buyer (as the case may be) on the market between these two parties, is justified by the fact that below the threshold of 30 % the effects on downstream markets will in general be limited. In addition, only having to consider the market between supplier and buyer makes the application of the Block Exemption Regulation easier and enhances the level of legal certainty, while the instrument of withdrawal (see paragraphs 71 to 87) remains available to remedy possible problems on other related markets.

2. Scope of the Block Exemption Regulation

(i) Definition of vertical agreements

(23) Vertical agreements are defined in Article 2(1) of the Block Exemption Regulation as 'agreements or concerted practices entered into between two or more undertakings each of which operates, for the purposes of the agreement, at a different level of the production or distribution chain, and relating to the conditions under which the parties may purchase, sell or resell certain goods or services'.

(24) There are three main elements in this definition:

— the agreement or concerted practice is between two or more undertakings. Vertical agreements with final consumers not operating as an undertaking are not covered;

More generally, agreements with final consumers do not fall under Article 81(1), as that article applies only to agreements between undertakings, decisions by associations of undertakings and concerted practices. This is without prejudice to the possible application of Article 82 of the Treaty;

— the agreement or concerted practice is between undertakings each operating, for the purposes of the agreement, at a different level of the production or distribution chain. This means for instance that one undertaking produces a raw material which the other undertaking uses as an input, or that the first is a manufacturer, the second a wholesaler and the third a retailer. This does not preclude an undertaking from being active at more than one level of the production or distribution chain;

— the agreements or concerted practices relate to the conditions under which the parties to the agreement, the supplier and the buyer, 'may purchase, sell or resell certain goods or services'. This reflects the purpose of the Block Exemption Regulation to cover purchase and distribution agreements. These are agreements which concern the conditions for the purchase, sale or resale of the goods or services supplied by the supplier and/or which concern the conditions for the sale by the buyer of the goods or services which incorporate these goods or services. For the application of the Block Exemption Regulation both the goods or services supplied by the supplier and the resulting goods or services are considered to be contract goods or services. Vertical agreements relating to all final and intermediate goods and services are covered.The only exception is the automobile sector, as long as this sector remains covered by a specific block exemption such as that granted by Commission Regulation (EC) No 1475/95[9]. The goods or services provided by the supplier may be resold by the buyer or may be used as an input by the buyer to produce his own goods or services.

(25) The Block Exemption Regulation also applies to goods sold and purchased for renting to third parties. However, rent and lease agreements as such are not cov-

ered, as no good or service is being sold by the supplier to the buyer. More generally, the Block Exemption Regulation does not cover restrictions or obligations that do not relate to the conditions of purchase, sale and resale, such as an obligation preventing parties from carrying out independent research and development which the parties may have included in an otherwise vertical agreement. In addition, Articles 2(2) to (5) directly or indirectly exclude certain vertical agreements from the application of the Block Exemption Regulation.

(ii) Vertical agreements between competitors

(26) Article 2(4) of the Block Exemption Regulation explicitly excludes from its application 'vertical agreements entered into between competing undertakings'. Vertical agreements between competitors will be dealt with, as regards possible collusion effects, in the forthcoming Guidelines on the applicability of Article 81 to horizontal cooperation[10]. However, the vertical aspects of such agreements need to be assessed under these Guidelines. Article 1(a) of the Block Exemption Regulation defines competing undertakings as 'actual or potential suppliers in the same product market', irrespective of whether or not they are competitors on the same geographic

---

[9] OJ L 145, 29.6.1995, p. 25.

[10] Draft text published in OJ C 118, 27.4.2000, p. 14.

market. Competing undertakings are undertakings that are actual or potential suppliers of the contract goods or services or goods or services that are substitutes for the contract goods or services. A potential supplier is an undertaking that does not actually produce a competing product but could and would be likely to do so in the absence of the agreement in response to a small and permanent increase in relative prices. This means that the undertaking would be able and likely to undertake the necessary additional investments and supply the market within 1 year. This assessment has to be based on realistic grounds; the mere theoretical possibility of entering a market is not sufficient[11].

(27) There are three exceptions to the general exclusion of vertical agreements between competitors, all three being set out in Article 2(4) and relating to non-reciprocal agreements. Non-reciprocal means, for instance, that while one manufacturer becomes the distributor of the products of another manufacturer, the latter does not become the distributor of the products of the first manufacturer. Non-reciprocal agreements between competitors are covered by the Block Exemption Regulation where (1) the buyer has a turnover not exceeding EUR 100 million, or (2) the supplier is a manufacturer and distributor of goods, while the buyer is only a distributor and not also a manufacturer of competing goods, or (3) the supplier is a provider of services operating at several levels of trade, while the buyer does not provide competing services at the level of trade where it purchases the contract services. The second exception covers situations of dual distribution, i.e. the manufacturer of particular goods also acts as a distributor of the goods in competition with independent distributors of his goods. A distributor who provides specifications to a manufacturer to produce particular goods under the distributor's brand name is not to be considered a manufacturer of such own-brand goods. The third exception covers similar situations of dual distribution, but in this case for services, when the supplier is also a provider of services at the level of the buyer.

(iii) Associations of retailers

(28) Article 2(2) of the Block Exemption Regulation includes in its application vertical agreements entered into by an association of undertakings which fulfils certain conditions and thereby excludes from the Block Exemption Regulation vertical agreements

---

[11] See Commission Notice on the definition of the relevant market for the purposes of Community competition law, OJ C 372, 9.12.1997, p. 5, at paras. 20–24, the Commission's Thirteenth Report on Competition Policy, point 55, and Commission Decision 90/410/EEC in Case No IV/32.009 – *Elopak/Metal Box-Odin*, OJ L 209, 8.8.1990, p. 15.

entered into by all other associations. Vertical agreements entered into between an association and its members, or between an association and its suppliers, are covered by the Block Exemption Regulation only if all the members are retailers of goods (not services) and if each individual member of the association has a turnover not exceeding EUR 50 million. Retailers are distributors reselling goods to final consumers. Where only a limited number of the members of the association have a turnover not significantly exceeding the EUR 50 million threshold, this will normally not change the assessment under Article 81.

(29) An association of undertakings may involve both horizontal and vertical agreements. The horizontal agreements have to be assessed according to the principles set out in the forthcoming Guidelines on the applicability of Article 81 to horizontal cooperation. If this assessment leads to the conclusion that a cooperation between undertakings in the area of purchasing or selling is acceptable, a further assessment will be necessary to examine the vertical agreements concluded by the association with its suppliers or its individual members. The latter assessment will follow the rules of the Block Exemption Regulation and these Guidelines. For instance, horizontal agreements concluded between the members of the association or decisions adopted by the association, such as the decision to require the members to purchase from the association or the decision to allocate exclusive territories to the members have to be assessed first as a horizontal agreement. Only if this assessment is positive does it become relevant to assess the vertical agreements between the association and individual members or between the association and suppliers.

(iv) Vertical agreements containing provisions on intellectual property rights (IPRs)

(30) Article 2(3) of the Block Exemption Regulation includes in its application vertical agreements containing certain provisions relating to the assignment of IPRs to or use of IPRs by the buyer and thereby excludes from the Block Exemption Regulation all other vertical agreements containing IPR provisions. The Block Exemption Regulation applies to vertical agreements containing IPR provisions when five conditions are fulfilled:

— The IPR provisions must be part of a vertical agreement, i.e. an agreement with conditions under which the parties may purchase, sell or resell certain goods or services;

— The IPRs must be assigned to, or for use by, the buyer;

— The IPR provisions must not constitute the primary object of the agreement;

— The IPR provisions must be directly related to the use, sale or resale of goods or services by the buyer or his customers. In the case of franchising where marketing forms the object of the exploitation of the IPRs, the goods or services are distributed by the master franchisee or the franchisees;

— The IPR provisions, in relation to the contract goods or services, must not contain restrictions of competition having the same object or effect as vertical restraints which are not exempted under the Block Exemption Regulation.

(31) These conditions ensure that the Block Exemption Regulation applies to vertical agreements where the use, sale or resale of goods or services can be performed more effectively because IPRs are assigned to or transferred for use by the buyer. In other words, restrictions concerning the assignment or use of IPRs can be covered when the main object of the agreement is the purchase or distribution of goods or services.

(32) The first condition makes clear that the context in which the IPRs are provided is an agreement to purchase or distribute goods or an agreement to purchase or provide services and not an agreement concerning the assignment or licensing of IPRs for the manufacture of goods, nor a pure

licensing agreement. The Block Exemption Regulation does not cover for instance:

— agreements where a party provides another party with a recipe and licenses the other party to produce a drink with this recipe;

— agreements under which one party provides another party with a mould or master copy and licenses the other party to produce and distribute copies;

— the pure licence of a trade mark or sign for the purposes of merchandising;

— sponsorship contracts concerning the right to advertise oneself as being an official sponsor of an event;

— copyright licensing such as broadcasting contracts concerning the right to record and/or the right to broadcast an event.

(33) The second condition makes clear that the Block Exemption Regulation does not apply when the IPRs are provided by the buyer to the supplier, no matter whether the IPRs concern the manner of manufacture or of distribution. An agreement relating to the transfer of IPRs to the supplier and containing possible restrictions on the sales made by the supplier is not covered by the Block Exemption Regulation.

This means in particular that sub-contracting involving the transfer of know-how to a subcontractor[12] does not fall within the scope of application of the Block Exemption Regulation. However, vertical agreements under which the buyer provides only specifications to the supplier which describe the goods or services to be supplied are covered by the Block Exemption Regulation.

(34) The third condition makes clear that in order to be covered by the Block Exemption Regulation the primary object of the agreement must not be the assignment or licensing of IPRs. The primary object must be the purchase or distribution of goods or services and the IPR provisions must serve the implementation of the vertical agreement.

(35) The fourth condition requires that the IPR provisions facilitate the use, sale or resale of goods or services by the buyer or his customers. The goods or services for use or resale are usually supplied by the licensor but may also be purchased by the licensee from a third supplier. The IPR provisions will normally concern the marketing of goods or services. This is for instance the case in a franchise agreement where the franchisor sells to the franchisee goods for resale and in addition licenses the franchisee to use his trade mark

and know-how to market the goods. Also covered is the case where the supplier of a concentrated extract licenses the buyer to dilute and bottle the extract before selling it as a drink.

(36) The fifth condition signifies in particular that the IPR provisions should not have the same object or effect as any of the hardcore restrictions listed in Article 4 of the Block Exemption Regulation or any of the restrictions excluded from the coverage of the Block Exemption Regulation by Article 5 (see paragraphs 46 to 61).

(37) Intellectual property rights which may be considered to serve the implementation of vertical agreements within the meaning of Article 2(3) of the Block Exemption Regulation generally concern three main areas: trade marks, copyright and know-how.

Trade mark

(38) A trade mark licence to a distributor may be related to the distribution of the licensor's products in a particular territory. If it is an exclusive licence, the agreement amounts to exclusive distribution.

Copyright

(39) Resellers of goods covered by copyright (books, software, etc.) may be obliged by the copyright holder only to resell under the condition that the buyer, whether another reseller or the end user,

---

[12] See Notice on subcontracting, OJ C 1, 3.1.1979, p. 2

shall not infringe the copyright. Such obligations on the reseller, to the extent that they fall under Article 81(1) at all, are covered by the Block Exemption Regulation.

(40) Agreements under which hard copies of software are supplied for resale and where the reseller does not acquire a licence to any rights over the software but only has the right to resell the hard copies, are to be regarded as agreements for the supply of goods for resale for the purpose of the Block Exemption Regulation. Under this form of distribution the licence of the software only takes place between the copyright owner and the user of the software. This may take the form of a 'shrink wrap' licence, i.e. a set of conditions included in the package of the hard copy which the end user is deemed to accept by opening the package.

(41) Buyers of hardware incorporating software protected by copyright may be obliged by the copyright holder not to infringe the copyright, for example not to make copies and resell the software or not to make copies and use the software in combination with other hardware. Such use-restrictions, to the extent that they fall within Article 81(1) at all, are covered by the Block Exemption Regulation.

Know-how

(42) Franchise agreements, with the exception of industrial franchise agreements, are the most obvious example where know-how for marketing purposes is communicated to the buyer. Franchise agreements contain licences of intellectual property rights relating to trade marks or signs and know-how for the use and distribution of goods or the provision of services. In addition to the licence of IPR, the franchisor usually provides the franchisee during the life of the agreement with commercial or technical assistance, such as procurement services, training, advice on real estate, financial planning etc. The licence and the assistance are integral components of the business method being franchised.

(43) Licensing contained in franchise agreements is covered by the Block Exemption Regulation if all five conditions listed in point 30 are fulfilled. This is usually the case, as under most franchise agreements, including master franchise agreements, the franchisor provides goods and/or services, in particular commercial or technical assistance services, to the franchisee. The IPRs help the franchisee to resell the products supplied by the franchisor or by a supplier designated by the franchisor or to use those products and sell the resulting goods or services. Where the franchise agreement only or primarily concerns licensing of IPRs, such an agreement is not covered by the Block Exemption Regulation, but it will be treated in a way similar to

those franchise agreements which are covered by the Block Exemption Regulation.

(44) The following IPR-related obligations are generally considered to be necessary to protect the franchisor's intellectual property rights and are, if these obligations fall under Article 81(1), also covered by the Block Exemption Regulation:

(a) an obligation on the franchisee not to engage, directly or indirectly, in any similar business;

(b) an obligation on the franchisee not to acquire financial interests in the capital of a competing undertaking such as would give the franchisee the power to influence the economic conduct of such undertaking;

(c) an obligation on the franchisee not to disclose to third parties the know- how provided by the franchisor as long as this know-how is not in the public domain;

(d) an obligation on the franchisee to communicate to the franchisor any experience gained in exploiting the franchise and to grant it, and other franchisees, a non-exclusive licence for the know-how resulting from that experience;

(e) an obligation on the franchisee to inform the franchisor of infringements of licensed intellectual property rights, to take legal action against infringers or to assist the franchisor in any legal actions against infringers;

(f) an obligation on the franchisee not to use know-how licensed by the franchisor for purposes other than the exploitation of the franchise;

(g) an obligation on the franchisee not to assign the rights and obligations under the franchise agreement without the franchisor's consent.

(v) *Relationship to other block exemption regulations*

(45) Article 2(5) states that the Block Exemption Regulation does 'not apply to vertical agreements the subject matter of which falls within the scope of any other block exemption regulation.' This means that the Block Exemption Regulation does not apply to vertical agreements covered by Commission Regulation (EC) No 240/96[13] on technology transfer, Commission Regulation (EC) No 1475/1995[14] for car distribution or Regulations (EEC) No 417/85[15] and (EEC) No 418/85[16] exempting vertical agreements concluded in

---

[13] OJ L 31, 9.2.1996, p. 2.
[14] OJ L 145, 29.6.1995, p. 25.
[15] OJ L 53, 22.2.1985, p. 1.
[16] OJ L 53, 22.2.1985, p. 5.

connection with horizontal agreements, as last amended by Regulation (EC) No 2236/97[17] or any future regulations of that kind.

3. Hardcore restrictions under the Block Exemption Regulation

(46) The Block Exemption Regulation contains in Article 4 a list of hardcore restrictions which lead to the exclusion of the whole vertical agreement from the scope of application of the Block Exemption Regulation. This list of hardcore restrictions applies to vertical agreements concerning trade within the Community. In so far as vertical agreements concern exports outside the Community or imports/re-imports from outside the Community see the judgment in *Javico* v. *Yves Saint Laurent*. Individual exemption of vertical agreements containing such hardcore restrictions is also unlikely.

(47) The hardcore restriction set out in Article 4(a) of the Block Exemption Regulation concerns resale price maintenance (RPM), that is agreements or concerted practices having as their direct or indirect object the establishment of a fixed or minimum resale price or a fixed or minimum price level to be observed by the buyer. In the case of contractual provisions or concerted practices that directly establish the resale price,

the restriction is clear cut. However, RPM can also be achieved through indirect means. Examples of the latter are an agreement fixing the distribution margin, fixing the maximum level of discount the distributor can grant from a prescribed price level, making the grant of rebates or reimbursement of promotional costs by the supplier subject to the observance of a given price level, linking the prescribed resale price to the resale prices of competitors, threats, intimidation, warnings, penalties, delay or suspension of deliveries or contract terminations in relation to observance of a given price level. Direct or indirect means of achieving price fixing can be made more effective when combined with measures to identify price-cutting distributors, such as the implementation of a price monitoring system, or the obligation on retailers to report other members of the distribution network who deviate from the standard price level. Similarly, direct or indirect price fixing can be made more effective when combined with measures which may reduce the buyer's incentive to lower the resale price, such as the supplier printing a recommended resale price on the product or the supplier obliging the buyer to apply a most- favoured-customer clause. The same indirect means and the same 'supportive' measures can be used to make maximum or recommended prices work as RPM. However, the provision of a list of

[17] OJ L 306, 11.11.97, p.12.

recommended prices or maximum prices by the supplier to the buyer is not considered in itself as leading to RPM.

(48) In the case of agency agreements, the principal normally establishes the sales price, as the agent does not become the owner of the goods. However, where an agency agreement falls within Article 81(1) (see paragraphs 12 to 20), an obligation preventing or restricting the agent from sharing his commission, fixed or variable, with the customer would be a hardcore restriction under Article 4(a) of the Block Exemption Regulation. The agent should thus be left free to lower the effective price paid by the customer without reducing the income for the principal[18].

(49) The hardcore restriction set out in Article 4(b) of the Block Exemption Regulation concerns agreements or concerted practices that have as their direct or indirect object the restriction of sales by the buyer, in as far as those restrictions relate to the territory into which or the customers to whom the buyer may sell the contract goods or services. That hardcore restriction relates to market partitioning by territory or by customer. That may be the result of direct obligations, such as the

obligation not to sell to certain customers or to customers in certain territories or the obligation to refer orders from these customers to other distributors. It may also result from indirect measures aimed at inducing the distributor not to sell to such customers, such as refusal or reduction of bonuses or discounts, refusal to supply, reduction of supplied volumes or limitation of supplied volumes to the demand within the allocated territory or customer group, threat of contract termination or profit pass-over obligations. It may further result from the supplier not providing a Community-wide guarantee service, whereby all distributors are obliged to provide the guarantee service and are reimbursed for this service by the supplier, even in relation to products sold by other distributors into their territory. These practices are even more likely to be viewed as a restriction of the buyer's sales when used in conjunction with the implementation by the supplier of a monitoring system aimed at verifying the effective destination of the supplied goods, e.g. the use of differentiated labels or serial numbers. However, a prohibition imposed on all distributors to sell to certain end users is not classified as a hardcore restriction if there is an objective justification related to the product, such as a general ban on selling dangerous substances to certain customers for reasons of safety or health. It implies that

[18] See, for instance, Commission Decision 91/562/EEC in Case No IV/32.737 – Eirpage, OJ L 306, 7.11.1991, p. 22, in particular point (6).

also the supplier himself does not sell to these customers. Nor are obligations on the reseller relating to the display of the supplier's brand name classified as hardcore.

(50) There are four exceptions to the hardcore restriction in Article 4(b) of the Block Exemption Regulation. The first exception allows a supplier to restrict active sales by his direct buyers to a territory or a customer group which has been allocated exclusively to another buyer or which the supplier has reserved to itself. A territory or customer group is exclusively allocated when the supplier agrees to sell his product only to one distributor for distribution in a particular territory or to a particular customer group and the exclusive distributor is protected against active selling into his territory or to his customer group by the supplier and all the other buyers of the supplier inside the Community. The supplier is allowed to combine the allocation of an exclusive territory and an exclusive customer group by for instance appointing an exclusive distributor for a particular customer group in a certain territory. This protection of exclusively allocated territories or customer groups must, however, permit passive sales to such territories or customer groups. For the application of Article 4(b) of the Block Exemption Regulation, the Commission interprets 'active' and 'passive' sales as follows:

— 'Active' sales mean actively approaching individual customers inside another distributor's exclusive territory or exclusive customer group by for instance direct mail or visits; or actively approaching a specific customer group or customers in a specific territory allocated exclusively to another distributor through advertisement in media or other promotions specifically targeted at that customer group or targeted at customers in that territory; or establishing a warehouse or distribution outlet in another distributor's exclusive territory.

— 'Passive' sales mean responding to unsolicited requests from individual customers including delivery of goods or services to such customers. General advertising or promotion in media or on the Internet that reaches customers in other distributors' exclusive territories or customer groups but which is a reasonable way to reach customers outside those territories or customer groups, for instance to reach customers in non-exclusive territories or in one's own territory, are passive sales.

(51) Every distributor must be free to use the Internet to advertise or to sell products. A restriction on the use of the Internet by distributors

could only be compatible with the Block Exemption Regulation to the extent that promotion on the Internet or sales over the Internet would lead to active selling into other distributors' exclusive territories or customer groups. In general, the use of the Internet is not considered a form of active sales into such territories or customer groups, since it is a reasonable way to reach every customer. The fact that it may have effects outside one's own territory or customer group results from the technology, i.e. the easy access from everywhere. If a customer visits the web site of a distributor and contacts the distributor and if such contact leads to a sale, including delivery, then that is considered passive selling. The language used on the website or in the communication plays normally no role in that respect. Insofar as a web site is not specifically targeted at customers primarily inside the territory or customer group exclusively allocated to another distributor, for instance with the use of banners or links in pages of providers specifically available to these exclusively allocated customers, the website is not considered a form of active selling. However, unsolicited e-mails sent to individual customers or specific customer groups are considered active selling. The same considerations apply to selling by catalogue. Notwithstanding what has been said before, the supplier may require quality standards for the use of the Internet site to resell his goods, just as the supplier may require quality standards for a shop or for advertising and promotion in general. The latter may be relevant in particular for selective distribution. An outright ban on Internet or catalogue selling is only possible if there is an objective justification. In any case, the supplier cannot reserve to itself sales and/or advertising over the Internet.

(52) There are three other exceptions to the second hardcore restriction set out in Article 4(b) of the Block Exemption Regulation. All three exceptions allow for the restriction of both active and passive sales. Thus, it is permissible to restrict a wholesaler from selling to end users, to restrict an appointed distributor in a selective distribution system from selling, at any level of trade, to unauthorised distributors in markets where such a system is operated, and to restrict a buyer of components supplied for incorporation from reselling them to competitors of the supplier. The term 'component' includes any intermediate goods and the term 'incorporation' refers to the use of any input to produce goods.

(53) The hardcore restriction set out in Article 4(c) of the Block Exemption Regulation concerns the restriction of active or passive sales to end users, whether professional end users or final consumers, by members of a selective

distribution network. This means that dealers in a selective distribution system, as defined in Article 1(d) of the Block Exemption Regulation, cannot be restricted in the users or purchasing agents acting on behalf of these users to whom they may sell. For instance, also in a selective distribution system the dealer should be free to advertise and sell with the help of the Internet. Selective distribution may be combined with exclusive distribution provided that active and passive selling is not restricted anywhere. The supplier may therefore commit itself to supplying only one dealer or a limited number of dealers in a given territory.

(54) In addition, in the case of selective distribution, restrictions can be imposed on the dealer's ability to determine the location of his business premises. Selected dealers may be prevented from running their business from different premises or from opening a new outlet in a different location. If the dealer's outlet is mobile ('shop on wheels'), an area may be defined outside which the mobile outlet cannot be operated.

(55) The hardcore restriction set out in Article 4(d) of the Block Exemption Regulation concerns the restriction of cross-supplies between appointed distributors within a selective distribution system. This means that an agreement or concerted practice may not have as its direct or indirect

object to prevent or restrict the active or passive selling of the contract products between the selected distributors. Selected distributors must remain free to purchase the contract products from other appointed distributors within the network, operating either at the same or at a different level of trade. This means that selective distribution cannot be combined with vertical restraints aimed at forcing distributors to purchase the contract products exclusively from a given source, for instance exclusive purchasing. It also means that within a selective distribution network no restrictions can be imposed on appointed wholesalers as regards their sales of the product to appointed retailers.

(56) The hardcore restriction set out in Article 4(e) of the Block Exemption Regulation concerns agreements that prevent or restrict end-users, independent repairers and service providers from obtaining spare parts directly from the manufacturer of these spare parts. An agreement between a manufacturer of spare parts and a buyer who incorporates these parts into his own products (original equipment manufacturer (OEM)), may not, either directly or indirectly, prevent or restrict sales by the manufacturer of these spare parts to end users, independent repairers or service providers. Indirect restrictions may arise in particular when the supplier of the spare

parts is restricted in supplying technical information and special equipment which are necessary for the use of spare parts by users, independent repairers or service providers. However, the agreement may place restrictions on the supply of the spare parts to the repairers or service providers entrusted by the original equipment manufacturer with the repair or servicing of his own goods. In other words, the original equipment manufacturer may require his own repair and service network to buy the spare parts from it.

4. Conditions under the Block Exemption Regulation

(57) Article 5 of the Block Exemption Regulation excludes certain obligations from the coverage of the Block Exemption Regulation even though the market share threshold is not exceeded. However, the Block Exemption Regulation continues to apply to the remaining part of the vertical agreement if that part is severable from the non-exempted obligations.

(58) The first exclusion is provided in Article 5(a) of the Block Exemption Regulation and concerns non-compete obligations. Non-compete obligations are obligations that require the buyer to purchase from the supplier or from another undertaking designated by the supplier more than 80% of the buyer's total purchases during the previous year of the contract goods and services and their substitutes (see the definition in Article 1(b) of the Block Exemption Regulation), thereby preventing the buyer from purchasing competing goods or services or limiting such purchases to less than 20% of total purchases. Where for the year preceding the conclusion of the contract no relevant purchasing data for the buyer are available, the buyer's best estimate of his annual total requirements may be used. Such non-compete obligations are not covered by the Block Exemption Regulation when their duration is indefinite or exceeds five years. Non-compete obligations that are tacitly renewable beyond a period of five years are also not covered by the Block Exemption Regulation. However, non-compete obligations are covered when their duration is limited to five years or less, or when renewal beyond five years requires explicit consent of both parties and no obstacles exist that hinder the buyer from effectively terminating the non-compete obligation at the end of the five year period. If for instance the agreement provides for a five-year non-compete obligation and the supplier provides a loan to the buyer, the repayment of that loan should not hinder the buyer from effectively terminating the non-compete obligation at the end of the five-year period; the repayment needs to be structured in equal or decreasing instalments and should not increase over

time. This is without prejudice to the possibility, in the case for instance of a new distribution outlet, to delay repayment for the first one or two years until sales have reached a certain level. The buyer must have the possibility to repay the remaining debt where there is still an outstanding debt at the end of the non- compete obligation. Similarly, when the supplier provides the buyer with equipment which is not relationship-specific, the buyer should have the possibility to take over the equipment at its market asset value at the end of the non-compete obligation.

(59) The five-year duration limit does not apply when the goods or services are resold by the buyer 'from premises and land owned by the supplier or leased by the supplier from third parties not connected with the buyer.' In such cases the non-compete obligation may be of the same duration as the period of occupancy of the point of sale by the buyer (Article 5(a) of the Block Exemption Regulation). The reason for this exception is that it is normally unreasonable to expect a supplier to allow competing products to be sold from premises and land owned by the supplier without his permission. Artificial ownership constructions intended to avoid the five-year limit cannot benefit from this exception.

(60) The second exclusion from the block exemption is provided for in Article 5(b) of the Block Exemption Regulation and concerns post term non-compete obligations. Such obligations are normally not covered by the Block Exemption Regulation, unless the obligation is indispensable to protect know-how transferred by the supplier to the buyer, is limited to the point of sale from which the buyer has operated during the contract period, and is limited to a maximum period of one year. According to the definition in Article 1(f) of the Block Exemption Regulation the know-how needs to be 'substantial', meaning 'that the know-how includes information which is indispensable to the buyer for the use, sale or resale of the contract goods or services'.

(61) The third exclusion from the block exemption is provided for in Article 5(c) of the Block Exemption Regulation and concerns the sale of competing goods in a selective distribution system. The Block Exemption Regulation covers the combination of selective distribution with a non-compete obligation, obliging the dealers not to resell competing brands in general. However, if the supplier prevents his appointed dealers, either directly or indirectly, from buying products for resale from specific competing suppliers, such an obligation cannot enjoy the benefit of the Block Exemption Regulation. The objective of the exclusion of this

obligation is to avoid a situation whereby a number of suppliers using the same selective distribution outlets prevent one specific competitor or certain specific competitors from using these outlets to distribute their products (foreclosure of a competing supplier which would be a form of collective boycott)[19].

5. No presumption of illegality outside the Block Exemption Regulation

(62) Vertical agreements falling outside the Block Exemption Regulation will not be presumed to be illegal but may need individual examination. Companies are encouraged to do their own assessment without notification. In the case of an individual examination by the Commission, the latter will bear the burden of proof that the agreement in question infringes Article 81(1). When appreciable anti-competitive effects are demonstrated, undertakings may substantiate efficiency claims and explain why a certain distribution system is likely to bring about benefits which are relevant to the conditions for exemption under Article 81(3).

6. No need for precautionary notification

(63) Pursuant to Article 4(2) of Council Regulation No 17 of 6 February 1962, First Regulation implementing Articles 85 and 86 of the Treaty[20], as last amended by Regulation (EC) No 1216/1999[21], vertical agreements can benefit from an exemption under Article 81(3) from their date of entry into force, even if notification occurs after that date. This means in practice that no precautionary notification needs to be made. If a dispute arises, an undertaking can still notify, in which case the Commission can exempt the vertical agreement with retroactive effect from the date of entry into force of the agreement if all four conditions of Article 81(3) are fulfilled. A notifying party does not have to explain why the agreement was not notified earlier and will not be denied retroactive exemption simply because it did not notify earlier. Any notification will be reviewed on its merits. This amendment to Article 4(2) of Regulation No 17 should eliminate artificial litigation before national courts and thus strengthen the civil enforceability of contracts. It also takes account of the situation where undertakings have not notified because they assumed the agreement was covered by the Block Exemption Regulation.

(64) Since the date of notification no longer limits the possibility of exemption by the Commission, national courts have to assess the

---

[19] An example of indirect measures having such exclusionary effects can be found in Commission Decision 92/428/EEC in Case No IV/33.542 – *Parfum Givenchy* (OJ L 236, 19.8.1992, p. 11).

[20] OJ 13, 21.2.1962, p. 204/62.

[21] OJ L 148, 15.6.1999, p. 5.

likelihood that Article 81(3) will apply in respect of vertical agreements falling within Article 81(1). If such likelihood exists, they should suspend proceedings pending adoption of a position by the Commission. However, national courts may adopt interim measures pending the assessment by the Commission of the applicability of Article 81(3), in the same way as they do when they refer a preliminary question to the Court of Justice under Article 234 of the EC Treaty. No suspension is necessary in respect of injunction proceedings, where national courts themselves are empowered to assess the likelihood of application of Article 81(3)[22].

(65) Unless there is litigation in national courts or complaints, notifications of vertical agreements will not be given priority in the Commission's enforcement policy. Notifications as such do not provide provisional validity for the execution of agreements. Where undertakings have not notified an agreement because they assumed in good faith that the market share threshold under the Block Exemption Regulation was not exceeded, the Commission will not impose fines.

7. Severability

(66) The Block Exemption Regulation exempts vertical agreements on condition that no hardcore

restriction, as set out in Article 4, is contained in or practised with the vertical agreement. If there are one or more hardcore restrictions, the benefit of the Block Exemption Regulation is lost for the entire vertical agreement. There is no severability for hardcore restrictions.

(67) The rule of severability does apply, however, to the conditions set out in Article 5 of the Block Exemption Regulation. Therefore, the benefit of the block exemption is only lost in relation to that part of the vertical agreement which does not comply with the conditions set out in Article 5.

8. Portfolio of products distributed through the same distribution system

(68) Where a supplier uses the same distribution agreement to distribute several goods/services some of these may, in view of the market share threshold, be covered by the Block Exemption Regulation while others may not. In that case, the Block Exemption Regulation applies to those goods and services for which the conditions of application are fulfilled.

(69) In respect of the goods or services which are not covered by the Block Exemption Regulation, the ordinary rules of competition apply, which means:

— there is no block exemption but also no presumption of illegality;

[22] Case C-234/89 *Delimitis* v. *Henninger Brau* [1991] ECR I-935, at paragraph 52.

— if there is an infringement of Article 81(1) which is not exemptable, consideration may be given to whether there are appropriate remedies to solve the competition problem within the existing distribution system;

— if there are no such appropriate remedies, the supplier concerned will have to make other distribution arrangements.

This situation can also arise where Article 82 applies in respect of some products but not in respect of others.

9. Transitional period

(70) The Block Exemption Regulation applies from 1 June 2000. Article 12 of the Block Exemption Regulation provides for a transitional period for vertical agreements already in force before 1 June 2000 which do not satisfy the conditions for exemption provided in the Block Exemption Regulation, but which do satisfy the conditions for exemption under the Block Exemption Regulations which expired on 31 May 2000 (Commissions Regulations (EEC) No 1983/83, (EEC) No 1984/83 and (EEC) No 4087/88). The Commission Notice concerning Regulations (EEC) Nos 1983/83 and 1984/83 also ceases to apply on 31 May 2000. The latter agreements may continue to benefit from these outgoing Regulations until

31 December 2001. Agreements of suppliers with a market share not exceeding 30% who signed with their buyers non-compete agreements with a duration exceeding five years are covered by the Block Exemption Regulation if on 1 January 2002 the non-compete agreements have no more than five years to run.

IV. WITHDRAWAL OF THE BLOCK EXEMPTION AND DISAPPLICATION OF THE BLOCK EXEMPTION REGULATION

1. Withdrawal procedure

(71) The presumption of legality conferred by the Block Exemption Regulation may be withdrawn if a vertical agreement, considered either in isolation or in conjunction with similar agreements enforced by competing suppliers or buyers, comes within the scope of Article 81(1) and does not fulfil all the conditions of Article 81(3). This may occur when a supplier, or a buyer in the case of exclusive supply agreements, holding a market share not exceeding 30%, enters into a vertical agreement which does not give rise to objective advantages such as to compensate for the damage which it causes to competition. This may particularly be the case with respect to the distribution of goods to final consumers, who are often in a much weaker position than professional buyers of intermediate goods. In the case of sales to final consumers, the disadvan-

tages caused by a vertical agreement may have a stronger impact than in a case concerning the sale and purchase of intermediate goods. When the conditions of Article 81(3) are not fulfilled, the Commission may withdraw the benefit of the Block Exemption Regulation under Article 6 and establish an infringement of Article 81(1).

(72) Where the withdrawal procedure is applied, the Commission bears the burden of proof that the agreement falls within the scope of Article 81(1) and that the agreement does not fulfil all four conditions of Article 81(3).

(73) The conditions for an exemption under Article 81(3) may in particular not be fulfilled when access to the relevant market or competition therein is significantly restricted by the cumulative effect of parallel networks of similar vertical agreements practised by competing suppliers or buyers. Parallel networks of vertical agreements are to be regarded as similar if they contain restraints producing similar effects on the market. Similar effects will normally occur when vertical restraints practised by competing suppliers or buyers come within one of the four groups listed in paragraphs 104 to 114. Such a situation may arise for example when, on a given market, certain suppliers practise purely qualitative selective distribution while other suppliers practise quantita-

tive selective distribution. In such circumstances, the assessment must take account of the anti-competitive effects attributable to each individual network of agreements. Where appropriate, withdrawal may concern only the quantitative limitations imposed on the number of authorised distributors. Other cases in which a withdrawal decision may be taken include situations where the buyer, for example in the context of exclusive supply or exclusive distribution, has significant market power in the relevant downstream market where he resells the goods or provides the services.

(74) Responsibility for an anti-competitive cumulative effect can only be attributed to those undertakings which make an appreciable contribution to it. Agreements entered into by undertakings whose contribution to the cumulative effect is insignificant do not fall under the prohibition provided for in Article 81(1)[23] and are therefore not subject to the withdrawal mechanism. The assessment of such a contribution will be made in accordance with the criteria set out in paragraphs 137 to 229.

(75) A withdrawal decision can only have ex nunc effect, which means that the exempted status of the agreements concerned will not be affected until the date at which the withdrawal becomes effective.

[23] Judgment in the Delimitis Case.

(76) Under Article 7 of the Block Exemption Regulation, the competent authority of a Member State may withdraw the benefit of the Block Exemption Regulation in respect of vertical agreements whose anti-competitive effects are felt in the territory of the Member State concerned or a part thereof, which has all the characteristics of a distinct geographic market. Where a Member State has not enacted legislation enabling the national competition authority to apply Community competition law or at least to withdraw the benefit of the Block Exemption Regulation, the Member State may ask the Commission to initiate proceedings to this effect.

(77) The Commission has the exclusive power to withdraw the benefit of the Block Exemption Regulation in respect of vertical agreements restricting competition on a relevant geographic market which is wider than the territory of a single Member State. When the territory of a single Member State, or a part thereof, constitutes the relevant geographic market, the Commission and the Member State concerned have concurrent competence for withdrawal. Often, such cases lend themselves to decentralised enforcement by national competition authorities. However, the Commission reserves the right to take on certain cases displaying a particular Community interest, such as cases raising a new point of law.

(78) National decisions of withdrawal must be taken in accordance with the procedures laid down under national law and will only have effect within the territory of the Member State concerned. Such national decisions must not prejudice the uniform application of the Community competition rules and the full effect of the measures adopted in implementation of those rules[24]. Compliance with this principle implies that national competition authorities must carry out their assessment under Article 81 in the light of the relevant criteria developed by the Court of Justice and the Court of First Instance and in the light of notices and previous decisions adopted by the Commission.

(79) The Commission considers that the consultation mechanisms provided for in the Notice on cooperation between national competition authorities and the Commission[25] should be used to avert the risk of conflicting decisions and duplication of procedures.

2. Disapplication of the Block Exemption Regulation

(80) Article 8 of the Block Exemption Regulation enables the Commission to exclude from the scope of the Block Exemption Regulation,

---

[24] Judgment of the Court of Justice in Case 14/68 *Walt Wilhelm and Others* v. *Bundeskartellamt* [1969] ECR 1, paragraph 4, and judgment in *Delimitis*.

[25] OJ C 313, 15.10.1997, p. 3, points 49 to 53.

by means of regulation, parallel networks of similar vertical restraints where these cover more than 50% of a relevant market. Such a measure is not addressed to individual undertakings but concerns all undertakings whose agreements are defined in the regulation disapplying the Block Exemption Regulation.

(81) Whereas the withdrawal of the benefit of the Block Exemption Regulation under Article 6 implies the adoption of a decision establishing an infringement of Article 81 by an individual company, the effect of a regulation under Article 8 is merely to remove, in respect of the restraints and the markets concerned, the benefit of the application of the Block Exemption Regulation and to restore the full application of Article 81(1) and (3). Following the adoption of a regulation declaring the Block Exemption inapplicable in respect of certain vertical restraints on a particular market, the criteria developed by the relevant case-law of the Court of Justice and the Court of First Instance and by notices and previous decisions adopted by the Commission will guide the application of Article 81 to individual agreements. Where appropriate, the Commission will take a decision in an individual case, which can provide guidance to all the undertakings operating on the market concerned.

(82) For the purpose of calculating the 50% market coverage ratio,

account must be taken of each individual network of vertical agreements containing restraints, or combinations of restraints, producing similar effects on the market. Similar effects normally result when the restraints come within one of the four groups listed in paragraphs 104 to 114.

(83) Article 8 does not entail an obligation on the part of the Commission to act where the 50% market-coverage ratio is exceeded. In general, disapplication is appropriate when it is likely that access to the relevant market or competition therein is appreciably restricted. This may occur in particular when parallel networks of selective distribution covering more than 50% of a market make use of selection criteria which are not required by the nature of the relevant goods or discriminate against certain forms of distribution capable of selling such goods.

(84) In assessing the need to apply Article 8, the Commission will consider whether individual withdrawal would be a more appropriate remedy. This may depend, in particular, on the number of competing undertakings contributing to a cumulative effect on a market or the number of affected geographic markets within the Community.

(85) Any regulation adopted under Article 8 must clearly set out its scope. This means, first, that the

Commission must define the relevant product and geographic market(s) and, secondly, that it must identify the type of vertical restraint in respect of which the Block Exemption Regulation will no longer apply. As regards the latter aspect, the Commission may modulate the scope of its regulation according to the competition concern which it intends to address. For instance, while all parallel networks of single-branding type arrangements shall be taken into account in view of establishing the 50% market coverage ratio, the Commission may nevertheless restrict the scope of the disapplication regulation only to non-compete obligations exceeding a certain duration. Thus, agreements of a shorter duration or of a less restrictive nature might be left unaffected, in consideration of the lesser degree of foreclosure attributable to such restraints. Similarly, when on a particular market selective distribution is practised in combination with additional restraints such as non-compete or quantity-forcing on the buyer, the disapplication regulation may concern only such additional restraints. Where appropriate, the Commission may also provide guidance by specifying the market share level which, in the specific market context, may be regarded as insufficient to bring about a significant contribution by an individual undertaking to the cumulative effect.

(86) The transitional period of not less than six months that the Commission will have to set under Article 8(2) should allow the undertakings concerned to adapt their agreements to take account of the regulation disapplying the Block Exemption Regulation.

(87) A regulation disapplying the Block Exemption Regulation will not affect the exempted status of the agreements concerned for the period preceding its entry into force.

V. MARKET DEFINITION AND MARKET SHARE CALCULATION ISSUES

1. Commission Notice on definition of the relevant market

(88) The Commission Notice on definition of the relevant market for the purposes of Community competition law[26] provides guidance on the rules, criteria and evidence which the Commission uses when considering market definition issues. That Notice will not be further explained in these Guidelines and should serve as the basis for market definition issues. These Guidelines will only deal with specific issues that arise in the context of vertical restraints and that are not dealt with in the general notice on market definition.

---

[26] OJ C 372, 9.12.1997, p.5.

2. The relevant market for calculating the 30% market share threshold under the Block Exemption Regulation

(89) Under Article 3 of the Block Exemption Regulation, it is in general the market share of the supplier that is decisive for the application of the block exemption. In the case of vertical agreements concluded between an association of retailers and individual members, the association is the supplier and needs to take into account its market share as a supplier. Only in the case of exclusive supply as defined in Article 1(c) of the Block Exemption Regulation is it the market share of the buyer, and only that market share, which is decisive for the application of the Block Exemption Regulation.

(90) In order to calculate the market share, it is necessary to determine the relevant market. For this, the relevant product market and the relevant geographic market must be defined. The relevant product market comprises any goods or services which are regarded by the buyer as interchangeable, by reason of their characteristics, prices and intended use. The relevant geographic market comprises the area in which the undertakings concerned are involved in the supply and demand of relevant goods or services, in which the conditions of competition are sufficiently homogeneous, and which can be distinguished from neighbouring geographic areas because, in particular, conditions

of competition are appreciably different in those areas.

(91) For the application of the Block Exemption Regulation, the market share of the supplier is his share on the relevant product and geographic market on which he sells to his buyers.[27] In the example given in paragraph 92, this is market A. The product market depends in the first place on substitutability from the buyers' perspective. When the supplied product is used as an input to produce other products and is generally not recognisable in the final product, the product market is normally defined by the direct buyers' preferences. The customers of the buyers will normally not have a strong preference concerning the inputs used by the buyers. Usually the vertical restraints agreed between the supplier and buyer of the input only relate to the sale and purchase of the intermediate product and not to the sale of the resulting product. In the case of distribution of final goods, what are substitutes for the direct buyers will normally be influenced or determined by the preferences of the final consumers. A distributor, as reseller, cannot ignore the

_____

[27] For example, the Dutch market for new replacement truck and bus tyres in the *Michelin* case (Case 322/81 *Nederlandsche Banden-Industrie Michelin* v. *Commission* [1983] ECR 3461), the various meat markets in the Danish slaughter-house case: Commission Decision 2000/42/EC in Case No IV/M.1313 – *Danish Crown/Vestjyske Slagterier*, OJ L 20, 25.1.2000, p. 1.

preferences of final consumers when he purchases final goods. In addition, at the distribution level the vertical restraints usually concern not only the sale of products between supplier and buyer, but also their resale. As different distribution formats usually compete, markets are in general not defined by the form of distribution that is applied. Where suppliers generally sell a portfolio of products, the entire portfolio may determine the product market when the portfolios and not the individual products are regarded as substitutes by the buyers. As the buyers on market A are professional buyers, the geographic market is usually wider than the market where the product is resold to final consumers. Often, this will lead to the definition of national markets or wider geographic markets.

(92) In the case of exclusive supply, the buyer's market share is his share of all purchases on the relevant purchase market.[28] In the example below, this is also market A.

(93) Where a vertical agreement involves three parties, each operating at a different level of trade, their market shares will have to be below the market share threshold of 30% at both levels in order to benefit from the block exemption. If for instance, in an agreement between a manufacturer, a whole-

saler (or association of retailers) and a retailer, a non-compete obligation is agreed, then the market share of both the manufacturer and the wholesaler (or association of retailers) must not exceed 30% in order to benefit from the block exemption.

(94) Where a supplier produces both original equipment and the repair or replacement parts for this equipment, the supplier will often be the only or the major supplier on the after-market for the repair and replacement parts. This may also arise where the supplier (OEM supplier) subcontracts the manufacturing of the repair or replacement parts. The relevant market for application of the Block Exemption Regulation may be the original equipment market including the spare parts or a separate original equipment market and after-market depending on the circumstances of the case, such as the effects of the restrictions involved, the lifetime of the equipment and importance of the repair or replacement costs[29].

---

[28] For an example of purchase markets, see Commission Decision 1999/674/EC in Case No IV/M.1221 – *Rewe/Meinl*, OJ L 274, 23.10.1999, p. 1.

[29] See for example *Pelikan/Kyocera* in XXV Report on Competition Policy, point 87, and Commission Decision 91/595/EEC in Case No IV/M.12 – *Varta/Bosch*, OJ L 320, 22.11.1991, p. 26, Commission Decision in Case No IV/M.1094 – *Caterpillar/Perkins Engines*, OJ C 94, 28.3.1998, p. 23, and Commission Decision in Case No IV/M.768 – *Lucas/Varity*, OJ C 266, 13.9.1996, p. 6.

See also *Eastman Kodak Co* v. *Image Technical Services, Inc et al*, Supreme Court of the United States, No 90 1029. See also point 56 of the Commission Notice on the definition of relevant market for the purposes of Community competition law.

(95) Where the vertical agreement, in addition to the supply of the contract goods, also contains IPR provisions – such as a provision concerning the use of the supplier's trademark – which help the buyer to market the contract goods, the supplier's market share on the market where he sells the contract goods is decisive for the application of the Block Exemption Regulation. Where a franchisor does not supply goods to be resold but provides a bundle of services combined with IPR provisions which together form the business method being franchised, the franchisor needs to take account of his market share as a provider of a business method. For that purpose, the franchisor needs to calculate his market share on the market where the business method is exploited, which is the market where the franchisees exploit the business method to provide goods or services to end users. The franchisor must base his market share on the value of the goods or services supplied by his franchisees on this market. On such a market the competitors may be providers of other franchised business methods but also suppliers of substitutable goods or services not applying franchising. For instance, without prejudice to the definition of such market, if there was a market for fast-food services, a franchisor operating on such a market would need to calculate his market share on the basis of the relevant sales figures of his franchisees on this market. If the franchisor, in addition to the business method, also supplies certain inputs, such as meat and spices, then the franchisor also needs to calculate his market share on the market where these goods are sold.

3. The relevant market for individual assessment

(96) For individual assessment of vertical agreements not covered by the Block Exemption Regulation, additional markets may need to be investigated besides the relevant market defined for the application of the Block Exemption Regulation. A vertical agreement may not only have effects on the market between supplier and buyer but may also have effects on downstream markets. For an individual assessment of a vertical agreement the relevant markets at each level of trade affected by restraints contained in the agreement will be examined:

(i)   For 'intermediate goods or services' that are incorporated by the buyer into his own goods or services, vertical restraints generally have effects only on the market between supplier and buyer. A non-compete obligation imposed on the buyer for instance may foreclose other suppliers but will not lead to reduced in-store competition downstream. However, in cases of exclusive supply the position of the buyer on his downstream market is also relevant because the buyer's foreclosing behaviour may only have appreciable negative effects if he has market power on the downstream market.

(ii) For 'final products' an analysis limited to the market between supplier and buyer is less likely to be sufficient since vertical restraints may have negative effects of reduced inter-brand and/or intra-brand competition on the resale market, that is on the market downstream of the buyer. For instance, exclusive distribution may not only lead to foreclosure effects on the market between the supplier and the buyer, but may above all lead to less intra-brand competition in the resale territories of the distributors. The resale market is in particular important if the buyer is a retailer selling to final consumers. A non-compete obligation agreed between a manufacturer and a wholesaler may foreclose this wholesaler to other manufacturers but a loss of in-store competition is not very likely at the wholesale level. The same agreement concluded with a retailer may however cause this added loss of in-store inter- brand competition on the resale market.

(iii) In cases of individual assessment of an 'after-market', the relevant market may be the original equipment market or the after-market depending on the circumstances of the case. In any event, the situation on a separate after-market will be evaluated taking account of the situation on the original equipment market. A less significant position on the original equipment market will normally reduce possible anti-competitive effects on the after-market.

4. Calculation of the market share under the Block Exemption Regulation

(97) The calculation of the market share needs to be based in principle on value figures. Where value figures are not available substantiated estimates can be made. Such estimates may be based on other reliable market information such as volume figures (see Article 9(1) of the Block Exemption Regulation).

(98) In-house production, that is production of an intermediate product for own use, may be very important in a competition analysis as one of the competitive constraints or to accentuate the market position of a company. However, for the purpose of market definition and the calculation of market share for intermediate goods and services, in-house production will not be taken into account.

(99) However, in the case of dual distribution of final goods, i.e. where a producer of final goods also acts as a distributor on the market, the market definition and market share calculation need to include the goods sold by the producer and competing producers

through their integrated distributors and agents (see Article 9(2)(b) of the Block Exemption Regulation). 'Integrated distributors' are connected undertakings within the meaning of Article 11 of the Block Exemption Regulation.

VI. ENFORCEMENT POLICY IN INDIVIDUAL CASES

(100) Vertical restraints are generally less harmful than horizontal restraints. The main reason for treating a vertical restraint more leniently than a horizontal restraint lies in the fact that the latter may concern an agreement between competitors producing identical or substitutable goods or services. In such horizontal relationships the exercise of market power by one company (higher price of its product) may benefit its competitors. This may provide an incentive to competitors to induce each other to behave anti- competitively. In vertical relationships the product of the one is the input for the other. This means that the exercise of market power by either the upstream or downstream company would normally hurt the demand for the product of the other. The companies involved in the agreement therefore usually have an incentive to prevent the exercise of market power by the other.

(101) However, this self-restraining character should not be overestimated. When a company has no market power it can only try to increase its profits by optimising its manufacturing and distribution processes, with or without the help of vertical restraints. However, when it does have market power it can also try to increase its profits at the expense of its direct competitors by raising their costs and at the expense of its buyers and ultimately consumers by trying to appropriate some of their surplus. This can happen when the upstream and downstream company share the extra profits or when one of the two uses vertical restraints to appropriate all the extra profits.

(102) In the assessment of individual cases, the Commission will adopt an economic approach in the application of Article 81 to vertical restraints. This will limit the scope of application of Article 81 to undertakings holding a certain degree of market power where inter-brand competition may be insufficient. In those cases, the protection of inter-brand and intra-brand competition is important to ensure efficiencies and benefits for consumers.

1. The framework of analysis

1.1. *Negative Effects of Vertical Restraints*

(103) The negative effects on the market that may result from vertical

restraints which EC competition law aims at preventing are the following:

(i) foreclosure of other suppliers or other buyers by raising barriers to entry;

(ii) reduction of inter-brand competition between the companies operating on a market, including facilitation of collusion amongst suppliers or buyers; by collusion is meant both explicit collusion and tacit collusion (conscious parallel behaviour);

(iii) reduction of intra-brand competition between distributors of the same brand;

(iv) the creation of obstacles to market integration, including, above all, limitations on the freedom of consumers to purchase goods or services in any Member State they may choose.

(104) Such negative effects may result from various vertical restraints. Agreements which are different in form may have the same substantive impact on competition. To analyse these possible negative effects, it is appropriate to divide vertical restraints into four groups: a single branding group, a limited distribution group, a resale price maintenance group and a market partitioning group. The vertical restraints within each group have largely similar negative effects on competition.

(105) The classification into four groups is based upon what can be described as the basic components of vertical restraints. In paragraphs 103 to 136, the four different groups are analysed. In 137 to 229, vertical agreements are analysed as they are used in practice because many vertical agreements make use of more than one of these components.

Single Branding Group

(106) Under the heading of 'single branding' come those agreements which have as their main element that the buyer is induced to concentrate his orders for a particular type of product with one supplier. This component can be found amongst others in non-compete and quantity-forcing on the buyer, where an obligation or incentive scheme agreed between the supplier and the buyer makes the latter purchase his requirements for a particular product and its substitutes only, or mainly, from one supplier. The same component can be found in tying, where the obligation or incentive scheme relates to a product that the buyer is required to purchase as a condition of purchasing another distinct product. The first product is referred to as the 'tied' product

and the second is referred to as the 'tying' product.

(107) There are four main negative effects on competition:

  (1) other suppliers in that market cannot sell to the particular buyers and this may lead to foreclosure of the market or, in the case of tying, to foreclosure of the market for the tied product;

  (2) it makes market shares more rigid and this may help collusion when applied by several suppliers;

  (3) as far as the distribution of final goods is concerned, the particular retailers will only sell one brand and there will therefore be no inter-brand competition in their shops (no in-store competition); and (4) in the case of tying, the buyer may pay a higher price for the tied product than he would otherwise do. All these effects may lead to a reduction in inter-brand competition.

(108) The reduction in inter-brand competition may be mitigated by strong initial competition between suppliers to obtain the single branding contracts, but the longer the duration of the non-compete obligation, the more likely it will be that this effect will not be strong enough to compensate for the reduction in inter-brand competition.

Limited Distribution Group

(109) Under the heading of 'limited distribution' come those agreements which have as their main element that the manufacturer sells to only one or a limited number of buyers. This may be to restrict the number of buyers for a particular territory or group of customers, or to select a particular kind of buyers. This component can be found amongst others in:

— exclusive distribution and exclusive customer allocation, where the supplier limits his sales to only one buyer for a certain territory or class of customers;

— exclusive supply and quantity-forcing on the supplier, where an obligation or incentive scheme agreed between the supplier and the buyer makes the former sell only or mainly to one buyer;

— selective distribution, where the conditions imposed on or agreed with the selected dealers usually limit their number;

— after-market sales restrictions which limit the component supplier's sales possibilities.

(110) There are three main negative effects on competition:

(1)   certain buyers within that market can no longer buy from that particular supplier, and this may lead in particular in the case of exclusive supply, to foreclosure of the purchase market, (2) when most or all of the competing suppliers limit the number of retailers, this may facilitate collusion, either at the distributor's level or at the supplier's level, and (3) since fewer distributors will offer the product it will also lead to a reduction of intra-brand competition. In the case of wide exclusive territories or exclusive customer allocation the result may be total elimination of intra-brand competition. This reduction of intra-brand competition can in turn lead to a weakening of inter-brand competition.

Resale Price Maintenance Group

(111) Under the heading of 'resale price maintenance' (RPM) come those agreements whose main element is that the buyer is obliged or induced to resell not below a certain price, at a certain price or not above a certain price. This group comprises minimum, fixed, maximum and recommended resale prices. Maximum and recommended resale prices, which are not hardcore restrictions, may still lead to a restriction of competition by effect.

(112) There are two main negative effects of RPM on competition:

(1)   a reduction in intra-brand price competition, and (2) increased transparency on prices. In the case of fixed or minimum RPM, distributors can no longer compete on price for that brand, leading to a total elimination of intra-brand price competition. A maximum or recommended price may work as a focal point for resellers, leading to a more or less uniform application of that price level. Increased transparency on price and responsibility for price changes makes horizontal collusion between manufacturers or distributors easier, at least in concentrated markets. The reduction in intra-brand competition may, as it leads to less downward pressure on the price for the particular goods, have as an indirect effect a reduction of inter-brand competition.

Market Partitioning Group

(113) Under the heading of 'market partitioning' come agreements whose main element is that the buyer is restricted in where he either sources or resells a particular product. This component can be found in exclusive

urchasing, where an obligation or incentive scheme agreed between the supplier and the buyer makes the latter purchase his requirements for a particular product, for instance beer of brand X, exclusively from the designated supplier, but leaving the buyer free to buy and sell competing products, for instance competing brands of beer. It also includes territorial resale restrictions, the allocation of an area of primary responsibility, restrictions on the location of a distributor and customer resale restrictions.

(114) The main negative effect on competition is a reduction of intra-brand competition that may help the supplier to partition the market and thus hinder market integration. This may facilitate price discrimination. When most or all of the competing suppliers limit the sourcing or resale possibilities of their buyers this may facilitate collusion, either at the distributors' level or at the suppliers' level.

1.2. Positive effects of vertical restraints

(115) It is important to recognise that vertical restraints often have positive effects by, in particular, promoting non-price competition and improved quality of services. When a company has no market power, it can only try to increase its profits by optimising its manufacturing or distribution processes. In a number of situations vertical restraints may be helpful in this respect since the usual arm's length dealings between supplier and buyer, determining only price and quantity of a certain transaction, can lead to a sub-optimal level of investments and sales.

(116) While trying to give a fair overview of the various justifications for vertical restraints, these Guidelines do not claim to be complete or exhaustive. The following reasons may justify the application of certain vertical restraints:

(1) To 'solve a 'free-rider' problem'. One distributor may free-ride on the promotion efforts of another distributor. This type of problem is most common at the wholesale and retail level. Exclusive distribution or similar restrictions may be helpful in avoiding such free-riding. Free-riding can also occur between suppliers, for instance where one invests in promotion at the buyer's premises, in general at the retail level, that may also attract customers for its competitors. Non-compete type restraints can help to overcome this situation of free-riding.

For there to be a problem, there needs to be a real free-rider issue. Free-riding between buyers can only occur on pre-sales services and not on after-sales services. The product will usually need to be relatively new or technically complex as the customer may otherwise very well know what he or she wants, based on past purchases. And the product must be of a reasonably high value as it is otherwise not attractive for a customer to go to one shop for information and to another to buy. Lastly, it must not be practical for the supplier to impose on all buyers, by contract, effective service requirements concerning pre-sales services.

Free-riding between suppliers is also restricted to specific situations, namely in cases where the promotion takes place at the buyer's premises and is generic, not brand specific.

(2)   To 'open up or enter new markets'. Where a manufacturer wants to enter a new geographic market, for instance by exporting to another country for the first time, this may involve special 'first time investments' by the distributor to establish the brand in the market. In order to persuade a local distributor to make these investments it may be necessary to pro-

vide territorial protection to the distributor so that he can recoup these investments by temporarily charging a higher price. Distributors based in other markets should then be restrained for a limited period from selling in the new market. This is a special case of the free-rider problem described under point (1).

(3)   The 'certification free-rider issue'. In some sectors, certain retailers have a reputation for stocking only 'quality' products. In such a case, selling through these retailers may be vital for the introduction of a new product. If the manufacturer cannot initially limit his sales to the premium stores, he runs the risk of being de-listed and the product introduction may fail. This means that there may be a reason for allowing for a limited duration a restriction such as exclusive distribution or selective distribution. It must be enough to guarantee introduction of the new product but not so long as to hinder large-scale dissemination. Such benefits are more likely with 'experience' goods or complex goods that represent a relatively large purchase for the final consumer.

(4) The so-called 'hold-up problem'. Sometimes there are client-specific investments to be made by either the supplier or the buyer, such as in special equipment or training. For instance, a component manufacturer that has to build new machines and tools in order to satisfy a particular requirement of one of his customers. The investor may not commit the necessary investments before particular supply arrangements are fixed.

However, as in the other free-riding examples, there are a number of conditions that have to be met before the risk of under-investment is real or significant. Firstly, the investment must be relationship-specific. An investment made by the supplier is considered to be relationship-specific when, after termination of the contract, it cannot be used by the supplier to supply other customers and can only be sold at a significant loss. An investment made by the buyer is considered to be relationship-specific when, after termination of the contract, it cannot be used by the buyer to purchase and/or use products supplied by other suppliers and can only be sold at a significant loss. An invest-ment is thus relationship-specific because for instance it can only be used to produce a brand-specific component or to store a particular brand and thus cannot be used profitably to produce or resell alternatives. Secondly, it must be a long-term investment that is not recouped in the short run. And thirdly, the investment must be asymmetric; i.e. one party to the contract invests more than the other party. When these conditions are met, there is usually a good reason to have a vertical restraint for the duration it takes to depreciate the investment. The appropriate vertical restraint will be of the non-compete type or quantity-forcing type when the investment is made by the supplier and of the exclusive distribution, exclusive customer allocation or exclusive supply type when the investment is made by the buyer.

(5) The 'specific hold-up problem that may arise in the case of transfer of substantial know-how'. The know-how, once provided, cannot be taken back and the provider of the know-how may not want it to be used for or by his competitors. In as far as the know-how was not readily available to the buyer, is

substantial and indispensable for the operation of the agreement, such a transfer may justify a non-compete type of restriction. This would normally fall outside Article 81(1).

(6) 'Economies of scale in distribution'. In order to have scale economies exploited and thereby see a lower retail price for his product, the manufacturer may want to concentrate the resale of his products on a limited number of distributors. For this he could use exclusive distribution, quantity forcing in the form of a minimum purchasing requirement, selective distribution containing such a requirement or exclusive purchasing.

(7) 'Capital market imperfections'. The usual providers of capital (banks, equity markets) may provide capital sub-optimally when they have imperfect information on the quality of the borrower or there is an inadequate basis to secure the loan. The buyer or supplier may have better information and be able, through an exclusive relationship, to obtain extra security for his investment. Where the supplier provides the loan to the buyer this may lead to non-compete or quantity forcing on the buyer. Where the buyer

provides the loan to the supplier this may be the reason for having exclusive supply or quantity forcing on the supplier.

(8) 'Uniformity and quality standardisation'. A vertical restraint may help to increase sales by creating a brand image and thereby increasing the attractiveness of a product to the final consumer by imposing a certain measure of uniformity and quality standardisation on the distributors. This can for instance be found in selective distribution and franchising.

(117) The eight situations mentioned in paragraph 116 make clear that under certain conditions vertical agreements are likely to help realise efficiencies and the development of new markets and that this may offset possible negative effects. The case is in general strongest for vertical restraints of a limited duration which help the introduction of new complex products or protect relationship-specific investments. A vertical restraint is sometimes necessary for as long as the supplier sells his product to the buyer (see in particular the situations described in paragraph 116, points (1), (5), (6) and (8).

(118) There is a large measure of substitutability between the

different vertical restraints. This means that the same inefficiency problem can be solved by different vertical restraints. For instance, economies of scale in distribution may possibly be achieved by using exclusive distribution, selective distribution, quantity forcing or exclusive purchasing. This is important as the negative effects on competition may differ between the various vertical restraints. This plays a role when indispensability is discussed under Article 81(3).

1.3. General rules for the evaluation of vertical restraints

(119) In evaluating vertical restraints from a competition policy perspective, some general rules can be formulated:

(1) For most vertical restraints competition concerns can only arise if there is insufficient inter-brand competition, i.e. if there exists a certain degree of market power at the level of the supplier or the buyer or both. Conceptually, market power is the power to raise price above the competitive level and, at least in the short term, to obtain supra-normal profits. Companies may have market power below the level of market dominance, which is the threshold for the application of Article 82. Where there are many firms competing in an unconcentrated market, it can be assumed that non-hardcore vertical restraints will not have appreciable negative effects. A market is deemed unconcentrated when the HHI index, i.e. the sum of the squares of the individual market shares of all companies in the relevant market, is below 1000.

(2) Vertical restraints which reduce inter-brand competition are generally more harmful than vertical restraints that reduce intra-brand competition. For instance, non-compete obligations are likely to have more net negative effects than exclusive distribution. The former, by possibly foreclosing the market to other brands, may prevent those brands from reaching the market. The latter, while limiting intra-brand competition, does not prevent goods from reaching the final consumer.

(3) Vertical restraints from the limited distribution group, in the absence of sufficient inter-brand competition, may significantly restrict the choices available to consumers. They are particularly harmful when

more efficient distributors or distributors with a different distribution format are foreclosed. This can reduce innovation in distribution and denies consumers the particular service or price-service combination of these distributors.

(4) Exclusive dealing arrangements are generally worse for competition than non-exclusive arrangements. Exclusive dealing makes, by the express language of the contract or its practical effects, one party fulfil all or practically all its requirements from another party. For instance, under a non-compete obligation the buyer purchases only one brand. Quantity forcing, on the other hand, leaves the buyer some scope to purchase competing goods. The degree of foreclosure may therefore be less with quantity forcing.

(5) Vertical restraints agreed for non-branded goods and services are in general less harmful than restraints affecting the distribution of branded goods and services. Branding tends to increase product differentiation and reduce substitutability of the product, leading to a reduced elasticity of demand and an increased possibility to raise price. The distinction between branded and non-branded goods or services will often coincide with the distinction between intermediate goods and services and final goods and services.

Intermediate goods and services are sold to undertakings for use as an input to produce other goods or services and are generally not recognisable in the final goods or services. The buyers of intermediate products are usually well-informed customers, able to assess quality and therefore less reliant on brand and image. Final goods are, directly or indirectly, sold to final consumers who often rely more on brand and image. As distributors (retailers, wholesalers) have to respond to the demand of final consumers, competition may suffer more when distributors are foreclosed from selling one or a number of brands than when buyers of intermediate products are prevented from buying competing products from certain sources of supply.

The undertakings buying intermediate goods or services normally have specialist departments or advisers who monitor developments in the supply market. Because they effect sizeable transactions, search costs are in general not prohibitive. A loss of intra-brand competition is therefore less important at the intermediate level.

(6) In general, a combination of vertical restraints aggravates their negative effects. However, certain combinations of vertical restraints are better for competition than their use in isolation from each other. For instance, in an exclusive distribution system, the distributor may be tempted to increase the price of the products as intra-brand competition has been reduced. The use of quantity forcing or the setting of a maximum resale price may limit such price increases.

(7) Possible negative effects of vertical restraints are reinforced when several suppliers and their buyers organise their trade in a similar way. These so-called cumulative effects may be a problem in a number of sectors.

(8) The more the vertical restraint is linked to the transfer of know-how, the more reason there may be

to expect efficiencies to arise and the more a vertical restraint may be necessary to protect the know-how transferred or the investment costs incurred.

(9) The more the vertical restraint is linked to investments which are relationship-specific, the more justification there is for certain vertical restraints. The justified duration will depend on the time necessary to depreciate the investment.

(10) In the case of a new product, or where an existing product is sold for the first time on a different geographic market, it may be difficult for the company to define the market or its market share may be very high. However, this should not be considered a major problem, as vertical restraints linked to opening up new product or geographic markets in general do not restrict competition. This rule holds, irrespective of the market share of the company, for two years after the first putting on the market of the product. It applies to all non-hardcore vertical restraints and, in the case of a new geographic market, to restrictions on active and

passive sales imposed on the direct buyers of the supplier located in other markets to intermediaries in the new market. In the case of genuine testing of a new product in a limited territory or with a limited customer group, the distributors appointed to sell the new product on the test market can be restricted in their active selling outside the test market for a maximum period of 1 year without being caught by Article 81(1).

1.4. Methodology of analysis

(120) The assessment of a vertical restraint involves in general the following four steps:

(1) First, the undertakings involved need to define the relevant market in order to establish the market share of the supplier or the buyer, depending on the vertical restraint involved (see paragraphs 88 to 99, in particular 89 to 95).

(2) If the relevant market share does not exceed the 30% threshold, the vertical agreement is covered by the Block Exemption Regulation, subject to the hardcore restrictions and conditions set out in that regulation.

(3) If the relevant market share is above the 30% threshold,

it is necessary to assess whether the vertical agreement falls within Article 81(1).

(4) If the vertical agreement falls within Article 81(1), it is necessary to examine whether it fulfils the conditions for exemption under Article 81(3).

1.4.1. Relevant factors for the assessment under Article 81(1)

(121) In assessing cases above the market share threshold of 30%, the Commission will make a full competition analysis. The following factors are the most important to establish whether a vertical agreement brings about an appreciable restriction of competition under Article 81(1):

(a) market position of the supplier;

(b) market position of competitors;

(c) market position of the buyer;

(d) entry barriers;

(e) maturity of the market;

(f) level of trade;

(g) nature of the product;

(h) other factors.

(122) The importance of individual factors may vary from case to case and depends on all other

factors. For instance, a high market share of the supplier is usually a good indicator of market power, but in the case of low entry barriers it may not indicate market power. It is therefore not possible to provide strict rules on the importance of the individual factors. However the following can be said:

Market Position of the Supplier

(123) The market position of the supplier is established first and foremost by his market share on the relevant product and geographic market. The higher his market share, the greater his market power is likely to be. The market position of the supplier is further strengthened if he has certain cost advantages over his competitors. These competitive advantages may result from a first mover advantage (having the best site, etc.), holding essential patents, having superior technology, being the brand leader or having a superior portfolio.

Market Position of Competitors

(124) The same indicators, that is market share and possible competitive advantages, are used to describe the market position of competitors. The stronger the established competitors are and the greater their number, the less risk there is that the supplier or buyer in question will be able to foreclose the market individu-

ally and the less there is a risk of a reduction of inter-brand competition. However, if the number of competitors becomes rather small and their market position (size, costs, R & D potential, etc.) is rather similar, this market structure may increase the risk of collusion. Fluctuating or rapidly changing market shares are in general an indication of intense competition.

Market Position of the Buyer

(125) Buying power derives from the market position of the buyer. The first indicator of buying power is the market share of the buyer on the purchase market. This share reflects the importance of his demand for his possible suppliers. Other indicators focus on the market position of the buyer on his resale market including characteristics such as a wide geographic spread of his outlets, own brands of the buyer/distributor and his image amongst final consumers. The effect of buying power on the likelihood of anti-competitive effects is not the same for the different vertical restraints. Buying power may in particular increase the negative effects in case of restraints from the limited distribution and market partitioning groups such as exclusive supply, exclusive distribution and quantitative selective distribution.

Entry Barriers

(126) Entry barriers are measured by the extent to which incumbent companies can increase their price above the competitive level, usually above minimum average total cost, and make supra-normal profits without attracting entry. Without any entry barriers, easy and quick entry would eliminate such profits. In as far as effective entry, which would prevent orerode the supra-normal profits, is likely to occur within one or two years, entry barriers can be said to be low.

(127) Entry barriers may result from a wide variety of factors such as economies of scale and scope, government regulations, especially where they establish exclusive rights, state aid, import tariffs, intellectual property rights, ownership of resources where the supply is limited due to for instance natural limitations[30], essential facilities, a first mover advantage and brand loyalty of consumers created by strong advertising. Vertical restraints and vertical integration may also work as an entry barrier by making access more difficult and foreclosing (potential) competitors. Entry barriers may be present at only the supplier or buyer level or at both levels.

---

[30] See Commission Decision 97/26/EC (Case No IV/M.619 – Gencor/Lonrho), (OJ L 11, 14.1.1997, p. 30).

(128) The question whether certain of these factors should be described as entry barriers depends on whether they are related to sunk costs. Sunk costs are those costs that have to be incurred to enter or be active on a market but that are lost when the market is exited. Advertising costs to build consumer loyalty are normally sunk costs, unless an exiting firm could either sell its brand name or use it somewhere else without a loss. The more costs are sunk, the more potential entrants have to weigh the risks of entering the market and the more credibly incumbents can threaten that they will match new competition, as sunk costs make it costly for incumbents to leave the market. If, for instance, distributors are tied to a manufacturer via a non-compete obligation, the foreclosing effect will be more significant if setting up its own distributors will impose sunk costs on the potential entrant.

(129) In general, entry requires sunk costs, sometimes minor and sometimes major. Therefore, actual competition is in general more effective and will weigh more in the assessment of a case than potential competition.

Maturity of the Market

(130) A mature market is a market that has existed for some time, where the technology used is well known and widespread and

ot changing very much, where there are no major brand innovations and in which demand is relatively stable or declining. In such a market negative effects are more likely than in more dynamic markets.

Level of Trade

(131) The level of trade is linked to the distinction between intermediate and final goods and services. As indicated earlier, negative effects are in general less likely at the level of intermediate goods and services.

Nature of the Product

(132) The nature of the product plays a role in particular for final products in assessing both the likely negative and the likely positive effects. When assessing the likely negative effects, it is important whether the products on the market are more homogeneous or heterogeneous, whether the product is expensive, taking up a large part of the consumer's budget, or is inexpensive and whether the product is a one-off purchase or repeatedly purchased. In general, when the product is more heterogeneous, less expensive and resembles more a one-off purchase, vertical restraints are more likely to have negative effects.

Other Factors

(133) In the assessment of particular restraints other factors may have to be taken into account. Among these factors can be the cumulative effect, i.e. the coverage of the market by similar agreements, the duration of the agreements, whether the agreement is 'imposed' (mainly one party is subject to the restrictions or obligations) or 'agreed' (both parties accept restrictions or obligations), the regulatory environment and behaviour that may indicate or facilitate collusion like price leadership, preannounced price changes and discussions on the 'right' price, price rigidity in response to excess capacity, price discrimination and past collusive behaviour.

1.4.2. Relevant factors for the assessment under Article 81(3)

(134) There are four cumulative conditions for the application of Article 81(3):

— the vertical agreement must contribute to improving production or distribution or to promoting technical or economic progress;

— the vertical agreement must allow consumers a fair share of these benefits;

— the vertical agreement must not impose on the undertakings concerned vertical restraints which are not indispensable to the attainment of these benefits;

— the vertical agreement must not afford such undertakings the possibility of eliminating competition in respect of a substantial part of the products in question.

(135) The last criterion of elimination of competition for a substantial part of the products in question is related to the question of dominance. Where an undertaking is dominant or becoming dominant as a consequence of the vertical agreement, a vertical restraint that has appreciable anti-competitive effects can in principle not be exempted. The vertical agreement may however fall outside Article 81(1) if there is an objective justification, for instance if it is necessary for the protection of relationship-specific investments or for the transfer of substantial know-how without which the supply or purchase of certain goods or services would not take place.

(136) Where the supplier and the buyer are not dominant, the other three criteria become important. The first, concerning the improvement of production or distribution and the promotion of technical or economic progress, refers to the type of efficiencies described inparagraphs 115 to 118. These efficiencies have to be substantiated and must produce a net positive effect. Speculative claims on avoidance of free-riding or general statements on cost savings will not be accepted. Cost savings that arise from the mere exercise of market power or from anti-competitive conduct cannot be accepted. Secondly, economic benefits have to favour not only the parties to the agreement, but also the consumer. Generally the transmission of the benefits to consumers will depend on the intensity of competition on the relevant market. Competitive pressures will normally ensure that cost-savings are passed on by way of lower prices or that companies have an incentive to bring new products to the market as quickly as possible. Therefore, if sufficient competition which effectively constrains the parties to the agreement is maintained on the market, the competitive process will normally ensure that consumers receive a fair share of the economic benefits. The third criterion will play a role in ensuring that the least anti-competitive restraint is chosen to obtain certain positive effects.

2. Analysis of specific vertical restraints

(137) Vertical agreements may contain a combination of two or more of the components of vertical restraints described in paragraphs 103 to 114. The most common vertical restraints and combinations of vertical restraints are analysed below following the methodology of

nalysis developed in paragraphs 120 to 136.

2.1. Single branding

(138) A non-compete arrangement is based on an obligation or incentive scheme which makes the buyer purchase practically all his requirements on a particular market from only one supplier. It does not mean that the buyer can only buy directly from the supplier, but that the buyer will not buy and resell or incorporate competing goods or services. The possible competition risks are foreclosure of the market to competing suppliers and potential suppliers, facilitation of collusion between suppliers in case of cumulative use and, where the buyer is a retailer selling to final consumers, a loss of in-store inter-brand competition. All three restrictive effects have a direct impact on inter-brand competition.

(139) Single branding is exempted by the Block Exemption Regulation when the supplier's market share does not exceed 30% and subject to a limitation in time of five years for the non-compete obligation. Above the market share threshold or beyond the time limit of five years, the following guidance is provided for the assessment of individual cases.

(140) The 'market position of the supplier' is of main importance to assess possible anti-competitive effects of non-compete obligations. In general, this type of obligation is imposed by the supplier and the supplier has similar agreements with other buyers.

(141) It is not only the market position of the supplier that is of importance but also the extent to and the duration for which he applies a non-compete obligation. The higher his tied market share, i.e. the part of his market share sold under a single branding obligation, the more significant foreclosure is likely to be. Similarly, the longer the duration of the non-compete obligations, the more significant foreclosure is likely to be. Non-compete obligations shorter than one year entered into by non-dominant companies are in general not considered to give rise to appreciable anti-competitive effects or net negative effects. Non-compete obligations between one and five years entered into by non-dominant companies usually require a proper balancing of pro- and anti-competitive effects, while non-compete obligations exceeding five years are for most types of investments not considered necessary to achieve the claimed efficiencies or the efficiencies are not sufficient to outweigh their foreclosure effect. Dominant companies may not impose non-compete obligations on their buyers unless they can objectively

justify such commercial practice within the context of Article 82.

(142) In assessing the supplier's market power, the 'market position of his competitors' is important. As long as the competitors are sufficiently numerous and strong, no appreciable anti-competitive effects can be expected. It is only likely that competing suppliers will be foreclosed if they are significantly smaller than the supplier applying the non-compete obligation. Foreclosure of competitors is not very likely where they have similar market positions and can offer similarly attractive products. In such a case foreclosure may however occur for potential entrants when a number of major suppliers enter into non-compete contracts with a significant number of buyers on the relevant market (cumulative effect situation). This is also a situation where non-compete agreements may facilitate collusion between competing suppliers. If individually these suppliers are covered by the Block Exemption Regulation, a withdrawal of the block exemption may be necessary to deal with such a negative cumulative effect. A tied market share of less than 5% is not considered in general to contribute significantly to a cumulative foreclosure effect.

(143) In cases where the market share of the largest supplier is below 30 % and the market share of the five largest suppliers (concentration rate (CR) 5) is below 50%, there is unlikely to be a single or a cumulative anti-competitive effect situation. If a potential entrant cannot penetrate the market profitably, this is likely to be due to factors other than non-compete obligations, such as consumer preferences. A competition problem is unlikely to arise when, for instance, 50 companies, of which none has an important market share, compete fiercely on a particular market.

(144) 'Entry barriers' are important to establish whether there is real foreclosure. Wherever it is relatively easy for competing suppliers to create new buyers or find alternative buyers for the product, foreclosure is unlikely to be a real problem. However, there are often entry barriers, both at the manufacturing and at the distribution level.

(145) 'Countervailing power' is relevant, as powerful buyers will not easily allow themselves to be cut off from the supply of competing goods or services. Foreclosure which is not based on efficiency and which has harmful effects on ultimate consumers is therefore mainly a risk in the case of dispersed buyers. However, where non-compete agreements are concluded with major buyers this may have a strong foreclosure effect.

(146) Lastly, 'the level of trade' is relevant for foreclosure. Foreclosure is less likely in case of an intermediate product. When the supplier of an intermediate product is not dominant, the competing suppliers still have a substantial part of demand that is 'free'. Below the level of dominance a serious foreclosure effect may however arise for actual or potential competitors where there is a cumulative effect. A serious cumulative effect is unlikely to arise as long as less than 50% of the market is tied. When the supplier is dominant, any obligation to buy the products only or mainly from the dominant supplier may easily lead to significant foreclosure effects on the market. The stronger his dominance, the higher the risk of foreclosure of other competitors.

(147) Where the agreement concerns supply of a final product at the wholesale level, the question whether a competition problem is likely to arise below the level of dominance depends in large part on the type of wholesaling and the entry barriers at the wholesale level. There is no real risk of foreclosure if competing manufacturers can easily establish their own wholesaling operation. Whether entry barriers are low depends in part on the type of wholesaling, i.e. whether or not wholesalers can operate efficiently with only the product concerned by the agreement (for

example ice cream) or whether it is more efficient to trade in a whole range of products (for example frozen foodstuffs). In the latter case, it is not efficient for a manufacturer selling only one product to set up his own wholesaling operation. In that case anti-competitive effects may arise below the level of dominance. In addition, cumulative effect problems may arise if several suppliers tie most of the available wholesalers.

(148) For final products, foreclosure is in general more likely to occur at the retail level, given the significant entry barriers for most manufacturers to start retail outlets just for their own products. In addition, it is at the retail level that non-compete agreements may lead to reduced in-store inter-brand competition. It is for these reasons that for final products at the retail level, significant anti-competitive effects may start to arise, taking into account all other relevant factors, if a non-dominant supplier ties 30% or more of the relevant market. For a dominant company, even a modest tied market share may already lead to significant anti-competitive effects. The stronger its dominance, the higher the risk of foreclosure of other competitors.

(149) At the retail level a cumulative foreclosure effect may also arise. When all companies have market shares below 30% a

cumulative foreclosure effect is unlikely if the total tied market share is less than 40 % and withdrawal of the block exemption is therefore unlikely. This figure may be higher when other factors like the number of competitors, entry barriers etc. are taken into account. When not all companies have market shares below the threshold of the Block Exemption Regulation but none is dominant, a cumulative foreclosure effect is unlikely if the total tied market share is below 30%.

(150) Where the buyer operates from premises and land owned by the supplier or leased by the supplier from a third party not connected with the buyer, the possibility of imposing effective remedies for a possible foreclosure effect will be limited. In that case intervention by the Commission below the level of dominance is unlikely.

(151) In certain sectors the selling of more than one brand from a single site may be difficult, in which case a foreclosure problem can better be remedied by limiting the effective duration of contracts.

(152) A so-called 'English clause', requiring the buyer to report any better offer and allowing him only to accept such an offer when the supplier does not match it, can be expected to have the same effect as a non-compete obligation, especially when the buyer has to reveal who makes the better offer. In addition, by increasing the transparency of the market it may facilitate collusion between the suppliers. An English clause may also work as quantity- forcing. Quantity-forcing on the buyer is a weaker form of non-compete, where incentives or obligations agreed between the supplier and the buyer make the latter concentrate his purchases to a large extent with one supplier. Quantity- forcing may for example take the form of minimum purchase requirements or non- linear pricing, such as quantity rebate schemes, loyalty rebate schemes or a two-part tariff (fixed fee plus a price per unit). Quantity-forcing on the buyer will have similar but weaker foreclosure effects than a non-compete obligation. The assessment of all these different forms will depend on their effect on the market. In addition, Article 82 specifically prevents dominant companies from applying English clauses or fidelity rebate schemes.

(153) Where appreciable anticompetitive effects are established, the question of a possible exemption under Article 81(3) arises as long as the supplier is not dominant. For non-compete obligations, the efficiencies described in paragraph 116, points 1 (free riding between suppliers), 4, 5 (hold-up problems)

and 7 (capital market imperfections) may be particularly relevant.

(154) In the case of an efficiency as described in paragraph 116, points 1, 4 and 7, quantity forcing on the buyer could possibly be a less restrictive alternative. A non-compete obligation may be the only viable way to achieve an efficiency as described in paragraph 116, point 5 (hold-up problem related to the transfer of know-how).

(155) In the case of a relationship-specific investment made by the supplier (see efficiency 4 in paragraph 116), a non-compete or quantity forcing agreement for the period of depreciation of the investment will in general fulfil the conditions of Article 81(3). In the case of high relationship-specific investments, a non-compete obligation exceeding five years may be justified. A relationship-specific investment could, for instance, be the installation or adaptation of equipment by the supplier when this equipment can be used afterwards only to produce components for a particular buyer. General or market-specific investments in (extra) capacity are normally not relationship-specific investments. However, where a supplier creates new capacity specifically linked to the operations of a particular buyer, for instance a company producing metal cans which creates new capacity to produce cans on the premises of or next to the canning facility of a food producer, this new capacity may only be economically viable when producing for this particular customer, in which case the investment would be considered to be relationship-specific.

(156) Where the supplier provides the buyer with a loan or provides the buyer with equipment which is not relationship-specific, this in itself is normally not sufficient to justify the exemption of a foreclosure effect on the market. The instances of capital market imperfection, whereby it is more efficient for the supplier of a product than for a bank to provide a loan, will be limited (see efficiency 7 in paragraph 116). Even if the supplier of the product were to be the more efficient provider of capital, a loan could only justify a non- compete obligation if the buyer is not prevented from terminating the non- compete obligation and repaying the outstanding part of the loan at any point in time and without payment of any penalty. This means that the repayment of the loan should be structured in equal or decreasing instalments and should not increase over time and that the buyer should have the possibility to take over the equipment provided by the supplier at its market asset value. This is without prejudice to the possibility, in case for example of a new point

of distribution, to delay repayment for the first one or two years until sales have reached a certain level.

(157) The transfer of substantial know-how (efficiency 5 in paragraph 116) usually justifies a non-compete obligation for the whole duration of the supply agreement, as for example in the context of franchising.

(158) Below the level of dominance the combination of non-compete with exclusive distribution may also justify the non-compete obligation lasting the full length of the agreement. In the latter case, the non-compete obligation is likely to improve the distribution efforts of the exclusive distributor in his territory (see paragraphs 161 to 177).

(159) Example of non-compete

The market leader in a national market for an impulse consumer product, with a market share of 40%, sells most of its products (90%) through tied retailers (tied market share 36%). The agreements oblige the retailers to purchase only from the market leader for at least four years. The market leader is especially strongly represented in the more densely populated areas like the capital. Its competitors, 10 in number, of which some are only locally available, all have much smaller market shares, the biggest having 12%. These 10

competitors together supply another 10% of the market via tied outlets. There is strong brand and product differentiation in the market. The market leader has the strongest brands. It is the only one with regular national advertising campaigns. It provides its tied retailers with special stocking cabinets for its product.

The result on the market is that in total 46% (36% + 10%) of the market is foreclosed to potential entrants and to incumbents not having tied outlets. Potential entrants find entry even more difficult in the densely populated areas where foreclosure is even higher, although it is there that they would prefer to enter the market. In addition, owing to the strong brand and product differentiation and the high search costs relative to the price of the product, the absence of in-store inter-brand competition leads to an extra welfare loss for consumers. The possible efficiencies of the outlet exclusivity, which the market leader claims result from reduced transport costs and a possible hold-up problem concerning the stocking cabinets, are limited and do not outweigh the negative effects on competition. The efficiencies are limited, as the transport costs are linked to quantity and not exclusivity and the stocking cabinets do not contain special know-how and are not brand specific. Accordingly, it is unlikely that the conditions for exemption are fulfilled.

(160) Example of quantity forcing

A producer X with a 40% market share sells 80% of its products through contracts which specify that the reseller is required to purchase at least 75% of its requirements for that type of product from X. In return X is offering financing and equipment at favourable rates. The contracts have a duration of five years in which repayment of the loan is foreseen in equal instalments. However, after the first two years buyers have the possibility to terminate the contract with a six-month notice period if they repay the outstanding loan and take over the equipment at its market asset value. At the end of the five-year period the equipment becomes the property of the buyer. Most of the competing producers are small, twelve in total with the biggest having a market share of 20%, and engage in similar contracts with different durations. The producers with market shares below 10% often have contracts with longer durations and with less generous termination clauses. The contracts of producer X leave 25% of requirements free to be supplied by competitors. In the last three years, two new producers have entered the market and gained a combined market share of

around 8%, partly by taking over the loans of a number of resellers in return for contracts with these resellers.

Producer X's tied market share is 24% (0,75 × 0,80 × 40%). The other producers' tied market share is around 25%. Therefore, in total around 49% of the market is foreclosed to potential entrants and to incumbents not having tied outlets for at least the first two years of the supply contracts. The market shows that the resellers often have difficulty in obtaining loans from banks and are too small in general to obtain capital through other means like the issuing of shares. In addition, producer X is able to demonstrate that concentrating his sales on a limited number of resellers allows him to plan his sales better and to save transport costs. In the light of the 25% non-tied part in the contracts of producer X, the real possibility for early termination of the contract, the recent entry of new producers and the fact that around half the resellers are not tied, the quantity forcing of 75% applied by producer X is likely to fulfil the conditions for exemption.

2.2. Exclusive distribution

(161) In an exclusive distribution agreement the supplier agrees to sell his products only to one distributor for resale in a particular

territory. At the same time the distributor is usually limited in his active selling into other exclusively allocated territories. The possible competition risks are mainly reduced intra-brand competition and market partitioning, which may in particular facilitate price discrimination. When most or all of the suppliers apply exclusive distribution this may facilitate collusion, both at the suppliers' and distributors' level.

(162) Exclusive distribution is exempted by the Block Exemption Regulation when the supplier's market share does not exceed 30%, even if combined with other non-hardcore vertical restraints, such as a non-compete obligation limited to five years, quantity forcing or exclusive purchasing. A combination of exclusive distribution and selective distribution is only exempted by the Block Exemption Regulation if active selling in other territories is not restricted. Above the 30% market share threshold, the following guidance is provided for the assessment of exclusive distribution in individual cases.

(163) The market position of the supplier and his competitors is of major importance, as the loss of intra-brand competition can only be problematic if inter-brand competition is limited. The stronger the 'position of the supplier', the more serious is the loss of intra-brand competition. Above the 30% market share threshold there may be a risk of a significant reduction of intra-brand competition. In order to be exemptable, the loss of intra-brand competition needs to be balanced with real efficiencies.

(164) The 'position of the competitors' can have a dual significance. Strong competitors will generally mean that the reduction in intra-brand competition is outweighed by sufficient inter-brand competition. However, if the number of competitors becomes rather small and their market position is rather similar in terms of market share, capacity and distribution network, there is a risk of collusion. The loss of intra-brand competition can increase this risk, especially when several suppliers operate similar distribution systems. Multiple exclusive dealerships, i.e. when different suppliers appoint the same exclusive distributor in a given territory, may further increase the risk of collusion. If a dealer is granted the exclusive right to distribute two or more important competing products in the same territory, inter-brand competition is likely to be substantially restricted for those brands. The higher the cumulative market share of the brands distributed by the multiple dealer, the higher the risk of collusion and the more inter-brand competition will be reduced.

Such cumulative effect situations may be a reason to withdraw the benefit of the Block Exemption Regulation when the market shares of the suppliers are below the threshold of the Block Exemption Regulation.

(165) 'Entry barriers' that may hinder suppliers from creating new distributors or finding alternative distributors are less important in assessing the possible anti-competitive effects of exclusive distribution. Foreclosure of other suppliers does not arise as long as exclusive distribution is not combined with single branding.

(166) Foreclosure of other distributors is not a problem if the supplier which operates the exclusive distribution system appoints a high number of exclusive distributors in the same market and these exclusive distributors are not restricted in selling to other non-appointed distributors. Foreclosure of other distributors may however become a problem where there is 'buying power' and market power downstream, in particular in the case of very large territories where the exclusive distributor becomes the exclusive buyer for a whole market. An example would be a supermarket chain which becomes the only distributor of a leading brand on a national food retail market. The foreclosure of other distributors may be aggravated in the case of multiple exclusive dealership. Such a case,

covered by the Block Exemption Regulation when the market share of each supplier is below 30%, may give reason for withdrawal of the block exemption.

(167) 'Buying power' may also increase the risk of collusion on the buyers' side when the exclusive distribution arrangements are imposed by important buyers, possibly located in different territories, on one or several suppliers.

(168) 'Maturity of the market' is important, as loss of intra-brand competition and price discrimination may be a serious problem in a mature market but may be less relevant in a market with growing demand, changing technologies and changing market positions.

(169) 'The level of trade' is important as the possible negative effects may differ between the wholesale and retail level. Exclusive distribution is mainly applied in the distribution of final goods and services. A loss of intra-brand competition is especially likely at the retail level if coupled with large territories, since final consumers may be confronted with little possibility of choosing between a high price/high service and a low price/low service distributor for an important brand.

(170) A manufacturer which chooses a wholesaler to be his exclusive

distributor will normally do so for a larger territory, such as a whole Member State. As long as the wholesaler can sell the products without limitation to downstream retailers there are not likely to be appreciable anti-competitive effects if the manufacturer is not dominant. A possible loss of intra-brand competition at the wholesale level may be easily outweighed by efficiencies obtained in logistics, promotion etc, especially when the manufacturer is based in a different country. Foreclosure of other wholesalers within that territory is not likely as a supplier with a market share above 30% usually has enough bargaining power not to choose a less efficient wholesaler. The possible risks for inter-brand competition of multiple exclusive dealerships are however higher at the wholesale than at the retail level.

(171) The combination of exclusive distribution with single branding may add the problem of foreclosure of the market to other suppliers, especially in case of a dense network of exclusive distributors with small territories or in case of a cumulative effect. This may necessitate application of the principles set out above on single branding. However, when the combination does not lead to significant foreclosure, the combination of exclusive distribution and single branding may be pro-competitive by increasing the incentive

for the exclusive distributor to focus his efforts on the particular brand. Therefore, in the absence of such a foreclosure effect, the combination of exclusive distribution with non-compete is exemptable for the whole duration of the agreement, particularly at the wholesale level.

(172) The combination of exclusive distribution with exclusive purchasing increases the possible competition risks of reduced intra-brand competition and market partitioning which may in particular facilitate price discrimination. Exclusive distribution already limits arbitrage by customers, as it limits the number of distributors and usually also restricts the distributors in their freedom of active selling. Exclusive purchasing, requiring the exclusive distributors to buy their supplies for the particular brand directly from the manufacturer, eliminates in addition possible arbitrage by the exclusive distributors, who are prevented from buying from other distributors in the system. This enhances the possibilities for the supplier to limit intra-brand competition while applying dissimilar conditions of sale. The combination of exclusive distribution and exclusive purchasing is therefore unlikely to be exempted for suppliers with a market share above 30% unless there are very clear and substantial efficiencies leading to lower prices to all final consumers. lack of such efficiencies

may also lead to withdrawal of the block exemption where the market share of the supplier is below 30%.

(173) The 'nature of the product' is not very relevant to assessing the possible anti-competitive effects of exclusive distribution. It is, however, relevant when the issue of possible efficiencies is discussed, that is after an appreciable anti-competitive effect is established.

(174) Exclusive distribution may lead to efficiencies, especially where investments by the distributors are required to protect or build up the brand image. In general, the case for efficiencies is strongest for new products, for complex products, for products whose qualities are difficult to judge before consumption (so-called experience products) or of which the qualities are difficult to judge even after consumption (so-called credence products). In addition, exclusive distribution may lead to savings in logistic costs due to economies of scale in transport and distribution.

(175) Example of exclusive distribution at the wholesale level

In the market for a consumer durable, A is the market leader. A sells its product through exclusive wholesalers. Territories for the wholesalers correspond to the entire Member State for small Member States, and to a region for larger Member States.

These exclusive distributors take care of sales to all the retailers in their territories. They do not sell to final consumers. The wholesalers are in charge of promotion in their markets. This includes sponsoring of local events, but also explaining and promoting the new products to the retailers in their territories. Technology and product innovation are evolving fairly quickly on this market, and pre-sale service to retailers and to final consumers plays an important role. The wholesalers are not required to purchase all their requirements of the brand of supplier A from the producer himself, and arbitrage by wholesalers or retailers is practicable because the transport costs are relatively low compared to the value of the product. The wholesalers are not under a non-compete obligation. Retailers also sell a number of brands of competing suppliers, and there are no exclusive or selective distribution agreements at the retail level. On the European market of sales to wholesalers A has around 50% market share. Its market share on the various national retail markets varies between 40% and 60%. A has between 6 and 10 competitors on every national market: B, C and D are its biggest competitors and are also present on each national market, with market shares varying between 20% and 5%. The remaining producers are national producers, with smaller market shares.

B, C and D have similar distribution networks, whereas the local producers tend to sell their products directly to retailers.

On the wholesale market described above, the risk of reduced intra-brand competition and price discrimination is low. Arbitrage is not hindered, and the absence of intra-brand competition is not very relevant at the wholesale level. At the retail level neither intra- nor inter-brand competition are hindered. Moreover, inter-brand competition is largely unaffected by the exclusive arrangements at the wholesale level. This makes it likely, if anti-competitive effects exist, that the conditions for exemption are fulfilled.

(176) Example of multiple exclusive dealerships in an oligopolistic market

In a national market for a final product, there are four market leaders, who each have a market share of around 20%. These four market leaders sell their product through exclusive distributors at the retail level. Retailers are given an exclusive territory which corresponds to the town in which they are located or a district of the town for large towns. In most territories, the four market leaders happen to appoint the same exclusive retailer ('multiple dealership'), often centrally located and rather specialised in the product. The remaining 20% of the national market is composed of small local producers, the largest of these producers having a market share of 5% on the national market. These local producers sell their products in general through other retailers, in particular because the exclusive distributors of the four largest suppliers show in general little interest in selling less well-known and cheaper brands. There is strong brand and product differentiation on the market. The four market leaders have large national advertising campaigns and strong brand images, whereas the fringe producers do not advertise their products at the national level. The market is rather mature, with stable demand and no major product and technological innovation. The product is relatively simple.

In such an oligopolistic market, there is a risk of collusion between the four market leaders. This risk is increased through multiple dealerships. Intra-brand competition is limited by the territorial exclusivity. Competition between the four leading brands is reduced at the retail level, since one retailer fixes the price of all four brands in each territory. The multiple dealership implies that, if one producer cuts the price for its brand, the retailer will not be eager to transmit this price cut to the final consumer as it would reduce its sales and profits made with the other brands. Hence, producers have a reduced interest in entering into price competition with one another. Inter-brand price competition exists mainly with the low brand image goods of the fringe producers. The possible efficiency arguments for (joint) exclusive distributors are limited, as the product is relatively simple, the resale does not require any specific investments or training and advertising is mainly carried out at the level of the producers.

Even though each of the market leaders has a market share below the threshold, exemption under Article 81(3) may not be justified and withdrawal of the block exemption may be necessary.

(177) Example of exclusive distribution combined with exclusive purchasing

Manufacturer A is the European market leader for a bulky consumer durable, with a market share of between 40% and 60% in most national retail markets. In every Member State, it has about seven competitors with much smaller market shares, the largest of these competitors having a market share of 10 %. These competitors are present on only one or two national markets. A sells its product through its national subsidiaries to exclusive distributors at the retail level, which are not allowed to sell actively into each other's territories. In addition, the retailers are obliged to purchase manufacturer A's products exclusively from the national subsidiary of manufacturer A in their own country. The retailers selling the brand of manufacturer A are the main resellers of that type of product in their territory. They handle competing brands, but with varying degrees of success and enthusiasm. A applies price differences of 10% to 15% between markets and smaller differences within markets. This is translated into smaller price differences at the retail level. The market is relatively stable on the demand and the supply side, and there are no significant technological changes.

In these markets, the loss of intra-brand competition results not only from the territorial exclusivity at the retail level but is aggravated by the exclusive purchasing obligation imposed on the retailers. The exclusive purchase obligation helps to keep markets and territories separate by making arbitrage between the exclusive retailers impossible. The exclusive retailers also cannot sell actively into each other's territory and in practice tend to avoid delivering outside their own territory. This renders price discrimination possible. Arbitrage by consumers or independent traders is limited due to the bulkiness of the product.

The possible efficiency arguments of this system, linked to economies of scale in transport and promotion efforts at the retailers' level, are unlikely to outweigh the negative effect of price discrimination and reduced intra-brand competition. Consequently, it is unlikely that the conditions for exemption are fulfilled.

2.3. Exclusive customer allocation

(178) In an exclusive customer allocation agreement, the supplier agrees to sell his products only to one distributor for resale to a particular class of customers. At the same time, the distributor is usually limited in his active selling to other exclusively allocated classes of customers. The possible competition risks are mainly reduced intra-brand competition and market partitioning, which may in particular facilitate price discrimination. When most or all of the suppliers apply exclusive customer allocation, this may facilitate collusion, both at the suppliers' and the distributors' level.

(179) Exclusive customer allocation is exempted by the Block Exemption Regulation when the supplier's market share does not exceed the 30% market share threshold, even if combined with other non-hardcore verti-

cal restraints such as non-compete, quantity-forcing or exclusive purchasing. A combination of exclusive customer allocation and selective distribution is normally hardcore, as active selling to end-users by the appointed distributors is usually not left free. Above the 30% market share threshold, the guidance provided in paragraphs 161 to 177 applies mutatis mutandis to the assessment of exclusive customer allocation, subject to the following specific remarks.

(180) The allocation of customers normally makes arbitrage by the customers more difficult. In addition, as each appointed distributor has his own class of customers, non-appointed distributors not falling within such a class may find it difficult to obtain the product. This will reduce possible arbitrage by non- appointed distributors. Therefore, above the 30% market share threshold of the Block Exemption Regulation exclusive customer allocation is unlikely to be exemptable unless there are clear and substantial efficiency effects.

(181) Exclusive customer allocation is mainly applied to intermediate products and at the wholesale level when it concerns final products, where customer groups with different specific requirements concerning the product can be distinguished.

(182) Exclusive customer allocation may lead to efficiencies, especially when the distributors are required to make investments in for instance specific equipment, skills or know-how to adapt to the requirements of their class of customers. The depreciation period of these investments indicates the justified duration of an exclusive customer allocation system. In general the case is strongest for new or complex products and for products requiring adaptation to the needs of the individual customer. Identifiable differentiated needs are more likely for intermediate products, that is products sold to different types of professional buyers. Allocation of final consumers is unlikely to lead to any efficiencies and is therefore unlikely to be exempted.

(183) Example of exclusive customer allocation

A company has developed a sophisticated sprinkler installation. The company has currently a market share of 40% on the market for sprinkler installations. When it started selling the sophisticated sprinkler it had a market share of 20% with an older product. The installation of the new type of sprinkler depends on the type of building that it is installed in and on the use of the building (office, chemical plant, hospital etc.). The company has appointed a number of distributors to sell and install the sprin-

kler installation. Each distributor needed to train its employees for the general and specific requirements of installing the sprinkler installation for a particular class of customers. To ensure that distributors would specialise the company assigned to each distributor an exclusive class of customers and prohibited active sales to each others' exclusive customer classes. After five years, all the exclusive distributors will be allowed to sell actively to all classes of customers, thereby ending the system of exclusive customer allocation. The supplier may then also start selling to new distributors. The market is quite dynamic, with two recent entries and a number of technological developments. Competitors, with market shares between 25% and 5%, are also upgrading their products.

As the exclusivity is of limited duration and helps to ensure that the distributors may recoup their investments and concentrate their sales efforts first on a certain class of customers in order to learn the trade, and as the possible anti-competitive effects seem limited in a dynamic market, the conditions for exemption are likely to be fulfilled.

2.4. Selective distribution

(184) Selective distribution agreements, like exclusive distribution agreements, restrict on the

one hand the number of authorised distributors and on the other the possibilities of resale. The difference with exclusive distribution is that the restriction of the number of dealers does not depend on the number of territories but on selection criteria linked in the first place to the nature of the product. Another difference with exclusive distribution is that the restriction on resale is not a restriction on active selling to a territory but a restriction on any sales to non-authorised distributors, leaving only appointed dealers and final customers as possible buyers. Selective distribution is almost always used to distribute branded final products.

(185) The possible competition risks are a reduction in intra-brand competition and, especially in case of cumulative effect, foreclosure of certain type(s) of distributors and facilitation of collusion between suppliers or buyers. To assess the possible anti-competitive effects of selective distribution under Article 81(1), a distinction needs to be made between purely qualitative selective distribution and quantitative selective distribution. Purely qualitative selective distribution selects dealers only on the basis of objective criteria required by the nature of the product such as training of sales personnel, the service provided at the point of sale, a certain range of the products being sold etc[31]. The application of such criteria does not put a direct limit on the number of dealers. Purely qualitative selective distribution is in general considered to fall outside Article 81(1) for lack of anti-competitive effects, provided that three conditions are satisfied. First, the nature of the product in question must necessitate a selective distribution system, in the sense that such a system must constitute a legitimate requirement, having regard to the nature of the product concerned, to preserve its quality and ensure its proper use. Secondly, resellers must be chosen on the basis of objective criteria of a qualitative nature which are laid down uniformly for all potential resellers and are not applied in a discriminatory manner. Thirdly, the criteria laid down must not go beyond what is necessary[32]. Quantitative selective distribution adds further criteria for selection that more directly limit the potential number of dealers by, for instance, requiring minimum or maximum sales, by fixing the number of dealers, etc.

---

[31] See for example judgment of the Court of First Instance in Case T-88/92 *Groupement d'achat Edouard Leclerc* v. *Commission* [1996] ECR II-1961.

[32] See judgments of the Court of Justice in Case 31/80 *L'Oreal* v. *PVBA* [1980] ECR 3775, paragraphs 15 and 16; Case 26/76 *Metro I* [1977] ECR 1875, paragraphs 20 and 21; Case 107/82 *AEG* [1983] ECR 3151, paragraph 35; and of the Court of First Instance in Case T-19/91 *Vichy* v. *Commission* [1992] ECR II-415, paragraph 65.

(186) Qualitative and quantitative selective distribution is exempted by the Block Exemption Regulation up to 30 % market share, even if combined with other non-hardcore vertical restraints, such as non-compete or exclusive distribution, provided active selling by the authorised distributors to each other and to end users is not restricted. The Block Exemption Regulation exempts selective distribution regardless of the nature of the product concerned. However, where the nature of the product does not require selective distribution, such a distribution system does not generally bring about sufficient efficiency enhancing effects to counterbalance a significant reduction in intra-brand competition. If appreciable anti-competitive effects occur, the benefit of the Block Exemption Regulation is likely to be withdrawn. In addition, the following guidance is provided for the assessment of selective distribution in individual cases which are not covered by the Block Exemption Regulation or in the case of cumulative effects resulting from parallel networks of selective distribution.

(187) The market position of the supplier and his competitors is of central importance in assessing possible anti-competitive effects, as the loss of intra-brand competition can only be problematic if inter-brand competition is limited. The stronger the position of the supplier, the more problematic is the loss of intra-brand competition. Another important factor is the number of selective distribution networks present in the same market. Where selective distribution is applied by only one supplier in the market which is not a dominant undertaking, quantitative selective distribution does not normally create net negative effects provided that the contract goods, having regard to their nature, require the use of a selective distribution system and on condition that the selection criteria applied are necessary to ensure efficient distribution of the goods in question. The reality, however, seems to be that selective distribution is often applied by a number of the suppliers in a given market.

(188) The position of competitors can have a dual significance and plays in particular a role in case of a cumulative effect. Strong competitors will mean in general that the reduction in intra-brand competition is easily outweighed by sufficient inter-brand competition. However, when a majority of the main suppliers apply selective distribution there will be a significant loss of intra-brand competition and possible foreclosure of certain types of distributors as well as an increased risk of collusion between those major suppliers.

The risk of foreclosure of more efficient distributors has always been greater with selective distribution than with exclusive distribution, given the restriction on sales to non-authorised dealers in selective distribution. This is designed to give selective distribution systems a closed character, making it impossible for non-authorised dealers to obtain supplies. This makes selective distribution particularly well suited to avoid pressure by price discounters on the margins of the manufacturer, as well as on the margins of the authorised dealers.

(189) Where the Block Exemption Regulation applies to individual networks of selective distribution, withdrawal of the block exemption or disapplication of the Block Exemption Regulation may be considered in case of cumulative effects. However, a cumulative effect problem is unlikely to arise when the share of the market covered by selective distribution is below 50%. Also, no problem is likely to arise where the market coverage ratio exceeds 50%, but the aggregate market share of the five largest suppliers (CR5) is below 50%. Where both the CR5 and the share of the market covered by selective distribution exceed 50%, the assessment may vary depending on whether or not all five largest suppliers apply selective distribution. The stronger the position of the competitors not applying selective distribution, the less likely the foreclosure of other distributors. If all five largest suppliers apply selective distribution, competition concerns may in particular arise with respect to those agreements that apply quantitative selection criteria by directly limiting the number of authorised dealers. The conditions of Article 81(3) are in general unlikely to be fulfilled if the selective distribution systems at issue prevent access to the market by new distributors capable of adequately selling the products in question, especially price discounters, thereby limiting distribution to the advantage of certain existing channels and to the detriment of final consumers. More indirect forms of quantitative selective distribution, resulting for instance from the combination of purely qualitative selection criteria with the requirement imposed on the dealers to achieve a minimum amount of annual purchases, are less likely to produce net negative effects, if such an amount does not represent a significant proportion of the dealer's total turnover achieved with the type of products in question and it does not go beyond what is necessary for the supplier to recoup his relationship-specific investment and/or realise economies of scale in distribution. As regards individual contributions, a supplier with a market share of less than 5% is in

APPENDIX V 393

general not considered to contribute significantly to a cumulative effect.

(190) 'Entry barriers' are mainly of
interest in the case of foreclosure
of the market to non-authorised
dealers. In general entry barriers
will be considerable as selective
distribution is usually applied by
manufacturers of branded products. It will in general take time
and considerable investment for
excluded retailers to launch their
own brands or obtain competitive supplies elsewhere.

(191) 'Buying power' may increase the
risk of collusion between dealers
and thus appreciably change the
analysis of possible anti-competitive effects of selective distribution. Foreclosure of the
market to more efficient retailers
may especially result where a
strong dealer organisation
imposes selection criteria on the
supplier aimed at limiting distribution to the advantage of its
members.

(192) Article 5(c) of the Block
Exemption Regulation provides
that the supplier may not
impose an obligation causing
the authorised dealers, either
directly or indirectly, not to sell
the brands of particular competing suppliers. This condition
aims specifically at avoiding
horizontal collusion to exclude
particular brands through the
creation of a selective club of
brands by the leading suppliers.

This kind of obligation is
unlikely to be exemptable when
the CR5 is equal to or above
50%, unless none of the suppliers imposing such an obligation
belongs to the five largest suppliers in the market.

(193) Foreclosure of other suppliers is
normally not a problem as long
as other suppliers can use the
same distributors, i.e. as long as
the selective distribution system
is not combined with single
branding. In the case of a dense
network of authorised distributors or in the case of a cumulative effect, the combination of
selective distribution and a non-
compete obligation may pose a
risk of foreclosure to other suppliers. In that case the principles
set out above on single branding
apply. Where selective distribution is not combined with a non-
compete obligation, foreclosure
of the market to competing suppliers may still be a problem
when the leading suppliers apply
not only purely qualitative selection criteria, but impose on their
dealers certain additional obligations such as the obligation to
reserve a minimum shelf-space
for their products or to ensure
that the sales of their products
by the dealer achieve a minimum percentage of the dealer's
total turnover. Such a problem is
unlikely to arise if the share of
the market covered by selective
distribution is below 50% or,
where this coverage ratio is
exceeded, if the market share of

the five largest suppliers is below 50%.

(194) Maturity of the market is important, as loss of intra-brand competition and possible foreclosure of suppliers or dealers may be a serious problem in a mature market but is less relevant in a market with growing demand, changing technologies and changing market positions.

(195) Selective distribution may be efficient when it leads to savings in logistical costs due to economies of scale in transport and this may happen irrespective of the nature of the product (efficiency 6 in paragraph 116). However, this is usually only a marginal efficiency in selective distribution systems. To help solve a free-rider problem between the distributors (efficiency 1 in paragraph 116) or to help create a brand image (efficiency 8 in paragraph 116), the nature of the product is very relevant. In general the case is strongest for new products, for complex products, for products of which the qualities are difficult to judge before consumption (so-called experience products) or of which the qualities are difficult to judge even after consumption (so-called credence products). The combination of selective and exclusive distribution is likely to infringe Article 81 if it is applied by a supplier whose market share exceeds 30% or in case of cumulative effects, even though active sales between the territories remain free. Such a combination may exceptionally fulfil the conditions of Article 81(3) if it is indispensable to protect substantial and relationship-specific investments made by the authorised dealers (efficiency 4 in paragraph 116).

(196) To ensure that the least anti-competitive restraint is chosen, it is relevant to see whether the same efficiencies can be obtained at a comparable cost by for instance service requirements alone.

(197) Example of quantitative selective distribution:

In a market for consumer durables, the market leader (brand A), with a market share of 35%, sells its product to final consumers through a selective distribution network. There are several criteria for admission to the network: the shop must employ trained staff and provide pre-sales services, there must be a specialised area in the shop devoted to the sales of the product and similar hi-tech products, and the shop is required to sell a wide range of models of the supplier and to display them in an attractive manner. Moreover, the number of admissible retailers in the network is directly limited through the establishment of a maximum number of retailers per number of inhabitants in each province or urban area. Manufacturer A has 6 competitors in this market. Its largest competitors, B, C and D, have market shares of respectively 25, 15 and 10%, whilst the other producers have smaller market shares. A is the only manufacturer to use selective distribution. The selective distributors of brand A always handle a few competing brands. However, competing brands are also widely sold in shops which are not member of A's selective distribution network. Channels of distribution are various: for instance, brands B and C are sold in most of A's selected shops, but also in other shops providing a high quality service and in hypermarkets. Brand D is mainly sold in high service shops. Technology is evolving quite rapidly in this market, and the main suppliers maintain a strong quality image for their products through advertising.

In this market, the coverage ratio of selective distribution is 35%. Inter- brand competition is not directly affected by the selective distribution system of A. Intra-brand competition for brand A may be reduced, but consumers have access to low service/low price retailers for brands B and C, which have a comparable quality image to brand A. Moreover, access to high service retailers for other brands is not foreclosed, since there is no limitation on the capacity of selected distributors

to sell competing brands, and the quantitative limitation on the number of retailers for brand A leaves other high service retailers free to distribute competing brands. In this case, in view of the service requirements and the efficiencies these are likely to provide and the limited effect on intra-brand competition the conditions for exempting A's selective distribution network are likely to be fulfilled.

(198) Example of selective distribution with cumulative effects:

On a market for a particular sports article, there are seven manufacturers, whose respective market shares are: 25%, 20%, 15%, 15%, 10%, 8% and 7%. The five largest manufacturers distribute their products through quantitative selective distribution, whilst the two smallest use different types of distribution systems, which results in a coverage ratio of selective distribution of 85%. The criteria for access to the selective distribution networks are remarkably uniform amongst manufacturers: shops are required to have trained personnel and to provide pre-sale services, there must be a specialised area in the shop devoted to the sales of the article and a minimum size for this area is specified. The shop is required to sell a wide range of the brand in question and to display the article in an attractive manner, the shop must be located in a commercial street, and this type of article must represent at least 30% of the total turnover of the shop. In general, the same dealer is appointed selective distributor for all five brands. The two brands which do not use selective distribution usually sell through less specialised retailers with lower service levels. The market is stable, both on the supply and on the demand side, and there is strong brand image and product differentiation. The five market leaders have strong brand images, acquired through advertising and sponsoring, whereas the two smaller manufacturers have a strategy of cheaper products, with no strong brand image.

In this market, access by general price discounters to the five leading brands is denied. Indeed, the requirement that this type of article represents at least 30% of the activity of the dealers and the criteria on presentation and pre-sales services rule out most price discounters from the network of authorised dealers. As a consequence, consumers have no choice but to buy the five leading brands in high service/high price shops. This leads to reduced inter-brand competition between the five leading brands. The fact that the two smallest brands can be bought in low service/low price shops does not compensate for this, because the brand image of the five market leaders is much better. Inter-brand competition is also limited through multiple dealership. Even though there exists some degree of intra-brand competition and the number of retailers is not directly limited, the criteria for admission are strict enough to lead to a small number of retailers for the five leading brands in each territory.

The efficiencies associated with these quantitative selective distribution systems are low: the product is not very complex and does not justify a particularly high service. Unless the manufacturers can prove that there are clear efficiencies linked to their network of selective distribution, it is probable that the block exemption will have to be withdrawn because of its cumulative effects resulting in less choice and higher prices for consumers.

2.5. Franchising

(199) Franchise agreements contain licences of intellectual property rights relating in particular to trade marks or signs and know-how for the use and distribution of goods or services. In addition to the licence of IPRs, the franchisor usually provides the franchisee during the life of the agreement with commercial or technical assistance. The licence and the assistance are integral components of the business

method being franchised. The franchisor is in general paid a franchise fee by the franchisee for the use of the particular business method. Franchising may enable the franchisor to establish, with limited investments, a uniform network for the distribution of his products. In addition to the provision of the business method, franchise agreements usually contain a combination of different vertical restraints concerning the products being distributed, in particular selective distribution and/or non-compete and/or exclusive distribution or weaker forms thereof.

(200) The coverage by the Block Exemption Regulation of the licensing of IPRs contained in franchise agreements is dealt with in paragraphs 23 to 45. As for the vertical restraints on the purchase, sale and resale of goods and services within a franchising arrangement, such as selective distribution, non-compete or exclusive distribution, the Block Exemption Regulation applies up to the 30% market share threshold for the franchisor or the supplier designated by the franchisor(33). The guidance provided earlier in respect of these types of restraints applies also to franchising, subject to the following specific remarks:

1) In line with general rule 8 (see paragraph 119), the more important the transfer of know-how, the more easily the vertical restraints fulfil the conditions for exemption.

2) A non-compete obligation on the goods or services purchased by the franchisee falls outside Article 81(1) when the obligation is necessary to maintain the common identity and reputation of the franchised network. In such cases, the duration of the non-compete obligation is also irrelevant under Article 81(1), as long as it does not exceed the duration of the franchise agreement itself.

(201) Example of franchising:

A manufacturer has developed a new format for selling sweets in so-called fun shops where the sweets can be coloured specially on demand from the consumer. The manufacturer of the sweets has also developed the machines to colour the sweets. The manufacturer also produces the colouring liquids. The quality and freshness of the liquid is of vital importance to producing good sweets. The manufacturer made a success of its sweets through a number of own retail outlets all operating under the same trade name and with the uniform fun image (style of layout of the shops, common advertising etc.). In order to expand sales the manufacturer started a franchising system. The franchisees are obliged to buy the sweets, liquid and colouring machine from the manufacturer, to have the same image and operate under the trade name, pay a franchise fee, contribute to common advertising and ensure the confidentiality of the operating manual prepared by the franchisor. In addition, the franchisees are only allowed to sell from the agreed premises, are only allowed to sell to end users or other franchisees and are not allowed to sell other sweets. The franchisor is obliged not to appoint another franchisee nor operate a retail outlet himself in a given contract territory. The franchisor is also under the obligation to update and further develop its products, the business outlook and the operating manual and make these improvements available to all retail franchisees. The franchise agreements are concluded for a duration of 10 years.

Sweet retailers buy their sweets on a national market from either national producers that cater for national tastes or from wholesalers which import sweets from foreign producers in addition to selling products from national producers. On this market the franchisor's products compete with other brands of sweets. The franchisor has a market share of 30% on the market for sweets sold to retailers. Competition comes from a number of national and international brands, sometimes produced by large diversified food companies. There are many potential points of sale of sweets in the form of tobacconists, general food retailers, cafeterias and specialised sweet shops. On the market for machines for colouring food the franchisor's market share is below 10%.

Most of the obligations contained in the franchise agreements can be assessed as being necessary to protect the intellectual property rights or maintain the common identity and reputation of the franchised network and fall outside Article 81(1). The restrictions on selling (contract territory and selective distribution) provide an incentive to the franchisees to invest in the colouring machine and the franchise concept and, if not necessary for, at least help to maintain the common identity, thereby offsetting the loss of intra- brand competition. The non-compete clause excluding other brands of sweets from the shops for the full duration of the agreements does allow the franchisor to keep the outlets uniform and prevent competitors from benefiting from its trade name. It does not lead to any serious foreclosure in view of the great number of potential outlets available to other sweet producers. The franchise agreements of this franchisor are likely to fulfil the conditions for exemption under Article 81(3) in as far as the obligations contained therein fall under Article 81(1).

2.6. Exclusive supply

(202) Exclusive supply as defined in Article 1(c) of the Block Exemption Regulation is the extreme form of limited distribution in as far as the limit on the number of buyers is concerned: in the agreement it is specified that there is only one buyer inside the Community to which the supplier may sell a particular final product. For intermediate goods or services, exclusive supply means that there is only one buyer inside the Community or that there is only one buyer inside the Community for the purposes of a specific use. For intermediate goods or services, exclusive supply is often referred to as industrial supply.

(203) Exclusive supply as defined in Article 1(c) of the Block Exemption Regulation is exempted by Article 2(1) read in conjunction with Article 3(2) of the Block Exemption Regulation up to 30% market share of the buyer, even if combined with other non-hardcore vertical restraints such as non-compete. Above the market share threshold the following guidance is provided for the assessment of exclusive supply in individual cases.

(204) The main competition risk of exclusive supply is foreclosure of other buyers. The market share of the buyer on the upstream purchase market is obviously important for assessing the ability of the buyer to 'impose' exclusive supply which forecloses other buyers from access to supplies. The importance of the buyer on the downstream market is however the factor which determines whether a competition problem may arise. If the buyer has no market power downstream, then no appreciable negative effects for consumers can be expected. Negative effects can however be expected when the market share of the buyer on the downstream supply market as well as the upstream purchase market exceeds 30%. Where the market share of the buyer on the upstream market does not exceed 30%, significant foreclosure effects may still result, especially when the market share of the buyer on his downstream market exceeds 30%. In such cases withdrawal of the block exemption may be required. Where a company is dominant on the downstream market, any obligation to supply the products only or mainly to the dominant buyer may easily have significant anti-competitive effects.

(205) It is not only the market position of the buyer on the upstream and downstream market that is important but also the extent to

and the duration for which he applies an exclusive supply obligation. The higher the tied supply share, and the longer the duration of the exclusive supply, the more significant the foreclosure is likely to be. Exclusive supply agreements shorter than five years entered into by non-dominant companies usually require a balancing of pro- and anti-competitive effects, while agreements lasting longer than five years are for most types of investments not considered necessary to achieve the claimed efficiencies or the efficiencies are not sufficient to outweigh the foreclosure effect of such long-term exclusive supply agreements.

(206) The market position of the competing buyers on the upstream market is important as it is only likely that competing buyers will be foreclosed for anti-competitive reasons, i.e. to increase their costs, if they are significantly smaller than the foreclosing buyer. Foreclosure of competing buyers is not very likely where these competitors have similar buying power and can offer the suppliers similar sales possibilities. In such a case, foreclosure could only occur for potential entrants, who may not be able to secure supplies when a number of major buyers all enter into exclusive supply contracts with the majority of suppliers on the market. Such a cumulative effect may lead to withdrawal of the benefit of the Block Exemption Regulation.

(207) Entry barriers at the supplier level are relevant to establishing whether there is real foreclosure. In as far as it is efficient for competing buyers to provide the goods or services themselves via upstream vertical integration, foreclosure is unlikely to be a real problem. However, often there are significant entry barriers.

(208) Countervailing power of suppliers is relevant, as important suppliers will not easily allow themselves to be cut off from alternative buyers. Foreclosure is therefore mainly a risk in the case of weak suppliers and strong buyers. In the case of strong suppliers the exclusive supply may be found in combination with non-compete. The combination with non-compete brings in the rules developed for single branding. Where there are relationship-specific investments involved on both sides (hold-up problem) the combination of exclusive supply and non-compete i.e. reciprocal exclusivity in industrial supply agreements is usually justified below the level of dominance.

(209) Lastly, the level of trade and the nature of the product are relevant for foreclosure. Foreclosure is less likely in the case of an intermediate product or where the product is homogeneous.

Firstly, a foreclosed manufacturer that uses a certain input usually has more flexibility to respond to the demand of his customers than the wholesaler/retailer has in responding to the demand of the final consumer for whom brands may play an important role. Secondly, the loss of a possible source of supply matters less for the foreclosed buyers in the case of homogeneous products than in the case of a heterogeneous product with different grades and qualities.

(210) For homogeneous intermediate products, anti-competitive effects are likely to be exemptable below the level of dominance. For final branded products or differentiated intermediate products where there are entry barriers, exclusive supply may have appreciable anti-competitive effects where the competing buyers are relatively small compared to the foreclosing buyer, even if the latter is not dominant on the downstream market.

(211) Where appreciable anti-competitive effects are established, an exemption under Article 81(3) is possible as long as the company is not dominant. Efficiencies can be expected in the case of a hold-up problem (paragraph 116, points 4 and 5), and this is more likely for intermediate products than for final products. Other efficiencies are less likely. Possible economies of scale in distribution (paragraph 116, point 6) do not seem likely to justify exclusive supply.

(212) In the case of a hold-up problem and even more so in the case of scale economies in distribution, quantity forcing on the supplier, such as minimum supply requirements, could well be a less restrictive alternative.

(213) Example of exclusive supply:

On a market for a certain type of components (intermediate product market) supplier A agrees with buyer B to develop, with his own know-how and considerable investment in new machines and with the help of specifications supplied by buyer B, a different version of the component. B will have to make considerable investments to incorporate the new component. It is agreed that A will supply the new product only to buyer B for a period of five years from the date of first entry on the market. B is obliged to buy the new product only from A for the same period of five years. Both A and B can continue to sell and buy respectively other versions of the component elsewhere. The market share of buyer B on the upstream component market and on the downstream final goods market is 40%. The market share of the component supplier is 35%. There are two other component suppliers with around 20–25% market share and a number of small suppliers.

Given the considerable investments, the agreement is likely to fulfil the conditions for exemption in view of the efficiencies and the limited foreclosure effect. Other buyers are foreclosed from a particular version of a product of a supplier with 35% market share and there are other component suppliers that could develop similar new products. The foreclosure of part of buyer B's demand to other suppliers is limited to maximum 40% of the market.

(214) Exclusive supply is based on a direct or indirect obligation causing the supplier only to sell to one buyer. Quantity forcing on the supplier is based on incentives agreed between the supplier and the buyer that make the former concentrate his sales mainly with one buyer. Quantity forcing on the supplier may have similar but more mitigated effects than exclusive supply. The assessment of quantity forcing will depend on the degree of foreclosure of other buyers on the upstream market.

2.7. Tying

(215) Tying exists when the supplier makes the sale of one product conditional upon the purchase of another distinct product from the supplier or someone designated by the latter. The first product is referred to as the tying product and the second is referred to as the tied product. If the tying is not objectively justified by the nature of the products or commercial usage, such practice may constitute an abuse within the meaning of Article 82[33]. Article 81 may apply to horizontal agreements or concerted practices between competing suppliers which make the sale of one product conditional upon the purchase of another distinct product. Tying may also constitute a vertical restraint falling under Article 81 where it results in a single branding type of obligation (see paragraphs 138 to 160) for the tied product. Only the latter situation is dealt with in these Guidelines.

(216) What is to be considered as a distinct product is determined first of all by the demand of the buyers. Two products are distinct if, in the absence of tying, from the buyers' perspective, the products are purchased by them on two different markets. For instance, since customers want to buy shoes with laces, it has become commercial usage for shoe manufacturers to supply shoes with laces. Therefore, the sale of shoes with laces is not a tying practice. Often combinations

---

[33] Judgment of the Court of Justice in Case C-333/94 P *Tetrapak v Commission* [1996] ECR I-5951, paragraph 37.

have become accepted practice because the nature of the product makes it technically difficult to supply one product without the supply of another product.

(217) The main negative effect of tying on competition is possible foreclosure on the market of the tied product. Tying means that there is at least a form of quantity-forcing on the buyer in respect of the tied product. Where in addition a non-compete obligation is agreed in respect of the tied product, this increases the possible foreclosure effect on the market of the tied product. Tying may also lead to supra-competitive prices, especially in three situations. Firstly, when the tying and tied product are partly substitutable for the buyer. Secondly, when the tying allows price discrimination according to the use the customer makes of the tying product, for example the tying of ink cartridges to the sale of photocopying machines (metering). Thirdly, when in the case of long-term contracts or in the case of after-markets with original equipment with a long replacement time, it becomes difficult for the customers to calculate the consequences of the tying. Lastly, tying may also lead to higher entry barriers both on the market of the tying and on the market of the tied product.

(218) Tying is exempted by Article 2(1) read in conjunction with Article 3 of the Block Exemption Regulation when the market share of the supplier on both the market of the tied product and the market of the tying product does not exceed 30%. It may be combined with other non-hardcore vertical restraints such as non-compete or quantity forcing in respect of the tying product, or exclusive purchasing. Above the market share threshold the following guidance is provided for the assessment of tying in individual cases.

(219) The market position of the supplier on the market of the tying product is obviously of main importance to assess possible anti-competitive effects. In general this type of agreement is imposed by the supplier. The importance of the supplier on the market of the tying product is the main reason why a buyer may find it difficult to refuse a tying obligation.

(220) To assess the supplier's market power, the market position of his competitors on the market of the tying product is important. As long as his competitors are sufficiently numerous and strong, no anti-competitive effects can be expected, as buyers have sufficient alternatives to purchase the tying product without the tied product, unless other suppliers are applying similar tying. In addition, entry barriers on the market of the tying product are relevant to

establish the market position of the supplier. When tying is combined with a non-compete obligation in respect of the tying product, this considerably strengthens the position of the supplier.

(221) Buying power is relevant, as important buyers will not easily be forced to accept tying without obtaining at least part of the possible efficiencies. Tying not based on efficiency is therefore mainly a risk where buyers do not have significant buying power.

(222) Where appreciable anti-competitive effects are established, the question of a possible exemption under Article 81(3) arises as long as the company is not dominant. Tying obligations may help to produce efficiencies arising from joint production or joint distribution. Where the tied product is not produced by the supplier, an efficiency may also arise from the supplier buying large quantities of the tied product. For tying to be exemptable, it must, however, be shown that at least part of these cost reductions are passed on to the consumer. Tying is therefore normally not exemptable when the retailer is able to obtain, on a regular basis, supplies of the same or equivalent products on the same or better conditions than those offered by the supplier which applies the tying practice. Another efficiency may exist where tying helps to ensure

a certain uniformity and quality standardisation (see efficiency 8 in paragraph 116). However, it needs to be demonstrated that the positive effects cannot be realised equally efficiently by requiring the buyer to use or resell products satisfying minimum quality standards, without requiring the buyer to purchase these from the supplier or someone designated by the latter. The requirements concerning minimum quality standards would not normally fall within Article 81(1). Where the supplier of the tying product imposes on the buyer the suppliers from which the buyer must purchase the tied product, for instance because the formulation of minimum quality standards is not possible, this may also fall outside Article 81(1), especially where the supplier of the tying product does not derive a direct (financial) benefit from designating the suppliers of the tied product.

(223) The effect of supra-competitive prices is considered anti-competitive in itself. The effect of foreclosure depends on the tied percentage of total sales on the market of the tied product. On the question of what can be considered appreciable foreclosure under Article 81(1), the analysis for single branding can be applied. Above the 30% market share threshold exemption of tying is unlikely, unless there are clear efficiencies that are transmitted, at least in part, to con-

sumers. Exemption is even less likely when tying is combined with non-compete, either in respect of the tied or in respect of the tying product.

(224) Withdrawal of the block exemption is likely where no efficiencies result from tying or where such efficiencies are not passed on to the consumer (see paragraph 222). Withdrawal is also likely in the case of a cumulative effect where a majority of the suppliers apply similar tying arrangements without the possible efficiencies being transmitted at least in part to consumers.

2.8. Recommended and maximum resale prices

(225) The practice of recommending a resale price to a reseller or requiring the reseller to respect a maximum resale price is – subject to the comments in paragraphs 46 to 56 concerning RPM – covered by the Block Exemption Regulation when the market share of the supplier does not exceed the 30% threshold. For cases above the market share threshold and for cases of withdrawal of the block exemption the following guidance is provided.

(226) The possible competition risk of maximum and recommended prices is firstly that the maximum or recommended price will work as a focal point for the resellers and might be followed by most or all of them. A second competition risk is that maximum or recommended prices may facilitate collusion between suppliers.

(227) The most important factor for assessing possible anti-competitive effects of maximum or recommended resale prices is the market position of the supplier. The stronger the market position of the supplier, the higher the risk that a maximum resale price or a recommended resale price leads to a more or less uniform application of that price level by the resellers, because they may use it as a focal point. They may find it difficult to deviate from what they perceive to be the preferred resale price proposed by such an important supplier on the market. Under such circumstances the practice of imposing a maximum resale price or recommending a resale price may infringe Article 81(1) if it leads to a uniform price level.

(228) The second most important factor for assessing possible anti-competitive effects of the practice of maximum and recommended prices is the market position of competitors. Especially in a narrow oligopoly, the practice of using or publishing maximum or recommended prices may facilitate collusion between the suppliers by exchanging information on the preferred price level and by

ducing the likelihood of lower resale prices. The practice of imposing a maximum resale price or recommending resale prices leading to such effects may also infringe Article 81(1).

2.9. Other vertical restraints

(229) The vertical restraints and combinations described above are only a selection. There are other restraints and combinations for which no direct guidance is provided here. They will however be treated according to the same principles, with the help of the same general rules and with the same emphasis on the effect on the market.

Appendix VI

COMMISSION NOTICE
on agreements of minor importance which do not appreciably
restrict competition under Article 81(1) of the Treaty
establishing the European Community (*de minimis*)[1]
(2001/C 368/07)
(Text with EEA relevance)

I

1. Article 81(1) prohibits agreements between undertakings which may affect trade between Member States and which have as their object or effect the prevention, restriction or distortion of competition within the common market. The Court of Justice of the European Communities has clarified that this provision is not applicable where the impact of the agreement on intra-Community trade or on competition is not appreciable.

2. In this notice the Commission quantifies, with the help of market share thresholds, what is not an appreciable restriction of competition under Article 81 of the EC Treaty. This negative definition of appreciability does not imply that agreements between undertakings which exceed the thresholds set out in this notice appreciably restrict competition. Such agreements

may still have only a negligible effect on competition and may therefore not be prohibited by Article 81(1)[2].

3. Agreements may in addition not fall under Article 81(1)because they are not capable of appreciably affecting trade between Member States. This notice does not deal with this issue. It does not quantify what does not constitute an appreciable effect on trade. It is however acknowledged that agreements between small and medium-sized under-takings, as defined in the Annex to Commission

---

[1] This notice replaces the notice on agreements of minor importance published in OJ C 372, 9.12.1997.

[2] See, for instance, the judgment of the Court of Justice in Joined Cases C-215/96 and C-216/96 Bagnasco (Carlos) v. Banca Popolare di Novara and Casa di Risparmio di Genova e Imperia (1999) ECR I-135, points 34–35. This notice is also without prejudice to the principles for assessment under Article 81(1) as expressed in the Commission notice 'Guidelines on the applicability of Article 81 of the EC Treaty to horizontal cooperation agreements', OJ C 3, 6.1.2001, in particular points 17-31 inclusive, and in the Commission notice 'Guidelines on vertical restraints', OJ C 291, 13.10.2000, in particular points 5–20 inclusive.

Recommendation 96/280/EC [3], are rarely capable of appreciably affecting trade between Member States. Small and medium-sized undertakings are currently defined in that recommendation as undertakings which have fewer than 250 employees and have either an annual turnover not exceeding EUR 40 million or an annual balance-sheet total not exceeding EUR 27 million.

4. In cases covered by this notice the Commission will not institute proceedings either upon application or on its own initiative. Where undertakings assume in good faith that an agreement is covered by this notice, the Commission will not impose fines. Although not binding on them, this notice also intends to give guidance to the courts andauthorities of the Member States in their application of Article 81.

5. This notice also applies to decisions by associations of undertakings and to concerted practices.

6. This notice is without prejudice to any interpretation of Article 81 which may be given by the Court of Justice orthe Court of First Instance of the European Communities.

---

[3] OJ L 107, 30.4.1996, p. 4. This recommendation will be revised. It is envisaged to increase the annual turnover threshold fromEUR 40 million to EUR 50 million and the annual balance-sheet total threshold from EUR 27 million to EUR 43 million.

II

7. The Commission holds the view that agreements between undertakings which affect trade between Member States do not appreciably restrict competition within the meaning of Article 81(1):

(a) if the aggregate market share held by the parties to the agreement does not exceed 10 % on any of the relevant markets affected by the agreement, where the agreement is made between undertakings which are actual or potential competitors on any of these markets (agreements between competitors) [4]; or

(b) if the market share held by each of the parties to the agreement does not exceed 15% on any of the relevant markets affected by the agreement, where the agreement is made between undertakings

---

[4] On what are actual or potential competitors, see the Commission notice 'Guidelines on the applicability of Article 81 of the EC Treaty to horizontal cooperation agreements', OJ C 3, 6.1.2001, paragraph 9. A firm is treated as an actual competitor if it is either active on the same relevant market or if, in the absence of the agreement, it is able to switch production to the relevant products and market them in the short term without incurring significant additional costs or risks in response to a small and permanent increase in relative prices (immediate supply-side substitutability). A firm is treated as a potential competitor if there is evidence that, absent the agreement, this firm could and would be likely to undertake the necessary additional investments or other necessary switching costs so that it could enter the relevant market in response to a small and permanent increase in relative prices.

which are not actual or potential competitors on any of these markets (agreements between non-competitors).

In cases where it is difficult to classify the agreement as either an agreement between competitors or an agreement between non-competitors the 10% threshold is applicable.

8. Where in a relevant market competition is restricted by the cumulative effect of agreements for the sale of goods or services entered into by different suppliers or distributors (cumulative foreclosure effect of parallel networks of agreements having similar effects on the market), the market share thresholds under point 7 are reduced to 5%, both for agreements between competitors and for agreements between non-competitors. Individual suppliers or distributors with a market share not exceeding 5% are in general not considered to contribute significantly to a cumulative foreclosure effect[5]. A cumulative foreclosure effect is unlikely to exist if less than 30% of the relevant market is covered by parallel (networks of) agreements having similar effects.

9. The Commission also holds the view that agreements are not restrictive of competition if the market shares do not exceed the thresholds of respectively 10%, 15% and 5% set out in point 7 and 8 during two successive calendar years by more than 2 percentage points.

10. In order to calculate the market share, it is necessary to determine the relevant market. This consists of the relevant product market and the relevant geographic market. When defining the relevant market, reference should be had to the notice on the definition of the relevant market for the purposes of Community competition law[6]. The market shares are to be calculated on the basis of sales value data or, where appropriate, purchase value data. If value data are not available, estimates based on other reliable market information, including volume data, may be used.

11. Points 7, 8 and 9 do not apply to agreements containing any of the following hardcore restrictions:

(1) as regards agreements between competitors as defined in point 7, restrictions which, directly or indirectly, in isolation or in combination with other factors under the control of the parties, have as their object [7]:

---

[5] See also the Commission notice 'Guidelines on vertical restraints', OJ C 291, 13.10.2000, in particular paragraphs 73, 142, 143 and 189. While in the guidelines on vertical restraints in relation to certain restrictions reference is made not only to the total but also to the tied market share of a particular supplier or buyer, in this notice all market share thresholds refer to total market shares.

[6] OJ C 372, 9.12.1997, p. 5.

[7] Without prejudice to situations of joint production with or without joint distribution as

(a) the fixing of prices when selling the products to third parties;

(b) the limitation of output or sales;

(c) the allocation of markets or customers;

(2) as regards agreements between non-competitors as defined in point 7, restrictions which, directly or indirectly, in isolation or in combination with other factors under the control of the parties, have as their object:

(a) the restriction of the buyer's ability to determine its sale price, without prejudice to the possibility of the supplier imposing a maximum sale price or recommending a sale price, provided that they do not amount to a fixed or minimum sale price as a result of pressure from, or incentives offered by, any of the parties;

(b) the restriction of the territory into which, or of the customers to whom, the buyer may sell the contract goods or services, except the following

restrictions which are not hardcore:

— the restriction of active sales into the exclusive territory or to an exclusive customer group reserved to the supplier or allocated by the supplier to another buyer, where such a restriction does not limit sales by the customers of the buyer,

— the restriction of sales to end users by a buyer operating at the wholesale level of trade,

— the restriction of sales to unauthorised distributors by the members of a selective distribution system, and

— the restriction of the buyer's ability to sell components, supplied for the purposes of incorporation, to customers who would use them to manufacture the same type of goods as those produced by the supplier;

(c) the restriction of active or passive sales to end users by members of a selective distribution system operating at the retail level of trade, without prejudice

defined in Article 5, paragraph 2, of Commission Regulation (EC) No 2658/2000 and Article 5, paragraph 2, of Commission Regulation (EC) No 2659/2000, OJ L 304, 5.12.2000, pp. 3 and 7 respectively.

to the possibility of prohibiting a member of the system from operating out of an unauthorised place of establishment;

(d) the restriction of cross-supplies between distributors within a selective distribution system, including between distributors operating at different levels of trade;

(e) the restriction agreed between a supplier of components and a buyer who incorporates those components, which limits the supplier's ability to sell the components as spare parts to end users or to repairers or other service providers not entrusted by the buyer with the repair or servicing of its goods;

(3) as regards agreements between competitors as defined in point 7, where the competitors operate, for the purposes of the agreement, at a different level of the production or distribution chain, any of the hardcore restrictions listed in paragraph (1) and (2) above.

12. (1) For the purposes of this notice, the terms 'under-taking', 'party to the agreement', 'distributor', 'supplier' and 'buyer' shall include their respective connected undertakings.

(2) 'Connected undertakings' are:

(a) undertakings in which a party to the agreement, directly or indirectly:

— has the power to exercise more than half the voting rights, or

— has the power to appoint more than half the members of the supervisory board, board of management or bodies legally representing the undertaking, or

— has the right to manage the undertaking's affairs;

(b) undertakings which directly or indirectly have, over a party to the agreement, the rights or powers listed in (a);

(c) undertakings in which an undertaking referred to in (b) as, directly or indirectly, the rights or powers listed in (a);

(d) undertakings in which a party to the agreement together with one or more of the undertakings referred to in (a), (b) or (c), or in which two or more of the latter undertakings, jointly have the rights or powers listed in (a);

(e) undertakings in which the rights or the powers listed in (a) are jointly held by:

— parties to the agreement or their respective

connected undertakings referred to in (a) to (d), or

— one or more of the parties to the agreement or one of more of their connected undertakings referred to in (a) to (d) and one or more third parties.

(3) For the purposes of paragraph 2(e), the market share held by these jointly held undertakings shall be apportioned equally to each undertaking having the rights or the powers listed in paragraph 2(a).

Index